Theoretical Ecology

Theoretical Ecology

Concepts and Applications

EDITED BY

Kevin S. McCann and Gabriel Gellner

Department of Integrative Biology, University of Guelph, Canada

OXFORD

UNIVERSITY PRESS

OXFORD
UNIVERSITY PRESS

Great Clarendon Street, Oxford, OX2 6DP,
United Kingdom

Oxford University Press is a department of the University of Oxford.
It furthers the University's objective of excellence in research, scholarship,
and education by publishing worldwide. Oxford is a registered trade mark of
Oxford University Press in the UK and in certain other countries

© Oxford University Press 2020

The moral rights of the authors have been asserted

First Edition published in 2020

Impression: 1

Published in the United States of America by Oxford University Press
198 Madison Avenue, New York, NY 10016, United States of America

British Library Cataloguing in Publication Data
Data available

Library of Congress Control Number: 2020930792

ISBN 978–0–19–882428–2 (hbk.)
ISBN 978–0–19–882429–9 (pbk.)

DOI: 10.1093/oso/9780198824282.001.0001

Printed and bound by
CPI Group (UK) Ltd, Croydon, CR0 4YY

Foreword

Robert D. Holt

The word "theory" in its broadest sense has to do with a framework of conceptual constructs that help explain or interpret phenomena in a particular domain (Pickett et al. 2007). The discipline of ecology has in some of its branches robust theory that is not particularly mathematical (Scheiner and Willig 2011). More narrowly construed, however, "theoretical ecology" pertains to the use of mathematical and computational models to explore ecological questions, ranging from individual behavior, through the intertwined complexities of communities, to even global-scale phenomena. This is the sense in which Robert May used the term in crafting the series of advanced texts titled "Theoretical Ecology," an influential lineage of volumes now stretching back nearly half a century. A historian of ecology could glean much insight into the development of ecology at its conceptual core by carefully perusing the contents of these volumes, starting with the first edition in 1976, and now manifest in the current fourth edition. May himself has played a central role in the maturation of theoretical ecology, and even in this volume nearly all the chapters cite one or more of his many papers and books.

As noted by the editors, comparing the table of contents of the timely and authoritative book you have before you, with the 1976 first edition, is quite revealing. They both start with a focus on single species dynamics and interactions among a small number of species, then build to multispecies ensembles before ending with applications, and are all written by leading authorities. But it is instructive to ponder the differences in emphases,

reflecting maturation of our discipline. In the current volume there is much more emphasis than in 1976 on the key role the internal structures of populations play in their dynamics, and on stochasticity, lags, and transient dynamics—all crucial ingredients in bringing to bear theory on important applied questions. There is much more emphasis in the current volume on aspects of ecological complexity that can be rendered as networks, on interactions among species, on parasites inflicting hosts, and on flows of individuals across space. A central theme in many chapters is elucidating the relationship between network structure, and the stability and robustness of ecological systems—an abiding theme in May's own research contributions.

In 1976, one chapter was on schistosomiasis; now, emphasis is placed on the community context of infectious disease. Applied issues (e.g., schistosomiasis as a case study) in 1976 were somewhat loosely tied to ecological theory, but in the present volume, issues such as the role of diversity in infectious disease dynamics, abiotic drivers of interspecific interactions, and the quest for early warning signals of impending radical change, squarely build on other areas of ecological theory. The 1976 volume nodded towards evolution, for instance, with discussions of bionomic strategies and sociobiology; the current volume includes themes such as adaptive dynamics as tools for examining trait evolution in a community context. One could well imagine that the fusion of ecology and evolution will become a central theme in yet future editions of this renowned text (see Pásztor et al. 2016 for a perceptive synthesis, grounding ecological theory on Darwinian principles).

In the final chapter in this volume, the editors reflect on likely "Areas of Current and Future Growth," specifically noting seasonal drivers of dynamics, ecosystem issues, coupled social-ecological systems, and grappling with the many dimensions of change in the world. In closing, I want to return to Robert May's own closing chapter in the third 2007 edition of *Theoretical Ecology* (co-edited with Angela McLean), titled "Unanswered questions and why they matter," which mulls on the consequences of the current largest driver of change on the planet—ourselves. May remarks on the startling singularity of our point in time, when over a few generations our species has burgeoned in numbers, with corresponding impacts on the planet. May cites an estimate that will reach 9 billion by 2050; the modal projection of today's demographic models worrisomely is even higher, at 9.8 billion. Back in 1800, well within the lifespan of many forest trees still standing, there were only 1 billion or so of us. May then remarks that by some estimates, we have already exceeded the "ecological footprint" of sustainability, and ends with reflections on "the aspiration of optimizing the preservation of our evolutionary heritage." The ethical goal of passing on to future generations some of the richness of biodiversity on our planet mandates a clear and rigorous understanding of the factors that govern their persistence and spatial arrangements and temporal fluxes, in the first place.

The ideas summarized in this splendid volume, carrying on the grand tradition Robert May established starting in 1976—from coexistence theory, to network analyses, to embracing stochasticity and lags, to grounding theory on an underpinning of key individual traits and subtle issues of population structure—are essential ingredients needed for such understanding. All active ecologists, from students to seasoned practitioners, would benefit from reading and digesting the chapters in this volume, and I applaud the editors and authors on the fruits of their labors.

References

Pásztor, L., Z. Botta-Dukát, G. Magyar, T. Czárán, and G. Meszéna. 2016. *Theory-based Ecology: A Darwinian Approach*. Oxford, UK: Oxford University Press.

Pickett, S. T. A., J. Kolasa, and C. G. Jones. 2007. *Ecological Understanding: The Nature of Theory and the Theory of Nature*. 2nd edition. Burlington NY: Academic Press, Elsevier.

Scheiner, S. M. and M. R. Willig. 2011. *The Theory of Ecology*. Chicago IL: University of Chicago Press.

Detailed table of contents

List of contributors

Karen C. Abbott Department of Biology, Case Western Reserve University, USA

Stefano Allesina Department of Ecology and Evolution, University of Chicago, USA

Jordi Bascompte Department of Evolutionary Biology and Environmental Studies, University of Zurich, Switzerland

Ulrich Brose German Centre for Integrative Biodiversity Resarch (iDiv) Halle-Jena-Leipzig and Friedrich-Schiller-University Jena, Germany

Emily J. Champagne Department of Integrative Biology, University of Guelph, Canada

Peter Chesson Ecology and Evolutionary Biology, University of Arizona, USA

Vasilis Dakos Institut des Sciences de l'Evolution de Montpellier, France

André M. de Roos Institute for Biodiversity and Ecosystem Dynamics, University of Amsterdam, the Netherlands

John M. Drake Odum School of Ecology and Center for the Ecology of Infectious Diseases, University of Georgia, USA

Antonio Ferrera Department of Evolutionary Biology and Environmental Studies, University of Zurich, Switzerland

Gabriel Gellner Department of Integrative Biology, University of Guelph, Canada

Dominique Gravel Department of Biology, University of Sherbrooke, Canada

Christopher Greyson-Gaito Department of Integrative Biology, University of Guelph, Canada

Jacopo Grilli Quantitative Life Sciences, International Centre for Theoretical Physics, Italy

Robert D. Holt Department of Biology, University of Florida, USA

Kazutaka Kawatsu Graduate School of Life Sciences, Tohoku University, Japan

Sonia Kéfi Institut des Sciences de l'Evolution de Montpellier, CNRS, France

Christopher A. Klausmeier Kellogg Biological Station, Michigan State University, USA

Thomas Koffel Kellogg Biological Station, Michigan State University, USA

Michio Kondoh Graduate School of Life Sciences, Tohoku University, Japan

Colin T. Kremer Kellogg Biological Station, Michigan State University, USA

François Massol Evo-Eco-Paléo Unit (EEP), University of Lille, France

Kevin S. McCann Department of Integrative Biology, University of Guelph, Canada

Suzanne M. O'Regan Department of Mathematics, North Carolina Agricultural and Technical State University, USA

Yutaka Osada Graduate School of Life Sciences, Tohoku University, Japan

T. Alex Perkins Department of Biological Sciences, University of Notre Dame, USA

Pejman Rohani Odum School of Ecology, Center for the Ecology of Infectious Diseases and Department of Infectious Diseases, College of Veterinary Medicine, University of Georgia, USA

Jason R. Rohr Department of Biological Sciences, University of Notre Dame, USA

Masayuki Ushio Hakubi Center, Kyoto University, Japan; Center for Ecological Research, Kyoto University, Japan; PRESTO, Japan Science and Technology Agency, Japan

David A. Vasseur Department of Ecology and Evolutionary Biology, Yale University, USA

CHAPTER 1

Introduction

Gabriel Gellner, Kevin S. McCann, and Emily J. Champagne

1.1 This book and its predecessors

First of all, we are absolutely honored to take over the next installment in this excellent series, *Theoretical Ecology: Principles and Applications*, first started by Lord Robert May (editions I and II), and most recently with the excellent update approximately a decade ago with both Lord May and Dr. Angela McLean (edition III). We were also pleased as this eminent series allowed us to easily garner a significant set of major players in theoretical ecology.

In some real sense, the chronology of this book series (1976 to the present), forms a snapshot of the history of theoretical ecology led by arguably theoretical ecology's most broadly impactful theoretician, Robert May. The first two books, *Theoretical Ecology I* and *Theoretical Ecology II* (TE1 and TEII), were replete with the theory of the times, reflected in much filled population ecology, competition, predator-prey interactions, and the occasional heavily researched area of these earlier times (e.g., island biogeography, succession). In these earlier books, species interactions are often functional group dependent (e.g., plant-arthropod, herbivore plant) as opposed to the more general consumer-resource theory, that has both looked generally at consumptive interactions (as C-R theory), and catalogued specific functional results to produce a more general theory for antagonistic interactions (see the excellent book by Murdoch, Briggs, and Nisbet 2013). In this respect, although May and McLean's TEIII differed significantly from the first two, it did not cover the more general

consumer-resource theory. It did, though, start to venture heavily into the applied aspect of theoretical and quantitative ecology with chapters on infectious disease, fisheries, food production, and associated ecology, conservation biology and climate change. While some of these have been around historically, collectively it does represent that theoretical/conceptual movement over the last twenty years towards the integration of fundamental and applied theory. Indeed, it is clear that applied issues can help push fundamental theory more solidly into species area. As an example, and discussed in the final chapter, current theory and empirical data are starting to really wrestle with seasonality (a longstanding issue that has never truly picked up steam) as climate change is altering seasons and the life histories of players within it (e.g., phenology). As such, the push to unpack seasonally integrated theory is growing because of looming climate change. To expand on the historical accounts of ecology in TEIII, this edition comes at the heels of increased use of and exposure to theoretical models for practicing ecologists. Trends over the last decade have shown major shifts towards data-driven multi-disciplinary ecology, and especially increased research addressing anthropogenic influences (McCallen et al. 2019). Theoretical ecology is more accessible than ever with the growing use of statistical software, machine learning and open-source data, and the new generation of technologically savvy ecologists are well-poised to take advantage. With recent shifts

Gellner, G., McCann, K. S., and Champagne, E. J., *Introduction* In: *Theoretical Ecology: Concepts and Applications*. Edited by: Kevin S. McCann and Gabriel Gellner, Oxford University Press (2020). © Oxford University Press.
DOI: 10.1093/oso/9780198824282.003.0001

in ecology towards unified theories, knowledge of emerging and foundational concepts at a theoretical scale will only become more important.

1.2 This book: Themes and directions

Similar, to the other books in this series, we have not made any attempt to cover all of the developed and emerging areas in theory. It is not that we would not want to, but rather that such a task is impossible to accomplish. Here, we decided to unpack some of the areas of growth during the last twenty years and include areas that were not covered in the previous books but have blossomed to play a significant role in theoretical ecology (e.g., energy flows, meta-community and meta-ecosystems, body size, network ecology, trait dynamics). Nonetheless, we still included a section of applied theory as it has, if anything, only increased in theoretical ecology, and looks poised to increase even more dramatically in the coming decades. For this reason, we followed May and McLean (2007) and included a brief final chapter highlighting current growth areas and areas we believe are on the cusp of taking off (e.g., seasonally motivated theory referred to previously). Curiously, while in the May and McLean (2007) book, we did not include a chapter on socio-ecological theory or food production. Both areas are currently growing massively. We do think there is excellent work in this area and no doubt believe that the next version of Theoretical Ecology (TEV) will have a well-developed chapter on each of these critical topics. In line with the previous contributions in this series, this book is written for upper level undergraduate students, graduate students, and researchers seeking synthesis and the state of the art in growing areas of interest in theoretical ecology.

In picking topics, we leaned towards areas that we feel have developed strongly in the last twenty years, which were not yet covered in TEIII and were not fully covered elsewhere (e.g., macroecological theory is covered here tangentially but is well discussed numerous books and reviews; see Brown, 1995). As an example, we included a chapter by Chesson on competition. While multispecies coexistence has long been around and was in the original three TE's, Chesson's work represent a major generalization of all these results and has been picked up by theory and empirical

ecologists alike. Similarly, ideas from researchers like Peter Yodzis (e.g., Yodzis and Innes, 1992) and Kooijman (Kooijman and Kooijman, 2000) have pushed using body size and metabolism as a major unifying empirical idea in theory—an area that has grown significantly in ecology (e.g., from consumer-resource theory or predator-prey theory to whole networks). These ideas have allowed for energetic interpretations for the dynamics (e.g., stability, cycles) and structure (e.g., the shape of biomass of Eltonian pyramids) of populations, communities and ecosystems. In a sense, this energetic approach has been used as a constraint-based approach to ecology where researchers are moving towards whole food web perspectives, as Robert May so famously did (May, 1973), but the more modern movement has begun to consider this under plausibly biological constraints not just May's "statistical universes." As such, this area, which is related to macro-ecology, appears in several of the chapters.

The book starts with several chapters that are collectively more about the building blocks for understanding dynamics of interacting species in time and space. Chesson, as discussed previously, uses longstanding Lotka–Volterra models to flesh out the mechanisms behind coexistence in Chapter 2. His work, as always, takes you to the core of the mechanisms that yield coexistence and make for an apt starting point; bridging the past to the future in an area that has resonated through the history of ecology. Similarly, Gellner et al. use Chapter 3 to look at the role energy and biological lags play in the dynamics of consumer-resource interactions. This chapter briefly reviews C-R theory but pays special emphasis to the potentially critical role of lags in the dynamics of ecological systems. Here, too, like Chesson we focus on the general rules that have come out of the theory that ultimately can be used as building blocks for understanding higher order species interactions. Like the previous two chapters, both areas within which resides much historical work, Karen Abbott does a wonderful job of revisiting the role of stochasticity in ecological dynamics giving the reader an intuitive understanding, by using pseudo-potentials, of how stochasticity operates on deterministic systems, and along the way paves us a theoretical means to understand how transients may play out in ecology (see Hastings et al., 2018 for an interesting perspective on transients in ecology). This chapter is followed by de Roos, who elegantly lays out how stage structure plays out in the dynamics and structure of ecological systems. As de Roos points out in Chapter 4, nature is replete with stage structure and yet much of community and food web theory ignore this at their peril. Interestingly, while Gellner and McCann argue that even basic theory suggests a role for lags, de Roos and work with colleague Lennart Persson and others has long understood that lags are critical (Roos and Persson, 2013). De Roos does a nice job of unpacking this relatively complex area in a simple and coherent manner.

The next five chapters are representative of a large growth area in theoretical ecology in the last few decades, much of this work extending theory beyond simple species interactions to whole networks. This area arguably has grown for several reasons. One, after showing that simple equilibrium community matrix models in ecology predicted that diversity, all equal, beget instability, Robert May argued for research on the dynamics of intermediate dimension species interaction models. Similarly, over the last few decades, research has pushed the role of networks and connectivity in science. In ecology—a world of vast and wildly complex connections—network theory has risen to play a significant research role and is undoubtedly here to stay in ecology. We start these whole systems approaches with Chapter 6, by Allesina and Grilli, which reviews a number of really nice developments in the matrix theory that have ultimately originated from May's work. Effectively, Allesina and Grilli have drawn from a large bed of matrix theory to put together a very complete picture of the answers behind community matrices that may be composed of a suite of underlying species interactions (e.g., competition, predation, or mutualism). The work of Allesina and others in the past decade, or so, has done much to reinvigorate this area first brought to bear by May (1973).

Following this chapter, in Chapter 7, Bascompte and Fererra examine mutualistic networks in ecology, an area of substantial growth in ecology over the last few decades and one where Bascompte and colleagues have played a significant role. For background work on the theory of mutualism at the

interaction and community-level, which has also grown, see Bronstein (2015) for an empirical and theoretical update. We then move to Chapter 8, by Kondoh and colleagues, on how communities and food webs respond structurally and dynamically in a variable world. This is an area of recent growth, and here Kondoh embraces variation in multi-species interactions, rather than assumes communities and food webs are static through time (e.g., accepts the idea that things like interaction strengths are far from static). It is interesting to note that modern developments have both further explored the dynamical understanding of equilibrium matrices first championed by May, while also simultaneously developing theory of how systems respond to stochasticity—an issue that has long been clear to empiricists. Uli Brose follows the Kondoh chapter and represents a lot of work that has attempted to use body size as a core trait that determines system structure and ultimately dynamics. This constraint-based ecology, as discussed earlier, has been in a lot of bioenergetically-driven theory. This is an idea that has forefathers, like Yodzis and Kooijman, and one that was not in the previous three TE volumes. Finally, these five chapters are capped off by Sonia Kéfi who reviews network ecology in general. As discussed, this has been an enormously active area, one that integrates with a lot of the previously mentioned areas (e.g., mutualistic networks, food webs), but is more concerned with the topological structure and not as directly concerned with dynamics.

The next two chapters represent areas of theoretical development that have only modest attachment to historical ideas. Very recently, researchers have pushed for following the dynamics of traits as they allow models/theory to be posed at a variety of scales from individual variation to species variation. While the body-size theory has been around for a while and is somewhat of an example of a trait-driven model, this research more directly follows traits rather than is parameterized by a trait. Some of this research push came out of strong empirical research programs that have found that individual variation was ubiquitous in systems. Again, this is another example of embracing variation both in tracking it and recognizing that systems "adapt" rapidly within a changing context. Klausmeier,

Kremer, and Koffel use their Chapter 11 to outline both how trait models can be embedded in the classical species interactions and also unpacking some of the implications of this trait-based research. In a sense, this trait-based dynamic research is related to the view of the complex adaptive system perspective put forth by Kondoh et al. That is, that systems change, behavior changes, traits change and in turn the interactions are continuously re-embedded within a changing matrix. Overall, the issue of directional change in a changing world is a theme that modern theory, perhaps pushed by global change, has moved considerably towards. The Klausmeier et al. chapter is then followed by Gravel and Massol and takes on the growth of meta-ecology. Here, by meta-ecology, I refer to the outgrowth from meta-population ecology (represented in the earlier TE books) where theory has first considered meta-community ecology and more recently extended to meta-ecosystem theory. This area considers the critical role that spatial connectivity, through dispersal and movement across space, plays on the dynamics of populations to whole ecosystems.

Finally, as with the last TE book by May and McLean, we turn to applied theory. This area has grown and continues to grow daily. We use the final few chapters to give a taste from applied theoretical ecology starting with the disease ecology, an area that has been in all TE books representing its longstanding place in ecological theory, before turning to climate change and the general problem of predicting collapse within a changing world (often called early warning signals in ecology).

Perkins and Rohr continue the long-standing narrative on disease ecology with a review of the effects of host diversity on diseases, as well as the current understanding around the coexistence of multiple strains or pathogens within a host community. Since much of the existing body of research on ecology focuses on single-pathogen, single-host systems, this branch of research could elucidate implications for public health, and policy in the face of global changes. Perkins and Rohr end by arguing for the implementation of underutilized aspects of ecological theory. Similarly,

in a very well executed chapter, Vasseur ties longstanding ideas from ecological theory (e.g., the role of carrying capacity, a surrogate from productivity) to synthesize and forecast the role temperature may play in population community models. Finally, work like that reviewed and synthesized by Vasseur on climate has been front and center in ecological theory, often suggesting for the potential of heightened instability and/or collapse in populations or communities. Since the last book, this emphasis on collapse, with clear empirical examples from the field emerging (e.g., dead zones increasing globally) has led to the development of theory predicting such collapse. Here, in a very clearly elucidated Chapter 15, John Drake and colleagues walk us through the still developing theory for early warning signals (EWS). EWS, an area that is used by scientists of all ilk (e.g., physics) revealing the intersecting applications of mathematics in many areas of science. Drake also visits the empirical and experimental data that is also rapidly being developed as the theory blazed through some of the major journals in science.

This book, in a greatly simplified sense, shows that ecological theory has thoroughly embraced complexity. The complexity of understanding the role of a noisy (and changing) abiotic world on a wildly connected Earth, where species connections defy longstanding spatial boundaries and aspects of the ecological hierarchy mix together to produce the diversity and functioning of ecosystems. It is worth noting that as we take over this series and reflect on where theoretical ecology has been and is going, that the fingerprints of Robert May's career as a theoretical ecologist are everywhere in this book and in the modern literature. His vision as a researcher, and his curiosity in so many realms of this endeavor have led him to be an enormously impressive force, not only in ecology but also in the influence ecology now plays on multiple disciplines like economics and human health. While still a young science, the work and efforts of Robert May have catapulted ecology into a modern era, where it is being taken very seriously, and is playing a role in structuring the development of humankind.

CHAPTER 2

Species coexistence

Peter Chesson

2.1 Introduction

How do we explain the remarkable diversity of living species on Earth? This question has long been an inspiration and a challenge to biologists. The structure and behavior of organisms, and the relationships between species, ever arouse wonder; but the questions of how and why can be enormously complex. Although the complexity of an organism reveals itself over time to the careful observer (Lawton 1999), the how and why of species diversity requires knowing the details of the interactions between species and the implications of these interactive relationships for the dynamics of populations, microevolution, and speciation. This web of relationships and its consequences is one of the most complex questions ever subject to scientific investigation.

Mathematical theory has long had prominent roles in sorting out the logical consequences of the interactions between species and generating hypotheses about diversity maintenance (Scudo and Ziegler 1978; Kingsland 1985). In this chapter, an important part of this endeavor is discussed, specifically how the interactions between species affect their ability to coexist. Species diversity at any one locality on Earth, in most fundamental terms, is the outcome of three key processes: speciation, immigration, and extinction. Species coexistence is about persistence of species in the presence of others, interacting with each other. But persistence is never forever, and so this question is really about how extinction is delayed. Moreover, it can also be about how immigrants establish (Shea and Chesson 2002), and how speciation is fostered by the interactions between individual organisms, both within and between species (Chesson and Huntly 1997). Species coexistence is thus a key question in the quest to explain the diversity of life.

There are many sorts of interactions between species. They include predator-prey relationships (Terborgh and Estes 2010; Chapter 3, this book) where one species is food of another, mutualistic relationships (Bronstein 2015; Chapter 7, this book) where each partner to the relationship provides something that another needs, and they can be competitive relationships (Birch 1957), where the interaction may be indirect through the effects that each species has on their shared environment. For any given species, its natural enemies (predators, herbivores, parasites, and diseases), have direct negative effects on its ability to persist, as do its competitors. In contrast, resources, such food species, water, and places to live, have direct positive effects (Andrewartha and Birch 1984). Local communities of organisms are generally considered to have a web of interactions, as illustrated in highly simplified form in Figure 2.1. Foodweb theory (Williams and Martinez 2000; Rossberg et al. 2006; Rossberg 2013) is an approach to understanding this web of interactions by studying who eats whom, as depicted by the downward dashed arrows in the figure. A food web can be envisaged as a set of intertwining food chains, where individual chains show pathways of energy and materials between trophic levels (feeding levels), e.g., the path $R_3 \rightarrow N_2 \rightarrow P_1 \rightarrow Q_1$ in Figure 2.1 consisting of four trophic levels.

Chesson, P., *Species coexistence* In: *Theoretical Ecology: Concepts and Applications*. Edited by: Kevin S. McCann and Gabriel Gellner, Oxford University Press (2020).
© Oxford University Press.
DOI: 10.1093/oso/9780198824282.003.0002

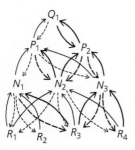

Figure 2.1 Idealized food web diagram. The letters R, N, P, and Q correspond to guilds in different trophic levels, with each subscripted letter being a species in that guild. The general expectation is that these trophic levels would represent plants, herbivores, carnivores, and a "top predator," but the development in the text does not adhere strictly to this interpretation. Curved arrows indicate effects of one species on another, defining feedback loops.

In his seminal work, "Homage to Santa Rosalia or Why Are There So Many Kinds of Animals?" G. E. Hutchinson (1959) pointed out that food chains tend to be short: mostly less than five trophic levels to very rarely ten trophic levels (Briand and Cohen 1987). But local communities often have hundreds if not thousands of species. To get such high numbers, one needs to understand the determinants of the average numbers of species per trophic level. Thus, Hutchinson's analysis has argued for focusing on how species in the same trophic level coexist with one another, potentially competing with one another for shared resources and interacting with each other indirectly through shared natural enemies, as depicted in Figure 2.1. Studies of species coexistence generally have this focus on species within the same trophic level with similar ecology. Using terminology originating with (Root 1967; Simberloff and Dayan 1991; Fauth et al. 1996), they belong to the same guild. In Figure 2.1, different letters are intended to identify different guilds, and in this chapter the N guild is intended as the guild of focus, although it will often be assumed that this guild has only two species. The R guild and the P guild are then respectively resources and natural enemies of the N guild. The notation N_2, R_1, etc., will do double duty as the name of the species and its density (numbers per unit area) at a specific locality.

Coexisting ecologically similar species have generally been regarded as requiring explanation, and the key, either implicitly or explicitly, to how high local diversity can be possible. More scientifically, lab systems and simple ecological models suggest that it is difficult for similar species to coexist (Hardin 1960; Roughgarden 1989). Yet, we see in nature many similar species persisting together over time in the same locality (Hubbell 2001). Species coexistence studies thus tend to focus on the detailed relationships between similar species that allow them to coexist (Saavedra et al. 2017). Although one might attempt to study entire food webs, and there is much theory and empirical work that does (Martinez et al. 2006, Amarasekare 2008; Berlow et al. 2009), these studies generally concern broad patterns and properties that allow the entire food web to persist. This chapter focuses on how members of the same guild can coexist stably (Chesson 2000b), which means that species show average tendencies to recover when they are perturbed to low density. As is shown here, this outcome depends on differences between species in how they interact with their shared environment. In contrast, the neutral theory of community ecology holds that species in the same guild have no important ecological differences (Hubbell 2001). Under neutral theory, species in the same guild to do not coexist stably, but instead ecological drift occurs: species' relative abundances change at random, and perturbations to low density are equally likely to be followed by further losses as they are by gains.

2.2 Models

Species interactions start at the level of the individual organisms. An organism modifies its environment, for instance, by consuming resources, and these environmental changes then affect other individuals. The links in Figure 2.1 show potential effects of consuming food resources. Species N_2 consumes R_3, but so do the other N species. This consumption by N_2 potentially reduces the abundance of R_3, in turn affecting the ability of individuals of N_2 to continue to obtain it (intraspecific competition), and also the abilities of individuals of both N_1 and N_3 to obtain it (interspecific competition). To understand species coexistence, we must consider the flow on effects of such competition to the growth of a species' population. An individual organism contributes to population growth through births and deaths depending on its circumstances at any given time, t. The average contribution of an individual per unit time to growth of the population is denoted $r_i(t)$ and is termed the per capita growth rate. In the simplest case, without any interactions, $r_i(t)$ would equal a constant, r_i^0, but with competitive interactions, $r_i(t)$ would be reduced relative to a maximum value, r_i^0, depending on the densities of each species competing with N_i. If each individual of N_j on a unit of area reduces $r_i(t)$ by a proportion α_{ij} of its maximum value r_i^0, then we see that $r_i(t)$ is

$$r_i(t) = r_i^0 \left(1 - \sum_{j=1}^{n} \alpha_{ij} N_j \right). \qquad (2.1)$$

Thus, $r_i(t)$ is a linear decreasing function of the densities of all species. The per capita effect of N_j on $r_i(t)$ is the competition coefficient, α_{ij} (more generally, "the interaction coefficient"), which is assumed to be either positive or zero. This is the Lotka–Volterra competition model (Chesson 2018) named after the ecological theory pioneers Alfred J. Lotka and Vito Volterra (Scudo and Ziegler 1978). In many accounts, the equation for $r_i(t)$ is written with α_{ij}/K_i replacing α_{ij}, where K_i is the carrying capacity (Box 2.1), but then the meaning of the α_{ij} changes and the results become more complex and unintuitive (Chesson 2000a).

Equation (2.1) gives the contribution of an individual, on average, to population growth, and so the total growth of the population is found by multiplying this individual-level contribution by the number

---

Box 2.1 Two-species coexistence in the Lotka–Volterra model

In the single-species case, the Lotka-Volterra competition Equation (2.1) specializes to the single-species logistic equation (May 1974),

$$r_i(t) = r_i^0 \left(1 - \alpha_{ii} N_i \right). \qquad (B2.1.1)$$

Thus, N_i must converge on its "carrying capacity," K_i, the single-species equilibrium, which, by definition, is the value of N_i for which the growth rate, Equation (B2.1.1), is 0. Thus,

$$K_i = 1/\alpha_{ii}. \qquad (B2.1.2)$$

Species N_i rises to K_i but cannot rise above it. Moreover, N_i and must fall towards K_i if initially above it because there $r_i(t) < 0$. The question is whether other species will make $r_i(t) < 0$ at all densities of species i and drive it extinct. In the case of just one other species, the system is driven by the pair of equations

$$r_i(t) = r_i^0 \left(1 - \alpha_{ii} N_i - \alpha_{ij} N_j \right), i = 1, 2, j \neq i, \qquad (B2.1.3)$$

which is just a shorthand for

$$\begin{aligned} r_1(t) &= r_1^0 \left(1 - \alpha_{11} N_1 - \alpha_{12} N_2 \right) \\ r_2(t) &= r_2^0 \left(1 - \alpha_{21} N_1 - \alpha_{22} N_2 \right). \end{aligned} \qquad (B2.1.4)$$

Because over time N_j must head towards $1/\alpha_{jj}$ or below, in the long run

$$r_i(t) \geq r_i^0 \left(1 - \frac{\alpha_{ij}}{\alpha_{jj}} - \alpha_{ii} N_i \right). \qquad (B2.1.5)$$

The right-hand side of this inequality can only be positive if

$$\frac{\alpha_{ij}}{\alpha_{jj}} < 1, \qquad (B2.1.6)$$

for only then is $1 - \alpha_{ij}/\alpha_{jj} > 0$. In that case $r_i(t)$ is positive over the range $0 < N_i < N_{i,\min}^*$, where

$$N_{i,\min}^* = \left(1 - \frac{\alpha_{ij}}{\alpha_{jj}} \right) K_i. \qquad (B2.1.7)$$

Hence N_i must increase until it is at least $N_{i,\min}^*$, and remain there, defining a minimum density for N_i, in the presence of N_j, as a fraction of its carrying capacity.

The species coexist if (B2.1.6) applies for both species as i with the other as j, i.e., if $\alpha_{12} < \alpha_{22}$ and $\alpha_{21} < \alpha_{11}$. Figure 2.2a illustrates this outcome, showing how each species rises above its $N_{i,\min}^*$ in the presence of the other species. This ability to increase from low density in the presence of the other species means that the species satisfy the invasibility criterion for species coexistence (Turelli 1978). The presence of a minimum positive density means they coexist in the sense of permanence, which is generally implied by invasibility in the two species case (Kang and Chesson 2010; Chesson 2018).

of individuals per unit area (the density) to give $r_i(t)N_i(t)$. In standard calculus notation, this total growth rate is

$$\frac{dN_i}{dt} = r_i^0 \left(1 - \sum_{j=1}^{n} \alpha_{ij}N_j\right) N_i, \qquad (2.2)$$

where it is understood that N_i and N_j are functions of time, even though t is not explicitly indicated on the right-hand side. Note that $r_i(t) = (dN_i/dt)/N_i$, which is the usual definition of the per capita growth rate.

Figure 2.2 gives the range of different predictions that the equations can have when the N guild has just two species. In Figure 2.2a, we see the species coexisting: they each converge on a positive value. However, in b one particular species dominates, and the other is driven extinct, while in c, the species with the smaller initial density is driven extinct, a case of contingent competitive exclusion. In this

simple two-species Lotka–Volterra model, these outcomes are all equilibrium outcomes: the system settles on an equilibrium, i.e., values of the densities at which the growth rates of all species are zero, as discussed in Boxes 2.1 and 2.2, and these equilibria are stable in the sense that if the densities are moved away from equilibrium, they move back over time.

Observations from nature, however, never look like Figure 2.2, because in nature populations fluctuate. Smooth change does not occur. So, what is the reality of these equations and their predictions? The traditional response is that settling on an equilibrium in a model means that the population fluctuates about the equilibrium in reality (May 1974). Adding more realism to a model, for instance, by adding environmental fluctuations, supports this view in some circumstances, but not in others, as we will see (Section 2.6 Role of environmental variation). For now, however, we can simply

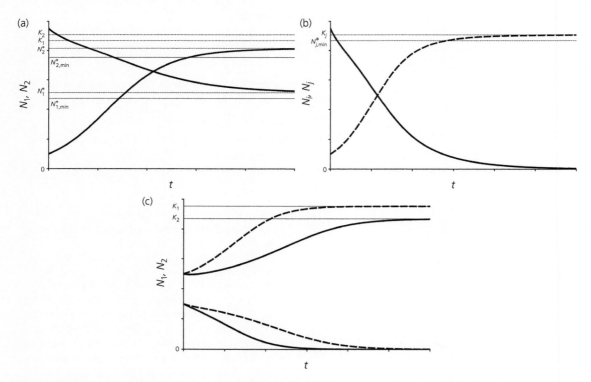

Figure 2.2 Density against time for two-species Lotka–Volterra. The quantities K_1, K_2, K_j are the carrying capacities, $N^*_{1,min}, N^*_{2,min}, N^*_{j,min}$, the minimum long term densities of the species in the presence of the other, and N^*_1 and N^*_2 are the densities in the two-species joint equilibrium. (a) Coexistence and convergence on the joint equilibrium, $\alpha_{21} < \alpha_{11}, \alpha_{12} < \alpha_{22}$; (b) exclusion of N_i by N_j, which rises to carrying capacity, $\alpha_{ij} > \alpha_{jj}, \alpha_{ji} < \alpha_{ii}$; (c) contingent exclusion with solid ($N_1(0)$ low, $N_2(0)$ high) and dashed lines ($N_1(0)$ high, $N_2(0)$ low) illustrating dependence of the outcome on the initial conditions, $\alpha_{21} > \alpha_{11}, \alpha_{12} > \alpha_{22}$.

Box 2.2 Isoclines, equilibrium, and outcomes

Figure 2.3 plots the species' densities against each other (curved lines) as they change over time for the same scenarios as Figure 2.2, but for a range of different initial points, $(N_1(0), N_2(0))$. In Figure 2.3a (coexistence), all these trajectories converge on a central equilibrium point defined by zero growth rates for both species. In Figure 2.3b, there is a dominant species, and no central equilibrium point. Instead, the system converges on the boundary equilibrium where N_j is at carrying capacity and $N_i = 0$. In Figure 2.3c, the central equilibrium point is unstable: all trajectories move away from it to one or other of the boundary equilibria, depending on the starting location of the trajectory.

The diagonal straight lines are the 0-growth isoclines, which define for each N_i a line of densities for which $r_i(t) = 0$. Thus, setting Equations (B2.1.4) to zero and rearranging gives

$$\alpha_{11}N_1 + \alpha_{12}N_2 = 1 \qquad (B2.2.1)$$

and

$$\alpha_{21}N_1 + \alpha_{22}N_2 = 1,$$

which define respectively the 0-growth isoclines for N_1 and N_2. As shown in the figures, trajectories cross N_2's isocline horizontally, and N_1's vertically. Moreover, a species has positive growth above its isocline, and negative growth below it. From these rules, it is possible to determine where the trajectories must go, and the outcomes depicted in these figures by rigorous argument.

The intersection of the isoclines defines zero growth for both species and hence an equilibrium point, (N_1^*, N_2^*), for the system (Figures 2.3a,c), as the simultaneous solution of equations (B2.2.1):

$$N_1^* = \frac{\alpha_{22} - \alpha_{12}}{\alpha_{11}\alpha_{22} - \alpha_{12}\alpha_{21}}, N_2^* = \frac{\alpha_{11} - \alpha_{21}}{\alpha_{11}\alpha_{22} - \alpha_{12}\alpha_{21}}. \qquad (B2.2.2)$$

In the case of coexistence, an algebraic rearrangement of these formulae leads to the expressions,

$$N_1^* = \frac{N_{1,\min}^*}{1 - \rho^2}, N_2^* = \frac{N_{2,\min}^*}{1 - \rho^2}. \qquad (B2.2.3)$$

Thus, when coexistence occurs, the equilibrium values are inflated by the common multiple $1/(1 - \rho^2)$ over the minimum values defined by invasion analysis (Box 2.1). Further meaning comes from rewriting $N_{i,\min}^*$ in terms of overall interaction, ρ, and average fitness ratios (Section 2.3) to give

$$N_1^* = \frac{1 - \rho\kappa_2/\kappa_1}{1 - \rho^2}K_1, N_2^* = \frac{1 - \rho\kappa_1/\kappa_2}{1 - \rho^2}K_2. \qquad (B2.2.4)$$

Thus, the equilibrium density of a species is an increasing function of its average fitness ratio. Moreover, the species with the larger average fitness has the higher density in the joint equilibrium, not absolutely, but relative to its carrying capacity.

---

note that when a model predicts convergence on a stable equilibrium, small environmental fluctuations would lead to fluctuations about the equilibrium (May 1974; Ripa et al. 1998), although large environmental fluctuations potentially destroy this picture.

The various outcomes in Figure 2.2 for the two-species case are determined quite simply and intuitively by the relationships between the competition coefficients, α (Table 2.1). Key is whether a species restricts its own growth more than it restricts the growth of the other species. If it does, it cannot become abundant enough to drive the other species extinct. Species N_j, (j is either 1 or 2), restricts its own growth according to its intraspecific competition coefficient, α_{jj}, and restricts the growth of the other species, N_i, according to its interspecific

competition coefficient α_{ij}. Thus, the key question is whether,

$$\alpha_{ij} < \alpha_{jj}, \qquad (2.3)$$

is true for N_i and N_j. When condition (2.3) holds, there is a well-defined positive minimum value, $N_{i,\min}^*$, that species i maintains in the presence of N_j (Box 2.1). These results now lead to a fundamental conclusion: stable coexistence occurs when the relationship (2.3) holds for both species in a two-species interaction $(j = 1, 2, i \neq j)$, (Table 2.1, upper-left cell). Moreover, as we will now see, this condition is also necessary for stable coexistence in the two-species Lotka–Volterra model.

When inequality (2.3) is violated, N_j can prevent N_i from increasing from low density. Then, if N_j is at its carrying capacity, K_j, the density it achieves

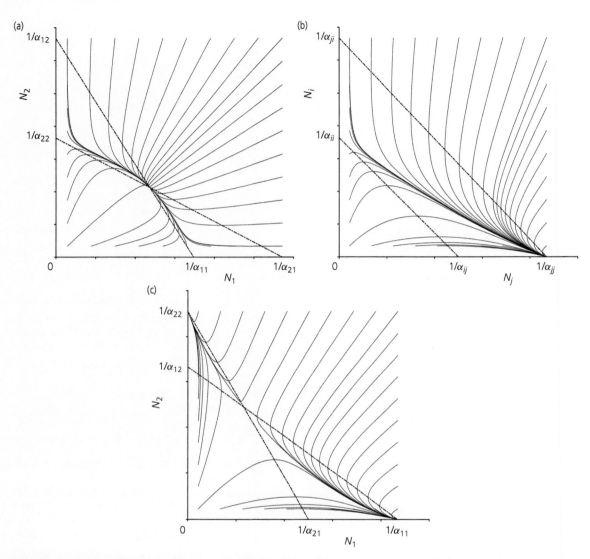

Figure 2.3 Phase space plots for two-species Lotka–Volterra. Thin curved lines are the trajectories of the community over time for a range of different starting values. Dashed lines are the 0-growth isoclines. In all cases, the isocline for N_i ends at $1/\alpha_{ii}$ on the N_i axis. (a) Coexistence and convergence on the central equilibrium point, $\alpha_{21} < \alpha_{11}, \alpha_{12} < \alpha_{22}$; (b) exclusion of N_i by N_j and convergence on the boundary equilibrium $(1/\alpha_{jj}, 0) = (K_j, 0), \alpha_{ij} > \alpha_{jj}, \alpha_{ji} < \alpha_{ii}$; (c) contingent exclusion and divergence from the central equilibrium to boundary equilibria, $\alpha_{21} > \alpha_{11}, \alpha_{12} > \alpha_{22}$.

when present alone, N_i will have negative growth, and head to extinction. In this way, N_j can keep N_i out of the system. Whether N_j can drive N_i extinct from other initial densities depends on whether $\alpha_{ii} > \alpha_{ji}$, i.e., whether N_i restricts its own growth more than it restricts the growth of N_j. If it does, then N_j can exclude N_i at low density, but N_i cannot

prevent N_j from increasing from low density. The ultimate outcome (Box 2.2), is that N_j will exclude N_i regardless of what their initial densities are (Table 2.1, lower left and upper right, and Figure 2.2b). If each species affects the other more strongly than itself ($\alpha_{11} < \alpha_{21}$ and $\alpha_{22} < \alpha_{12}$), each species can prevent the other from increasing

Table 2.1 Outcomes in two-species Lotka–Volterra competition.

	$\alpha_{21} < \alpha_{11}$	$\alpha_{21} > \alpha_{11}$
$\alpha_{12} < \alpha_{22}$	Stable equilibrial coexistence	N_1 excludes N_2
$\alpha_{12} > \alpha_{22}$	N_2 excludes N_1	The first to arrive excludes the second

Boundary cases

$\alpha_{ij} = \alpha_{jj}, \alpha_{ji} < \alpha_{ii}$: N_j excludes N_i;

$\alpha_{ij} = \alpha_{jj}, \alpha_{ji} > \alpha_{ii}$: N_i excludes N_j;

$\alpha_{21} = \alpha_{11}, \alpha_{12} = \alpha_{22}$: neutral coexistence.

from low density. The outcome is contingent competitive exclusion: whichever species has the initial density advantage excludes the other (Figure 2.2c). However, because the concept of an "initial" time for a community is rarely meaningful in nature, this case is better interpreted as meaning that the first species to colonize excludes the other.

2.3 Overall interaction and average fitness differences

Whether a species limits its own growth more than it limits the growth of the other species is determined by the overall amount of interaction that the two species have, and how much they differ in their adaptation to their common environment, i.e., their relative average fitnesses, as species. These quantities can be calculated from the relative limitation ratio

$$\gamma_{ij} = \frac{\alpha_{ij}}{\alpha_{jj}}, \tag{2.4}$$

which measures just how much N_j limits N_i compared with how much it limits itself. In particular, the condition $\gamma_{ij} < 1$ is just a restatement of inequality (2.3). Overall interaction is the geometric mean relative limitation ratio (Chesson 2012),

$$\rho = \sqrt{\gamma_{ij}\gamma_{ji}}, \tag{2.5}$$

combining relative limitation of N_i by N_j and relative limitation of N_j by N_i. Interspecific and intraspecific interactions are evenly balanced if $\rho = 1$, while $\rho < 1$, means intraspecific interactions are dominant, and $\rho > 1$ means that interspecific interactions are dominant.

Relative average fitness, κ_j/κ_i, measures inequality in relative limitation as

$$\frac{\kappa_j}{\kappa_i} = \sqrt{\gamma_{ij}/\gamma_{ji}}, \tag{2.6}$$

with a value larger than one meaning that N_j gets the better outcome from the relationship.

Naturally, the relative limitation ratios, γ_{ij}, can be recovered from relative average fitness and overall interaction,

$$\gamma_{ij} = \frac{\kappa_j}{\kappa_i}\rho, \tag{2.7}$$

allowing an especially informative restatement of the condition (2.3) for N_i to avoid exclusion by N_j as

$$\frac{\kappa_j}{\kappa_i}\rho < 1. \tag{2.8}$$

This means that the ability of N_j to exclude N_i depends on how much fitter N_j is than N_i multiplied by how much they interact. If they do not interact much, then naturally N_j has to be quite a lot fitter than N_i to exclude it. Requiring inequality (2.8) to hold for $j = 1, 2, i \neq j$, leads to the coexistence condition,

$$\rho < \frac{\kappa_1}{\kappa_2} < \frac{1}{\rho}, \tag{2.9}$$

i.e., that the relative average fitness must lie between the interaction measure, and its reciprocal for coexistence to occur, which is exactly equivalent to the previous conditions, $\alpha_{11} > \alpha_{21}$ and $\alpha_{22} > \alpha_{12}$ (Chesson and Kuang 2008). The κ ratio and ρ also determine how abundant the coexisting species are relative to their carrying capacities. In particular, the species with the larger average fitness has the

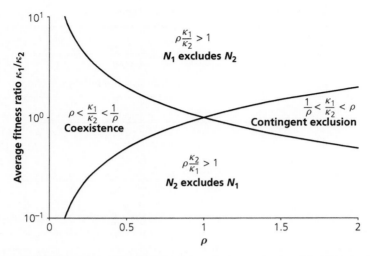

Figure 2.4 Coexistence region in the two-species Lotka–Volterra model in terms of ratios of average fitness and overall interaction. Coexistence, contingent exclusion, and determinate exclusions are the indicated regions bounded by the curves. Note that the ratios of average fitness are on the log-scale, which makes the diagram symmetric in the two species, as it should be because $\kappa_1/\kappa_2 = 10$ is an equivalent advantage to species 1 as $\kappa_1/\kappa_2 = 10^{-1}$ is to species 2. Note that $10^0 = 1$.

higher equilibrium density relative to its carrying capacity (Box 2.2).

Coexistence condition (2.9) and its converses lead to a convenient graphical representation of coexistence and exclusion conditions (Figure 2.4) revealing the tension between the amount of interaction, ρ, and the average fitness ratio κ_1/κ_2. For small ρ, the species can differ widely in average fitness yet still coexist. For ρ near 1, but still less than 1, the coexistence region narrows towards equality. Then, only if the species have very similar average fitness is it possible for them to coexist. For $\rho > 1$, no coexistence is possible because inequalities (2.9) cannot both be satisfied. Instead, the region between the lines of Figure 2.4 for $\rho > 1$ is defined by the inequalities

$$\frac{1}{\rho} < \frac{\kappa_1}{\kappa_2} < \rho, \tag{2.10}$$

and there $\rho\kappa_j/\kappa_i > 1$, regardless of which species is j and which is i. This is the region of contingent exclusion. The dominance of interspecific competition over intraspecific competition in this region means that whenever N_i is too low relative to N_j, it becomes overwhelmed by total interspecfic competition, $\alpha_{ij}N_j$, and must head towards extinction. Outside this region, but with $\rho > 1$, one of the two

species has such a large disadvantage in average fitness that no initial advantage in density can save it from ultimate exclusion.

The magnitude of ρ defines the strength of coexistence in two senses. Small values mean that the range of average fitness ratios allowing coexistence is high. It also means that for any given average fitness ratios, the rate at which species recover from low density is high because from Box 2.1, inequality (B2.1.5), this recovery rate approaches $r_i^0\left(1 - \alpha_{ij}/\alpha_{jj}\right) = r_i^0\left(1 - \rho\kappa_j/\kappa_i\right)$ for low N_i.

2.4 Competition for resources

How do species compete? MacArthur's (1970) resource-competition model, provides one concept (Box 2.3). It focuses on the lower two trophic levels, N and R, of Figure 2.1, where the members of the N guild interact by competition for the resource species R. In this model, overall interaction, ρ, can be understood as overlap between species in resource consumption, as illustrated in Figure 2.5. There, the "utilization function," c_{il}, defining the per capita rate at which R_l is consumed by species N_i, is plotted against l for each of two N species. The resource label l is assumed to indicate

Box 2.3 Density dependence from resources

Under MacArthur's (1970) resource-competition model, growth rates of N species are simply linear increasing functions of their resources, the members of the R guild:

$$r_i(t) = \frac{1}{N_i}\frac{dN_i}{dt} = \sum_{l=1}^{n_R} v_l c_{il} R_l - \mu_i. \qquad (B2.3.1)$$

The quantity $c_{il}R_l$ is the total consumption per unit time of resource l, by an individual of species N_i, on average, and the parameters v_l give the values of the resources, for example as food energy. The final parameter, μ_i, is the resource maintenance requirement, i.e., the total amount of resource that must be consumed per unit time to balance metabolic losses and ultimate death. More generally, there is a conversion constant from resource value to consumer in these equations, but it has no effect on the results and so has been omitted (Chesson 2018).

Dynamics of the resources are given by their per capita growth rate equations,

$$\frac{1}{R_l}\frac{dR_l}{dt} = r_l^R\left(1 - \alpha_l^R R_l\right) - \sum_{j=1}^{n} N_j c_{jl}, \qquad (B2.3.2)$$

showing how the resources regenerate according to the logistic model through the term $r_l^R(1 - \alpha_l^R R_l)$, and experience mortality from the N guild through the sum of the $N_j c_{jl}$. Note that as (B2.3.1) and (B2.3.2) are per capita growth, they both imply that $N_j c_{jl} R_l$ units of R_l are consumed by the entire N_j population per unit time.

Whenever the joint equilibrium, found by equating (B2.3.1) and (B2.3.2) to zero, is positive for all N and R species, and is unique, it is globally stable (Case and Casten 1979; Chesson 2018), i.e., it is approached asymptotically from all nonzero initial values of the N and R species. Uniqueness requires that the utilization functions be linearly independent (Chesson 1990), i.e., the utilization function of no species can be formed by linearly combining the utilization functions of other species. This means that when there are just two N species, these functions cannot be proportional like those in Figure 2.5b.

If resources were not consumed, they would rise to their carrying capacities, $K_l^R = 1/\alpha_l^R$. Thus, substituting K_l^R for R_l in (B2.3.1) gives the maximum benefit from resources,

$$h_i = \sum_l c_{il}v_l K_l^R, \qquad (B2.3.3)$$

which is achieved in the absence of competition. However, because resources are consumed, the actual benefit from resources is lower. To understand how much, MacArthur

(1970) assumed that R dynamics are much faster than N dynamics. This means that the N guild can be treated as fixed in (B2.3.2), and R_l converges on the slowly changing N-dependent equilibrium

$$R_l^*(\mathbf{N}) = K_l^R\left(1 - \sum_{j=1}^{n} N_j c_{jl}/r_l^R\right). \qquad (B2.3.4)$$

Substituting $R_l^*(\mathbf{N})$ for R_l in (B2.3.1) gives

$$r_i(t) = \left[h_i - \sum_{j=1}^{n} \sigma_{ij}^R N_j\right] - \mu_i, \qquad (B2.3.5)$$

where the term in [] is the actual benefit from resources as a reduction from its maximum value, h_i, due to resource competition. The quantity σ_{ij}^R is a constant, given as

$$\sigma_{ij}^R = \sum_l c_{il}\frac{v_l K_l^R}{r_l^R}c_{jl}, \qquad (B2.3.6)$$

and measures the strength of the feedback loops from N_j through each resource l, to N_i. This quantity naturally includes the maximum total value, $v_l K_l^R$, of each resource, and how rapidly resources regenerate, r_l^R.

The growth rates (B2.3.5) are Lotka–Volterra competition equations because they are linear decreasing functions of the N densities, but they give specific formulae for the parameters based on an explicit mechanism of competition. Comparing the standard form (2.1) with (B2.3.5) gives the formulae

$$r_i^0 = h_i - \mu_i \text{ and } \alpha_{ij} = \sigma_{ij}^R / (h_i - \mu_i). \qquad (B2.3.7)$$

Of most importance, ρ and the κ's can now be defined explicitly in terms of resource competition parameters. From (B2.3.7) and (2.5),

$$\rho_{ij} = \frac{\sigma_{ij}^R}{\sqrt{\sigma_{ii}^R}\sqrt{\sigma_{jj}^R}}. \qquad (B2.3.8)$$

Note that σ_{ij}^R is symmetric in i and j, which means that ρ_{ij} is too. Thus, when dealing with guilds of just two species, the subscripts are not necessary. The average fitnesses, κ, are defined in absolute terms as

$$\kappa_i = \frac{h_i - \mu_i}{\sqrt{\sigma_{ii}^R}}, \qquad (B2.3.9)$$

continued

Box 2.3 *Continued*

---

which is the maximum net resource benefit to N_i, divided by $\sqrt{\sigma_{ii}^R}$, a measure of its sensitivity to resource competition (Chesson 2018).

The validity of the Lotka–Volterra competition equations (B2.3.5) as an adequate description of the dynamics of the N guild, depends on two things. First is the assumption that the R guild has much faster dynamics than the N guild. Second is the implicit assumption that $R_l^*(\mathbf{N})$ is positive and therefore a valid R_l density for the relevant N range. The more limited goal of correct predictions about coexistence

and exclusion within the N guild is much less restrictive, only requiring R_l to be positive at the joint equilibrium of N and R. This means that an R species should only be included in the calculations of the coefficients (B2.3.3) and (B2.3.6) if it has positive density at the joint equilibrium. With this exclusion, the conclusions are valid due to the fact that the joint equilibrium is globally stable. The only complication is that as parameter values are changed, care must be taken in the calculation of key quantities such as the κ's and ρ's to be sure that only R species present at the equilibrium are included (Abrams 1998; Chesson 2018).

---

something meaningful, such as resource species body size, allowing resources to be arranged along a linear axis. These utilization functions define the resource niches of the species both in terms of how species are affected by their environment (the upward arrows in Figure 2.1, the "response niche" *sensu* (Chesson 2000a)), and how they affect it (the downward arrows in Figure 2.1, the "effect niche" *sensu* (Chesson 2000a)) because c_{il} determines both the reward to N_i from R_l and the cost to R_l from N_i. Thus, the overlap of the curves in Figure 2.5 is a graphical indication of niche overlap. Figure 2.5a shows partial overlap between the two N species, with N_1 focusing on smaller resource species relative to N_2, perhaps because N_2 has a larger body size than N_1, allowing it to consume larger food species (Morton and Law 1997; Leaper and Huxham 2002). In Figure 2.5b the curves are in direct proportion to each other, meaning that resource niche overlap is complete, but with different heights depicting N_2 as a generally faster consumer of resources than N_1.

Box 2.3 now shows that overall interaction, ρ, measures niche overlap in terms of the resource utilization functions. A value of 1 means complete overlap, and that interspecific competition for resources is as important as intraspecific competition. A value of zero means no overlap, and correspondingly no interspecific competition. Overlap cannot be greater than 1, as one would intuitively expect for an overlap measure. However, a modified MacArthur model, with different effect

and response niches, does allow overlap to be greater than 1 (Chesson 2018). In the calculation of ρ, resources are weighted by how easily they can be reduced by consumption and by their values to the consumer species (Box 2.3). For instance, a slowly regenerating resource would be reduced sharply by increases in consumer density and would corresponding sharply reduce the growth rates of the species in the N guild. Thus, it would have high weight, and more still if it were also valuable.

The average fitness κ reflects the ability of a species to harvest resources above its maintenance requirement, which is the rate of resource consumption needed to achieve zero per capita growth. Thus, larger consumption leads to positive growth, and smaller consumption to population decline. Finally, there is a timescale adjustment in the measurement of κ reflecting the sensitivity of the species to competition. This adjustment explicitly involves the overall magnitude of the species' utilization function, but can be reflective of such issues as life history, for instance, with slower, low-metabolism species being less sensitive, and so less responsive to changes in resource density (Chesson 2018).

The bottom line here is that niche overlap ρ measures how similar the species are in their use of resources, without regard to how well they are able to meet their resource needs. Thus, it does not compare the efficiency of resource consumption between N species or how much competition they can tolerate. The average fitnesses include

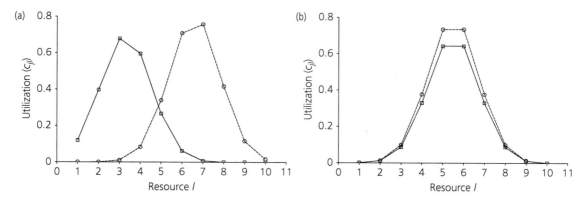

Figure 2.5 Utilization functions depicting resource niches. The two curves are c_{jl} against l, the resource, for $j = 1$ and $j = 2$, and represent the resource niches of these two members of the N guild. (a) partial overlap ($\rho < 1$). (b) full overlap ($\rho = 1$).

this missing information. Dissimilarity in resource use, "resource partitioning"(Schoener 1974), gives a low value of ρ and therefore a broad range of average fitness ratios compatible with coexistence, as shown at the left end of Figure 2.4. In this case, strong and weak competitors can coexist. In very simple terms, ρ measures how similar the species are in their use of the environment, and the average fitnesses measure their abilities in making use of it. Dissimilarity in use of environment favors coexistence, but dissimilarity in ability favors exclusion. This conclusion continues to hold as we add more dimensions of a species' niche to the discussion, including natural enemies and the physical environment. Although the key features of the story do not change as the situation becomes more complex and elaborate, in these more complex situations we can come to see how different components of the niche interact with each other.

2.5 Role of natural enemies

Natural enemies (guild P, standing for predators and herbivores, parasites and pathogens, in Figure 2.1) can create density feedback loops with very similar effects to feedback loops through resources. Holt (1977) termed these effects *apparent competition*, but to Nicholson (1937) they were simply a form of competition. To understand these effects in terms of Figure 2.1, we can trace out feedback loops from N_2 to P_1, and then back to each of N_1, N_2, and N_3. A high value of N_2 allows

P_1 to build up in abundance, meaning that it can then inflict more damage on N_2 (intraspecific apparent competition), as well as on N_1 and N_3 (interspecific apparent competition). Box 2.4 now shows how such effects contribute to the coefficients α_{ij} in a long-timescale interpretation of Equation (2.1). Niche overlap ρ and average fitnesses κ are extended to include natural enemy effects. Most important, the two-species coexistence condition (2.9), as graphed in Figure 2.4, still applies. In particular, coexistence is strongest with small values of niche overlap, and similar average fitness.

Key quantities defining natural enemy effects are the attack rates, a_{im}, which give the per capita rate at which each P_m kills N_i. They define the natural enemy niche, see Figure 2.6. Just as with resources, species may partially overlap with respect to which natural enemies affect them, see Figure 2.6a, or fully overlap, as in Figure 2.6b. Of most importance, partitioning of natural enemies can occur exactly in parallel with partitioning of resources, thereby promoting coexistence (Chesson and Kuang 2008). With both resource and natural enemy niches, two mechanisms of coexistence potentially occur in a given setting, with a key question being their interactions.

Niche relationships under joint resource and natural enemy niches can be considered by grouping panels in Figures 2.5 and 2.6 in various combinations. For instance, Figure 2.5a with Figure 2.6b gives partial resource overlap, with complete natural enemy overlap, while Figure 2.5b with Figure 2.6a gives the opposite scenario. Overall

Box 2.4 Modeling the effects of natural enemies

MacArthur's resource-competition equations from Box 2.3 can be expanded to include the P guild, the natural enemies of the N guild, as well (Chesson and Kuang 2008). Equation (B2.3.1) becomes,

$$r_i(t) = \frac{1}{N_i}\frac{dN_i}{dt} = \sum_{l=1}^{n_R} v_l c_{il} R_l - \sum_{m=1}^{n_P} a_{im} P_m - \mu_i. \quad \text{(B2.4.1)}$$

Thus, natural enemies increase the mortality rate of the consumer species in proportion to natural enemy abundances at the attack rates a_{im} for natural enemy P_m on N_i. The dynamics of the predators are defined by the equation

$$\frac{1}{P_m}\frac{dP_m}{dt} = r_m^P\left(1 - \alpha_m^P P_m\right) + \sum_{j=1}^{n} w N_j a_{jm}, \quad \text{(B2.4.2)}$$

where w is the unit value of consumer species to the predator, assumed to be same for each consumer species. The natural enemies are also assumed to have logistic dynamics in the absence of the focal N guild. This means they must be supported additionally by species outside the focal N guild. If this expanded model has a unique equilibrium with positive densities for all N, R, and P species, it is globally stable (Chesson 2018).

These augmented equations once again allow reduction to Lotka–Volterra-competition form for the N guild by equating (B2.4.2) to zero, solving for an equilibrium natural enemy density, $P_m^*(\mathbf{N})$, in terms of the N species, and substituting it and $R_j^*(\mathbf{N})$ from Box 2.3 into Equation (B2.4.1) to give

$$r_i(t) = \left(h_i - \eta_i - \sum_{j=1}^{n} \sigma_{ij} N_j\right) - \mu_i \quad \text{(B2.4.3)}$$

Here η_j is minimum mortality from natural enemies. Mortality above the minimum is accounted for in $\sigma_{ij} = \sigma_{ij}^R + \sigma_{ij}^P$, with

$$\sigma_{ij}^P = \sum_m a_{im} \frac{w K_m^P}{r_m^P} a_{jm}, \quad \text{(B2.4.4)}$$

summarizing feedback from N_j to N_i through each of the natural enemy species. The weights $w K_m^P / r_m^P$ reflect the

ability of P_m to increase in response to consuming species of the N guild.

These new Lotka–Volterra competition equations would accurately describe the dynamics of the N guild, with the same caveats about resource extinctions as in Box 2.3, if both the R guild and the P guild had fast dynamics relative to the N guild. Although such an assumption might be adequate for a P guild of pathogens and parasites, it is not likely to be adequate if it includes predators or herbivores. However, like the equations of Box 2.3, these equations still provide accurate conclusions about coexistence of the species in the N guild, with same caveats about getting the resources right. There is no similar concern about natural enemy species because their alternative hosts or prey outside the N guild prevent their extinction.

Table 2.2 Critical summary quantities in the three-level Lotka–Volterra model.

$\sigma_{ij}^R = \sum_l c_{il} \frac{v_l K_l^R}{r_l^R} c_{jl}$	density-dependent feedback through resources, species j to species i
$\sigma_{ij}^P = \sum_m a_{im} \frac{w K_m^P}{r_m^P} a_{jm}$	density-dependent feedback through natural enemies, species j to species i
$\rho = \frac{\sigma_{ij}^R + \sigma_{ij}^P}{\sqrt{\sigma_{ii}^R + \sigma_{ii}^P}\sqrt{\sigma_{jj}^R + \sigma_{jj}^P}}$	niche overlap through resources and natural enemies
$h_i = \sum_l c_{il} v_l K_l^R$	maximum harvesting rate
$\eta_i = \sum_m a_{im} K_m^P$	minimum mortality from natural enemies
$\kappa_i = \frac{h_i - \eta_i - \mu_i}{\sqrt{\sigma_{ii}^R + \sigma_{ii}^P}}$	species i's average fitness
$\rho^R = \frac{\sigma_{ij}^R}{\sqrt{\sigma_{ii}^R}\sqrt{\sigma_{jj}^R}}$	overlap through resources
$\rho^P = \frac{\sigma_{ij}^P}{\sqrt{\sigma_{ii}^P}\sqrt{\sigma_{jj}^P}}$	overlap through natural enemies
$u_i^R = \frac{\sqrt{\sigma_{ii}^R}}{\sqrt{\sigma_{ii}^R + \sigma_{ii}^P}}$	relative strength of intraspecific resource competition
$u_i^P = \frac{\sqrt{\sigma_{ii}^P}}{\sqrt{\sigma_{ii}^R + \sigma_{ii}^P}}$	relative strength of intraspecific apparent competition

niche overlap ρ can be calculated for any pair of species N_i and N_j in terms of overlap ρ^P (natural enemies alone), and overlap ρ^R (resources alone), according to the formula,

$$\rho = u_i^R u_j^R \rho^R + u_i^P u_j^P \rho^P, \quad (2.11)$$

(Chesson 2018), where the coefficients u_i^R and u_i^P measure respectively the relative strengths of resource and apparent competition for N_i on a scale of 0 to 1 as given in Table 2.2. This means that ρ might be determined mostly by ρ^R or mostly by ρ^P independently of what the ρ^R and

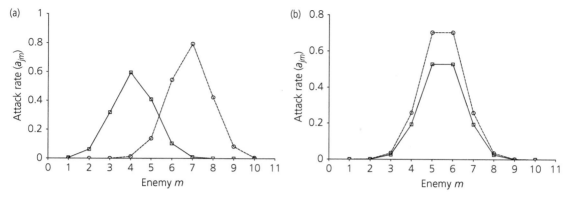

Figure 2.6 Attack rates depicting natural enemy niches. The two curves are a_{jm} against m, the natural enemy, and for $j = 1$ and $j = 2$, and represent the natural enemy niches of two members of the N guild. Natural enemies come from the P guild. (a) partial overlap ($\rho < 1$). (b) full overlap ($\rho = 1$).

ρ^P values are. For instance, ρ would equal ρ^P in the event that resource densities were unaffected by consumption, for example, if they regenerated extremely rapidly. On the other hand, ρ would equal ρ^R if natural enemies did not increase in response to increases in the N species because they were supported primarily by alternative prey even though causing substantial mortality to the N guild.

The relative strengths have the property,

$$u_i^R u_j^R + u_i^P u_j^P \leq 1, \qquad (2.12)$$

with equality to 1 when both species have the same relative apparent competition strength (Chesson 2018). In this case, the overlap measure ρ is intermediate between ρ^R and ρ^P. As a consequence, the strength of coexistence is similarly intermediate between the two. If ρ^R and ρ^P are approximately equal to each other, then the overall ρ value is just their approximate common value, e.g., Figure 2.5a with Figure 2.6a or Figure 2.5b with Figure 2.6b. In the first case coexistence is strongly promoted, but in the second, coexistence would not be possible because their niches overlap completely. In contrast, combining Figure 2.5a with Figure 2.6b means that the coexistence promoting effect of resource partitioning in Figure 2.5a would be undermined by strong natural enemy overlap in Figure 2.6b. Then, coexistence would be nearly impossible if apparent competition were strong relative to resource competition. On the other hand,

strong resource competition relative to apparent competition would promote coexistence because ρ would be close to ρ^R, which would be small. Combining Figure 2.5b with Figure 2.6a would lead to the opposite pattern with coexistence by natural enemy partitioning being undermined by strong resource competition. Figure 2.7 shows how these various scenarios play out.

When N guild species differ in relative apparent competition strength, the species can be considered to partition the major interactions that affect them, with one species being more affected by natural enemies and the other by resources ("partitioning between resource and natural enemy niches"). In that case, the sum of the weights according to inequality (2.12) would be strictly less than 1. This means in particular that there could be complete natural enemy niche overlap and complete resource niche overlap (Figure 2.5b combined with Figure 2.6b), and yet a region of coexistence would be possible. The relative strengths, would, however, have to be very different for a strong effect. Moreover, although, natural enemy partitioning and resource partitioning readily extend beyond two species to give multispecies coexistence, that possibility does not exist when partitioning is between resource and natural enemy niches, not within them (Chesson 2018).

Natural enemies affect, not just niche overlap ρ, but also average fitnesses, κ (Box 2.4), which is especially important when natural enemies might

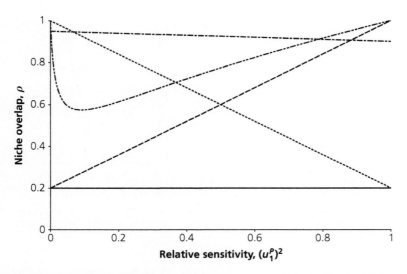

Figure 2.7 Niche overlap ρ as a function of relative strength of apparent competition. The relative strength of apparent competition, u_1^P, for N_1, is given on the scale of $\left(u_1^P\right)^2$ because on that scale the change in ρ is linear for $u_1^P = u_2^P$. The case $u_1^P = u_2^P$ is given by the solid line ($\rho^R = \rho^P = 0.2$, coexistence strength invariant in u_1^P), long-dash upward sloping line ($\rho^R = 0.2$, $\rho^P = 1$, coexistence strength decreasing in u_1^P), short-dash downward sloping line ($\rho^R = 1$, $\rho^P = 0.2$, coexistence strength increasing with u_1^P), and mixed-dash slightly downward sloping line ($\rho^R = 0.95$, $\rho^P = 0.9$, coexistence strength weak and almost invariant in u_1^P). The mixed dash curved line is the case where N_1 and N_2 are oppositely affected by natural enemies and competition equivalent to $(c_{1l}/a_{1m}) / (c_{2l}/a_{2m}) = 10$, with $\rho^R = \rho^P = 1$, and shows that stable coexistence depends on intermediate relative strength of apparent competition.

affect some species more strongly than others. In particular, this will be the case for partitioning between resource and natural enemy niches, which means that the effects of natural enemies on average fitness must be considered too. Naturally, natural enemies reduce average fitness (Box 2.4), and if the species are differentially sensitive to apparent competition, the average fitness of the more sensitive species is reduced more. Thus, for partitioning between resource and natural enemy niches, the more sensitive species will also have its average fitness reduced by natural enemies, with the potential that the average fitness ratio would be pushed outside the coexistence region unless compensated for in some way. There is a common hypothesized way in which compensation could happen: a competition-defense tradeoff (Viola et al. 2010; Mortensen et al. 2018). Under this hypothesis, one species would be more sensitive to apparent competition because it would not be well defended against natural enemies but would have a low maintenance requirement making it tolerant of natural enemies. The other species would

not be sensitive to apparent competition because it invests in defenses, leading to a high maintenance requirement. As a result, average fitness need not be dissimilar, allowing coexistence to occur when differential sensitivity of the species to resource and apparent competition leads to a low value of ρ.

2.6 Role of environmental variation

Species can differ in their times of most intense resource uptake (Hutchinson 1961; Armstrong and McGehee 1976; Abrams 1984; Klausmeier 2010; Chesson et al. 2013; Li and Chesson 2016), thus partitioning resources in time. In terms of MacArthur's resource-competition model, the utilization functions are time-dependent (Box 2.5):

$$c_{il}(t) = \bar{c}_{il}E_i(t), \qquad (2.13)$$

where $\bar{c}_{il}$ is the temporal average of $c_{il}(t)$, and $E_i(t)$ is a multiplicative deviation from this average reflecting temporal change in the physical environment, such as diurnal and seasonal variation, or random variation reflecting the unpredictability of

Box 2.5 Modeling the effects of temporal variation

When resource consumption varies over time, MacArthur's resource-competition equations (Box 2.3) are simply modified to have the utilization functions, c_{il}, change with time:

$$r_i(t) = \sum_{l=1}^{n_R} v_l c_{il}(t) R_l(t) - \mu_i,$$ (B2.5.1)

(Li and Chesson 2016). To understand trends in population growth, $r_i(t)$ must be integrated over time. Because, $r_i(t) = (1/N_i)\,dN_i/dt = d\ln N_i/dt$, the time integral is

$$\ln N_i(T) - \ln N_i(0) = \int_0^T r_i(t)dt.$$ (B2.5.2)

Thus, the trend in $\ln N_i$ over the time interval $(0, T)$ is determined by the average growth rate,

$$\bar{r}_i = \frac{1}{T}\int_0^T r_i(t)dt,$$ (B2.5.3)

which satisfies the formula,

$$\bar{r}_i = \frac{1}{T}\sum_{l=1}^{n_R}\int_0^T v_l c_{il}(t) R_l(t)dt - \mu_i.$$ (B2.5.4)

Letting $T \to \infty$, the average covers the full range of fluctuations that can occur.

For analytical conclusions, resource dynamics are now assumed both faster than the consumer dynamics and the dynamics of environmental change, i.e., faster than the fluctuations in the $c_{il}(t)$. Expressing $R_l(t)$ in terms of the $N_j(t)$, following Equation (B2.3.4), and substituting back in (B2.5.4),

$$\bar{r}_i = \left(\bar{h}_i - \sum_{j=1}^n \overline{\sigma_{ij}^R N_j}\right) - \mu_i.$$ (B2.5.5)

The overbars mean the temporal average, as in Equation (B2.5.4). They are averages over the now time-dependent maximum harvesting rate, $h_i(t)$, and density-weighted feedback loop strength, $\sigma_{ij}^R(t)N_j(t)$. Because the average of a product is the product of the averages, plus their covariance (Chesson et al. 2005),

$$\overline{\sigma_{ij}^R N_j} = \overline{\sigma_{ij}^R}\cdot\overline{N_j} + \mathrm{cov}\left(\sigma_{ij}^R, N_j\right).$$ (B2.5.6)

The covariance in (B2.5.6) is a complication that can be avoided by assuming that the timescale of the dynamics of the N guild is long relative to the timescale of environmental

change. Then $\sigma_{ij}^R(t)$ and $N_i(t)$ no longer have any temporal covariance, and (B2.5.5) reduces to

$$\bar{r}_i = \left[\bar{h}_i - \sum_{j=1}^n \overline{\sigma_{ij}^R}\cdot\overline{N_j}\right] - \mu_i$$ (B2.5.7)

(Li and Chesson 2016). Invasibility analysis, as discussed in Box 2.1, now shows that the two-species coexistence region is once again defined by inequalities (2.9), with ρ and κ now defined as in Table 2.3.

To see how temporal niches and resource niches combine, they first must be distinguished with the model

$$c_{il}(t) = \bar{c}_{il}E_i(t).$$ (B2.5.8)

This means that each species has periods of lower and higher foraging activity, but there is no specific time when a species focuses on one food type versus another. With this model, it follows that feedback loop intensity $\overline{\sigma_{ij}^R}$ splits into a product, $\hat{\sigma}_{ij}^R \cdot \overline{E_iE_j}$, with $\hat{\sigma}_{ij}^R$ being feedback intensity for average utilization functions. We can now define a measure of overlap between species in foraging activity equivalent to overlap in resource use as ρ^E (Table 2.3). Then niche overlap ρ splits into the product of two separate overlaps

$$\rho = \rho^R \cdot \rho^E.$$ (B2.5.9)

Table 2.3 Critical quantities for the effects of temporal variation.

Quantity	Description
$\bar{h}_i = \sum_{l=1}^{n_R}\bar{c}_{il}v_lK_l^R$	Average harvesting rate
$\overline{\sigma_{ij}^R} = \sum_{l=1}^{n_R}\overline{c_{il}c_{jl}}\frac{v_lK_l^R}{r_l^R}$	Average feedback from N_j to N_i
$\rho = \frac{\overline{\sigma_{ij}^R}}{\sqrt{\overline{\sigma_{ii}^R}}\cdot\sqrt{\overline{\sigma_{jj}^R}}}$	Overall niche overlap
$\kappa_i = \left(\bar{h}_i - \mu_i\right)/\sqrt{\overline{\sigma_{ii}^R}}$	Average fitness
$\hat{\sigma}_{ij}^R = \sum_{l=1}^{n_R}\bar{c}_{il}\frac{v_lK_l^R}{r_l^R}\bar{c}_{jl}$	Feedback from N_j to N_i not accounting for temporal variation
$\rho^R = \frac{\hat{\sigma}_{ij}^R}{\sqrt{\hat{\sigma}_{ii}^R}\sqrt{\hat{\sigma}_{jj}^R}}$	Resource overlap not accounting for temporal variation
$\rho^E = \frac{\overline{E_iE_j}}{\sqrt{\overline{E_i^2}}\cdot\sqrt{\overline{E_j^2}}}$	Temporal overlap

weather (Chesson et al. 2004; Levine and Rees 2004; Klausmeier 2010; Chesson et al. 2013; Kelly et al. 2013; Schwinning and Kelly 2013; Holt and Chesson 2014; and Li and Chesson 2016). The temporal pattern of $E_i(t)$ for a species then represents its temporal niche. In some cases, such patterns can be related directly to specific temporal variation in environmental factors, for example, temperature, or moisture (Chesson et al. 2013; Holt and Chesson 2014). The assumption here is that environmental variation can be modelled as stationary, i.e., as having well-defined means and variances that do not change on some longer timescale. Although it is now possible to develop ecological theory with nonstationary variation and so take into account long-term environmental change (Chesson 2017), it is beyond the scope of this chapter.

Box 2.5, now gives a long-timescale version of Lotka–Volterra dynamics applicable to a variable environment, with coexistence conditions given once more by inequalities (2.9) in terms of niche overlap and species average fitnesses. To obtain this particular version of Lotka–Volterra dynamics, three timescales are treated as distinct. First, resources are assumed to have rapid dynamics, followed on a longer timescale by

environmental change, and finally dynamics of the species in the N guild. With environmental variation, average fitnesses involve a mean over time of environmental states. Most important, niche overlap, ρ, is the product of resource overlap and temporal overlap:

$$\rho = \rho^R \rho^E. \qquad (2.14)$$

This result means that the joint partitioning of resources and time leads to a joint niche overlap smaller than either separate overlap alone. For instance, if they were both .5 separately, the joint overlap would be just a quarter, and the opportunities for coexistence would be dramatically increased. Note that if there were only one resource, $\rho^R = 1$, temporal partitioning ($\rho^E < 1$) could promote coexistence alone (Figure 2.8), and it could do so even if the variation in the environment were random (Li and Chesson 2016). This outcome, therefore, is contrary to the equilibrium prediction that with a single resource only one N species could persist in the long run. More generally, it is contrary to the idea that adding environmental variation to a deterministic model leads to fluctuations about the equilibrium predicted by the deterministic model. Instead, these results show that the number of

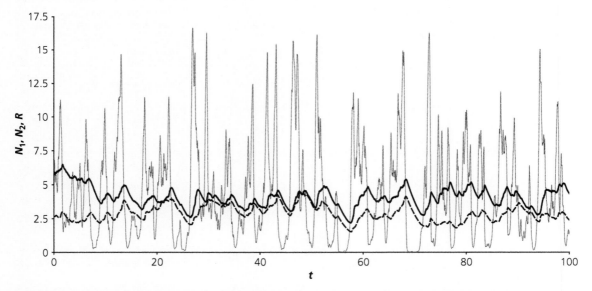

Figure 2.8 Coexistence with temporal niches in a stochastic environment. Simulation of MacArthur's resource-competition model in an environment fluctuating stochastically, but independently affecting N_1 and N_2, showing long-term stable coexistence on a single resource, and thus depending only on temporal partitioning. Solid line, N_1; dashed line, N_2; thin dotted line, R.

species predicted to persist in the long run can in fact increase when environmental variation causes fluctuations in resource uptake. Although differing greatly from the deterministic prediction, this outcome is in line with the classical prediction of Hutchinson (1961), although not exactly as he envisioned it (Li and Chesson 2016).

2.7 Discussion

The question of species coexistence hinges on why the most fit species in a guild does not increase in density until it squeezes the other species out. At the simplest level, the most fit species cannot do this when the species differ sufficiently in the way they use the environment, generating greater density feedback within species than between species. Models help us get into the key details. In the two-species Lotka–Volterra competition model, coexistence is very simply determined by an intuitive and fundamental idea: if each species limits itself more than it limits the other species, neither species can drive the other extinct, and they coexist. This idea is simply expressed in terms of the interaction coefficients as $\alpha_{ij} < \alpha_{jj}$, or in terms of their ratio, the relative interaction coefficient, as $\gamma_{ij} < 1$. In the multispecies case, a species N_i can be driven extinct by the collective action of the other species, but this collective action can never be more than the sum of their relative interactions, γ_{ij}, with N_i (Box 2.6). Thus, multispecies coexistence is guaranteed when these sums are less than 1 for each N_i. However, this conservative criterion does not account for reduction of the collective action of a group of species by their negative interactions with each other, i.e., by indirect effects (Chesson 2018). Box 2.6 shows how such indirect effects can be fully accounted for by generalizations of the relative interaction coefficient and niche overlap. Although these fundamental concepts extend, their exploration in the multispecies case is as yet quite limited (Chesson 2018).

Relative limitation ratios measure the ratio of density feedback, between species versus within species, and mechanistic models allow these coefficients to be specified in terms of the relationships between ecological niches, specifically niche overlap and average fitnesses. Niche overlap is based on measuring the association between species

of the density feedback loops, and thus depends on how much two species share the same mediators of feedback, here being specific resources, natural enemies, and foraging times. Average fitnesses involve various density-independent aspects of the niche, not directly involved with feedback loops, such as the maintenance requirements in the MacArthur models, in addition to traits that are involved with feedback, such as resource uptake rates. Similarity of average fitnesses involves tradeoffs: performing well in one aspect of the niche coincides with performing poorly in another (Tilman and Snell-Rood 2014). Tradeoffs can naturally arise with foraging traits in animals, such as beaks and teeth (Dayan and Simberloff 2005), optimized for only narrow size ranges of food resources. In plants, tradeoffs can arise from architecture optimized for different kinds of light, water, and nutrient conditions or specific soil layers and properties (Schwinning and Sala 2004; Mayfield and Levine 2010; Tilman and Snell-Rood 2014). Already mentioned is tradeoffs in life-history traits, such as individual growth and maintenance requirements as in the competition-defense tradeoff (2.5 Role of natural enemies, previously mentioned).

In the two-species case, there is a simple bottom line: if species have low niche overlap, i.e., do not interact very much, tradeoffs do not have to be very precise, that is species do not have to have similar average fitnesses to coexist. But if niche overlap is high, these tradeoffs are highly constrained. In multispecies cases, this same conclusion is true when there is little structure to the matrix of niche overlaps, for example in the case of diffuse interactions where niche overlaps are similar for different pairs of species (Chesson 2000a; Chesson 2018). Low niche overlap is generally favorable to coexistence in the multispecies case, but coexistence can also involve high niche overlaps for some species, with indirect effects having key roles in coexistence (Box 2.6). For example, strong negative effects of N_j on N_i can be counteracted by strong negative effects of N_k on N_j when N_k and N_i have little direct interaction, i.e., low pairwise niche overlap (Chesson 2018).

Multiple mechanisms of coexistence can be considered in terms of how different components of the niche contribute to niche overlap. Overall niche overlap is a linear combination of separate overlaps

Box 2.6 Multispecies guilds

With more than two species in the N guild, new issues arise, but previous concepts are preserved in extended form. The relative limitation ratios, $\gamma_{ij} = \alpha_{ij}/\alpha_{jj}$, remain key to coexistence (Chesson 2018), but now the requirement $\gamma_{ij} < 1$, for each N_i and N_j, is not sufficient. A partial generalization is the requirement

$$\sum_{j=1, j\neq i}^{n} \gamma_{ij} < 1, \qquad \text{(B2.6.1)}$$

which means that N_i maintains a minimum positive density in the long run, just as $\gamma_{ij} < 1$ implies in the two-species case (Box 2.1). If (B2.6.1) is true for all N_i, they all coexist (Chesson 2018). Unlike the two-species case, however, (B2.6.1) for each N_i is not a necessary condition. It is merely sufficient, because the left-hand side of (B2.6.1) is the sum of the effects that other species would have on N_i if they were at their carrying capacities. Interactions between the species, however, means that these other species will generally be below their carrying capacities in the long run, diminishing their overall effects on N_i. Such interactions between species that modify their effects on another species are termed "indirect effects."

A full accounting for indirect effects is available for the Lotka–Volterra equations derived from MacArthur's consumer-resource model, for any of the forms discussed in this chapter. It is most informatively expressed in terms of average fitnesses κ and niche overlaps ρ. For multiple species, there is a matrix $\mathbf{P}$ of ρ's, one for each pair of species:

$$\mathbf{P} = \begin{pmatrix} 1 & \rho_{12} & \cdot & \cdot & \rho_{1n} \\ \rho_{21} & 1 & \cdot & \cdot & \rho_{2n} \\ \cdot & \cdot & \cdot & \cdot & \cdot \\ \cdot & \cdot & \cdot & \cdot & \cdot \\ \rho_{n1} & \rho_{n2} & \cdot & \cdot & 1 \end{pmatrix}, \qquad \text{(B2.6.2)}$$

where self-overlaps are $\rho_{ii} = 1$. The ith row, $\boldsymbol{\rho}_i = (\rho_{i1}, \rho_{i2}, \ldots \rho_{in})$, of $\mathbf{P}$, with $\rho_{ii} = 1$ omitted, gives the overlap of each species with N_i. The submatrix, $\mathbf{P}^{\{-i\}}$, obtained by deleting the ith row and column of $\mathbf{P}$, describes the overlaps between the members of the N guild excluding N_i, and the column vector $\boldsymbol{\kappa}^{\{-i\}}$ consists of their average fitnesses. In these terms, the two-species requirement $\gamma_{ij} < 1$, for N_i to increase from low density, is given as $\rho \kappa_j/\kappa_i < 1$, and generalizes to

$$\boldsymbol{\rho}_i \left(\mathbf{P}^{\{-i\}} \right)^{-1} \boldsymbol{\kappa}^{\{-i\}}/\kappa_i < 1, \qquad \text{(B2.6.3)}$$

where $\left(\mathbf{P}^{\{-i\}} \right)^{-1}$ is the inverse of the matrix $\mathbf{P}^{\{-i\}}$ and accounts for indirect effects under the assumption that the N guild comes to a positive equilibrium without N_i (Chesson 2018). If these other guild members do not interact with each other, and therefore have only direct effects on N_i, $\mathbf{P}^{\{-i\}}$ is the identity matrix and (B2.6.3) is equivalent to (B2.6.1). This criterion (B2.6.3) leads to a generalization, $\hat{\gamma}_i$, of γ_{ij}, defining the collective relative limitation of N_i with its multiple competitors,

$$\hat{\gamma}_i = \boldsymbol{\rho}_i \left(\mathbf{P}^{\{-i\}} \right)^{-1} \boldsymbol{\kappa}^{\{-i\}}/\kappa_i. \qquad \text{(B2.6.4)}$$

Just like the two-species case, $r_i^0 \left(1 - \hat{\gamma}_i \right)$ defines the rate at which N_i increases from low density, while the other guild members are at the equilibrium they have in its absence. Finally, it is possible to define a collective overlap measure, or a collective overall interaction measure, for a given species N_i with its competitors. This measure combines the pairwise overlaps from $\boldsymbol{\rho}_i$ adjusting for indirect effects to give,

$$\hat{\rho}_i = \sqrt{\boldsymbol{\rho}_i \left(\mathbf{P}^{\{-i\}} \right)^{-1} \boldsymbol{\rho}_i'}, \qquad \text{(B2.6.5)}$$

where $\boldsymbol{\rho}_i'$ is the transpose of $\boldsymbol{\rho}_i$.

To apply these results, the equations $r_j(t) = 0, j \neq i$, can be solved simultaneously to give the joint equilibria of the other guild members in terms of N_i, just as R_l (Box 2.3) and P_m (Box 2.4) were solved in terms of the N guild previously. On substituting back into Equation (2.1) using the parameter relationships $\alpha_{ij} = \alpha_{jj}\gamma_{ij} = \left(1/K_j \right) \rho_{ij}\kappa_j/\kappa_i$, an equation for $r_i(t)$ in logistic form is obtained:

$$r_i(t) = r_i^0 \left(1 - \hat{\gamma}_i \right) \left[1 - \left(\frac{1 - \hat{\rho}_i^2}{1 - \hat{\gamma}_i} \right) \frac{N_i}{K_i} \right]. \qquad \text{(B2.6.6)}$$

This equation defines the feedback from N_i to itself passing through the entire N guild. It defines an equilibrium value

$$N_i^* = \left(\frac{1 - \hat{\gamma}_i}{1 - \hat{\rho}_i^2} \right) K_i, \qquad \text{(B2.6.7)}$$

which is the value of N_i at the joint equilibrium of the entire guild, as a direct generalization of the two-species formulae (B2.2.4). A critical question is when Equation (B2.6.6) is valid. Strictly speaking, it only applies when the dynamics of N_i are indeed slow relative to the other species. Here this means, r_i^0 is much less than the maximum growth rates of the other species, which can apply only to one member of the N guild. Also, it requires the equilibria of other members to be positive as functions of N_i, which necessary restricts the range of N_i values for which it makes sense. Indeed, if the other species do not have a joint equilibrium in the absence of N_i, then (B2.6.6) is not valid for N_i near zero. However, as a result of indirect effects, it is possible for (B2.6.7) to be positive for each N_i even when some subsets of the N guild do not have positive joint equilibria (Chesson 2018). Indeed, (B2.6.6) always has the correct interpretation of defining the joint equilibrium (B2.6.7), implying also that (B2.6.6) always validly defines feedback from N_i to itself through all of the N guild near the equilibrium whenever all species have positive densities at the joint equilibrium.

These formulae give insight into how a positive joint equilibrium comes about. Most important, a positive value for all species at the joint equilibrium means globally stable coexistence (Chesson 1990). At a coarse level, this formula reveals that coexistence in the multispecies case involves the same issues as the two-species case, with small overlaps and similar κ's favoring coexistence. At a subtler level, the detailed structure of the matrix $\mathbf{P}$ is important, as this determines the kinds of indirect effects revealed by $\left(\mathbf{P}^{(-i)}\right)^{-1}$, to expect, with the potential that specific patterns in the $\mathbf{P}$ matrix combine with average fitness patterns to allow coexistence when neither overlaps nor average fitness differences are necessarily small (Chesson 2018).

of resource and natural enemy niches. Most commonly, this means that coexistence strength for the combined mechanisms is intermediate between the strengths of the separate mechanisms. In particular, high natural enemy overlap may cause exclusion even though the species partition resources, because high natural enemy overlap increases niche overlap overall. This finding is at odds with an intuitive view of natural enemies as promoting coexistence because they reduce the effect of competition (Connell 1970). However, when resources are partitioned, the effect of competition is to cause greater within-species than between-species density dependence, which is undermined by natural enemies that are not partitioned. On the other hand, when natural enemies are partitioned, they promote coexistence.

The combination of resource partitioning and temporal partitioning seriously contrasts with the combination of resource partitioning and natural enemy partitioning because with temporal and resource partitioning the joint overlap is the product of the separate overlaps. Hence, the joint overlap is always smaller than either separate overlap, and indeed, the two mechanisms strongly reinforce each other. Similar reinforcement has been observed in models of temporal variation in recruitment coupled with resource partitioning (Chesson 1994), and in also models of spatial partitioning coupled with natural enemy partitioning (Stump and Chesson 2015). What distinguishes these models? In these models with reinforcement,

each time or spatial location defines its own density feedback loops through resources or natural enemies. As a consequence, the number of ways in which species differ becomes the product of the separate ways in which they differ. However, resources and natural enemies are assumed here in section 2.5 to operate independently, and it is the similarity of the union of the resource and natural enemy niches that counts in ρ, not their product.

The approach to species coexistence in this chapter using Lotka–Volterra models has permitted a unified quantitative treatment of the different mechanisms, resource partitioning, natural enemy partitioning and temporal partitioning. The basic ideas of feedback loops, density dependence, tradeoffs, average fitnesses and niche overlap appear in one form or another in many different modeling frameworks, often tailored to specific guilds of organisms (Tilman 1982; Bonsall et al. 2002; Amarasekare 2003; Kuang and Chesson 2010; Muller-Landau 2010; Letten et al. 2017; Wilson et al. 1999), or specific kinds of environment (Connolly and Roughgarden 1999; Chesson et al. 2004; Klausmeier 2010). It has not been possible to consider all the different mechanisms proposed for species coexistence, with spatial mechanisms (Chesson 2000b; Hart et al. 2017), including spatial partitioning (Amarasekare 2003), being an important class of mechanisms omitted, although they are the subject of Chapter 12. Temporal partitioning discussed here has been mostly developed in the literature under the heading of "the storage effect," because under this mechanism, a population can be regarded as storing the gains of favorable periods to fuel future growth (Li and Chesson 2016). Another important class of temporal mechanisms require nonlinearities in per capita growth rates, not available in Lotka–Volterra models (Armstrong and McGehee 1980; Chesson 1994; Yuan and Chesson 2015; Kuang and Chesson 2008; Miller et al. 2011). Multispecies coexistence, through the complexity of indirect effects, adds another dimension to the study of species coexistence. Box 2.6 provides one approach from models based on the key concepts of niche overlap and average fitnesses, but these concepts are not so well defined for multispecies models outside the MacArthur framework used here (Chesson 2018), which has spawned alternative approaches (Barabas et al. 2016; Grilli et al. 2017; Saavedra et al. 2017; Levine et al. 2017).

Although stochastic temporal variation promotes coexistence in the models considered here, other outcomes are possible. For example, having maintenance requirements, rather than resource uptake rates, fluctuate over time in these models causes population fluctuations with no coexistence promoting effect (Chesson and Huntly 1997; Li and Chesson 2016). Population fluctuations are inevitable due to environmental fluctuations and other factors, and if too severe in small populations can lead to extinctions (May 1974).

In general, even though a coexistence mechanism may be present, extinction eventually occurs (Danino et al. 2018). Thus, species coexistence should not be taken literally as forever. Instead, it is about delaying the inevitable species losses, whether the mechanism of extinction is severe population fluctuations, climate change, evolutionary change, invasion of other species or some other cause. But also, species coexistence mechanisms are key to community assembly (HilleRisLambers et al. 2012) and reassembly (Ignace and Chesson 2014), the processes by which newly arriving species may colonize a locality, entering the local community, and sometimes causing exclusion of previous residents. Finally, species coexistence mechanisms are at the heart of ecological speciation, the process by which segments of a population may develop different niches with a genetic basis, ultimately becoming reproductively isolated (Nosil 2012). In these ways, species coexistence mechanisms are a key component of the explanation of the amazing diversity of life on Earth.

Acknowledgments

This work was supported by NSF grant DEB-1353715.

References

Abrams, P. (1984). Variability in resource consumption rates and the coexistence of competing species. *Theoretical Population Biology* 25: 106–24.

Abrams, P. A. (1998). High competition with low similarity and low competition with high similarity: Exploitative and apparent competition in consumer-resource systems. *The American Naturalist* 152: 114–28.

Amarasekare, P. (2003). Competitive coexistence in spatially structured environments: A synthesis. *Ecology Letters* 6: 1109–22.

Amarasekare, P. (2008). Spatial dynamics of foodwebs. *Annual Review of Ecology, Evolution, and Systematics* 39: 479–500.

Andrewartha, H. G. and L. C. Birch. (1984). *The Ecological Web: More on the Distribution and Abundance of Animals*. Chicago: Chicago University Press.

Armstrong, R. A. and R. McGehee. (1976). Coexistence of species competing for shared resources. *Theoretical Population Biology* 9: 317–28.

Armstrong, R. A. and R. McGehee. (1980). Competitive exclusion. *The American Naturalist* 115: 151–70.

Barabas, G., M. J. Michalska-Smith, and S. Allesina. (2016). The effect of intra- and interspecific competition on coexistence in multispecies communities. *American Naturalist* 188: E1–E12.

Berlow, E. L., J. A. Dunne, N. D. Martinez, P. B. Stark, R. J. Williams, and U. Brose. (2009). Simple prediction of interaction strengths in complex food webs. *Proc Natl Acad Sci U S A* 106: 187–91.

Birch, L. C. (1957). The meanings of competition. *American Naturalist* 91: 5–18.

Bonsall, M. B., M. P. Hassell, and G. Asefa. (2002). Ecological trade-offs, resource partitioning, and coexistence in a host-parasitoid assemblage. *Ecology* 83: 925–34.

Briand, F. and J. Cohen. (1987). Environmental correlates of food chain length. *Science* 238: 956–60.

Bronstein, J. L. 2015. *Mutualism*. Oxford, UK: Oxford University Press.

Case, T. J. and R. G. Casten. (1979). Global stability and multiple domains of attraction in ecological systems. *The American Naturalist* 113: 705–14.

Chesson, P. (1990). MacArthur's consumer-resource model. *Theoretical Population Biology* 37: 26–38.

Chesson, P. (1994). Multispecies competition in variable environments. *Theoretical Population Biology* 45: 227–76.

Chesson, P. (2000a). Mechanisms of maintenance of species diversity. *Annual Review of Ecology and Systematics* 31: 343–66.

Chesson, P. (2000b). General theory of competitive coexistence in spatially varying environments. *Theoretical Population Biology* 58: 211–37.

Chesson, P. (2012). Species competition and predation. In R. A. Meyers, (ed.) *Encyclopedia Of Sustainability Science And Technology*. New York: Springer, pp. 10061–85.

Chesson, P. (2017). AEDT: A new concept for ecological dynamics in the ever-changing world. *PLoS Biology* 15(5): e2002634.

Chesson, P. (2018). Updates on mechanisms of maintenance of species diversity. *Journal of Ecology* 106: 1773–94.

Chesson, P., M. J. Donahue, B. A. Melbourne, and A. L. W. Sears. (2005). Scale transition theory for understanding mechanisms in metacommunities. In M. Holyoak, M. A. Leibold, and R. D. Holt, eds. *Metacommunities: Spatial Dynamics and Ecological Communities*. Chicago: The University of Chicago Press, pp. 279–306.

Chesson, P., R. L. E. Gebauer, S. Schwinning, N. Huntly, K. Wiegand, M. S. K. Ernest, A. Sher, A. Novoplansky, and J. F. Weltzin. (2004). Resource pulses, species interactions and diversity maintenance in arid and semi-arid environments. *Oecologia* 141: 236–57.

Chesson, P., and N. Huntly. (1997). The roles of harsh and fluctuating conditions in the dynamics of ecological communities. *The American Naturalist* 150: 519–53.

Chesson, P., N. J. Huntly, S. H. Roxburgh, M. Pantastico-Caldas, and J. M. Facelli. (2013). The storage effect: Definition and tests in two plant communities. In C. K. Kelly, M. G. Bowler, and G. A. Fox, (eds.) *Temporal Dynamics and Ecological Process*. New York: Cambridge University Press, pp. 11–40.

Chesson, P., and J. J. Kuang. (2008). The interaction between predation and competition. *Nature* 456(7219): 235–8.

Connell, J. H. (1970). On the role of natural enemies in preventing competitive exclusion in some marine animals and rainforest trees. In P. J. den Boer and G. Gradwell, editors. *Dynamics of Populations*. Wageningen: Centre for Agricultural Publishing and Documentation, pp. 298–312.

Connolly, S. R. and J. Roughgarden. (1999). Theory of marine communities: Competition, predation, and recruitment-dependent interaction strength. *Ecological Monographs* 69: 277–96.

Danino, M., D. A. Kessler, and N. M. Shnerb. (2018). Stability of two-species communities: Drift, environmental stochasticity, storage effect and selection. *Theoretical Population Biology* 119: 57–71.

Dayan, T., and D. Simberloff. (2005). Ecological and community-wide character displacement: the next generation. *Ecology Letters* 8: 875–94.

Fauth, J. E., J. Bernardo, M. Camara, W. J. Resetarits, J. Van-Buskirk, and S. A. McCollum. (1996). Simplifying the jargon of community ecology: A conceptual approach. *American Naturalist* 147: 282–6.

Grilli, J., G. Barabás, M. J. Michalska-Smith, and S. Allesina. (2017). Higher-order interactions stabilize dynamics in competitive network models. *Nature* 548: 210–13.

Hardin, G. (1960). The competitive exclusion principle. *Science*: 131(3409): 1292–7.

Hart, S. P., J. Usinowicz, and J. M. Levine. (2017). The spatial scales of species coexistence. *Nature Ecology & Evolution* 1: 1066–73.

HilleRisLambers, J., P. B. Adler, W. S. Harpole, J. M. Levine, and M. M. Mayfield. (2012). Rethinking community assembly through the lens of coexistence theory. *Annual Review of Ecology, Evolution, and Systematics* 43: 227–48.

Holt, G. and P. Chesson. (2014). Variation in moisture duration as a driver of coexistence by the storage effect in desert annual plants. *Theoretical Population Biology* 92: 36–50.

Holt, R. D. (1977). Predation, apparent competition, and the structure of prey communities. *Theoretical Population Biology* 12: 197–229.

Hubbell, S. P. (2001). *The Unified Neutral Theory of Biodiversity And Biogeography*. Princeton, NJ: Princeton University Press.

Hutchinson, G. E. (1959). Homage to Santa Rosalia or why are there so many kinds of animals? *The American Naturalist* 93: 145–59.

Hutchinson, G. E. (1961). The paradox of the plankton. *The American Naturalist* 95: 137–45.

Ignace, D. D. and P. Chesson. (2014). Removing an invader: Evidence for forces reassembling a Chihuahuan Desert ecosystem. *Ecology* 95: 3203–12.

Kang, Y. and P. Chesson. (2010). Relative nonlinearity and permanence. *Theoretical Population Biology* 78: 26–35

Kelly, C. K., M. G. Bowler, and G. A. Fox, (eds.) (2013). *Temporal Dynamics and Ecological Process*. New York: Cambridge University Press.

Kingsland, S. E. (1985). *Modeling Nature: Episodes in the History of Population Ecology*. 1st edition. Chicago, Illinois: Chicago University Press.

Klausmeier, C. A. (2010). Successional state dynamics: A novel approach to modeling nonequilibrium foodweb dynamics. *Journal of Theoretical Biology* 262: 584–95.

Kuang, J. J. and P. Chesson. (2008). Predation-competition interactions for seasonally recruiting species. *The American Naturalist* 171: E119–E133.

Kuang, J. J. and P. Chesson. (2010). Interacting coexistence mechanisms in annual plant communities: Frequency-Dependent predation and the storage effect *Theoretical Population Biology* 77: 56–70.

Lawton, J. H. (1999). Are there general laws in ecology? *OIKOS* 84: 177–92.

Leaper, R. and M. Huxham. (2002). Size constraints in a real food web: Predator, parasite and prey body-size relationships. *OIKOS* 99: 443–56.

Letten, A. D., P. J. Ke, and T. Fukami. (2017). Linking modern coexistence theory and contemporary niche theory. *Ecological Monographs* 87: 161–77.

Levine, J. M., J. Bascompte, P. B. Adler, and S. Allesina. (2017). Beyond pairwise mechanisms of species coexistence in complex communities. *Nature* 546: 56–64.

Levine, J. M. and M. Rees. (2004). Effects of temporal variability on rare plant persistence in annual systems. *American Naturalist* 164: 350–63.

Li, L. and P. Chesson (2016). The effects of dynamical rates on species coexistence in a variable environment: The paradox of the plankton revisited. *The American Naturalist* 188: E46–E58.

MacArthur, R. (1970). Species packing and competitive equilibrium for many species. *Theoretical Population Biology* 1: 1–11.

Martinez, N. D., Williams, R. J., Dunne, J. A. (2006). Diversity, complexity, and persistence in large model ecosystems. In: Pascual M, Dunne J (eds.) *Ecological Networks: Linking Structure to Dynamics in Food Webs.* New York: Oxford University Press, pp. 163–85.

May, R. M. (1974). *Stability And Complexity In Model Ecosystems.* 2nd edition. Princeton, NJ: Princeton University Press.

Mayfield, M. M. and J. M. Levine. (2010). Opposing effects of competitive exclusion on the phylogenetic structure of communities. *Ecology Letters* 13: 1085–93.

Miller, A. D., S. H. Roxburgh, and K. Shea. (2011). How frequency and intensity shape diversity-disturbance relationships. *Proceedings of the National Academy of Sciences of the United States of America* 108: 5643–48.

Mortensen, B., K. C. Abbott, and B. Danielson. (2018). Defensive tradeoffs are not prerequisites to plant diversity in a two species model. *OIKOS* 127: 63–72.

Morton, R. D. and R. Law. (1997). Regional species pools and the assembly of local ecological communities. *Journal of Theoretical Biology* 187: 321–31.

Muller-Landau, H. C. (2010). The tolerance-fecundity trade-off and the maintenance of diversity in seed size. *Proceedings of the National Academy of Sciences of the United States of America* 107: 4242–7.

Nicholson, A. J. (1937). The role of competition in determining animal populations. *Journal of the Council for Scientific and Industrial Research* (Australia) 10: 101–06.

Nosil, P. (2012). *Ecological Speciation.* Oxford: Oxford University Press.

Ripa, J., P. Lundberg, and V. Kaitala. (1998). A general theory of environmental noise in ecological food webs. *American Naturalist* 151: 256–63.

Root, R. B. (1967). The niche exploitation pattern of the blue-gray gnatcatcher. *Ecological Monographs* 37: 317–50.

Rossberg, A. G. (2013). *Food Webs and Biodiversity: Foundations, Models, Data.* Chichester: Wiley.

Rossberg, A. G., H. Matsuda, T. Amemiya, and K. Itoh. (2006). Food webs: Experts consuming families of experts. *Journal of Theoretical Biology* 241: 552–63.

Roughgarden, J. (1989). The structure and assembly of communities. In J. Roughgarden, R. M. May, and S. A. Levin, (eds.) *Perspectives In Ecological Theory.* Princeton, N.J: Princeton University Press, pp. 203–26.

Saavedra, S., R. P. Rohr, J. Bascompte, O. Godoy, N. J. B. Kraft, and J. M. Levine. (2017). A structural approach for understanding multispecies coexistence. *Ecological Monographs* 87: 470–86.

Schoener, T. W. (1974). Resource partitioning in ecological communities. *Science* 185: 27–39.

Schwinning, S. and C. K. Kelly. (2013). Plant competition, temporal niches and implications for productivity and adaptability to climate change in water-limited environments. *Functional Ecology* 27: 886–97.

Schwinning, S. and O. E. Sala. (2004). Hierarchy of responses to resource pulses in arid and semi-arid ecosystems. *Oecologia* 141: 211–20.

Scudo, F. M. and J. R. Ziegler. (1978). *The Golden Age of Theoretical Ecology.* New York: Springer.

Shea, K. and P. Chesson. (2002). Community ecology theory as a framework for biological invasions. *Trends in Ecology and Evolution* 17: 170–6.

Simberloff, D. and T. Dayan. (1991). The guild concept and the structure of ecological communities. *Annual Review of Ecology and Systematics* 22: 115–43.

Stump, S. M. and P. Chesson. (2015). Distance-responsive predation is not necessary for the Janzen-Connell hypothesis. *Theoretical Population Biology* 106: 60–70.

Terborgh, J. and J. A. Estes. (2010). *Trophic Cascades: Predators, Prey, and the Changing Dynamics of Nature* Washington, D.C: Island Press.

Tilman, D. (1982). *Resource Competition and Community Structure.* Princeton, New Jersey: Princeton University Press.

Tilman, D. and E. C. Snell-Rood. (2014). Diversity breeds complementarity. *Nature* 515: 45.

Turelli, M. (1978). Does environmental variability limit niche overlap? *Proceedings of the National Academy of Science, USA* 75: 5085–9.

Viola, D. V., E. A. Mordecai, A. G. Jaramillo, S. A. Sistla, L. K. Albertson, J. S. Gosnell, B. J. Cardinale, and J. M. Levine. (2010). Competition-Defense tradeoffs and the maintenance of plant diversity. *Proceedings of the National Academy of Sciences of the United States of America* 107: 17217–22.

Williams, R. J. and N. D. Martinez. (2000). *Simple rules yield complex food webs. Nature* 404: 180–3.

Wilson, W. G., C. W. Osenberg, R. J. Schmitt, and R. M. Nisbet. (1999). Complementary foraging behaviors allow coexistence of two consumers. *Ecology* 80: 2358–72.

Yuan, C. and P. Chesson. 2015. The relative importance of relative nonlinearity and the storage effect in the lottery model. *Theoretical Population Biology* 105: 39–52.

CHAPTER 3

The synergistic effects of interaction strength and lags on ecological stability

Gabriel Gellner, Kevin S. McCann, and Christopher Greyson-Gaito

3.1 Introduction

Theoretical ecologists have developed a relatively deep understanding of how growth rates and interaction strengths influence population dynamics (May 1975, 1976) to whole food webs (May 1973a; Rooney et al. 2006; Allesina and Tang 2012; Gellner and McCann 2016). At the same time, mathematical biologists, including ecologists, have historically examined the role of lags on the stability of simple to more complex models generally concluding that delays are often destabilizing (e.g., Blythe, Nisbet, and Gurney 1982.; De Roos and Persson 2001) but not always (e.g., see Beddington and May 1975). Nonetheless, while lags have been explored mathematically (Cooke and Grossman 1982) and frequently in stage-structured ecological modules (De Roos and Persson 2001), little work has looked at the synergistic role of interaction strength and lags in food webs and ecosystems. This is all the more surprising because nature is replete with lags (see Box. 3.1 for examples). In this chapter, we explore the interaction between growth rates (i.e., r, per capita maximal growth) and lags as well as interaction strength where interaction strength will be defined as a flux-based metric that is strongly related to a consumer's numerical response or growth rate (see Box. 3.2).

Here, we will concentrate largely both on the classical eigenvalue defined metric of stability and the more empirical coefficient of variation (hereafter CV) metric asking the empirical question of how growth rates, or a related flux-based metric of interaction strength (hereafter IS) (Nilsson and McCann 2016) influence the relative stability of models (e.g., we will experimentally manipulate growth rate and/or IS and follow a given stability metric seeing where the system is more or less stable). Recent work has argued cogently that multiple metrics of stability can yield different answers and so where appropriate we will comment on alternative stability metrics (Donohue et al. 2013; Arnoldi, Loreau, and Haegeman 2016). Nonetheless, our goal is to compare modern results to classical results and so we will largely stick to the classical longstanding eigenvalue metric for simplicity and clarity. It is perhaps appropriate to reflect on the role of lags in ecological models in this series historically edited by Robert May since lags were one of the areas May explored (May 1973b, 1975, 1976; Beddington and May 1975) although research on lags in general did not take off near as much as his work on IS and stability (May 1973).

Here, we argue that like May's work on interaction strength, which has yielded considerable

Gellner, G., McCann, K. S., and Greyson-Gaito, C., *The synergistic effects of interaction strength and lags on ecological stability* In: *Theoretical Ecology: Concepts and Applications*. Edited by: Kevin S. McCann and Gabriel Gellner, Oxford University Press (2020). © Oxford University Press.
DOI: 10.1093/oso/9780198824282.003.0003

Box 3.1 Lags in models and nature

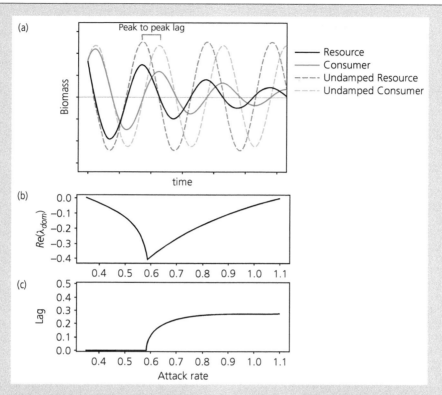

Figure B.3.1.1 A) Calculations of implicit lag on oscillatory solutions follow Bulmer (Bulmer 1974). We do the same calculations on oscillatory decay (solid curves) by using the eigenvector expansion depicted by dashed curves (Hirsch, Smale, and Devaney 2004). Note the eigenvector expansion peaks and valleys (solid decaying solutions) line up perfectly with eigenvectors expansion suggesting Bulmer (1974) calculations on approximation are valid. **B)** Maximum eigenvalue response to changing maximum attack rate. Ultimately high attack rates yield less stable population dynamic responses. **C)** Lag changes with changing attack rate. Note, lags tend to increase with declining stability.

Bulmer, M. G. (1974). A statistical analysis of the 10-year cycle in Canada. *Journal Animal Ecology* 43: 701.

Lags, or delays as defined in much mathematical literature, are responses to conditions that occurred sometime in the past. As a result of this definition, discrete mathematical models are an example of explicitly lagged models whereby this year's population density (N_{t+1}) is a function of last year's (N_t). Similarly, the delayed logistic model—a continuous model—embodies a lag in the response to carrying capacity:

$$dN/dt = rN\left(1 - N(t - \tau)/K\right), \qquad (B.3.1)$$

since here the response to density dependence occurs τ years ago.

Ecological systems are replete with lagged influences. This year's breeding density is a function of last years' breeding density. Ontogeny imposes lags to maturity; indeed, lags exist between all different life history stages and so stage structure in populations drive lagged effects—an area well known by population biologists (see Chapter 5 by Andre de Roos). Starvation takes time, and so this form of mortality, is lagged relative to previous resource conditions. Similarly,

continued

Box 3.1 *Continued*

consumers or predators grow at a rate lagged relative to their resource/prey conditions. At the ecosystem scale, the process of decomposition delays nutrient returns back to the grazer food web. These delays can depend on how labile or recalcitrant the dead material is, and so can be either quick or extremely long lags. There are lags in the response to abiotic conditions, good spring conditions, for example, can alter plant productivity over the course of a growing season (note, phenology shifts due to global change are generally shifts to lags that can be important for dynamics). In summary, we have only scratched the surface here, but lagged effects are ubiquitous in nature.

In the previous section we discussed two types of lagged mathematical models, discrete and delayed ordinary differential equations (e.g., delayed logistic model). In both cases, these mathematical equations explicitly model a lag. We refer to these types of lags in theory as **explicit lags.**

Nonetheless, the nature of dynamic responses to conditions are such that many of our models have within them **implicit lags**. A classic example of this comes from the consumer-resource model as discussed in the text. For sustained oscillations lags are calculated following Bulmer (1974). Figure B.3.1.1 outline how we measure implicit lags for decaying oscillations (Figure B.3.1.1A). Effectively we use eigenvector expansion to approximate the oscillation (dashed curves) that show synchronicity with the decaying solution thus allowing us to use Bulmer (1974) on the expansion. Figure B.3.1.1B,C then show the maximum eigenvalue response of the consumer to increasing maximum attack rates (Figure B.3.1.1B) in the Rosenzweig-MacArthur model and the associated calculated implicit lag response (Figure B.3.1.1C). Note, that depending on the parameter conditions that this lagged response changes. See main text for discussion.

research and significant increases in our understanding of diversity and stability (Allesina and Tang 2012, 2015; Gellner and McCann 2016; Maser, Guichard, and McCann 2007; McCann 2000; Rooney et al. 2006), there exists similar unexplored potential in furthering our understanding of the dynamical implication of lags on growth and interaction strength. The subtle aspect of lags in mathematical models, and indeed in nature, is that they may be embedded implicitly in the dynamics (see Box. 3.1). As an example, in well-studied consumer-resource (hereafter C-R) models like the Rosenzweig–MacArthur model, when a consumer population rises and falls in an oscillation, it does so with a lag to the resource dynamics (Figure 3.1B in Box 3.1). This lag is not explicitly written into the equation of the model but rather is an outcome of the dynamics of the rate equations. Implicit lags, perhaps because they are so deeply intertwined in the dynamics and hard to tease apart, have not been well explored mathematically, or theoretically, although we recognize and consider their effects frequently in time series analysis of empirical results (Turchin and Taylor 1992).

This chapter largely seeks to review existing theoretical literature and motivate the notion

that biological lags, both explicit and implicit, are relevant and are ultimately needed to complete a stability theory that allows a full understanding of population dynamics in populations to whole ecosystems. Further, we argue that beneath much of what we have already learned about the role of growth and interaction strengths on ecological stability, lies a very important role for lags. A role that promises to develop potent ways of understanding how feedbacks at different timescales (e.g., consumer-resource versus whole ecosystem feedbacks) may ultimately influence the stability of nature's complex networks. Understanding lags, since we are altering them considerably in a changing world (e.g., phenology; see Edwards and Richardson 2004; Cleland et al. 2007), is critical.

In what follows, we start from simple population models and review how biomass growth rates (r) in population models interact with lags (discretely modeled or delayed) to promote population overshoots (i.e., where population densities show damped oscillations or sustained oscillations thus overshooting the equilibrium) and variation-driven population dynamic instability. We then use the simple ideas from the simplest case of an implicit lag—a C-R model (see Box. 3.1)—arguing that the similarity between the experimental results of the single dimensional population dynamic model (with an explicit lag) and C-R dynamics (with a single implicit lag) are not coincidence—lags are interacting in both cases with growth rates (flux-based interaction strengths in the (C-R) model) in a similar manner to produce instability. This interaction between growth rates (and interaction strength) and lag is therefore expected and fundamental in that we can then consider how nature may operate to exaggerate this lag effect (hereafter, called **lag excitation**) or interfere with this lag effect (hereafter, **lag interference**). We then highlight some theoretical examples of the interactions between interaction strength and lags revisiting old results in terms of the potential roles lags are likely playing. We end by arguing there is much room for future theoretical and empirical results in unpacking the role of lags across scales in the dynamics and stability of whole ecological systems.

3.2 Population models: The interactive role of growth and lags

To explore the role of lags it is informative to start with the simplest building block of food webs and ecosystems, the population model without structure. Here, let us review how growth rates influence stability in a number of population models both unlagged and lagged. Note, that growth rates in a population model are akin to the positive interaction strengths in consumer-resource interactions (see Box 3.2) and so, this will allow us to create a coherent perspective on lags (through growth rates) from population model to whole ecosystem models.

Let us start with the most basic and common of population models. The logistic population model (e.g., $dN/dt = rN(1 - N/K)$ and ask how maximum growth rate, r, impacts the stability (return times, eigenvalues) of the model. It is simple to solve for the eigenvalue of the equilibrium at K (carrying capacity) to see that the return time is $-r$ (Figure 3.1A). This suggests that the population, N, returns to the carrying capacity after a tiny perturbation at rate, $-r$. Larger r means faster return time. The system becomes more stable with increased growth. Metrics of non-local stability from a stochastic

version of this model (e.g., continuous random normally distributed perturbations where we follow the coefficient of variation) yield similar answers (Figure 3.1B). In this latter case, the rapid returns tighten the noisy dynamics around the equilibrium. The point being increased growth rates broadly stabilize these dynamics. From the perspective of lags, there are no lags in this very simple model. A system without lags, at least the very simple single dimensional system, has the property that growth rate decreases return times and bounds dynamics more tightly around K. Note, one can devise structured stochasticity that may defy this result, but it is a very non-generic form of stochasticity that would do this—the answer of increased stability is quite robust.

While we have shown this with the simple logistic other forms of unstructured population models of single dimension that contain a carrying capacity yield the same result (Gellner and McCann 2016). Thus, in summary, our first main point is that in unlagged population models, increased growth rate is only stabilizing. From a stability perspective, then, there is no cost to growth rate in these simple models without lags. This is a very simple result, but it is very informative from the perspective of lags. As an example, one might conjecture that even in any higher dimensional model (e.g., food web) that have no lags (implicit or explicit; Box 3.1), then increased growth rates, or increased interaction strengths (see Box 3.2 which equates growth rates with flux-based interaction strengths) ought to drive increased stability as well (i.e., remove oscillations). If we imagine the multi-species case without lags, we have to be careful though as there is at least one caveat. That is, in the multi-species case, increasing growth rates to a consumer without lags may not drive oscillatory instability if our result from the simple continuous logistic are general, but it still may lead to the suppression of one or a few resources to extremely low and therefore non-persistent densities. In this case, we might expect the return time away from the equilibrium to be quite rapid (e.g., C rebounds rapidly due to the high growth rates until C is very close to its equilibrium value) and then the dynamics slow down enormously once the resource equilibrium is close to the suppressed

Box 3.2   Growth rates and a simple flux-based metric of interaction strength

In a simple population model ($dN/dt = rN - (rN^2)/K$; see mass balance Box Figure B.3.2A), r, the per maximum per capita growth rate governs the flux rate into the biomass pool (i.e., positive rN term). Effectively this tells us the growth potential of this population N. Similarly, a consumer-resource (C-R) model, the growth potential for the consumer is $eCF(R)$; where $F(R)$ is the functional response (e.g., type II is $a_{max}R/(R + R_0)$); e is conversion efficiency of resource

biomass into consumer biomass; a_{max} is the maximal attack rate; R_0 is the half saturation density. This is shown in the mass balance diagram for the consumer-resource model (see Box B.3.2B) as an influx term akin to the rN term of the population model. Note, flux-based interaction strength has frequently been linked to the coupling terms (i.e., the negative functional response in the C-R mass balance model and the positive numerical response term discussed previously). There have been variants on the appropriate form from total biomass flux to per capita but nonetheless all of these metrics, in a sense, encapsulate the growth potential of the consumer in a manner that is consistent with the growth potential of r in the population models. Here, we define interaction strength as the following:

$$IS_{CR} = \frac{eF(R)}{CR}$$
$$IS_{RC} = \frac{F(R)}{CR}.$$

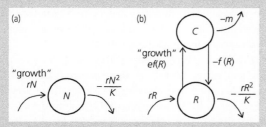

Figure B.3.2.1 Mass balance models showing underlying fluxes for a standard population model **A)** and a consumer-resource model. **B)** Growth rate fluxes into population model are similar to the numerical response flux of the consumer resource interaction in that both are the "growth" terms of the underling dynamical system.

Cleland, E., Chuine, I., and Menzel, A. et al. (2007). Shifting plant phenology in response to global change. *Trends in Ecology and Evolution* 22: 357–65.

By making the previous per coupling term (i.e., CR), this interaction strength metric effectively defines interaction strength as the expected instantaneous frequency of C-R collisions in unit space. Doing this, makes the relationship to maximum growth rate, r, clear. For example, following the positive interaction strength of a type I functional response in a model experiment means that we follow the key consumer growth parameters, ea_{max}—both terms that drive the size of the flux into the following consumer box as r does for the population model.

near zero resource equilibrium value (this is a case where different stability metrics may yield different answers as warned by (Arnoldi, Loreau and Haegeman 2016; Donohue et al. 2016). So, even here, under the assumption of no lags, one would expect instability with large interaction strengths, though it would occur not by wild oscillations but by the complete loss of an interior equilibrium (i.e., an R pushed to zero densities and a bifurcation). Nonetheless, our conjecture from the single species models without lags suggests we would see strong stabilization with increased interaction strengths (i.e., no oscillation) until a species nears a bifurcation point signaling the loss of an entire equilibrium (e.g., via a transcritical bifurcation). This result occurs, for example, in multispecies models with subsidies whereby oscillations are suppressed but

suppression drives instability (Huxel and McCann 1998; Takimoto, Iwata, and Murakami 2002). We argue later that multiple resources being out-of-phase can effectively remove the lag as seen by a generalist consumer and this may in fact be what is going in a constant or out-of-phase seasonal subsidies.

The next question we consider is what do lags do to the previous simple models? Lags, as discussed in Box. 3.1 enter either through the application of discrete equations or through a delayed differential equation model. Either way, the lag suddenly drives a very different dynamic response. Figure 3.2A shows the response of increasing r for the discrete Ricker model which is similar in biological assumptions to the continuous logistic model but with a lag of one (May 1975,

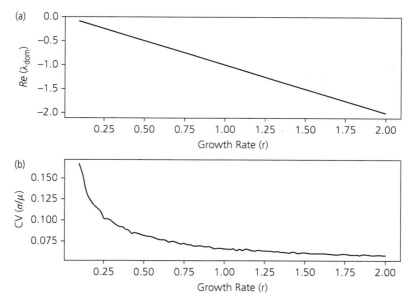

Figure 3.1 A) Maximum real eigenvalue (estimate of return time) from continuous deterministic logistic model with changes in the intrinsic growth rate (r). **B)** Coefficient of variation for continuous stochastic logistic model with changes in the intrinsic growth rate (r).

1976; Levin and May 1976). Generally, all discrete models explicitly have a lag. For low to moderate growth rates (i.e., r), the population stability is increased as before, but for higher growth rates the population stability is decreased (Figure 3.2A,B). Indeed, at some point the equilibrium becomes unstable and produces wild cycles and even chaos (Figure 3.2B), the variation in these non-equilibrium dynamics grow in size with increases in r. Note, the point at which increases in r become destabilizing (identified in Figure 3.2A) is also the point where the eigenvalues for the discrete model become negative (but absolute value less than 1) suggesting fluctuating decay to the equilibrium. A similar answer occurs for delayed logistic models with the eigenvalue becoming complex (meaning the population density overshoots on its way to the equilibrium in discrete models; (May 1973b)). Thus, lags in simple population models are inspiring instability for strong maximal growth rates. The result can be phrased as follows: a lag plus increased growth rate ultimately drives instability, delaying return times and ultimately inspiring wildly varying population fluctuations. Stochastic results measuring CV readily yield the same

qualitative answer under these same conditions (Figure 3.2C).

Note, research has recently phrased this first stabilizing phase dominated by negative real eigenvalues and increasing stability as **non-excitable dynamics** (growth rates do not inspire fluctuations only quicker return times) and the overshooting dynamic phase (i.e., both oscillatory decay and fluctuations) as **excitable dynamics** (growth rates tend to inspire increased overshot and fluctuations and so growth excites dynamics). These results suggest that we may expect similar responses in systems with implicit lags (e.g., the base building block of all food webs, the C-R interaction). We now go beyond a single population model by adding a consumer. This increase in dimension effectively allows us to add a single implicit delay to the logistic model via the consumer response—that is, the consumer can now have an implicit lagged response to resource growth as discussed previously, although the extent to which it expresses itself will depend on the parameters as discussed in Box. 3.1. This time, we will investigate how a flux-based interaction strength metric (defined in Box. 3.2; also see (Nilsson and McCann 2016), that

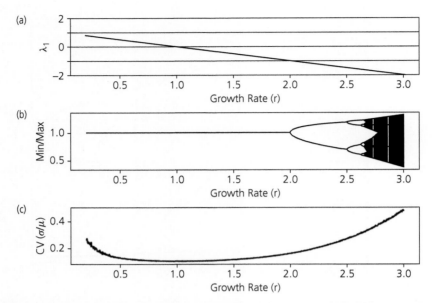

Figure 3.2 A) Maximum real eigenvalue (estimate of return time) for different growth rate (r) values from discrete Ricker model, which is a discrete analog to the continuous logistic model. Discrete eigenvalues are stable when $|\lambda| < 1$ and fluctuating decay when negative. **B)** Bifurcation diagram (i.e., local maxima and minima on the attractor) across the same range in growth rates (r), **C)** Coefficient of variation for discrete stochastic Ricker model with changes in the intrinsic growth rate (r). Note, CV directionally consistent with eigenvalue.

is qualitatively similar to how r influences stability in single population models. We expect similarities to the previous lagged population model.

3.3 Consumer-Resource models: The interactive role of IS and lags

To keep our synthesis consistent, we ask how altering consumer growth potential, or similarly interaction strength (e.g., increasing e and a) alter the stability of C-R interactions. Figure 3A–3D shows the response for the simple type I, and II functional response for both maximum eigenvalue and a stochastically forced case where we measure CV. All show the characteristic bi-phasic stability responses as already predicted and all transition at precisely the point the eigenvalues switch from real to complex. The result thus suggests again the following: *lag plus relatively high growth rates (here, high IS_{CR}) yields increasingly less stable dynamic outcome. The implicit lag expressing itself with the onset of complex eigenvalues and overshoot dynamics.*

Box. 3.1. discusses this latter result of lags expressing themselves to different extents with changing C-R population dynamics (see Figure B.3.1.1). Here, the implicit lag (calculations discussed in Box 3.1) reveals itself effectively with the onset of oscillatory decays and starts off at exactly ½. After which, as attack rate increases the lag decreases until becoming the familiar ¼ lag at the Hopf bifurcation (Figure B.3.1.1B,C). After the Hopf, and the creation of sustained oscillations, the lag grows (here via further increases in maximum attack rate, a). Again, this suggests that there is a complex interplay between interaction strength (also growth rate of numerical response) and lag. It is beyond this scope of this chapter but is tempting to argue that for weak decays the consumer population is relatively slow in terms of growth potential and unresponsive, so it weakly tracks the resource driving a large lag. This lag decreases as the decaying oscillatory overshoot gets stronger right until it becomes sustained oscillations (at the Hopf), after which increased attack rates drive stronger oscillations with more overshoot and again leads to increasing lags. To our knowledge, no one has

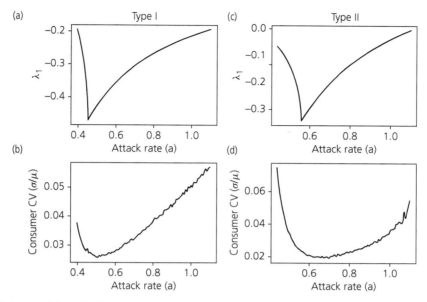

Figure 3.3 A) Maximum real eigenvalue for continuous deterministic Rosenzweig–MacArthur consumer – resource model with a Type I foraging response. **B)** Coefficient of variation for continuous stochastic Rosenzweig-MacArthur model with a Type I foraging response. **C)** Maximum real eigenvalue for continuous deterministic Rosenzweig–MacArthur model with a Type II foraging response. **D)** Coefficient of variation for continuous stochastic Rosenzweig–MacArthur model with a Type II foraging response.

tracked this interplay between interaction strength and lag and it potentially is a very interesting result that requires more thought. As a starting point, we argue that both lag and interaction strength work together to produce oscillations, and therefore, altering either (i.e., increasing interaction strength or increasing lags) has the potential to drive cycles. Similarly, then, muting either may act to stabilize.

Recent slow-fast separation of timescales potentially shed some light on this issue. Kooi and Poggiale (2018) examined a Rosenzweig–MacArthur consumer-resource model by making the timescale of the consumer slow (overall dynamics are a scaler of a small rate, ε such that $dC/dt = \varepsilon F(C,R)$) relative to the resource. This effectively reduces the numerical response (growth rate of the consumer, or interaction strength as defined here) and the mortality or loss rate simultaneously and does so without altering the isoclines. In a sense, this is a mathematical experiment, where we hold the "energy flux" (i.e., isoclines) constant while we change the response ability of the consumer. The rate, ε, when small or near 0 dramatically reduces the ability for the consumer to "track" to changes

in resources. As they vary ε, they are effectively increasing the implicit lag of the consumer and this eventually produces a canard explosion or wild oscillatory dynamics. As such, the lag (and not the change in energy flow) through the interaction produces wild oscillations. This is far from a proof that implicit lags are operating but it is an enticing model experiment using elegant mathematics suggesting that the implicit lag plays a large role in the oscillatory dynamics. The non-responsiveness of the consumer, or the lagged response, contributes to instability in and of itself.

To this point, we have considered very simple scenarios between lags and growth or interaction strength and our answer to this is simple, lags inspire or play a role in producing instability in population and consumer-resource interactions. These results importantly allow us to ask new questions that could provide major insights into how nature operates to maintain relatively stable systems or how nature may under some conditions inspire fluctuating dynamic outcomes. Since nature is replete with lags, and a lag in of itself is pivotal to the dynamics, the previous considerations on lags behooves us to consider how multiple lags can interact to alter dynamics. Two obvious cases emerge: i) **lag excitation** where lags interact with each other to further excite the population dynamics (e.g., two consumer-resource oscillations in food chain coupled to produce chaotic dynamics), and ii) in contrast there may be situations where multiple lags can interact to effectively mute lags (**lag interference**) or even cancel each other out entirely (**lag cancellation**; or complete lag interference). To our knowledge, this latter idea is not well considered in the theoretical literature and given the enormous number of natural lags in real ecological systems this is a surprising hole in theory. We now motivate some possible example of both cases.

3.4 Lag excitation and lag interference

While largely undiscussed in ecological theory to our knowledge, mathematicians and engineers have employed delays to understand how to control dynamical outcomes in many applied systems. This interest has led to examples of where the addition of delays in dynamical systems can excite period-doubling to chaos or, under the proper conditions, do the exact opposite—that is, drive period-doubling reversals to stable equilibria (e.g., see Xu and Chung, 2003 results on the van der Pol-Duffy Oscillator). In an interesting and rare ecological example, MacDonald (1986a) showed using a mathematical eliminant technique that proved in two-species interactions that two lags under certain constraints can cancel each other out to generate a stable equilibrium. Although complete lag cancellation is extreme, the more continuous version of lag interference (whereby a lag mutes or reduces the effect of another lag or lags) remains a more general possible outcome in dynamical systems. Ecological theory has a reasonably long history of considering lags (Caswell 1972; Levin and May 1976; May and Oster 1976), but the ideas of MacDonald (1986a) seem to have not played much of a role in this theory. As an example, the literature has yet to ask what ecological structures and conditions yield lag interference in stage structured interaction, food webs or whole ecosystems (i.e., enhanced stability)?

To understand the role of delays, it is interesting to note that engineers have developed an area commonly referred to as "control theory," the objective of which is to regulate systems dynamics via what they sometimes refer to as feedback stabilization or lag stabilization (e.g., Fiagbedzi and Pearson 1986). One of the major results of control theory with respect to lag stabilization occurs from delayed feedback loops whereby the scale of the delayed feedback (i.e., a lagged response of the outputs feedback) interferes with the lags in the main system. A review of control theory is beyond this chapter but presents a potentially enticing perspective for looking for biological structure within feedbacks that may help govern the stability of complex food webs and ecosystems. Curiously, this control perspective is metaphorically consistent with nutrient feedbacks, via decomposition, that can show lagged response back into the green world food chain that can enhance stability in the classical food chain (to be discussed further). We now look at some existing results within the framework that lags, explicit or implicit, may be exciting or inhibiting other lags dynamically.

3.5 Asynchrony as a form of lag interference?

Rooney et al. (2006b) found that under certain conditions, a large mobile top predator that coupled into separate energy pathways, or channels, could make a food web very top heavy without the usual cost of instability (Rip and McCann 2011). They also showed through simulation techniques that this stabilization result tended to occur because the pathways fell out of phase with each other allowing the top consumer to effectively surf these waves in time and space. Recalling that single C-R interaction, when oscillating or showing oscillatory decay, has a consumer roughly ¼ lagged behind resource dynamics then in this situation, all else equal, we have a consumer behaviorally responding potentially to two different lags. If these resources are completely out-of-phase (i.e., lag each other by ½; see Figure 3.4) then we have what wave theory in physics calls complete destructive interference (Figure 3.4)—the waves cancel each other out. Given a generalist predator that consumes across these

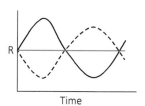

(A) Destructive Interference

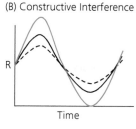

(B) Constructive Interference

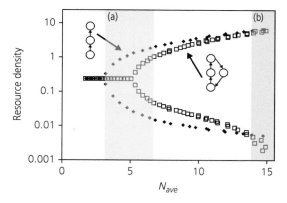

Figure 3.4 A) Two resources are completely out-of-phase (i.e., lag of 0.5) summing together to produce no resource oscillations (red curve is summed waves) for a consumer that perfectly consumes them according to density. This wave interference is called destructive interference (or lag cancellation) in wave theory. **B)** Two resources are in phase (i.e., lag of < 0.5) such that they sum together to produce more resource oscillations (i.e., amplify the summed wave; red curve is summed waves). This wave interference is called constructive interference (or lag excitation) in wave theory. The consumer would be "excited" if it consumed according to resource density in the latter case.

Figure 3.5 Bifurcation of the resource density (R) across a range of average nutrient inputs (N_{ave}). When a food chain contains a detrital recycling (open boxes) they bifurcate to cycles at higher productivity (N_{ave}) than communities without detrital recycling (solid boxes), highlighted in section (a) in blue. The amplitude of resource cycles expands further, and densities reach closer to zero, in communities with a detrital motif, highlighted in section (b) in pink.

out-of-phase prey then the impact of the implicit consumer lag is muted or entirely canceled if it can switch from one prey to another effectively surfing the resource waves perfectly in time (Figure 3.4). Note, consistent with this literature we define interference here as the destructive case where two difference resources sum to lower or equal variance as one of the resources (Figure 3.4A; note, Figure 3.4B is constructive interference where resources add up to more variation together). The issue is more complex if we have a consumer playing a role in driving how out-of-phase these two resources are but nonetheless the consumer, when faced with resources that are out-of-phase, tends to gain same stability from this destructive resource interference (McCann and Rooney 2009).

A second arguably more interesting result occurs in the ecosystem models championed by the theoretician Donald DeAngelis (DeAngelis 1992; DeAngelis et al. 1989) where ecosystem level feedbacks can drive both stability and instability relative to classical food web theory that ignores these larger scale feedbacks. As discussed previously, this is similar to the negative feedback controls discussed by engineers interested in maintaining stability in automated machines. Here, though, nature under certain conditions appears to be able to create its own control feedback.

As an example, McCann (2011) showed that relative to a simple N-C-R interaction without an ecosystem feedback (Figure 3.5; R dynamics shown) that an ecosystem model that has a detrital feedback (i.e., D recycles nutrients back to N) can interfere with the R dynamics in a manner that promotes the stability of the C-R interaction. Let us start with the case that the N-C-R model is producing cycles (Figure 3.5; redrawn from McCann 2011) and then use the same parameter values (for parameter matching technique see McCann 2011), but now for a model with detrital recycling. If we consider a low detrital recycling rate, d_D (Figure 3.5A), then we see that the inclusion of the detritus feedback stabilizes the cycle relative to N-C-R case. Effectively what is happening here is that as R goes down from C overconsumption the nutrients are recycled back into N with a lag that makes the correlation between N and R negative. In other words, the detrital lag means that when R is declining N is increasing—note, this mean N is adding growth to R to reduce its decline relative to the N-C-R case. Similarly, the lag also means that as R is increasing N is low and so it reduces the growth rate of R and therefore reduces the overshoot of C and mutes the rise of R. Thus, this detrital feedback mutes the cycle relative to the N-C-R case—the detrital lag under low recycling rates acts like a feedback control of engineering.

Now, if we continue to increase the recycling rate, d_D, we effectively alter this feedback and can reverse the result driving lag excitation of the C-R oscillation (Figure 3.5B). In this case as R declines N is now also declining approximately in tandem with R. This positive correlation magnifies the R decline while the increasing R stage is fueled further by an increasing and high N that increases the overall growth of the C-R interaction. Thus, under high recycling rate the nutrients have fallen into phase with R and "excited" the C-R interaction (Figure 3.5B). This excitation means that the C-R cycle is now larger than the N-C-R case, so we have arguably lag excitation. This result appears to quite robustly occur although more work is required (DeAngelis 1992; McCann 2011). Food web theory has largely ignored ecosystem models and more work bridging these areas remains.

3.6 Summary

Populations, consumer-resource interactions and whole systems show that generally strong growth rates, and strong interactions, lead to instability (May 1973b; Rip and McCann 2011; Gellner and McCann 2016). A close look at these results suggest that lags play an important role such that without lags growth rates do not manifest as instability. Indeed, in simple continuous logistic population models, without a lag, increased growth rates only increase stability (reduced return times and reduced CV). Here, we have looked at population, consumer-resource and food web literature and suggested that underneath many results lie an important role for lags of different lengths (both explicit and implicit in the models) to generate instability when coupled to strong growth rates or strong energy fluxes through interactions. Despite an early theoretical focus on explicit lags (Wangersky and Cunningham 1957; May 1973b; Levin and May 1976; MacDonald 1986a). the role lags play in food webs and species interactions remains not well understood. Specifically, we argue here that the notion that multiple lags can interfere with each other (lag interference) to mute dynamic instabilities, or exaggerate each other, to further destabilize and excite dynamics (lag excitation) seems little considered since MacDonald (1986).

Research has argued that weak interactions can often re-route energy away from strong interactions to mute and stabilize their influence in food webs (May 1973a; McCann, Hastings, and Huxel 1998). This has led to the search for food web structure that harbors weak interactions that may play a major role in stabilizing ecosystems—structures that produce weak interactions include metabolic constraints (Otto, Rall, and Brose 2007), spatial compartments (McCann, Rasmussen, and Umbanhowar 2005; Rooney et al. 2006), omnivory (Emmerson and Yearsley 2004; Gellner and McCann 2012), generalists (Gross et al. 2009), and weak feedback loops (Neutel et al. 2002), note these feedbacks operate akin to the control theory discussed previously). If lags can interfere or excite interactions altering stability, then further research on the role of lags may point to novel structures that play a role in mediating stability and the maintenance of diversity of complex ecosystems.

References

Allesina, S. and Tang, S. (2012). Stability criteria for complex ecosystems. *Nature* 483: 205–8.

Allesina, S. and Tang, S. (2015). The stability complexity relationship at age 40: A random matrix perspective. *Population Ecology* 57: 63–75.

Arnoldi J. F., Loreau M., and Haegeman B. (2016). Resilience, reactivity and variability: A mathematical comparison of ecological stability measures. *Journal of Theoretical Biology* 389: 47–59.

Beddington J. R. and May R. M. (1975). Time delays are not necessarily destabilizing. *Mathematical Biosciences* 27: 109–17.

Blythe, S. P., Nisbet, R. M., and Gurney, W. S. C. (1982). Instability and complex dynamic behaviour in population models with long time delays. *Theoretical Population Biology* 22: 147–76.

Caswell, H. A. (1972). Simulation study of a time lag population model. *Journal of Theoretical Biology* 34: 419–39.

Cleland, E., Chuine, I., and Menzel, A. et al. (2007). Shifting plant phenology in response to global change. *Trends Ecol.*

Cooke, K. L. and Grossman, Z. (1982). Discrete delay, distributed delay and stability switches. *Journal Mathematical Analysis Applications* 86: 592–627.

DeAngelis, D. L. (1992.) *Dynamics of Nutrient Cycling and Food Webs*. London: Chapman and Hall.

DeAngelis, D. L., Mulholland, P. J., and Palumbo, A. V. et al. (1989). Nutrient dynamics and food-web stability. *Annual Review of Ecology and Systematics* 20: 71–95.

Donohue, I., Hillebrand, H., and Montoya, J. M. et al. (2016). Navigating the complexity of ecological stability. *Ecology Letters* 19, 1172–85.

Donohue, I., Petchey, O. L., and Montoya, J. M. et al. (2013). On the dimensionality of ecological stability. *Ecology Letters* 16: 421–9.

Edwards, M. and Richardson, A. (2004). Impact of climate change on marine pelagic phenology and trophic mismatch. *Nature* 430: 881.

Emmerson, M. and Yearsley, J. M. (2004). Weak interactions, omnivory and emergent food-web properties. *Proceedings of the Royal Society B: Biological Sciences* 271: 397–405.

Fiagbedzi, Y. and Pearson, A. (1986). Feedback stabilization of linear autonomous time lag systems. *IEEE Transactions on Automatic Control* 31: 847–55.

Gellner, G. and McCann, K. (2012). Reconciling the omnivory-stability debate. *American Naturalist* 179: 22–37.

Gellner, G. and McCann, K. S. (2016). Consistent role of weak and strong interactions in high- and low-diversity trophic food webs. *Nature Communications* 7: 11180.

Gross, T., Rudolf, L., Levin, S. A. et al. (2009). Generalized models reveal stabilizing factors in food webs. *Science* 325: 747–50.

Huxel, G. R. and McCann, K. (1998). Food web stability: The influence of trophic flows across habitats. *American Naturalist* 152: 460–9.

Kooi B. W. and Poggiale, J. C. (2018) Modelling, singular perturbation and bifurcation analyses of bitrophic food chains. *Mathematical Biosciences* 301: 93–110.

Levin, S. A. and May, R. M. (1976). A note on difference-delay equations. *Theoretical Population Biology* 9: 178–87.

MacDonald, N. (1986a). Two delays may not destabilize although either delay can. *Mathematical Biosciences* 82: 127–40.

Maser, G. L., Guichard, F., and McCann, K. S. (2007). Weak trophic interactions and the balance of enriched metacommunities. *Journal Theoretical Biology* 247: 337–45.

May, R. M. (1973a). Stability *and Complexity in Model Ecosystems*. Princeton: Princeton University Press.

May, R. M. (1973b). Time-Delay versus stability in population models with two and three trophic levels. *Ecology* 54: 315–25.

May, R. M. (1975). Biological populations obeying difference equations: Stable points, stable cycles, and chaos. *Journal Theoretical Biology* 51: 511–24.

May, R. M. (1976). Simple mathematical models with very complicated dynamics. *Nature* 261: 459–67.

May, R. M. and Oster, G. F. (1976). Bifurcations and dynamic complexity in simple ecological models. *Am Nat* 110: 573–99.

McCann, K., Hastings, A., and Huxel, G. R. (1998). Weak trophic interactions and the balance of nature. *Nature* 395: 794–8.

McCann, K. S. (2000). The diversity-stability debate. *Nature* 405: 228–33.

McCann, K. S. (2011). [OUP-CE8] *Food Webs*. Princeton: Princeton University Press.

McCann, K. S., Rasmussen, J. B., and Umbanhowar, J. (2005). The dynamics of spatially coupled food webs. *Ecology Letters* 8.

McCann, K. S. and Rooney, N. (2009). The more food webs change, the more they stay the same. *Philosophical Transactions Royal Society Londondon B: Biological Sciences* 364: 1789–801.

Neutel, A. -M., Heesterbeek, J. A. P., and De Ruiter P. C. et al. (2002). Stability in real food webs: weak links in long loops. *Science* 296: 1120–3.

Nilsson, K. A. and McCann, K. S. (2016). Interaction strength revisited—clarifying the role of energy flux for food web stability. *Theoretical Ecology* 9: 59–71.

Otto, S. B., Rall, B. C., and Brose, U. (2007). Allometric degree distributions facilitate food-web stability. *Nature* 450: 1226–9.

Rip, J. M. K. and McCann, K. S. (2011). Cross-ecosystem differences in stability and the principle of energy flux. *Ecology Letters* 14: 733–40.

Rooney, N., McCann K., and Gellner, G. et al. (2006). Structural asymmetry and the stability of diverse food webs. *Nature* 442: 265–9.

De Roos, A. M. and Persson, L. (2001). Physiologically structured models—from versatile technique to ecological theory. *Oikos* 94: 51–71.

Takimoto, G., Iwata, T., and Murakami, M. (2002). Seasonal subsidy stabilizes food web dynamics: Balance in a heterogeneous landscape. *Ecological Research* 17: 433–9.

Turchin, P. and Taylor, A. D. (1992). Complex Dynamics in Ecological Time Series. *Ecology* 73: 289–305.

Wangersky, P. J. and Cunningham, W. J. (1957). Time lag in prey-predator population models. *Ecology* 38: 136–9.

Xu, J. and Chung, K. W. (2003). Effects of time delayed position feedback on a van der Pol–Duffing oscillator. *Physica D Nonlinear Phenomena* 180: 17–39.

CHAPTER 4

Non-equilibrium dynamics and stochastic processes

Karen C. Abbott

4.1 Introduction to stochasticity and transients

The concept of the *equilibrium* is central in ecology (May 1974) (see Glossary for definitions of italicized words and phrases). As species interact, indirect effects and nonlinear feedbacks are ubiquitous, and it is instructive to consider if and how these processes settle out—how they equilibrate. For example, understanding how the interactions between a focal species and its resources, natural enemies, mutualists, and competitors jointly govern its population size is a useful way to distill a lot of ecological complexity into a single, concrete prediction. However, the equilibrium is largely a theoretical construct (DeAngelis and Waterhouse 1987; Ives 1995): it constitutes the hypothetical outcome that we would expect if a collection of interactions and feedbacks were allowed to play out undisturbed and in a constant environment. Because real populations rarely, if ever, experience such undisturbed, constant conditions, we must recognize that the dynamics we observe in nature and in many experiments often reflect something other than the equilibrium state (Bjørnstad and Grenfell 2001; Hastings 2001, 2004).

Dynamics that occur before a system has equilibrated are called *transient dynamics*, and they are observed when the initial conditions—the state of the system at the start of an experiment or at the beginning of an observation window—are away from the equilibrium conditions (Hastings 2004). This can occur for two non-mutually exclusive reasons. First, the system may have been disturbed and has not yet had time to return to equilibrium. This is the case if a natural population or community was perturbed away from equilibrium before observations began, or when an experiment is initiated in a non-equilibrium state (Figure 4.1a) (Briggs and Borer 2005). Another way initial conditions and equilibrium conditions can differ is if the equilibrium has recently changed, due for example to global change, and the system has not yet fully tracked this change (Figure 4.1b) (Davis 1986). In addition, an ecological system may be away from equilibrium simply because it is subject to continual *stochastic* perturbations that prevent it from ever fully and permanently settling onto an equilibrium (Figure 4.1c) (Higgins et al. 1997; Lande et al. 2003; Vellend et al. 2014).

Despite all the reasons for ecological systems to exist away from equilibrium, ecological theory is strongly grounded in quantitative methods for characterizing equilibrium behaviors. The staple of theoretical ecology is *linear stability analysis*, which classifies the dynamics of an ecological system that is close to, but not exactly at, equilibrium. It is based on a linear approximation to the true dynamics near equilibrium (usually written in the form of a Jacobian matrix), and determines whether this approximation exhibits exponential decay in the size of the displacement from

Abbott, K. C., *Non-equilibrium dynamics and stochastic processes* In: *Theoretical Ecology: Concepts and Applications*. Edited by: Kevin S. McCann and Gabriel Gellner, Oxford University Press (2020). © Oxford University Press.
DOI: 10.1093/oso/9780198824282.003.0004

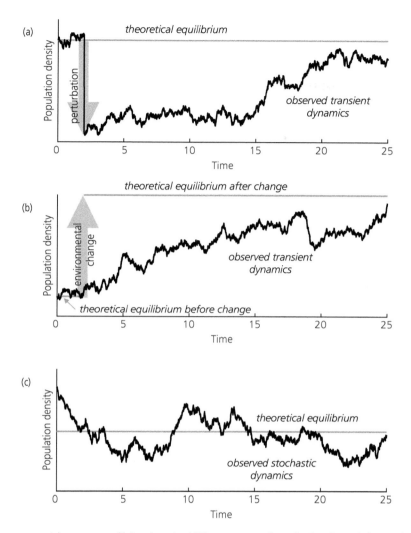

Figure 4.1 Three reasons we might see non-equilibrium dynamics. (a) The system state (here, the size of a particular population) was perturbed away from equilibrium and has not yet returned during the course of our observations. (b) The system was at equilibrium, but the equilibrium changed and the system has not finished tracking this change. (c) The system is as much at equilibrium as it ever will be; stochasticity is continually exciting transient cycles rather than allowing the system to settle onto the equilibrium density marked by the gray line.

equilibrium—meaning the system is approaching the equilibrium and thus the equilibrium is called *stable*—or exponential growth in the displacement from what would then be labeled an *unstable equilibrium*. Details can be found in textbooks such as Otto and Day (2007). The key point is that the linear approximation that forms the basis of this analysis is only valid when the system is close to equilibrium, and thus its results only provide information about the system around equilibria. It tells us whether a population or community near an equilibrium point will approach that point or move away, and how quickly; the analysis tells us almost nothing about what it will do in all other circumstances.

With so many common ways for populations and communities to exist far from equilibrium (Figure 4.1), it is tempting to conclude that linear stability analysis is of no use. However, decades of theoretical insights that are based on linear stability analysis reveal that this would be wrong. Foundational ideas like the roles of inter- and intraspecific competition in species coexistence, the paradox of enrichment, and the burnout of host-parasite cycles were derived using linear stability analysis and have proven robust (Nicholson and Bailey 1935; MacArthur and Levins 1967; Rosenzweig 1971). Still, there are clearly limits to what classic theoretical approaches can do, and theory for non-equilibrium contexts remains profoundly underdeveloped in ecology.

Without an adequate understanding of non-equilibrium phenomena, we risk misinterpreting empirical observations and experiments. For example, when a particular species' or community's equilibrium changes in response to warming, the system may not take a straight path from the old, pre-warming equilibrium to the new one. Instead, the initial transient change could be in the opposite direction from the eventual equilibrium change, and proper interpretation of the effects of warming requires researchers to distinguish between initial and long-term responses (Gilbert et al. 2014). Similarly, an understanding of whether a degraded ecosystem is in an alternative stable state or a long transient is vital to determining if and how recovery to the more desirable pre-collapse state is possible (Frank et al. 2011). With continued development of non-equilibrium theory, our ability to properly interpret data and design experiments to avoid the pitfalls of conflating equilibrium and non-equilibrium systems will continue to improve.

Possible applications for non-equilibrium theory are vast, but this chapter will focus on two specific challenges in the study of *non-equilibrium systems*: quantifying stability, and predicting regime shifts. The central message is that stochasticity and transient dynamics actually reveal much more about the system being studied than we would otherwise see (Coulson et al. 2004; Boettiger 2018). This is in stark contrast to the common sentiment that stochasticity and transients obscure our ability to understand underlying interactions and feedbacks. Progress toward meeting the two key challenges has come from refining how we study and interpret the hypothetical construct of an undisturbed system in

a constant environment, not by setting this construct aside. Fortuitously, theoretical ecology's long history with equilibrium dynamics sets us up well for a future of better understanding non-equilibrium dynamics.

4.2 Challenge 1: Stability in stochastic ecological systems

Many basic and applied ecological question can be framed as questions about stability, in some form. "Stability," indeed, takes many forms; ecologists mean many different things when using that word (Grimm et al. 1992; Grimm and Wissel 1997). We may consider a population to be stable when its size has small temporal variance, when its range boundaries are relatively constant, or when it has a low risk of extinction. We may consider a community to be stable when its species composition, total biomass, or function is fairly constant, or resists change, or returns quickly to its previous state following perturbation (Ives and Carpenter 2007). The proliferation of ways to quantify stability (Ives and Carpenter 2007) and words used to describe these measures (Grimm and Wissel 1997) reflects the reality that ecological stability is a multi-faceted problem, and different facets are more important in different contexts and for different questions. The key to success is to choose a stability metric carefully, and to think critically about what it can and cannot tell you about your system.

4.2.1 Why is this a challenge for non-equilibrium systems?

Linear stability analysis gives a clear and direct measure of stability, in terms of whether and how quickly a system will return to an equilibrium state after a small, isolated perturbation. Because it only applies in the immediate neighborhood of the equilibrium, it is a very localized measure of stability ("local" here meaning nearby in *state space*). The challenge is that the dynamics of real systems are likely to explore areas of state space that are not local to an equilibrium point. By definition, this is the situation for non-equilibrium systems. It is still useful to think about the stability of various ecological states, but the familiar local measures of stability won't be very informative. Instead, we need to think about stability in a more global way. Across all of the state space that a system's dynamics are likely to cover, what states or configurations are most stable—most strongly attracting, most likely, or most persistent? For all its virtues, linear stability analysis has nothing to offer us here.

The *potential function*, which provides a global quantification of stability, solves this problem in some situations (see e.g., Dennis et al. 2016). The potential function is the "landscape" in the familiar analogy depicted in Figure 4.2. If we imagine the current state of the system as a ball, the landscape describes its dynamics through time—i.e., how the ball will roll. Peaks on the landscape occur at unstable equilibrium states and wells occur at stable equilibria. A ball exactly at equilibrium (dark circles in Figure 4.2) will not roll; it will remain at equilibrium indefinitely unless perturbed. A ball that is away from equilibrium (light colored circles) will roll until it reaches a stable equilibrium at the base of a well. In this framework, the landscape itself—the black curve in Figure 4.2—is the potential function. Because it maps the movements of a ball at any point in the state space, it provides global information about which states are most likely, and how readily a perturbation will cause the system to switch from one state to another (Beisner et al. 2003).

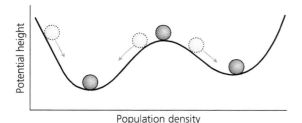

Figure 4.2 Illustration of a potential function for a hypothetical population. The x-axis is the one-dimensional state space and the y-axis gives the height of the potential function, U. Dark balls are situated at equilibrium points and will not roll unless perturbed. Light balls are not at equilibrium and will roll downhill toward stable equilibrium states. The steepness of the slope indicates how quickly stable equilibrium will be approached, and the depth of each well indicates how much perturbation is needed for the ball to exit to another well.

Mathematically, the potential function is the function $U(\mathbf{N})$ that satisfies $\frac{d\mathbf{N}}{dt} = -\frac{dU}{dN}$, where $\mathbf{N}$ is a vector of state variables (e.g., the list of population densities for all species present) and $\frac{d\mathbf{N}}{dt} = f(\mathbf{N})$ is a differential equation model describing the deterministic skeleton (that is, the dynamics we would predict in the absence of perturbations). The potential has been evoked in two ways in ecology: it has been used in its formal mathematical sense (e.g., Livina et al. 2010; Dennis et al. 2016), and it has been used as an analogy (e.g., Scheffer and Carpenter 2003; Beisner et al. 2003). The latter is more common, because while the ball-rolling-on-a-landscape analogy is broadly useful, the function $U(\mathbf{N})$ itself frequently does not exist for multi-species models (Guttal and Jayaprakash 2008, 2009; Dennis et al. 2016). Any system whose dynamics are influenced by something besides a strict "downhill" pull lacks a potential function. For example, consumer-resource systems have a tendency to oscillate, as the consumer population grows in response to a high resource population, causes the resource to crash, then crashes itself in response, allowing the resource population to recover and restart the cycle (Murdoch et al. 2003). Even when a stable equilibrium point exists—so that in the absence of additional perturbations these cycles would get smaller in amplitude through time until both consumer and resource populations level out—the approach to equilibrium is not strictly "downhill". Instead of rolling straight to the equilibrium, like in Figure 4.3a, the system approaches the equilibrium point by spiraling toward it, as in Figure 4.3b. Because the potential function $U(\mathbf{N})$ can only describe downhill movement, not circulatory movement, such a function does not exist for systems like 4.3b. Oscillations due to consumer-resource and other interactions are ubiquitous (Elton 1924; Hanski et al. 1993; Kendall et al. 1998, 1999; Barraquand et al. 2017; Myers 2018), so it is not surprising that potential functions do not exist for most ecological systems with two or more state variables.

This is unfortunate, because the shape of this landscape gives us exactly the kind of global information about stability that we want for understanding non-equilibrium systems. From it, we can extract many of the facets of stability that we care about: risk of extinction, distribution of

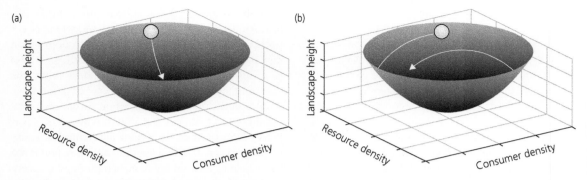

Figure 4.3 Comparison of systems that do (a) and do not (b) have a potential function. The x, y-plane is the 2-dimensional state space, and the z-axis gives the height of the landscape that the potential function is supposed to map. In both panels, there is a stable equilibrium point at the base of the well, where consumer and resource coexist. In (a), this equilibrium is approached directly—the ball rolls straight downhill, meaning that consumer and resource densities change concurrently to map a straight path from initial conditions to stable equilibrium. In (b), the species undergo damping oscillations toward equilibrium. The landscape in (a) would represent a true potential, since dynamics proceed strictly downhill; the landscape in (b) would not. The dynamics shown in (b) are typical of consumer-resource systems.

states we expect to see and how readily the system can shift between them, how strongly a system near a particular equilibrium will resist changing if perturbed, and more (Xu et al. 2014, Dennis et al. 2016). So, what can we do when we're studying a non-equilibrium system that doesn't have a potential function?

4.2.2 A way forward

As it turns out, the true potential function, $U(\mathbf{N})$ as defined previously, is not the only mathematical object that provides us with a global view of dynamics that can be used to understand stability in stochastic and other non-equilibrium systems. Related formalisms, such as the quasi-potential (Freidlin and Wentzell 2012), offer a promising response to the challenge (Zhou et al. 2012, Nolting and Abbott 2015).

The quasi-potential (Figure 4.4), which can be found numerically (Cameron 2012; Moore et al. 2015, 2016) even when a true potential function does not exist, shares much of the same intuitive interpretation as the potential. Both describe the tendency of the system state to move toward wells that represent stable ecosystem configurations. Unlike dynamics on a true potential, however, this downhill gradient in the quasi-potential only partially describes how the system will change.

Another set of rules, which we can derive after computing the shape of the quasi-potential surface (Nolting and Abbott 2015), describes any circulation at constant quasi-potential elevation. If Figure 4.3b represents a consumer-resource system spiraling toward a stable equilibrium point at the bottom of the bowl, the quasi-potential surface describes the steepness of the bowl and thus represents net downward movement, whereas the circulatory component represents the counterclockwise movements of the ball.

The quasi-potential represents stochastic, non-equilibrium dynamics by using information about the system's deterministic interactions and feedbacks, which drive the system toward a stable equilibrium, to derive a measure of how "difficult" it is for stochasticity to push the system against this flow (i.e., uphill). The height of the quasi-potential surface at any particular point in the state space, relative to the height of the deepest trough, measures how much of a push from stochasticity would be needed for the ball to move up to this spot. Therefore, an equilibrium in a deeper well is more stable, in the stochastic sense. In fact, well shape and barrier height have long been recognized as better descriptors of stochastic stability than that provided by linear stability analysis (Holling 1973), but they haven't been used frequently as stability metrics since they were previously unquantifiable for most ecological models.

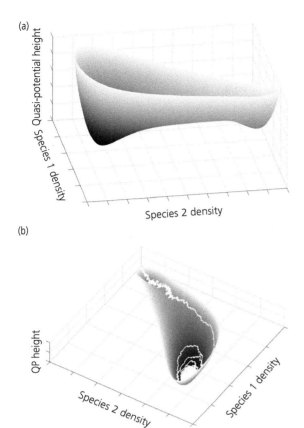

(a)

Quasi-potential height

Species 1 density

Species 2 density

(b)

QP height

Species 2 density

Species 1 density

Figure 4.4 (a) An example of a quasi-potential for a consumer-resource model. The *x, y* coordinates give the ecosystem state (here, the population densities of the two species) and wells correspond to alternative stable states. The surface describes the tendency of the state to "roll downhill" with respect to the *z*-axis. Both wells have a stable equilibrium at the base, but the shallower well is much less stable in the sense that a much more modest "uphill" perturbation is needed for the system to transition from the shallow to the deep well than vice versa. (b) The same quasi-potential, shown from a different viewpoint. The white trace shows one realization of a stochastic version of this model, beginning in the top corner, traveling into the shallower well, then eventually transitioning to the deeper well. Notice that the populations spiral toward the stable state at the base of this well. The system's full dynamics are therefore due to the combined effect of the downhill tendency represented in the surface itself, an additional circulatory component that causes the populations to spiral, and stochastic perturbations.

Model from Steele and Henderson 1981.

Extending beyond the strict definition of the potential (i.e., $U(\mathbf{N})$ such that $\frac{d\mathbf{N}}{dt} = -\frac{dU}{d\mathbf{N}}$) and considering its generalized counterparts affords

us many benefits. First, it extends a powerful visualization tool for understanding stochastic dynamics (i.e., the ability to map surfaces like the one pictured in Figure 4.4) to a substantially broader range of applications (systems that lack a potential, including those with limit cycles and other non-point attractors). Second, it allows us to measure the stability of different states (different wells or other points in state space) that considers the possibility of large perturbations rather than purely local ones. In other words, it offers a global view of stability not given by linear stability analysis. As a consequence, comparing quasi-potential heights at different equilibria gives a far superior measure of relative stability than comparing dominant eigenvalues (Nolting and Abbott 2015). For instance, a stable equilibrium point would be considered only weakly stable in the local sense if linear stability analysis reveals a slow return rate following a small perturbation. However, this slow return rate simply reflects that a (quasi-)potential well has relatively flat curvature right at its base. If this same well is very deep, the equilibrium will be very stable in the global sense— a system in this well is very likely to stay there. In a system that is dominated by non-equilibrium dynamics, due for example to stochasticity, the local curvature of the base of the well (the information given by linear stability analysis) is much less relevant than the shape of the entire well (the information given by the potential and its extensions).

While progress toward applying the quasi-potential and related approaches to ecology is exciting, these methods are currently fairly limited. The computational methods for deriving a quasi-potential are only fully developed for systems with very simple noise structures (Nolting and Abbott 2015), and computation becomes cumbersome with larger numbers of species. Methods for discrete-valued state variables (e.g., numbers of individuals, rather than a continuous measure of population density) are currently under development (A. Strang, unpublished work). Applications to discrete time systems would also be very useful. Despite its infancy, this approach is promising and continued work on extending the concept of the potential to a wider range of systems should be fruitful.

4.2.3 Lesson from Challenge 1: Non-equilibrium dynamics strengthen ecological understanding

When a system is at, or near, a stable equilibrium, we only have the opportunity to observe the location of that equilibrium. In non-equilibrium systems, we are given the opportunity to observe dynamics over a broad region of state space. The stable equilibria are still there and, given a long enough window of observation, we should still see them. We'll also see how the system moves between them and what it does when it's far from equilibrium. Obviously, non-equilibrium dynamics reveal a lot more about the system. The trick is to find ways to interpret and analyze this information, and doing so will generally require less reliance on local, equilibrium-focused descriptors.

4.3 Challenge 2: Predicting regime shifts

The possibility that an ecological system can shift suddenly and unexpectedly from its historical state to a new and very different state, perhaps with no imminent shift back, is a great cause for alarm (Scheffer et al. 2001; Beisner et al. 2003; Scheffer 2009). Ecologists have largely sought to understand this phenomenon through the analysis and application of deterministic models that have alternative stable states (multiple stable equilibria under a single set of conditions, as in Fig. 4.5a) (May 1977; Scheffer and Carpenter 2003). Understanding and predicting regime shifts that occur when one of these stable states disappears (Figure 4.5b) is the subject of Chapter 15. Regime shifts of this type are caused by changes in the equilibrium characteristics of a system in response to changing conditions. So, what about regime shifts in non-equilibrium systems?

4.3.1 Why is this a challenge for non-equilibrium systems?

Regime shifts can occur when a system crosses a local bifurcation or "tipping point" at which one stable state disappears or loses stability (Figure 4.5b), when a disturbance causes a system that was in one regime (e.g., at equilibrium) to enter another dynamical regime (Figure 4.5c; the transition in

Figure 4.4b is another example of this type), or when a long transient dynamic ends and either another transient or the equilibrium dynamics begin (Figure 4.5d) (Beisner et al. 2003; Scheffer and Carpenter 2003; Sharma et al. 2015). Regime shifts caused by non-equilibrium phenomena—long transient dynamics and stochastic perturbations—can occur in completely different ways than regime shifts caused by local bifurcations. Early warning signals associated with an approach to bifurcation, or post-hoc explanations for a regime shift that are predicated on the notion that a local bifurcation was crossed, will not apply to transient and stochasticity-related regime shifts (Boettiger and Hastings 2013, Dutta et al. 2018). Therefore, an entirely different approach is needed for these situations (Boettiger and Hastings 2012, Hastings et al. 2018).

4.3.2 A way forward

Some regime shifts due to transient dynamics are highly predictable (Hastings et al. 2018). Consider long transients caused by a *saddle*—a type of unstable equilibrium point (Box 4.1). At any equilibrium, stable or unstable, the system by definition does not change (its rate of change is 0); it follows that the dynamics near, but not right at, any equilibrium will change but will do so slowly (rate of change is close to 0). Therefore, escape from an unstable equilibrium from very nearby is expected to be slow. Saddles are an interesting type of unstable equilibrium because although they are ultimately repelling (the system state will change to move away from the saddle), they are attracting in some direction (Cushing et al. 1998; Henson et al. 1999). For example, most consumer-resource systems have saddle points at total extinction (both consumer and resource abundance = 0) and at the resource species' carrying capacity in the absence of the consumer (Murdoch et al. 2003). Usually if the consumer and resource can coexist, these points are unstable; however, both are temporarily attracting. When consumer density is high and resource density is low, the consumer will crash—this moves the system toward total extinction. However, because this extinction state is unstable, once the system is near it (i.e., once the

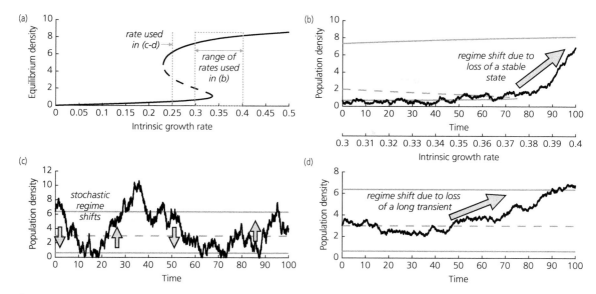

Figure 4.5 Three different ways that regime shifts can occur. (a) Equilibrium population size plotted against an important driver (here, intrinsic growth rate) for a hypothetical population. This system has two tipping points (bifurcations) at which a stable equilibrium state (solid line) disappears. (b) An example of a regime shift caused by changing conditions (gradual increase in growth rate from 0.3 to 0.4 over the time frame plotted) that drive the system across a tipping point. The gray lines show the equilibria given the current conditions (taken from panel (a) and replotted on the lower x-axis), and the black line is a time series. The system had been in one regime (the lower stable equilibrium) and shifts to another (the upper stable equilibrium) as the bifurcation is crossed. (c) An example of regime shifts caused by stochastic perturbations. Even though conditions aren't changing (the growth rate is held constant at 0.25 here, which has three equilibria shown by the gray lines), the system is switching stochastically between the two stable regimes. (d) An example of a regime shift due to a long transient ending. Again, growth rate is held constant at 0.25. The initial state of the system is near the unstable equilibrium (a saddle). Because the dynamics are slow near this equilibrium, the system state can remain near it for a meaningful amount of time. When it eventually converges to a stable state, we see a shift from the transient regime to the upper stable regime.

consumer population has crashed), the system will then move away. With consumers scarce, the resource species will grow toward its carrying capacity. This is the other saddle. Again, this is ultimately unstable so rather than fully converging on the resource's carrying capacity, the system will again move away after this approach.

What happens next depends on the consumer-resource system's equilibrium dynamics. In some cases, the consumer and resource can ultimately coexist at a stable point equilibrium and the system will next tend to approach this equilibrium, provided no new perturbations change its course. In these systems, the dynamics near the saddles are unambiguously transient dynamics. In other cases, consumers and resource coexist in a stable limit cycle at equilibrium, in which overexploitation at high consumer and resource densities causes a crash in both species, followed by sequential transits by the saddle points at two-species extinction and

at the resource's carrying capacity as described previously, before recovery to high densities and another crash to restart the cycle. In this latter situation, the limit cycle itself represents the *equilibrium* dynamics of the system. If the system lingers near the saddles as a natural part of this cycle, it is unclear whether the dynamics near these saddles ought to be labeled as transient dynamics. However, semantics aside, if transits past the saddles are slow enough that we might mistake them for stable equilibria in time series data, it can be useful to think of them as transient states on timescales shorter than the duration of a full cycle (Ludwig et al. 1978; Hastings et al. 2018).

Transits past saddle points have been called "saddle fly-bys" in the literature (e.g., Cushing et al. 2003), although we recently proposed (Hastings et al. 2018) to call them "crawl-bys" to emphasize that they can be quite slow relative to the time it takes to switch from one saddle to another (Box 4.1).

Box 4.1 Introduction to saddle points

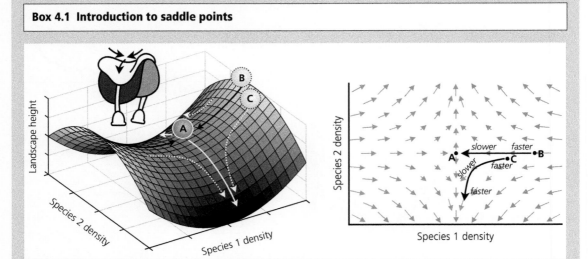

Figure B4.1   Illustrations of a two-species saddle point (see Box 4.1 text for details.)

A saddle point—labeled "A" in both following diagrams—is an equilibrium point that is attracting from some directions but ultimately repelling, much like a marble rolling on a horse's saddle would first roll downhill toward the center of the seat (the center is at first attracting), but then roll off the side (ultimately repelling). Both panels in Figure B4.1 illustrate a two-species saddle point, using the ball-on-a-landscape framework (left) or as a vector field, where gray arrows depict the speed and direction of change in two-dimensional state space (right). If the system is exactly at the saddle point, A, it will remain there because the saddle is an equilibrium. If the system is exactly aligned with the direction from which the saddle is attracting (point B), it will approach A and then stay there. However, in real-world systems subject to stochasticity, neither of these hypothetical cases is likely. Instead, we are more likely to see something like the dynamics from point C, in which the system first moves toward the saddle but, after this approach, moves away in a different

direction. (Where the system goes next after moving away depends on what other phenomena exist in the state space. It may approach a stable equilibrium point, another saddle, or something else like a stable limit cycle. It could even loop back to move past this same saddle again. These diagrams don't extend far enough out into state space for us to know what the particular system depicted here will do next.)

There are two important aspects of saddle points to note here. First, it is significant that the system approaches the saddle even though it is ultimately unstable. Second, notice that the landscape on the left flattens out as it approaches the saddle. This is necessary because the surface must be perfectly flat at the saddle point itself (since it is an equilibrium). As a result, the dynamics near the saddle are slower than dynamics elsewhere in state space, where the surface is steeper. This slowing down can keep the system in a transient state near the saddle point for extended periods of time (e.g., Figure 4.5d).

Therefore, a cycling system like this shows repeated shifts between regimes, each regime corresponding to one of the saddles. The dynamics within each of these regimes are transient, because although the system is relatively static for a meaningful time period, it is not actually at equilibrium and will eventually leave even without any external perturbation. Even though these are non-equilibrium regimes, if we know where the saddles are in consumer-resource state space and

we understand the process that drives the system toward and then away from these saddles, we know the cause of, and can predict the timing of, the shifts.

Our ability to predict the specific timing and nature of regime shifts depends on their underlying cause. When regime shifts are due to stochastic perturbations that bump a system from one regime to another (as in Figure 4.5c), the timing of any specific shift is random. However, we can still make

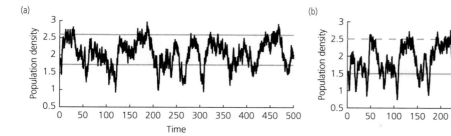

Figure 4.6 Example time series for the prey population in a stochastic predator-prey model. Both time series show two regimes (one near the prey's carrying capacity at 2.5, corresponding to the top gray line, and one corresponding to predator-prey coexistence, lower gray line) with stochastic shifts between them. In (a), both of these regimes are stable. In (b), the equilibrium at the prey's carrying capacity is a saddle and coexistence is stable. Model from Freedman and Wolkowicz 1986.

strong predictions about the expected frequency of shifts and the states the system will shift between. If we have a quasi-potential, we can compute the expected transition rates from one well to another directly from the depth of the current well, the height of the intervening peak, and the intensity of stochastic perturbations being exerted on the system (Bouchet and Reygner 2016; Nolting and Abbott 2015). Thus, even when the exact timing of regime shifts is fundamentally unpredictable, an understanding of the global stability properties of a system gives us direct insight into the expected frequency of shifts.

In addition to knowing how often stochastic regime shifts occur, it is crucial to understand which regimes the system is likely to be switching between. A common assumption, whether made implicitly or explicitly, is that shifts will occur between stable states (wells). Thus, knowing the locations and shapes of these wells is important. Also important, though frequently neglected, is knowing the location and characteristics of saddles for the reasons mentioned previously. Stochastic perturbations that place a system near a saddle, or at a state from which the saddle is attracting, may stay in the vicinity of that saddle for a meaningful amount of time (Cushing et al. 1998; Henson et al. 1999; Abbott and Nolting 2017). Generally speaking, when the flat area around a saddle point on the (quasi-)potential landscape is broader and less steep, the stochastic dynamics should stay in the vicinity of the saddle longer (Cushing et al. 1998). That is, a ball can be jostled around the plateau for longer before eventually rolling back into a well.

Recognizing this role of saddles is again hugely insightful. Stochastic dynamics like those depicted in Figure 4.6, where a system is clearly switching between two regimes (marked by horizontal lines), are usually attributed to the presence of two stable equilibria. In fact, in the equilibrium worldview, this is the only reasonable explanation. However, only Figure 4.6a fits this paradigm. In Figure 4.6b, only one of the regimes is stable and the other is a saddle. Failing to consider the importance of non-equilibrium dynamics would prevent us from understanding the regime shifts in Figure 4.6b.

These are just examples, and they only scratch the surface. Not all transients are caused by slow transits past a saddle, and not all systems will include a saddle amidst the regimes visited in stochastic regime shifts (Hastings et al. 2018). Other situations will require other approaches. Nevertheless, these examples illustrate that even for non-equilibrium systems, it can still be possible to derive a basic understanding of which regimes will likely appear, the relative frequency with which we should observe different regimes and, crucially, the expected rate at which regime shifts should occur. Although research on non-equilibrium regime shifts has lagged behind efforts to understand bifurcation-based regime shifts, continued work should pay off.

4.3.3 Lesson from Challenge 2: Unstable equilibria can reveal a lot about non-equilibrium dynamics

The influence of unstable equilibria is often dismissed as negligible. Although a system that is precisely at an unstable equilibrium would hypothetically remain there until perturbed, perturbations of course abound. With the possible exception of an unstable extinction state, we generally pay little attention to unstable equilibria.

However, the examples here reveal that when we expand to consider non-equilibrium dynamics, both unstable and stable equilibria can have an influence. Even though a non-equilibrium system is, by definition, not at any of these equilibria, knowing where they are in state space is enormously important. So too is knowing from which, if any, states they are (even transiently) attracting. Conveniently, standard off-the-shelf methods—starting with linear stability analysis itself!—is what we need to make many of these characterizations (Cushing et al. 1998). We simply have to consider a bit more carefully which aspects of a system's equilibrium behavior are informative, and not de facto ignore states that are not asymptotically stable.

4.4 Building on these lessons to confront future challenges

Although most standard theoretical approaches emphasize the role of deterministic density dependence in creating and maintaining equilibrium dynamics, it is widely recognized that ecological processes are inherently stochastic and that transient dynamics are likely common over relevant time scales. Our ability to interpret experimental and observational data accurately relies on the completeness of our theory, so it is important to continue to grow non-equilibrium theory to complement the large body of equilibrium-based theory in ecology. The examples in this chapter show how new insights can arise when classic ideas (stability and regime shifts) are reframed in a non-equilibrium way. The examples also revealed two general lessons: that non-equilibrium dynamics strengthen ecological understanding, and that unstable equilibria can have a strong and predictable influence on non-equilibrium dynamics. These lessons show that although intuition may suggest that stochasticity and transient phenomena

should obscure ecological understanding, they can actually strengthen it when viewed through the appropriate lens (Boettiger 2018).

To build on these lessons and continue to expand our understanding of non-equilibrium systems, we must increase our comfort with non-equilibrium concepts and embrace the mindset that stochastic and transient dynamics are tractable rather than hopelessly unpredictable. This change is likely to occur naturally over time, as more ecologists confront non-equilibrium problems and our catalog of successes continues to grow. For theoretical ecologists, investing effort in the study of stochastic models and methods for their analysis, and gaining a deep understanding of the dynamical structures that drive stochastic and transient dynamics, should be fruitful. For empirical ecologists, considering non-equilibrium explanations for observed dynamics will lead to more robust study designs, hypothesis tests, and sensitivity analyses.

To meet the quantitative challenges involved in studying non-equilibrium systems, interdisciplinary research is likely to be key. Non-equilibrium systems figure prominently in subdisciplines of physics (Kamenev 2011; Bressloff and Newby 2014), mathematics (Ludwig 1975; Kuehn 2015), and chemistry (Ge and Qian 2010), and many of the examples used in this chapter build directly on results from other fields (e.g., Freidlin and Wentzell 2012; Cameron 2012). Deep cross-disciplinary communication is notoriously difficult, making it challenging to identify research and researchers in other fields with close connections to problems in ecology. The reverse is also true: it is difficult for researchers in other fields to deeply understand the nature of ecological questions because we tend to communicate our questions through framing that will be unfamiliar. Despite these challenges, research that crosses disciplinary boundaries will likely pay off here, as it does elsewhere in ecology.

The equilibrium has long been a central paradigm in ecology, and it continues to serve us well. Expanding our use of non-equilibrium concepts will be an important avenue to new insights that complement and extend what we gain from equilibrium-based theory.

References

Abbott, K. C. and Nolting, B. C. (2017). Alternative (un)stable states in a stochastic predator-prey model. *Ecological Complexity* 32(Part B): 181–95.

Barraquand, F., Louca, S., Abbott, K. C. et al. (2017). Moving forward in circles: Challenges and opportunities in modelling population cycles. *Ecology Letters* 20(8): 1074–92.

Beisner, B. E., Haydon, D. T., and Cuddington, K. M. (2003). Alternative stable states in ecology. *Frontiers in Ecology and the Environment* 1(7): 376–82.

Bjørnstad, O. N. and Grenfell, B. T. (2001). Noisy clockwork: Time series analysis of population fluctuations in animals. *Science* 293(5530): 638–43.

Boettiger, C. (2018). From noise to knowledge: How randomness generates novel phenomena and reveals information. *Ecology Letters* 21(8): 1255–67.

Boettiger, C. and Hastings, A. (2012). Quantifying limits to detection of early warning for critical transitions. *Journal of the Royal Society Interface* 9(75): 2527–39.

Boettiger, C. and Hastings, A. (2013). No early warning signals for stochastic transitions: Insights from large deviation theory. *Journal of the Royal Society Interface* 280(1766): 20131372.

Bouchet, F. and Reygner, J. (2016). Generalisation of the Eyring–Kramers transition rate formula to irreversible diffusion processes. *Annales Henri Poincaré* 17(12): 3499–532.

Bressloff, P. C. and Newby, J. M. (2014). Path integrals and large deviations in stochastic hybrid systems. *Physical Reviews E* 89: 042701.

Briggs, C. J. and Borer, E. T. (2005). Why short-term experiments may not allow long-term predictions about intraguild predation. *Ecological Applications* 15(4): 1111–17.

Cameron, M. K. (2012). Finding the quasipotential for non-gradient SDEs. *Physica D* 241(18): 1532–50.

Coulson, T., Rohani, P., and Pascual, M. (2004). Skeletons, noise and population growth: The end of an old debate? *Trends in Ecology and Evolution* 19(7): 359–64.

Cushing, J. M., Costantino, R. F., Dennis, B., Desharnais, R. A., and Henson, S. M. (2003). *Chaos in Ecology: Experimental Nonlinear Dynamics*. Oxford: Academic Press/Elsevier.

Cushing, J., Dennis, B., Desharnais, R. A., and Costantino, R. F. (1998). Moving toward an unstable equilibrium: Saddle nodes in population systems. *Journal of Animal Ecology* 67(2): 298–306.

Davis, M. B. (1986). Climatic instability, time lags, and community disequilibrium. In J. Diamond and T. J. Case (eds.), *Community Ecology*, pp. 269–84. New York: Harper & Row.

DeAngelis, D. L. and Waterhouse, J. C. (1987). Equilibrium and nonequilibrium concepts in ecological models. *Ecological Monographs* 57(1): 1–21.

Dennis, B., Assas, L., Elaydi, S., Kwessi, E., and Livadiotis, G. (2016). Allee effects and resilience in stochastic populations. *Theoretical Ecology* 9(3): 323–35.

Dutta, P. S., Sharma, Y., and Abbott, K. C. (2018). Robustness of early warning signals for catastrophic and noncatastrophic transitions. *Oikos* 127(9): 1251–63.

Elton, C. S. (1924). Periodic fluctuations in the number of animals: Their causes and effects. *Journal of Experimental Biology* 2(1): 119–63.

Frank, K. T., Petrie, B., Fisher, J. A. D., and Leggett, W. C. (2011). Transient dynamics of an altered large marine ecosystem. *Nature* 477: 86–9.

Freedman, H. I. and Wolkowicz, G. S. K. (1986). Predator-prey systems with group defence: the paradox of enrichment revisited. *Bulletin of Mathematical Biology* 48(5/6):493–508.

Freidlin, M. I. and Wentzell, A. D. (2012). *Random Perturbations of Dynamical Systems*, volume 260 of *A Series of Comprehensive Studies in Mathematics*. 3rd edition. Heidelberg: Springer.

Ge, H. and Qian, H. (2010). Non-equilibrium phase transition in mesoscopic biochemical systems: From stochastic to nonlinear dynamics and beyond. *Journal of the Royal Society Interface* 8(54): 107–16.

Gilbert, B., Tunney, T. D., McCann, K. S. et al. (2014). A bioenergetic framework for the temperature dependence of trophic interactions. *Ecology Letters* 17(8): 902–14.

Grimm, V. and Wissel, C. (1997). Babel, or the ecological stability discussions: An inventory and analysis of terminology and a guide for avoiding confusion. *Oecologia* 109(3): 323–34.

Grimm, V., Schmidt, E., and Wissel, C. (1992). On the application of stability concepts in ecology. *Ecological modelling* 63(1–4): 143–61.

Guttal, V. and Jayaprakash, C. (2008). Changing skewness: An early warning signal of regime shifts in ecosystems. *Ecology Letters* 11(5): 450–460.

Guttal, V. and Jayaprakash, C. (2009). Spatial variance and spatial skewness: leading indicators of regime shifts in spatial ecological systems. *Theoretical Ecology* 2(1): 3–12.

Hanski, I., Turchin, P. V., Korpimaki, E., and Henttonen, H. (1993). Population oscillations of boreal rodents: Regulation by mustelid predators leads to chaos. *Nature* 364: 232–5.

Hastings, A. (2001). Transient dynamics and persistence of ecological systems. *Ecology Letters* 4(3): 215–220.

Hastings, A. (2004). Transients: The key to long-term ecological understanding? *Trends in Ecology and Evolution* 19(1): 39–45.

Hastings, A., Abbott, K. C., Cuddington, K. et al. (2018). Transient phenomena in ecology. *Science* 361(6406): eaat6412.

Henson, S. M., Costantino, R. F., Cushing, J. M., Dennis, B., and Desharnais, R. A. (1999). Multiple attractors, saddles, and population dynamics in periodic habitats. *Bulletin of Mathematical Biology* 61(6): 1121–49.

Higgins, K., Hastings, A., Sarvela, J. N., and Botsford, L. W. (1997). Stochastic dynamics and deterministic skeletons: Population behavior of Dungeness crab. *Science* 276(5317): 1431–5.

Holling, C. S. (1973). Resilience and stability of ecological systems. *Annual Review of Ecology and Systematics* 4: 1–23.

Ives, A. R. (1995). Measuring resilience in stochastic systems. *Ecological Monographs* 65(2): 217–233.

Ives, A. and Carpenter, S. R. (2007). Stability and diversity of ecosystems. *Science* 317(5834): 58–62.

Kamenev, A. (2011). *Field Theory of Non-Equilibrium Systems*. Cambridge: Cambridge University Press.

Kendall, B. E., Prendergast, J., and Bjørnstad, O. N. (1998). The macroecology of population dynamics: Taxonomic and biogeographic patterns in population cycles. *Ecology Letters* 1(3): 160–4.

Kendall, B. E., Briggs, C. J., Murdoch, W. W. et al. (1999). Why do populations cycle? A synthesis of statistical and mechanistic modeling approaches. *Ecology* 80(6): 1789–805.

Kuehn, C. (2015). *Multiple Time Scale Dynamics*. New York: Springer.

Lande, R., Engen, S., and Sæther, B. E. (2003). *Stochastic Population Dynamics in Ecology and Conservation*. Oxford: Oxford University Press.

Livina, V. N., Kwasniok, F., and Lenton, T. M. (2010). Potential analysis reveals changing number of climate states during the last 60 kyr. *Climate of the Past* 6(1): 77–82.

Ludwig, D., Jones, D., and Holling, C. S. (1978). Qualitative analysis of insect outbreak systems: The spruce budworm and forest. *Journal of Animal Ecology* 47(1): 315–32.

Ludwig, D. (1975). Persistence of dynamical systems under random perturbations. *SIAM Review* 17(4): 605–40.

MacArthur, R. H. and Levins, R. (1967). The limiting similarity, convergence, and divergence of coexisting species. *American Naturalist* 101(921): 377–85.

May, R. M. (1974). *Stability and Complexity in Model Ecosystems*. Princeton: Princeton University Press.

May, R. M. (1977). Thresholds and breakpoints in ecosystems with a multiplicity of stable states. *Nature* 269: 471–7.

Moore, C. M., Stieha, C. R., Nolting, B. C., Cameron, M. K., and Abbott, K. C. (2015). *QPot:* Quasi-potential analysis for stochastic differential equations. https://cran.r-project.org/web/packages/QPot/index.html.

Moore, C. M., Stieha, C. R., Nolting, B. C., Cameron, M. K., and Abbott, K. C. (2016). QPot: An R package for stochastic differential equation quasi-potential analysis. *The R Journal* 8(2): 19–38.

Murdoch, W. W., Briggs, C. J., and Nisbet, R. M. (2003). *Consumer-Resource Dynamics*. Princeton: Princeton University Press.

Myers, J. H. (2018). Population cycles: Generalities, exceptions and remaining mysteries. *Proceedings of the Royal Society B* 285(1875): 20172841.

Nicholson, A. J. and Bailey, V. A. (1935). The balance of animal populations. Part I. *Proceedings of the Zoological Society of London* 105(3): 551–98.

Nolting, B. C. and Abbott, K. C. (2015). Balls, cups, and quasi-potentials: Quantifying stability in stochastic systems. *Ecology* 97(4): 850–64.

Otto, S. and Day, T. (2007). *A Biologist's Guide to Mathematical Modeling in Ecology and Evolution*. Princeton: Princeton University Press.

Rosenzweig, M. L. (1971). Paradox of enrichment: Destabilization of exploitation ecosystems in ecological time. *Science* 171(3969): 385–7.

Scheffer, M., Carpenter, S., Foley, J. A., Folke, C., and Walker, B. (2001). Catastrophic shifts in ecosystems. *Nature* 413: 591–6.

Scheffer, M. (2009). *Critical Transitions in Nature and Society*. Princeton: Princeton University Press.

Scheffer, M. and Carpenter, S. R. (2003). Catastrophic regime shifts in ecosystems: linking theory to observation. *Trends in Ecology and Evolution* 18(12): 648–56.

Sharma, Y., Abbott, K. C., Dutta, P. S., and Gupta, A. K. (2015). Stochasticity and bistability in insect outbreak dynamics. *Theoretical Ecology* 8(2): 163–74.

Steele, J. H. and Henderson, E. Q. (1981). A simple plankton model. *American Naturalist* 117(5): 676–91.

Vellend, M., Srivastava, D. S., Anderson, K. M. et al. (2014). Assessing the relative importance of neutral stochasticity in ecological communities. *Oikos* 123(12): 1420–30.

Xu, L., Zhang, F., Zhang, K., Wang, E., and Wang, J. (2014). The potential and flux landscape theory of ecology. *PLoS ONE* 9(1): e86746.

Zhou, J. X., Aliyu, M. D. S., Aurell, E., and Huang, S. (2012). Quasi-potential landscape in complex multistable systems. *Journal of the Royal Society Interface* 9(77): 3539–53.

CHAPTER 5

The impact of population structure on population and community dynamics

André M. de Roos

5.1 Introduction

In a book on theoretical ecology a chapter on structured population models will inevitably, but perhaps unjustly, stand out, as so much of current theory in population ecology is based on unstructured rather than on structured models. Every student in ecology will, at some point, have studied the seminal models for competition and predation introduced by Lotka (1925) and Volterra (1926). Far fewer students, however, will have encountered structured population models, such as the age-structured model introduced by Sharpe and Lotka (1911) or the age-structured matrix model proposed by Leslie (1945). Text books in general ecology (Begon et al. 2005) discuss unstructured population models in quite some detail, while even text books in theoretical ecology (Yodzis 1989) may devote only a few subsections to structured models.

The term structured population models itself is used rather loosely for a wide variety of different models. For the purpose of this chapter, the term hence needs a more precise definition, as it is simply impossible to discuss all types of structured population models. Unstructured population models effectively treat all individuals in the population as identical, such that it is only necessary to keep track of the total population abundance, in terms of the number of individuals, their density, or their total biomass. But the birth and death rates that

ultimately determine the changes in the number of individuals in a population are never the same for all individuals. An individual always starts out life as a juvenile, incapable of reproduction or replication, whatever species the individual belongs to. Birth and death rates thus vary with the age of the individual, its developmental stage, spatial location or its genotype, among many other factors. In a very general sense, any population dynamic model that takes differences between individuals into account can be referred to as structured. However, in this chapter, I will restrict myself to discussing models that account for differences between individuals resulting from the developmental process that individuals go through during their life history. "Ontogenetically structured population models" would be an appropriate name for this class of models, referring to the ontogeny or individual life history that the models are aimed to capture. Instead, in the literature ontogenetically structured population models are indicated as age-structured, stage-structured, size-structured or physiologically structured population models. In what follows, I will use the general term structured population model and in particular the abbreviation SPM to indicate models that account for differences between individuals arising from their ontogeny and thereby explicitly exclude models that account for the spatial, genetic, behavioral or any other type of structure of a population.

de Roos, A. M., *The impact of population structure on population and community dynamics* In: *Theoretical Ecology: Concepts and Applications.* Edited by: Kevin S. McCann and Gabriel Gellner, Oxford University Press (2020). © Oxford University Press. DOI: 10.1093/oso/9780198824282.003.0005

5.2 State concepts in SPMs

All SPMs have at their core a model representation of the individual life history. This life history representation may be more or less detailed and more data-driven or more model-based, but structured population models in effect are based on data or assumptions about the individual life history. They translate this individual-level representation to the population level by bookkeeping operations. Population dynamics, therefore, truly emerges from the individual life history processes. In contrast, unstructured population models are based on mathematical functions that describe the population dynamic processes themselves as a function of population-level quantities such as densities or biomasses. Unstructured models are thus based on population-level assumptions. Structured and unstructured population models can therefore also be classified as individual-based versus population-based approaches of modelling ecological dynamics.

The first step when modelling any system, be it a community, a population, or an individual, is to identify the quantities that characterize the state of the system. These state variables have to be chosen such that they capture all relevant information about the history of the system to determine its dynamics and hence its future. In unstructured population models the choice of the state of the system only requires a choice between representing populations by their numerical densities or their biomass. The state of the system is then determined by the (numerical or biomass) abundance of all the populations that the unstructured model accounts for. The dynamics of the system, that is the growth of the populations and their interactions, subsequently has to be specified (modelled) dependent on the state variables (abundances of all populations). In SPMs the choice of the state of the system is more complex, because the basis of such models is formed by a representation or model of the individual life history, whereas the aim of the SPM is to describe the changes in populations. To capture these different levels of biological organization Metz and Diekmann (1986) introduced the distinction between the state of an individual, also referred to as *individual* or *i-state*, the state of the population, referred to as *population* or *p-state*, and the state of the environment that the individuals live in (*environmental* or *E-state*).[1]

The concepts of *i-*, *p-*, and *E*-state are fundamental and powerful (Metz and Diekmann 1986; Metz and de Roos 1992; Caswell and John 1992; Caswell 2001). To formulate a SPM, we have to start asking the question which characteristics, quantities or traits of the individual organism play the most important role in its life history and have the largest impact on its birth and death rate. Is it the age of the individual? Then the *i*-state would be made up by individual age and we would end up with an age-structured model. More often, however, the body size of an individual is the most important life history trait of an individual, such that body size is the appropriate choice for the *i*-state and a size-structured population model would result. Given a choice of the individual state, the choice of the population or *p*-state is rather straightforward as the distribution, be it a discrete distribution or a continuous density function, over all possible *i*-states.

More important than the choice of the *p*-state, is arguably the choice of the environmental or *E*-state. This choice forces us to consider which factors have an influence on the individual's reproduction, mortality, and development, apart from its own traits. Are there no factors other than the individual state variables (age or size) influencing the life history processes (reproduction, mortality and development)? In that case, the individual is apparently living in a constant environment, its life history is independent of any external factors and in particular independent of population density. Abiotic factors like temperature that vary over time can influence the individual life history and hence be part of the environmental state. But temperature is generally not changed by the individuals in a population themselves and their life history will hence unfold in a time-varying environment, but again, independent of any population impact. However, if individuals would compete with other individuals for example for nesting sites, the

---

[1] For clarity I use environmental or *E*-state, even though from a system theory point of view the use of "state" is not appropriate (Metz and de Roos 1992).

reproductive success of an individual will depend on how many competitors there are around. In this case, the environmental or E-state would have to include as an E-state variable the number of individuals in the population that are competing for the nest sites. As yet another example, if the life history processes depend on food availability in the environment and the individuals of the population together are capable of depleting this food availability through their foraging, food density would be an appropriate choice as E-state variable.

These last two examples of possible E-states both give rise to a feedback of the population on the individual life history, in other words, they involve density dependence. However, the first example, competition for nest sites, is a direct form of density dependence, whereas, in the second example, competition for food, the density dependence operates indirectly through a quantity (food density) other than population abundance itself, but whose dynamics is influenced by the population. The premise of distinguishing the i-, p-, and E-state is that density dependence or population feedback always operates through the E-state. Vice versa, if the environment (E-state) is unaffected by the population the life history of an individual unfolds in a way that is independent of other individuals in the environment.

The extensive discussion of the individual and environmental state emphasizes the need to carefully think about the biology of the system we want to study when formulating a SPM. What individual traits influence the individual life history? What are the most important elements of the environment that individuals are facing during their life? Given their basis in individual life history and combined with the concept of environmental or E-state, SPMs allow for a faithful representation of the ecology of the system in a population dynamic model. Many examples of structured population models in the literature, however, account for density dependence by simply making the individual birth, death or development rate a function of the (numerical) abundance of the population. This is obviously a simplifying assumption, which may not correctly reflect how density dependence operates mechanistically in the modelled ecological system (except when density

dependence operates through some form of direct competition for example for nest sites or through interference competition) and which may thus lead to misleading results. In short, one form of density dependence is not necessarily the same as the other, often the devil is in the details.

5.3 Types of structured population models

A SPM can either describe the changes in the state of a population continuously through time or can describe the state of the structured population at discrete points in time only. Similarly, the individual state variable that is adopted in the model can be continuous or discrete. For example, with age as a continuous i-state variable every individual in the population will be characterized by its age, which may adopt any positive value. Alternatively, all individuals can be grouped into a limited number of distinct age classes. Often, four different types of SPMs are recognized based on the choice between discrete and continuous representation of the time and the i-state variable in the model (Caswell et al. 1997 see Table 5.1).

For each of these four types of SPMs, a different mathematical framework is used to formulate the model: matrices, integral projection equations, ordinary or delay differential equations, and partial differential equations.

Matrix models (Caswell 2001) classify individuals in discrete stages on the basis of their i-state variable (age or size). If k such stages are distinguished, the population state is a vector $(n_1(t), \ldots, n_k(t))^T$ representing the number of individuals in each of the stages. The model then describes the dynamics of the structured population using a population projection matrix $\mathbf{A}$ by:

$$
\begin{pmatrix} n_1(t+1) \\ \vdots \\ n_k(t+1) \end{pmatrix} = \mathbf{A} \begin{pmatrix} n_1(t) \\ \vdots \\ n_k(t) \end{pmatrix}
$$

$$
= \begin{pmatrix} a_{11} & \cdots & a_{1k} \\ \vdots & \ddots & \vdots \\ a_{k1} & \cdots & a_{kk} \end{pmatrix} \begin{pmatrix} n_1(t) \\ \vdots \\ n_k(t) \end{pmatrix}
$$

$$(5.1)$$

Table 5.1 Types of structured population models (adapted from Caswell et al. (1997) with references to monographs about them).

		Time dynamics	
		Discrete	Continuous
Individual state representation	Discrete	Matrix models (Caswell 2001)	Stage-structured models (Murdoch et al. 2003)
	Continuous	Integral projection models (Ellner et al. 2016)	Physiologically structured population models (de Roos and Persson 2013)

Each of the elements a_{ij} of the population projection matrix **A** describes the number of individuals that will be in stage i at time $t + 1$ per individual in stage j at time t.

In integral projection models (IPMs; Rees et al. 2014; Ellner et al. 2016) individuals are characterized by a continuous i-state variable z, often referring to the individual body size. The population state in IPMs is a density function $n(t, z)$ representing the density of individuals with i-state z at time t. The integral of $n(t, z)$ over the interval from a to b:

$$\int_a^b n(t, z) \ dz$$

equals the number of individuals with an i-state in the interval $[a, b]$. IPMs describe the dynamics of the population with an integral equation, which in its simplest form can be written as:

$$n(t + 1, z) = \int_\Omega \left(F\left(z, z'\right) + S\left(z'\right) G\left(z, z'\right) \right) n\left(t, z'\right) \ dz'$$

$$(5.2)$$

In this equation the function $G(z, z')$ represents the probability that an individual with i-state z' at time t will have i-state z at time $t + 1$, $S(z')$ is the probability that an individual with i-state z' at time t survives till time $t + 1$ and the function $F(z, z')$ models the density of offspring with an i-state z produced between time t and time $t + 1$ by an individual with i-state z'. The interpretation of the function $F(z, z')$, and similarly the function $G(z, z')$, is analogous to the interpretation of $n(t, z)$ in that the integral

$$\int_a^b F\left(z, z'\right) \ dz$$

equals the number of offspring with an i-state in the interval $[a, b]$ produced between time t and $t + 1$ by an individual with i-state z' at time t.

Continuous-time stage-structured models can be described by a system of ordinary or delay-differential equations (Nisbet and Gurney 1983; Murdoch et al. 2003). For example, consider a model with only 2 stages, juveniles and adults with densities $J(t)$ and $A(t)$ at time t, respectively. The population dynamics can then be described by a system of two ordinary differential equations (ODEs; see for examples de Roos et al. 2007; Schreiber and Rudolf 2008):

$$\frac{dJ}{dt} = \beta A - \gamma J - \mu J$$
$$\frac{dA}{dt} = \gamma J - \mu A$$

$$(5.3)$$

In these ODEs the parameter β represents the per capita reproduction rate (fecundity) of an adult individual, γ the per capita maturation rate of a juvenile individual and μ the per capita mortality rate of juveniles and adults. This formulation in terms of ODEs, however, assumes that every juvenile individual, irrespective how long time they have spent in the juvenile stage, has a probability per unit time to mature equal to γ. The probability distribution for the juvenile stage duration τ then follows an exponential distribution with a mean equal to $1/\gamma$.

Alternatively, the dynamics of the population can be described by a system of delay-differential equations (DDEs; see for examples Nisbet and Gurney 1983; de Roos and Persson 2003):

$$\frac{dJ}{dt} = \beta A(t) - \beta A(t - \tau)\, e^{-\mu\tau} - \mu J(t)$$
$$\frac{dA}{dt} = \beta A(t - \tau)\, e^{-\mu\tau} - \mu A(t) \tag{5.4}$$

This formulation assumes that all individuals that are born at time t all mature at the same time after exactly τ time units. The juvenile stage duration is therefore for all individuals the same. The recruitment rate to the adult stage at time t therefore equals the birth rate τ time units prior, $\beta A(t - \tau)$, multiplied by the probability that an individual survives its juvenile period, $e^{-\mu\tau}$.

Like IPMs physiologically structured population models (PSPMs) also characterize an individual by a continuous i-state variable, for example, the individual body size s. The population state is, in that case, a density function $n(t, s)$ representing the density of individuals with body size s at time t. The integral

$$\int_{s_1}^{s_2} n(t, s)\, ds$$

equals the number of individuals with a body size in the range s_1 to s_2. Classically, in a PSPM the population dynamics is described by a partial differential equation (PDE) of the form:

$$\frac{\partial n(t, s)}{\partial t} + \frac{\partial g(s) n(t, s)}{\partial s} = -\mu(s) n(t, s) \tag{5.5}$$

in which the function $g(s)$ represents the growth rate in body size of an individual with size s and $\mu(s)$ represents the mortality rate of such an individual. To complete the model specification the PDE has to be supplemented with a boundary condition of the form:

$$g(s_b)\, n(t, s_b) = \int_{s_b}^{\infty} \beta(s) n(t, s)\, ds \tag{5.6}$$

Here it is assumed that newborn individuals have a size at birth equal to s_b and the function $\beta(s)$ represents the rate at which offspring is produced by an individual with body size s. The boundary condition matches the total rate at which offspring is produced by the population (right-hand side of the equation) to the rate at which individuals enter the possible body size range at the lower end (left-hand side of the equation). The partial differential equation (5.5) with its boundary condition (5.6) is often referred to as the McKendrick–von Foerster equation. However, with body size as i-state variable it was first studied by Bell and Anderson (1967) and introduced into ecology by Sinko and Streifer (1967, 1969).

The equations presented previously for matrix, integral projection, stage-structured, and physiologically structured population models are the simplest representatives of these four types of SPMs. More complex examples of matrix models can be found in Caswell (2001), of IPMs in Ellner et al. (2016 for IPMs), of stage-structured models in Murdoch et al. (2003), and of PSPMs in Metz and Diekmann (1986) and de Roos and Persson (2013). These four types of SPMs, however, differ not just in their mathematical formulation, but also in some subtle, more biological aspects.

Data-driven or function-based life history model: Discrete-time SPMs (matrix and IPMs) are formulated in terms of quantities that can be directly measured in experiments or collected empirically. The matrix elements a_{ij} in Equation (5.1), for example, are identical to or constructed from (i) the i-state of an individual at time $t + 1$ given its i-state at time t, (ii) its survival probability and (iii) the number of offspring it produces between time t and $t + 1$. These quantities are all directly measurable. The model of the individual life history in discrete-time SPMs is therefore often data-driven, consisting of generalized linear or additive models fitted to the life history observations.

In contrast, continuous-time SPMs are formulated in terms of *rates of change*, more specifically the vital rates, i.e., the reproduction, development and mortality rate. These vital rates are not directly measurable and can only be inferred indirectly from the quantities that discrete-time SPMs use directly as input: the i-state of individuals at time $t + 1$ given their state at time t, their probability to survive and the number of offspring they produce during this time interval. A continuous-time SPM is therefore usually formulated by choosing a priori specific functional forms for the vital rates as functions of the i-state of the individual and possibly the environmental state. For example, a common assumption in PSPMs with body size as i-state variable is that growth in body size follows von Bertalanffy growth with growth rate,

$$g(s) = K (s_\infty - s)$$

in which $g(s)$ represents the rate of change in body size s, s_∞ is the ultimate size an individual can reach, and the parameter K characterizes how rapidly this ultimate size is approached. Appropriate values for the parameters in these vital rate functions are subsequently inferred from experimental or empirical observations. Furthermore, these functions for the vital rates often have a mechanistic basis. Many continuous-time size-structured models are, for example, based on an underlying model for the energy acquisition and use of an individual. The assumptions about energy acquisition and use implemented in such a dynamic energy budget model (Kooijman 1993; Kooijman 2010; Lika and Nisbet 2000) then translate into functional forms of the individual growth rate in body size and reproduction rate as a function of body size and food availability in the environment. With a mechanistic basis for the vital rate functions the model for the individual life history is also easily extended to conditions for which measurements are not directly available. So it is rather straightforward to make the rates in a dynamic energy budget model temperature dependent using established rules for the scaling of physiological rates with temperature (Kooijman 2010; Lindmark et al. 2019). In discrete-time, data-driven SPMs accounting for temperature dependence in the life history model requires demographic observations of individuals at different temperatures.

Linear and non-linear models: The dynamics of linear population models is independent of the population state itself, whereas in non-linear models the population state has an influence on the dynamics. Linear, density-independent SPMs always lead in the long run to exponential growth of the population, irrespective of the type of SPMs that is used. In principle, all four different types of SPMs also allow for density dependence in population dynamics, but they differ in how they account for such density dependence. A good example of how density dependence tends to be incorporated in

data-driven, discrete-time SPMs is provided by Childs et al. (2011), who present a density dependent integral projection model (IPM) for Soay sheep. The life history model in this IPM is constructed by fitting generalized linear and additive models to observations of survival, fecundity and changes in body size at three different densities of the population. This results in a phenomenological representation of density dependence, which does not specify the mechanism by which such density dependence occurs. It also does not consider whether the population density (to which all individuals contribute equally) is an appropriate measure for the strength of the density dependence or that individuals in different stages contribute to a different extent to this density dependence.

In contrast, continuous-time SPMs tend to be far more explicit and mechanistic about the form of density dependence. For example, the model for cannibalistic interactions in a single fish population analysed by Claessen et al. (2000) models explicitly the basic resource that all cannibalistic individuals compete for, the impact of each of the cannibalistic individuals on this basic resource dependent on its body size, the mortality imposed by cannibalistic individuals of particular body sizes on smaller-sized conspecifics and the energy gains that cannibalistic individuals derive from eating their conspecifics. Density dependence thus occurs in this model through different mechanisms, exploitative competition for a shared resource and cannibalism, and both mechanisms are explicitly accounted for in the model in a functional, non-phenomenological manner.

Deterministic or stochastic individual development: The four types of SPMs differ in the extent to which they can and do represent variation between individuals that at one particular time have the same i-state value (for example, individuals that are born at the same time with the same i-state). Individual development in PSPMs is always deterministic and hence variation will never arise between two individuals born with the same i-state at the same time. At the other extreme, the premise of IPMs is that individuals with the same current i-state will exhibit variation in their i-state at the next time step. Matrix and continuous-time stage-structured models can account for variation in individual development, more specifically individual stage duration, but can also be formulated to exclude any such variation (see de Valpine et al. 2014 for an excellent discussion of this topic). The two systems of differential equations (5.3) and (5.4) exemplify how different formulations can capture either an exponential distribution of the juvenile stage duration or a fixed juvenile stage duration in an otherwise identical stage-structured population model. Different implementations may thus differ in the individual life history that SPMs represent, and the model results should hence also be carefully interpreted in the light of such possible differences.

Ecological complexity and mathematical tractability: Matrix models, IPMs, stage-structured models and PSPMs differ in the level of complexity in the life history and the ecological interactions of individuals that they can and tend to handle. In matrix models, IPMs and stage-structured models individuals are usually distinguished from each other by a single trait, commonly age, size, or stage (but see Caswell et al. 2018 for a recent synthesis of age x stage classified matrix models). The majority of matrix models and IPMs model a single population in a density-independent setting (but see Table 1 in Rees et al. 2014 for exceptions). These models are hence more geared toward demographic analysis, that is to studying the growth rate and structure of a population in relation to the rates of individual reproduction, development and mortality, as well as the sensitivity of population growth rate and structure in response to changes in these vital rates. In contrast, virtually all continuous-time stage-structured models and PSPMs are non-linear or density dependent. In PSPMs individuals are furthermore frequently characterized by more than a single *i*-state variable (e.g., de Roos et al. 1990; Persson et al. 1998; Claessen et al. 2000; de Roos et al. 2002). Continuous-time SPMs are hence more geared toward analyzing the interactions between individuals of the same or different species. The flip side of the complexity that the different model types can handle is the ease of their analysis. To analyze linear, density-independent matrix models the substantial power of linear algebra can be brought to bear. This allows for numerous, demographic aspects to be studied using matrix models. For IPMs something similar holds, as following their formulation and parameterization these models are usually discretized into a large matrix model for analysis. Non-linear, continuous-time SPMs are by comparison more difficult to analyze and in practice often studied only with numerical simulations of the dynamics at particular parameter values. A more powerful and more complete analysis of model dynamics is possible using the theory on bifurcations in non-linear dynamical systems (Kuznetsov 1998). Bifurcation analysis is however up to now only used to a limited extent to assess the generality and robustness of observed dynamics in ecological models. Methods for bifurcation analysis of continuous-time stage-structured models in terms of delay-differential equations (Engelborghs et al. 2002) and PSPMs (Kirkilionis et al. 2001; Diekmann et al. 2003; de Roos 2008) have been developed in recent years as well. These methods form the basis for a recently developed software package to analyze bifurcations in the ecological and evolutionary dynamics of PSPMs (de Roos 2018a), which only requires as input the functions describing development, reproduction and mortality of individuals throughout their life history and functions describing the interactions of these individuals with their environment.

Summarizing, both discrete- and continuous-time SPMs have at their core a model representation of the individual life history, but as discussed previously, they differ in a number of aspects, including in how they represent the life history. The different types of SPMs therefore also serve different purposes and have different strengths and weaknesses. It would be quite ridiculous to claim that one particular framework is better than the other, each of the four types of SPMs is better at something than the others. Roughly speaking, matrix and integral projection models are better suited to analyse life history observations, infer their implications and explore the consequences of variability of individual development between otherwise identical individuals on population growth. On the other hand, continuous-time SPMs, in particular PSPMs, allow for mechanistic representations of individual-level processes, like energetics and in particular the interactions of an individual organism with its environment, including individuals of the same or other populations. They are therefore better suited to analyse how particular mechanisms or aspects of the life history or ecology of an individual would affect the population and community dynamics.

5.4 Ecological consequences of changing population structure

Recent years have seen two prominent developments in the field of structured population modelling: first, integral projection models (IPMs) have become more and more popular with an increasing number of new applications (see Rees et al. 2014; Ellner et al. 2016 for examples). Second, physiologically structured population models (PSPMs) have been used to analyze the consequences of ontogenetic development as a fundamental life history process for population dynamics and community structure (de Roos and Persson 2013). These latter studies have revealed the importance of the population composition or size-structure and the changes therein with changing ecological conditions for the dynamics and persistence of species. In this section I will provide a summary of the highlights of this newly emerging body of ecological theory and a discussion of how this body of theory adds to or contrasts with predictions of unstructured models.

As pointed out in an earlier section physiologically structured population models (PSPMs) can account for substantial complexity in individual life history and the ecological interactions of the individual with its environment. A range of life history and ecological scenario's has been analyzed using PSPMs: consumer-resource interactions, in which consumers forage on a single shared resource throughout life with consumer reproduction occurring continuously (de Roos et al. 1990; de Roos et al. 2008; de Roos et al. 2013) or as discrete pulses in time (Persson et al. 1998; de Roos and Persson 2001); consumers exploiting multiple resources throughout life (Schellekens et al. 2010; Nakazawa 2011; van Leeuwen et al. 2013; Wollrab et al. 2013; Nakazawa 2015) or adaptively switching between different resources (de Roos et al. 2002); dynamics and community structure of cannibalistic (Claessen et al. 2000) and tritrophic systems with one (de Roos and Persson 2002) or multiple size-selective predators (de Roos

et al. 2008); among others. This variety might lead one to expect a lot of rather specific insights into dynamics and community structure, but surprisingly some very general understanding has emerged.

5.4.1 Juvenile and adult-driven population cycles

Most PSPMs studied to date characterize individuals by their body size and use a model of individual energetics to describe the somatic growth and reproduction of individuals at different body sizes. In these dynamic energy budget (DEB) models energy assimilation from food equals energy allocation to growth, reproduction and metabolic maintenance. DEB models generally predict growth rate and ultimate body size to be determined by food availability (Kooijman and Metz 1984; Kooijman 2010; Persson et al. 1998; Lika and Nisbet 2000), as is representative for the growth patterns of invertebrate and ectotherm vertebrate species. Only one energy budget model has been published that considers growth in structural mass (excluding energy reserves) and ultimate size to be genetically determined (de Roos et al. 2009; de Roos and Persson 2013), which would better reflect the growth patterns of mammals and birds. Growth in total body mass (including reserves) and reproduction, however, are in all DEB models dependent on food availability and on individual body size. Individuals at different body sizes may hence respond differently to changes in food availability, which has implications for population dynamics.

Consider, for example, a scenario in which small, juvenile individuals are more efficient foragers than adults in the sense that there are low food densities at which adults have a negative energy balance while juveniles can still ingest sufficient food to meet their metabolic maintenance requirements. Reproduction will then halt at low food densities that allow juvenile growth in body size to continue. In consumer-resource systems this type of juvenile-adult asymmetry leads to cycles in population density with reproduction only occurring when juvenile biomass is low and stopping as soon as the increasing density of juveniles suppresses food availability to too low levels (see Figure 5.1, left panel). The intraspecific interactions among differently sized consumers thus cause the reproduction to become pulsed in time. Furthermore, as a result of these reproduction pulses the (juvenile) population becomes dominated by a single cohort of individuals that is born within a short period of time. Alternatively, when small, juvenile individuals have higher maintenance requirements per unit biomass than adults, population cycles also emerge as a

consequence of juvenile-adult asymmetry. In this case, adults reproduce continuously, but juvenile growth slows down when adult density becomes too high (see Figure 5.1, right panel). High adult densities hence slow down the juvenile maturation rate, leading to a decrease in adult density and in reproduction. In turn, the decrease in reproduction causes the juvenile density to decline and the cyclic dynamics to restart. Besides the difference between pulsed and continuous reproduction juvenile- and

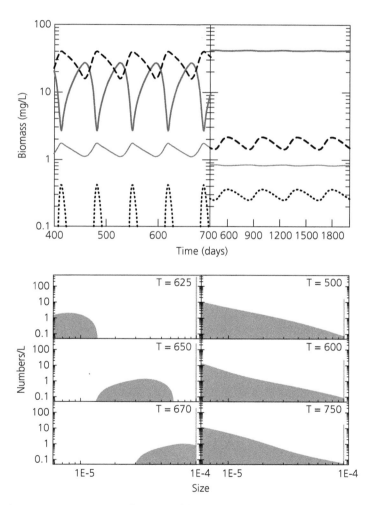

Figure 5.1 Population cycles emerge as a consequence of consumer life history. *Top*: Two types of population cycles emerge as a consequence of the consumer life history, when either juvenile (*left*) or adult (*right*) consumers can withstand lower resource densities. Panels show densities of juvenile (*thick solid line*), adult (*thick dashed line*) and resource biomass (*thin solid line*) as well as daily biomass production through reproduction (*dotted line*). *Bottom*: Changes over time in population size distribution in the two types of population cycles shown in the top panels.

Panels redrawn with permission from de Roos and Persson (2013, Figures 9.2 and 9.3, respectively).

adult-driven cycles (Figure 5.1) differ from each other in a range of aspects, including the amplitude of the cycles, the duration of the juvenile period and the adult lifespan (de Roos and Persson 2003; de Roos and Persson 2013).

These population cycles are caused by the asymmetry in the energetics between juveniles and adults. The ingestion rate and maintenance requirements of an individual determine, together with the efficiency with which ingested food is assimilated and converted into new tissue, how much new biomass an individual of a particular body size produces at a given food density through growth and reproduction. Because of the juvenile-adult asymmetry there are food densities at which either juveniles or adults are just staying alive without contributing to consumer population growth. The asymmetry may be only stage-dependent or may occur between any two individuals with a different body size, the two types of cycles show up irrespectively and occur with both continuous and pulsed reproduction of consumers (Persson et al. 1998; de Roos and Persson 2003; de Roos and Persson 2013; Persson and de Roos 2013). Population cycles due to within-stage or between-stage interactions have been extensively studied in continuous-time stage-structured models as well (Gurney et al. 1980; Nisbet and Gurney 1982; Nisbet and Gurney 1983; Gurney and Nisbet 1985). They are also referred to as "single-generation" cycles, because throughout a cycle the population is dominated by a single generation of individuals (Gurney and Nisbet 1985). The juvenile- and adult-driven cycles shown in Figure 5.1 are in essence equivalent to single-generation cycles, although in continuous-time stage-structured models the single-generation cycles have not been linked to the energetic asymmetry between individuals in different stages.

5.4.2 Biomass overcompensation

The occurrence of juvenile- or adult-driven population cycles, originating from the asymmetry in energetics between juveniles and adults or more generally between individuals of different body sizes, is one of the two general findings that have emerged from the analysis of PSPMs, in which individuals are characterized by their body size. The

second general finding is the occurrence of biomass overcompensation (de Roos et al. 2007; de Roos and Persson 2013), which term refers to the phenomenon that the biomass of a particular size-class of individuals or of the entire population increases as opposed to decreases with an increase in mortality experienced by the individuals (see Figure 5.2). Biomass overcompensation is also a consequence of the asymmetry in energetics between individuals in different stages or with different body sizes. Consider for example that juvenile consumers are more efficient foragers than adults and hence have a more positive energy balance (see Figure 5.2, top-left and bottom row). This would imply that at low food availability adult reproduction is very limited or even stops, whereas juvenile growth and maturation can still progress. In a consumer-resource equilibrium at low consumer mortality adult reproduction would hence constitute a more severe bottleneck in consumer life history which contributes more to controlling the population at equilibrium than juvenile growth and maturation. If consumer mortality would be slightly higher, the total consumer biomass in equilibrium will be lower and resource density will consequently be higher. Because of the reproduction bottleneck, the higher resource density leads to a larger, relative increase in the rate at which newborn consumers are produced, than in the rate at which juveniles mature and recruit to the adult stage. This difference in response between the recruitment rate to and the maturation rate out of the juvenile stage exceeds the increased loss rate due to the higher mortality and thus leads to a higher equilibrium biomass density of juvenile individuals despite the higher mortality they experience.

Analysis of simple size-structured population models have revealed that even a little bit of asymmetry between juveniles and adults is sufficient to result in biomass overcompensation or juvenile- or adult-driven population cycles (de Roos et al. 2013; Persson and de Roos 2013). These analyses have also shown that the two most important conditions for *symmetry* in energetics between juveniles and adults to occur are: (*i*) mortality is size- and stage-independent and (*ii*) the mass-specific, per-unit biomass production rate of new biomass through somatic growth and reproduction is the same for

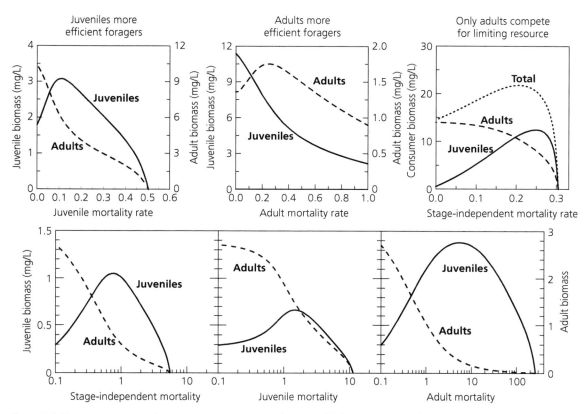

Figure 5.2 Biomass overcompensation emerges as a consequence of consumer life history. *Top:* Types of biomass overcompensation that emerge as a consequence of the consumer life history, when either juvenile (*left*) or adult (*middle*) consumers are more efficient foragers or when only adults compete for a limiting resource (*right*). *Bottom:* Biomass overcompensation in response to increases in stage-independent (*left*), juvenile (*middle*) and adult mortality (*right*) in case juveniles are more efficient foragers than adults. Solid and dashed lines refer to juvenile and adult biomass densities, respectively.

Panels redrawn with permission from de Roos and Persson (2013, Figure 3.5 and 3.6), and de Roos et al. (2007, Figure 1).

individuals of all body sizes (de Roos et al. 2013). The latter condition holds when the quantity

$$\frac{g(s, R) + \beta(s, R)s_b}{s} \quad (5.7)$$

is independent of body size s, where $g(s, R)$ and $\beta(s, R)$ equal the growth rate in body size and the fecundity, respectively, at size s and resource density R. Only when these symmetry conditions hold, will an increase in individual mortality leave the population size distribution unchanged, and will the life history processes not result in population cycles. In other words, only in case of ontogenetic symmetry in energetics will population structure not play a role whatsoever and will the results of PSPMs be equivalent to the results of unstructured population models for species interactions. The insights from those unstructured population models therefore apply under these limiting conditions of ontogenetic symmetry in energetics.

Biomass overcompensation does not refer to a temporary or transient increase in the biomass of a particular stage but is an equilibrium phenomenon. It, moreover, can occur irrespective of the type of increase in mortality, whether this increase is the same for all individuals, or whether only specific stages or size classes experience the increased mortality (Figure 5.2, bottom row). Effectively, it is the increase in equilibrium food density that causes the biomass overcompensation, while the increased mortality is only the means to increase this equilibrium food density and this occurs irrespective of whether the mortality increase is stage- or size-dependent or not. Abrams (Abrams and Matsuda 2005; Abrams 2009) was the first to propose that population density could increase with increasing mortality and dubbed this the "Hydra" effect. Biomass overcompensation resembles the Hydra effect but differs from it in some important aspects (Schröder et al. 2014). Most importantly, the Hydra effect deals with the number of individuals in a population and does not distinguish between small juveniles and large adults. In contrast, biomass overcompensation deals with stage-specific or total population biomass and comes about because of an increase in energetic efficiency of consumers at higher mortality levels. Maintenance requirements play a crucial role in this higher efficiency at higher mortality rates (de Roos 2018b). In consumer-resource systems at low consumer mortality most of the resource ingested by consumers is spent on maintenance costs for all consumers together and only little is used effectively for either juvenile growth and maturation or for adult reproduction. With an increase in consumer mortality the loss to maintenance requirements is smaller and the ratio between effective production and ingestion, either the reproduction rate per unit of ingested resource by adults or the maturation rate per unit of ingested resource by juveniles, increases. This increased efficiency subsequently leads to overcompensation in either juvenile or adult biomass. The two life history elements that are sufficient for such overcompensation to occur are differences between juveniles and adults and significant energy requirements to cover metabolic maintenance costs (de Roos 2018b).

5.4.3 Community consequences of biomass overcompensation

In unstructured models of ecological communities, a competitor or a predator of a particular focal population only changes its density, usually in a negative manner. In PSPMs, however, competitors and predators of a focal population not only change its overall density but also its population structure. Furthermore, competitors or predators may not affect all individuals in the focal population

equally but only have an impact on a subset of them. For example, predation mortality tends to be much higher for smaller than for larger sized individuals of a prey population. Because of biomass overcompensation predation on a specific size range of prey individuals may result in an increase in the biomass of this particular size class of prey (cf. Figure 5.2, bottom-middle panel). In contrast to the negative impact of predators on their prey population that is intuitively expected on the basis of unstructured models, size-selective predators can change the size-structure of their prey population and thus have a positive effect on the availability of their own prey. Through this positive feedback, biomass overcompensation in a prey population has ramifications for the persistence of species at higher trophic levels that feed on the prey as it gives rise to the presence of alternative stable community states or facilitation among predators. These effects are absent in case of ontogenetic symmetry and hence quite distinct from existing unstructured theory about basic trophic modules.

Consider for example a tritrophic food chain consisting of a basic resource, a consumer or prey and a predator population. Unstructured population models predict the occurrence of a unique community equilibrium under all conditions, whereby the length of the food chain increases with the productivity of the basic resource and decreases with the mortality rate of the top predator (Oksanen et al. 1981). Alternative stable states therefore do not occur (McCann and Yodzis 1995). In contrast, if the prey population is size-structured and predators would only forage on juvenile prey, biomass overcompensation in juvenile prey would lead to the occurrence of alternative stable community states, one with and one without predators, for certain ranges of basic resource productivity or predator mortality rates (Figure 5.3). Biomass overcompensation in juvenile prey occurs when juveniles have a greater energy efficiency, because they have higher ingestion rates relative to their energetic needs. When predators are absent and juvenile prey do not experience increased mortality relative to adults, the prey population is then dominated by adults, while juvenile biomass is relatively low due to low adult population fecundity (Figure 5.2; bottom-middle panel). If a

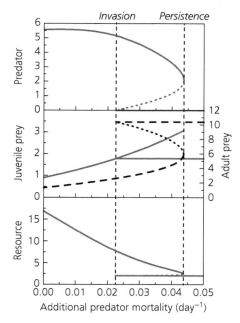

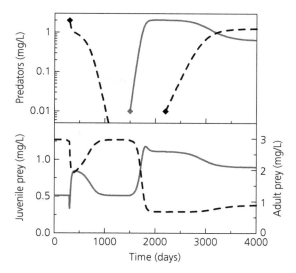

Figure 5.3 Emergent Allee effect for predators in a stage-structured food chain. Changes in equilibrium biomass of basic resource (*bottom*), juvenile (*middle, solid lines*) and adult prey (*middle, dashed lines*), and top predator (*top panels*) with increasing predator mortality in excess of background levels. Predators forage exclusively on juvenile prey. Stable equilibria are indicated with solid or dashed lines, unstable equilibria with dotted lines. For mortality rates between 0.023 and 0.044, one unstable and two stable equilibria co-occur.

Panels redrawn with permission from de Roos and Persson (2013, Figure 4.4).

Figure 5.4 Emergent facilitation between generalist and stage-specific predators in a stage-structured food chain. Invasion dynamics of a generalist (*top, solid lines*) and a stage-specific predator of juvenile prey (*top, dashed lines*) into an equilibrium of resource, juvenile (*bottom, solid lines*), and adult prey (*bottom, dashed lines*). Generalist and specialist predators forage equally on both juvenile and adult prey and exclusively on juvenile prey, respectively. Invasion of juvenile-specialized predators at $t = 300$ into the prey-only equilibrium is unsuccessful, despite the high initial density, whereas generalist predators can invade successfully even from low density ($t=1500$). Generalist predator invasion allows for subsequent, successful invasion of specialist predators from low density ($t = 2200$).

Panels redrawn with permission from de Roos and Persson (2013, Figure 5.1).

predator that selectively feeds on juvenile prey is present, though, the predation mortality it imposes on juvenile prey causes an overcompensatory increase in juvenile prey biomass (Figure 5.2; bottom-middle panel). In an equilibrium with predators the juvenile prey biomass is therefore higher as opposed to lower than in an equilibrium without predators (Figure 5.3). This change in the size-structure of the prey population induced by predation mortality allows for the occurrence of alternative community states with and without predators. As a consequence, once present the predator may persist at higher mortality rates than those for which it would be able to invade an equilibrium community state from which it is absent. The phenomenon that predators through predation change the size-structure of their prey

population and thus promote their own food availability has been termed an emergent Allee effect because it is based on purely exploitative predation of prey (de Roos and Persson 2002), in contrast to most mechanisms causing Allee effects.

Biomass overcompensation in prey populations may also lead to positive effects among predators of the same prey that differ in the range of body sizes of prey they select, a phenomenon referred to as *emergent predator facilitation*. This facilitation can occur between stage-specific predators that forage on two entirely different stages of prey or between a generalist predator that forages on all prey stages and a stage-specific predator foraging on either juvenile or adult prey only (Figure 5.4). For example, in case juveniles have a greater energy efficiency due to higher ingestion rates relative to their energetic needs, the increase in juvenile biomass with mortality is independent of the size-selectivity of the mortality (Figure 5.2; bottom panels). Analogous to how the increase in juvenile biomass with juvenile mortality forms the basis of the emergent Allee effect discussed previously, the increase with either stage-independent or adult-specific mortality forms the basis of emergent facilitation. Through this juvenile biomass overcompensation a generalist predator can increase the food availability for a predator foraging on juvenile prey only and allow this juvenile-specialized predator to invade under conditions that do not allow for its invasion in the absence of the generalist predator (Figure 5.4). Persistence of the predator feeding only on juveniles may then crucially depend on the presence of the generalist predator. If juvenile and adult prey individuals feed on different resources, predator facilitation may also be bidirectional, in that both predators need each other to persist (mutual predator facilitation) (de Roos and Persson 2013).

Ontogenetic asymmetry between juveniles and adults of the same species may not only come about through intrinsic differences in energetic efficiency between the stages but may also arise because the stages feed on different resources that have different productivities. Schreiber and Rudolf (2008) showed that alternative stable states could occur in case the juveniles and adults of a consumer species feed on different resources. The alternative community states differ in that they are either dominated by juveniles, in case juvenile resource is in short supply and maturation is more resource limited than fecundity, or by adults if adult resource is in short supply and consequently fecundity is more resource limited than maturation. Gradual changes in either juvenile or adult resource supply can in this case lead to abrupt regime shifts. For example, a gradual increase in juvenile resource supply will induce an abrupt shift from a juvenile-dominated consumer-resource equilibrium at low juvenile resource supply to an adult-dominated consumer-resource equilibrium at high juvenile resource supply. A predator feeding only on juvenile consumers will be able to establish itself in the consumer-resource equilibrium occurring at low juvenile resource supply (Figure 5.5). Once established, the predator will keep the juvenile biomass

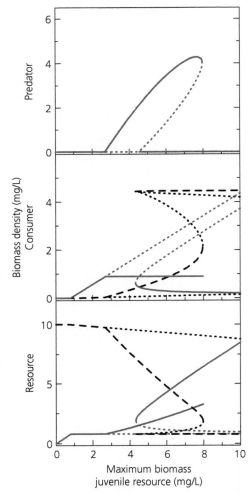

Figure 5.5 Emergent predator exclusion in a stage-structured food chain with different resources for juvenile and adult prey. Changes in equilibrium biomass of basic resources (*bottom*), consumer (prey, *middle*), and juvenile-specialized predator (*top panels*) with increasing maximum density of resource 1, foraged on by juvenile consumers. Solid lines refer to juvenile consumer biomass or their exclusive resource 1; dashed lines to adult consumer biomass or their exclusive resource 2. Consumers experience a complete niche shift from resource 1 to resource 2 at maturation. Stable equilibria are indicated with solid or dashed lines; unstable equilibria with dotted lines.

Panels redrawn with permission from de Roos and Persson (2013, Figure 6.6).

constant when productivity of the juvenile resource increases, while juvenile resource density and adult consumer biomass increase, and adult resource density decreases with this change in productivity (Figure 5.5). The ratio between juvenile and adult consumer biomass therefore decreases, which will lead to an abrupt shift to the adult-dominated consumer-resource equilibrium at high productivity of the juvenile resource. In this adult-dominated equilibrium state the juvenile biomass density is too low for the juvenile-specialized predator to survive. In contrast to unstructured food chain models, which predict that increasing productivity of the basic resource increases the density of the top predator, the ontogenetic niche shift in the prey makes the predator go extinct with increasing productivity of the resource that its main prey, juvenile consumers, is foraging on. This phenomenon is also referred to as *emergent predator exclusion* (Persson and de Roos 2013).

These examples of consequences of ontogenetic asymmetry in energetics between juveniles and adults for community structure represent only three of the many possible feeding modules. The phenomena are considered emergent (emergent Allee effect, emergent facilitation and emergent predator exclusion) because they arise as a consequence of the life history processes of the prey, in particular the biomass overcompensation that results from the ontogenetic asymmetry in energetics between juvenile and adult prey, whereas the community effect occurs at the higher trophic level of the predators exploiting this prey. In all feeding modules analyzed so far, the changes in size distribution that predators induce in their prey population readily give rise to the occurrence of alternative stable states (de Roos and Persson 2013).

5.5 Interfacing theory and data

A current trend in theoretical ecology is that models are to an increasing extent required to have a tight link to empirical and experimental data. This is especially true for structured population models as they necessarily include more detail and hence require more assumptions about the individual life history than unstructured population models. However, unlike the other types of structured populations models PSPMs also offer a larger scope for confronting model predictions with empirical or

experimental data. PSPMs are built on a function-based life-history model, in which the life history is shaped by environmental variables that in turn are influenced by the dynamics of the population abundance and composition. Model predictions about the individual life history are therefore to a considerable extent shaped by this population feedback on life history and only loosely related to the underlying model assumptions. As a consequence, PSPMs generate virtually independent predictions at both the individual as well as the population level that can be confronted with data to determine the relevance of the generated model results (de Roos and Persson 2001). For example, if an equilibrium state occurs under certain conditions in a size-structured population model, the model not only generates predictions about the total population abundance or biomass, but also about its size-distribution, whether it is stunted or not, and about the ratio of juveniles and adults in the population. In addition to these population level predictions, the model also generates predictions about the shape of the growth curve as a function of age that the individuals follow in the equilibrium state, about the duration of their juvenile period and the maximum size they reach in their life.

Persson et al. (2007) used this predictive capacity of PSPMs at both the individual and population level to test whether the abrupt changes in the fish community of Lake Takvatn (Norway) following a short period of culling of the dominant fish species in the lake, Arctic char (*Salvelinus alpinus*), represented a shift between two alternative stable states of the fish community. Before the experimental manipulation the fish community was dominated by Arctic char, ever since brown trout (*Salmo trutta*), a predator of juvenile Arctic char, had gone extinct decades earlier. Because the high density of Arctic char in the lake meant that individual char only reached medium body sizes around 20 cm, it was decided in view of the importance of char for sport fisheries to cull the population during a period of four years. This short-term manipulation of the char population resulted in a reduction in the density of Arctic char and an unexpected recovery of the brown trout population (Figure 5.6, top-left panel), which has by now persisted for over 20 years (Persson et al. 2013). In

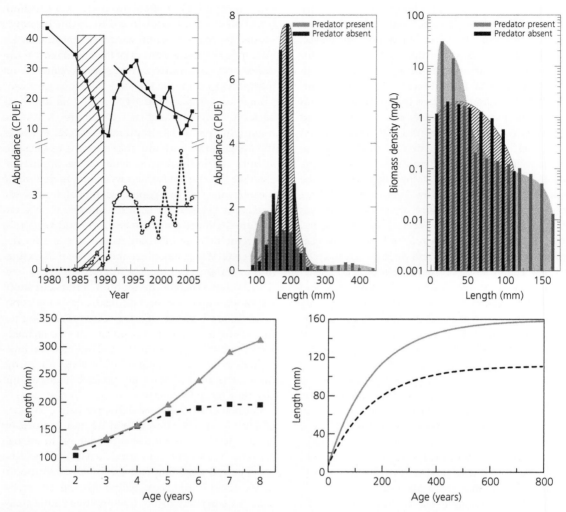

Figure 5.6 Confronting model predictions of the fish community dynamics in Lake Takvatn with empirical data. *Top, left*: Changes in the abundance (catch per unit effort defined as capture per gill net per 24 hours) of brown trout (*open circles, dashed line*) and Arctic char (*closed squares, solid line*) in Lake Takvatn, 1980–2006. Heavy fishing of Arctic char took place from 1984 to 1989 (*hatched area*). Thin, solid curves starting in 1991 represent trend lines. *Top, middle*: Size distribution of Arctic char in Lake Takvatn in 1980 (predator absent; *black bars and hatched convex hull*) and 1994 (predator present; *grey bars and filled convex hull*). *Top, right*: Prey size-distribution in the two alternative stable community states with (*grey bars and filled convex hull*) and without predators (*black bars and hatched convex hull*) as predicted by a generic tritrophic food-chain model of a basic resource, a size-structured consumer and a top-predator foraging on small-sized consumers only (see de Roos and Persson 2013, pp. 136–45). *Bottom, left*: Average individual growth curves of Arctic char in Lake Takvatn before (*black closed squares and dashed line*) and after the culling period (*grey closed triangles and solid line*). *Bottom, right*: Individual growth curves of consumers in the two alternative stable community states with (*grey solid line*) and without predators (*black dashed line*) shown in the top-right panel.

Top-left, top-middle, top-right and bottom-left panels redrawn and adapted with permission from de Roos and Persson (2013 Figure 4.17, 4.19, 4.10 and 4.18, respectively) using data from Persson et al. (2007).

this new community state predation of brown trout prevents severe intraspecific competition among char, such that individual growth in body size is no longer limited by strong density dependence and individuals reach larger sizes (sometimes up to 50 cm; Figure 5.6, bottom-left panel). Due to their larger sizes and the reduced intraspecific competition the total reproduction rate of the Arctic char population has increased leading to an increase in density of Arctic char smaller than 15 cm. In the presence of a dominant brown trout population, the density of both small and large Arctic char individuals was therefore substantially higher than in the absence of predators (Figure 5.6, top-middle panel), even though Arctic char smaller than 15 cm constitute the main prey of brown trout. The experimental observations regarding the change in individual growth curves and population size-distribution are in line with the qualitative predictions of a generic tritrophic food-chain model of a basic resource, a size-structured consumer and a top-predator foraging on small-sized consumers only (see de Roos and Persson 2013, pp. 136–45), even though the latter model is not specifically parameterized for the Arctic char-brown trout interaction and comparison between modelled and observed size distributions is difficult because of the difference in catchability of individuals of different body sizes. On the basis of a confrontation of seven different model predictions with the empirical data Persson et al. (2007) argued that the fish communities before and after the culling of Arctic char represented two alternative stable states, brought about by an emergent Allee effect in brown trout.

5.6 On generality and model specificity

A chapter on SPMs can not ignore the question whether or not the model results derived from a SPM are general or not and in particular whether they are more or less general than results from unstructured population models. Theoretical results are only relevant if they apply to a range of systems and situations. Unstructured population models are often considered more general than structured models, as the latter make more explicit and more system-specific assumptions about the individual life history (Holling 1966;

May 2001; Evans et al. 2013). The background for this view is two-fold: First, unstructured population models tend to be based on fewer assumptions and often involve fewer functions and parameters and are therefore considered to apply to a wider variety of systems. This view is inspired by May's (2001) plea for a strategic modelling approach that "sacrifices precision in an effort to grasp at general principles … to provide a conceptual framework for the discussion of broad classes of phenomena". As a second reason, for unstructured population models it is often possible to derive analytical results, whereas structured population models can often only be analyzed using numerical techniques. Numerical results are considered less general, as they depend on the particular values of the model parameters for which the results have been derived.

It can, however, also be argued that unstructured population models poorly represent ecological systems, as they consider all individuals identical and thus model populations essentially as collections of elementary particles. Unstructured models have even inspired classic textbooks in ecology to define population dynamics as "the variations in time and space in the sizes and densities of populations," where population density is defined as "the numbers of individuals per unit area" (Begon et al. 2005; Turchin 2013). This perspective again emphasizes changes in numbers of individuals and neglects differences between them. Therefore, in the current ecological paradigm population dynamics arises only as a consequence of two processes: individual reproduction and mortality. And yet, life history is the most fundamental feature that sets individual organisms apart from elementary particles in physics or molecules in chemistry. Individual development throughout life history constitutes an essential and uniquely ecological process. Furthermore, individual development is unlike other factors, such as for example spatial heterogeneity or genetic variability, that may be argued to influence population dynamics. The impact of both spatial heterogeneity and genetic variability can be controlled and even eliminated by choosing an appropriate, experimental setup. In fact, some of the most classic ecological experiments (Tilman 1982) have been carried out in well-stirred chemostats or using parthenogenetic species (McCauley and Murdoch 1990). In contrast, individual development can never be eliminated by any experimental design, as it is in fact the first process that invariably takes place after the birth of an individual, before reproduction and mortality will ever occur. In my opinion, individual development is therefore also a constituent part of population dynamics just like reproduction and mortality. Structured population models are based on this premise that not only reproduction and mortality, but also individual development shapes the dynamics of a population and that the population is not equivalent to just the number of its individuals, but that the composition or structure of the population (the distribution of the individuals over the possible individual states) is equally important, a fact that is supported by numerous ecological studies (e.g., Olson et al. 2001; Klemetsen et al. 2002). I therefore in general do support May's plea for a strategic modelling approach, but at the same time argue that ignoring individual development in population and community models may be an unjustified oversimplification.

5.7 Outlook

Undoubtedly, the individual life history of a species plays a very important role in its ecology and its evolution. Nonetheless, current ecological theory, in particular theory about population interactions and community dynamics, accounts only to a limited extent for the influence of life history as it is mostly based on unstructured models. Similarly, evolutionary theory about individual life history is often based on a density-independent, fitness-maximization principle and mostly ignores the ecological interactions that shape an individual's life history. Analysis of evolutionary dynamics within an ecological context involving intra- and interspecific interactions is possible using the framework of Adaptive Dynamics (Metz et al. 1996; Dieckmann 1997), but only few adaptive dynamics studies up to now have considered more detailed life histories. Physiologically structured population models (PSPMs) offer ample possibilities to address general questions about the consequences of individual life history on ecological and evolutionary dynamics, in particular facilitated by the recent development of software for their analysis (de Roos 2018a). These developments allow for addressing exciting and novel ecological and evolutionary questions in the years to come. However, as a cautionary closing note it is important to consider the desired complexity of a PSPM. When formulating a PSPM one often has a particular ecological scenario or system in mind that one wants to capture in the model. It is then quite easy to give in to the natural tendency to tailor the model more and more to this ecological situation, by incorporating an increasing amount of detail (something I also do too often). However, making more detailed assumptions greatly limits the generality of the model predictions. I therefore advocate a certain middle ground of model complexity, in which certain qualitative features of the individual life history are captured by the model with reference to a range of ecological systems, while all the time carefully weighing the benefits of incorporating further aspects of a life history against the costs of a decrease in generality of its results. Furthermore, once a particular pattern emerges from a PSPM with detailed assumptions the generality of the pattern and its mechanistic causes can be investigated by simplifying the PSPM, while preserving the elements that are involved in generating the pattern. For example, juvenile and adult-driven population cycles were first described as results from a model that mimicked in quite some detail the foraging of roach (*Rutilus rutilus*) on zooplankton. Later studies, however, with much more simplified models (de Roos and Persson 2003; Persson and de Roos 2013) revealed that these cycles occurred commonly whenever there is a competitive asymmetry between juveniles and adults. Similarly, biomass overcompensation was first found in a consumer-resource model, in which the consumer population was characterized by a complete size distribution (de Roos and Persson 2002), but was later on shown to also occur in stage-structured models (de Roos et al. 2007; de Roos 2018b), provided that juvenile and adult individuals differ in their energetic requirements, i.e., there is asymmetric competition for resources between them, and metabolic maintenance costs require a significant amount of energy. I would argue that this approach of model simplification is necessary and greatly benefits the generality of the developed theory.

References

Abrams, P. A. (2009). When does greater mortality increase population size? The long history and diverse mechanisms underlying the hydra effect. *Ecology Letters* 12(5): 462–74.

Abrams, P. A. and Matsuda, H. (2005). The effect of adaptive change in the prey on the dynamics of an exploited predator population. *Canadian Journal of Fisheries and Aquatic Science* 62(4): 758–66.

Begon, M., Townsend, C. R., and Harper, J. L., (2005). *Ecology: From Individuals To Ecosystems*. 4th edition. Oxford: Blackwell Publishing.

Bell, G. I. and Anderson, E. C. (1967). Cell growth and division. I. A mathematical model with applications to cell volume distributions in mammalian suspension cultures. *Biophysical Journal* 7: 329–51.

Caswell, H. (2001). *Matrix Population Models*. 2nd edition. Sunderland, MA: Sinauer Associates.

Caswell, H. and John, A. M. (1992). From the individual to the population in demographic models. In D. L. DeAngelis and L. J. Gross (eds.), *Individual-Based Models and Approaches in Ecology: Populations, Communities and Ecosystems*. New York: Chapman-Hall, pp. 36–61.

Caswell, H., de Vries, C., Hartemink, N., Roth, G., and van Daalen, S. F. (2018). Age × stage-classified demographic analysis: A comprehensive approach. *Ecological Monographs* 17: 310–25.

Caswell, H., Nisbet, R. M., de Roos, A. M., and Tuljapurkar, S. (1997). Structured-population models: Many methods, a few basic concepts. In S. Tuljapurkar and H. Caswell (eds.), *Structured-Population Models in Marine, Terrestrial, and Freshwater Systems*. Boston, MA: Springer, pp. 3–17.

Childs, D. Z., Coulson, T. N., Pemberton, J. M., Clutton-Brock, T. H., and Rees, M. (2011). Predicting trait values and measuring selection in complex life histories: reproductive allocation decisions in Soay sheep. *Ecology Letters* 14(10): 985–92.

Claessen, D., de Roos, A. M., and Persson, L. (2000). Dwarfs and giants: Cannibalism and competition in size-structured populations. *American Naturalis* 155(2): 219–37.

de Roos, A. M. (2008). Demographic analysis of continuous-time life-history models. *Ecology Letters* 11: 1–15.

de Roos, A. M. (2018a). PSPM analysis: A package for numerical analysis of physiologically structured population models. Available at: https://bitbucket.org/amderoos/pspmanalysis/R.

de Roos, A. M. (2018b). When individual life history matters: conditions for juvenile-adult stage structure effects on population dynamics. *Theoretical Ecology* 11(4): 397–416.

de Roos, A. M. and Persson, L. (2003). Competition in size-structured populations: Mechanisms inducing cohort formation and population cycles. *Theoretical Population Biology* 63(1): 1–16.

de Roos, A. M. and Persson, L. (2001). Physiologically structured models—from versatile technique to ecological theory. *Oikos* 94(1): 51–71.

de Roos, A. M. and Persson, L. (2013). *Population and Community Ecology Of Ontogenetic Development*. Princeton, NJ: Princeton University Press.

de Roos, A. M. and Persson, L. (2002). Size-dependent life-history traits promote catastrophic collapses of top predators. *Proceedings of the National Academy of Sciences* 99(20): 12907–12.

de Roos, A. M., Metz, J. A. J., Evers, E., and Leipoldt, A. (1990). A size dependent predator-prey interaction: Who pursues whom? *Journal of Mathematical Biology* 28: 609–43.

de Roos, A. M., Schellekens, T., van Kooten, T., van de Wolfshaar, K., Claessen, D., and Persson, L. (2007). Food-dependent growth leads to overcompensation in stage-specific biomass when mortality increases: The influence of maturation versus reproduction regulation. *American Naturalist* 170: E59–E76.

de Roos, A. M., Leonardsson, K., Persson, L. and Mittelbach, G. G. (2002). Ontogenetic niche shifts and flexible behavior in size-structured populations. *Ecological Monographs* 72(2): 271–92.

de Roos, A. M., Galic, N., and Heesterbeek, H. (2009). How resource competition shapes individual life history for nonplastic growth: Ungulates in seasonal food environments. *Ecology* 90(4): 945–60.

de Roos, A. M., Metz, J. A. J., and Persson, L., (2013). Ontogenetic symmetry and asymmetry in energetics. *Journal of Mathematical Biology* 66(4-5): 889–914.

de Roos, A. M., Schellekens, T., van Kooten, T., and Persson, L. (2008). Stage-specific predator species help each other to persist while competing for a single prey. *Proceedings of the National Academy of Science*, 105(37): 13930–5.

de Roos, A. M., Schellekens, T., van Kooten, T., van de Wolfshaar, K. E., Claessen, D., and Persson, L. (2008). Simplifying a physiologically structured population model to a stage-structured biomass model. *Theoretical Population Biology* 73(1): 47–62.

de Valpine, P., Scranton, K., Knape, J., Ram, K., and Mills, N. J. (2014). The importance of individual developmental variation in stage-structured population models. *Ecology Letters* 17(8):1026–38.

Dieckmann, U. (1997). Can adaptive dynamics invade? *Trends in Ecology and Evolution* 12(4): 128–31.

Diekmann, O., Gyllenberg, M., and Metz, J. A. J. (2003). Steady-state analysis of structured population models. *Theoretical Population Biology* 63(4): 309–38.

Ellner, S. P., Childs, D. Z., and Rees, M. (2016). *Data-driven Modelling of Structured Populations*. Cham: Springer.

Engelborghs, K., Luzyanina, T., and Roose, D. (2002). Numerical bifurcation analysis of delay differential equations using DDE-BIFTOOL. *ACM Trans. Math. Softw.* 28(1): 1–21.

Evans, M. R., Grimm, V., Johst, K., Knuuttila, T., de Langhe, R., Lessells, C. M., Merz, M., O'Malley, M. A., Orzack, S. H., Weisberg, M., Wilkinson, D. J., Wolkenhauer, O., and Benton, T. G. (2013). Do simple models lead to generality in ecology? *Trends in Ecology and Evolution* 28(10): 578–83.

Gurney, W. S. C., and Nisbet, R. M. (1985). Fluctuation periodicity, generation separation, and the expression of larval competition. *Theoretical Population Biology* 28(2): 150–80.

Gurney, W. S. C., Blythe, S. P., and Nisbet, R. M. (1980). Nicholson's blowflies revisited. *Nature* 287(5777): 17–21.

Holling, C. S. (1966). The strategy of building models of complex systems. In K. E. D. Watt, (ed.) *System Analysis in Ecology*. New York: Academic Press, pp. 195–214.

Kirkilionis, M. A., Diekmann, O., Lisser, B., Nool, M., de Roos, A. M., and Sommeijer, B. P. (2001). Numerical continuation of equilibria of physiologically structured population models. I. Theory. *Mathematical Models and Methods in Applied Sciences* 11(6): 1101–27.

Klemetsen, A., Amundsen, P. -A., Grotnes, P. E., Knudsen, R., Kristoffersen, R., and Svenning, M. -A. (2002). Takvatn through 20 years: Long-term effects of an experimental mass removal of Arctic charr, *Salvelinus alpinus*, from a subarctic lake. *Environmental Biology of Fishes* 64: 39–47.

Kooijman, S. A. L. M. (2010). *Dynamic Energy Budget Theory for Metabolic Organisation*. Cambridge: Cambridge University Press.

Kooijman, S. A. L. M. (1993). *Dynamic Energy Budgets in Biological Systems*. Cambridge: Cambridge University Press.

Kooijman, S. A. L. M. and Metz, J. A. J. (1984). On the dynamics of chemically stressed populations: The deduction of population consequences from effects on individuals. *Ecotoxicology and Environmental Safety* 8: 254–74.

Kuznetsov, Y. A. (1998). *Elements of Applied Bifurcation Theory*. 2nd edition. New York: Springer.

Leslie, P. H. (1945). On the use of matrices in certain population mathematics. *Biometrika*, 33(3): 183–212.

Lika, K. and Nisbet, R. M. (2000). A dynamic energy budget model based on partitioning of net production. *Journal of Mathematical Biology*, 41(4): 361–86.

Lindmark, M., Ohlberger, J., Huss, M., and Gårdmark, A. (2019). Size-based ecological interactions drive food web responses to climate warming. *Ecology Letters*, 22(5): 778–86.

Lotka, A. J. (1925). *Elements of Physical Biology*. Baltimore, MD: Williams and Wilkins.

May, R. M., 2001. *Stability and Complexity in Model Ecosystem*. Princeton, NJ: Princeton University Press.

McCann, K. and Yodzis, P. (1995). Bifurcation structure of a 3-species food-chain model. *Theoretical Population Biology*, 48(2): 93–125.

McCauley, E. and Murdoch, W. W. (1990). Predator-prey dynamics in environments rich and poor in nutrients. *Nature*, 343: 455–57.

Metz, J. A. J. and de Roos, A. M. (1992). The role of physiologically structured population models within a general individual-based modelling perspective. In D.L. DeAngelis and L. J. Gross (eds.), *Individual-Based Models and Approaches in Ecology: Populations, Communities and Ecosystems*. New York: Chapman-Hall, pp. 88–111.

Metz, J. A. J. and Diekmann, O. (1986). *The Dynamics of Physiologically Structured Populations*. Heidelberg: Springer-Verlag.

Metz, J. A. J., Geritz, S. A. H., Meszéna, G., Jacobs, F. J. A., and van Heerwaarden, J. S. (1996). Adaptive dynamics, a geometrical study of the consequences of nearly faithful reproduction. In S. J. van Strien and S. M. Verduyn-Lunel (eds.), *Stochastic and Spatial Structures of Dynamical Systems*. Amsterdam: KNAW Verhandelingen, pp. 183–231.

Murdoch, W. W., Briggs, C. J., and Nisbet, R. M. (2003). *Consumer-Resource Dynamics*. Princeton, NJ: Princeton University Press.

Nakazawa, T. (2011). Alternative stable states generated by ontogenetic niche shift in the presence of multiple resource use. *Plos One* 6(2): e14667.

Nakazawa, T. (2015). Ontogenetic niche shifts matter in community ecology: A review and future perspectives. *Population Ecology* 57(2): 347–54.

Nisbet, R. M. and Gurney, W. S. C. (1982). *Modelling Fluctuating Populations*. New York: Wiley and Sons.

Nisbet, R. M. and Gurney, W. S. C. (1983). The systematic formulation of population models for insects with dynamically varying instar duration. *Theoretical Population Biology* 23(1): 114–35.

Oksanen, L., Fretwell, S. D., Arruda, J., and Niemela, P. (1981). Exploitation ecosystems in gradients of primary productivity. *American Naturalist* 118: 240–61.

Olson, M. H., Green, D. M., and Rudstam, L. G. (2001). Changes in yellow perch (*Perca flavescens*) growth associated with the establishment of a walleye (*Stizostedion vitreum*) population in Canadarago Lake, New York (USA). *Ecology of Freshwater Fish* 10(1): 11–20.

Persson, L. and de Roos, A.M. (2013). Symmetry breaking in ecological systems through different energy efficiencies of juveniles and adults. *Ecology* 94(7): 1487–98.

Persson, L., Amundsen, P. -A., de Roos, A. M., Klemetsen, A., Knudsen, R., and Primicerio, R. (2007). Culling prey promotes predator recovery—Alternative states in a whole-lake experiment. *Science* 316(5832): 1743–46.

Persson, L., Amundsen, P. -A., de Roos, A. M., Knudsen, R., Primicerio, R., and Klemetsen, A. (2013). Density-dependent interactions in an Arctic char—brown trout system: Competition, predation, or both? *Canadian Journal of Fisheries and Aquatic Science* 70(4): 610–16.

Persson, L., Leonardsson, K., de Roos, A. M., Gyllenberg, M., and Christensen, B. (1998). Ontogenetic scaling of foraging rates and the dynamics of a size-structured consumer-resource model. *Theoretical Population Biology* 54(3): 270–93.

Rees, M., Childs, D. Z., and Ellner, S. P. (2014). Building integral projection models: A user's guide. *Journal of Animal Ecology* 83(3): 528–45.

Schellekens, T., de Roos, A. M., and Persson, L. (2010). Ontogenetic diet shifts result in niche partitioning between two consumer species irrespective of competitive abilities. *American Naturalist* 176(5): 625–37.

Schreiber, S. and Rudolf, V. H. W. (2008). Crossing habitat boundaries: Coupling dynamics of ecosystems through complex life cycles. *Ecology Letters* 11(6): 576–87.

Schröder, A., van Leeuwen, A., and Cameron, T. C. (2014). When less is more: positive population-level effects of mortality. *Trends in Ecology and Evolution* 29(11): 614–24.

Sharpe, F. R. and Lotka, A. J. (1911). A problem in age-distributions. *Philosophical Magazine* 21: 435–38.

Sinko, J. W. and Streifer, W. (1967). A new model for age-size structure of a population. *Ecology* 48: 910–18.

Sinko, J. W. and Streifer, W. (1969). Applying models incorporating age-size structure of a population to *Daphnia*. *Ecology* 50: 608–15.

Tilman, D. (1982). *Resource Competition and Community Structure*. Princeton, NJ: Princeton University Press.

Turchin, P. (2013). *Complex Population Dynamics*. Princeton, NJ: Princeton University Press.

van Leeuwen, A., Huss, M., Gårdmark, A., Casini, M., Vitale, F., Hjelm, J., Persson, L., and de Roos, A. M. (2013). Predators with multiple ontogenetic niche shifts have limited potential for population growth and top-down control of their prey. *American Naturalist* 182(1): 53–66.

Volterra, V. (1926). Variazioni e fluttuazioni del numero d'individui in specie animali conviventi. *Memorie della R. Accademia dei Lincei* 2: 31–113.

Wollrab, S., de Roos, A. M., and Diehl, S. (2013). Ontogenetic diet shifts promote predator-mediated coexistence. *Ecology* 94(12): 2886–97.

Yodzis, P. (1989). *Introduction to Theoretical Ecology*. New York: Harper and Row.

CHAPTER 6

Models for large ecological communities—a random matrix approach

Stefano Allesina and Jacopo Grilli

6.1 Introduction

The pioneering work of Lotka (1956) and Volterra (1926) launched a concerted effort to mathematize the dynamics of natural populations. Since then, much progress has been made in the analysis of models describing a single population or a few interacting populations. The simple models by Lotka and Volterra have been enriched by considering life histories, size-structured populations (Tuljapurkar and Caswell 2012), and their diffusion in space (Cantrell and Cosner 2004); current models often include complex, nonlinear functional forms (Arditi and Ginzburg 2012), difference and partial differential equations, time lags, external forcing due to varying environmental conditions, and stochasticity (Lande et al. 2003). Because of the great interest in the mathematics of population dynamics, ecologists have played a fundamental role in the development of this field in the last fifty years, including seminal applications of chaos (May 1976; Hastings et al. 1993) and bifurcation theory (Scheffer et al. 2009) to natural phenomena.

The analysis of simple ecological communities paid off, leading to modern coexistence theory (Chesson 2000), the concepts of limiting similarity and niche partitioning (Abrams 1983), trophic cascades (Pace et al. 1999), and a wealth of other fundamental ideas in ecology and evolutionary biology.

Analyzing larger ecological communities, however, has proven more difficult. When the number of interacting populations in a community is greater than three, the study of the dynamical system becomes prohibitively difficult, leaving ecologists to rely on large numerical simulations, rather than attempting to understand the system using mathematical analysis.

In this chapter, we review classic and more recent studies that attempted to build a mathematical framework for understanding the dynamics of large ecological communities. In particular, we are going to focus on the use of random matrices to describe ecological problems. A random matrix is a matrix whose elements are random variables. As such, instead of studying a given matrix, results obtained using the methods reviewed here describe the "typical behavior" of an entire class of matrices whose entries are sampled from some given distribution.

The use of random matrices in ecology dates back to the seminal work of May (1972), who shook long-held beliefs by proving that a sufficiently large or complex ecological community would not be able to recover from perturbations. May's work has been extended by numerous studies, refining the original formulation of a "random ecosystem" to include a statistical description of the way species interact

Allesina, S. and Grilli, J., *Models for large ecological communities—a random matrix approach* In: *Theoretical Ecology: Concepts and Applications.*
Edited by: Kevin S. McCann and Gabriel Gellner, Oxford University Press (2020). © Oxford University Press.
DOI: 10.1093/oso/9780198824282.003.0006

(e.g., consumption, competition, mutualism), food web structure, meta-population dynamics, and many other features of natural communities.

As we will see, random matrix theory is particularly suited for the task of modeling large ecological communities, by virtue of three facts: i) it typically considers very large (infinite) matrices, and as such is a good starting point for studying highly speciose communities; ii) many results are "universal," i.e., hold for a wide range of parameterizations, meaning that a single result we can shed light on a variety of ecological problems, sometimes quite distant from each other; iii) the theory is currently experiencing a vigorous growth in mathematics, with new results being produced at a very fast pace—by studying increasingly sophisticated models, new ecological questions can be addressed with this toolbox.

To set the stage for the chapter, we describe May's original contribution in some detail. We then review the history of random matrix theory, and discuss what it means to solve a problem in this area. We show how classic results in random matrices inform ecological theory, and review applications using more sophisticated, structured random matrices. We list other areas of ecology that can benefit from a random matrix approach, and conclude with a list of open problems whose solution would considerably advance our understanding of large ecological communities.

6.2 May's stability criterion

In the late 1960s, computing became cheap and powerful enough to allow numerical explorations of a variety of natural phenomena. In 1970, two researchers from the Biological Computer Laboratory at the University of Illinois, Mark R. Gardner and W. Ross Ashby, investigated whether and when a "large" dynamical system would be stable (Gardner and Ashby 1970). Importantly, they considered systems in which each of the S "agents" in a community are randomly connected with only a fraction of the other agents, and the interactions between the agents are encoded in a matrix. They called the proportion of realized connections (i.e., the proportion of nonzero elements in the matrix)

the "connectance" of the system—a term that is still used today. For their results, presented in a single page in *Nature*, they considered random matrices of size 4, 7, and 10, and varied the number of nonzero coefficients (all sampled independently from a uniform distribution ranging from −1 to 1) to probe the effect of the size and connectance of the matrix on its "stability" (i.e., whether all the eigenvalues of the matrix had negative real part, see Box 6.1). They measured the probability of stability of a matrix given its size and connectance, and found a striking result: when crossing a critical level of connectance, systems rapidly moved from being "almost certainly stable" to "almost certainly unstable," with a sudden transition.

While Gardner and Ashby thought of airports, social networks and neural systems when writing their manuscript, their results were about to shake community ecology at its core.

In the post-World War Two era, community ecology was greatly influenced by cybernetics, thermodynamics, and information theory (McIntosh 1980). Using these tools, theoretical ecologists attempted to make sense of the networks of ecological interactions between species which had been appearing with increasing frequency in the literature. Following the observations by Elton and Odum, Robert H. MacArthur (1955) proposed the idea that the multiplicity of pathways connecting resources to consumers in complex ecological networks would buffer these systems against fluctuations: if one of the channels bringing energy from producers to a given species were to go dry, other channels would take its place, thereby mitigating the effect of environmental fluctuations on the dynamics of populations (Kingsland 1995). This theory was in good agreement with observation (McCann 2000): rich ecosystems are less prone to invasion than those encompassing only a handful of species, and the fluctuations in population abundances seem to be more constrained in richer ecosystems.

In 1972, the work of Robert M. May challenged these beliefs, through the first application of random matrix theory in ecology (May 1972). May recognized that the work of Gardner and Ashby was relevant for the study of the local asymptotic stability of ecological communities around equilibrium,

---

Box 6.1 Local asymptotic stability

The dynamics of an ecological community are often described using a system of nonlinear differential equations:

$$\frac{dx_i(t)}{dt} = f_i\left(\mathbf{x}(t)\right), \tag{6.7}$$

where x_i is the density of species i at time t, and $\mathbf{x}(t)$ is the vector collecting the densities of all of the species. The function f_i details how the growth of species i is affected by the species in the community. In general, this system of equations can lead to very complicated dynamics, but here we concentrate on the simplest case: equilibrium dynamics. An equilibrium $\mathbf{x}^*$ is a vector of densities such that:

$$\left.\frac{dx_i}{dt}\right|_{\mathbf{x}^*} = f_i\left(\mathbf{x}^*\right) = 0 \forall i. \tag{6.8}$$

A given system might have a multitude of equilibria. When the system is resting at an equilibrium point, it will remain there unless it is perturbed away from it. Local stability analysis is a method to probe whether a system that is perturbed infinitesimally away from an equilibrium will eventually return to it, or rather move away from it. The analysis is based on the Jacobian matrix of the system $\mathbf{J}$, whose elements are defined as:

$$J_{ij} = \frac{\partial f_i(\mathbf{x})}{\partial x_j}. \tag{6.9}$$

Each element of this matrix is therefore a function, whose value depends on $\mathbf{x}$. When we evaluate the Jacobian matrix at an equilibrium point $\mathbf{x}^*$, we obtain the so-called "community matrix" $\mathbf{M}$:

$$\mathbf{M} = \mathbf{J}|_{\mathbf{x}^*}. \tag{6.10}$$

Note that, although each system has a unique Jacobian matrix, there are as many community matrices as there are equilibria. The community matrix details the effect of increasing density of one species on the growth rate of any other species around the equilibrium point.

The most notable property of the community matrix is that its eigenvalues determine the stability of the equilibrium $\mathbf{x}^*$: if all the eigenvalues have negative real part, then the system will eventually return to the equilibrium after sufficiently small perturbations; conversely, if any of the eigenvalues have positive real part, the system will move away from the equilibrium whenever perturbed. Therefore, depending on the sign of the "rightmost" eigenvalue of $\mathbf{M}$, λ_1, we can determine the stability of $\mathbf{x}^*$:

$$\text{Re}\left(\lambda_1\right) \begin{cases} < 0 \rightarrow \mathbf{x}^* \text{ is stable} \\ > 0 \rightarrow \mathbf{x}^* \text{ is unstable} \end{cases} \tag{6.11}$$

Local asymptotic stability means that the equilibrium is stable with respect to infinitesimal perturbations ("local"), and that returning to the equilibrium could take a long time ("asymptotic"). Ecologists have also studied stronger forms of stability (e.g., "global stability," meaning that all trajectories lead to the same equilibrium).

(Box 6.1) and, in another very short article in *Nature*, proved that sufficiently large and connected ecological systems would inevitably be dynamically unstable.

May considered an unspecified system of first-order, nonlinear differential equations describing the interactions between a set of S species. Such a system would be difficult to study for sufficiently large S: depending on the parameters and the initial conditions, the trajectories of the community could end up in one of many dynamical attractors, leading to fixed points, limit cycles, or chaos. The difficulty of this problem is compounded by the fact that there is no universally accepted, canonical set of equations describing interacting populations, and that even for a specific functional form, measuring empirically all the parameters needed to investigate

the dynamics of a large community is unfeasible from a practical standpoint.

May's brilliant intuition was to jump over these difficulties altogether, and assume that an unspecified dynamical system is resting at an equilibrium point. Around the equilibrium, dynamics can be approximated using a linear system of equations, making the mathematical analysis straightforward.

Suppose that a system of S species is resting at the equilibrium $\mathbf{x}^*$ (with every component $x_i^* > 0$, a condition known as "feasibility"). If unperturbed, the system would remain at the equilibrium point forever. But what if it were slightly perturbed? Would it go back to the equilibrium, or rather move away from it? In the case of an infinitesimal perturbation $\Delta\mathbf{x}(0)$, we can track the evolution of the perturbation in time by approximating the dynamics using a linear system of equations:

$$\frac{d\Delta\mathbf{x}(t)}{dt} = \mathbf{M}\Delta\mathbf{x}(t), \tag{6.1}$$

where $\mathbf{M}$ is the "community matrix" of the system at equilibrium (see Box 6.1). Inspecting the eigenvalues and eigenvectors of $\mathbf{M}$ is sufficient to determine the stability of $\mathbf{x}^*$: for each direction encoded by an eigenvector of $\mathbf{M}$, the system moves towards the equilibrium if the corresponding eigenvalue has a negative real part, while it moves away from it if the real part of the eigenvalue is positive; the magnitude of the real part of the eigenvalue measures the speed at which the system approaches or moves away from the equilibrium, while the imaginary part measures the oscillations of the trajectory. Therefore, an equilibrium point is stable if all the eigenvalues of the corresponding community matrix have negative real part, and is unstable otherwise.

Of course, to determine exactly the community matrix $\mathbf{M}$, one would need to know the functional form, measure all of the parameters and initial conditions, and compute the equilibrium $\mathbf{x}^*$—this becomes impossibly daunting when communities are large. May took a different route, and modeled $\mathbf{M}$ as a random matrix.

The diagonal elements of $\mathbf{M}$ measure "self-regulation" (e.g., density dependence due to finite resources). Suppose species are not interacting with each other at all: then the matrix $\mathbf{M}$ would only have nonzero coefficients on the diagonal, and therefore the system would be stable if, and only if, all the diagonal coefficients were negative (the eigenvalues of $\mathbf{M}$ would be exactly its diagonal elements). When we add the interactions between species, the element M_{ij} measures the effect of species j on i around the equilibrium. Naturally, not all species affect each other directly. May first set the proportion of interacting species to C (connectance), and, whenever two species interacted, he then sampled the interaction strength from a distribution with mean 0 and variance σ^2. These rules define the community matrix as a random matrix with $M_{ii} = -d$, measuring the strength of self-regulation, and M_{ij} being zero with probability $(1 - C)$, and sampled independently from a distribution $\mathcal{X}$ with mean zero and variance σ^2 otherwise. With this

definition in place, one can probe how the size of the matrix S, the connectance C, and the variance σ^2 influence the stability of the system.

In Figure 6.1, we plot the eigenvalues of such a matrix: the eigenvalues are approximately uniformly distributed in a circle, and therefore knowing the center and radius of the circle is sufficient to determine the stability of the system. Because the matrix $\mathbf{M}$ has $-d$ on the diagonal, the circle is centered at $(-d, 0)$; for stability the radius r needs to be small enough, so that $r - d < 0$ (all eigenvalues would then fall in the negative half-plane). By applying a simple result from random matrix theory (discussed later), May computed the radius to be $r \approx \sqrt{SC\sigma^2}$, thereby providing a simple criterion for the stability of the system:

$$\sqrt{SC\sigma^2} < d. \tag{6.2}$$

If the stability criterion is satisfied, then the system is almost surely stable, while if it is not, it almost surely unstable (Figure 6.1). This result sheds light on the numerical experiment of Gardner and Ashby, who had found a sharp transition from stability to instability when varying connectance: May's result showed that changing the size of the system or the variance of the nonzero coefficients would have a similar effect (Figure 6.1).

By proving this simple result, May challenged the notion that more complex ecological communities would be intrinsically more stable: take a stable community, and increase its size, connectance, or the variance of the interaction strengths—eventually, the system will cross a critical level, and become unstable. This argument set in motion the so-called "complexity-stability" debate, which populated the literature for the following decades (McCann 2000): fundamentally, May showed that complex systems are not stable because they are complex, but rather that if they are stable it is despite being complex.

May's work is a good illustration of three paradigmatic aspects of random matrix theory. First, by using random matrices, May was able to show that for the stability of a random ecological community constructed as detailed earlier, only two quantities matter: the strength of the self-regulation, $-d$, and the "system's complexity," $\sqrt{SC\sigma^2}$ —changing the size, connectance, or variance has the same effect

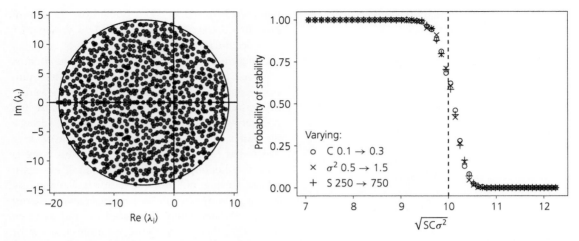

Figure 6.1 *Left*: location of the eigenvalues of a 1000 × 1000 matrix with connectance 0.2, nonzero coefficients sampled independently from a normal distribution with mean zero and variance $\sigma^2 = 1$, and diagonal coefficients $d = -5$. The eigenvalues are approximately uniformly distributed in a circle with center $(d, 0)$ and radius $\sqrt{SC\sigma^2}$. *Right*: starting with $S = 500$, $C = 0.2$, $\sigma^2 = 1$, and $d = -10$, we vary either the size (+), connectance (°) or the variance (×), and for each parameterization we produce 500 random matrices. The *y*-axis reports the probability of stability measured as the proportion of the matrices that were stable for a given parameterization. The *x*-axis reports the corresponding $\sqrt{SC\sigma^2}$. As predicted by May's stability criterion, whenever this quantity approaches d, the probability of stability rapidly decreases from about 1 to about 0. The transition is sharper for larger matrices.

on the stability of the system, so that two random matrices with the same "complexity" have the same stability properties. Second, May did not specify the distribution $\mathcal{X}$ from which the interactions are sampled, but rather only considered its mean and variance. This result, as many others in random matrix theory, is in fact "universal": it applies to any distribution $\mathcal{X}$ with the same mean and variance, irrespective of its shape. As such, May's result describes a very large class of random matrices, rather than any specific matrix. Third, the result only applies to large systems (technically, what matters is that SC is sufficiently large)—the result is useful to understand the behavior of large and dense, rather than small and sparse, systems.

In the following sections, we will show how this first result can be extended by considering more complicated models of random matrices.

6.3 Random matrices

A random matrix is simply a matrix whose coefficients are random variables, rather than fixed quantities. A random matrix *ensemble* is a probability

distribution over the possible matrices that can be produced by sampling random matrices.

Provided with a (diagonalizable) matrix, finding its eigenvalues and eigenvectors is a mechanical process, and there are many algorithms that one can use to solve this problem. Random matrix theory studies the probability distribution over the eigenvalues and eigenvectors of a matrix *ensemble*, often describing their typical behavior.

While the study of random matrices in statistics dates back ninety years (Wishart 1928), their use in the sciences was brought to the fore by Eugene Wigner, who, in a series of papers in the 1950s, modeled the energy spectra of heavy atomic nuclei, where a large number of neutrons and protons interact in a complex way (Wigner 1967). In quantum physics, the energy levels for these nuclei can be seen as the eigenvectors of the Hamiltonian operator, which can be expressed as a (large) symmetric matrix. Instead of calculating the energy levels from first principles, Wigner attempted to describe them statistically using random matrices, with great success (reviewed in Dyson 1962). Freeman Dyson's description of the problem is fitting for ecology as well—just substitute the word "nucleus" with "ecological community," and "particles" with "species":

what is here required is a new kind of statistical mechanics, in which we renounce exact knowledge not of the state of a system but of the nature of the system itself. We picture a complex nucleus as a "black box" in which a large number of particles are interacting according to unknown laws. (Dyson 1962)

Since then, random matrices have been used in many branches of physics: from solid state physics to quantum chromodynamics, from optics to quantum gravity. Beyond physics (and ecology), the use of random matrices has been instrumental in numerical analysis (Wishart 1928), number theory (Hughes et al. 2000), control theory (Chow et al. 1975), and theoretical neuroscience (Sompolinsky et al. 1988).

The objective of random matrix theory is to study the properties of (typically large) random matrices: the distribution of eigenvalues, eigenvectors, and the spacing between eigenvalues have all received much attention. For ecological applications, the distribution of the eigenvalues (called the "empirical spectral distribution," ESD) of random matrices is the property that has found the most applications. Simply put, this density function measures the probability of observing an eigenvalue with a given value. For simple cases, the full distribution can be derived, while for more complicated random matrices, one can concentrate on finding its support (i.e., the region where there is a non-zero probability of observing an eigenvalue, in the limit of large matrices), which is still relevant for the study of stability (Box 6.1). In Box 6.2 we list the main mathematical tools that are used to derive the spectral density or its support analytically: we include a brief description and pointers to the primary literature.

Often, the spectral density is characterized by few (i.e., a finite number in the limit of large matrices) outliers, which appear as isolated eigenvalues. These outliers might have a strong effect on stability, and, interestingly, can be computed very easily from the structure of the matrix. We analyze these cases in the following sections.

While identifying the spectral distribution is a well-defined problem for matrices of any size, very

often random matrix theory is developed in the limit of large (infinite) sized matrices. This choice turns out to be convenient because random matrix ensembles are often *self-averaging*: the relative fluctuations around the average behavior becomes smaller and smaller as the size increases. When this property holds, the spectrum of large matrices converges to the average behavior. Moreover, a large class of random matrix ensembles are *universal*: the spectral density, in the limit of large sizes, depends only on a few moments of the probability distribution from which the matrix elements are drawn. For instance, the spectral density of a symmetric matrix with independent elements depends only on the mean and variance of the distribution, and not on further moments (skewness, kurtosis, etc.).

In the following sections, we describe the spectral density of random matrices of increasing complexity. In all cases, solving the density provides directly applicable ecological insight, by highlighting which parameters determine the shape of the distribution, and therefore which properties of the ecological community are important for determining dynamics.

6.4 Fundamental results

In this section, we briefly review some of the most fundamental laws in random matrix theory. For a more rigorous mathematical introduction to the topic, we recommend the book by Bai and Silverstein (2010). For a more hands-on approach, we suggest instead the book by Livan et al. (2018).

Diagonal elements: before listing some of the laws for random matrices, we discuss the special role played by self-regulation in determining stability.

The sum of the diagonal elements of a matrix (its *trace*) is also the sum of its eigenvalues: $\sum_i M_{ii} = \text{tr}(\mathbf{M}) = \sum_i \lambda_i$. As such, adding a constant diagonal to a matrix results in a shift of all its eigenvalues: if $M'_{ii} = M_{ii} + d$, then the eigenvalues of $\mathbf{M'}$ are the same as those of $\mathbf{M}$, all shifted of d. This means that, for any system, we can always achieve stability by increasing self-regulation to all species, and therefore illuminates the special role self-regulation played in May's contribution. Because the effect of adding a constant diagonal is

---

Box 6.2 Tools for solving random matrix problems

The main object of study of random matrix theory is the spectral density, which can be formally defined as

$$\mu(\lambda) = E\left(\frac{1}{n}\sum_{i=1}^{n}\delta(\lambda - \lambda_i)\right), \quad (6.12)$$

where $\{\lambda_1, \lambda_2, \ldots, \lambda_n\}$ are the eigenvalues of a random matrix of size n, $E(\cdot)$ is the average over the random matrix ensemble and $\delta(\cdot)$ is the Dirac delta function. This formula holds for Hermitian matrices, which have only real eigenvalues, but can be extended to the non-Hermitian case (Sommers et al. 1988). While this definition is formally correct, it is not directly usable for computing the spectral density.

It is convenient to define

$$\mathcal{G}(z) = E\left(\frac{1}{n}\sum_{i=1}^{n}\frac{1}{z - \lambda_i}\right) = E\left(\frac{1}{n}\text{tr}(z\mathbf{I} - \mathbf{M})^{-1}\right),$$
$$(6.13)$$

which is more amenable to analytical treatment. One can in fact compute the spectral density (using Livan et al. 2018):

$$\mu(\lambda) = \frac{1}{\pi}\lim_{\epsilon \to 0^+}\text{Im}\,\mathcal{G}(\lambda + i\epsilon) \quad (6.14)$$

The complex function $\mathcal{G}(z)$ is called resolvent and is the central object of study of random matrix theory.

Method of moments

The average of the spectral density (i.e., the average eigenvalue) is simply given by the expectation of $\text{tr}(\mathbf{M})/n$. Similarly, we have that the k-th moment of the spectral density is given by

$$E\left(\lambda^k\right) := \int d\lambda\,\mu(\lambda)\,\lambda^k = E\left(\frac{1}{n}\sum_{i=1}^{n}\lambda_i^k\right) = \frac{1}{n}E\left(\text{tr}\left(\mathbf{M}^k\right)\right).$$
$$(6.15)$$

By computing all these moments one can reconstruct the spectral density. For a review of the application of the method of moments to random matrices see Kirsch and Kriecherbauer (2016).

Replica method and cavity method

Statistical mechanics studies systems with a large number of interacting degrees of freedom from a probabilistic point of view. It can be shown (Livan et al. 2018) that the resolvent can be computed as the correlation function of continuous degrees of freedom whose interactions is defined by a random matrix. This correspondence allows to use standard techniques borrowed from statistical mechanics of disordered systems. In particular, the resolvent can be written as

$$\mathcal{G}(z) = \frac{1}{n}E\left(\text{tr}(z\mathbf{I} - \mathbf{M})^{-1}\right) = \frac{1}{n}\frac{\partial}{\partial z}E\left(\log\det(z\mathbf{I} - \mathbf{M})\right)$$
$$=: \frac{2}{n}\frac{\partial}{\partial z}E\left(\log Z(z)\right) \quad (6.16)$$

The statistical mechanics analogy comes from the fact that, using the properties of the Gaussian integral, $Z(z)$ can be interpreted as a *partition function*

$$Z(z) := \sqrt{\det(z\mathbf{I} - \mathbf{M})} = \int d^n\mathbf{x}\,e^{-\frac{1}{2}\mathbf{x}\cdot(z\mathbf{I} - \mathbf{M})\cdot\mathbf{x}} \quad (6.17)$$

Averaging Z over the randomness of the matrix $\mathbf{M}$ would be a relatively simple problem: we could exchange the average over $\mathbf{M}$ with the integral over $\mathbf{x}$ in Equation 6.17, compute the average of the exponential and then integrate over $\mathbf{x}$. Unfortunately, in Equation 6.16, it appears the average of $\log Z$ instead of Z. The replica method exploits the formula

$$\log Z = \lim_{n \to 0}\frac{Z^n - 1}{n}, \quad (6.18)$$

where Z is the partition function, to calculate the average of $\log Z$ (which is a complicated problem), by reducing the problem to the calculation of Z^n (with integer n, which is much easier). This is equivalent to averaging over n copies of the system (from which the name replicas). This method has been applied to compute the spectral density of different random matrix ensembles (Kanzieper 2001; Livan et al. 2018) and to the non-Hermitian case (Sommers et al. 1988).

The cavity method assumes that the random matrix has a tree structure (there are no loops) to write consistency equation for the derivatives of $\log Z$. While this method is only exact under the assumption of a tree structure, it provides the correct result also for large dense random matrices. The cavity method has been successfully applied for a broad range of random matrix ensembles (Rogers et al. 2008; Rogers and Castillo 2009; Grilli et al. 2016; Gibbs et al. 2018).

Free probability

Free probability studies random variables when multiplication is not commuting (e.g., for matrices, where $\mathbf{AB}$ is generally different from **BA**). Since random matrices are not commuting, the spectral density of the sum of two random matrices is not given by a simple convolution of the spectral densities of the two. Free probability allows to write the resolvant of the sum as a proper combination of the resolvants of the two matrices (Mingo and Speicher 2017; Livan et al. 2018). For standard random variables, the cumulant generating function of a sum of two random variables is the sum of the two cumulant generating functions. In free probability the role of the cumulant generating function is replaced by the so-called R-transform. The R-tranform is a complex function $\mathcal{R}(z)$ that can be obtained from the resolvant as

$$\mathcal{R}(z) = \mathcal{G}^{-1}(z) - \frac{1}{z}. \qquad (6.19)$$

The R-transform of the sum of two matrices **A** + **B** is simply the sum of the two resolvants,

$$\mathcal{R}_{\mathbf{A}+\mathbf{B}}(z) = \mathcal{R}_{\mathbf{A}}(z) + \mathcal{R}_{\mathbf{B}}(z). \qquad (6.20)$$

Similarly, free probability can be applied to obtain the spectral density of the product of random matrices (Mingo and Speicher 2017).

Non-Hermitian matrices

Non-Hermitian matrices have complex eigenvalues. The spectral density needs therefore to be defined over the complex plane

$$\mu(x,y) = E\left(\frac{1}{n}\sum_{i=1}^{n} \delta(x - \mathrm{Re}(\lambda_i))\, \delta(y - \mathrm{Im}(\lambda_i))\right). \qquad (6.21)$$

Given the presence of the product of two Dirac delta functions, we cannot use translate directly the formula for the resolvant to the non-Hermitian case. One way to define a resolvant which applies to the non-Hermitian case is to introduce quaternions. Quaternions are a number system that extends complex numbers. An important feature of quaternions is that the algebra is not commutative. A quaternion q can be written as $q = z + wj$, where z and w are complex numbers. The properties $j^2 = -1$ and $ij = -ji$ fully define the algebra of quaternions.

The quaternionic resolvant is defined as the quaternionic function (Rogers 2010),

$$\mathcal{G}(q) = \frac{1}{n}E\left(\sum_{i=1}^{n}(q - \lambda_i)^{-1}\right), \qquad (6.22)$$

where q is a quaternion and the λs are complex eigenvalues. The spectral density can be obtained as (Rogers 2010),

$$\mu(x,y) = \frac{1}{2\pi}\lim_{\epsilon \to 0^+}\left(\frac{\partial}{\partial x} + i\frac{\partial}{\partial y}\right)\mathcal{G}(x + iy + \epsilon j). \qquad (6.23)$$

trivial, in most articles using random matrices the diagonal is taken to be 0.

Symmetric matrices—Wigner's semicircle law: a Wigner matrix is an $S \times S$ random matrix **X** where all the coefficients X_{ij} in the upper-triangular part (i.e., $i < j$) are independent, identically distributed random variables, and $X_{ij} = X_{ji}$ (i.e., the matrix is symmetric). The diagonal coefficients X_{ii} have mean zero and finite variance, while the off-diagonal elements have mean zero and unit variance ($E[X_{ij}] = 0$, $E[X_{ij}^2] = 1$). Then, as $S \to \infty$, the empirical spectral distribution of $\mathbf{M}/\sqrt{S}$ (i.e., of the matrix in which all the coefficients have been divided by the $\sqrt{S}$) converges almost surely to the Wigner's semicircular distribution:

$$\mu(\lambda) = \begin{cases} \frac{1}{2\pi}\sqrt{4 - \lambda^2} & \text{if } \lambda \in [-2,2] \\ 0 & \text{otherwise.} \end{cases} \qquad (6.3)$$

Importantly, we have not defined the distribution of the X_{ij}: as long as the coefficients have mean zero, and unit variance, the result holds (universality).

This result can be used to approximate the leading ("rightmost") eigenvalue of a random symmetric matrix. If the size of the matrix is S, the diagonal coefficients are zero, and the upper-triangular coefficients are sampled independently from a distribution with mean zero and variance σ^2, then $\lambda_1 \approx 2\sqrt{S\sigma^2}$. Note that the result holds when the size of the matrix is infinite; for finite matrices, fluctuations can lead some eigenvalues to fall outside of the semi-circle, which is another problem studied in random matrix theory (Tao and Vu 2012).

Non-symmetric matrices—circular law: take a non-symmetric, $S \times S$ random matrix in which all coefficients X_{ij} are i.i.d. random variables with $E[X_{ij}] = 0$ and $E[X_{ij}^2] = 1$. Then, as $S \to \infty$, the ESD of $\mathbf{X}/\sqrt{S}$ converges to the circular law:

$$\mu(\lambda) = \begin{cases} \frac{1}{\pi} & \text{if } (\text{Re}(\lambda))^2 + (\text{Im}(\lambda))^2 \leq 1 \\ 0 & \text{otherwise.} \end{cases} \quad (6.4)$$

This result can be used to calculate the radius of the eigenvalue distribution of the matrices studied by May: when the off-diagonal coefficients M_{ij} are 0 with probability $1 - C$ and are sampled independently from a distribution with mean 0 and variance σ^2 with probability C, we have that $E[M_{ij}] = 0$ and $E[M_{ij}^2] = C\sigma^2$. This means that if we were to divide the coefficients of $\mathbf{M}$ by $\sqrt{C\sigma^2}$ we would recover the unit variance, and the matrix would follow the circular law when S is large. Armed with this, we can calculate the radius: if the radius of $\mathbf{M}/\sqrt{SC\sigma^2}$ converges to 1 when the matrix is large, then the radius of $\mathbf{M}$ is approximately $\sqrt{SC\sigma^2}$. For stability, we need a sufficiently negative diagonal ($\sqrt{SC\sigma^2} - d < 0$), yielding May's stability criterion.

Bivariate distribution—elliptic law: in ecological communities, the effect of species i on j and that of j on i are typically not independent: in the case of competition between species, we expect them both to be negative; for consumption, if one is positive, the other is negative, and so forth. A more refined model of a random matrix would therefore sample interactions in pairs from a bivariate distribution. The elliptic law can be applied to this case.

Take a non-symmetric, $S \times S$ random matrix in which the pairs of coefficients (X_{ij}, X_{ji}) are sampled independently from a bivariate distribution defined by a vector of means $m = (0,0)^t$ and a covariance matrix $\Sigma = \begin{pmatrix} 1 & \rho \\ \rho & 1 \end{pmatrix}$. Then, as $S \to \infty$, the ESD of $\mathbf{X}/\sqrt{S}$ converges to the elliptic law:

$$\mu(\lambda) = \begin{cases} \frac{1}{\pi(1-\rho^2)} & \text{if } \frac{(\text{Re}(\lambda))^2}{(1+\rho)^2} + \frac{(\text{Im}(\lambda))^2}{(1-\rho)^2} \leq 1 \\ 0 & \text{otherwise.} \end{cases} \quad (6.5)$$

Note that, when $\rho = 0$, the elliptic law reduces to the circular law. Using the elliptic law, Allesina and Tang (2012) were able to extend May's criterion to ecological networks with different mixtures of interaction types (Box 6.3).

Covariance matrices—Marchenko–Pastur's law: the last law we are going to consider in this section deals with covariance matrices, which often appear in both ecological and statistical literature.

Take a $p \times n$ rectangular matrix $\mathbf{X}$, with $p < n$ and i.i.d. coefficients with $E[X_{ij}] = 0$ and $E[X_{ij}^2] = 1$. When $n \to \infty$, the ratio $p/n \to y$ (i.e., the number of rows and columns grow proportionally). Then the eigenvalue distribution of the scaled covariance matrix $\mathbf{S} = \frac{1}{n}\mathbf{X}\mathbf{X}'$ converges to:

$$\mu(\lambda) = \begin{cases} \frac{1}{2\pi\lambda y}\sqrt{\left((1+\sqrt{y})^2 - \lambda\right)\left(\lambda - (1-\sqrt{y})^2\right)} \\ \qquad\qquad \text{if } (1-\sqrt{y})^2 \leq \lambda \leq (1+\sqrt{y})^2 \\ \qquad\qquad 0 \quad \text{otherwise.} \end{cases}$$

$$(6.6)$$

Small-rank perturbations of random matrices: all the basic results listed previously consider matrices whose coefficients have mean zero. Clearly, this is rarely the case in ecological systems, and therefore for applications we need to incorporate the possibility of nonzero means. While in general one cannot compute the distribution of the eigenvalues of a sum of two matrices $\mathbf{M} = \mathbf{A} + \mathbf{B}$ from the eigenvalues of the two matrices, this calculation is possible whenever $\mathbf{A}$ has small-rank (i.e., few nonzero eigenvalues, or a finite amount in the limit of infinitely large sizes) and $\mathbf{B}$ is a large random matrix. In this case, the distribution of the eigenvalues of $\mathbf{B}$ will be composed by a bulk, defined by the spectrum of $\mathbf{B}$, and (possibly) a few outlier eigenvalues, matching closely the nonzero eigenvalues of $\mathbf{A}$ (a correction is needed when the coefficients of $\mathbf{B}$ are correlated, (O'Rourke and Renfrew 2014)).

Applications to stability: Figure 6.2 shows numerical examples for the laws examined in this section, while Box 6.3 and Box 6.4 report two examples showing how these tools can be used to assess the stability of ecological systems.

Box 6.3 Stability criteria for correlated entries

The original result by Robert May (1972) applies to a community with random interaction types: the elements M_{ij} and M_{ji} are sampled independently, and therefore one can have arbitrary combinations of signs. For instance, given a connectance C, a fraction $C^2/4$ of the interactions is expected to be mutualistic (corresponding to a $(+, +)$ pair), a fraction $C^2/4$ competitive (a $(-, -)$ pair) and a fraction $C(1 - C)/2$ commensalistic (a $(+, 0)$ pair). It is therefore natural to ask what is the effect of having a single interaction type represented, or having different types in arbitrary proportions.

The effect of interaction types (which translate into constraints on the signs of the elements of the community matrix) is, unexpectedly, remarkably simple (Allesina and Tang 2012). The spectrum of the corresponding random matrix depends only on three key parameters: the mean, the variance and the correlation between off-diagonal elements. Note that different interaction types influence the value of mean, variance and correlation. For instance, mutualistic interactions correspond to positive mean and positive correlation, competitive interactions produce negative mean and positive correlation, while antagonistic interactions are characterized by a negative correlation.

More formally, we can consider the following model. With probability C an interaction between two species is present.

If the interaction is not present the corresponding pair of coefficients (M_{ij}, M_{ji}) is set to $(0, 0)$, otherwise, (M_{ij}, M_{ji}) is sampled from a bivariate distribution $\mathcal{X}$ with identical marginal means μ, marginal variances σ^2 and correlation ρ. The diagonal elements are set to $-d$.

Since the spectrum of random matrices is *universal*, it does not depend on the choice of the bivariate distribution X, but only on C, d, μ, σ and ρ. It is simple to observe that

$$E[M_{ij}] = C\mu,$$

$$E[M_{ij}^2] = C\left(\sigma^2 + (1 - C)\mu^2\right),$$

$$E[M_{ij}M_{ji}] = \rho\sigma^2 + (1 - C)\mu^2. \tag{6.24}$$

The bulk of eigenvalues is therefore described by the elliptic law centered in $-d - E[M_{ij}]$. There is also an outlier eigenvalue, which takes value $-d + SE[M_{ij}]$. The condition for stability reads then

$$-d + \max\left\{SE[M_{ij}], -E[M_{ij}] + \sqrt{SE[M_{ij}^2]}\left(1 + \frac{E[M_{ij}M_{ji}]}{E[M_{ij}^2]}\right)\right\}. \tag{6.25}$$

6.5 Structured random matrices

In the previous section, we have discussed the properties of random matrices without any underlying structure: the pairs of entries (M_{ij}, M_{ji}) were all sampled independently from the same distribution. Real ecological networks are quite distant from this idealized case. For example, empirically we find that some species interact with few others (specialists) and others with many (generalists). Similarly, often species can be organized into groups such that interactions are frequent within groups, and infrequent among groups (modularity)—for example, in a stratified lake we find that benthic organisms tend to interact with other bottom-dweller organisms, while pelagic species with other organisms that are close to the surface. Moreover,

ecological networks are often structured by species' traits—the adage of "big fish eat small fish" being one example.

All these features translate into peculiar organizations of ecological interactions, collectively known as "network structure." Historically, applications of random matrices to ecology have been criticized exactly because of this fact: the lack of structure made it difficult to see how the highly idealized cases described previously would fare once more complications had been included. Recent progress in the mathematics of random matrices opened the door to the study of "structured random matrices," and in this section we provide a few pointers to contemporary work in this area. All these results can be seen as special cases—as of today, there is not a general theory of structured random matrices,

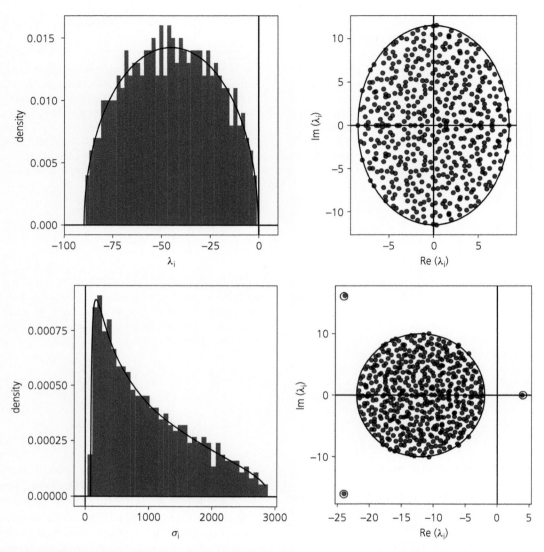

Figure 6.2 *Top-left*: Wigner's Semicircle Law: the plot shows the histogram of the eigenvalues of a symmetric matrix **M** with 500 rows and columns, diagonal elements $M_{ii} = -45$, and off-diagonal elements sampled independently from a standard normal distribution. The histogram is well-described by the semicircle law (line). *Top-right*: Elliptic Law. The plot shows the eigenvalues of a matrix **M** of size 500 with diagonal elements equal to zero, and off-diagonal elements sampled in pairs. With probability C, the pair (M_{ij}, M_{ji}) is sampled from a bivariate normal distribution with means zero, unit variances and correlation -0.75; with probability $1 - C$ both coefficients are zero. The eigenvalues are approximately uniform in an ellipse in the complex plane. *Bottom-Left*: Marchenko-Pastur Law. The histogram of the singular values of a 1000×500 random matrix with entries sampled independently from a standard normal follows the distribution studied by Marchenko and Pastur. *Bottom-right*: Small-rank perturbation of a random matrix. A random matrix, as those studied by May ($S = 500$, $C = 0.2$, $\sigma^2 = 1$, $d = -12$), follows the circular law. When we add to this matrix another matrix of rank three (small circles), we can calculate the location of the bulk (large circle), and the three outliers.

Box 6.4 The stability of random competitive communities

To show how fundamental results in random matrix theory can be used to solve ecological problems, we are going to consider a simple case: we have S species, competing for shared resources. In particular, the matrix **A** accounts for the interactions between the species. Each species is characterized by a growth rate, r_i, and dynamics following the Generalized Lotka–Volterra model:

$$\frac{dx_i(t)}{dt} = x_i \left(r_i + \sum_j A_{ij} x_j \right) \qquad (6.26)$$

The Jacobian of the system evaluated at the equilibrium **x*** is simply $M_{ij} = A_{ij} x_i^*$. When the interactions are symmetric ($A_{ij} = A_{ji}$) we have that, if the equilibrium is feasible ($x_i^* > 0 \forall i$), then it is stable if and only if **A** is stable.

Now suppose that $A_{ii} = -d$, while the upper triangular coefficients A_{ij} (with $j > i$) are sampled independently from a uniform distribution between -1 and 0 and the lower triangular coefficients have correlation ρ with the upper triangular. Which is the minimum value of d needed for stability?

To solve the problem we need to recognize that the eigenvalues of the matrix **M**, with elements $M_{ij} = A_{ij} x_i^*$, defines the stability of a feasible fixed point **x***. We can therefore translate this problem into a random matrix theory problem. Given a random matrix **A** and a positive random vector **x***, what is the distribution of eigenvalues of the matrix **M**?

It turns out that the solution can in fact be obtained analytically using the cavity method (Gibbs et al. 2018) in the case $\rho = 0$. In particular, the support of eigenvalues is given by the solution λ of

$$\int dx P(x) \frac{x^2}{|\lambda - xd|} = 1, \qquad (6.27)$$

where $P(x)$ is the distribution of the population abundance. Remarkably, one can easily observe that the community matrix **M** is expected to be stable if and only if **A** is stable. This result can be extended, via numerical analysis, to the case $\rho \neq 0$, showing, somewhat unexpectedly, that the results obtained in the linear case apply trivially to a relevant non-linear scenario (the GLV equations), provided the existence of a fixed point.

---

but rather a collection of results for particular cases. On the bright side, all of these examples have direct ecological relevance.

Food webs: when analyzing aquatic food webs, a striking pattern emerges: the size of an organism is a strong determinant of its diet. This notion has been encoded in the "cascade" model (Cohen et al. 1986) for food web structure, in which species are ordered by size (or trophic level) and each species can feed on the preceding—but not subsequent—species. The random matrix that would arise in this case is special in that all of the positive interactions (effects of prey on predators) would be confined to the lower-triangular part of the matrix, while the negative ones to the upper-triangular part. As shown in Figure 6.3, this structure greatly alters the spectrum of the matrix, which does not simply follow the elliptic law. The spectrum is composed of a bulk of eigenvalues (in an ellipse) and a few outlier eigenvalues lying close to a circumference in the complex plane. Importantly, as demonstrated by Allesina et al. (2015), the orientation of the outlier eigenvalues depends on the relative strength

of positive and negative interactions: if negative interactions are stronger than the positive ones, then stability is enhanced; if the reverse is true, then the outlier eigenvalues determine stability, and the system will oscillate widely.

Degree distribution In natural ecosystems, some species establish many more interactions than others. In a random-matrix context, this amounts to studying matrices in which the location of the nonzero coefficients is determined by the adjacency matrix **A** of the underlying ecological network (where $A_{ij} = 1$ stands for an interaction between species i and j), where the *degree distribution* is broad. Much progress has been made in this area for the case in which the nonzero coefficients are i.i.d. random variables. In this case, the eigenvalues still fall in a circle in the complex plane, but the density is not uniform (as in the circular law), but rather concentrated around the origin (Figure 6.4). Yan et al. (2017) derived a stability criterion for the case of heterogeneous degrees, and in mathematics Cook et al. (2018) proved independently a more general case.

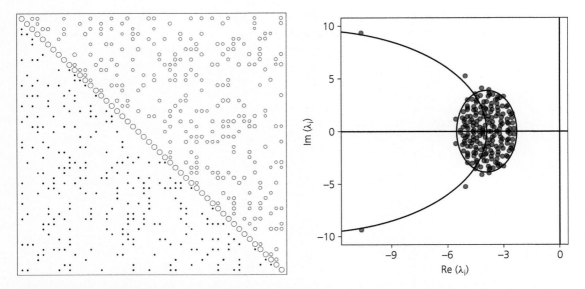

Figure 6.3 *Left*: When species are consuming each other such that large bodied species prey upon smaller-bodied ones, the random matrix is structured. The negative coefficients (open circles, size proportional to their strength) are confined to the upper-triangular part of the matrix, while the positive ones (filled circles), to the lower-triangular part. *Right*: This pattern strongly influences the spectrum of the random matrix, which is now composed of a bulk of eigenvalues falling in an ellipse, and a few outlier eigenvalues that are located close to a circumference (line in the plot). The whole spectrum can be derived using the methods developed in Allesina et al. (2015).

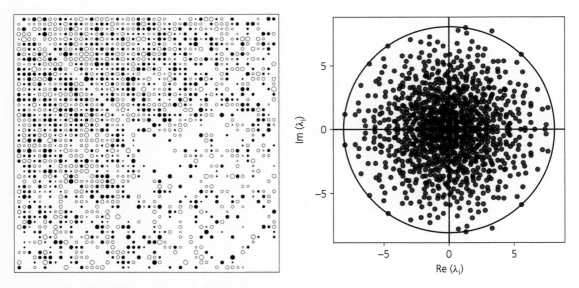

Figure 6.4 *Left*: In natural communities, some species interact with very many other species (generalists), while others with very few (specialists). If we build a random matrix in which each species establishes a different number of interactions, and the interactions are sampled independently from a distribution with mean zero and unit variance (*Left*: positive interactions represented by filled circles, negative by open circles; the size of the circle is proportional to interaction strengths), then the eigenvalues still fall in a circle in the complex plane, but the distribution is not uniform (Right). The radius of the circle can be found using the results of Cook et al. (2018).

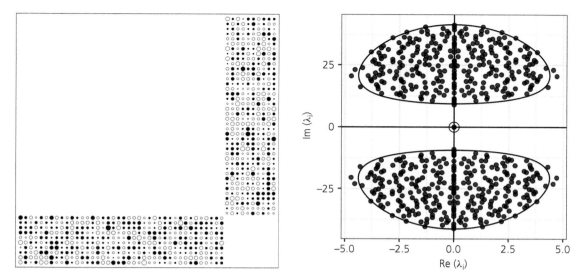

Figure 6.5 *Left*: Species are divided into two groups of different sizes, and interactions only connect species across groups (bipartite structure); when species interact, the coefficients are sampled from a bivariate normal distribution with means zero, unit variances, and correlation −0.75. *Right*: in this case, the spectrum departs dramatically from the elliptic law, but the location of the eigenvalues can be computed applying the method developed by Grilli et al. (2016).

Block-structured matrices One of the most studied concepts in networks is that of modularity (Newman and Girvan 2004): often, nodes in complex networks can be grouped such that the bulk of interactions are found between members of the same group, and few interactions connect nodes across groups. In ecology, the idea that a modular structure would be conducive to stability was already highlighted in May's original study (May 1972), but it was only recently that new results in random matrix theory allowed for a thorough calculation (Grilli et al. 2016). The spectrum of block-structured matrices can differ dramatically from that of unstructured ones (Figure 6.5). For species divided into two groups, Grilli et al. (2016) showed that an organization in modules can be either stabilizing or destabilizing, depending on the moments of the distribution of interaction strengths.

Species abundances In the Generalized Lotka–Volterra model (Box 6.4), the community matrix takes a particularly simple form: $M_{ij} = A_{ij}x_i^*$, where A_{ij} is the effect of species j on the growth of i and x_i^* is the equilibrium value of species i. In matrix form, we can write $\mathbf{M} = D(\mathbf{x}^*)\mathbf{A}$, where $D(\cdot)$ defines a diagonal matrix given a vector. Previously, we

have studied $\mathbf{M}$ directly as a random matrix. However, one could define $\mathbf{A}$ as a random matrix of species interaction, $\mathbf{x}^*$ as a (positive) random vector of species abundances at equilibrium, and study their product $\mathbf{M}$ using new methods in random matrix theory. For a given definition of the interaction matrix $\mathbf{A}$, one can then probe how the distribution of species abundances ($\mathbf{x}^*$) influences stability. This calculation was recently performed by Gibbs et al. (2018), who found that if $\mathbf{A}$ is stable, then almost any species-abundance distribution has no effect on stability. The same conclusion was found by Stone (2018) using a different method.

Spatial networks Finally, so far we have considered "closed" ecological communities, in which new species cannot enter the system. Using a random-matrix approach, Gravel et al. (2016) have studied the case in which several ecological communities are linked by dispersal, resulting in a stabilization of the "meta-ecosystem" when dispersal is intermediate. Interestingly, the mathematical treatment of this problem has strong parallels with the case in which we let self-regulation vary among species. The results of Barabás et al. (2017) showed that food webs cannot have stable equilibria unless the majority of species exhibit strong self-regulation, again finding that intermediate levels of self-regulation were the most conducive to stability.

The previous examples show that the random-matrix approach to ecological dynamics illustrated in this chapter is experiencing a rapid growth, and that many special cases of ecological network structure have been solved. While tackling arbitrary ecological network structures is still beyond what can be accomplished with current mathematical tools, these results provide a solid foundation upon which more complex results can be built.

6.6 Other applications

In the previous sections, we dealt with the problem of the local asymptotic stability of large ecological communities, which was historically the first application of random matrix theory in ecology. However, many other ecological problems can be expressed using matrices, eigenvalues and eigenvectors. Here we briefly introduce some of the ecological problems where a random-matrix approach could yield interesting insights.

Spread of diseases in contact network: two seemingly distant ecological problems turn out to have the same mathematical formulation, and random matrices can help make sense of them both.

Take n individuals, with each being in one of two states: S, susceptible to a disease, or I infected with the disease and infectious. If the individuals can recover and become susceptible again, we speak of an S-I-S model. In the simplest model of this kind, infected individuals randomly transmit the disease to susceptible individuals. A more refined model is one in which the contacts between individuals are encoded in a network, or equivalently in its adjacency matrix $\mathbf{A}$. An infected node/individual can transmit to the nodes it connects to, and these to their neighbors, and so forth. One of the main questions in this setting is to determine whether an epidemic outbreak will occur, and how the probability of an epidemic is mediated by the structure of the contact network. Under simple assumptions, the possibility of an epidemic depends on the largest eigenvalue of the matrix $\mathbf{A}$, the transmission rate

among neighboring individuals, and the recovery rate (Pastor-Satorras et al. 2015). If we think of $\mathbf{A}$ as a (structured) random network, then we can write criteria for the epidemic threshold reminiscent of May's stability criterion.

Metapopulation persistence: now turn to a landscape in which there are n patches of suitable habitat, and in each patch the species of interest is either present or absent. The patches are connected by dispersal, with colonization turning empty patches into occupied ones, and (local) extinctions playing the opposite role. Then we can think of patches as "susceptible" to colonization or already "infected," drawing a parallel with the S-I-S system presented previously. The parallel runs much deeper than one would imagine: the formula derived by Hanski and Ovaskainen (2000) for the survival of a metapopulation is exactly the same as that of Van Mieghem et al. (2009) for the occurrence of epidemics, with the network of dispersal playing the role of the contact network for disease spread.

Exploiting this parallel, Grilli et al. (2015) derived the conditions for the persistence of a metapopulation in a "random fragmented landscape," in which patches of suitable habitat are randomly arranged in a d-dimensional landscape.

Feasibility: biological models need to be robust: if the nature of an outcome relies on the "fine-tuning" of parameters, then the relevance for biology is very limited, as biological parameters are known to vary quite substantially in time, space, and among individuals and populations. When examining population dynamics and coexistence of ecological communities, one can ask for which range of parameters would we expect coexistence, a type of calculation known as sensitivity analysis (Barabás et al. 2014).

When considering the Generalized Lotka–Volterra model described in Box 6.4, a question on sensitivity and robustness would be to ask for which subspace of matrices $\mathbf{A}$ and growth rates $\mathbf{r}$ would a feasible equilibrium exist (i.e., an equilibrium $\mathbf{x}^*$ such that all species have positive density). The simplest case is that in which we are provided with a fixed matrix $\mathbf{A}$, and we want to measure the space of growth rates leading to feasibility (Rohr et al. 2014). Because the scaling of the growth rates does not matter (only their relative strengths), we can assume that they lie on a unit (hyper-)sphere ($\sum r_i^2 = 1$), in which case the problem becomes equivalent to measuring a solid angle in S dimensions. Similarly, one can fix the growth rates, and let the matrix be random, and measure the probability of feasibility in this setting (Stone 2016). Finally, one can let both the growth rates and the matrix be random, and measure the expected region of coexistence using random matrix theory (Grilli et al. 2017).

In fact, one can go a step further, and investigate how many species would coexist under Lotka–Volterra dynamics when all of the parameters are sampled from given distributions (Serván et al. 2018). Taking the parameters to be random allows one to identify the main drivers of species richness, abundance distribution, and dynamics (Barbier et al. 2018).

Network structure: ecologists are building larger and larger networks to describe the interactions between species. Networks are complex objects, and are difficult to characterize using a few values. The wealth of network metrics that has been proposed over the years is a testament to the difficulty of this problem. In physics and mathematics, *spectral graph theory* is becoming a standard way to examine large networks (Van Mieghem 2010). Basically, each network can be mapped to a matrix, and the eigenvalues and eigenvectors completely characterize the matrix (and thus, the network). In practice, a cursory examination of the eigenvalues of the adjacency matrix of a network (or other matrices associated with the network, such as the Laplacian) can yield insights on the large-scale structure of the network, including the presence of modules, a hierarchical organization, and the degree distribution.

Clearly, random matrix theory would allow to predict the typical spectrum of networks possessing a given set of properties, providing a framework to characterize large-scale patterns in ecological networks.

6.7 Open problems and conclusions

We have shown that a random matrix approach can yield important insights in theoretical ecology. In this area, random matrices can serve two main

purposes: i) be used to produce cogent null-models for ecological network structure; ii) identify which parameters matter the most for the dynamics of large communities. Notably, this approach complements the classic analysis of small ecological systems, by providing a means to examine large communities using a new mathematical toolbox.

We have illustrated some of the basic results in the theory of random matrices, and showcased a number of applications using structured random matrices. The vast number of results might give the illusion of a senescent subfield, in which all that could be done has been done already, and what has not been done is either incredibly difficult or impossible to do. This characterization would be very far from reality: new tools are appearing in the mathematical literature at a very fast pace, and most of them have direct applicability in ecology and biology in general. Moreover, several fundamental problems are still outstanding.

Take the circular law: we have mentioned in passing that for this result to hold the number of nonzero coefficients per row/column must be sufficiently high (i.e., should go to infinity when the size of the matrix goes to infinity). In many biological networks, even when we consider a large number of nodes, the number of interactions per species will be capped: when $S \to \infty$, $SC \to k$. What happens to the spectrum in this case? In Figure 6.5 we show that, when each species entertains the same number of interactions (five in the Figure), then the spectrum, rather than describing a circle in the complex plane, resembles a diamond. Moreover, one can show that in this case the result is not universal: different distributions of the nonzero coefficients (say all with mean zero and unit variance) will yield different spectra. As of today, a characterization of this case is completely open.

Similarly, extending the results on structured random matrices to more complex cases would also be needed for applications. For example, in Figure 6.6 we draw the spectrum of a tri-trophic system, in which producers are consumed by herbivores, and carnivores consume herbivores and other carnivores. Though the spectrum looks reasonably simple, its actual shape is unknown at the moment.

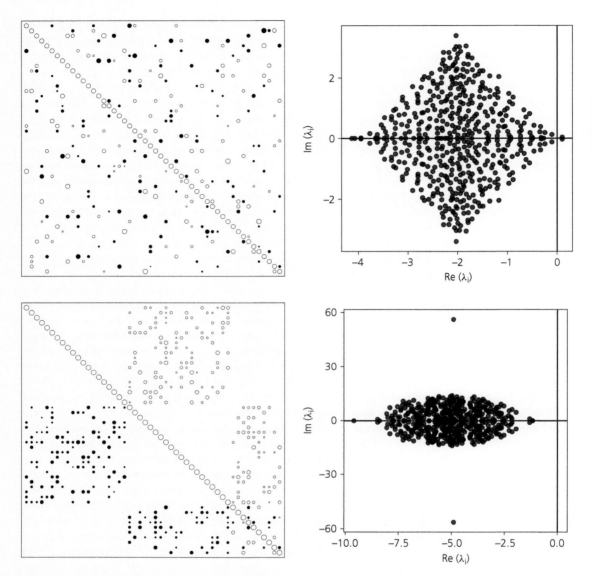

Figure 6.6 *Top*: When each species interacts with a small, fixed number of other species, the spectrum departs strongly from the circular law, leading to an interesting diamond shape in the complex plane. The exact shape of the spectrum, and the effect of the distribution of coefficients on the shape are an open problem in random matrix theory. *Bottom*: More complex cases of structured random matrices have not been studied yet. For example, the panels show the structure (Left) and spectrum (Right) of a tri-trophic system, in which species are either producers, herbivores, or carnivores. The spectrum looks reasonably simple to study, and yet its characterization is an open problem.

In summary, random matrices provide theoretical ecologists with a new, vast toolbox to tackle problems dealing with highly speciose ecological communities. Though the application of random matrix theory to ecology dates back to the seminal work of May, all the other results presented here were derived in the past seven years. As such, this research area is moving at a very fast pace, and has the potential to influence many sub-discipline of ecology and biology in general.

References

Abrams, P. (1983). The theory of limiting similarity. *Annual Review of Ecology and Systematics* 14(1): 359–76.

Allesina, S., Grilli, J., Barabás, G., Tang, S., Aljadeff, J., and Maritan, A. (2015). Predicting the stability of large structured food webs. *Nature Communications* 6: 7842.

Allesina, S. and Tang, S. (2012). Stability criteria for complex ecosystems. *Nature* 483(7388): 205–8.

Arditi, R. and Ginzburg, L. R. (2012). *How Species Interact: Altering the Standard View on Trophic Ecology*. Oxford: Oxford University Press.

Bai, Z. and Silverstein, J. W. (2010). *Spectral Analysis of Large Dimensional Random Matrices*. (Vol. 20). New York: Springer.

Barabás, G., Michalska-Smith, M. J., and Allesina, S. (2017). Self-regulation and the stability of large ecological networks. *Nature Ecology and Evolution* 1(12): 1870–5.

Barabás, G., Pásztor, L., Meszéna, G., and Ostling, A. (2014). Sensitivity analysis of coexistence in ecological communities: theory and application. *Ecology Letters* 17(12): 1479–94.

Barbier, M., Arnoldi, J.-F., Bunin, G., and Loreau, M. (2018). Generic assembly patterns in complex ecological communities. *Proceedings of the National Academy of Sciences* 115(9): 2156–61.

Cantrell, R. S. and Cosner, C. (2004). *Spatial Ecology via Reaction-Diffusion Equations*. *Chichester*: New York: John Wiley and Sons.

Chesson, P. (2000). Mechanisms of maintenance of species diversity. *Annual Review of Ecology and Systematics* 31(1): 343–66.

Chow, G. C. et al. (1975), *Analysis and Control of Dynamic Economic Systems*. New York: John Wiley and Sons.

Cohen, J., Briand, F., and Newman, C. (1986). A stochastic theory of community food webs. III. Predicted and observed lengths of food chains. *Proc. R. Soc. Lond. B* 228(1252): 317–53.

Cook, N., Hachem, W., Najim, J., and Renfrew, D. (2018). Non-Hermitian random matrices with a variance profile (I): Deterministic equivalents and limiting ESDs. *Electronic Journal of Probability* 23 paper no. 110.

Dyson, F. J. (1962). Statistical theory of the energy levels of complex systems. I. *Journal of Mathematical Physics* 3(1): 14056.

Gardner, M. R. and Ashby, W. R. (1970). Connectance of large dynamic (cybernetic) systems: Critical values for stability. *Nature* 228(5273): 784.

Gibbs, T., Grilli, J., Rogers, T., and Allesina, S. (2018). Effect of population abundances on the stability of large random ecosystems. *Physical Review E* 98(2): 022410.

Gravel, D., Massol, F., and Leibold, M. A. (2016). Stability and complexity in model meta-ecosystems. *Nature Communications* 7: 12,457.

Grilli, J., Adorisio, M., Suweis, S., Barabás, G., Banavar, J. R., Allesina, S., and Maritan, A. (2017). Feasibility and coexistence of large ecological communities. *Nature Communications* 8: 14,389.

Grilli, J., Barabás, G., and Allesina, S. (2015). Metapopulation persistence in random fragmented landscapes. *PLoS Computational Biology* 11(5): e1004251.

Grilli, J., Rogers, T., and Allesina, S. (2016). Modularity and stability in ecological communities. *Nature Communications* 7: 12,031.

Hanski, I. and Ovaskainen, O. (2000). The metapopulation capacity of a fragmented landscape. *Nature* 404(6779): 755.

Hastings, A., Hom, C. L., Ellner, S., Turchin, P., and Godfray, H. C. J. (1993). Chaos in ecology: Is Mother Nature a strange attractor? *Annual Review of Ecology and Systematics* 24(1): 1–33.

Hughes, C. P., Keating, J. P. et al. (2000). Random matrix theory and the derivative of the Riemann zeta function. *Proceedings of the Royal Society of London A: Mathematical, Physical and Engineering Sciences* 456: 2611–27.

Kanzieper, E. (2001). Random matrices and the replica method. *Nuclear Physics B* 596(3): 548–66.

Kingsland, S. E. (1995). *Modeling Nature*. Chicago: University of Chicago Press.

Kirsch, W. and Kriecherbauer, T. (2016). Sixty years of moments for random matrices. In Gesztesy et al. (eds.), *Non-Linear Partial Differential Equations, Mathematical Physics, and Stochastic Analysis*. Zurich: European Mathematical Society Publishing House, pp. 349–79.

Lande, R., Engen, S., and Saether, B.-E. (2003). *Stochastic Population Dynamics in Ecology and Conservation*. Oxford: Oxford University Press on Demand.

Livan, G., Novaes, M., and Vivo, P. (2018). *Introduction to Random Matrices: Theory and Practice*. Cham: Springer.

Lotka, A. J. (1956). *Elements of Mathematical Biology*, New York: Dover.

MacArthur, R. (1955). Fluctuations of animal populations and a measure of community stability. *Ecology* 36(3): 533–6.

May, R. M. (1972). Will a large complex system be stable? *Nature* 238(5364): 413.

May, R. M. (1976). Simple mathematical models with very complicated dynamics. *Nature* 261(5560): 459.

McCann, K. S. (2000). The diversity–stability debate. *Nature* 405(6783): 228.

McIntosh, R. P. (1980). The background and some current problems of theoretical ecology. *Synthese* 43(2): 195–255.

Mingo, J. A. and Speicher, R. (2017). *Free Probability and Random Matrices*. (Vol. 4). New York: Springer.

Newman, M. E. and Girvan, M. (2004). Finding and evaluating community structure in networks. *Physical Review E* 69(2): 026113.

O'Rourke, S. and Renfrew, D. (2014). Low rank perturbations of large elliptic random matrices. *Electronic Journal of Probability* 19, paper no. 43.

Pace, M. L., Cole, J. J., Carpenter, S. R., and Kitchell, J. F. (1999). Trophic cascades revealed in diverse ecosystems. *Trends in Ecology and Evolution* 14(12): 483–8.

Pastor-Satorras, R., Castellano, C., Van Mieghem, P., and Vespignani, A. (2015). Epidemic processes in complex networks. *Reviews of Modern Physics* 87(3): 925.

Rogers, T. (2010). Universal sum and product rules for random matrices. *Journal of Mathematical Physics* 51(9): 093304.

Rogers, T. and Castillo, I. P. (2009). Cavity approach to the spectral density of non-Hermitian sparse matrices. *Physical Review E* 79(1): 012101.

Rogers, T., Castillo, I. P., Kühn, R., and Takeda, K. (2008). Cavity approach to the spectral density of sparse symmetric random matrices. *Physical Review E* 78(3): 031116.

Rohr, R. P., Saavedra, S., and Bascompte, J. (2014). On the structural stability of mutualistic systems. *Science* 345(6195): 1,253,497.

Scheffer, M., Bascompte, J., Brock, W. A., Brovkin, V., Carpenter, S. R., Dakos, V., Held, H., Van Nes, E. H., Rietkerk, M., and Sugihara, G. (2009). Early-warning signals for critical transitions. *Nature* 461(7260): 53.

Serván, C. A., Capitán, J. A., Grilli, J., Morrison, K. E., and Allesina, S. (2018). Coexistence of many species in random ecosystems. *Nature Ecology and Evolution* 2(8): 1237.

Sommers, H., Crisanti, A., Sompolinsky, H., and Stein, Y. (1988). Spectrum of large random asymmetric matrices. *Physical Review Letters* 60(19): 1895.

Sompolinsky, H., Crisanti, A., and Sommers, H.-J. (1988). Chaos in random neural networks. *Physical Review Letters* 61(3): 259.

Stone, L. (2016). The Google matrix controls the stability of structured ecological and biological networks. *Nature Communications* 7: 12,857.

Stone, L. (2018). The feasibility and stability of large complex biological networks: a random matrix approach. *Scientific Reports* 8(1): 8246.

Tao, T. and Vu, V. (2012). Random matrices: The universality phenomenon for Wigner ensembles. *Modern Aspects of Random Matrix Theory* 72: 121–72.

Tuljapurkar, S. and Caswell, H. (2012). *Structured-Population Models in Marine, Terrestrial, and Freshwater Systems*. (Vol. 18.) New York: Springer Science and Business Media.

Van Mieghem, P. (2010). *Graph Spectra for Complex Networks*. Cambridge: Cambridge University Press.

Van Mieghem, P., Omic, J., and Kooij, R. (2009). Virus spread in networks. *IEEE/ACM Transactions on Networking (TON)* 17(1): 1–14.

Volterra, V. (1926). Fluctuations in the abundance of a species considered mathematically. *Nature* 118: 558–60.

Wigner, E. P. (1967). Random matrices in physics. *SIAM Review* 9(1): 1–23.

Wishart, J. (1928). The generalised product moment distribution in samples from a normal multivariate population. *Biometrika* 20A (1/2): 32–52.

Yan, G., Martinez, N. D. and Liu, Y.-Y. (2017), Degree heterogeneity and stability of ecological networks. *Journal of The Royal Society Interface* 14(131): 20, 170, 189.

CHAPTER 7

A structural theory of mutualistic networks

Jordi Bascompte and Antonio Ferrera

7.1 Introduction

Mutualistic interactions among free-living species such as those between plants and their animal pollinators or seed dispersers have shaped much of biodiversity on Earth. Ironically, however, mutualism did not play a major role in the theoretical agenda until recently. The first theoretical approaches to mutualistic interactions considered those interactions as ill-behaved, leading towards runaway dynamics with abundances growing to infinity (e.g., May 1981). A second round of models attempted to bring biological realism by considering density-dependence effects as a way to stabilize mutualism. These models focussed on pairs of highly specific interactions, mimicking work on iconic interactions such as those between senita cactus and its pollinating seed-eating moth and looked at mutualism from the point of view of consumer-resource dynamics (see, e.g., Holland et al. 2002). An alternative way to stabilize the dynamics of mutualistic systems was by considering the mutualist interaction embedded within other interaction types (Ringel et al. 1996). These authors already showed that, in this broader context, mutualism may stabilize ecological interactions, thus reversing the conclusion of the earlier models that seem to suggest mutualism should be rare in nature.

In parallel, a different generation of models was studying the role of spatial structure in gene flow and local adaptation of mutualistic interactions (Nuismer et al. 2004). This work showed that spatial structure affects the outcome of local interactions, maintains allelic polymorphism, and leads to trait mismatching. This theoretical approach was key to the development of the geographic mosaic theory of coevolution, which sustains that the outcome of species interactions changes across habitat patches as a function of the set of copollinators inhabiting each of these patches. This results in some patches acting as truly coevolutionary hotspots and others acting as coevolutionary coldspots (Thompson 2005).

The concept of diffuse coevolution (Iwao and Rausher 1997) and the discussion about the degree of specialization of pollinators (Waser et al. 1996) started moving into the community context of plant-animal interactions. Specifically, Iwao and Rausher (1997) presented a set of conditions for coevolution to be pairwise, rather than diffuse. Namely, susceptibilities to different herbivore species should be uncorrelated, the presence of a herbivore should not affect the amount of damage caused by another herbivore, and the impact of one herbivore on plant fitness should not depend on the absence or presence of other herbivores. These authors proceeded by presenting an experimental design to partition the total effect of one herbivore on plant fitness into components that can be understood as pairwise or diffuse. Waser et al. (1996), in a highly influential paper, asked

Bascompte, J. and Ferrera, A., *A structural theory of mutualistic networks* In: *Theoretical Ecology: Concepts and Applications.* Edited by: Kevin S. McCann and Gabriel Gellner, Oxford University Press (2020). © Oxford University Press.
DOI: 10.1093/oso/9780198824282.003.0007

whether plant-pollinator interactions are eminently specialized (as many authors assumed at the time) or generalist. They concluded that the large majority are eminently generalized and came up with an explanation.

Delving deeper into the structure of interactions, Bascompte et al. (2003) described the community-wide patterns in plant-animal mutualistic networks (Figure 7.1). Mutualistic interactions amongst free-living species are organized in a nested pattern, with specialist plants, for example, interacting with proper subsets of the animals that more generalist plants interact with (see also Vázquez and Aizen (2004) for an equivalent result). This was received with interest by some evolutionary biologists as it helped dispelling the idea that coevolution among free-living species has to lead to either highly specific one-on-one interactions or highly diffuse assemblages intractable to analysis (Thompson 2005). Specifically, despite the complexity of these networks, they can be described by an apparently simple rule.

Bascompte et al. (2003) already discussed the potential implications of this community-wide pattern for community robustness and coevolution, but these were quite speculative ideas. More formal explorations had to wait for the development of a conceptual framework similar to the one existing for predation and competition. The first such attempt came up three years after in the context of a similar analysis of weighted networks for which there was empirical information not only on who-interacts-with-whom, but on the strength of this interaction (Bascompte et al. 2006a).

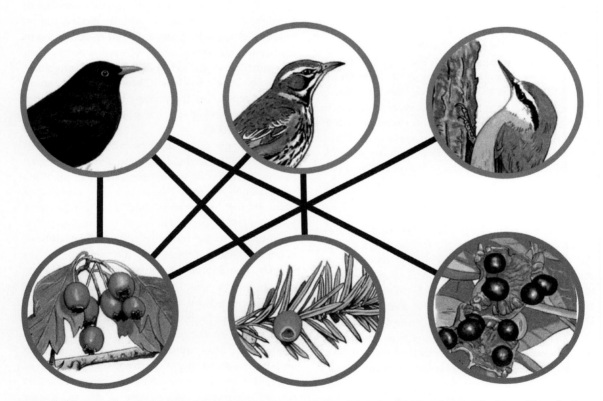

Figure 7.1 The interactions of mutual benefit between fruiting plants and their seed dispersers shape complex networks of mutual dependencies. The feasibility and persistence of these communities, the topic of this chapter, depend on the balance between competition within sets and mutualism between sets. Drawing by J. Pérez-Rojas illustrating a subset of a seed-dispersal community in Nava de las Correhuelas, Cazorla, South East Spain compiled by P. Jordano (network *M_SD*_021 from www.web-of-life.es). Bird species are, from left to right, *Turdus merula, Turdus iliacus,* and *Sitta europaea*. Plant species are, from left to right, *Crataegus monogyna, Taxus bacatta, and Paeonia officinalis*.

In what follows, we provide a chronological account of the major steps in building a theory of mutualistic networks. The purpose is threefold. First, it will provide a short summary of a fast-growing field. Second, it may help to link different approaches to better understand to what degree conclusions depend on their assumptions and limitations. Third, it will illustrate a structural stability approach to community ecology.

7.2 A purely dynamic stability approach to mutualistic networks

7.2.1 Early models

Bascompte et al. (2006a) reported that mutualistic networks are built from weak and asymmetric links among species. Indeed, the majority of interactions are really weak with only a few strong ones. In such rare cases, the strong dependence of a plant on an animal was accompanied by a much weaker dependence of the animal on that plant. They then proceeded by exploring the dynamical implications of these patterns. This was the starting point of a series of community models of mutualistic networks that have been refined through the last few years. The approach followed by the authors was quite simplistic. Their model included two sets of species that interacted via mutualism, but lacked interspecific competition among species within a set, assumed linear functional responses, and, more importantly, considered that all animal species interacted with all plant species. The model, an extension of the two-species mutualistic model by Robert May and others (May 1981; Ringel et al. 1996), read as follows:

$$\frac{dN_i^{(P,A)}}{dt} = r_i^{(P,A)}N_i^{(P,A)} - \left(\beta_0^{(P,A)}\right)_i\left(N_i^{(P,A)}\right)^2$$
$$+ \sum_{j=1}^{S^{(A,P)}} \gamma_{ij}^{(P,A)}N_i^{(P,A)}N_j^{(A,P)}, \qquad (7.1)$$

where $N_i^{(P)}$ and $N_j^{(A)}$ represent the abundances of plant i and animal j, respectively; $r_i^{(P,A)}$ are the growth rates of plant/animal i; $\left(\beta_0^{(P,A)}\right)_i$ are the intraspecific competition coefficients for plant/animal i; $\gamma_{ij}^{(P,A)}$ represent the per-capita effect of the mutualistic interaction of animal/plant j on

plant/animal i in the limit of very small biomasses, and $S^{(P,A)}$ is the number of plant/animal species. Here, we will be using the notation of Bastolla et al. (2009) (see also Table 7.1).

For the sake of analytical simplification, Bascompte et al. (2006a) further assumed a mean field assumption in which all species within each set are equivalent to one another ($r_i^{(P,A)} = r^{(P,A)}$, $\left(\beta_0^{(P,A)}\right)_i = \beta_0^{(P,A)}$, $\gamma_{ij}^{(P,A)} = \gamma^{(P,A)}$). This simplified system has a non-trivial coexistence solution that will be both feasible (i.e., all species have positive abundances) and locally stable (i.e., the system will return to the solution after an infinitesimally small perturbation of the densities; Figure 7.2) if, and only if:

$$\gamma^{(P)}\gamma^{(A)} < \frac{\beta_0^{(P)}\beta_0^{(A)}}{S^{(P)}S^{(A)}}, \qquad (7.2)$$

provided that all parameters are positive. Positive growth rates can be assumed for facultative mutualism as those describing pollination and seed dispersal.

The previous condition is quite similar to May's condition for the stability of a randomly built model ecosystem (May 1972), which can be written as:

$$\gamma < \frac{1}{\sqrt{SC}}, \qquad (7.3)$$

where γ, S, and C are the average interaction strength, number of species, and connectivity (i.e., fraction of realized interactions), respectively.

7.2.2 Adding non-linear functional responses

As noted, the previous result appears in the context of a highly simplified model. The first highlighted omission was the lack of a saturating functional response representing that the benefits to mutualists saturate with the densities of their mutualistic partners, a point made by Holland et al. (2006) and later explored in more detail in Okuyama and Holland (2008). Their model can be written as:

$$\frac{dN_i^{(P,A)}}{dt} = r_i^{(P,A)}N_i^{(P,A)} - \left(\beta_0^{(P,A)}\right)_i\left(N_i^{(P,A)}\right)^2$$
$$+ \sum_{j=1}^{S^{(A,P)}} \frac{\gamma_{ij}^{(P,A)}N_i^{(P,A)}N_j^{(A,P)}}{1 + \sum_k h_{ik}^{(P,A)}\gamma_{ik}^{(P,A)}N_k^{(A,P)}}. \qquad (7.4)$$

Table 7.1 Symbols used in this chapter.

Symbol	Description
$N_i^{(P,A)}$	Abundance density of (Plant/Animal) species i
$r_i^{(P,A)}$	Growth rate of (Plant/Animal) species i
$\beta^{(P,A)}$	Competition matrix for Plants/Animals, with elements $\left(\beta^{(P,A)}\right)_{ij}$
$\left(\beta_0^{(P,A)}\right)_i$	Intraespecific competition for (Plant/Animal) species i, $\left(\beta_0^{(P,A)}\right)_i = \beta_{ii}^{(P,A)}$
$\rho^{(P,A)}$	Interspecific niche overlap coefficient for mean field Plants/Animals competition matrix.
$\tilde{\rho}^{(P,A)}$	Effective Interspecific niche overlap coefficient for effective mean field Plants/Animals competition matrix
$\gamma^{(P,A)}$	Mutualist matrix for Plants/Animals, with elements $\left(\gamma^{(P,A)}\right)_{ij}$
$C^{(P,A)}$	Effective competition matrix for Plants/Animals
$p_i^{(P,A)}$	Effective growth rate of (Plant/Animal) species i
$S_i^{(P,A)}$	Number of (Plant/Animal) species
$\bar{S}_i^{(P,A)}$	Expected biodiversity scale for (Plant/Animal) set.
I	Identity matrix
$h^{(P,A)}$	Handling time for Plants/Animals.
$\lambda_1(B)$	Highest eigenvalue of matrix B ordered as $\mathfrak{R}(\lambda_1) \geq \mathfrak{R}(\lambda_2) \geq \cdots \geq \mathfrak{R}(\lambda_n)$, where $\mathfrak{R}(\lambda_i)$ is the real part of eigenvalue λ_i
$\bar{\sigma}(B)$	Highest singular value of matrix B, ordered as $\bar{\sigma} = \sigma_1 \geq \sigma_2 \geq \cdots \geq= \underline{\sigma}$

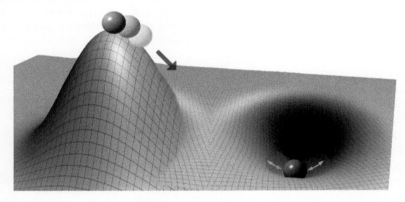

Figure 7.2 This cartoon illustrates the concept of linear stability, which has been central to the development of theoretical ecology, including some of the results here discussed on mutualistic networks. In this mechanical analogy, the ball rests at an equilibrium both in the left and the right. The scenario on the left depicts an unstable solution: the ball will roll away following an infinitesimally small perturbation. The scenario on the right, in turn, depicts a stable solution: the ball will return to its original equilibrium after suffering such a small perturbation. Global stability extends this definition for the case of any arbitrary perturbation (not just infinitesimally small). Note that, in this approach, one assesses the stability of a solution given an arbitrary set of parameter values and assumes that perturbations only affect the state variable (i.e., the density of the population), but not any parameter such as growth rates. This is a particular dimension of stability that will be complemented by the one of structural stability.

Note that, although this looks somewhat different to the original equations appearing in Okuyama and Holland (2008), both models are completely equivalent. The non-linear term on the right-hand side (RHS) represents the saturation of the beneficial effects of mutualism on population growth. It corresponds to a Holling type II functional response, which for a two-species case reads $f(N_1, N_2) = (\gamma N_1 N_2) / (1 + h\gamma N_2)$. The constant h represents a handling time and in the large N limit bounds the maximum contribution from mutualism to the growth rates of N_1 to $1/h$, preventing it from diverging. The summation factor in the denominator of the third term in Equations (7.4) incorporates the total density of species that interact with mutualist i, while the h_{ik} corresponds to a species dependent handling time. Consequently, $1/h_{ik}$ now yields the maximum benefit for species i of the mutualistic interactions with species k.

In a first paper, Holland et al. (2006) used a simplified version of Model (7.4) that still assumed equivalence amongst all species within a set as in Bascompte et al. (2006a). In that work, the authors claimed that non-linear functional responses were enough to ensure community persistence, thus downplaying the role of network structure. While this result is generally correct, this does not mean Condition (7.2) does not play a role in their model, though. What Holland et al. (2006) missed is that there are two qualitatively different sets of solutions (what later on will be called weak and strong mutualistic regimes), and that Condition (7.2) represents the boundary between such solutions (Bascompte et al. 2006b).

The comment by Holland et al. (2006) and the subsequent response by Bascompte et al. (2006b) played an important role in further expanding the theory of mutualistic networks in the direction of bringing more realism. The follow-up by Okuyama and Holland (2008) was based on a numerical simulation of the full Model (7.4) to find its stable equilibrium points and analyse their resilience. Resilience is defined as the rate of return to the equilibrium following an infinitesimally small perturbation. Denote by $\Re(\lambda_i)$ the real part of eigenvalue λ_i of the Jacobian matrix, computed at the equilibrium solution. The system's resilience is then determined by the highest such $\Re(\lambda_i)$ —the system's spectral abscissa as defined later on. Through that approach, Okuyama and Holland (2008) found that although resilience is largely independent of nestedness in general, nestedness slightly increase resilience when mutualistic strengths are small and asymmetric and connectivity is small. This is the set of conditions observed in nature in most cases (Bascompte et al. 2006a). Most of their simulations, though, seem to take place in a region of parameter space where strong mutualism, and hence nonlinear response, ought to hold. In this regime, they find that community resilience is enhanced by increasing

species richness and connectivity, and through strong, symmetric interaction strengths of highly nested networks. The fact that only a minor set of simulations are run in the weakly coupling regime, however, makes it difficult to compare with other research which has centered on the weakly interacting regime. This will become clearer later on.

7.2.3 Adding interspecific competition within sets

The model by Bastolla et al. (2009) originally arose as an attempt to incorporate both non-linear functional responses—as in Holland et al. (2006) and Okuyama and Holland (2008)—and interspecific competition, while at the same time remaining within an analytical framework as in Bascompte et al. (2006a). The addition of competition is important, as the effects of network structure on mutualistic networks should be understood as affecting the relative balance between competition and facilitation. The model subsequently became the field standard for studies of mutualistic networks (e.g., James et al. 2012; Suweis et al. 2013). It reads as follows:

$$\frac{dN_i^{(P,A)}}{dt} = r_i^{(P,A)}N_i^{(P,A)} - \sum_{j=1}^{S(P,A)}\beta_{ij}^{(P,A)}N_i^{(P,A)}N_j^{(P,A)}$$
$$+ \sum_{k=1}^{S(A,P)}\frac{\gamma_{ik}^{(P,A)}N_i^{(P,A)}N_k^{(A,P)}}{1+h^{(P,A)}\sum_{l=1}^{S(A,P)}\gamma_{il}^{(P,A)}N_l^{(A,P)}},$$
$$(7.5)$$

where symbols are as in the previous equation (see also Table 7.1), and the handling times $h^{(P,A)}$ are taken to be the same for each set of species. As with the previous two papers, the functional response is given by a Holling Type II term.

Direct competition between species i and j is indicated by $-\beta_{ij}^{(P,A)}N_i^{(P,A)}N_j^{(P,A)}$ for plants and animals, respectively, and the competition matrices $\beta_{ij}^{(P,A)}$ are assumed to be of mean field form for both sets. This means that all interspecific competitive interactions are assumed to be of equal intensity within each set. Likewise, all intraspecific competitive interaction coefficients are assumed to be equal and normalized to $\beta_{ii}^{(P,A)}=1$ for all species. That is,

$$\beta_{ij}^{(P,A)} = \rho^{(P,A)} + \left(1-\rho^{(P,A)}\delta_{ij}\right), \qquad (7.6)$$

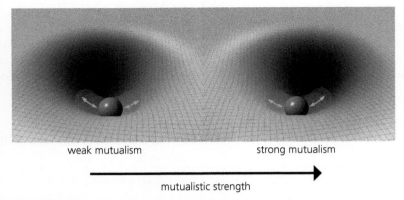

weak mutualism   strong mutualism

mutualistic strength

Figure 7.3 As mutualistic strength is increased, the weak mutualistic regime loses stability and a new solution, the strong mutualism, becomes stable. In this transition some species may become extinct. Both Bascompte et al. (2006a) and Bastolla et al. (2009) focussed on the weak regime, while the conditions considered in posterior papers sometimes correspond to the strong regime.

where δ_{ij} is the Kronecker's Delta (1 if $i = j$, 0 otherwise). We defer to Section 7.3.1 for a discussion about the ecological implications of this choice.

Bastolla et al. (2009) found two different types of analytical solutions to Equations (7.5) (Figure 7.3). The first one, referred to as *weak mutualism* and the focus of Bastolla et al.'s result, is characterized by small equilibrium biomasses $N \ll 1/h\gamma$. In that regime, we may expand the $(1 + h\gamma N)^{-1}$ factor in the denominator of the functional response in powers of $h\gamma N$. The linear response regime is then analytically recovered as a valid approximation, corresponding simply to the zeroth order term in the series expansion. The second type of fixed point, referred to as *strong mutualism*, corresponds to equilibrium biomasses N of order $1/h\gamma$. In this case, the previously mentioned power expansion can not be performed, but it is still possible to obtain analytical expressions by using the fact that the handling time h is small compared with the typical intrinsic time of growth $1/r$ (whence terms of order hr may be neglected with respect to $h\gamma N$).

In the weak mutualism regime, and using the linear functional response approximation, the fixed point equations for the plant set (for instance) can be rewritten at the dominant order in h as

$$\sum_j C_{ij}^{(P)} N_j^{(P)} = p_i^{(P)}, \qquad (7.7)$$

with an equivalent expression for the animals. Note that these equations are formally equivalent to

those corresponding to the fixed points of a purely competitive system. Therefore, the matrix $C_{ij}^{(P)}$ will be referred to as the *effective competition* matrix for plants, whereas $p_i^{(P)}$ will be denoted as the *effective growth rates* for the plant set. At order zero in h, they are given by:

$$C_{ij}^{(P)} = \beta_{ij}^{(P)} - \sum_{kl} \gamma_{ik}^{(P)} \left(\beta_{kl}^{(A)} \right)^{(-1)} \gamma_{lj}^{(A)}, \qquad (7.8)$$

$$p_i^{(P)} = r_i^{(P)} + \sum_{kl} \gamma_{ik}^{(P)} \left(\beta_{kl}^{(A)} \right)^{(-1)} r_l^{(A)}. \qquad (7.9)$$

The use of the effective competition framework is one of the key insights that can be found of Bastolla et al. (2009). Two important points should be emphasized here. The first one is that, as is clear from these two expressions, *this formalism is a conceptual extension of the direct competition matrix which allows us to incorporate the indirect competitive effects generated by the mutualistic interaction into the common framework of competition theory*. The second point is that a direct implication of this approach would seem to be that *the direct competition matrix should only account for competitive effects arising from limiting factors not explicitly present in the model (e.g., sunlight, water, and nutrients)*. Indeed, if the competitive effects generated by the mutualistic interaction were incorporated into the direct competition matrix, they would be accounted for twice as would become apparent when constructing the effective competition matrix.

We may now proceed to the analysis of the dynamical stability of the solutions. If the mutualistic network is fully connected, it may be seen that a necessary condition for the local stability of a fully feasible system is that the relation,

$$\gamma_0^{(P)}\gamma_0^{(A)} < \beta_0^{(P)}\beta_0^{(A)}\left(\rho^{(A)} + \frac{1-\rho^{(A)}}{S^{(A)}}\right)\left(\rho^{(P)} + \frac{1-\rho^{(P)}}{S^{(P)}}\right),$$
(7.10)

must be satisfied. This generalizes the result by Bascompte et al. (2006a) represented by Equation (7.2), becoming identical in the limit of vanishing interspecific competition. Notice that for non-null interspecific competition parameters $\rho^{(P,A)}$, the maximum value of mutualistic interaction strengths in the weak mutualism regime do not need to vanish for large communities (large $S^{(P)}$ and $S^{(A)}$) as was the case for systems where competition is not present (see Condition (7.2)). In this large community limit, the interaction strengths are now limited by

$$\gamma_0^{(P)}\gamma_0^{(A)} < \beta_0^{(P)}\beta_0^{(A)}\rho^{(A)}\rho^{(P)}.$$
(7.11)

Crucially, note how in the simultaneous limit of large $S^{(P,A)}$ and $\rho^{(P,A)} \to 0$ the weak mutualism regime tends to become unstable. We will come back to this result later on. For mutualistic interactions stronger than Equation (7.10) the weak mutualism fixed point is not stable, at which point the strong mutualism fixed point becomes stable.

7.3 A structural stability approach to mutualistic networks

An important aspect of the paper by Bastolla et al. (2009), beyond the previous study of dynamic stability of weak and strong mutualistic regimes, is that it built on the concept of structural stability which had previously been used by Bastolla and colleagues in the analysis of exclusively competitive communities (Bastolla et al., 2005a,b).

The concept of structural stability has formed part of the general study of the behavior of dynamical systems for quite some time (Wiggins, 1990, see Box 7.1 for a general definition and a historical perspective). In the context of this chapter, structural stability is defined in a narrower sense as follows. A system will be considered structurally stable against changes in the components of the vector

of growth rates for as long as it shows continuous existence of solutions which remain simultaneously dynamically stable and fully feasible (Roberts 1974; Vandermeer 1975; Rohr et al. 2014; Stone 2016). The incorporation of this important concept constitutes a turning point in the study of mutualism. Indeed, structural stability provides an interesting framework to address the limits on the number of coexisting species and the robustness of mutualistic communities.

In order to put structural stability in context, consider that robustness in ecology has been traditionally treated through two main approaches, each with its own limitations as we will see later on. Numerical simulations usually parametrize a model and measure the fraction of initial species surviving a certain number of iterations. Analytical methods, on the other hand, have mainly relied on the concept of local (asymptotic) stability. As already noted, this essentially finds a solutions of the model for an arbitrary choice of parameter values, and looks at whether the system will return to this equilibrium after an infinitesimally small perturbation of the state dynamical variable (densities). Obviously however perturbations may also affect the parameters of the model, such as growth rates or mutualistic interaction strengths. Hence, the picture provided by looking only at perturbations of dynamical variables is incomplete.

7.3.1 Preliminary work on the limits to the number of coexisting species in purely competitive systems

An important set of papers by Ugo Bastolla and collaborators laid the foundations for a new approach to mutualistic networks (Bastolla et al. 2005a,b). In the first of these papers, the authors addressed the case of purely competitive communities and tried to develop a natural scale in the number of coexisting species that the system can pack before becoming destabilized by environmentally induced fluctuations in the growth rates. Since the formalism presented in those papers will constitute an integral part of later developments, it pays to look at it in some detail in order to understand their power and limitations.

Bastolla et al. (2005a,b) started by studying a purely competitive system with a Competition

Box 7.1 Structural stability

A system is said to be structurally stable if its dynamical behavior (i.e., limit cycles, character and number of its fixed points, etc) is not altered by a smooth change on the value of its parameters or structure of the model itself (Wiggins 1990). Structural stability has a long tradition in several fields of research. Most notably, it is at the core of René Thom's Catastrophe Theory (Thom 1994) and in its arguably most successful derivation, namely the study of tipping points in complex systems (Scheffer et al. 2001). In developmental biology, Alberch (1989) and Goodwin (1990) championed a structuralist approach that shifted the emphasis from a functional, historical explanation to an internalist explanation based on dynamical principles. Thus, Alberch would answer the question of why the limb of tetrapods has remained invariant for such a long evolutionary time by saying that such a structure is simply the one compatible with a broader range of developmental conditions (Alberch 1989: Figure 7.4).

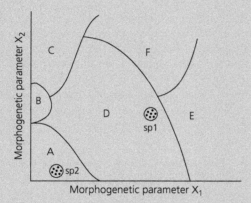

Figure 7.4 The figure represents the structuralist approach in developmental biology championed by Pere Alberch and colleagues. It depicts an ideal morphogenetic space with dots in the circles representing the individuals of a hypothetical population. Although the morphogenetic parameters may change, this will not result in a change in phenotype as long as the values are constrained to each of the domains, e.g., A and D. Only when the morphogenetic change pushes the individual towards the threshold (e.g., from D to E), there is a resulting change in phenotype. Under this structuralist view, some structures or phenotypes are more evolutionary conserved than others because they are compatible with a broader range of developmental conditions. Some populations, such as number 1, are close to the boundary and therefore more prone to experience an abrupt change in phenotype. Redrawn from from Alberch (1989).

In turn, control engineers had been developing the concept of a "robust plant," i.e., a plant able to function within the specified tolerance levels in spite of unknown noise and disturbances that may affect either the plant's input, or its inner workings, or both, at least from the 70s. In this regard, it is fascinating that some of the most outstanding figures in that field of engineering soon turned to ecology as a fertile ground in which their ideas could be put to test, obviously not from the point of view of an operator controlled plant, but rather considering it as a natural system that ought to be robust "by construction" in order to withstand the inevitable environmental perturbations. For instance, Siljak (1978, 1991), Vidyasagar (1981), and Kaszkurewicz and Bhaya (2000), to name but the most salient examples, dedicated entire chapters in their books to studying the system described by the Lotka–Volterra equations. From a physical perspective, Ilya Prigogine also discussed the implications of structural stability for such ecological models in the context of innovation and the appearance of new species into the system (Prigogine 1980). Furthermore, it is important to realize that these authors come from a field in which complex systems formed by a large number of coupled units are common, hence they were also equipped with the tools to study the network perspective. It bears noting, however, that in their case the paramount demand on the system was that it maintained dynamical stability in the face of the external disturbances, without much concern for its feasibility. This being said, the criteria developed for instance by Siljak (1991) around the concept of *connective stability* are several steps beyond the standard results ensuring global dynamical stability that have been used in Ecology for quite sometime now.

The factor that ended up dooming these efforts into a relative and undeserved obscurity was first and foremost a lack of contact with practitioner ecologists. This had the twin effects of, on one hand setting the problem up in terms of species configurations that in many cases felt very contrived from the ecological perspective. And on the other hand, for the most part the mathematical apparatus involved was also alien for a typical ecologist, and evolved in directions that kept increasing the intellectual distance between the two fields. On top of this, mainstream ecological theory was very much aligned with the concept of linear stability (Justus 2014: Figure 7.2). Some worth mentioning exceptions are ecologists that long ago noted that the conditions for stability are not sufficient and that one should also look at the conditions for feasibility (Roberts 1974; Vandermeer 1975; Case 1990).

Matrix assumed to be of mean field form. This approximation is expected to hold when there is a set of nutrients on which all species are simultaneously dependent in the same fashion. The essence of the mean field approximation rests in assuming that all species are strictly equivalent to each other. Specifically, all interspecific interactions β_{ij} have the same value and all intraspecific interactions are also equal to one another—and normalized to $\beta_{ii} = 1$. A direct implication of these two facts is that a mean field competition matrix for S species has actually only two different eigenvalues. Namely, the largest one (λ_1) with multiplicity one and λ_2 with multiplicity $S - 1$. One has, in particular,

$$\lambda_1 = S\rho + (1 - \rho) \tag{7.12}$$

and

$$\lambda_2 = \lambda_3 = \cdots = \lambda_n = 1 - \rho. \tag{7.13}$$

Furthermore, since the number of species (hence the trace of β, $\mathrm{Tr}(\beta)$) is fixed, one can extract one eigenvalue from the other. Hence for a fixed number of species there is actually only one eigenvalue left as a free parameter in the model. This is a key observation: *for a fixed number of species the mean field assumption reduces all the degrees of freedom normally associated to a matrix to just one, ρ.* Thus in the mean field approximation either ρ or the value of any of the two distinct matrix eigenvalues can be used to completely characterize the dynamics of the system represented by the matrix. We note also that Equation (7.12) is equivalent to

$$\rho = \frac{\lambda_1 - 1}{S - 1}. \tag{7.14}$$

We now go back to Bastolla et al. (2005a,b). The authors first take advantage of the previously mentioned property of mean field matrices to develop a coexistence condition for a set of competing species under environmentally induced changes in the growth rates r_i. In particular, let us consider the distribution of growth rates r_i comprising the growth rates vector $\mathbf{r}$, its average value $\langle \mathbf{r} \rangle$ and second momentum $\langle \mathbf{r}^2 \rangle = (1/S) \sum_i r_i^2$. Then an inequality can be found which sets a limit in the maximal variance allowed in the distribution of the r_i under external perturbations: in order to maintain full feasibility (i.e., $N_i > 0$ for all species), this variance must be below a certain ratio which can be expressed solely in terms of S and ρ. Namely,

$$\frac{\langle \mathbf{r}^2 \rangle - \langle \mathbf{r} \rangle^2}{\langle \mathbf{r} \rangle^2} \leq \frac{\lambda_2}{\lambda_1} = \frac{1}{\left(S/\bar{S} + 1 \right)}, \tag{7.15}$$

where we have substituted the expressions for λ_1 and λ_2 previously and we have defined the quantity,

$$\bar{S} = \frac{\lambda_2}{\rho} = \frac{1 - \rho}{\rho}. \tag{7.16}$$

$\bar{S}$, which is fixed solely by ρ, provides a good natural scale for the expected biodiversity associated to a competitive system with a mean field competition matrix. If the number of species S is much larger than $\bar{S}$, the allowed variability in r becomes very small and the condition of coexistence becomes rather stringent—the ecosystem is *tightly packed* and consequently *not very robust* under environmentally induced variations in the vector of growth rates r. On the other hand, if S is much smaller than $\bar{S}$, the allowed range of variation in growth rates becomes large and the coexistence condition is not a stringent factor. In this case, we say that the system is *loosely packed* and *very robust* against perturbations in the vector of growth rates (see Bastolla et al. 2005a,b). For this reason we will refer to $\bar{S}$ as the *predicted biodiversity scale*.

The most salient characteristic of the previous expressions is that ρ increases as λ_1 grows towards its maximum possible value, S (equivalently, $\bar{S}$ decreases to zero as ρ grows towards 1). Conversely, ρ decreases as λ_1 decreases towards 1 ($\bar{S}$ increases to become very large as ρ decreases towards 0). Hence, the largest λ_1 is, the smallest is the associated biodiversity scale of the system.

After examining the exact mean field case the authors in Bastolla et al. (2005a,b) turn to study matrices $\tilde{C}$ that are not necessarily of mean field type. Again, a coexistence condition under perturbations to the growth rates can be found and expressed by an inequality. Also as before, this expression places an upper limit on the allowed variability of the growth rates in terms of a ratio

---

Box 7.2 Extension to nearly mean field matrices

Let us examine the case where the competition matrix $\tilde{C}$ is not necessarily of mean field type any more. Note that for technical reasons, however, we will still assume $\tilde{C}_{ii} = 1$. Likewise, the matrices at hand will still be required to be symmetric, positive definite, and with strictly positive elements. In this case, it can be shown that in order to ensure coexistance of all species, the vector of growth rates has to satisfy (Equation 7.29 in Bastolla et al. (2005a) after neglecting extinction thresholds):

$$\sum_{\alpha=2}^{S} \frac{(r^{\alpha})^2}{(r^1)^2} \kappa_\alpha \leq 1, \tag{7.35}$$

where r^α is the component of $\mathbf{r}$ along the eigendirection associated to λ_α. Here we have called $\kappa_\alpha = \lambda_1/\lambda_\alpha$, the "condition coefficient" corresponding to λ_α. Note how each component along the different eigendirections of the competition matrix is multiplied by its corresponding condition coefficient.

To simplify this expression, we now substitute all the condition coefficients by the smallest one, κ_2, and use the fact that $\sum_{\alpha=2}^{S} (r^\alpha)^2 = \|\mathbf{r}\|^2 - (r^1)^2$. Thus, we obtain,

$$\frac{\sum_i r_i^2 - (r^1)^2}{(r^1)^2} \leq \frac{\lambda_2}{\lambda_1}, \tag{7.36}$$

where r_i is now the growth rate of species i. This inequality shows that unless $\lambda_2/\lambda_1 \simeq 1$, $\mathbf{r}$ needs to be largely parallel

to the Perron vector of C in order to ensure coexistence of all species.

An important issue must be brought up at this point, however. Let us assume that Equation (7.35) is tight. Then the inequality resulting by substituting all the s_α by s_2 will still be tight if and only if all the s_α are at least approximately equal. That is, Inequality (7.36) will be tight if and only if the condition

$$\lambda_2 \simeq \lambda_3 \simeq \cdots \simeq \lambda_n \tag{7.37}$$

is satisfied. Indeed, let us imagine that this is not the case, and that there are large differences between the λ_α's and λ_2. Then, we will generally have $1/\kappa_2 = \lambda_2/\lambda_1 \gg \lambda_n/\lambda_1 = 1/\kappa_n$. But, if $1/\kappa_2 \gg 1/\kappa_n$, the RHS of (7.36), which is $1/\kappa_2$, will in fact be much larger than what the sum $\sum_{\alpha=2}^{S}(r^\alpha)^2/(r^1)^2$ is really allowed to be if it is to satisfy Inequality (7.35).

Equivalently, if Relation (7.37) is not satisfied, then the Expression (7.35) places a much tighter limit on the variability of $\mathbf{r}$ than Equation (7.36). Thus, in this case the RHS of (7.36), which is supposed to set the upper limit to the variability of $\mathbf{r}$, would in fact never be attainable by the LHS. It follows then that in this circumstance Expression (7.36), although still necessary, ceases to provide a sufficient condition to ensure coexistence of all species in the system. We conclude then that *the RHS of (7.36) will faithfully represent the allowed variance in the distribution of r_i while maintaining full feasibility only if Relation (7.37) holds.*

---

of quantities which can be computed from $\tilde{C}$ (see Box 7.2 for some more details of this derivation). This time around, though, the condition on the growth rates can be written in terms of the allowed variability in the modulus of $\mathbf{r}$ with respect to its component, r^1, along the principal (Perron) vector of the competition matrix $\tilde{C}$ —the *competition load* of the system in the original notation or the *structural vector* as generalized later on. This reads now,

$$\frac{\sum_i r_i^2 - (r^1)^2}{(r^1)^2} \leq \frac{\lambda_2}{\lambda_1}. \tag{7.17}$$

We must note at this point that, for this inequality to be meaningful, $\tilde{C}$ must be such that the condition,

$$\lambda_2\left(\tilde{C}\right) \simeq \lambda_3\left(\tilde{C}\right) \simeq \cdots \simeq \lambda_n\left(\tilde{C}\right) \tag{7.18}$$

is satisfied. That this expression must hold is dictated because if this were not the case then the Inequality (7.17) would cease to be tight, in which case it would not be a sufficient condition to ensure coexistence of all species any longer (see Box 7.2 for a lengthier discussion of this issue).

We may now define a parameter analogous to the mean field niche overlap parameter ρ, the "equivalent mean field inter-specific competition" $\tilde{\rho}$

$$\tilde{\rho} = \frac{\lambda_1(\tilde{C}) - 1}{S - 1}, \tag{7.19}$$

which the reader should compare to Equation (7.14). In other words, $\tilde{\rho}$ behaves *as if* it was the inter-specific competition parameter of an (equivalent) mean field matrix. With this definition Condition (7.18) becomes

$$\lambda_2\left(\tilde{C}\right) \simeq \lambda_3\left(\tilde{C}\right) \simeq \cdots \simeq \lambda_n\left(\tilde{C}\right) \simeq 1 - \tilde{\rho}. \quad (7.20)$$

where we have used $\mathrm{Tr}\left[\tilde{C}\right] = S$. Again, as in the exact mean field case, a typical scale of biodiversity for the system $\bar{S}$ may be defined in terms of $\tilde{\rho}$

$$\bar{S} = \frac{1 - \tilde{\rho}}{\tilde{\rho}}. \quad (7.21)$$

Provided then that $\lambda_2 \simeq 1 - \tilde{\rho}$, as per Condition (7.20) again, one may rewrite inequality (7.17) as

$$\frac{\sum_i r_i^2 - \left(r^1\right)^2}{\left(r^1\right)^2} \leq \frac{1}{S/\bar{S} + 1}, \quad (7.22)$$

and we again have a relation between the maximal variability in **r** and the number of species present in the system as was the case for exact mean field matrices. Again, the larger is $\lambda_1\left(\tilde{C}\right)$ the larger is $\tilde{\rho}$. Therefore the smaller $\tilde{\rho}$ is, the larger both $\bar{S}$ and the allowed variance in the growth rates vector with respect to the structural vector are. Hence, the smaller the typical number of species that can stably coexist in a purely competitive system, and the less robust the system is.

The reader should now compare Equations (7.19) and (7.20) with their exact mean field counterparts, Equations (7.13) and (7.14). It becomes readily apparent that the former equations amount to requesting that $\tilde{C}$ be a weak perturbation around an exact mean field matrix. The result of this exercise seems inescapable: *the extension of the mean field results to a non-exactly mean field system $\tilde{C}$ is meaningful only if $\tilde{C}$ is sufficiently close to being mean field to begin with.* Only under this proviso may we fully characterize the system solely in terms of $\tilde{\rho}$ as in the exact mean field case. In particular, the existence of a biodiversity scale describable by a single parameter, as embodied by the Identification (7.21), only makes sense for matrices that are weak perturbations around the mean field limit.

Lastly, it is not hard to use the previous developments to obtain an estimate for the maximal number of species that can coexist given a certain level of environmental variability $0 \leq \Delta \leq 1$. For matrices that are weak perturbations around the

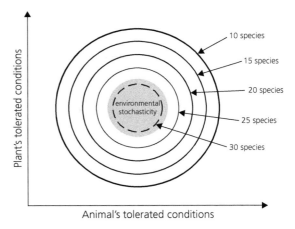

Figure 7.5 The figure sketches the underlying structural stability approach used by Bastolla and colleagues both in the original competitive systems (Bastolla et al. 2005a,b) and its extension to mutualistic networks (Bastolla et al. 2009). The axes represent some idealized conditions (e.g., values of growth rates in parameter space). This approach assumes that there is a certain level of environmental stochasticity the system has to cope with (grey circle). As more species are packed, the range of conditions (volume of parameter space) compatible with their stable coexistence shrinks. At some point, one can not pack more species (thirty in this example) as the range of conditions compatible with their coexistence is smaller than the range of environmental variability. The analytical approach estimates this maximum number of species or biodiversity scale.

mean field case, and for large S, the expression is (neglecting threshold populations; Bastolla et al. (2005a,b)):

$$S_{max} \leq 1 + \bar{S}\left(\frac{1 - \Delta}{\Delta}\right) \sim \bar{S}\left(\frac{1 - \Delta}{\Delta}\right), \quad (7.23)$$

where the last step is valid only for large communities. For large competitive overlap close to unity ($\bar{S} \to 0$) or large environmental variability ($\Delta \to 1$), only one species can survive in the long run. If both the overlap and the environmental variability are small, on the other hand, the maximal number of species can be rather large (Figure 7.5). Note how $\bar{S}$ sets again the scale for the maximum number of allowed species, *provided of course that Δ is fixed*. We will come back to this comment.

We conclude therefore that the meaningfulness of the generalization beyond the exact mean field of the concept of typical biodiversity scale $\bar{S}$ entirely depends on the relevant matrix being close enough to a mean field form. Furthermore, it should be clear that the process by which the results on $\bar{S}$ are obtained is completely equivalent in a formal sense to first defining an "equivalent mean field matrix" $C_{ii}^{emf} = 1, C_{ij}^{emf} = \tilde{\rho}$, with $\tilde{\rho}$ given by Equation (7.19), then substituting C by its approximation C^{emf}. Hereafter, the process of substituting a competition matrix by its related equivalent mean field form will be referred to as "performing an equivalent mean field approximation."

7.3.2 Limits to the number of coexisting species in systems with competition plus mutualism

The core idea behind Bastolla et al. (2009) is the extension of the structural results on the biodiversity of competitive systems as described previously to the more complex setting of two groups of species interacting by way of direct competition within sets plus mutualism between sets. The key insight here is that this can be done, at least in some cases, by using the effective competition formalism previously described and performing an equivalent mean field approximation to the effective competition matrices. Furthermore, this framework will allow us to compute the net effect of the mutualistic interaction on biodiversity.

Indeed, note that as it is clear from Equations (7.9), the effective competition matrix becomes the direct competition matrix if we set $\lambda^{(P,A)} = 0$. To obtain explicit analytical expressions, Bastolla et al. (2009) considered, in line with the previous approach, direct competition matrices of mean field type as in Equation (7.6). Thus, we start from the baseline limit to the number of coexisting species defined by Equation (7.16) with $\rho = \rho^{(P)}$—for plants for instance. We can then incorporate mutualism between plants and animals and quantify the new limit to biodiversity. First, both for the case when γ is mean field itself and for small γ we compute the effective competition matrix including the effect of mutualism. Next, we perform a mean field approximation to it. Lastly, for a given value of environmental noise, the maximum eigenvalue of the effective competition matrix will then provide a limit to biodiversity through Equations (7.19), (7.21), and (7.23).

Let us first consider a fully connected mutualistic network where all plants interact with all animals. Note that in this case performing a mean field approximation to the effective competition is fully justified since the mutualist matrices are also of mean field type. The effective interspecific competition $\tilde{\rho}_{mut}^{(P)}$ is related to the direct competition without mutualism as follows:

$$\tilde{\rho}_{mut}^{(P)} = \frac{\rho^{(P)} - a^{(P)}}{1 - a^{(P)}}, \qquad (7.24)$$

where $a^{(P)}$ is a parameter defined in Bastolla et al. (2009) which is proportional to the strength of mutualistic interactions. Stable solutions exist for $a^{(P)} < \rho^{(P)}$, whence $\tilde{\rho}_{mut}^{(P)}$ must be smaller than $\rho^{(P)}$. This means that mutualism always reduces the effective interspecific competition in a fully connected plant-animal network, hence one should expect to find that fully connected competitive plus mutualistic networks allow for higher biodiversity than their purely competitive counterparts. The predicted maximum number of plant species in the presence of mutualism, $\bar{S}_{mut}^{(P)}$ indeed becomes (Bastolla et al. 2009):

$$\bar{S}_{mut}^{(P)} = \frac{1 - \tilde{\rho}_{mut}^{(P)}}{\tilde{\rho}_{mut}^{(P)}} = \frac{\bar{S}^{(P)}}{1 - a^{(P)}/\rho^{(P)}}, \qquad (7.25)$$

which is strictly greater than $\bar{S}^{(P)}$, proving that fully connected mutualistic networks increase the number of coexisting species by reducing the effective interspecific competition. The reader should note that $\tilde{\rho}_{mut}^{(P)}$ has been defined so far only for the fully connected case.

One can now proceed to asses how the mutualistic effect is shaped by the structure of the network when departing from the extreme of a fully connected case. The effective competition matrix in the previous case contained constant terms describing an average identical effect of one species on another. Now, however, the elements of the effective competition matrix $C_{ij}^{(P)}$ are different and can be written as (Bastolla et al. 2009):

$$\frac{C_{ij}^{(P)}}{(1 - \rho^{(P)})} = \delta_{ij} + \frac{1}{\bar{S}^{(P)}} + R\left(\frac{1}{S^{(A)} + \bar{S}^{(A)}} n_i^{(P)} n_j^{(P)} - n_{ij}^{(P)}\right), \qquad (7.26)$$

where δ_{ij} is the Kronecker's Delta as before, R is the mutualism-to-competition ratio (Supplementary Equation 22 in Bastolla et al. 2009), and $n_i^{(P)}$, $n_j^{(P)}$, and $n_{ij}^{(P)}$ are the number of interactions of plant species i, of plant species j, and the shared interactions between both species, respectively. Importantly, the RHS of Equation (7.26) decreases with the nestedness of the mutualistic network. Indeed, a nested network maximizes the overlap in interactions between any two species i and j (term $-n_{ij}^{(P)}$ in Equation 7.26) in relation to the number of interactions of both species (terms $n_i^{(P)}$ and $n_j^{(P)}$ in Equation 7.26). As a consequence, under visual inspection nestedness reduces the effective interspecific competition $\tilde{\rho}$ for a given distribution of number of interactions across plant species and fixed parameters. Since according to Definition (7.21) the predicted biodiversity scale for plant species increases with decreasing $\tilde{\rho}$, the model predicts that the more nested the matrix is, the higher the typical biodiversity scale.

To explicitly quantify the increase in biodiversity due to the nested architecture of mutualistic networks (from the baseline of an exclusively competitive system), Bastolla et al. (2009) first defined a normalized effective competition matrix $B_{ij}^{(P)} = C_{ij}^{(P)}/\sqrt{C_{ii}^{(P)}C_{jj}^{(P)}}$ to ensure unit diagonal entries, as required by the previous formalism. They then computed the derivative of the first eigenvalue of this normalized matrix with respect to the mutualism-to-competition ratio in the vicinity of $\gamma = 0$. By using Equations (7.19) and (7.21), this is immediately translated into the derivative of the expected biodiversity scale (or equivalently, via Equation (7.23), the derivative of the maximum number of coexisting species) with respect to γ around $\gamma = 0$. The result is that, around $\gamma = 0$, the typical scale biodiversity supported by the system generally increases as γ grows.

This analysis shows that while mutualism always increases the expected number of coexisting species in fully connected networks, its effect is variable in structured networks. Thus, mutualism may increase the effective competition and reduce biodiversity for low nestedness if the number of shared interactions is quite low. Mutualism can also decrease biodiversity if direct competition is strong so that the predicted maximum number of species in the absence of mutualism, $\bar{S}^{(A)}$ and $\bar{S}^{(P)}$, are small. The architecture of mutualistic networks, therefore, highly conditions the sign and magnitude of the effect of mutualism on the number of coexisting species. Nestedness maximizes the number of species given a fixed number of interactions.

To fully understand the relationship with later results, it is important to note the key limitations of Bastolla et al. (2009)'s approach. These can be divided in two types. The first one encompasses potential problems with the applicability of the results of Bastolla et al. (2005a,b) in the context of effective competition matrices due to the technical requirements involved. The second one has to do with limitations of the approach used in Bastolla et al. (2005a,b) itself that are inherited by Bastolla et al. (2009).

Regarding the first limitation, and as was noted, the extension developed in Bastolla et al. (2005a,b) of the competitive load formalism to a general matrix B non strictly mean field requires that B be symmetric, with non-negative elements, and defined positive. Note that *prima facie* the normalized effective competition matrices $B^{(P,A)}$ need not satisfy some of these requirements. An extension to the non-symmetric competition matrices case of the main Inequality (7.36) was however carried out later on in Rohr et al. (2013) and also in Rohr et al. (2014). It ensured positive definitness via the use of $C^T C$ and imposed non-negative elements of $C^T C$. As could have been expected, the essential features of (7.21) carry out to this more general setting.

The second limitation of Bastolla et al. (2009) stems from the fact that, as discussed previously, the approach followed by Bastolla et al. (2005a,b) to establish the biodiversity scale $\bar{S}$ beyond the pure mean field case is only meaningful when the matrices analysed are themselves weak perturbations around the mean field. This does not hamper the internal logic of the paper since, on one hand, in the the fully connected mutualistic case the mutualistic matrices were also mean field themselves. On the other hand, the perturbative expansion of $\lambda_1(B^{(P)})$ for less than fully connected networks is carried out in the vicinity of $\gamma = 0$.

In this regime, it is sensible to expect that the mutualistic matrices will act as a small perturbation around the mean field competition matrices. Nonetheless, it is still important to keep in mind that the regime covered by the authors corresponds to that of very weak mutualistic interaction acting as a small perturbation to the direct competitive matrices of mean field type. One could argue, however, that these weak dependencies are in agreement with the pattern observed in nature as noted previously (Bascompte et al. 2006a).

The paper by Bastolla et al. (2009) was followed by several papers. Allesina and Tang (2012) and Suweis et al. (2013) focussed on the local stability of the mutualistic model, while James et al. (2012) re-examined the limits on the number of coexisting species. We will next briefly describe these papers.

Allesina and Tang (2012) explored the local stability of nested mutualistic networks using a random matrix approach. Specifically, they extended May (1972)'s approach (threshold for stability provided by Equation (7.3)) to incorporate more realistic interaction arrangements between species. The yardstick against which to establish which configurations are more stable than others is as follows: assume that we order the eigenvalues of the community matrix A by their real parts such that $\lambda_1 < \lambda_2 < \ldots < \lambda_n < 0$, where the λ_i refers only to the real part of the respective eigenvalue. We will refer to λ_n as the spectral abscissa. Under the logic that $\lambda_n < 0$ is a necessary condition for local stability, the authors use the size of the spectral abscissa as the criterium to compare the stability of different systems. Thus, they assume that a system a with a spectral abscissa λ_n^a is more stable than system b if $\lambda_n^a < \lambda_n^b$. Applying this criterium, the authors find that for random matrices, the pure predator-prey case increases the stability of the network, whilst the mutualist/competitive random mix decreases its stability.

They then proceed to study purely mutualistic (i.e., no competition present) bipartite networks, both with and without nested structure. In this context the authors found that weak interaction strengths increase local stability (compatible with Equation (7.2), and for obvious reasons) while nestedness tends to decrease local stability. The latter result needs some explanation and it seems at

odds with related work finding a stabilizing role of network structure.

There are two issues at work here. First, and crucially, Allesina and Tang (2012) consider only mutualism but not competition. However, we already know from Equation (7.11) that mutualism without the presence of interspecific competition tends to destabilize the weakly interacting regime for large systems. In other words: mutualism must be understood as a mechanism to compensate for competition. That this destabilizing effect should be even more pronounced if the architecture is nested should come as no surprise since nestedness is, essentially, a mechanism to enhance the mutualistic effect of countering competition.

Second, from a conceptual point of view there is the issue that the spectral abscissa of the community matrix is, generally speaking, not the sole factor determining the stability of the system. Indeed, it is important here to distinguish between two different concepts: the necessary condition for local stability on the one hand, and the size of the maximal perturbation that the system can absorb before loosing local stability (the so-called *distance to instability*) on the other hand. It is of course the case that negativity of λ_n is a necessary condition for local stability. But it is however wrong to generally assume that the value of the spectral abscissa gives a correct measurement of the system's distance to instability. Indeed, that this is generally not the case has been known to control engineers for quite some time (see Hinrichsen and Pritchard (2005), Section 5.4), and in fact λ_n coincides with the distance to instability only for the case of normal matrices. It follows then that the qualitative ordering criterium stated previously, "System a is more stable than System b if $\lambda_n^a < \lambda_n^b$," turns out to be correct only if matrices A and B are normal. Note however that this is generally not the case for the random matrices used by the authors in their computations.

The second manuscript building from Bastolla et al. (2009) was that by Suweis et al. (2013). These authors focused mostly (although not exclusively) in the weakly interacting regime. The first main conclusion of their work was that although nested networks remain stable, they tend to be less resilient than the equivalent randomization. This means that the networks take more time to recover from a perturbation. This seems to differ from the previous result by Okuyama and Holland (2008) that, as noted, reported that although resilience is largely independent of nestedness in general, nestedness does increase resilience (albeit the effect is small) when mutualism strengths are small and asymmetric and connectivity is small. Although apparently different, the two sets of results are perhaps not that different as Suweis et al. (2013) coincide with Okuyama and Holland (2008) in that it is when mutualistic strengths are small that network architecture has a major effect. For strongly interacting systems the effect of structure vanishes. Keep in mind also, that for these large values we may have already entered the strong mutualistic regime, a problem that we will see again in relation to the paper by James et al. (2012). On the other hand, the fact that Okuyama and Holland (2008) had a rather small set of simulations in the weakly coupled regime makes the comparison of the detailed results difficult (as previously mentioned).

While nested networks may remain less resilient but still stable, Suweis et al. (2013) imply a higher difference in abundances between the most generalists and the most specialists species, and they show that it is the abundance of the rarest species which determines the resilience of the community. Note, however, that this result is obtained only in the limit in which both interspecific competition and mutualistic interaction are very small when compared to intra-specific self-limitation (i.e., well below 5% in relative value). Furthermore, the same caveats exposed regarding the spectral abscissa and the distance to instability apply here, although in this case the authors correctly coach their result in terms of the system's resiliency (i.e., its rate of return to equilibrium), rather than in terms of whether the system is locally stable (i.e., whether it will return to the equilibrium point following an infinitesimally small perturbation).

Since they posit that nested mutualistic networks have higher spectral abscissas (controlled by the rarest species) and are less resilient than non-nested networks, Suweis et al. (2013) then move to propose that the optimization principle by which nested networks would ultimately arise is that of maximizing species abundances. Under this point of view, the network architecture would not be generated by optimal stability considerations, and whatever associated stability the network may have it would be a consequence of the system's tendency to increase species abundances (Suweis et al. 2013). This consitutes a very intriguing possibility. Note that, under a similar argument, Bastolla et al. (2009) had shown that a nested network would automatically arise if new species entering the community tend to interact with partners in a way that minimizes their competitive loads—hence maximizing their abundances.

Turning now to the numerical study by James et al. (2012), these authors claimed that nestedness does not necessarily increase the number of coexisting species, thus challenging the result by Bastolla et al. (2009). This apparent contradiction can be traced back to two problems with their approach, one regarding the correct analytical expression for the maximum number of species, the other with the confounding effect of parametrization of the model. We next explain briefly these two points, which in turn, lead to further refinements of the framework of structural stability and additional insight into the role of network structure.

Regarding the choice of the right equation, James et al. (2012) missguided their criticism by incorrectly applying the expression for the biodiversity scale, Equation (7.25), obtained for the fully connected case, to obtain the maximum allowed biodiversity S_{max} of empirical, sparse networks. Indeed, to obtain a general formula for the maximum biodiversity in the effective competition framework for non-fully connected systems, one needs to take into account that the growth rate vector components must now be taken from the *effective growth rates* vector. Furthermore, note that $\bar{S}$ only sets the scale for S_{max} provided that the environmental variability Δ is fixed. Otherwise, S_{max} is also a function of the variability of the effective growth rates components (see Equation (7.23) and subsequent discussion). The effective growth rates are similar across species in fully connected networks since they have the same number of interactions. Real networks, however, show a strong heterogeneity in the number of interactions across species, and therefore in the components of their vector of effective growth rates. Rohr et al. (2013) showed that once using the right expressions for non-fully connected, real networks, the predicted upper bound of biodiversity is much closer to the observed values. In the process, Rohr et al. (2013) expanded Bastolla et al.'s (2009) method (originally requiring symmetric competitive matrices with positive elements) to the general case of asymmetric effective competition matrices.

The second pitfall of James et al. (2012)'s approach has to do with the effect of parametrization. As shown by Rohr et al. (2014), depending on the choice of parameter values, one can show that nestedness increases persistence, nestedness decreases persistence, and nestedness does not affect persistence. Conclusions that arise from studies that use arbitrary values in intrinsic growth rates are not about the effects of network architecture on species coexistence, but about which network architecture maximizes species persistence for that specific choice of parameter values. James et al. parametrized growth rates from the same distribution across all species. However, as was already noted in the Supplementary Material of Bastolla et al. (2009: Section 6.2) and then again by Pascual-García and Bastolla (2017), growth rates in feasible systems are negatively correlated with the mutualistic degree. As a consequence, James et al.'s approach produced unfeasible equilibria with much higher probability for mutualistic than for competitive systems, which is at the heart of their conclusion that mutualism reduces the number of coexisting species.

From a geometric point of view, the previous problem stands from realizing that there are two important interrelated aspects. One is the range of parameter values compatible with the stable persistence of all species (structural stability) for a given architecture. The second aspect is how close a given choice of parameter values puts the system to the boundary of this fully feasible domain. This distinction was clearly made by the late developmental biologist Pere Alberch in his phenotype-genotype maps (Alberch, 1989, Figure 4). Therefore, the idea to disentangle properly the two effects (role of network architecture and that of parameterization) is to find the center of this feasibility domain and then explore its volume.

7.3.3 Robustness of mutualistic networks

Rohr et al. (2014) were interested in studying the role of network structure in the robustness of the network in the face of perturbations of the growth

rates. The authors used again model (5) of Bastolla et al. (2009) but now adding a trade-off between the strength of the mutualistic interaction (i.e., the per-capita effect of a species on the per-capita growth rate of their mutualistic partners) and the number of partners a species has—as already suggested in Bastolla et al. (2009). This mutualistic trade-off modulates the extent to which species that interact with a few others do so strongly, while species which interact with many partners do it weakly, an observation justified on empirical grounds (Margalef 1968; Vázquez et al. 2007). Rohr et al. (2014) assume that the trade-offs take the form $\gamma_{ij} = (\gamma_0 y_{ij}) / (k_i^\delta)$, where $y_{ij} = 1$ if species i and j interact and zero otherwise; k_i is the number of interactions of species i; γ_0 represents the level of mutualistic strength, and δ corresponds to the mutualistic trade-off. As for the community matrix, this is taken to be, in its most general form,

$$B_{nl} := \begin{bmatrix} \beta_{ij}^{(P)} & -\dfrac{\gamma_{ij}^{(P)}}{1+h\sum_k \gamma_{ik}^{(P)} A_k} \\ -\dfrac{\gamma_{ij}^{(A)}}{1+h\sum_k \gamma_{ik}^{(A)} P_k} & \beta_{ij}^{(A)} \end{bmatrix}, \quad (7.27)$$

where as in previous work the authors assume that the direct competition matrices are of mean field type. Note that as $h \to 0$ we recover the linear functional response regime—which we will denote as B_l.

Rohr et al. first proceed to investigate the conditions which any feasible equilibrium point needs to satisfy in order to be globally stable in the space of positive densities. Global stability of a solution within a given domain D determines whether a system returns to the equilibrium after a perturbation of the variables *of any given magnitude*, with the requirement only that the perturbation does not take the system outside the domain D. As such, it is a more general concept than that of local stability. These conditions had been solved for Lotka–Volterra equations in the linear response regime, but not in general. In the linear response regime, it is well known that the system will be globally stable under quenched (this is very sudden and time-independent) perturbations provided that B_l is diagonally stable (Goh 1977; Takeuchi et al. 1978). That is, there is a diagonal matrix D with positive elements such that $DB_l + B_l^T D$ is positive definite. In this regard, the authors state a conjecture asserting that any matrix of the form B_l is locally stable if and only if it is also diagonally stable. If the conjecture holds, establishing global stability becomes equivalent to establishing local stability. Since the direct competition matrices are defined positive, it follows that B_l must be locally stable in a neighborhood around $\gamma_0 = 0$ by continuity. The authors then find by numerical simulations that local stability is maintained all the way up to a critical value $\gamma_0 = \gamma_c$. The exact critical value will depend on the value of the interspecific competition strength ρ, but roughly speaking, one may take $\gamma_c \sim \rho$. Hence, if the conjecture is valid, we have that weak mutualist solutions in the range $0 \leq \gamma_0 \lesssim \gamma_c$ are all globally stable.

The authors then proceed to examine the dynamical stability in the non-linear case of density-dependent functional responses. This boils down to showing that the stability conditions for the linear case also hold when considering B_{nl} instead of B_l. But note how B_{nl} differs from the equivalent matrix containing all interaction terms in the linear case (B_l) only in the off-diagonal block with B_{nl} having a decreased mutualistic strength with respect to the linear response form. This implies that the critical value of mutualistic strength for the nonlinear Lotka–Volterra system is larger or equal than the critical value for the linear system. Therefore, the critical value γ_c derived from the linear Lotka–Volterra system is already a sufficient condition to grant the global stability of any feasible equilibrium in the nonlinear case, which converges to the result by Bascompte et al. (2006a) discussed in Equation 7.2.

Once the global dynamical stability of solutions is stablished, Rohr et al. (2014) studied whether a given stable solution is feasible. Obviously, the conditions that ensure either the former or the latter status are not the same. They proceed by analytically estimating the center of the feasibility domain by generalizing to the non-symmetric case the formalism for symmetric competition matrices developed in Bastolla et al. (2005a,b). The shift from symmetric to non-symmetric matrices is accomplished by switching from the spectral decomposition of symmetric competition matrices to the Singular Value Decomposition (SVD) of the effective competition matrices for both plants and animals. Note how in Bastolla et al. (2005a,b) the *competitive load vector*,

corresponding to the principal (Perron) vector of the symmetric competition matrix, was at the center of the feasibility domain. The direct translation of this result into the SVD formalism is that two *structural vectors*, corresponding now to the two different principal (Perron) singular vectors—the right one and left one—of each effective competition matrix $C^{(P,A)}$, will lie at the center of the domain. These *structural vectors* therefore correspond to a direct generalization of the competitive load vector of Bastolla et al. (2005a,b).

In the process, the authors obtain a generalization of the coexistance inequality previously obtained for symmetric non-mean field matrices by Bastolla et al. (2005a,b) to the non-symmetric, SVD based case. This now reads,

$$\frac{\sum_{k=1}^{S} <\mathbf{u}_{eff}^k \mid \mathbf{p}_{eff}><\mathbf{v}_{eff}^k \mid \mathbf{p}_{eff}> - <\mathbf{u}_{eff}^1 \mid \mathbf{p}_{eff}><\mathbf{v}_{eff}^1 \mid \mathbf{p}_{eff}>}{<\mathbf{u}_{eff}^1 \mid \mathbf{p}_{eff}><\mathbf{v}_{eff}^1 \mid \mathbf{p}_{eff}>}$$
$$\leq \frac{\sigma_2}{\sigma_1}, \tag{7.28}$$

where $\left\{\mathbf{u}_{eff}^k\right\}$, $\left\{\mathbf{v}_{eff}^k\right\}$ correspond to the left and right singular basis of the relevant effective competition matrix, $\mathbf{p}_{eff}$ is the vector of effective growth rates, $\mathbf{u}_{eff}^1$, $\mathbf{v}_{eff}^1$ are the two structural (Perron) vectors of the effective competition matrix, and σ_1, σ_2 its highest and second highest singular values. The reader may note how the previous inequality is a direct generalization of the symmetric case previously described. Note how if $\mathbf{p}_{eff}$ is collinear with either $\mathbf{u}_{eff}^1$ or $\mathbf{v}_{eff}^1$, its corresponding solution will automatically be fully feasible. Furthermore, any solution with a vector of effective growth rates possessing minimal sum of angles subtended with these two vectors (i.e, bisecting them) will lie at the center of the feasibility domain for each set of species and will be able to tolerate the strongest deviation before leaving the feasibility domain, namely, before one or more species go extinct.

Once the center of the feasibility domain has been located, the authors determine the boundaries of the domain by numerically perturbing the vector of effective growth rates from its value at the center of the domain and quantifying the amount of variation tolerated by the solution before one species goes extinct (Figure 7.6). Thus, the main steps in this procedure, given a matrix B_l will be: i) switch

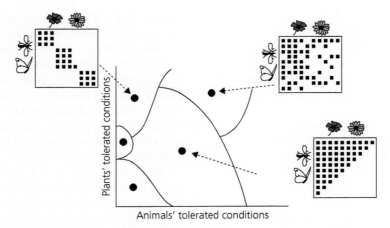

Figure 7.6 A structural stability approach to measuring robustness in mutualistic networks. This is directly related to the interpretation in development biology illustrated in Figure 7.4. Here, parameter space is represented by two idealized axis representing conditions for both plants and animals (e.g., growth rates). Some network structures, e.g., the nested structure on the right may have a wider range of parameter combinations compatible with the stable coexistence of all species. In order to quantify this, however, one has to account for the confounding factor of having the system close to a boundary. Redrawn from Rohr et al. (2014).

to the effective competition matrix formalism, ii) determine the corresponding structural vectors and centers of the feasibility domain for each set of species, iii) establish by numerical simulations the size of the full feasibility domain by computing the maximal angle subtended by a perturbed vector of effective growth rates with the central directions before loosing species, and iv) finally transform back from the effective competition to the B_l frame to obtain the results in the ecologically meaningful set of growth rates.

With these methods to estimate both the global stability and feasibility of the mutualistic model, Rohr et al. (2014) explored the role of network architecture in modulating the range in parameter space compatible with both feasibility and global stability (all species persisting in a stable way). Specifically, they used the partial fitted values from a binomial regression of the fraction of surviving species on nestedness (N), mean mutualistic strength ($\bar{\gamma}$), and mutualistic trade-off (δ), while controlling for the deviations from the structural vectors of intrinsic growth rates ($\eta_{(A)}, \eta_{(P)}$). These partial fitted values are the contribution of network architecture to the logit of the probability of species persistence, and in turn, these values are positively proportional to the size of the feasibility domain. Through this procedure, Rohr et al.

(2014) concluded that network architecture had a large influence of structural stability. In particular, the structure that maximizes structural stability corresponds to: i) a maximal level of nestedness, ii) a small (sub-linear) mutualistic trade-off, and iii) a high level of mutualistic strength within the constraint of any feasible solution being globally stable (Equation 7.2). Interestingly enough, this network architecture maximizing structural stability corresponds to the structure found in the majority of mutualistic networks. Specifically, in eighteen out of twenty-three networks ($P = 0.004$, binomial test), the observed network architectures induce more than half the value of the maximum net effect on structural stability. The architecture of mutualistic networks, therefore, tends to maximize the range of parameter space—structural stability—for species coexistence (Rohr et al. 2014).

The key limitation of Rohr et al. (2014) is that Inequality (7.28) is, much like its predecessor (18), only tight when $\sigma_2 \simeq \sigma_3 \simeq \cdots \simeq \sigma_n$ (the reader should remember Condition (7.20) in this regard). That is, (7.28) is tight when all subdominant singular values are approximately equal and we are close to the mean field situation. In the present work, however, and unlike that of Bastolla et al. (2009), this fact does not limit the paper conclusions. This is due to the fact that Rohr et al. (2014) do not use the value of the RHS of the inequality to find the maximal value that the LHS can take while ensuring full feasibility. Rather, they start by recognizing that the LHS of Equation (7.28) implies that the structural vectors play a privileged role in defining the center of the feasibility domain, and then use exclusively the LHS to find that center. They subsequently find the maximal values of the deviation from this center, not from the inequality itself, but rather from numerical simulations. Hence whether the RHS is tight or not is ineffectual.

An analysis of structural stability equivalent to that by Rohr et al. (2014) was done by Grilli et al. (2017). Essentially, they found that the structure of empirical mutualistic networks has a positive effect on feasibility. Although their results indicate that this is mainly driven by the number and mean strength of interactions, nestedness contributes to feasibility and may be relevant in the cases where interaction strengths are constrained. Interestingly, these authors did not only estimate the size of the feasibility domain, but also its shape. Indeed, the structure of mutualistic networks was also found to affect the shape of this feasibility domain in the sense of making it more heterogeneous: the volume of parameter space is larger in some directions and smaller in others. This means that, even when the total volume may be larger than expected for a random matrix, the system may be more susceptible to certain directions of perturbations (Grilli et al. 2017). From a methodological point of view, these interesting findings are based on the analysis of random matrices, so it is worth considering the potential limitations of such an approach. As already noted by the authors, the properties of random $S \times S$ matrices are valid *only* in the large S limit (i.e., read $S \gg 10^4$). Since such large networks do not occur in the real world, the authors validate their analytical predictions for smaller networks by performing a large number of simulations over a large number of randomized parametrizations. In this way, the large S predictions are recovered *on average* even for networks in which S is not large. The downside of this procedure, though, is that the variability across individual runs must necessarily still be rather large for networks with S as low as fifty or one hundred. As a consequence, the conceptual case for considering

the random model as a null hypothesis would seem somewhat weak (in this sense note that this criticism may also be applied to Allesina and Tang (2012) previously mentioned). One interesting possibility that deserves further attention in this regard is that nestedness could be a way to achieve a feasible domain volume equal or larger than the average random case while at the same time avoiding the variability necessarily associated to small random networks.

Similarly to the paper by Allesina and Tang (2012), Valdovinos et al. (2016) also reported a negative effect of nestedness on species persistence (i.e., fraction of initial species persisting at the end of the numerical simulations after perturbing the system). It must be emphasized again, though, that they include competition only at the plant level. Pollinator species do not compete amongst them for any other external resources in their model. As explained previously, however, one would indeed expect nestedness to decrease persistence in these conditions and for large systems (see comments following Equation (7.11)). The authors then show that by including adaptive foraging they recover the positive effect of nestedness on persistence. In other words, it is possible that adaptive foraging may have a positive effect on the system's stability by reducing excessive niche overlap, much like the introduction of trade-offs does. Thus, this result goes precisely along the same direction as the suggestion in Bastolla et al. (2009)'s Supp. Mat. that trade-offs in the species interactions ought to be introduced in order to further stabilize the system.

Lastly, the paper by Pascual-García and Bastolla (2017) tries to answer both the comment by James et al. to Bastolla et al. (2009) and to Rohr et al. (2014). They do so both on analytical grounds and with an extensive set of numerical simulations. Their main conclusion would seem to reconcile at some extent the differing results of James et al. (2012) and of Rohr et al. (2014) by stating that nested mutualistic networks indeed increase structural stability, but only if the direct competition parameter ρ is below a critical value ρ^c.

From the analytical point of view, Pascual-García and Bastolla (2017) start by introducing a new version of the coexistence condition. This states that in order to have positive abundances in a purely competitive system, with a strictly nonnegative competition matrix which has unit diagonal elements ($C_{ii} = 1$), every species i must satisfy as a sufficient condition (after neglecting extinction thresholds),

$$\eta_i(p) = 1 - \frac{p_i}{p^1 v_i^1} \le \frac{1}{\left(S/\bar{S} + 1\right)}, \qquad (7.29)$$

where the η_i are called the vulnerability factors (guild superscripts are omitted here). This expression can be seen to also hold under a more general definition of the equivalent mean field competition parameter, valid also for the case of competition matrices whose diagonal elements have not been normalized to unity,

$$\tilde{\rho} = \frac{1}{S-1}\left(\frac{\lambda_1(C)}{Tr(C)/S} - 1\right). \qquad (7.30)$$

The authors employ this latter expression for $\tilde{\rho}$, but this does not seem to change the conceptual landscape. Standard equivalent mean field identification (see Section 7.3.1),

$$\bar{S} = \frac{1 - \tilde{\rho}}{\tilde{\rho}} \qquad (7.31)$$

and condition,

$$\lambda_i \simeq \frac{Tr(C)}{S}(1 - \tilde{\rho}) \; \forall i \ge 2 \qquad (7.32)$$

must be employed to obtain (7.29). The paper then follows the expected scheme of an equivalent mean field approximation as discussed earlier in this chapter. Assuming direct competition matrices of mean field form with parameter ρ, the effective competition matrix C for each set of species is computed. Subsequently, its first eigenvalue λ_1 is analytically calculated in order to perform an equivalent mean field approximation to C by computing an equivalent niche overlap $\tilde{\rho}$ via Equation (7.30). Having obtained $\tilde{\rho}$ we can now compute the associated biodiversity scale $\bar{S} = \bar{S}(\tilde{\rho})$ as per Equation (7.31). From Equation (7.29) then, for C close enough to being mean field (so that (7.32) holds and the inequalities are tight) this should provide us with a good approximation to the scale of biodiversity supported by the original system. As usual in the standard equivalent mean field scheme, $\bar{S}$ decreases as $\tilde{\rho}$ increases.

After computing C and $\lambda_1(C)$ and substituting their values into (30) an expression for $\tilde{\rho}$ (denoted as ρ^{eff} in the paper) is finally reached:

$$\tilde{\rho} \approx \rho + \xi\left(\rho - \rho^c\right), \qquad (7.33)$$

where both ξ and ρ^c are positive parameters that may be computed from the effective competition matrix C. This expression constitutes the main analytical support to the authors claim that "Mutualism supports biodiversity when direct competition is weak." Note how only if the direct competition parameter ρ is such that $\rho < \rho^c$ then $\tilde{\rho} < \rho$ and mutualism decreases $\tilde{\rho}$, whereas if $\rho > \rho^c$ we will always have $\tilde{\rho} < \rho$. According to these comments, one would then expect that in the latter case mutualism will decrease the scale of biodiversity supported by the system.

The limitations in the paper by Pascual-García and Bastolla (2017) are, as expected, mostly inherited from the equivalent mean field substitution approach. First, as already discussed several times, not only the accuracy of the approach, but also the correctness of associating a biodiversity scale as per Identification (7.31) critically depend on the matrices under consideration (the effective competition matrices in this case) being weak perturbations around the mean field direct competition. In particular Condition (7.32) must hold for this set of Inequalities (7.29) to be not just tight (hence both necessary *and* sufficient to ensure coexistence), but also correct in the sense that it is only if (7.32) holds that $\bar{S}$, as already defined, appears in the RHS of (7.29). Thus the concept of the predicted biodiversity scale itself as embodied by (7.31), holds any meaning only for matrices C which are approximately of mean field type, strictly nonnegative and symmetric. It is only in this case that Equation (7.32) is justified, $\bar{S}$ is meaningful, and the inequalities are tight.

This limitation is compounded by the fact that the expression used to compute $\lambda_1(C)$ (provided in the original text following it, Equation (7.24)) is valid only for matrices C for which all rows have equal row sum, as is the case if C is mean field. It is well known however that, unless the system is fully connected, nested matrices are characterized by having not just large, but the largest possible variability in row sums (Mahadev and Peled 1995). It follows that any real impact that a nested arquitechture would have on the dynamics must necessarily be largely (if not completely) diluted before the given approach becomes valid, or else we will be lead astray by an erroneous determination of λ_1. Hence, if correct, the result would be valid only in the immediate vicinity of direct mean field competition matrices, where $\gamma \simeq 0$.

7.4 Concluding remarks

The previous development tried to navigate across the recent papers on the structural stability of weakly interacting mutualistic networks by relating the different contributions and separating what could be considered a core of common conclusions from the particular limitations due to the either the assumptions or the approach of each work.

A first conclusion at this stage in the development of the field is that requiring dynamical stability under external perturbations seems to push the system in a direction in configuration space which is opposite to that required to maintain full feasibility under those same perturbations. To see how this comes about, let us start by defining q as the ratio of interspecific competition to mutualistic interaction strength, i.e., $q^{(P,A)} = \rho^{(P,A)}/\gamma^{(P,A)}$. We may then rewrite Condition (7.11) for dynamical stability of large ecosystems in the weakly interacting regime as

$$q^{(P)}q^{(A)} > 1. \qquad (7.34)$$

Assuming to simplify the discussion that $q^{(P)} = q^{(A)} = q$, this expression clearly establishes a limiting value $q_{lim} = 1$ such that for $q \leq q_{lim}$ the system will loose its dynamical stability. Let us then use q as a proxy to measure the system's distance to instability (akin to the spectral abscissa λ_n in the work of Allesina and Tang (2012)). Then, it follows that $q_{lim} \to 0$ as $\rho \to 0$ and $q \to q_{lim}$ as $\gamma \to \rho$. The first of the two results coincides with Allesina and Tang (2012): mutualism tends to destabilize the system in the absence of interspecific competition. The second result, however, implies that even if one starts in the regime $\gamma \ll \rho$ ($q \gg 1$), increasing the mutualistic strength tends to decrease the resistance of dynamical stability to external perturbations. Note that this essentially coincides with Suweis et al. (2013) if one

assumes that lowering q is akin to lowering the system's resilience, a not altogether unreasonable point of view. This last result, however, is in marked contrast with the conclusions of both Bastolla et al. (2009) and Rohr et al. (2014). Namely, that if $\gamma \ll \rho$ then increasing γ together with increasing nestedness, which is in essence a mechanism to enhance mutualism, increases the ability of the system to maintain full feasibility, and increase its biodiversity even in the presence of external perturbations. Network architecture has a major effect when mutualistic strengths are small. Note that the analytical results in Bastolla et al. (2009) are constrained to the $q \gg 1$ egime, but the simulations in Rohr et al. (2014) hold all the way down to $q \to q_{lim}$.

In light of the previous considerations, we end up with the following summary. It would appear that the final state of the system will be a compromise between two conflicting tendencies. At $q \gg 1$ dynamical stability is ensured. The system's priority in this regime is to ensure its full feasibility and enhance its biodiversity, and to that end both mutualism and nestedness are beneficial (Bastolla et al. 2009; Rohr et al. 2014). In this domain of small mutualistic strength, network architecture becomes more relevant. As q decreases, however, dynamical stability constraints become a relevant factor. The system is close to being destabilized (Valdovinos et al. 2016), or looses resilience (Suweis et al. 2013) by the combination of mutualism plus nestedness. Hence, mechanisms designed to lessen the impact of nestedness on the dynamical stability of the system come into play. These may correspond to either the trade-offs suggested in Bastolla et al. (2009) and explored in Rohr et al. (2014), or their more sophisticated equivalent, the adaptive foraging explored by Valdovinos et al. (2016). Whether these mechanisms alone will suffice to maintain the system stable while simultaneously optimally persistent all the way down to $q = q_{lim}$ is unclear at the moment. Finally, if γ grows beyond the γ_c associated to q_{lim}, the weakly coupled system looses its dynamical stability (Rohr et al. 2014), giving rise to the strong mutualist regime (Bastolla et al. 2009).

Some of the caveats associated to this synthesis have been abundantly mentioned previously. On the side of the dynamical stability, the spectral abscissa (and much less so q, for obvious reasons) is not a proper measurement of the system's distance to instability. Furthermore, in all likelihood, such a measure will need to include not just the lowest eigenvalue/singular value, but some combination of the smallest and the largest. On the side of the system's feasibility, it is clear that the available analytical results for non-fully connected networks are only valid in the vicinity of $\gamma \simeq 0$, i.e., $q \gg 1$, and mean field direct competition matrices. It is evident that more work is needed in this direction. Finally, note also that a critical assumption behind these analytical developments is that of a mean field direct competition matrix. How much real competitive systems depart from this is still unclear, but more attention is now being placed to this topic (Barabás et al. 2016; Levine et al. 2017; Saavedra et al. 2017).

More importantly from a conceptual standpoint, the previously expressed view is predicated on the assumption that maintaining both full feasibility and dynamical stability is of paramount importance to the system. However, only a better knowledge of all the relevant factors involved in the system's dynamical stability will, eventually, assess the appropriateness of such an assumption. Likewise, it would be foolhardy to assume that the concept of structural stability, as it now comprises the system constantly maintaining full feasibility, has reached its definitive form; after all, one may wonder whether it is that costly to the system to loose a rare specialist species. It follows, therefore, that we need to better understand the impact in the system of *not* maintaining either dynamical stability or full feasibility or both, but instead maintaining the average total biomass.

One advantage of the structural approach here developed is that it allows to translate trophic interactions into the framework of competitive theory. Another advantage is that it is an approach that is well suited as a framework to study global environmental change as this is large and directional (rather than infinitesimally small) and it affects growth rates and interaction strengths besides affecting species densities (Justus 2008). This may serve to reconcile a growing body of empirical evidence showing effects of global environmental change on species interactions (e.g., Tylianakis et al. 2008).

References

Alberch, P. (1989). The logic of monsters: Evidence for internal constraint in development and evolution. *Geobios* 22: 21–57.

Allesina, S. and Tang, S. (2012). Stability criteria for complex ecosystems. *Nature* 483: 205–8.

Barabás, G., J Michalska-Smith, M., and Allesina, S. (2016). The effect of intra- and interspecific competition on coexistence in multispecies communities. *The American Naturalist* 188: E1–E12.

Bascompte, J., Jordano, P., Melian, C. J., and Olesen, J. M. (2003). The nested assembly of plant-animal mutualistic networks. *Proceedings of the National Academy of Science* 100: 9383–7.

Bascompte, J., Jordano, P. and Olesen, J. M. (2006a). Asymmetric coevolutionary networks facilitate biodiversity maintenance. *Science* 312: 431–3.

Bascompte, J., Jordano, P., and Olesen, J. M. (2006b). Response to Comment on "Asymmetric Coevolutionary Networks Facilitate Biodiversity Maintenance. *Science (New York, N.Y.)* 313: 1887c–1897c.

Bastolla, U., Fortuna, M. A., Pascual-García, A., Ferrera, A., Luque, B., and Bascompte, J. (2009). The architecture of mutualistic networks minimizes competition and increases biodiversity. *Nature* 458: 1018–20.

Bastolla, U., Lassig, M., Manrubia, S., and Valleriani, A. (2005a). Biodiversity in model ecosystems, I: Coexistence conditions for competing species. *Journal of Theoretical Biology* 235: 521–30.

Bastolla, U., L.ssig, M., Manrubia, S. C. and Valleriani, A. (2005b). Biodiversity in model ecosystems, II: Species assembly and food web structure. *Journal of Theoretical Biology* 235: 531–9.

Case, T. J. (1990). Invasion resistance arises in strongly interacting species-rich model competition communities. *Proceedings of the National Academy of Sciences* 87: 9610–14.

Goh, B. S. (1977). Global stability in many-species systems. *The American Naturalist* 111: 135–43.

Goodwin, B. C. (1990). Structuralism in biology. *Science Progress* 74: 227–43.

Grilli, J., Adorisio, M., Suweis, S., Barábas, G., Banavar, J. R., Allesina, S., and Maritan, A. (2017). Feasibility and coexistence of large ecological communities. *Nature Communications* 8: 523.

Hinrichsen, D. and Pritchard, A. (2005). *Mathematical Systems Theory I: Modelling, State Space Analysis, Stability and Robustness*. Springer, Heidelberg.

Holland, J. N., DeAngelis, D. L., and Bronstein, J. L. (2002). Population dynamics and mutualism: Functional responses of benefits and costs. *The American Naturalist* 159: 231–44.

Holland, J. N., Okuyama, T., and DeAngelis, D. L. (2006). Comment on "Asymmetric coevolutionary networks facilitate biodiversity maintenance." *Science (New York, N.Y.)* 313: 1887b.

Iwao, K. and Rausher, M. D. (1997). Evolution of plant resistance to multiple herbivores: Quantifying diffuse coevolution. *The American Naturalist* 149: 316–35.

James, A., Pitchford, J. W., and Plank, M. J. (2012). Disentangling nestedness from models of ecological complexity. *Nature* 487: 227–30.

Justus, J. (2014). Ecological and Lyapunov Stability. *Philosophy of Science* 75: 421–36.

Kaszkurewicz, E. and Bhaya, A. (2000). *Matrix Diagonal Stability in Systems and Computation*. Boston: Birkhauser.

Levine, J. M., Bascompte, J., Adler, P. B., and Allesina, S. (2017). Beyond pairwise mechanisms of species coexistence in complex communities. *Nature* 546: 56–64.

Mahadev, N. V. R. and Peled, U. (1995). *Threshold Graphs and Related Topics*. North Holland: Annals of Discrete Mathematics, Volume 56.

Margalef, R. (1968). *Perspectives in Ecological Theory*. Chicago: University of Chicago Press.

May, R. (1972). Will a large complex system be stable? *Nature* 238: 413–14.

May, R. M. (1981). Models for two interacting populations. In: *Theoretical Ecology. Principles and Applications*, May, R. M. (ed.). Oxford: Oxford University Press, pp. 78–104.

Nuismer, S., Thompson, J. and Gomulkiewicz, R. (2004). Gene flow and geographically structured coevolution. *Proceedings of the Royal Society of London B* 266: 605–9.

Okuyama, T. and Holland, J. N. (2008). Network structural properties mediate the stability of mutualistic communities. *Ecology Letters* 11: 208–16.

Pascual-García, A. and Bastolla, U. (2017). Mutualism supports biodiversity when the direct competition is weak. *Nature Communications* 8: 14, 326.

Prigogine, I. (1980). *From Being to Becoming. Time and Complexity in the Physical Sciences*. San Francisco: W. H. Freeman and Company.

Ringel, M., Hu, H. H., Anderson, G., and Ringel, M. S. (1996). The stability and persistence of mutualisms embedded in community interactions. *Theoretical Population Biology* 50: 281–97.

Roberts, A. (1974). The stability of a feasible random ecosystem. *Nature* 251: 607–8.

Rohr, R. P., Fortuna, M. A., Luque, B., and Bascompte, J. (2013). Nestedness in mutualistic networks. arXiv:1301.3651v1 [q-bio.PE] 16 Jan 2013: 1–2.

Rohr, R. P., Saavedra, S. and Bascompte, J. (2014). On the structural stability of mutualistic systems. *Science* 345: 497–1, 253.

Saavedra, S., Rohr, R. P., Bascompte, J., Godoy, O., Kraft, N. J. B., and Levine, J. M. (2017). A structural approach for understanding multispecies coexistence. *Ecological Monographs* 87: 470–86.

Scheffer, M., Carpenter, S., Foley, J. A., Folke, C., and Walker, B. (2001). Catastrophic shifts in ecosystems. *Nature* 413: 591–6.

Siljak, D. D. (1978). *Large-scale Dynamic Systems: Stability and Structure*. Amsterdam: North Holland.

Siljak, D. D. (1991). *Decentralized Control of Complex Systems*. New York: Dover.

Stone, L. (2016). The Google matrix controls the stability of structured ecological and biological networks. *Nature Communications* 7: 1–7.

Suweis, S., Simini, F., Banavar, J. R., and Maritan, A. (2013). Emergence of structural and dynamical properties of ecological mutualistic networks. *Nature* 500: 449–52.

Takeuchi, Y., Adachi, N., and Tokumaru, H. (1978). Global stability of ecosystems of the generalized volterra type. *Mathematical Biosciences* 42: 119–36.

Thom, R. (1994). *Structural Stability and Morphogenesis*. Boston: Addison-Wesley.

Thompson, J. N. (2005). *The Geographic Mosaic of Coevolution*. Chicago: Chicago University Press.

Tylianakis, J. M., Didham, R. K., Bascompte, J., and Wardle, D. A. (2008). Global change and species interactions in terrestrial ecosystems. *Ecology Letters* 11: 1351–63.

Valdovinos, F. S., Brosi, B. J., Briggs, H. M., Moisset de Espanés, P., Ramos-Jiliberto, R., and Martinez, N. D. (2016). Niche partitioning due to adaptive foraging reverses effects of nestedness and connectance on pollination network stability. *Ecology Letters* 19: 1277–86.

Vandermeer, J. H. (1975). Interspecific competition: A new approach to the classical theory. *Science (New York, N.Y.)* 188: 253–5.

Vázquez, D. P. and Aizen, M. A. (2004). Asymmetric specialization: A pervasive feature of plant-pollinator interactions. *Ecology* 85: 1251–7.

Vázquez, D. P., J Melián, C., M Williams, N., Blüthgen, N. R., Krasnov, B., and Poulin, R. (2007). Species abundance and asymmetric interaction strength in ecological networks. *Oikos* 116: 1120–7.

Vidyasagar, M. (1981). *Input-Output Analysis of Large-Scale Interconnected Systems*. Lecture Notes in Control and Information Sciences, vol. 29, Heidelberg: Springer.

Waser, N. M., Chittka, L., Price, M. V., Williams, N. M., and Ollerton, J. (1996). Generalization in pollination systems, and why it matters. *Ecology* 77: 1043–60.

Wiggins, S. (1990). *Introduction to Applied Nonlinear Dynamical Systems and Chaos*. Heidelberg: Springer.

CHAPTER 8

Theoretical ecology, concepts, and applications: A data-driven approach to complex ecological systems

Michio Kondoh, Kazutaka Kawatsu, Yutaka Osada, and Masayuki Ushio

8.1 Interspecific interactions and ecological dynamics

8.1.1 Population dynamics and interspecific interactions

What causes the population dynamics we observe in nature? Why can so many species coexist despite the theoretically predicted instability of many-species system? How will an ecological community respond to ongoing climate change and other anthropogenic disturbances? These questions encompassing ecological dynamics are all relevant to, and therefore will not be fully answered without understanding interspecific interactions, which are the major driving force of population dynamics. We start this chapter by introducing the definition of interspecific interactions and how they are related to ecological dynamics.

There are two kinds of "interspecific interactions" that must be clearly distinguished to avoid unnecessary confusion (Goldberg 1996); namely, individual-level and population-level interactions. The former are represented by the various behaviors of

individuals, including killing, chasing, and food or shelter provisioning to individuals of another species. In comparison, the latter are not a directly observable behavior, rather, they are a causality between the population density of different species inferred through changes to population density. The presence of interactions at the individual level does not necessarily means the presence of interactions the population level. Yet, population-level, dynamic interactions are based on individual-level, behavioral interactions (Hassell and May 1985; Tilman 1987; Sutherland 1996; Anholt 1997; Fryxell and Lundberg 1998).

Population dynamics are the dynamical changes in the population density of a species, which are driven by the three processes, birth, death, and migration:

$$x_{t+1} = x_t + (\text{birth}) - (\text{death}) \pm (\text{migration}) \quad (8.1)$$

where x_t is the population density of species X at time t. These three processes are influenced by behavioral and physiological states of only species X and other species. If any of the three processes of

Kondoh, M., Kawatsu, K., Osada, Y., and Ushio, M., *Theoretical ecology, concepts, and applications: A data-driven approach to complex ecological systems*
In: *Theoretical Ecology: Concepts and Applications*. Edited by: Kevin S. McCann and Gabriel Gellner, Oxford University Press (2020). © Oxford University Press.
DOI: 10.1093/oso/9780198824282.003.0008

species X are influenced by the existence or density of species Y at time t, the future density of species X density (x_{t+1}) should be affected by the current density of species Y (y_t). In mathematical terms, this is expressed as: $x_{t+1} = f_x(x_t, y_t)$. Any terms in function f_x that represent the effect of y_t are called interspecific interactions from species Y to X. An interspecific interaction is a causal relationship between the density of coexisting species, making it essential to understand a community as a system.

An interspecific interaction between a pair of species may be studied by evaluating how one species responds to forced changes in the density or presence/absence of the other species. Inspired by theoretical studies of Lotka (1925) and Volterra (1926), the Russian biologist, Georgii Frantsevich Gause conducted a series of experiments using small organisms, including protozoa and yeast. The author compared the population dynamics of these two species cultivated separately and in a mixed population (Gause 1934). In the experiments using protozoa, *Paramecium aurelia* in a separated culture persisted for more than three weeks, but when placed in a mixed population with *P. caudatum* its numbers declined within a week. By analyzing the time-series data in light of the Lotka–Volterra model, Gause showed that the population growth rate of *P. caudatum* decreased with increasing *P. aurelia* density. The author concluded that this decline in population growth is caused by competition for the resource bacteria, *Bacillus pyocyaneus*. A well-controlled manipulative experiment allowed the interspecific interaction to be identified, and the quantification of its impact on community dynamics. However, the same approach is not directly applicable to studying natural communities, which are usually open and subject to continuous disturbances of different types. Consequently, they are unlikely to remain around the stable equilibrium resulting in their being inhabited by a much greater number of interacting species.

This chapter is separated into four sections. In the remaining part of this Section 8.1, we explain the link between interspecific interactions and ecological dynamics. In Section 8.2, we identify the fundamental difficulties in studying interspecific interactions and their consequences in dynamics

empirically, especially in the field. In Section 8.3, we propose a data-driven approach that could be provided by using nonlinear dynamical theory as an alternative to traditional theories. In Section 8.4, we review some intriguing properties of interspecific interactions revealed by the recent studies with the modern data-driven approaches.

8.1.2 Community dynamics and interspecific interactions

Interspecific interactions drive community dynamics. When species X influences the density of species Y, it is considered to be the transmission of an "effect" from the former to the latter (Wootton 1994; Higashi and Nakajima 1995). Therefore, the affecting and affected species, X and Y, are referred to as donor and recipient species, respectively. For some types of interactions (prey-predator interactions, for example), two interacting species might act as both recipient and donor species at the same time. When there are more than three species, transmissions of interspecific effects might become more complicated, as such effects are further transmitted to other species through interspecific interactions. When this type of indirect transmission of effects occurs among species that are not directly interacting, it is called an indirect effect. In the presence of indirect effects, the structure of the interaction network (or who interacts with whom) determines the paths through which an effect spreads over the community, contributing towards determining endogenous community dynamics (May 1973; Chen and Cohen 2001; Kondoh 2003; de Ruiter et al. 1995, 2005) and community responses to exogenous disturbances (Higashi and Nakajima 1995; Brose et al. 2005; Montoya et al. 2009; Novak et al. 2011; Tunny et al. 2017).

The structure of the interspecific interaction network affects the dynamics of the endogenous community. A good example derives from studies of random communities. Consider a community consisting of S species, any pairs of which are interacting with probability C (connectance). The dynamics of species i is given as an ordinary differential equation describing the growth rate of a population, $dx_i/dt = F_i(X)$, where X is a vector representing the community state, or a set of densities for each species, $\{x_1, x_2, x_3, \ldots, x_S\}$. If the system is at an equilibrium, i.e., $F(X^*) = 0$, the local dynamics around the equilibrium can be approximated as linear dynamics, $\mathrm{d}X/\mathrm{d}t = A \cdot X$, where A is an $S \times S$ Jacobian matrix evaluated at equilibrium, in which each element describes the partial derivatives with respect to the density of species j, $A_{ij} = \left[\partial F_i / \partial X_j\right]_{X^*}$. Using random network theory, it is predicted that an equilibrium, X^*, is asymptotically stable if the product of species richness (S) and connectance (C) is smaller than a threshold value, α^2/σ^2, where interaction strength is assumed to follow a normal distribution, $N(0, \sigma^2)$, and α represents the strength of self-regulation force (May 1973). In other words, if network complexity (SC) is large enough, the addition of a small perturbation to the system will grow and shift the system away from the original state; otherwise, the system state will eventually return to the original equilibrium.

The prediction of destabilizing complexity contradicted the expectations of ecologists, leading to the so-called complexity-stability debate over the last few decades (McCann 2000; Landi et al. 2018). Many theoretical studies have been carried out, some of which confirm the controversial prediction, while others overturned it. Yet, this debate also provides a very general insight, that is, the complexity-stability effect of demographic interactions could be changed, or even reversed, by adding small modifications to the model setting, such as functional responses, interaction types, and density dependence (May 1973; Allesina and Tang 2012; Mougi and Kondoh 2012, 2016; Mougi 2017; Kawatsu and Kondoh 2018). Allesina and Tang (2012) showed that the sign structure of an interaction could shift the position of the instability threshold. An antagonistic community is where interacting species generate positive and negative effects on each other, and it is more stable and has a higher instability threshold compared to competitive networks, followed by a mutualistic community, in which interacting species enhance each other. Kawatsu and Kondoh (2018) theoretically showed that the way that the interaction strength responds to density changes is a key determinant of the complexity-stability effect. If negative interspecific effects are more density dependent than positive interspecific effects,

then increasing complexity stabilizes community dynamics. In comparison, if negative effects are less density dependent, the complexity-stability relationship becomes negative. The high sensitivity of the complexity-stability relationship to the detailed model settings of interaction strength confirms that interspecific interactions are an essential component for understanding endogenous community dynamics.

Theory predicts that the way that ecosystems respond to perturbations is influenced by the interaction network (Yodzis 1996; Brose et al. 2005; Montoya et al. 2009; Novak et al. 2011; Tunny et al. 2017). For example, let us consider the question of how the density of a given prey responds to a small increase in the density of its predator. If prey-predator pairs are isolated from the surrounding ecosystem and are at an equilibrium (which is not realistic), an increase in predator density should always cause prey density to decrease. However, this relationship might be no longer true if the pair is embedded in a larger community network (Yodzis 2000). An increase in predator density often leads to an increase in prey density, according to simulations, as the community surrounding the pair provides an indirect effect and could reverse the net effect from negative to positive. Similarly, the community response to the removal of a species is dependent on the interaction network structure (O'Gorman and Emmerson 2009). Consider a keystone predator for which the suppression of a competitive resource species allows the coexistence of many resource species. A theoretical study showed that the keystone effect could be altered if embedded in a larger community network and if related to the community that surrounds the community module of the keystone species and its resource species (Brose et al. 2005). These examples demonstrate that understanding the dynamics of an isolated interacting species pair is different to understanding their dynamics when embedded in a larger ecosystem.

Thus, how do we test the theoretically predicted effects of interaction networks on community stability and responses to external disturbances under natural conditions? One possible approach is to invest effort towards obtaining a detailed understanding of actual interspecific interactions and structures of interaction networks. In fact, several studies have been conducted along this line in the last two decades. There have been attempts to describe the realistic shapes of functional responses (Spalinger and Hobbs 1992; Vucic-Pestic et al. 2010), to identify the many types of existing interactions and to describe their structure as a single phenomenon (Pocock et al. 2012; Kéfi et al. 2016), and to evaluate the interaction strength and its arrangement within a community (de Ruiter et al. 1995). However, despite intensive studies on individual interactions and their organization, few empirical studies have determined the structure of the community network and related it to the observed dynamics of many-species communities (but see Ushio et al. 2018). Difficulty in accomplishing this objective arises from the very nature of interspecific interactions, the diversity in behavioral mechanisms, scale-dependency, and spatiotemporal variability.

8.2 Nature of population-level interspecific interactions

8.2.1 Diversity in behavioral mechanisms

Measuring interspecific interaction has been a major challenge in ecology (Berlow et al. 1999; Wootton and Emmerson 2005), partly due to the diversity of behavioral mechanisms behind given interspecific interactions (Scharf et al. 2008; Kawatsu and Kishi 2018). Some of the diverse behaviors that might give rise to population-level interactions include exploitative competition, interference, predation, herbivory, parasitism, and various forms of mutualistic interactions, such as shelter or food provision, seed dispersal, pollination, and protection against predators. Furthermore, new kinds of interactions are continuously discovered, such as ecosystem engineering (i.e., environmental modifications by a species that affects resource availability for another species; Erwin 2008) and the interspecific transmission of information (Lima 1998; Goodale et al. 2010; Farine et al. 2015). An ecological community can be viewed as a network of direct contact and information mediated interactions (Takabayashi and Dicke 1996; Yoneya and Takabayashi 2014), where a donor

species might affect its recipient species through multiple mechanisms (Scharf et al. 2008).

Given the diversity of individual-level interactions, their population-level integration, which is an interspecific demographic interaction, is not likely to be static, but should be inherently dynamic and condition dependent (Bronstein 1994). This is because any factors that change the relative strength of different behavioral mechanisms can induce variability to population-level interactions. In addition, scale-dependency might arise from any interactions that induce spatial or temporal variability of population-level interactions. Interspecific interactions might be continuously modified by biological processes, such as physiological state, ontogenetic niche shift, and evolution, which cause interspecific interactions to vary temporally. These sections focus on the scale dependency and dynamic nature of interspecific interactions.

8.2.2 Scale dependency of interspecific interactions

Population-level interactions are scale-dependent (de Roos et al. 1991; Wootton and Emmerson 2005). Most main driver of population dynamics varies depending on spatial and temporal scales. For example, the relative importance of migration (immigration or emigration) in population dynamics (Hanski 1994; Nathan et al. 2008) should be greater at a smaller spatial scale, because a larger area has shorter boundary length and the expected proportion of individuals that cross the boundary should be smaller. As a result, the demographic impact of a given species on another species should vary with changing spatial or temporal scales. A good example of this is the interaction between barnacles and mussels in rocky intertidal systems (Kawai and Tokeshi 2006). Two different interactions might occur between the two species; namely, competition for limited resources and space and facilitation through weakening physiological stresses. However, the relative contribution of the two interactions depends on its spatial scale; specifically, competition has a dominant effect at a local scale, while facilitation has a dominant effect at a larger spatial scale, where continuous local extinctions and colonization occur.

The spatial and temporal heterogeneity of the environment is another source of scale dependency (Wootton and Emmerson 2005), with ecologists showing that such spatial variations of environments promote the stable coexistence of competing species (Amarasekare 2003, 2008). Consider mutually connected local habitats with environmental heterogeneity, in which two speciesare competing for limited resources. Even in the case that those two species are unable to coexist in the same local habitat, they might coexist for a long period at a larger spatial scale, with inferior-to-superior relationship of the competition differing across different environments (Amarasekare 2003). Thus, the strength of interspecific competition might be scale-dependent in heterogeneous environments. Local competitive exclusions in individual local habitats represent strong competition in the same habitat. However, at a larger spatial scale, the two species are spatially segregated, and their encounters are less frequent, suggesting weakened competition (Shoemaker and Melbourne. 2016; Hart et al. 2017). Thus, the strength of competition is dependent on spatial scale.

A similar argument should apply to the case where competing species are temporally segregated for temporal variations of limiting resources (Levins 1979; Carothers and Jaksic 1984). Consider two species that compete for limited resources and cannot coexist at the same time. However, if the two species have different phenology or differ in the timing of resource use, they might coexist over a longer time scale. Some theories and empirical studies demonstrate that such temporal niche partitioning facilitates the coexistence of competitors (Schoener 1974; Albrecht and Gotelli 2001; Richards 2002). Temporal scale-dependency of interspecific interactions might contribute to the coexistence of species, as well as spatial scale-dependency.

8.2.3   Dynamic nature of interspecific interactions

Interspecific interactions vary with time and space, even after they are fixed at the spatiotem-poral scale. However, migration, behavioral/ physiological plasticity, ontogenetic niche shifts, and evolutionary processes also drive the spatiotemporal variability.

Movement, a major driver of population dynamics, is a source of the spatiotemporal variation of interspecific interactions. Most animal organisms move around to search for resources and reproductive partners. Bears broaden their range of activities in fall to intensify foraging effort in preparation for hibernation (inner-habitat movement; Noyce and Garshelis 2011). Predator fishes move between benthic and pelagic habitat in a lake food web (inter-habitat movement or migration; vander Zanden and Vadeboncoeur 2002). These movements affect the encounter rates of interspecific species, altering the interaction strength at the population level. Furthermore, movement should influence the spatial scale at which interspecific interactions are transmitted to a third species. The presence of widely moving organisms, for example, mediates indirect interactions between species that are spatially segregated (Takimoto et al. 2009).

Behavioral and physiological plasticity also influence the spatiotemporal variability of interspecific interactions. Organisms modify their foraging and defense behavior in response to changing densities of its potential prey and predator species. The predatory fish Poecilia reticulatus modifies its attack times on Drosophila and tubificid worms depending on relative availability of these prey species (Mardoch et al. 1975). Grasshoppers hide themselves in the presence of actively hunting spiders (Schmitz 2008). Tadpoles develop plastic morphological defenses in response to an increase in predation risk (Kishida and Nishimura 2004). This adaptive plasticity alters the strength of interactions and might modify dominant interspecific interactions, both spatially and temporally, in the community. In most cases, behavioral (or physiological) processes appear to cause changes in interspecific interactions over shorter time scales compared to demographic and evolutionary processes, resulting in local adaptations. Yet, this phenomenon does not mean that the spatial scale of interactions caused by behavioral processes is limited to local ones. Massive and pulsed migration of interacting resource easily spreads to the community dynamics at a broad spatial scale (allochthonous subsidy; Polis et al. 1997). Furthermore, engineering in the environment surrounding a given species might noticeably alter resource availability for another species (ecosystem engineering; Hastings et al. 2007).

Temporally regular events, such as seasonal changes or developmental stages also drive spatiotemporal changes in interspecific interactions. One such example is ontogenetic niche shifts, which are changes in resource or habitat use due to metamorphosis or migration between habitats during development (Nakazawa 2015). Ecologists have demonstrated that behavioral, morphological, and physiological changes experienced by an organism during its life history lead to changes in its interactions with other species, including access to food resources and predation risks. Insects and amphibians that exhibit major changes in their niche after metamorphosis are good examples of this phenomenon. Adult fishes tend to have a broader range of prey than larval fishes, due to relaxed mouth-size constraints (Olson 1996). In the presence of ontogenetic niche shifts, the interactions of focal species with other species tend to vary with the proportion of individuals present at different developmental stages. Consequently, if the length of each developmental stage is flexible with environmental conditions, then so are interspecific interactions (Takimoto 2003; de Roos et al 2002). If the ontogenetic niche shifts of individuals are synchronized, the timing of interspecific interactions might be subject to abrupt and massive changes.

Evolutionary processes also modify interspecific interactions (Yoshida et al. 2003; Hairston Jr. et al. 2005). Recent studies have shown that rapid evolution, which influences interspecific interactions, arises at the time scale of ecological process. For example, laboratory microcosm experiments demonstrated that algal prey rapidly evolve defensive traits in response to increased rotifer density, to weaken the strength of trophic interactions with rotifers (Hairston Jr. et al. 2005; Kasada et al. 2014). The time scale of evolutionary process of organisms with short generation time, such as microbes, might match to the time scale of ecological processes of long generation time organisms (King et al. 2016). Furthermore, the evolutionary modification

of interspecific interactions could provide insights on how interspecific interactions are responding to ongoing anthropogenic environmental changes (Winder and Schindler 2004).

8.3 How to study interspecific interactions in nature

8.3.1 Identifying population-level interactions

Given the important role of interspecific interactions as a driver of community dynamics, it is necessary to identify and quantify (e.g., determining the sign and strength) interspecific interactions to understand community dynamics. However, population-level interactions (not individual-level interactions) are not visible, with direct observation being impossible in most cases (Freilich et al. 2018). This raises the question of how to document condition-dependent interspecific interactions to understand the consequences of these interactions on dynamics. Thus, we present a brief review of the two typical major methodologies used to identify and quantify interspecific interactions in the field: i) direct observations of behavioral interactions, and ii) manipulative field experiments. Based on this review, we identify the inherent difficulties of these methodologies.

8.3.2 Identification of interactions based on behavior by individuals

It is possible to use visible behavioral interactions (i.e., demographic interactions) to identify interspecific interactions in the field (see Clare 2014 for its modern form using eDNA). Indeed, this method is very popular for easily visible interactions, such as prey-predator interactions, pollination, and seed-dispersal. Behavior-based identification of interactions are investigated using several methods, including the direct field observations of interactive behaviors or their marks and indirect investigations, such as stomach content analysis, fecal analysis and biotracer analysis (e.g., stable isotopes and fatty acids; Layman et al. 2012; Kelly and Scheibling 2012). These methods often provide strong evidence for interspecific interactions that take place at the individual level.

However, of note, two major difficulties exist when translating individual-level interactions to demographic interactions. First, it is not straightforward to translate the magnitude of individual behavior to that of demographic effects. For example, when conducting diet analyses, such as stomach content analysis and fecal analysis, it is possible to estimate the proportion of prey species eaten, but it might not be possible to estimate the absolute magnitude of demographic effects. In addition, there is a risk of error in estimating the strength of interactions due to different rates of information accumulating among species (e.g., digestive efficiency varies between diets and dynamically changes within an individual or a species). Second, while many types of behavioral interactions exist in nature, we usually do not know a priori what behavioral interactions exist and which is the most important behavior driving population dynamics. Thus, to evaluate the demographic effect appropriately, multiple interactions must be recorded to understand community dynamics and to translate the identified behavioral interactions to demographic effects in a comparable way (Kéfi et al. 2016). However, this is an extremely difficult task to complete, especially in systems with many species.

Direct observation of individual-level interactions often needs major labour effort, especially when interacting species are not abundant in a given survey area. If the observation probabilities of species X and Y are independent and are represented by small values of P_X and P_Y, respectively, then the encounter rate between the two species will be as low as $P_X \times P_Y$. Moreover, an important demographic interaction could be overlooked when using direct observations, as less frequent behavior is not necessarily less important in driving demographic interactions. For example, an interspecific interaction that is essential for reproduction might only be observed during a limited period of a species' life history. This issue could be overcome by using appropriate, long-lasting marks of target interactions that might also accumulate, such as feces and biotracers. However, fecal and biotracer analyses only provide information of trophic interactions, and do not capture all facets of interspecific interactions. In addition, long-lasting marks tend to obscure the timing that the interaction occurred, which could be disadvantageous when tracing temporally varying interactions.

8.3.3 Manipulative field experiments

To evaluate a population-level effect between species, manipulative field experiments could be used (Paine 1966). When two species interact at the population level, a change to the density of the donor species should, by definition, alter the density of the recipient species. Thus, interspecific interactions could be quantified by measuring the magnitude of change in population density of recipient species after manipulating the abundance of donor species. The best-known manipulative field experiment is the intertidal community experiments conducted by Paine (1966, 1969). In these experiments, Paine artificially removed starfish, the top predator of the system, from the intertidal community and showed that this action resulted in a rapid increase in *Mytilus*, and the decline (almost to extinction) of most benthic algae, chitons, and limpets. This dramatic change was attributed to *Mytilus* being released from the predation pressure of starfish, which increased competition for space or food.

There are, however, some major limitations in using a manipulative experiment to study population-level interactions between species (Wootton and Emmerson 2005). First, the observed response might be caused by indirect effects that are not easily distinguished from direct interactions (Bender et al. 1984; Yodzis 1996). To quantify the interaction strength of species pairs accurately, the variables that might cause indirect effects, such as interspecific interactions other than the target interaction and population densities of other species, should be carefully controlled. Additional experiments or observations and careful consideration by experts are required to explain the actual (behavioral) mechanism that causes the demographic effect identified. Second, a population-level interaction often exhibits condition-dependency (see Sections 8.2–8.3; Bronstein 1994); consequently, it might change with the experimental setting being used. To obtain a complete understanding of the interaction, the evaluation should be conducted under a variety of environmental settings, which is extremely effort demanding. Third, demographic interactions might be scale-dependent, with it being difficult to evaluate population-level interactions (see Section 8.2.2). Because considerable time is required to detect or quantify interspecific effects after manipulative perturbations, the temporal scale of the identified interaction is accordingly limited, which might be a strong limitation when interaction strength or sign rapidly change over time (Deyle et al. 2016b; Ushio et al. 2018). Fourth, the greatest problem when using manipulative experiments is the difficulty in simultaneously evaluating multiple interactions of the same system. Ecological theory shows that the organization of the interaction network and its re-organization in response to external perturbations are essential for elucidating ecological dynamics. To understand such dynamics, temporal changes of multiple interactions must be evaluated simultaneously. If the dynamics of individual interactions or species are estimated separately, a knowledge gap exists.

8.4 Modern Data-Driven approach to interspecific interactions

8.4.1 Estimating population-level interactions from time-series data

In this section, a time-series data-driven approach is proposed as an alternative and/or complement to traditional interpretations based on individual-level interactions. Previous studies have attempted to use ecological time-series data to infer population-level interactions (e.g., Ives et al. 2003; Turchin 2003). However, these studies tended to be based on simplified assumptions, such as that dynamics is close to an equilibrium state or follows a specific dynamic model, like the Lotka–Volterra equation. Consequently, it was difficult to apply these studies to real, complex ecosystems, as we do not know which interactions are the major drivers of ecological dynamics. Thus, an approach is needed that facilitates the model-free analysis of community dynamics by capturing the real ecological system as a nonlinear dynamic system that is not at equilibrium. The objective is to extract as much information as possible from real ecological data, such as identifying population-level interspecific interactions, estimating their signs and magnitudes, and evaluating dynamic properties (such as stability).

An ecological community is a multivariate dynamic system; thus, an ecological time-series could be regarded as the dynamic output of specific mechanisms behind the system. Such time-series form a unique set of states and trajectories in a multi-dimensional space, where each coordinate represents the density of each species in the community. The set of rules describing which states becomes which state in the next step (the geometric set of state vectors) is called an attractor. An important property of dynamical ecosystems with interacting species is that time-series data of single species contains the dynamical information of other species interacting with it. Using this property, the theory of nonlinear dynamical systems suggests that one could reconstruct a shadow version of the original attractor (i.e., an attractor topologically identical to the original one; Takens' theorem; Takens 1981). More specifically, a shadow attractor could be reconstructed by projecting the original attractor to a state space with E dimensional time-delayed coordinates of an observed species X, in which a state vector contains E time-lagged species states or densities. In other words, $\{x_t, x_{t-\tau}, \ldots, x_{t-(E-1)\tau}\}$, where x_t is the population density of the species X at time t and τ is the time steps to use delayed coordinates. This procedure is called state-space reconstruction (SSR) and, by choosing a sufficiently large E ($E \geq 2D + 1$, where D is the true dimension of the original attractor; Whitney 1936; Takens 1981), the shadow attractor preserves the essential dynamical properties of the original attractor, such as neighbor points and their trajectories.

Takens' theorem and the related SSR theories (Takens 1981; Sauer et al. 1991; Deyle and Sugihara 2011) form the basis of a promising framework called empirical dynamic modelling (EDM). EDM is a tool used to analyze interspecific interactions from observed ecological time-series data (Sugihara et al. 2012; Deyle et al. 2013, 2016b; Ye et al. 2015a, 2015b; Ushio et al. 2018). The EDM framework consists of various analytical tools based on two fundamental techniques, simplex projection

(Sugihara and May 1990) and S-map (sequential locally weighted global linear map, Sugihara 1994). These two tools implement similar algorithms to forecast nonlinear time series by using information about the behavior of the nearest neighbours of a target point in a reconstructed attractor. That is, trajectories of nearest neighbours should be similar to those of the target point (if state space is appropriately reconstructed), allowing the future of the target to be predicted. Then, based on simplex projection and S-map, the two tools [Convergent Cross Mapping (CCM, Sugihara et al. 2012) and multivariate S-map (Dixon et al. 1999; Deyle et al. 2016b)] were developed. These tools allowed (population-level) interspecific interactions in ecological communities to be identified and quantified from time-series data alone.

8.4.2 Convergent cross mapping and multivariate S-map

CCM is a technique used to identify population-level interactions (causality) from the time-series data of focal donors and recipient species (Sugihara et al. 2012). Consider a simple two-species (X and Y) system. According to Takens' theorem and extended theorem by Sauer et al. (1991), the two attractors reconstructed from either X alone or Y alone map one-to-one to the original attractors, as they are involved in the same dynamic system. Therefore, the two reconstructed attractors should also map one-to-one to each other. Thus, it follows that one could identify the interaction between X and Y by testing the one-to-one mapping of reconstructed attractors (cross-mapping). In practice, the one-to-one mapping of two reconstructed attractors is checked by looking at whether the cross-map skill (i.e., forecasting skill by cross-mapping) of the donor-species state from the recipient-species improves when the number of reference data is increased (i.e., the time-series data used to reconstruct recipient species attractor; Sugihara et al. 2012). This practice is based on the expectation that, as the number of time-series data increases, the points that are reconstructed in the recipient attractor become denser. As a result, we are able to find the states of recipient-species that are closer to

the focal time point from the reference data, leading to the improvement (or convergence) of the cross-mapping skills. The convergence of the cross-map skill (which is the origin of the CCM) is a criterion used to distinguish true demographic effects from the correlation that might arise without causalities. For example, if the dynamics of two variables are forced by the same external factors, they might be correlated with each other, but the cross-map skill should not converge, as the reconstructed manifolds do not map one-to-one with each other. The CCM is a useful tool for detecting "true" demographic causality in ecological communities.

The EDM framework also provides a practical method (i.e., the multivariate S-map) for quantifying the time-changing effects of interspecific interactions in terms of partial derivatives, $\partial[\text{recipient-species' density}]/\partial[\text{donor-species' density}]$ (Sugihara 1994; Dixon et al. 1999; Deyle and Sugihara 2011; Deyle et al. 2016b). The multivariate S-map is an extension of the S-map (Sugihara 1994), which is another fundamental EDM tool that facilitates nonlinear forecasting by leveraging information about the behavior of nearest neighbours. In the S-map procedure, a linear model $\mathbf{C}$ is sequentially generated to predict the future value of a target time point t^* from observed time series data (Sugihara 1994; Deyle et al. 2013). More specifically, a linear model that predicts the t_p future density of species X becomes:

$$x_{t*+t_p} = C_{t*} \cdot \mathbf{Z}_{t*}{}^{\mathrm{T}}, \qquad (8.2)$$

where $\mathbf{Z}_{t*}$ is an $E+1$ dimensional row vector that combines a time independent constant z with the state vector X_{t*}, i.e., $\{z, x_t, x_{t-\tau}, \ldots, x_{t-(E-1)\tau}\}$ (T indicates the transpose) and $\mathbf{C}_{t*}$ is also an $E+1$ dimensional coefficient vector $\{c_0, c_1, \ldots, c_E\}$. Because the value of z is usually set to 1.0, c_0 corresponds to the model intercept. The coefficient vector $\mathbf{C}_{t*}$ is obtained as the SVD (singular value decomposition) solution to the equation, $\mathbf{B}_{t*} = \mathbf{A}_{t*} \cdot \mathbf{C}_{t*}$, in which $\mathbf{B}_{t*}$ is an n-dimensional of the value $w_i \cdot x_{ti+tp}$ (n is the number of points in the reconstructed attractor) and $\mathbf{A}_{t*}$ is an $n \times (E+1)$ dimensional matrix of $w_i \cdot \mathbf{Z}_{ti}$. Note that, in the S-map procedure, an ith element of $\mathbf{B}_{t*}$ and $\mathbf{A}_{t*}$ is weighted by the value w_i, which is based on the distance between $\mathbf{X}_{ti}$ and $\mathbf{X}_{t*}$ as:

$$w_i = \exp\left(-\theta \frac{\|X_{ti} - X_{t^*}\|}{\bar{d}}\right), \qquad (8.3)$$

where $\bar{d}$ is the average distance from target point t^*. Parameter θ determines the nonlinearity of the reconstructed attractor, because the points closer to the target are given greater weighting when $\theta > 0$ (Sugihara 1994; Deyle et al. 2016b). Importantly, the obtained $\mathbf{C}_{t^*}$ is approximated to coefficients (or Jacobian) at target time t^* for each column in the $\mathbf{Z}_{t^*}$. Of note, an interspecific effect is defined as the magnitude of change in the density of the recipient species caused by a change to the density of the donor species. Thus, the magnitude of the interspecific interaction could be estimated by using the multivariate attractor, including causal variable(s) instead of time-delayed coordinates (Deyle et al. 2016b).

8.4.3 Application of EDM to interaction network studies

EDM tools have been applied to ecological time series for a variety of purposes, including forecasting ecological dynamics, determining causal variables, and inferring mechanisms that drive ecological dynamics (Deyle et al. 2013; van Nes et al. 2015; Ye et al. 2015a,b; Deyle et al. 2016a,b; McGowan et al. 2017; Nakayama et al. 2018; Ushio et al. 2018; Kawatsu and Kishi 2018). The applications (the CCM and multivariate S-map method) that facilitate the identification and quantification of interactions represent potential tools to study population-level interspecific interactions in ecological systems.

Important properties of interspecific interactions are scale-dependency and spatiotemporal variability. The multivariate S-map method allows one to track temporally varying population-level interactions, which are defined for a given scale of an ecological community (Deyle et al. 2016b). Application of the multivariate S-map method to the time series of marine and lake communities (the Baltic Sea mesocosm and Sparkling Lake; Beatrix et al. 2003; Benincà et al. 2008; Benincà et al. 2009; Figure 1) led to biologically reasonable estimations of interaction strength. For example, the influence of a prey (nanoflagellates) on a predator (calanoid

copepods) was estimated to be positive through time (i.e., prey-predator interaction), while the influence of a second grazer (rotifers) on calanoid copepods was estimated to be negative through time (i.e., competition). In the Baltic Sea mesocosm, for example, the intensity of competition between two predators, rotifers and calanoid copepods (measured as $\partial[\text{calanoid density}]/\partial[\text{rotifer density}]$) strengthened as the intensity of food limitation (measured by $\partial[\text{calanoid density}]/\partial[\text{nanoflagellate density}]$) strengthened, supporting ecological theory (Figure 8.1b,c).

As shown in Section 8.3, multiple individual-level interactions might simultaneously give rise to population-level interspecific interactions. EDM tools could be used to identify multiple individual-level mechanisms underlying observed population-level interactions. For example, EDM was used in experiments to investigate competition between two bean beetles, *Callosobruchus chinensis* and *C. maculatus*. These experiments were used as a model system to study interspecific competition and its effect on population dynamics (Figure 8.2). Although two types of interactions (resource competition and reproductive interference) are the two major drivers of population dynamics (Bellows and Hassell 1984; Ishii and Shimada 2008; Kishi et al. 2009; Kishi 2015), it is difficult to distinguish their relative importance in driving community dynamics through manipulative experiments or observation of individual-level behaviors alone (Scharf et al. 2008). Kawatsu and Kishi (2018) used the multivariate S-map method and lagged CCM, which is a type of CCM that accounts for delayed responses (Ye et al. 2015b) in the time series. Using two studies that performed laboratory competition experiments (Ishii and Shimada 2008; Kishi et al. 2009), the authors successfully identified which interaction drive population dynamics. This insight was made possible by looking at how the timing of the two interactions affects population dynamics. Reproductive interference directly affects adult individuals of the same (due to the increased mortality) and/or next generation (due to reduced fecundity). In comparison, resource competition occurs among larvae; thus, its effect is observed in the number of adults present in the next generation. Thus, it is possible to determine which interaction

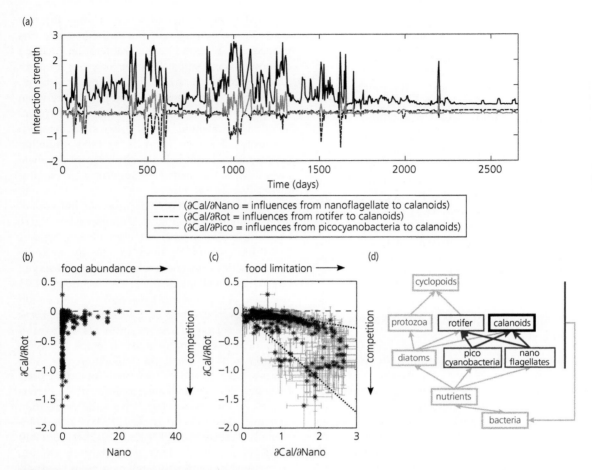

Figure 8.1 Dynamic interactions in the Baltic Sea mesocosm.

is the major driver of population dynamics by estimating when interspecific effects take place (Kawatsu and Kishi 2018).

Researchers have recently become interested in applying EDM to more species-rich, natural ecological communities. Ushio et al. (2018) used EDM to a twelve-year dataset containing fortnightly observations of a natural fish community consisting of fifteen dominant species in Maizuru Bay, Japan. The study detected fourteen interspecific interactions between the dominant species by CCM, and showed that the fourteen interspecific interactions, which were calculated by the multivariate S-map method, fluctuated in a manner consistent with nonlinear dynamic systems, even in a natural fish community (Figure 8.3a,b). In addition, the

authors developed a method to measure time-varying stability based on local Lyapunov stability ("dynamic stability" in Ushio et al. 2018; Figure 3c) for the dynamics in non-equilibrium nonlinear systems (such as natural ecological communities). The results showed that both interspecific interactions and community stability changed through time. Moreover, causal inference (CCM) between the fluctuating stability of the community and interspecific interactions demonstrated the dominance of weak interactions and higher species diversity. These findings supported theoretical suggestions that these phenomena are mechanisms that drive community dynamics (McCann et al. 1998; Bascompte et al. 2005; Downing et al. 2014), being associated with higher dynamic stability

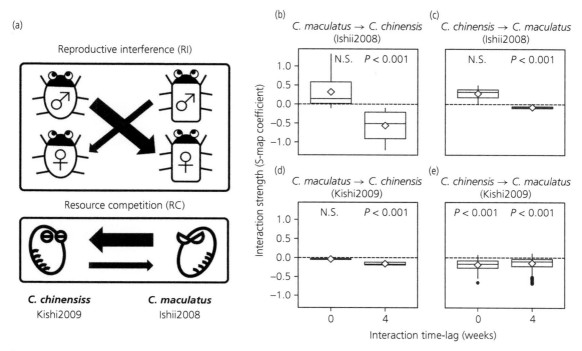

Figure 8.2 Bean-beetle experimental systems and their interactions.

and smaller population fluctuations in natural fish community.

Population-level interactions have either positive or negative effects. Because traditional community ecology focuses on competition and trophic interactions as the major drivers (Menge and Sutherland 1976; Kotler and Holt 1989), negative interspecific effects tend to be detected; however, studies on mutualistic interactions are increasing (Morales-Castilla et al. 2015). However, knowledge remains limited about their relative proportions and strength in nature. Two empirical studies show that positive interactions are as abundant as negative ones. In the lake ecosystem, cyclopoids tend to have a positive demographic effect on calanoids, despite both species supposedly competing over the same resources (Deyle et al. 2016b). In a coastal fish community, eight out of fourteen identified interactions were positive when averaged over the twelve-year observation period (Ushio et al. 2018). This is an interesting finding that cannot be achieved by traditional approaches; yet, the generality of this finding should be examined in

the future by applying a similar analysis to other ecosystems.

Both Deyle et al. (2016b) and Ushio et al. (2018) empirically confirmed that temporal fluctuations and context dependency are the rule of interspecific interactions. In the lake ecosystem, the interspecific effect of cyclopoids on calanoids fluctuates between positive and negative, with the negative effect being associated with predatory fish abundance, possibly because fish mediate mutualism between the two grazers. The interactions identified in the coastal ecosystem also fluctuated; some interactions showed switches in their signs. Further, there was a clear seasonal pattern in which weak interactions became more dominant during summer compared to winter. The major causes of these fluctuations require examination in the future. Yet, the conditions driving these fluctuations might not be limited. For instance, the experimental study of Kawatsu and Kishi (2018) showed that demographic interspecific interactions change depending on conditions, even in an experimental system where identical pairs of bean beetle species

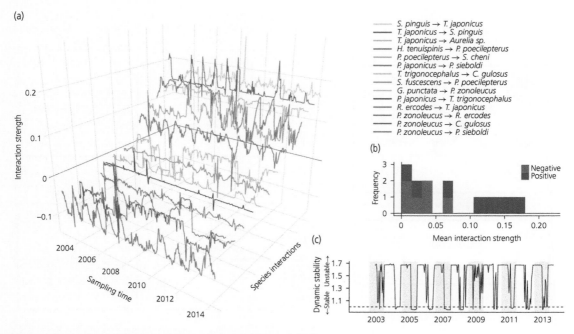

Figure 8.3 Fluctuating interactions and dynamic stability of a natural ecological community.

8.5 Conclusion and future directions

Interspecific interactions are the main driver of community dynamics; consequently, identifying and quantifying them is an essential part of studying community dynamics. However, population-level interactions are scale- and condition-dependent, exhibiting spatiotemporal variation, making it difficult to capture them fully through effort-demanding traditional methods, such as behavior-based approaches and field manipulative experiments. Here, we show that combining long-term monitoring data, which inherently contains dynamic mechanistic information, and sophisticated time-series analysis tools, which allow information to be extracted from the data, could serve as a powerful approach for identifying and quantifying interspecific interactions in real ecosystems.

This approach is ideal because, regardless of the actual mechanism involved, it facilitates the correct detection and quantification of population-level interactions that give rise to the ecological dynamics in question. Thus, we do not need to know or assume which behavior actually drives population dynamics. For example, if available time-series data of the dynamics of the target population has a small spatial scale or short temporal scale (e.g., the time interval is sufficiently short to fall within the lifetime of an individual) and is mainly driven by migration, the interaction detected by the time-series analysis would be the one arising from the modification of migration. In contrast, if the available time-series data has a large spatial scale or long temporal scale, then changes to the population would be mainly driven by birth and death processes; thus, the interaction detected by the same method would be the one arising from the modification of birth-death processes. The important point is to start with the observed ecological dynamics to be explained and to make minimal assumptions that the system is a deterministic dynamical system. By so doing, it is possible to avoid making a priori assumptions about the major driver of dynamics, behavioral/physiological basis of interaction, functional shape of demographic interactions, and so on. Thus, the data of ecological dynamics reveals the causes of ecological dynamics.

As the present approach provides limited information about the actual individual-level mechanisms behind population-level interspecific interactions, linking them remains challenging. For instance, population-level interactions might be caused by multiple individual-level interactions and their combinations simultaneously. Time-series data contain information on the affecting variables, effect size, and its sign, but do not contain information on the type of behavioral/physiological mechanism causing the interaction. In contrast, the behavior-based approach has an advantage in studying the behavioral/physiological basis of individual-level interactions. Therefore, combining the behavioral-based approach and data-driven approach represents a promising way to investigate individual-level mechanisms of a population-level interactions (Kawatsu and Kishi 2018). Specifically, basic information such as donor species and effect sign, could help with identifying the exact behavioral/physiological basis of focal demographic interactions.

Of note, the presented approach has some limitations because it is data-driven. First, time-series data must be sampled with equal intervals and must satisfy some stationarity. In other words, it must be a process for which moments, such as mean and variance, do not change over time (Chang et al. 2017). Thus, if applying the data-driven approach to non-stationary time-series data, the data must be transformed to be stationary, as in traditional time-series analysis (Box et al. 1994; Hsieh et al. 2008). Another serious limitation is the quality and quantity of the time-series being analyzed. For example, at least 35–40 data points are required for EDM analysis (Sugihara et al. 2012); however, more points are needed depending on the observation and process noises of dynamic systems (Chang et al. 2017). Also, it might be difficult meet the time-series length requirement for long-term, wide area ecological studies. To avoid these limitations, it would be useful to leverage time-series data from similar dynamic systems, as natural replicates. It might also be possible to combine time-series data that are different but dynamically similar, to

generate single, longer time series data (Hsieh et al. 2008; Clark et al. 2015; Kawatsu and Kishi 2018).

The usefulness of time-series analysis in studying ecological systems demonstrates that ecological monitoring data contain far more information than previously thought. An appropriate analysis of the temporal changes of population densities helps forecasting, conducting causality tests, and evaluating effect sizes. Given the increasing importance of understanding ecological systems, long-term monitoring of ecosystems is important because sufficient volumes of time-series data are required to identify interactions with other species. However, the amount of information that can be obtained from the data depends on the analytical technique. For example, when examining temporal correlations in the density of two populations, pseudo-correlation might lead to incorrect interpretations (e.g., mirage correlation; Sugihara et al. 2012). In addition to long-term monitoring data, a sophisticated technique is required that allows us to extract more ecological information than previously thought possible. For example, a causality test that allows causal relationships to be detected from time-series data, such as CCM, could inform us of what drives the dynamics of populations observed in nature. Evaluation of spatial and temporal variability of interspecific interactions and their influence on dynamic stability could provide greater insights on why species are able to coexist. Such information could provide us strategies to cope with ongoing biodiversity loss and its impact on humanity.

References

Albrecht, M. and Gotelli, N. J. (2001). Spatial and temporal niche partitioning in grassland ants. *Oecologia* 126: 131–41.

Allesina, S. and Tanga, S. (2012). Stability criteria for complex ecosystems. *Nature* 483: 205–8.

Amarasekare, P. (2003). Competitive coexistence in spatially structured environments: A synthesis. *Ecol Lett* 6: 1109–22.

Amarasekare, P. (2008). Spatial dynamic of foodwebs. *Annu Rev Ecol Evol Syst* 39: 479–500.

Anholt, B. R. (1997). How should we test for the role of behaviour in population dynamics. *Evol Ecol* 11: 633–40.

Bascompte, J., Melián, C. J., and Sala, E. (2005). Interaction strength combinations and the overfishing of a marine food web. *Proc Natl Acad Sci USA* 102: 5443–7. DOI: 10.1073/pnas.0501562102.

Beatrix, E. B., Anthony, R. I., and Stephen, R. C. (2003). The effects of an exotic fish invasion on the prey communities of two lakes. *J Anim Ecol* 72: 331–42. DOI: 10.1046/j.1365–2656.2003.00699.x.

Bellows, T. S. and Hassell, M. P. (1984). Models for Interspecific Competition in Laboratory Populations of Callosobruchus. *Spp. J Anim Ecol* 53: 831–48. DOI: 10.2307/4662

Bender, E. A., Case, T. J., and Gilpin, M. E. (1984). Perturbation experiments in community ecology: theory and practice. *Ecology* 65: 1–13.

Benincà, E., Huisman, J., Heerkloss, R., Jöhnk, K. D., Branco, P., Van Nes, E. H., Scheffer, M., and Ellner, S. P. (2008). Chaos in a long-term experiment with a plankton community. *Nature* 451: 822.

Benincà, E., Klaus, D. J., Heerkloss, R., and Huisman J. (2009). Coupled predator–prey oscillations in a chaotic food web. *Ecol Lett* 12: 1367–78. DOI: 10.1111/j.1461–0248.2009.01391.x.

Berlow, E. L., Navarrete, S. A., Briggs, C. J., Power, M. E., and Menge, B. A. (1999). Quantifying variation in the strengths of species interactions. *Ecology* 80: 2206–24.

Box, G. E. P., Jenkins, G. M., and Reinsel G. C. (1994) Time Series Analysis: Forecasting and Control. 3rd edition. Englewood Cliffs: Prentice-Hall Inc.

Bronstein, J. L. (1994). Conditional outcome of mutualistic interactions. *Trends in Ecology and Evolution* 9: 214–17.

Brose, U., Berlow, E. L., and Martinez, N. D. (2005). Scaling up keystone effects from simple to complex ecological networks. *Ecol Lett* 8: 1317–25.

Carothers, J. H. and Jaksic, F. M. (1984). Time as a niche difference: the role of interference competition. *Oikos* 42: 403–6.

Chang, C. W., Ushio, M., and Hsieh, C. -H. (2017). Empirical dynamic modeling for beginners. *Ecological Research* 32: 785–96.

Chen, X. and Cohen, J. E. (2001). Transient dynamics and food-web complexity in the Lotka–Volterra cascade model. *Proceedings of the Royal Society B: Biological Sciences* 268: 869–77.

Clare, E. L. (2014). Molecular detection of trophic interactions: emerging trends, distinct advantages, significant considerations and conservation applications. *Evol Appl.* 7: 1144–57.

Clark, A.T., Ye, H., Isbell, F., Deyle, E. R., Cowles, J., Tilman, G. D., and Sugihara, G. (2015). Spatial convergent cross mapping to detect causal relationships from short time series. *Ecology* 96: 1174–81.

de Ruiter, P. C., Neutel, A. -M., and Moore, J. C. (1995). Energetics, patterns of interaction strengths, and stability in real ecosystems. *Science* 269: 1257–60.

de Ruiter, P. C., Wolters, V., Moore, J. C., and Winemiller, K. O. (2005). Food web ecology: Playing Jenga and beyond. *Science* 309: 69–71.

de Roos, A. M. and Wilson, E. (1991). Mobility versus density-limited predator-prey dynamics on different spatial scales. *Proceedings of the Royal Society B: Biological Sciences* 246: 117–22.

de Roos, A. M., Leonardsson K, Persson L, Mittelbach GG (2002) Ontogenetic niche shifts and flexible behavior in size-structured populations. *Ecol Monogr* 72: 271–292.

Deyle, E. R., Fogarty, M., Hsieh C. H., Kaufman, L., MacCall, A. D., Munch, S. B., Perretti, C. T., Ye, H., and Sugihara, G. (2013). Predicting climate effects on Pacific sardine. *Proc Natl Acad Sci U S A* 110: 6430–5. DOI: 10.1073/pnas.1215506110.

Deyle, E. R., Maher, M. C., Hernandez, R. D., Basu S., and Sugihara G. (2016a). Global environmental drivers of influenza. *Proc Natl Acad Sci* 113: 13081–6. DOI: 10.1073/pnas.1607747113

Deyle, E. R., May, R. M., Munch, S. B., and Sugihara, G. (2016b). Tracking and forecasting ecosystem interactions in real time. *Proc R Soc B Biol Sci* 283: 20152258. DOI: 10.1098/rspb.2015.2258

Deyle, E. R. and Sugihara, G. (2011). Generalized theorems for nonlinear state space reconstruction. *PLoS One* 6: e18295. DOI: 10.1371/journal.pone.0018295

Dixon, P.A., Milicich, M. J., and Sugihara, G. (1999). Episodic fluctuations in larval supply. *Science* 283: 1528–30.

Downing, A. L., Brown, B. L., and Leibold, M. A. (2014). Multiple diversity-stability mechanisms enhance population and community stability in aquatic food webs. *Ecology* 95: 173–84.

Erwin, D. H. (2008). Macroevolution of ecosystem engineering, niche construction and diversity. *Trends Ecol. Evol.* 23: 304–10.

Farine, D. R., Aplin, L. M., Sheldon, B. C., and Hoppitt, W. (2015). Interspecific social networks promote information transmission in wild songbirds. *Proceedings of the Royal Society B: Biological Sciences* 282(20): 142, 804.

Freilich, M. A., Wieters, E., Broitman, B. R., Marquet, P. A., and Navarrete S. A. (2018). Species co-occurrence networks: Can they reveal trophic and non-trophic interactions in ecological communities? *Ecology* 99: 690–9.

Fryxell, J. M. and Lundberg, P. (1998). *Individual Behavior and Community Dynamics*. London: Chapman and Hall.

Gause, G. F. (1934). *The Struggle for Existence*. Baltimore: Williams & Wilkins.

Goldberg, D. E. (1996). Competitive ability: Definitions, contingency and correlated traits. *Philosophical Transactions of The Royal Society B* 351: 1377–85.

Goodale, E., Beauchamp, G., Magrath, R. D., Nieh, J. C., and Ruxton, G. D. (2010). Interspecific information transfer influences animal community structure. *Trends Ecol. Evol.* 25: 354–61.

Hairston, Jr. N. G., Ellner, S. P., Geber, M. A., Yoshida, T., and Fox, J. A. (2005). Rapid evolution and the convergence and evolutionary time. *Ecol Lett* 8: 1114–27.

Hanski, I. (1994). Spatial scale, patchiness and population dynamics on land. *Philos. Trans. R. Soc. London Ser. B.* 343: 19–25.

Hassell, M. P. and May, R. M. (1985). From individual behaviour to population dynamics. In *Behavioural Ecology*, Sibly R. M. and Smith R. H. (eds.), Oxford: Blackwell, pp. 3–32.

Hastings, A., Byers, J. E., Crooks, J. A., Cuddington, K., Jones, C. G., Lambrinos, J. G., Talley, T. S., and Wilson, W. G. (2007). Ecosystem engineering in space and time. *Ecol Lett* 10: 153–64.

Hart, S. P., Usinowicz, J., and Levine, J. M. (2017). The spatial scales of species coexistence. *Nature Ecology and Evolution* 1: 1066–73.

Higashi, M. and Nakajima, H. (1995). Indirect effects in ecological interaction networks I. The chain rule approach. *Mathematical Biosciences* 130: 99–128.

Ishii, Y., Shimada, M. (2008). Competitive exclusion between contest and scramble strategists in Callosobruchus seed–beetle modeling. *Popul Ecol* 50: 197–205. DOI: 10.1007/s10144-008-0080-x.

Ives, A. R., Dennis, B., Cottingham, K. L., and Carpenter, S. R. (2003). Estimating community stability and ecological interactions from time-series data. *Ecological Monographs* 73: 301–30.

Kasada, M., Yamamichi, M., and Yoshida, T. (2014). Form of an evolutionary tradeoff affects eco-evolutionary dynamics in a predator–prey system. *Proceedings of the National Academy of Sciences of the United States of America* 111: 16, 035–40.

Kawai, T. and Tokeshi, M. (2006). Asymmetric coexistence: Bidirectional abiotic and biotic effects between goose barnacles and mussels. *J Anim Ecol* 75: 928–41.

Kawatsu, K. and Kishi, S. (2018). Identifying critical interactions in complex competition dynamics between bean beetles. *Oikos* 127: 553–60 DOI: 10.1111/oik.04103

Kawatsu, K. and Kondoh, M. (2018). Density-dependent interspecific interactions and the complexity-stability relationship. *Proceedings of the Royal Society B*, 285: 20180698.

Kéfi, S., Miele, V., Wieters, E. A., Navarrete, S. A., and Berlow, E. L. (2016). How structured is the entangled bank? The surprisingly simple organization of multiplex ecological networks leads to increased persistence and resilience. *PLOS Biology* 14: e1002527. DOI:10.1371/journal.pbio.100252

Kelly, J. R. and Scheibling, R. E. (2012). Fatty acids as dietary tracers in benthic food webs. *Mar Ecol Prog Ser* 446: 1–22.

King, K. C., Brockhurst, M. A., Vasieva, O., Paterson, S., Betts, A., Ford, S. A., Frost, C. L., Horsburgh, M. J., Haldenby, S., and Hurst, G. D. D. (2016). Rapid evolution of microbe -mediated protection against pathogens in a worm host. *ISME J.* 10: 1915–24.

Kishi, S., Nishida, T., and Tsubaki, Y. (2009). Reproductive interference determines persistence and exclusion in species interactions. *J Anim Ecol* 78: 1043–9. DOI: 10.1111/j.1365–2656.2009.01560.x

Kishi, S. (2015). Reproductive interference in laboratory experiments of interspecific competition. *Popul Ecol* 57: 283–92. DOI: 10.1007/s10144-014-0455-0

Kishida, O. and Nishimura, K. (2004). Bulgy tadpoles: Inducible defense morph. *Oecologia* 140: 414–21.

Kondoh, M. (2003). Foraging adaptation and the relationship between food-web complexity and stability. *Science* 299: 1388–91.

Kotler, B. P. and Holt, R. D. (1989). Predation and competition: The interaction of two types of species interactions. *Oikos* 54: 256–60.

Landi, P., Minoarivelo, H. O., Brännström, Å., Hui C., and Dieckmann, U. (2018). *Population Ecology* 60: 319–45. https://doi.org/10.1007/s10144-018-0628-3.

Layman, C. A., Araujo M. S., Boucek, R., Hammerschlag-Peyer, C. M., Harrison, E., Jud, Z. R., Matich, P., Rosenblatt, A. E., Vaudo, J. J., Yeager, L. A., Post, D. M., and Bearhop, S. (2012). Applying stable isotopes to examine food-web structure: An overview of analytical tools. *Biol Rev* 87: 545–62.

Levins, R. (1979). Coexistence in a variable environment. *American Naturalist* 114: 765–83.

Lima, S. L. (1998). Nonlethal effects in the ecology of predator-prey interactions. *BioScience* 48: 25–34.

Lotka, A. J. (1925) *Elements of Physical Biology*. Baltimore: Wiliams and Wilkins.

Mardoch, W. W., Avery, S., and Smith M. E. B. (1975). Switching in predatory fish. *Ecology* 56: 1094–105.

May, R. M. (1973). *Stability and Complexity in Model Eco Systems*. Princeton, NJ: Princeton University Press.

May, R. M. (1973). *Stability and Complexity in Model Ecosystems*. Princeton University Press, Princeton.

McCann, K. S. (2000). The diversity-stability debate. *Nature* 405: 228–33.

McCann, K., Hastings, A., and Huxel, G. R. (1998). Weak trophic interactions and the balance of nature. *Nature* 395: 794–8. DOI: 10.1038/27427.

McGowan, A. J., Deyle, R. E., Ye, H., et al. (2017). Predicting coastal algal blooms in southern California. *Ecology* 98: 1419–33. DOI: 10.1002/ecy.1804.

Menge, B. A. and Sutherland, J. P. (1976). Species diversity gradients: Synthesis of the roles of predation, competition and temporal heterogeneity. *Am. Nat.* 110: 351–69.

Montoya, J. M., Woodward, G., Emmerson, M. C., and Solé, R. V. (2009). Press perturbations and indirect effects in real food webs. *Ecology* 90: 2426–33.

Morales-Castilla, I., Matias, M. G., Gravel, D., Araújo, M. B. (2015). Inferring biotic interactions from proxies. *Trends Ecol Evol* 30: 347–56.

Mougi, A. and Kondoh, M. (2012). Diversity of interaction types and ecological community stability. *Science* 337: 349–51.

Mougi, A., Kondoh, M. (2016). Food-web complexity, meta-community complexity and community stability. *Scientific Reports* 6: 24478.

Nakayama, S. -I., Takasuka, A., Ichinokawa, M., and Okamura, H. (2018). Climate change and interspecific interactions drive species alternations between anchovy and sardine in the western North Pacific: Detection of causality by convergent cross mapping. *Fish Oceanogr* 27: 312-322. DOI: 10.1111/fog.12254.

Nakazawa, T. (2015). Ontogenetic niche shifts matter in community ecology: A review and future perspectives. *Population Ecology* 57: 347–54.

Nathan, R., Getz, W. M., Revilla, E., Holyoak, M., Kadmon, R., Saltz, D., and Smouse, P. E. (2008). A movement ecology paradigm for unifying organismal movement research. *Proc Natl Acad Sci USA*. 105: 19052–9. DOI: 10.1073/pnas.0800375105.

Novak, M., Wootton, J. T., Doak, D. F., Emmerson, M., Estes, J. A., and Tinker, M. T. (2011). Predicting community responses to perturbations in the face of imperfect knowledge and network complexity. *Ecology* 92: 836–46.

Noyce, K. V. and Garshelis D. L. (2011). Seasonal migrations of black bears (Ursus americanus): Causes and consequences. *Behav Ecol Sociobiol* 65: 823–35.

O'Gorman, E. J., Emmerson, M. C. (2009). Perturbations to trophic interactions and the stability of complex food webs. *Proc Natl Acad Sci U S A* 106: 13, 393–8.

Olson, M. H. (1996). Ontogenetic niche shifts in largemouth bass: Variability and consequences for first-year growth. *Ecology* 77: 179–90.

Paine, R. T. (1966). Food web complexity and species diversity. *Ame Nat* 100: 65–75.

Paine, R. T. (1969). A note on trophic complexity and community stability. *Ame Nat* 103: 91–3.

Pocock, M. J. O., Evans, D. M., and Memmott, J. (2012). The robustness and restoration of a network of ecological networks. *Science* 335: 973–7.

Polis, G. A., Anderson, W. B., and Holt, R. D. (1997). Toward an integration of landscape and food web ecology: The dynamics of spatially subsidized food webs. *Ann Rev Ecol Syst* 28: 289–316.

Richards, S. A. (2002). Temporal partitioning and aggression among foragers; modelling the effects of stochasticity and individual state. *Behavioural Ecology* 13: 427–38.

Sauer, T., York, J. A., and Casdagli, M. (1991). Embedology. *Journal of Statistical Physics* 65: 579–616.

Scharf, I., Filin, I., and Ovadia, O. (2008). An experimental design and a statistical analysis separating interference from exploitation competition. *Population Ecology* 50: 319–324.

Schmitz, O. J. (2008). Effects of predator hunting mode on grassland ecosystem function. *Science* 319: 952–54.

Schoener, T. W. (1974). Resource partitioning in ecological communities. *Science* 185: 27–38.

Shoemaker, L. G. and Melbourne, B. A. (2016). Linking metacommunity paradigms to spatial coexistence mechanisms. *Ecology* 97: 2436–46.

Spalinger, D. E. and Hobbs N. T. (1992). Mechanisms of foraging in mammalian herbivores: New models of functional response. *The American Naturalist* 140: 325–48.

Sugihara, G. (1994). Nonlinear forecasting for the classification of natural time series. *Philos Trans R Soc A Math Phys Eng Sci* 348: 477–95. DOI: 10.1098/rsta.1994.0106.

Sugihara, G., May, R. M. (1990). Nonlinear forecasting as a way of distinguishing chaos from measurement error in a data series. *Nature* 344: 734–41.

Sugihara, G., May, R., Ye, H., Hsieh C. H., Deyle, E., Fogarty, M., and Munch, S. (2012). Detecting causality in complex ecosystems. *Science* 338: 496–500. DOI: 10.1126/science.1227079.

Sutherland, W. J. (1996). *From Individual Behaviour to Population Ecology*. Oxford: Blackwell.

Takabayashi, J. and Dicke M. (1996). Plant-carnivore mutualism through herbivore-induced carnivore attractants. *Trends Plant Sci* 1: 109–13

Takens F. (1981). Dynamical Systems and Turbulence, Warwick 1980. Lecture Notes in Mathematics. Berlin: Springer, pp. 366–81.

Takimoto, G. (2003). Adaptive plasticity in ontogenetic niche shifts stabilizes consumer-resource dynamics. *The American Naturalist* 162: 93–109.

Takimoto, G., Iwata, T., and Murakami M. (2009). Timescale hierarchy determines the indirect effects of fluctuating subsidy inputs on in situ resources. *The American Naturalist* 173: 200–11.

Tilman, D. (1987). The importance of the mechanisms of interspecific competition. *The American Naturalist* 129: 769–74.

Tunney, T. D., Carpenter, S. R., and Vander Zanden, M. J. (2017). The consistency of a species' response to press perturbations with high food web uncertainty. *Ecology* 98: 1859–68.

Turchin, P. (2003). *Complex Population Dynamics: A Theoretical/Empirical Synthesis*. Princeton, New Jersey: Princeton University Press.

Ushio, M., Hsieh, C. -H., Masuda, R., Deyle, E. R., Ye, H., Chang, C. W., Sugihara, G., and Kondoh, M. (2018). Fluctuating interaction network and time-varying stability of a natural fish community. *Nature* 554: 36–03.

Vander Zanden, M. J. and Vadeboncoeur, Y. (2002). Fishes as integrators of benthic and pelagic food webs in lakes. *Ecology* 83: 2152–61.

van Nes, E. H., Scheffer, M., Brovkin, V., Lenton, T. M., Ye, H., Deyle, E., and Sugihara G. (2015). Causal feedbacks in climate change. *Nat Clim Chang* 5: 445–8. DOI: 10.1038/nclimate2568.

Vucic-Pestic, O., Rall, B. C., Kalinkat G., and Brose, U. (2010). Allometric functional response model: Body masses constrain interaction strengths. *Journal of Animal Ecology* 79: 249–256.

Volterra, A. (1926). Variazioni e fluttuazoni del numero d'individui in specie animali onviventi. *Mem Acad Lincei Roma* 2: 31–113.

Whitney H. (1936). Differentiable manifolds. *Ann Math* 37: 645–80.

Winder, M. and Schindler, D. E. (2004). Climate change uncouples trophic interactions in an aquatic ecosystem. *Ecology* 85: 2100–06.

Wootton, J. T. (1994). The nature and consequences of indirect effects on ecological communities. *Annual Review of Ecology and Systematics* 25: 443–66.

Wootton, J. T. and Emmerson, M. (2005). Measurement of interaction strength in nature. *Annu. Rev. Ecol. Evol. Syst.* 36: 419–44

Ye, H., Beamish, R. J., Glaser, S. M., Grant, S. C. H., Hsieh, C. -H., Richards, L. J., Schnute, J. T., Sugihara G. (2015a). Equation-free mechanistic ecosystem forecasting using empirical dynamic modeling. *Proc Natl Acad Sci USA* 112: E1569-E1576. DOI: 10.1073/pnas.1417063112.

Ye, H., Deyle, E. R., Gilarranz, L. J., and Sugihara, G. (2015b). Distinguishing time-delayed causal interactions using convergent cross mapping. *Sci Rep* 5: 14750.

Yodzis P. (1996). Food webs and perturbation experiments: Theory and practice. In G. A. Polis, and K. O. Winemiller (eds.), *Food Webs: Integration of Patterns and Dynamics*. New York Chapman & Hall, Inc., pp. 192–200.

Yoneya K. and Takabayashi J. (2014). Plant-plant communication mediated by airborne signals: Ecological and plant physiological perspectives. *Plant Biotechnology* 31: 409–416.

Yoshida, T., Jones, L. E., Ellner, S. P., Fussmann, G. F., and Hairston N. G. Jr. (2003). Rapid evolution drives ecological dynamics in a predator-prey system. *Nature* 424: 303–6.

CHAPTER 9

Trait-based models of complex ecological networks

Ulrich Brose

9.1 Modeling complex ecological networks

Most natural communities comprise between dozens and hundreds of species that are engaged in hundreds to thousands of interactions. These interactions weave complex networks and couple most of the species in a community within pathways of few links. This pattern of species interwoven in networks of interactions has often been described by Darwin's classic description of natural communities as entangled banks. Over many decades, the more detailed description and quantitative modeling of this entangled-bank type of communities has been restricted to few food-web ecologists and some naturalists. However, the accelerating effects of global change on ecological communities have created a rising demand to provide a mechanistic and predictive understanding of ecosystem responses that also includes a realistic level of natural diversity (i.e., the number of species in a community) and complexity (the number of links or the linkage density in a community).

For a long time, this demand has mainly been addressed by two types of ecological modeling. The first type is represented by simplified community models that ignore the coupling of species by their interactions. This approach creates direct links between global change parameters and community variables such as diversity or abundance distributions. Despite some success in relating causes

and effects, this approach has remained limited in the possibility to predict future changes as it can only assume constant and static community and interaction structures, because they are not explicitly included in these models and thus cannot change. The second type of approach employs interaction modules of few species and low complexity to model population dynamics. The range in complexity of these models ranges from simple consumer-resource pairs to food chains or omnivory motifs. These models provide substantial mechanistic insight into the processes that drive natural communities, but they cannot predict community patterns in diversity or abundance distributions.

Hence, these two types of ecological modeling have been leaving a substantial gap that needed to be filled by ecological network models. These models include the full diversity of natural communities in terms of the number of species and the variety of interactions between them. Therefore, they combine mechanistic modeling of species' interactions with potential predictions of community patterns such as diversity and abundance distributions. While this approach offers a desirable combination of mechanistic understanding with community-level predictions, it has been hampered for decades by the requirement to provide an adequate set of parameters for each population and each interaction. A typical set of population model parameters includes

Brose, U., *Trait-based models of complex ecological networks* In: *Theoretical Ecology: Concepts and Applications*. Edited by: Kevin S. McCann and Gabriel Gellner, Oxford University Press (2020). © Oxford University Press.
DOI: 10.1093/oso/9780198824282.003.0009

at least growth rates, maximum feeding rates, and death or metabolic rates for each population as well as parameters of interaction strength and assimilation rates for each interaction. Tedious measurements of these parameters are certainly possible for species modules such as predator-prey pairs or food chains, but the higher diversity (i.e., the number of species) and complexity (i.e., the number of interactions between species) of natural communities prevents any systematic measurements of species and interaction parameters for network models. For instance, the food web of the Antarctic Weddell Sea (Jacob et al. 2011) comprises 488 species and 16,220 feeding links between (Figure 9.1). The requirement of two parameters per interaction and at least three parameters for each species renders a systematic empirical parametrization of a food-web model for this community impossible.

The initial solution for this chronic hunger for parameters was establishing random parameterization protocols. Analyses of random interaction networks have provided substantial insights into how network structure constrains the dynamics and survival of populations. For instance, classic network analyses showed that increases in the diversity (the number of nodes) or complexity (the connection probability between pairs of species) of networks cause a destabilization of the dynamics (May 1972) that can potentially lead to extinctions. Counter to the prior paradigm, this suggests that higher diversity and complexity in natural communities does not lead to higher stability. However, the classic modeling results also showed that the destabilizing effects of diversity and complexity could be ameliorated by decreasing strengths of the interactions between the species (May 1972).

The central question that has been arising was thus how natural communities can maintain their stability and structural integrity despite their high diversity and complexity. Some seminal studies identified the characteristics of natural communities that are responsible for their stability. The main findings showed that the network structure and interaction strengths of the links are not random. First, natural food webs are not well described by random network structures, as they do not engage randomly in their interactions. Interestingly, this non-random structure of the natural food webs provides a substantial increase in stability when

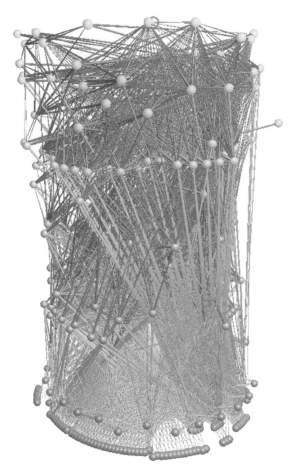

Figure 9.1 The food web of the Antarctic Weddell Sea (Jacob et al. 2011) with 488 species and 16,220 feeding interactions. This includes autotrophs such as phytoplankton at the base (red nodes), herbivores such as zooplankton (orange nodes) and predators across multiple trophic levels (yellow nodes). The complex structure of this food web includes a high number of interaction modules (e.g., food chains) that are interwoven.

compared to random networks (Yodzis 1981). This finding has triggered a quest for the non-random rules that govern who interacts with whom in natural communities and yield the non-random network structures. Specifically, structural niche models showed that species in natural communities are hierarchically ordered and higher ranked species predominantly feed on lower ranked species (Cohen and Briand 1984; Williams and Martinez 2000). Secondly, the strengths of interactions are also non-randomly distributed across the species of the network, which yields an additional gain in stability compared to random networks (De Ruiter et al. 1995).

These results suggest that non-random network structures and interaction strengths need to be taken into account when modeling ecological networks. The centrally important question was, thus, how to predict realistic network structures and interaction strengths while avoiding unrealistically labor-intensive measurements of these parameters in natural communities. The use of easily accessible species traits offers a potential solution for this problem. In natural communities, many aspects of food-web structure and interaction strengths are strongly linked to the average body masses of the species (Peters 1983; Emmerson and Raffaelli 2004; Woodward et al. 2005; Brose et al. 2006a; Brose 2010). Therefore, body mass has been used as a primary trait to predict the model parameters of network structure and population dynamics. In the following, this approach is described in more detail.

9.2 Allometric population models

In classic models, the dynamics of population densities are driven by the parameters of growth, feeding and either death (models of population abundance) or metabolism (models of population biomass). Interestingly, these parameters follow power-law relationships with the species body masses (see Figure 9.2 for an example), which are referred to as allometric scaling relationships (Peters 1983). The allometric scaling of metabolic rates were subsequently explained by the fractal structure of the species' physiological transport networks (West et al. 1999), which was more recently intensively debated. Irrespective of the mechanistic processes that are considered responsible, most approaches consider power-laws as the most appropriate relationships (but see Chapter 10 on allometries that are more complex). As metabolic rates provide the fuel for most other organismal process, a dominance of three-quarter power-law scaling relationships for most biological processes including those of the population-dynamic models was generally assumed (Brown et al. 2004). Consequently, these allometric scaling relationships were used to parameterize a generic bioenergetic population dynamic model (Yodzis and Innes 1992). The approach is based on general scaling relationships of a biological rate such as the metabolic rate with body mass (Figure 9.2, grey data points fitted by the black regression line). Subsequently, the regression model can be used to predict the biological rate of species based on their body masses, which

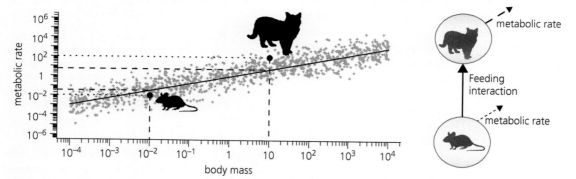

Figure 9.2 The relationship between metabolic rates and body mass (plot on the left, grey dots, arbitrary data) is often well described by a power-law relationship (black line). This relationship can be used to predict the metabolic rate of a species based on the body mass as shown for the mouse and the fox as examples (dashed lines). As many of the metabolic rates deviate from the regression line (residual variation), there is a discrepancy between the allometric predictions of metabolic rates (dashed lines) and the real metabolic rates (dotted lines). The allometric approach is thus trading generality across species and ease of application against accuracy in predicting metabolic rates of specific species. This approach can thus be used to generate general relationships across species (and body-mass classes), whereas detailed predictions of specific species' rates (and population dynamics) suffer from uncertainty. The allometrically-predicted metabolic rates can parameterize consumer-resource models such as that of the interaction between fox and mouse (plot on the right, size of the metabolic rate arrows corresponds to y-axis values of their predicted metabolic rates). Similar allometric approaches can be used to predict other physiological rates (e.g., death rate, maximum feeding rate) or interaction parameters (e.g., attack rates), which yields fully-parameterized population dynamic models.

parameterizes a population dynamic model (see Figure 9.2 for an example).

Initially, this allometric population dynamic model was used to generalize dynamics according to dimensionless consumer-resource body-mass ratios across species pairs that differ substantially in their masses from bacteria to whales (Yodzis and Innes 1992). These generalized dynamics were subsequently used to understand the stability of populations embedded in small modules. These studies showed the biologically reasonable conditions for chaotic dynamics in tri-trophic food chains (McCann and Yodzis 1994) and how they could be stabilized by the addition of an omnivorous link between the top and intermediate species (McCann and Hastings 1997). This solution to preventing extinctions by unbounded population oscillations was later extended to a general result that weak trophic interaction links in small modules can generally withdraw energy out of strongly oscillating chains, which creates increased probabilities of population persistence (McCann et al. 1998). In consumer-resource interactions, as the most simple building blocks of modules as well as complex food webs, population stability is generally undermined by any process that increases the energy flux from the resource to the consumer relative to the consumer loss rates (Rip and McCann 2011). Hence, stabilizing processes in enriched systems with strong oscillations thus increases the consumer loss rates (relative to the energy flux from the resource to the consumer) and prevents a pattern of top-heaviness (high consumer-to-resource biomass ratio). These approaches employed small modules of interaction populations to gain highly general mechanistic insights in processes that govern population stability and persistence. Nevertheless, these results still required scaling up to the diversity and complexity that characterizes natural communities.

9.3 Allometric models of complex communities: The Yodzis and Innes approach

Classic food-web studies illustrated the pattern that the stability of these complex networks is much higher than that of random networks due to natural food-web structures (Yodzis 1981) and natural distributions in interaction strengths across the links (De Ruiter et al. 1995). However, one centrally important question remained: why do natural communities possess network structures and interaction strength distributions that beget stability? This pattern of naturally stable networks becomes even more astonishing when considering that the likelihood of these stable configurations is extremely low (Gross et al. 2009) and that it requires systematic correlations between interaction strength parameters (Brose 2010). This patterning in the organization of natural communities required a structuring principle based on first principles, which was found to lay in the constraints of consumer and resource body masses on interaction strengths and food-web structure. Allometric rules yield non-random distributions of interaction strengths across the links of complex food webs, which increase their stability (Emmerson and Raffaelli 2004). The explanation for this pattern is that predator-prey interactions are subject to very simple yet highly general constraints that predators need to outpace, overwhelm, and ingest their prey (Brose 2010). These general principles cause that across different ecosystem types predators are systematically larger than their prey (Brose et al. 2006a). Implementing this general pattern of predator-prey body-mass ratios caused a substantial increase in the probability of population persistence from ~40% under random body-mass distributions to more than 90% under natural body-mass distributions (Brose et al. 2006b). This result indicated that the non-random pattern of predators being systematically larger than their prey might be an explanation of why natural food webs are constrained into patterns of interaction structures that beget stability. Moreover, the body-mass structure of natural food webs also turned negative relationships between their diversity (i.e., the number of species or nodes of the networks) or complexity (i.e., connectance or the connection probability between any pair of species in the network) and stability into neutral to slightly positive relationships (Brose et al. 2006b; Rall et al. 2008). Eventually, this implies that the diversity and complexity of natural communities does not undermine their stability as suggested by earlier theoretical studies.

These results opened up possibilities for a realistic understanding of the dynamic processes in complex natural food webs. The modeling approach required defining the network structure of who eats whom (the binary links of the network) and a population dynamic model. In the first approaches, the structure of the networks followed the niche model (Williams and Martinez 2000) that ordered species along an arbitrary niche axis and imposed systematic feeding niches of predators feeding predominantly on lower ranked species. These niche-model networks were combined with the allometric population dynamic model (Yodzis and Innes 1992) to yield dynamic complex networks (Brose et al. 2006b; Rall et al. 2008). In addition to direct effects of the predator-prey body-mass ratios, implementations of these models also showed the stability of the complex networks' profits from the compartmentalization (Stouffer and Bascompte 2011) and the relative frequency of some food-web modules (Stouffer and Bascompte 2010). Most of these stabilizing effects of food-web architecture and body-mass structure can be related to decreasing interaction strengths from the base to the top of the food webs (Kartascheff et al. 2009), which is explained by the combination of decreases in per unit biomass feeding rates with body mass (Rall et al. 2012), and increases in body mass along the trophic levels of complex food webs (Riede et al. 2011). This explanation for the strong body-mass effects is consistent with the principle of decreasing energy fluxes relative to consumer loss rates along trophic levels (Rip and McCann 2011), which links the dynamic stability of complex food webs to mechanistically understood consumer-resource population dynamics.

9.4 More complex allometries

The allometric models of natural food webs suggested that the dynamics of these complex systems are highly dependent on the interaction strength pattern that are quantified by functional responses. The original bioenergetics model of population dynamics (Yodzis and Innes 1992) included some simplifying assumptions such as

an inverse allometric scaling of handling time and attack rate, which is not supported by empirical data (Vucic-Pestic et al. 2010; Rall et al. 2012). Instead, empirical data suggested that handling time is well approximated by a power law scaling with predator body mass, whereas attack rates follow hump-shaped relationships with predator-prey body-mass ratios. This pattern is consistent with the notion that predators have an optimal prey size that yields maximal attack rates. These attack rates decrease towards predator-prey body-mass ratios that are smaller or larger, which causes a hump-shaped relationship between attack rates and predator-prey body-mass ratios (Brose et al. 2008; Kalinkat et al. 2013). These hump-shaped relationships between attack rates and predator-prey body-mass ratios were implemented in a bioenergetic population dynamic model that kept the other traditional power-law scaling relationships to show that it correctly predicts the body-mass ratios of natural predator-prey pairs (Kalinkat et al. 2013). This result suggested that the network structure of natural food webs and the population dynamics of their predator-prey pairs could be successfully predicted by the same model. This opened up a fundamental possibility to use the body masses of the species in a community to predict their interaction topology (who eats whom) as well as the dynamics of their population densities. However, the centrally important question was whether such an extremely reductionist approach of predicting food-web structure and population dynamics by body mass as a single super trait could be adequate in predicting empirical patterns. While the tests of these models are still in their infancy, one pioneering study used the allometric-trophic network approach to predict the interactions and their strengths in a small module of three predators and one basal species (Schneider et al. 2012). Despite the simplicity of this approach that was based on body masses as the only species traits, the predictions of the model were highly consistent with laboratory experiments that systematically removed the species to measure their interaction strengths (Schneider et al. 2012). These results illustrate that body masses can act as the dominant traits in natural food webs that organize their structure as well as their interaction strengths.

9.5 Modeling the temperature-dependence of network dynamics

Many of the effects of body masses on population dynamics go through their allometric constraints on the physiological rates of metabolism, growth and feeding as described by classic allometric scaling relationships (Peters 1983; Yodzis and Innes 1992) and the Metabolic Theory of Ecology (West et al. 1997; Brown et al. 2004). As ambient temperature has been used as the second important driver variable of metabolic scaling relationships (Gillooly et al. 2001), it has also been implemented in population dynamic models to analyse its effects on population stability (Vasseur and McCann 2005; Gilbert et al. 2014). Consistent with the principle of energy flux (Rip and McCann 2011), the effects of temperature on population stability are highly dependent on the relative strength in the changes in metabolism and consumption of the predators (Vasseur and McCann 2005; Fussmann et al. 2014). Interestingly, a meta-study showed that the increases in feeding with warming are systematically much lower than those in metabolism (Fussmann et al. 2014). Hence, the energy loss rates of predators (metabolic rates) are more accelerated under warming than their energy gains (feeding rates). This yields predictions of increasing population stability (smaller oscillations) but predator extinctions at high temperatures due to starvation, which were confirmed by laboratory experiments (Fussmann et al. 2014). These results were confirmed for simulations of tri-trophic food chains, where the detrimental effects of warming could be counteracted by nutrient enrichment (Binzer et al. 2012). Interestingly, these results obtained for small food-web modules can also provide an explanation for the increased extinction rates in complex food webs under warming (Binzer et al. 2016). Together, the studies on empirical temperature scaling relationships, population dynamics in small food-web modules and complex food webs have provided a systematic and generic insight into how the warming of natural ecosystems is likely to change the diversity and composition of natural species communities. This is providing an example how to address the consequences of global change drivers for the structure, dynamics and stability of complex natural communities by combining trait-based, allometric food web models with empirically derived effects of the global change driver on the network nodes and links.

9.6 Outlook

The trait-based approach to model complex ecological networks illustrated in this chapter provides a flexible toolbox to address theoretical and applied questions. This flexibility includes accounting for non-linear or other more complex scaling relationships between the species' biological rates and their traits, such as body mass. For instance, the hump-shaped scaling between predator-prey body-mass ratios and attack rates was included in the functional response of the models (Kalinkat et al. 2013). Similarly, curved or hump-shaped relationships between metabolic rates and body mass (Kolokotrones et al. 2010; Ehnes et al. 2011) could be included in the models. Additionally, also rates that change during the time series such as adaptive foraging rates can be realized with limited effort (Kondoh 2003; Heckmann et al. 2012). This flexibility in the model structure concerning how species traits affect the biological rates creates a broad applicability as it allows dovetailing the model to the specificications of the system studied.

Future studies could thus systematically include other important species traits such as their movement type, the species' functional groups, and the dimensionality of the interactions. There are substantial differences in the realized maximum and exploratory speeds between species of different movement types (running, flying, swimming) and functional groups such as predators, herbivores, and decomposers (Hirt et al. 2017a,b). The maximum speed is realized during the chases of attack and escape, whereas the much slower exploratory speed characterizes the search behavior of predators. Hence, both types of speed and their variation across species of different movement types and functional groups could have strong implications for the dynamics of complex food webs.

In addition to species traits, ecosystem characteristics can also have profound consequences for species interactions. For instance, the dimensionality of the ecosystem, 2D or 3D, has a strong effect on the attack rates of predator-prey interactions, which has severe knock-on effects on their dynamic stability (Pawar et al. 2012). Future studies could thus implement these effects of interaction dimensionality in models of complex communities to understand their consequences for community patterns and dynamics.

Natural communities do not only comprise numerous trophic interactions, they can include even more non-trophic interactions that contribute substantially to the structure of the entangled bank (Kefi et al. 2015). These non-trophic interaction can change the structure and strength of the food-web links substantially (Kefi et al. 2012), which can have substantial impact on the community dynamics up to changes between alternative stable states (Kefi et al. 2016a,b). Ultimately, the combination of different types of interaction networks, such as those formed by trophic and non-trophic interactions, compose multilayer or multiplex networks (Pilosof et al. 2017) that could also be parametrized by species traits. This is opening up an exciting research agenda of realistically modeling natural communities while accounting for the full complexity of their interaction structures.

Many of the modeling approaches described in this chapter have focused on understanding how processes and traits drive population dynamics and persistence in complex food webs. Some more recent studies have started to use the biomass fluxes through the links of the food webs (De Ruiter et al. 1994) to calculate ecosystem functions (Barnes et al. 2018). For instance, the sum over all biomass fluxes to herbivores and carnivores characterizes the ecosystem functions herbivory and carnivory, respectively (Barnes et al. 2018). Similarly, the strength of the flow in nutrients from abiotic pools into plants can also be used to calculate primary production in complex ecological networks (Wang and Brose 2018). Using the approach of trait-based energy flux calculations (Barnes et al. 2018), these studies have shown that primary production and other ecosystem functions in complex food webs are driven by the maximum trophic level (or maximum body mass) that is realized in the network (Wang and Brose 2018) and the diversity of the animal community (Schneider et al. 2016). This

novel application of quantitative food-web analyses allows for more detailed and mechanistic analyses of how community structure and diversity drive ecosystem functioning.

The combination of trophic interactions between species with their spatial processes of trait-based movement between different habitat patches can greatly modify the stability of food-web modules (McCann et al. 2005) or complex networks (Gravel et al. 2016). Despite the tremendous importance of spatial processes for ecological patterns, the study of trait-based food webs is still in its infancy. Most studies coupling trophic dynamics with movement between habitat patches have been restricted to interaction modules of few species such food chains or omnivory motifs (Koelle and Vandermeer 2005; Amarasekare 2007; Liao et al. 2017). These studies have shown that trait-based dispersal abilities of species can modify their coexistence probabilities substantially (Amarasekare 2006), which can increase the length of food chains (Holt 2002) and the species diversity of the food webs (Amarasekare 2008). A more systematic combination of complex food webs with trait-based dispersal functions is thus likely to be a fruitful avenue for an improved understanding of natural community structures and ecosystem functions (Massol et al. 2011).

The research directions outlined above offer great possibilities to improve our understanding of dynamic processes in the complex networks that characterize natural communities. The body mass and temperature constraints on species interactions and their population dynamics represent first steps towards achieving realistic models of complex ecological networks. However, only the systematic improvement of these models by including effects of other species traits, non-trophic interactions and spatial processes is likely to yield accurate models that would allow for realistic forecasting of ecological dynamics (Petchey et al. 2015). Despite arguably being quite complex, these ecological network models will close the lingering gap between mechanistic models of simple food-web modules and community models without species interactions. Eventually, these models enable the study of global change effects on populations, communities and ecosystem functioning while also accounting for the indirect effects between species that are coupled by their interactions. In a world challenged by global change, these trait-based network models can provide a mechanistic and predictive understanding of ecosystem responses that also includes a realistic level of natural diversity and complexity.

References

Amarasekare, P. (2006). Productivity, dispersal and the coexistence of intraguild predators and prey. *J. Theor. Biol.* 243: 121–33.

Amarasekare, P. (2007). Spatial dynamics of communities with intraguild predation: The role of dispersal strategies. *Am. Nat.* 170: 819–31.

Amarasekare, P. (2008). Spatial dynamics of foodwebs. *Annu. Rev. Ecol. Evol. Syst.* 39: 479–500.

Barnes, A. D., Jochum, M., Lefcheck, J. S., Eisenhauer, N., Scherber, C., O'Connor, M. I., et al. (2018). Energy Flux: The link between multitrophic biodiversity and ecosystem functioning. *Trends Ecol. Evol.* 33: 186–97.

Binzer, A., Guill, C., Brose, U., and Rall, B. C. (2012). The dynamics of food chains under climate change and nutrient enrichment. *Philos. Trans. R. Soc. B Biol. Sci.* 367: 2935–44.

Binzer, A., Guill, C., Rall, B. C., and Brose, U. (2016). Interactive effects of warming, eutrophication and size structure: Impacts on biodiversity and food-web structure. *Glob. Change Biol.* 22: 220–7.

Brose, U. (2010). Body-mass constraints on foraging behaviour determine population and food-web dynamics. *Funct. Ecol.* 24: 28–34.

Brose, U., Ehnes, R., Rall, B., Vucic-Pestic, O., Berlow, E., and Scheu, S. (2008). Foraging theory predicts predator-prey energy fluxes. *J. Anim. Ecol.* 77: 1072–8.

Brose, U., Jonsson, T., Berlow, E., Warren, P., Banasek-Richter, C., Bersier, L., et al. (2006a). Consumer-resource body-size relationships in natural food webs. *Ecology* 87: 2411–17.

Brose, U., Williams, R. J., and Martinez, N. D. (2006b). Allometric scaling enhances stability in complex food webs. *Ecol. Lett.* 9, 1228–36.

Brown, J. H., Gillooly, J. F., Allen, A. P., Savage, V. M., and West, G. B. (2004). Toward a metabolic theory of ecology. *Ecology* 85, 1771–89.

Cohen, J. E. and Briand, F. (1984). Trophic links of community food webs. *Proc. Natl. Acad. Sci. U. S. Am. Biol. Sci.* 81: 4105–09.

De Ruiter, P., Neutel, A. -M., and Moore, J. C. (1995). Energetics, patterns of interaction strengths, and stability in real ecosystems. *Science* 269: 1257–60.

De Ruiter, P. C., Neutel, A. M., and Moore, J. C. (1994). Modeling food webs and nutrient cycling in agroecosystems. *Trends Ecol. Evol.* 9: 378–83.

Ehnes, R. B., Rall, B. C., and Brose, U. (2011). Phylogenetic grouping, curvature and metabolic scaling in terrestrial invertebrates. *Ecol. Lett.* 14: 993–1000.

Emmerson, M. C. and Raffaelli, D. (2004). Predator-prey body size, interaction strength and the stability of a real food web. *J Anim Ecol* 73: 399–409.

Fussmann, K. E., Schwarzmüller, F., Brose, U., Jousset, A., and Rall, B. C. (2014). Ecological stability in response to warming. *Nat. Clim. Change* 4: 206–10.

Gilbert, B., Tunney, T. D., McCann, K. S., DeLong, J. P., Vasseur, D. A., Savage, V., et al. (2014). A bioenergetic framework for the temperature dependence of trophic interactions. *Ecol. Lett.* 17: 902–14.

Gillooly, J. F., Brown, J. H., West, G. B., Savage, V. M., and Charnov, E. L. (2001). Effects of size and temperature on metabolic rate. *Science* 293: 2248–51.

Gravel, D., Massol, F., and Leibold, M. A. (2016). Stability and complexity in model meta-ecosystems. *Nat. Commun.*, 7: 12,457.

Gross, T., Rudolf, L., Levin, S. A., and Dieckmann, U. (2009). Generalized models reveal stabilizing factors in food webs. *Science* 325: 747–50.

Heckmann, L., Drossel, B., Brose, U., and Guill, C. (2012). Interactive effects of body-size structure and adaptive foraging on food-web stability. *Ecol. Lett.* 15: 243–50.

Hirt, M. R., Jetz, W., Rall, B. C., and Brose, U. (2017a). A general scaling law reveals why the largest animals are not the fastest. *Nat. Ecol. Evol.* 1: 1116–22.

Hirt, M. R., Lauermann, T., Brose, U., Noldus, L. P. J. J., and Dell, A. I. (2017b). The little things that run: A general scaling of invertebrate exploratory speed with body mass. *Ecology* 98: 2751–7.

Holt, R. D. (2002). Food webs in space: On the interplay of dynamic instability and spatial processes. *Ecol Res Ecol Res* 17: 261–73.

Jacob, U., Thierry, A., Brose, U., Arntz, W. E., Berg, S., Brey, T., et al. (2011). The Role of Body Size in Complex Food Webs: A Cold Case. In Belgrano, A. (ed.) *Advances in Ecological Research, The Role of Body Size in Multispecies Systems.* Cambridge, Mass: Academic Press, pp. 181–223.

Kalinkat, G., Schneider, F. D., Digel, C., Guill, C., Rall, B. C., and Brose, U. (2013). Body masses, functional responses and predator–prey stability. *Ecol. Lett.* 16: 1126–34.

Kartascheff, B., Heckmann, L., Drossel, B., and Guill, C. (2009). Why allometric scaling enhances stability in food web models. *Theor. Ecol.* 3: 195–208.

Kefi, S., Berlow, E. L., Wieters, E. A., Joppa, L. N., Wood, S. A., Brose, U., et al. (2015). Network structure beyond food webs: Mapping non-trophic and trophic interactions on Chilean rocky shores. *Ecology* 96: 291–303.

Kefi, S., Berlow, E. L., Wieters, E. A., Navarrete, S. A., Petchey, O. L., Wood, S. A., et al. (2012). More than a meal ... integrating non-feeding interactions into food webs. *Ecol. Lett.* 15: 291–300.

Kefi, S., Holmgren, M., and Scheffer, M. (2016a). When can positive interactions cause alternative stable states in ecosystems? *Funct. Ecol.* 30: 88–97.

Kefi, S., Miele, V., Wieters, E. A., Navarrete, S. A., and Berlow, E. L. (2016b). How structured is the entangled bank? The surprisingly simple organization of multiplex ecological networks leads to increased persistence and resilience. *Plos Biol.* 14: e1002527.

Koelle, K. and Vandermeer, J. (2005). Dispersal-induced desynchronization: From metapopulations to metacommunities. *Ecol. Lett.* 8: 167–75.

Kolokotrones, T., Savage, V., Deeds, E. J., and Fontana, W. (2010). Curvature in metabolic scaling. *Nature* 464: 753–6.

Kondoh, M. (2003). Foraging adaptation and the relationship between food-web complexity and stability. *Science* 299: 1388–91.

Liao, J., Bearup, D., Wang, Y., Nijs, I., Bonte, D., Li, Y., et al. (2017). Robustness of metacommunities with omnivory to habitat destruction: Disentangling patch fragmentation from patch loss. *Ecology* 98: 1631–9.

Massol, F., Gravel, D., Mouquet, N., Cadotte, M. W., Fukami, T., and Leibold, M. A. (2011). Linking community and ecosystem dynamics through spatial ecology. *Ecol. Lett.* 14: 313–23.

May, R. M. (1972). Will a large complex system be stable? *Nature* 238: 413–14.

McCann, K. and Hastings, A. (1997). Re-evaluating the omnivory-stability relationship in food webs. *Proc. R. Soc. Lond. Ser. B-Biol. Sci.* 264: 1249–54.

McCann, K. and Yodzis, P. (1994). Biological conditions for chaos in a three-species food chain. *Ecology* 75: 561–4.

McCann, K. S., Hastings, A., and Huxel, G. R. (1998). Weak trophic interactions and the balance of nature. *Nature* 395: 794–8.

McCann, K. S., Rasmussen, J. B., and Umbanhowar, J. (2005). The dynamics of spatially coupled food webs. *Ecol. Lett.* 8: 513–23.

Pawar, S., Dell, A. I., and Savage, V. M. (2012). Dimensionality of consumer search space drives trophic interaction strengths. *Nature* 486: 485–9.

Petchey, O. L., Pontarp, M., Massie, T. M., Kefi, S., Ozgul, A., Weilenmann, M., et al. (2015). The ecological forecast horizon, and examples of its uses and determinants. *Ecol. Lett.* 18: 597–611.

Peters, R. H. (1983). *The Ecological Implications of Body Size.* New York: Cambridge University Press.

Pilosof, S., Porter, M. A., Pascual, M., and Kefi, S. (2017). The multilayer nature of ecological networks. *Nat. Ecol. Evol.* 1: UNSP 0101.

Rall, B. C., Brose, U., Hartvig, M., Kalinkat, G., Schwarzmüller, F., Vucic-Pestic, O., et al. (2012). Universal temperature and body-mass scaling of feeding rates. *Philos. Trans. R. Soc. B Biol. Sci.* 367: 2923–34.

Rall, B. C., Guill, C., and Brose, U. (2008). Food-web connectance and predator interference dampen the paradox of enrichment. *Oikos* 117: 202–13.

Riede, J. O., Brose, U., Ebenman, B., Jacob, U., Thompson, R., Townsend, C. R., et al. (2011). Stepping in Elton's footprints: A general scaling model for body masses and trophic levels across ecosystems. *Ecol. Lett.* 14: 169–78.

Rip, J. M. K. and McCann, K. S. (2011). Cross-ecosystem differences in stability and the principle of energy flux. *Ecol. Lett.* 14: 733–40.

Schneider, F. D., Brose, U., Rall, B. C., and Guill, C. (2016). Animal diversity and ecosystem functioning in dynamic food webs. *Nat. Commun.* 7: 12, 718.

Schneider, F. D., Scheu, S., and Brose, U. (2012). Body mass constraints on feeding rates determine the consequences of predator loss. *Ecol. Lett.* 15: 436–43.

Stouffer, D. B. and Bascompte, J. (2010). Understanding food-web persistence from local to global scales. *Ecol. Lett.* 13: 154–61.

Stouffer, D. B. and Bascompte, J. (2011). Compartmentalization increases food-web persistence. *Proc. Natl. Acad. Sci.* 108: 3648–52.

Vasseur, D. A. and McCann, K. S. (2005). A mechanistic approach for modeling temperature-dependent consumer-resource dynamics. *Am. Nat.* 166: 184–98.

Vucic-Pestic, O., Rall, B., Kalinkat, G., and Brose, U. (2010). Allometric functional response model: Body masses constrain interaction strengths. *J. Anim. Ecol.* 79: 249–56.

Wang, S. and Brose, U. (2018). Biodiversity and ecosystem functioning in food webs: The vertical diversity hypothesis. *Ecol. Lett.* 21: 9–20.

West, G. B., Brown, J. H. and Enquist, B. J. (1997). A general model for the origin of allometric scaling laws in biology. *Science* 276: 122–6.

West, G. B., Brown, J. H., and Enquist, B. J. (1999). The fourth dimension of life: Fractal geometry and allometric scaling of organisms. *Science* 284: 1677–80.

Williams, R. J. and Martinez, N. D. (2000). Simple rules yield complex food webs. *Nature* 404: 180–3.

Woodward, G., Ebenman, B., Ernmerson, M., Montoya, J. M., Olesen, J. M., Valido, A., et al. (2005). Body size in ecological networks. *Trends Ecol. Evol.* 20: 402–9.

Yodzis, P. (1981). The stability of real ecosystems. *Nature* 289: 674–6.

Yodzis, P. and Innes, S. (1992). Body size and consumer-resource dynamics. *Am Nat* 139: 1151–75.

CHAPTER 10

Ecological networks: From structure to dynamics

Sonia Kéfi

10.1 Brief introduction

Ecological systems are undeniably complex, including many species interacting in different ways with each other (e.g., predation, competition, facilitation, parasitism). One way of visualizing, describing, and studying this complexity is to represent these complex systems as networks. Ecological networks can be of different types, depending on the nature of the nodes and links involved, but in the most common case, nodes are typically species and links are interactions between these species. For example, food webs are networks of who eats whom among the species of a community. Mutualistic networks are networks of mutualistic interactions between species, such as networks of plants and their pollinators.

The study of these networks entails describing their structure, i.e., the way the nodes are connected to each other, understanding the rules governing this structure, and assessing how network structure drives ecological dynamics. Studies on different types of ecological networks have suggested that they exhibit structural regularities, i.e., common structural properties, which in turn affect network dynamics and resilience to perturbations.

Although the use of networks to represent ecological communities dates back to the early stages of the discipline, in the last two decades data has been collected at a faster rate and better resolution. Simultaneously, metrics are continuously developed to better characterize network structure, and numerical simulations of mathematical models have allowed investigating how network structure and dynamics are related. This has led to rapid progress in our understanding of ecological networks. We are reaching a more comprehensive and realistic description of ecological communities and their complexity. Combined with mathematical modeling, ecological network studies have contributed to the understanding of the mechanisms underlying the emergence of current ecological communities (species assemblages, species traits, and network structure), and of the response of ecological communities to natural gradients and to ongoing and future global change.

After defining networks in general, and ecological networks more specifically, this chapter presents recent results regarding the structure of different types of ecological networks, and what is known about their dynamics and resilience. Recent developments and challenges related to the study of ecological networks are highlighted. Understanding what precisely makes ecological systems stable remains one of the greatest challenges of ecology in the current context of global change. Addressing some of the current limitations of ecological networks could help improve our understanding and prediction ability of ecological communities. In particular, ecological network theory needs to further integrate different interaction types in the same framework (i.e., multi-layer networks) and to better account for the variability of these multi-layer networks in space and time.

Kéfi, S., *Ecological networks: From structure to dynamics* In: *Theoretical Ecology: Concepts and Applications*. Edited by: Kevin S. McCann and Gabriel Gellner, Oxford University Press (2020). © Oxford University Press.
DOI: 10.1093/oso/9780198824282.003.0010

10.2 What is a network?

Because of the explosion of information due to the Internet and the telecommunications in the nineties, as well as the improvement of computer power, a field targeting the study of complex systems and their emergent properties has boomed: network science (Watts and Strogatz 1998; Albert et al. 1999, 2000; Barabási and Albert 1999). Networks have since then been used at an accelerated rate in many different disciplines, including physics, social sciences, and biology (see Newman 2010 for an overview).

Networks (or *graphs*) are abstract representations of a system describing its components, the *nodes* (or *vertices*) and the relationships between them, the *links* (or *edges*) (Figure 10.1 left panel; Newman 2010). This network representation allows describing a large variety of systems with a common language.

In a *unipartite* network, all nodes are of the same type (e.g., species) and links (e.g., species interactions) can occur between any pairs of nodes (Figure 10.1 left panel). Food webs are often represented as unipartite networks (e.g., de Ruiter et al. 1995). A *bipartite network* is a particular type of network in which the nodes can be divided in two disjoint groups such that each link connects a node from one group to a node of another group (nodes have "colors"; Figure 10.1 middle panel, here with white and black nodes) but links among nodes of the same type do not occur. A typical example of bipartite networks are plant-pollinator networks, with

the nodes being either plants or pollinators, and the links being the pollination interactions (Jordano 1987). This can be generalized to *multipartite networks*, where more than two types of nodes can be considered, e.g., plants, pollinators, and herbivores, with pollination links between pollinators and plants, and herbivory links between herbivores and plants (e.g., Pocock et al. 2012). Real systems are often interconnected in many different ways, making it difficult to describe these systems with a single network. To account for this source of complexity, a new framework is currently developing in network science, focusing on the study of *multilayer networks*, a set of layers, each containing a network (Figure 10.1 right panel; Boccaletti et al. 2014; Kivelä et al. 2014; Pilosof et al. 2017). In ecology, such layers can correspond to different interaction types between a given set of species, different snapshots in time (each layer is a network snapshot taken at a different moment in time), or different locations in space (each layer is a network evaluated at a different location in space).

The links that connect the nodes of a network can be *directed* (Figure 10.2A1) or *undirected* (Figure 10.2A2). For example, pollination interactions are typically directed from a pollinator (the source of the interaction) to a flower (the target of the interaction). Note that feeding interactions are directed as well and can be represented as arrows going from predators to their prey (i.e., from the source to the target of the interaction) or as arrows going from prey to their predator when they are assumed to represent the flows of matter in the food web—

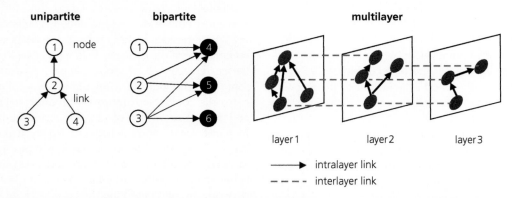

Figure 10.1 Examples of unipartite (left), bipartite (center), and multilayer (right) networks. Links that connect nodes within a layer are intralayer links whereas links that connect nodes across layers are interlayer links (dashed lines).

both representations can be found in the ecological literature. Other networks have undirected links, such as species co-occurrence networks (if species i is at the same location of species j, species j is also at the same location as species i).

A network is often represented by its *adjacency matrix* (Figure 10.2A2, B2). For a network of N nodes, the adjacency matrix has N rows and N columns with $A_{ij} = 0$ if j has no effect on i, and $A_{ij} \neq 0$ otherwise. Links can be binary (presence/absence or 0/1; we then talk about *qualitative or topological networks*) or weighted (measure of frequency or strength of the interaction; we then talk about *quantitative networks*). These values are the elements of the adjacency matrix. In an undirected network $A_{ij} = A_{ji}$ and the matrix is symmetric

(Figure 10.2B2). In a directed network A_{ij} can be different from A_{ji}; in a binary food web data set for example, A_{12} would be 1 if species 2 is a predator of species 1, but A_{21} would then be 0 (Figure 10.2A2).

Networks are one way of describing complex systems, visualizing and quantifying their structure, as well as evaluating the relationships between structure and dynamics. Their framework provides a common language to describe diverse complex systems and a set of tools to analyze them. A number of choices need to be made when we represent a system as a network (such as the level of description chosen for the nodes, the type of links included, etc.); these choices determine the type of information that can be extracted, the type of questions that can be explored, and the type of tools that can be

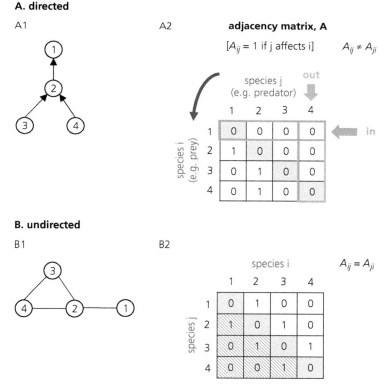

Figure 10.2 Typical representations of unipartite networks (on the left; using two simple 4-node networks as an illustration), with their corresponding adjacency matrix (on the right). Example of a directed (top row) and of an undirected (bottom row) network. In this example, all species are represented along the rows and columns. In case of directed links, the matrix elements contain information about who affects whom; here columns represent the species seen as a predator and the rows the species seen as a prey. This means that $A_{ij} = 1$ if species j is a predator of species i. Row i corresponds to the incoming links of species i (in orange in panel A2) and column i contains the outgoing links of species i (in green in panel A2). In case of undirected links, the adjacency matrix is symmetric (the white upper right cells contain identical information as the dashed bottom left cells in panel B2).

used. The first steps are therefore to decide what are the nodes and links in the system of interest and to collect the corresponding data. The following part presents the types of networks commonly studied in ecology.

10.3 Networks in ecology

Because of their inherent interconnectedness, ecological communities can quite naturally be described as networks, in which nodes typically represent species, individuals, or spatial locations, and links can indicate interactions between species or individuals as well as flows of energy, nutrients or individuals between locations (Table 10.1). Because topological networks (i.e., networks with only presence-absence information on the link, but no quantitative information on the strength of the link; see Section 10.2) are easier to assemble from empirical data, the bulk of published ecological networks are described by binary (rather than weighted) adjacency matrices (Figure 10.2A2, B2).

10.3.1 Interaction networks

Although different types of networks are used in ecology (see e.g., Borrett et al. 2014: Table 1), the ones that are the most widely used are so-called *interaction networks* in which the nodes are species and the links represent interactions between these species (Figure 10.3). Any type of interaction between two species may be considered to build such a network: trophic (i.e., feeding; Figure 10.3A) or non-trophic (e.g., competition, mutualism, facilitation, interference; Figure 10.3B,C). Food webs are networks of who eats whom in an ecosystem (Pimm 1982; Cohen et al. 1993) and have been the most common type of ecological networks studied so far in ecology (Berlow et al. 2004; Ings et al. 2009). Networks describing other interaction types have been investigated as well, such as host-parasitoid (Henri and Van Veen 2011), host-parasite (Lafferty et al. 2006), plant-plant facilitation (Verdú and Valiente-Banuet 2008), competition (Soliveres et al. 2015) and mutualistic networks. These latter have attracted increasing attention in the last two decades (e.g., pollination and seed dispersal; Jordano 1987; Bascompte et al. 2003; Jordano et al. 2003; Olesen et al. 2008).

Typical data sets of such interaction networks contain the lists of the species present in a given community and a list of the interactions between these species (i.e., filling in the adjacency matrix of Figure 10.2A2, B2). This can be done based on direct observations (e.g., observation of the consumption of an individual of one species by the individual of another species, observation of the visit of a pollinator on a given flower), indirect observations (e.g., gut content analysis to infer trophic links, pollen analysis to infer pollination links, stable isotopes, meta-barcoding, environmental DNA) or inference (based on traits, abundance, or similarity to another species whose diet is known).

Table 10.1 Typical types of ecological networks studied.

Network	Node	Link	E.g., of references
Interaction network	species, group of species	Inter-specific interaction (competition, predation, parasitism, mutualism, etc.)	(Jordano 1987; Dunne 2006; Lafferty et al. 2006; Verdú and Valiente-Banuet 2008)
Social network	Individuals	Social contact	(Hasenjager and Dugatkin 2015)
Spatial network (metacommunity, metapopulation, metaecosystem)	Local population/habitat fragment	Transfer of matter, individuals (dispersal), resources	(Hagen et al. 2012)
Co-occurrence network	Individuals, species	Co-occurrence in the same locality or physical contact (spatial overlap)	(Araújo et al. 2011; Morueta-Holme et al. 2016)

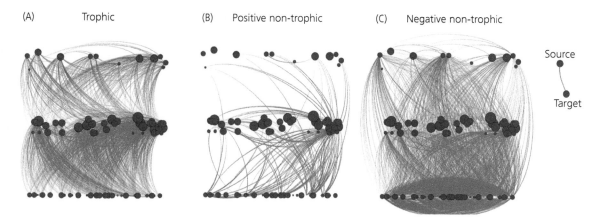

Figure 10.3 Example of three interaction networks for the Chilean web, which counts more than 100 species of the intertidal coast of central Chile, as well as feeding interactions (on the left), positive non-feeding links (such as facilitation for recruitment or refuge provisioning; in the middle) and negative non-feeding links (such as competition for space or predator interference; on the right) between these species. Nodes are organized vertically by trophic level (primary producers at the bottom and predators at the top) and horizontally randomly. Figure from Kéfi et al. (2015). The size of the nodes is proportional to the trophic degree of the species (i.e. how many feeding links the species has). The same species are represented in each network but the links represent a different interaction type in each of the three panels.

10.3.2 Toward multi-layer interaction networks

Traditionally, different interaction types have been studied in isolation from each other, and ecological networks most often contain information about a single interaction type at a time (Berlow et al. 2004; Ings et al. 2009; Kéfi et al. 2012). However, because species interact with each other in many different ways in nature, there has recently been a growing interest in the literature devoted to the description and understanding of networks combining different interaction types (e.g., Melián et al. 2009; Olff et al. 2009; Pocock et al. 2012; Kéfi et al. 2015). Furthermore, ecological network data is typically a snapshot of a community in time and space. Most ecological networks are, therefore, static descriptions of a given community, and very few studies have analyzed their temporal and spatial variability (Olesen et al. 2008; Trøjelsgaard and Olesen 2016). This requires obtaining different snapshots of an ecological community at different times or at different locations, thereby building *multi-layer networks* (Figure 10.1 right panel). Such multi-layer networks—in which layers represent either different interaction types, different times, or different locations—represent a new avenue of research in interaction networks (Pilosof et al. 2017).

Describing temporal and spatial variations in ecological networks—the changes in species but also in links—may provide insights into the mechanisms that generate these networks and their structure, as well as the mechanisms that provide resilience to ecological communities.

10.3.3 Other types of ecological networks

Spatial networks

In a spatial network, nodes (e.g., habitat patches) are locations in space (Figure 10.4). The links define the connections among the patches due to dispersal, nutrient flows, or other processes (Dale and Fortin 2010). Links can be directional or bidirectional. They can be binary or accounting for e.g., geographical distances between the patches. Nodes can have additional attributes such as the size or the shape of the patch. Patches can be classified as sinks or sources (depending on the population growth rate locally). So far, most work has been done on meta-populations, although recent theory has included the meta-community (McCann et al. 2005) as well as the meta-ecosystem concepts (Gravel et al. 2016). [See Chapter 12 of this book for more details about these types of networks.]

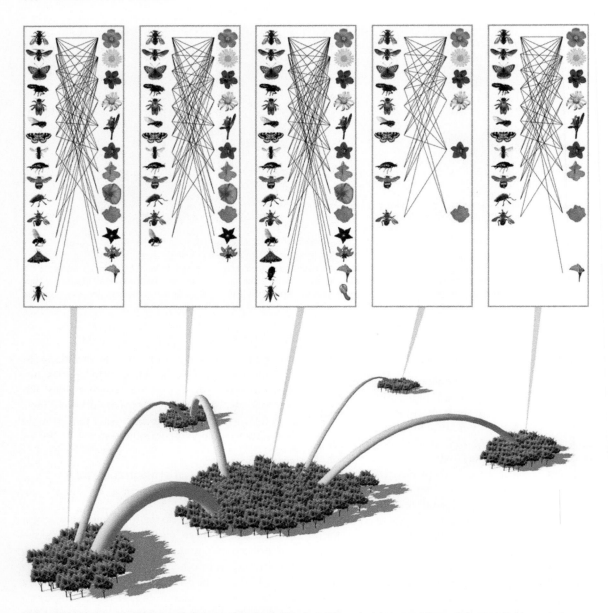

Figure 10.4 Example of ecological networks in space. Patches: habitat fragments, each of them containing a whole network of interactions. Connections between patches are due to species dispersal.

Figure from Hagen et al. (2012).

Co-occurrence networks

Co-occurrence networks use data to infer the presence of a link between two species. Nodes are species, and a link is present when two species are found in the same site (Araújo et al. 2011; Morueta-Holme et al. 2016) or if two individuals were found next to each other in space more frequently than expected by chance (Saiz and Alados 2011).

Because data collection of species interactions requires extensive efforts, co-occurrence networks have sometimes been used to reconstruct interaction networks. The development of the methods to do such reconstructions has a long history and keeps being refined (Sanderson and Pimm 2015), but the intuitive idea is that significantly positive species associations could be considered evidence of positive interactions, while significantly negative associations are assumed to reflect negative (competitive) interactions (Morueta-Holme et al. 2016). Therefore, in these networks, links have signs, plus or minus respectively, for positive or negative spatial associations. Limitations regarding the use of significant spatial associations as proxies for species interactions have recently been discussed in the literature (e.g. Barner et al. 2018; Freilich et al. 2018). Indeed, there are many reasons why we may not be able to reconstruct species interactions from species spatial associations, in particular because species interactions are not the only process driving species co-occurrence.

10.3.4 Broad questions asked in ecological networks

One of the long-lasting challenges in ecology is to understand how and why so many species can coexist in an ecosystem but also how and when these communities are stable, especially in the face of current global change. Robert May demonstrated, in the early seventies, that model communities with many species were in general less stable than model communities with fewer species (May 1973). In other words, the more complex an ecological community (i.e., with many species and links), the less likely it is to be stable, according to May's model analyses.

These results stimulated decades of research on ecological networks to decipher how the diverse and complex communities observed in nature could persist. At least part of the answer lies in the fact that, in May's communities, the location and the intensity of the links between the species were picked randomly. Indeed, the challenge for ecologists has been to find out in which ways

natural communities differ from random ones, and how these non-random structural properties contribute to the dynamics and stability of complex ecological communities. [See Chapter 6 in this book for more information on May's approach and recent developments]. This paved the way for numerous studies on the structure of ecological communities, especially food webs. Are there structural regularities or universal patterns in ecological networks? What are the drivers of species interactions and network structure (e.g., relative roles of traits, habitat and phylogeny)?

In the nineties, there was a shift of interest from identifying the cause of the emergence and maintenance of species diversity to investigating the consequences of this diversity for ecosystem functioning (Loreau 2010). This happened because of the increasing awareness of the growing species extinction rates, which raised the questions of the ability of ecological communities to maintain the services they provide to human populations despite the loss of species. What are the consequences of the observed network structures in terms of species diversity, community functioning, and stability to perturbations (e.g., species extinctions, habitat fragmentation, climate change)?

To sum up, different network types are studied in ecology, the most common ones so far being networks of interactions between species, among which feeding interactions have attracted the most attention so far (i.e., food webs). Lots of studies have been devoted to the description of the structure of these networks. The following parts present general structural measures of networks before focusing on the structure of ecological networks.

10.4 Quantifying networks structure

Fundamental network descriptors are the number of nodes (S), the number of links (L), and the connectance (fraction of realized links, i.e., L/S^2). Topological properties of networks can be divided in *local* (from a single node perspective, i.e., a node and its nearest neighbors) and *global* properties (from the whole network perspective, i.e., describing the structure of the entire network). Here are a few properties commonly used in ecological networks (see Dunne 2006; Newman 2010; Delmas et al. 2019 for more thorough reviews).

10.4.1 Local network descriptors

A key property of a node is its *degree*, i.e., its number of links with other nodes in the network. For a directed network, the sum of the adjacency matrix's rows and columns provides the *incoming* and *outgoing* degrees $k_i = \sum_j A_{ij}$, $k_i^{out} = \sum_j A_{ji}$ (see Figure 10.5A2). For an undirected network, the degree of a node is the sum over either the rows or the columns: $k_i = \sum_j A_{ji} = \sum_i A_{ji}$. In-degree (i.e., the number of resources in a food web) is also called the *generality*, and the out-degree (i.e., the number of consumers in a food web) is also called *vulnerability* in the ecological literature. The total degree of a node is the sum of its in- and out-degrees. Species with a high degree are generalists whereas species with a low degree are specialists (e.g., Memmott et al. 2004).

A convention is to refer to species that do not eat other organisms as "basal" species. In food webs, those are typically primary producers. A species' *trophic level* indicates how many nodes away along the food chain a given species is from basal species. Basal species are at trophic level one, and their consumers are at higher levels (Figure 10.5A1). While this is straight-forward in food chains, calculating a species trophic level is more challenging in complex food webs where consumers can eat species that belong to different trophic levels, and where trophic levels are therefore not necessarily discrete. In complex food webs, several measures of trophic levels have been proposed in the literature. For example, the *prey-averaged trophic level* of a species is calculated as one plus the mean trophic level of all of the species resources, where the trophic level of a resource is the chain length from the resource to a basal species (Williams and Martinez 2004).

Centrality describes the ability of a particular node to influence other nodes in the network. Centrality is one of the ways of measuring how important a given node is in a network. There are several measures of centrality (e.g., degree centrality, closeness centrality, betweenness centrality). For example,

betweenness centrality assumes that a node is more central if many shortest paths pass through the node (see Section 10.4.3 for a definition of shortest path).

10.4.2 Quasi-local network descriptors (intermediate description level)

Motifs are unique *n*-node sub-graphs of a network ("recurrent, significant patterns of interconnection" (Milo et al. 2002)); they are sometimes referred to as the "building blocks" of a network. The relative frequency of different *n*-node sub-graphs, or *modules*, contains information about the structure of the overall network. A question is whether certain modules are over- (or under-) represented in a given network (Milo et al. 2002), i.e., more (or less) frequent than expected in a random network. Motifs are over-represented modules, and they represent typical relationships between the nodes of the network. These motifs differ among network types (Milo et al. 2002). An example of a typical three-species motif in food webs in the tritrophic food chain (where species A eats species B which eats species C) (Stouffer et al. 2007).

The *clustering coefficient* is the probability that any two neighbors of a given node are themselves connected by a link. For a node *i* of degree k_i, the local clustering coefficient is $C_i = \frac{2L_i}{k_i(k_i-1)}$ where L_i is the number of links between the k_i neighbors of node *i*. C_i is between 0 and 1. C_i measures the *local link density*. $C_i = 0$ means that there are no links between *i*'s neighbors, $C_i = 1$ means that all *i*'s neighbors link to each other. This metrics informs about whether species are organized in small connected subsets of species.

10.4.3 Global network descriptors

The *degree distribution*, p_k, provides the probability that a randomly selected node in the network has degree *k*. $p_k = \frac{N_k}{N}$ with N_k the number of nodes with degree *k* and $\sum_k p_k = 1$ (see Figure 10.5A3). While the degree of a species provides information about how generalist the species is, the degree distribution shows how degree values (i.e., how the

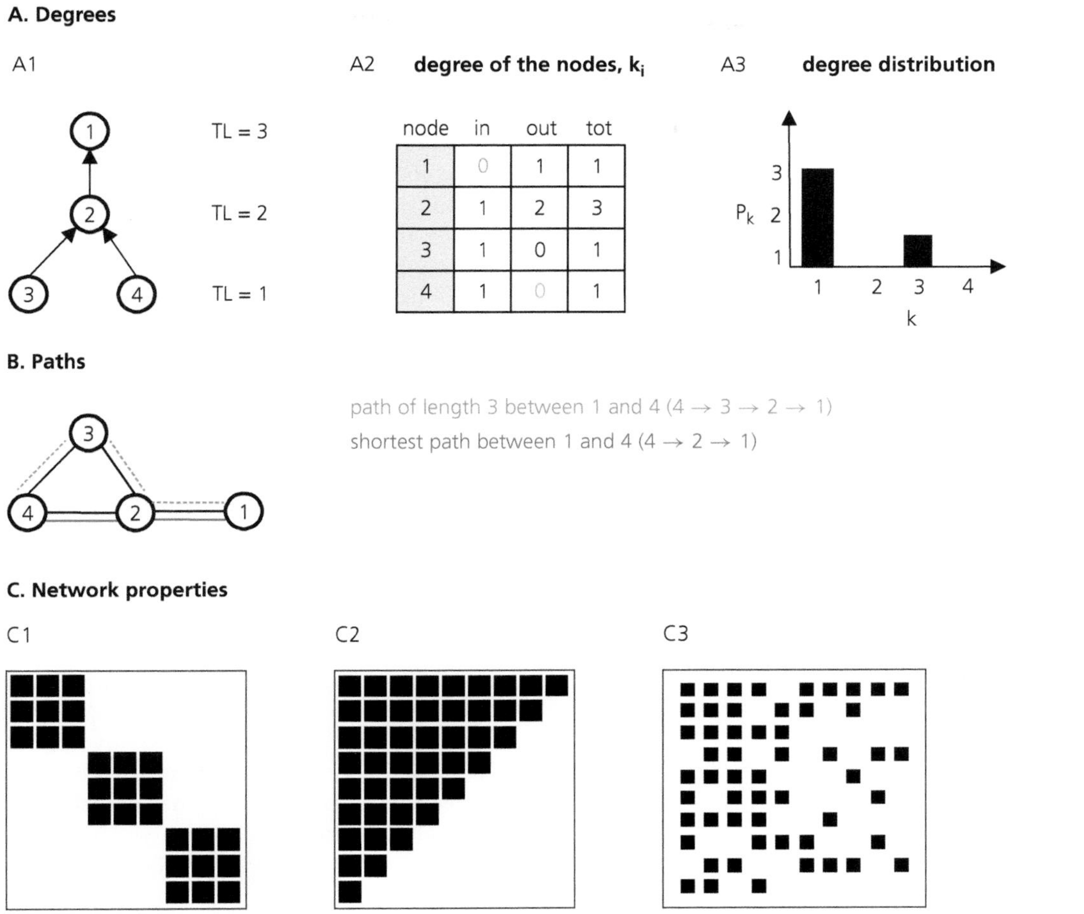

A. Degrees

A1

TL = 3

TL = 2

TL = 1

A2   **degree of the nodes, k_i**

node	in	out	tot
1	0	1	1
2	1	2	3
3	1	0	1
4	1	0	1

A3   **degree distribution**

B. Paths

path of length 3 between 1 and 4 ($4 \rightarrow 3 \rightarrow 2 \rightarrow 1$)

shortest path between 1 and 4 ($4 \rightarrow 2 \rightarrow 1$)

C. Network properties

C1

C2

C3

Figure 10.5 Cartoon representation of a few network properties. A. Example of a simple directed network. On the right, TL indicates the trophic level of the nodes. A2) in-, out- and total degree of each node of network A1. In orange, 0 is the in-degree of node 1 obtained by summing the elements of row 1 of the adjacency matrix on Figure 10.2A2. In green, 0 is the out-degree of species 4 obtained by summing the elements of column 4 of the adjacency matrix in Figure 10.2A2) Number of nodes, P_k, whose degree is k in network A1. B. Example of a path (in purple) and of the shortest path (in red) between node 1 and 4 in a non-directed network. C. Caricature representation of a modular (C1), nested (C2) or random (C3) matrix (black squares represent an interaction between a pair of species).

number of links) are spread among the species of the community. In steeper distributions, there is a larger disparity between the degrees of the different species. The degree distribution allows identifying important species such as keystone species, whose extinctions could have disproportionate effects on the whole community (Solé and Montoya 2001).

A *path* is a route that runs along the links of a network visiting each node only once (Figure 10.5B, purple path). The path's length is the number of links the patch contains, i.e., the number of links

separating two nodes. The *shortest path* is the path between two nodes with the fewer number of links (d_{ij} or d) (Figure 10.5B, red path). It can be used as a measure of distance between two nodes. In an undirected network $d_{ij} = d_{ji}$, but not in a directed network. The *average path length* is the average distance between all pairs of nodes in the network. We talk about a cycle when the path has the same start and end node.

A *community* is a group of nodes that are more connected to each other than to other nodes outside the community (Figure 10.5C1). In other words, a community is a locally dense connected sub-graph in a network. The objective of community detection is to estimate the number and the size of the communities in a network.

Modularity is metric which has been proposed to achieve partitioning a network in non-overlapping groups of highly interacting nodes (i.e., in communities). Modularity is defined by comparing the density of links between the nodes of a given group to the density of links between the same nodes in a randomly rewired network (Newman 2006). A modularity close to 0 indicates that there is no significant community structure. A higher modularity implies a better partition of the network. The idea is therefore to find the partition of the network that maximizes modularity. A series of algorithms exist to achieve that (Fortunato 2010; Fortunato and Hric 2016).

Another approach to find groups of nodes in a network consists in gathering nodes that are the most similar in terms of their connectivity patterns: nodes of the same group are not necessarily more connected with each other than with the rest of the network but they share the same connectivity pattern, i.e., they are connected to similar partners in similar ways. In particular, a class of models called *Stochastic Block Models* is dedicated to such task (Newman and Leicht 2007; Daudin et al. 2008). While the modularity analysis finds subsets of interdependent groups of nodes, the Stochastic Block Model approach identifies nodes that play a similar role in the network.

Nestedness was originally defined in the context of island biogeography; it measures patterns of how generalists and specialists interact (Bascompte et al. 2003). In a nested network, the links of specialist nodes are subsets of the links of more generalist nodes (Figure 10.5C2).

10.4.4 Extensions to multilayer networks

Metrics quantifying the structure of multilayer networks are on their way to be developed in ecology (Melián et al. 2009; Fontaine et al. 2011; Pocock et al. 2012; Kéfi et al. 2016). Recent advances in network science have produced tools to study community structure in time developing networks (Mucha et al. 2010), spatial networks (Miele et al. 2014) and more generally multi-layer networks (Boccaletti et al. 2014; Kivelä et al. 2014; Pilosof et al. 2017). The idea is then to use the information contained in the different layers of the network to quantify structure. For example, groups identified using the Stochastic Block Model approach on a multiplex network would identify species that have a similar connectivity patterns in all the different layers. Such an approach applied on the Chilean web identified fourteen groups of species that were similar in terms of their feeding, facilitation, and competition links (Kéfi et al. 2016).

10.5 Structural properties of ecological networks

Food webs and the study of their structure have a long history in ecology, but they have recently attracted a renewed interest with the emergence of improved data and the arrival of new statistical tools (see Chapter 2 in Pascual and Dunne 2006 for an overview and historical perspective on this). One of the old questions in the study of food web structure has been to determine whether there are universal patterns (across ecosystem types and geographical locations), and if so, to identify the processes that drive these patterns. It turns out that there are common structural properties, but that these differ from other interaction types. The next part presents some of these common properties identified for the most commonly studied interaction networks, namely food webs and mutualistic networks (Ings et al. 2009).

10.5.1 Food webs

Compared to other networks, food webs tend to be species poorer, have a relatively high connectance, a low clustering coefficient (Dunne et al. 2002), a short path length with the average mean distance between two species being two links (Williams et al. 2002), and they tend to be *disassortative* (Newman 2002), i.e., have a low probability that nodes with a high degree connect to other nodes with high degrees. Discussions about whether there are scale-invariant properties (i.e., properties which do not depend on the number of species) in food webs are still ongoing (see Chapter 2 in Pascual and Dunne 2006).

Food webs, moreover, tend to be organized into communities, i.e., groups of species that interact preferentially with each other and less with the rest of the network (Moore and William Hunt 1988; Krause et al. 2003; Rezende et al. 2009).

The distribution of interaction strengths was found to be non-random, with strong top-down effects of consumers on their resources at lower trophic levels and strong bottom up effects of resource on their consumers at higher trophic levels (de Ruiter et al. 1995). Moreover, food webs are characterized by many weak and a few strong interactions (McCann et al. 1998), and weak interactions tend to be concentrated in long loops (Neutel et al. 2002).

There does not seem to be a consensus about what food web degree distributions look like, but they tend to differ from what is expected in random networks (i.e., a Poisson distribution), and they tend to have heavy tails that decay faster than power laws (e.g., truncated power laws or exponentials) (Camacho et al. 2002; Dunne et al. 2002; Jordano et al. 2003; Montoya et al. 2006).

The niche model

Interestingly, relatively simple models are able to generate realistic structures of food webs. The *niche model* is one such model that is frequently used (Williams and Martinez 2000). The niche model has two key parameters: the number of species and the connectance (i.e., the fraction of realized links) of the web. Each species is assigned a uniformly random *niche value* (n_i), which determines its position along a line (Figure 10.6). Each species is then assigned a feeding range r_i. The center of this feeding range c_i is chosen to be smaller than the species niche value n_i (see next part for the interpretation of this, e.g., in terms of body size). A species consumes all species found in its feeding range (i.e., in that segment of the line). The feeding range therefore determines the width of species trophic niches. This relatively simple model is able to produce food web structures

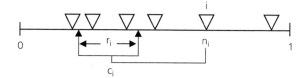

Figure 10.6 Diagram of the niche model. Species niche values, n_i, are represented by a triangle. C_i is the center of the feeding range of species i (typically smaller than n_i) and r_i is its width. Species i is assumed to eat all the species whose niche value end up in its feeding range. Figure redrawn from Williams and Martinez (2000).

comparable to those observed in data (Williams and Martinez 2000). Variations as well as updates of the niche model have been proposed (Allesina et al. 2008; Williams et al. 2010).

Body size and food web structure

Body size is a fundamental trait of organisms, related to many activities and biological rates (Brown et al. 2004). Predators (excluding pathogens, parasites, and parasitoids) have been found to be one to three orders of magnitude larger than their prey in terms of body size (Woodward et al. 2005; Brose et al. 2006a). Body size is thereby a strong driver of food web structure: it creates a hierarchical structure, in which species consume prey smaller than themselves.

In the niche model previously mentioned (Figure 10.6), the niche space of the community is collapsed into a single axis, and studies have explored the ecological meaning of such a single niche dimension. Because it creates a hierarchical ordering of feeding niches, body size is a candidate for this single niche dimension (Williams and Martinez 2000) and has been extensively used to parametrize dynamical food web models (see upcoming Section 10.6 on dynamics and Chapter 9 of this book; Yodzis and Innes 1992; Brose et al. 2006a).

While predators are usually larger than their prey, parasitoids and pathogens are typically smaller than their host (Brose et al. 2006a). This breaks down the organizing principles on which e.g., the niche model is based. Extensions of the niche model have been suggested in the literature to account for both feeding and parasitic interactions (Warren et al. 2010).

10.5.2 Mutualistic webs

Plant-animal mutualistic networks have been mostly described as bipartite webs, with two types of nodes—plants and animals—and links between these two groups. They have been shown to be highly structured.

One common property is the heterogeneity in the number of connections per species: most species have a few connections while a few have a large number of links (specialists vs generalists) (Jordano et al. 2003). As a consequence, degree distributions are heavy-tailed but with a truncation because of physical constraints on the number of interactions per species (e.g., due to morphological or phenological mismatch between the interaction partners), the so-called "forbidden links" (Jordano et al. 2003).

Species traits are known to play a key role in whether species can and do interact (Bartomeus et al. 2016). Trait mismatch may for example explain many forbidden links. For instance, short-tongued pollinators cannot reach the nectar in long-corolla flowers, and therefore pollinate them (Nilsson 1988; Stang et al. 2006; Olesen Jens M. et al. 1991).

Plant-animal mutualistic networks moreover tend to be more nested than expected by chance (Bascompte et al. 2003). This means that specialists interact with a subset of the species with which more generalist species interact. There is therefore a core of generalist plants and animals that interact with each other and concentrate a large number of interactions in the web. This also means that specialist species interact with the most generalist ones. They are also asymmetrical, so that if a plant depends strongly on an animal species, the animal depends weakly on the plant (Bascompte et al. 2006). [See Chapter 7 of this book for more detailed information about mutualistic networks and their structure.]

To conclude, the last decades of studies of ecological network's structure suggest that food webs and mutualistic networks have specific structural properties. Among others, food webs seem to be more modular while plant-pollinators tend to be more nested than expected by chance. A question that these results raise is: what are the functional consequences of the observed structures? The next part presents results of dynamical models investigating the consequence of network structural properties for their dynamics.

10.6 From the structure to the dynamics of ecological networks

What are the consequences of the structural properties of ecological networks in terms of species coexistence, productivity and communities' ability to respond to perturbations? In the seventies and the years after, the concept of stability was dominated by the local stability analysis used by Robert May in his influential book and papers (May 1973). During the nineties, the questions about stability were increasingly transformed into questions about the response of ecological communities to perturbations: loss of species, changes in environmental conditions such as climate or habitat fragmentation, for example.

Stability can be assessed using a purely structural approach, i.e., without dynamics, informed solely by network structure. The principle is to evaluate the impact of the removal of nodes on the network's integrity. If the removal of a single node can have a limited effect, the removal of several could break the network. Co-extinction analysis (or "knock-out" simulations) consists in sequentially removing species (one at a time) in a network and counting the number of secondary extinctions following the loss of each species. A classical rule in food webs for example is to assume that all species that have no resource anymore go extinct as well. Such an approach can be used to assess network *robustness*. This can be done in several ways, e.g., by looking at the shape of the extinction pattern curve (displaying the fraction of secondary extinctions as a function of the fraction of primary extinctions) (Memmott et al. 2004), or by evaluating the fraction of primary species loss that leads to at least 50% of total species loss (Dunne et al. 2002). Such simulations suggest that food webs are much more robust to random species extinctions than to targeted extinctions of well-connected species (Dunne et al. 2002). Dunne et al. (2002) moreover found that food web robustness increases with increasing connectance. In plant pollinator networks, the order of pollinator loss has an effect as well on plant extinctions, but not as importantly as in food webs (Memmott et al. 2004).

Shifting from a structural to a dynamical description of ecological networks allows addressing the question of how food web structure relates to ecosystem stability in a richer way. Dynamical simulations have long been limited to ecological configurations with a few species (e.g., study of modules of interactions), assuming that populations are close to, or at, equilibrium (e.g., linear stability analysis) and that relationships between species are linear (e.g., Type I functional response in Lotka–Volterra models). These studies have considerably improved our understanding of the drivers of community dynamics and stability. Only recently has the improvement in computer power allowed relaxing these simplifying assumptions, and in particular simulating the dynamics of species-rich ecological networks. Extensions of Lotka–Volterra equations to multi-species communities have been mapped to food web data to investigate the role of food web structure and interaction strengths on species persistence (e.g., de Ruiter et al. 1995), but these typically still assume linear relationships. Yodzis and Innes (1992) developed a bioenergetic model of population dynamics with nonlinear functional responses. This can be combined with either food web data or generative models of complex food webs (such as the niche model) to run dynamical simulations of food webs with a realistic structure (e.g., Brose et al. 2006b). In such complex nonlinear models, one issue is the parametrization of the model, but allometric scaling of many biological rates to species body masses can be used to parametrize these models. [See Chapter 9 of this book for more details about trait-based models.]

These dynamical models have proven to be useful to explore the dynamical constraints on network structure as well as the structural constraints on dynamics (Brose et al. 2006b; Thébault and Fontaine 2010; Stouffer and Bascompte 2011; Kéfi et al. 2016). For example, it has been argued that the organization of food webs in communities contributed to reduce the spread of perturbations by containing them within the communities, thereby increasing food webs' ability to withstand perturbations (Thébault and Fontaine 2010; Stouffer and Bascompte 2011). de Ruiter and colleagues (1995) showed that taking empirical interaction strength values into account increased the local stability of ecological communities in comparison with random interaction strength values. The importance of body size has also been highlighted in studies which have shown that size structured

food webs have a higher persistence (i.e., a higher fraction of species surviving at the end of simulations; Brose et al. 2006b; Otto et al. 2007). Exploration of predator–prey body mass ratios in the nonlinear dynamics of complex food webs has shown that increasing predator–prey body mass ratios increased persistence up to a saturation level that is reached when predators are ten to one hundred times larger than their prey. These body mass ratios are consistent with those observed in empirical data (Brose et al. 2006b; Otto et al. 2007). This suggests that the body mass structure of natural food webs could enhance their stability.

The fact that mutualistic networks tend to be more nested than expected by chance seems to increase species persistence and community resilience, evaluated as the speed of return to equilibrium after a perturbation (Bastolla et al. 2009; Thébault and Fontaine 2010). [See Chapter 7 for more information.]

Dynamical models have only recently started investigating ecological networks simultaneously including several interaction types (e.g., Goudard and Loreau 2008; Gross 2008; Melián et al. 2009; Allesina and Tang 2012; Kéfi et al. 2012, 2016; Mougi and Kondoh 2012; Sauve et al. 2014; Lurgi et al. 2016; Miele et al. 2019), showing that the presence, the relative abundance and the structure of the different interaction types could affect species diversity, community dynamics, functioning and response to environmental perturbations.

In summary, the combination of empirical patterns and dynamical models has revealed that not only the complexity but also the structure of the links were important determinant of the stability of ecological networks. While both data and models have so far focused on single layer networks, the description and analysis of ecological networks with multiple layers has gained recent interest.

10.7 Challenges

Ecological networks are a fast-expanding topic in the ecological literature with interesting promises toward improving our understanding of the drivers of community dynamics and resilience but also a number of challenges ahead. Here is a selection of a few of them.

Improving the quality of the data as well as the number of ecological data sets available is key for detecting network structure and inferring dynamics. The change in data quality across the years has hindered the description of network structure, and especially the identification of possible universal patterns (Dunne 2006).

The vast majority of the data sets currently available are presence/absence data and do not include interaction strengths. Early on, Yodzis (1981) showed that incorporating realistic interaction strengths (i.e., studying structured interaction matrices) increased the stability of May's community matrices. More recent research suggested that the non-random pattern of strong and weak links is important for stability (de Ruiter et al. 1995; Neutel et al. 2002). Moreover, interaction strengths are known to vary in time and with environmental and biological context. One path forward is to start getting beyond presence/absence data in ecological networks and to attempt at getting a better understanding of interaction strengths, their drivers, structure and dynamics (see Berlow et al. (2004) for a review on this point).

A number of species, species groups or ecosystem compartments have been neglected in ecological networks, notably parasites and detritus that are nonetheless known to play a fundamental role in many ecosystems (Moore et al. 2004; Lafferty et al. 2006). Further research in that direction is needed and has started to emerge.

Studying networks combining different interaction types would contribute to a more comprehensive but also a more complex view of ecological communities (Kéfi et al. 2012). It is more generally time to go beyond the snapshot analysis of ecological networks, describing ecological communities at an arbitrary temporal and spatial scale. The importance of considering communities within a spatial context has been highlighted (Holt 2002; McCann et al. 2005; Amarasekare 2008) and is particularly relevant to understand the effects of spatial perturbations such as habitat loss or fragmentation. Most published food webs are constructed from summary data, ignoring possible important seasonal and ontogenetic changes. The assumption of constancy of food web structure

is indeed often violated. A number of studies have explicitly investigated temporal changes in networks (Winemiller 1990; Woodward et al. 2002; Olesen et al. 2008; McLaughlin et al. 2010; Pilosof et al. 2013), but lots of work along these lines remains to be done. To achieve this, research in ecological networks can benefit from network studies outside of ecology, but it can also contribute to it, by providing novel insight due to our mechanistic understanding of ecological systems.

Because network data collection is time consuming and can be expensive, learning how to infer interactions from proxies is a promising avenue of research (e.g., Bartomeus et al. 2016). One way to do that is to build minimal mathematical models of network assembly that succeed in creating networks with a realistic structure. The niche model is probably the most successful such model for food webs (Williams and Martinez 2000). Similar approaches have been proposed for mutualistic interactions as well (Saavedra et al. 2009). Another way consists in identify biological properties that determine whether an interaction between two species is likely to take place or not. This question has for example been explored by searching for correlations between structural patterns and biological attributes. For example, the abundance of interacting species can help estimate the probability of interactions between two species (Vázquez et al. 2009). Certain traits can determine species that can or cannot interact (Bartomeus et al. 2016). In food webs, body size is an important driver of trophic interactions (Woodward et al. 2005), but traits can also constrain the possibility of an interaction to happen (Jordano et al. 2003; Olesen Jens M. et al. 2011). Closely related species often share similar traits, so phylogeny can also help predict species interactions (Ives et al. 2006).

Finally, the role of evolution in shaping ecological network organization still remains largely open (Loeuille and Loreau 2005; Guill 2010). Models of network assembly that incorporate evolutionary processes have started shedding light on how evolution may affect the organization of food webs (Loeuille and Loreau 2005; Guill 2010) but also of mutualistic and competitive communities (Loeuille 2010).

10.8 Conclusion

After decades of work on the topic, understanding the emergence and persistence of complex ecological systems remains a puzzle. Ecological networks are indeed difficult to measure and model. The manipulation of large systems in nature is often impossible; the modeling of simplified ecological systems may not be scalable to larger, more realistic ones; and the modeling of complex systems has its own challenges, in particular because of the number of parameters needed. Work of the last decades has provided increasing ecological network data of increasing quality and extent. Moreover, plausible structure, nonlinear relationships, realistic interaction strengths and trait dependencies have been incorporated in ecological network models, which start providing a more realistic picture—and therefore understanding—of the relation between the structure of ecological networks on the one hand and their dynamics and stability on the other hand. This may eventually help predicting the consequences of biodiversity loss and understanding the steps needed to preserve ecological communities in a rapidly changing world. There are clearly still many gaps to bridge before ecological models become truly predictive, but they can already help us identify important stabilizing and destabilizing factors for ecological communities.

References

Albert, R., Jeong, H., and Barabási, A. -L. (1999). Internet: Diameter of the World-Wide Web. *Nature* 401: 130–1.

Albert, R., Jeong, H., and Barabási, A.-L. (2000). Error and attack tolerance of complex networks. *Nature* 406: 378–82.

Allesina, S., Alonso, D., and Pascual, M. (2008). A general model for food web structure. *Science* 320: 658–61.

Allesina, S. and Tang, S. (2012). Stability criteria for complex ecosystems. *Nature* 483: 205–8.

Amarasekare, P. (2008). Spatial Dynamics of Foodwebs. *Annu. Rev. Ecol. Evol. Syst.* 39: 479–500.

Araújo, M. B., Rozenfeld, A., Rahbek, C., and Marquet, P. A. (2011). Using species co-occurrence networks to assess the impacts of climate change. *Ecography* 34: 897–908.

Barabási, A. -L. and Albert, R. (1999). Emergence of scaling in random networks. *Science* 286: 509–12.

Barner, A. K., Coblentz, K. E., Hacker, S. D., and Menge, B. A. (2018). Fundamental contradictions among observational and experimental estimates of non-trophic species interactions. *Ecology* 99: 557–66.

Bartomeus, I., Gravel, D., Tylianakis, J. M., Aizen, M. A., Dickie, I. A., and Bernard-Verdier, M. (2016). A common framework for identifying linkage rules across different types of interactions. *Funct. Ecol.* 30: 1894–1903.

Bascompte, J., Jordano, P., Melián, C. J., and Olesen, J. M. (2003). The nested assembly of plant–animal mutualistic networks. *Proc. Natl. Acad. Sci.* 100: 9383–7.

Bascompte, J., Jordano, P., and Olesen, J. M. (2006). Asymmetric Coevolutionary Networks Facilitate Biodiversity Maintenance. *Science* 312: 431–3.

Bastolla, U., Fortuna, M. A., Pascual-García, A., Ferrera, A., Luque, B., and Bascompte, J. (2009). The architecture of mutualistic networks minimizes competition and increases biodiversity. *Nature* 458: 1018–20.

Berlow, E. L., Neutel, A. -M., Cohen, J. E., De Ruiter, P. C., Ebenman, B., Emmerson, M., et al. (2004). Interaction strengths in food webs: Issues and opportunities. *J. Anim. Ecol.* 73: 585–98.

Boccaletti, S., Bianconi, G., Criado, R., del Genio, C. I., Gómez-Gardeñes, J., Romance, M., et al. (2014). The structure and dynamics of multilayer networks. *Phys. Rep.* 544: 1–122.

Borrett, S., Moody, J., and Edelmann, A. (2014). The rise of network ecology: Maps of the topic diversity and scientific collaboration. *Ecol. Model.* 293(111): 1271–17.

Brose, U., Jonsson, T., Berlow, E. L., Warren, P., Banasek-Richter, C., Bersier, L. -F., et al. (2006a). Consumer–resource body-size relationships in natural food webs. *Ecology* 87: 2411–17.

Brose, U., Williams, R. J., and Martinez, N. D. (2006b). Allometric scaling enhances stability in complex food webs. *Ecol. Lett.* 9: 1228–36.

Brown, J. H., Gillooly, J. F., Allen, A. P., Savage, V. M., and West, G. B. (2004). Toward a metabolic theory of ecology. *Ecology* 85: 1771–89.

Camacho, J., Guimerà, R., and Nunes Amaral, L. A. (2002). Robust patterns in food web structure. *Phys. Rev. Lett.* 88: 228,102.

Cohen, J. E., Pimm, S. L., Yodzis, P. and Saldana, J. (1993). Body sizes of animal predators and animal prey in food webs. *J. Anim. Ecol.* 62(1)67–78, https://www.jstor.org/stable/pdf/5483.pdf?seq=1.

Daudin, J-J., Picard, F., and Robin, S. A. (2008). Mixture Model for Random Graphs. Stat Comput.18: 173–83, DOI: 10.1007/s11222-007-9046-7, https://link.springer.com/article/10.1007/s11222-007-9046-7.

Dale, M. R. T. and Fortin, M. -J. (2010). From graphs to spatial graphs. *Annu. Rev. Ecol. Evol. Syst.* 41: 21–38.

Delmas, E., Besson, M., Brice, M.-H., Burkle, L. A., Riva, G. V. D., Fortin, M.-J., et al. (2019). Analysing ecological networks of species interactions. *Biol. Rev.* 94: 16–36.

Dunne, J. A. (2006). The network structure of food webs. In *Ecological Networks: Linking Structure to Dynamics in Food Webs*. Oxford: Oxford University Press, pp. 27–86.

Dunne, J. A., Williams, R. J., and Martinez, N. D. (2002). Food-web structure and network theory: The role of connectance and size. *Proc. Natl. Acad. Sci.* 99: 12,917–22.

Fontaine, C., Guimarães, P. R., Kéfi, S., Loeuille, N., Memmott, J., van der Putten, W. H., et al. (2011). The ecological and evolutionary implications of merging different types of networks. *Ecol. Lett.* 14: 1170–81.

Fortunato, S. (2010). Community detection in graphs. *Phys. Rep.* 486: 75–174.

Fortunato, S. and Hric, D. (2016). Community detection in networks: A user guide. *Phys. Rep.*, 659: 1–44, https://www.sciencedirect.com/science/article/abs/pii/S0370157316302964.

Freilich, M. A., Wieters, E., Broitman, B. R., Marquet, P. A., and Navarrete, S. A. (2018). Species co-occurrence networks: Can they reveal trophic and non-trophic interactions in ecological communities? *Ecology* 99: 690–9.

Goudard, A. and Loreau, M. (2008). Nontrophic interactions, biodiversity, and ecosystem functioning: An interaction web model. *Am. Nat.* 171: 91–106.

Gravel, D., Massol, F. and Leibold, M. A. (2016). Stability and complexity in model meta-ecosystems. *Nat. Commun.* 7: 12,457.

Gross, K. (2008). Positive interactions among competitors can produce species-rich communities. *Ecol. Lett.* 11: 929–36.

Guill, C. (2010). A model of large-scale evolution of complex food webs. *Math. Model. Nat. Phenom.* 5: 139–58.

Hagen, M., Kissling, W. D., Rasmussen, C., De Aguiar, M. A. M., Brown, L. E., Carstensen, D. W., et al. (2012). Biodiversity, species interactions and ecological networks in a fragmented world. In Jacob, U. and Woodward, G. (eds.), *Advances in Ecological Research, Global Change in Multispecies Systems Part 1*. Cambridge, Massachusetts: Academic Press, 89–210, DOI: 10.1101/686451.

Hasenjager, M. J. and Dugatkin, L. A. (2015). Social network analysis in behavioral ecology. In Naguib, M., Brockmann, H. J., Mitani, J. C., Simmons, L. W., Barrett, L., Healy, S., et al. (eds.), *Advances in the Study of Behavior*. Cambridge, Massachusetts: Academic Press, pp. 39–114, DOI: 10.1101/686451.

Henri, D. C. and Van Veen, F. J. F. (2011). Body size, life history and the structure of host–parasitoid networks. In Belgrano, A. (ed.), *Advances in Ecological Research, The Role of Body Size in Multispecies Systems*. Cambridge, Massachusetts: Academic Press, pp. 135–80.

Holt, R. D. (2002). Food webs in space: On the interplay of dynamic instability and spatial processes. *Ecol. Res.* 17: 261–73.

Ings, T. C., Montoya, J. M., Bascompte, J., Blüthgen, N., Brown, L., Dormann, C. F., et al. (2009). Ecological networks—beyond food webs. *J. Anim. Ecol.* 78: 253–69.

Ives, A. R., Godfray, H. C. J., Heard, A. E. S. B., and Losos, E. J. B. (2006). Phylogenetic analysis of trophic associations. *Am. Nat.* 168: E1–E14.

Jordano, P. (1987). Patterns of mutualistic interactions in pollination and seed dispersal: Connectance, dependence asymmetries, and coevolution. *Am. Nat.* 129: 657–77.

Jordano, P., Bascompte, J., and Olesen, J. M. (2003). Invariant properties in coevolutionary networks of plant–animal interactions. *Ecol. Lett.* 6: 69–81.

Kéfi, S., Berlow, E. L., Wieters, E. A., Joppa, L. N., Wood, S. A., Brose, U., et al. (2015). Network structure beyond food webs: Mapping non-trophic and trophic interactions on Chilean rocky shores. *Ecology* 96: 291–303.

Kéfi, S., Berlow, E. L., Wieters, E. A., Navarrete, S. A., Petchey, O. L., Wood, S. A., et al. (2012). More than a meal … integrating non-feeding interactions into food webs. *Ecol. Lett.* 15(4): 291–300.

Kéfi, S., Miele, V., Wieters, E. A., Navarrete, S. A., and Berlow, E. L. (2016). How structured is the entangled bank? The surprisingly simple organization of multiplex ecological networks leads to increased persistence and resilience. *PLOS Biol.* 14: e1002527.

Kivelä, M., Arenas, A., Barthelemy, M., Gleeson, J. P., Moreno, Y., and Porter, M. A. (2014). Multilayer networks. *J. Complex Netw.* 2(3): 203–71.

Krause, A. E., Frank, K. A., Mason, D. M., Ulanowicz, R. E., and Taylor, W. W. (2003). Compartments revealed in food-web structure. *Nature* 426: 282–85.

Lafferty, K. D., Dobson, A. P., and Kuris, A. M. (2006). Parasites dominate food web links. *Proc. Natl. Acad. Sci.* 103: 11, 211–16.

Loeuille, N. (2010). Influence of evolution on the stability of ecological communities. *Ecol. Lett.* 13: 1536–45.

Loeuille, N. and Loreau, M. (2005). Evolutionary emergence of size-structured food webs. *Proc. Natl. Acad. Sci.* 102: 5761–6.

Loreau, M. (2010). From populations to ecosystems. In Simon A. Levin and Henry S. Horn (eds.), *Monographs in Population Biology*. Princeton: Princeton University Press.

Lurgi, M., Montoya, D., and Montoya, J. M. (2016). The effects of space and diversity of interaction types on the stability of complex ecological networks. *Theor. Ecol.*, early view.

May, R. M. (1973). *Stability and Complexity in Model Ecosystems*. Princeton: Princeton University Press.

McCann, K., Hastings, A., and Huxel, G. R. (1998). Weak trophic interactions and the balance of nature. *Nature* 39: 794.

McCann, K. S., Rasmussen, J. B., and Umbanhowar, J. (2005). The dynamics of spatially coupled food webs. *Ecol. Lett.* 8: 513–23.

McLaughlin, O. B., Jonsson, T. and Emmerson, M. (2010). Temporal variability in predator-prey relationships of a forest floor food web. *Adv. Ecol. Res.* 42: 171–264.

Melián, C. J., Bascompte, J., Jordano, P., and Krivan, V. (2009). Diversity in a complex ecological network with two interaction types. *Oikos* 118: 122–30.

Memmott, J., Waser, N. M., and Price, M. V. (2004). Tolerance of pollination networks to species extinctions. *Proc. R. Soc. Lond. B Biol. Sci.* 271: 2605–11.

Miele, V., Picard, F., and Dray, S. (2014). Spatially constrained clustering of ecological networks. *Methods Ecol. Evol.* 5: 771–79.

Miele, V., Guill, C., Ramos-Jiliberto, R., and Kéfi, S. (2019). Non-trophic interactions strengthen the diversity-functioning relationship in an ecological bioenergetic network model. *PLOS Comput. Biol.* 15: e1007269.

Milo, R., Shen-Orr, S., Itzkovitz, S., Kashtan, N., Chklovskii, D., and Alon, U. (2002). Network motifs: Simple building blocks of complex networks. *Science* 298: 824–7.

Montoya, J. M., Pimm, S. L., and Solé, R. V. (2006). Ecological networks and their fragility. *Nature* 442: 259–64.

Moore, J. C., Berlow, E. L., Coleman, D. C., de Ruiter, P. C., Dong, Q., Hastings, A., et al. (2004). Detritus, trophic dynamics and biodiversity. *Ecol. Lett.* 7: 584–600.

Moore, J. C. and William Hunt, H. (1988). Resource compartmentation and the stability of real ecosystems. *Nature* 333: 261–3.

Morueta-Holme, N., Blonder, B., Sandel, B., McGill, B. J., Peet, R. K., Ott, J. E., et al. (2016). A network approach for inferring species associations from co-occurrence data. *Ecography* 39: 1139–50.

Mougi, A. and Kondoh, M. (2012). Diversity of interaction types and ecological community stability. *Science* 337: 349–51.

Mucha, P. J., Richardson, T., Macon, K., Porter, M. A., and Onnela, J. -P. (2010). Community structure in time-dependent, multiscale, and multiplex networks. *Science* 328: 876–8.

Neutel, A. -M., Heesterbeek, J. A. P., and Ruiter, P. C. de. (2002). Stability in real food webs: Weak links in long loops. *Science* 296: 1120–3.

Newman, M. E. J. (2010). *Networks: An Introduction*. 1 edition. New York: Oxford University Press.

Newman, M. E. J. (2002). Assortative mixing in networks. *Phys. Rev. Lett.* 89: 208, 701.

Newman, M. E. J., Leicht, E. A. (2007). Mixture models and exploratory analysis in networks Proceedings of the National Academy of Sciences 104(23): 9564–69; DOI: 10.1073/pnas.0610537104 https://www.pnas.org/content/104/23/9564.

Nilsson, L. A. (1988). The evolution of flowers with deep corolla tubes. *Nature* 334: 147.

Olesen, J. M., Bascompte, J., Dupont, Y. L., Elberling, H., Rasmussen, C., and Jordano, P. (2011). Missing and forbidden links in mutualistic networks. *Proc. R. Soc. B Biol. Sci.* 278: 725–32.

Olesen, J. M., Bascompte, J., Elberling, H., and Jordano, P. (2008). Temporal dynamics in a pollination network. *Ecology* 89: 1573–82.

Olff, H., Alonso, D., Berg, M. P., Eriksson, B. K., Loreau, M., Piersma, T., et al. (2009). Parallel ecological networks in ecosystems. *Philos. Trans. R. Soc. B Biol. Sci.* 364: 1755–79.

Otto, S. B., Rall, B. C., and Brose, U. (2007). Allometric degree distributions facilitate food-web stability. *Nature* 45: 1226–9.

Pascual, M. and Dunne, J. A. (2006). *Ecological Networks: Linking Structure to Dynamics in Food Webs*. Oxford: Oxford University Press.

Pilosof, S., Fortuna, M. A., Vinarski, M. V., Korallo-Vinarskaya, N. P., and Krasnov, B. R. (2013). Temporal dynamics of direct reciprocal and indirect effects in a host-parasite network. *J. Anim. Ecol.* 82: 987–96.

Pilosof, S., Porter, M. A., Pascual, M., and Kéfi, S. (2017). The multilayer nature of ecological networks. *Nat. Ecol. Evol.* 1: 0101.

Pimm, S. L. (1982). *Food Webs*. Chicago, USA: University of Chicago Press.

Pocock, M. J. O., Evans, D. M., and Memmott, J. (2012). The robustness and restoration of a network of ecological networks. *Science* 335: 973–7.

Rezende, E. L., Albert, E. M., Fortuna, M. A., and Bascompte, J. (2009). Compartments in a marine food web associated with phylogeny, body mass, and habitat structure. *Ecol. Lett.* 12: 779788.

de Ruiter, P. C., Neutel, A. -M., and Moore, J. C. (1995). Energetics, patterns of interaction strengths, and stability in real ecosystems. *Science* 269: 1257–60.

Saavedra, S., Reed-Tsochas, F., and Uzzi, B. (2009). A simple model of bipartite cooperation for ecological and organizational networks. *Nature* 457: 463–6.

Saiz, H. and Alados, C. L. (2011). Effect of Stipa tenacissima L. on the structure of plant co-occurrence networks in a semi-arid community. *Ecol. Res.* 26: 595–603.

Sanderson, J. G. and Pimm, S. L. (2015). *Patterns in Nature: The Analysis of Species Co-Occurrences*. Chicago: The University of Chicago Press.

Sauve, A. M. C., Fontaine, C., and Thébault, E. (2014). Structure–stability relationships in networks combining mutualistic and antagonistic interactions. *Oikos* 123: 378–84.

Solé, R. V. and Montoya, M. (2001). Complexity and fragility in ecological networks. *Proc. R. Soc. Lond. B Biol. Sci.* 26: 2039–45.

Soliveres, S., Maestre, F. T., Ulrich, W., Manning, P., Boch, S., Bowker, M. A., et al. (2015). Intransitive competition is widespread in plant communities and maintains their species richness. *Ecol. Lett.* 18: 790–8.

Stang, M., Klinkhamer, P. G. L., and Meijden, E. V. D. (2006). Size constraints and flower abundance determine the number of interactions in a plant–flower visitor web. *Oikos* 112: 111–21.

Stouffer, D. B. and Bascompte, J. (2011). Compartmentalization increases food-web persistence. *Proc. Natl. Acad. Sci.* 108: 3648–52.

Stouffer, D. B., Camacho, J., Jiang, W., and Amaral, N. L. A. (2007). Evidence for the existence of a robust pattern of prey selection in food webs. *Proc. R. Soc. B Biol. Sci.* 27: 1931–40.

Thébault, E. and Fontaine, C. (2010). Stability of ecological communities and the architecture of mutualistic and trophic networks. *Science* 329: 853–6.

Trøjelsgaard, K. and Olesen, J. M. (2016). Ecological networks in motion: micro- and macroscopic variability across scales. *Funct. Ecol.* 30: 1926–35.

Vázquez, D. P., Chacoff, N. P., and Cagnolo, L. (2009). Evaluating multiple determinants of the structure of plant–animal mutualistic networks. *Ecology* 90: 2039–46.

Verdú, M. and Valiente-Banuet, A. (2008). The nested assembly of plant facilitation networks prevents species extinctions. *Am. Nat.* 172: 751–60.

Warren, C. P., Pascual, M., Lafferty, K. D., and Kuris, A. M. (2010). The inverse niche model for food webs with parasites. *Theor. Ecol.* 3: 285–94.

Watts, D. J. and Strogatz, S. H. (1998). Collective dynamics of "small-world" networks. *Nature* 393: 440–2.

Williams, R. J., Anandanadesan, A., and Purves, D. (2010). The probabilistic niche model reveals the niche structure and role of body size in a complex food web. *Plos One* 5: e12092.

Williams, R. J., Berlow, E. L., Dunne, J. A., Barabási, A. -L., and Martinez, N. D. (2002). Two degrees of separation in complex food webs. *Proc. Natl. Acad. Sci.* 9: 12, 913–16.

Williams, R. J. and Martinez, N. D. (2000). Simple rules yield complex food webs. *Nature* 404: 180–3.

Williams, R. J. and Martinez, N. D. (2004). Limits to trophic levels and omnivory in complex food webs: Theory and data. *Am. Nat.* 163: 458–68.

Winemiller, K. O. (1990). Spatial and temporal variation in tropical fish trophic networks. *Ecol. Monogr.* 60: 331–67.

Woodward, G., Ebenman, B., Emmerson, M., Montoya, J. M., Olesen, J. M., Valido, A., et al. (2005). Body size in ecological networks. *Trends Ecol. Evol.* 20: 402–9.

Woodward, G., Jones, J. I., and Hildrew, A. G. (2002). Community persistence in Broadstone Stream (U.K.) over three decades. *Freshw. Biol.* 47: 1419–35.

Yodzis, P. (1981). The stability of real ecosystems. *Nature* 289: 674–6.

Yodzis, P. and Innes, S. (1992). Body-size and consumer-resource dynamics. *Am. Nat.* 139: 1151–73.

CHAPTER 11

Trait-based ecological and eco-evolutionary theory

Christopher A. Klausmeier, Colin T. Kremer, and Thomas Koffel

11.1 Overview of trait-based ecology and evolution

11.1.1 Why trait-based ecology?

Ecological systems are complex, consisting of a diversity of organisms whose growth, reproduction, and interactions are often nonlinear. Furthermore, these processes occur over multiple scales of organization and in environments that are heterogeneous in space and time. Theoretical ecologists have long pursued ways to simplify this complexity by identifying, describing, and exploring the essential features that drive ecological processes and patterns (Levin 1992). One such approach, trait-based ecology, offers a potent way of studying the theoretical underpinnings of diversity, while balancing reductionism and reality. This emerging paradigm unites new and old ideas behind a common focus: that by reducing our representation of individuals, populations, or species to their most essential characteristics—functional traits—we can better understand ecological systems.

Trait-based approaches cut across organization scales from the behavioral and physiological up to the population, community, and ecosystem levels, making it possible to study a range of fundamental questions. For example, the performance of a population of individuals within a given ecological setting might be revealed by considering the traits of an average individual, such as its life history,

behavior, and physiology. Similarly, the distribution of an entire species across a range of environments might be understood by considering its mean trait values, across individuals and populations (although trait variation also matters; Violle et al. 2012; Enquist et al. 2015). Traits can also be used to characterize a range of interactions between species, yielding insights into coexistence, trophic interactions, and ultimately the diversity and composition of entire communities. In turn, representing whole communities using features of their collective trait distributions, rather than focusing in detail on the identity of their constituent species, can reveal general patterns of succession (e.g., Terseleer et al. 2014) and the influence of climate (e.g., Wieczynski et al. 2019). Critical properties of ecosystems (productivity, stability, etc.) may also be related to the traits (or functions) of the communities they support (e.g., Díaz and Cabido 2001; Roscher et al. 2012; Polley et al. 2013). Finally, trait-based approaches have the potential to integrate ecological and evolutionary perspectives, due to their common focus on functional traits (or phenotypes) and measures of fitness. This makes it possible to consider both the ecological consequences of evolutionary trait change and the capacity of ecological forces to impose selection and drive evolution.

Trait-based approaches are valuable to ecological theory, offering both qualitative and quantitative insights. Qualitatively, trait-based studies can

Klausmeier, C. A., Kremer, C. T., and Koffel, T., *Trait-based ecological and eco-evolutionary theory* In: *Theoretical Ecology: Concepts and Applications*. Edited by: Kevin S. McCann and Gabriel Gellner, Oxford University Press (2020). © Oxford University Press.
DOI: 10.1093/oso/9780198824282.003.0011

uncover the mechanisms that drive ecological processes, informing the structure of the equations used to develop a model or theory. Quantitatively, these studies also provide the parameters of equations by measuring rates, efficiencies, and other key traits. Consequently, trait-based theories are often inherently mechanistic, due to their focus on function; this contrasts with other theoretical techniques for modeling diverse communities such as constructing random community matrices or interaction networks (May 2001; Allesina and Tang 2012; Barbier et al. 2018). To avoid biologically non-sensical results, many ecological theories invoke one or more tradeoffs (Kneitel and Chase 2004). Often these tradeoffs represent reasonable assumptions, which may nevertheless lack a strong empirical foundation. Trait-based studies have the potential to provide new and quantitative insights into the tradeoffs that constrain the strategies used when competing for resources, avoiding predation, timing reproduction, *etc.* (Edwards et al. 2011). Furthermore, in an era where ecologists are increasingly challenged to quantitatively predict how species, communities, and ecosystems will respond to environmental change, a focus on species traits is essential. Trait-based approaches are being used to anticipate shifts in species distributions, community composition, and ecosystem function driven by environmental change (Suding et al. 2008; Thomas et al. 2012). They can also be used to predict which species are likely to become harmful invaders outside their native ranges (Van Kleunen et al. 2010; Drenovsky et al. 2012), and to identify alternative targets for conservation, such as focusing on the preservation of functional biodiversity. Collectively, these examples give an indication of the value of trait-based approaches both for advancing basic theory as well as testing and applying theory in real ecological systems.

11.1.2 What are traits?

Traits can be defined as measurable properties of individual organisms; we are particularly interested in *functional traits*, those that affect performance and ultimately fitness (McGill et al. 2006; Violle et al. 2007). There are many different kinds of traits, reflecting the chemical composition, physiology, morphology, genetics, and behavior of organisms.

Traits determine how a given individual functions within its environment (e.g., its capacity to tolerate temperature or toxins) as well as how it interacts with other individuals or species (e.g., its ability to compete for resources or escape from predators). Traits may characterize how an organism is affected by its environment (often called "response" traits), how it influences its environment ("effect" traits), or both (Díaz and Cabido 2001; Lavorel and Garnier 2002; Violle et al. 2007). Mathematically, traits can be characterized as discrete, categorical, continuous, or even function-valued (Gomulkiewicz et al. 2018).

Numerous reviews have identified the functional traits most relevant to different groups of organisms (e.g., phytoplankton, Litchman and Klausmeier 2008; zooplankton, Litchman et al. 2013; plants, Westoby et al. 2002; Reich et al. 2003; insects, Poff et al. 2006), while considering relationships among traits, and how traits inform our understanding of ecology. Some of these studies categorize traits according to their type (life history, behavioral, physiological, morphological) and ecological function (reproduction, resource acquisition, predator avoidance). Given the vast number of possible traits, it is often useful to organize them into hierarchies, recognizing that the value of "high level" traits is determined by combinations of a large number of lower level traits. For example, while size might strongly influence an individual's fitness, size itself is the product of other traits, ranging from how an individual develops and forages, to the level of individual genes. Establishing the relationships between traits across such hierarchies, including eventually bridging the genotype/phenotype gap, remains an active and important area of research.

11.1.3 Historical survey of trait-based theories

The foundations of trait-based ecology long predate its emergence as an identifiable paradigm. Even the very earliest attempts to use mathematics to describe and study ecological processes invoked relationships that depended on parameters representing the traits of populations and species. For example, logistic growth (Verhulst 1845) depends on a population's intrinsic growth rate and strength of intraspecific competition, and predatory-prey dynamics (Lotka 1920, Volterra 1926) are governed by traits including the growth rate of the prey, and the attack rate, conversion efficiency, and mortality rate of the predator. Corresponding efforts to parameterize such models engaged empiricists in quantifying these, and many other traits across different species and under different conditions. Lotka (1920) explicitly identified some parameters Q with "the character of each species", what we would now call their traits, and noted that these would change over time. Elsewhere (Lotka 1912, 1934), he suggested that within-species trait variation could be modeled as a distribution of phenotypes, whose evolution would be subject to the same processes that determine population dynamics. However, this remained only a signpost for future work, because Lotka and others took these traits as constants to focus on population dynamics.

These traditional ecological models lay a solid foundation for trait-based approaches, by linking model parameters with the traits of organisms. Trait-based approaches take this one step further, by focusing on traits as key model outputs rather than just inputs. That is, traits are not fixed parameters but dynamic variables subject to change, typically by some adaptive processes. This opens up a whole new range of questions that can be addressed.

Optimization theory was one of the first trait-based theories in ecology and evolution (Parker and Maynard Smith 1990), with many notable, broad fields of application. *Life history theory* addresses questions such as optimal clutch size and the timing of life history events, assuming trade-offs between demographic traits such as survival, growth and reproduction (Stearns 1992, Roff 2002). *r/K selection* is an example linking suites of traits to the environment (MacArthur and Wilson 1967). *Optimal foraging theory* is another a well-developed field (Stephens and Krebs 1986), where traits are the effort spent foraging on different resources. These traits are typically assumed to be optimized on a rapid, behavioral timescale. Classic results include the marginal value theorem for patch use (Charnov 1976), the zero-one rule for substitutable resources (Emlen 1966), and the μ/f rule for balancing foraging gains and predator risk (Gilliam and Fraser 1987). *Eco-physiology* addresses resource allocation to different physiological systems (e.g., Bazzaz and Grace 1997; Klausmeier et al. 2004).

Although optimization theory is a central organizing theory in many areas of ecology and evolution, it has been criticized on various grounds (summarized in Maynard Smith 1978). One limitation of optimality approaches is that they assume that the payoff depends only on the strategy played by an individual. However, for ecological interactions that occur within and between species, the payoff of a strategy often depends on what strategy other individuals are playing. *Game theory* was designed to investigate such situations, originally in economics (Von Neumann and Morgenstern 1944; Nash 1951) and later imported to biology (Maynard Smith and Price 1973), where it became a standard approach to studying animal behavior (Maynard Smith 1982). The concept of an optimum strategy is replaced by the *evolutionarily stable strategy* (ESS), a strategy that cannot be improved on once it is adopted by an entire population. Many applications of game theory in behavioral ecology consider a discrete set of strategies, so the payoffs can be assembled in a matrix, but continuous strategy spaces are also possible.

Another body of trait-based theory, concerning competition for a spectrum of substitutable resources, dominated community ecology theory in the 1970s. Species differ in their resource utilization curves, which are related to a trait such as body or beak size, averaged at the species level. This underlying mechanistic model is then translated into a Lotka–Volterra competition model, where a species' carrying capacity depends on its trait and the competition coefficients depend on the difference in species' traits. MacArthur and Levins (1967) first used such a model to examine *limiting similarity*: how similar two resident species must be to prevent an intermediate species from invading. This approach was soon extended to a large number of species evenly spaced along the trait axis. Roughgarden (1972, 1979) showed that an unlimited number of species can coexist in an idealized deterministic setting, but May and MacArthur (1972) found a limit to diversity in randomly varying environments. This result was criticized on mathematical (Turelli 1978) and ecological grounds (Abrams 1983), and the theory of limiting similarity fell out of fashion by the 1980s. Despite this history, these one-dimensional Lotka–Volterra models are still widely used in trait-based eco-evolutionary modeling. We now know much more about the conditions that lead to continuous species packing versus a discrete number of coexisting species (Barabás et al. 2012).

One reaction to the disenchantment with this niche-based Lotka–Volterra theory was a shift to more mechanistic models of competition that explicitly include the resources for which species compete (Tilman 1982), although, the niche-based Lotka–Volterra was originally formulated as an explicit resource-consumer model (MacArthur 1970; Chesson 1990). Extended to include apparent competition through shared predators and stressors, this *contemporary niche theory* employs a graphical approach to determine community structure based on Zero Net Growth Isoclines (ZNGIs), which summarize the response of organisms to the environment, and impact vectors, which summarize the effect of organisms on the environment (Chase and Leibold 2003). Because these models are more mechanistic, the species parameters have direct ecological meaning, so can be considered traits. A common form of trait-based analysis of these models involves depicting a large number of species' ZNGIs and impact vectors, which can be used to determine community structure along environmental gradients (Tilman 1982; Chase and Leibold 2003). Recently we have extended this approach using ZNGI and impact vector envelopes to consider a continuum of strategies (Koffel et al. 2016). However, these graphical approaches restrict the number of limiting factors to two or three, capping the diversity that can emerge.

In the late 1980s and 1990s, two independent groups—one American (Brown and Vincent 1987), one European (Metz et al. 1996)—proposed a trait-based theoretical framework that allows for the emergence of community structure, termed *adaptive dynamics* (Geritz et al. 1998). These approaches combine ideas from evolutionary game theory and community ecology. In particular, they show how game theory's payoff can be identified with Darwinian fitness, which is described as the *per capita* population growth rate in a community ecological model. This general formulation provided analytical tools that could be applied to arbitrary ecological interactions

(i.e., not restricted to Lotka–Volterra models), which led to a flood of applications (Section 11.2.3). The original formulation of adaptive dynamics makes a number of restrictive assumptions, such as a separation of time scales between ecology and evolution, small mutations, and asexual populations; however, it can be seen as a particular case within a constellation of closely related theoretical frameworks (Abrams 2001; Section 11.3).

One other framework from the 1980s and 1990s worth mentioning is that of *community assembly theory*. In this purely ecological framework, species from a finite or infinite regional species pool are repeatedly introduced to a local community (Post and Pimm 1983; Rummel and Roughgarden 1985; Law and Morton 1993; Morton and Law 1997). Upon successful invasion, the new state of the community is computed and another random species is introduced from the regional species pool. Three outcomes are possible: the community is uninvasible, a recurrent assembly cycle occurs, or community assembly continues indefinitely along different trajectories (Morton and Law 1997). Furthermore, alternative outcomes are possible for a given set of parameters (Law and Morton 1993). Although any model of species interactions could be used, Lotka–Volterra models are typical; many applications employ trait-based models of competition (Rummel and Roughgarden 1985) or food web assembly (Morton and Law 1997) to define species interactions. The community assembly framework shares many similarities with adaptive dynamics—trait-based formulations of interactions, use of invasion criteria, separation of time scales between invasions, and uninvasible states as a long-term outcome—but these literatures have remained largely separate.

11.1.4 Overview of rest of chapter

Clearly, there is a rich history of trait-based theoretical approaches in ecology and evolution. In the rest of this chapter, we describe how trait-based models are set up and analyzed from the perspective of adaptive dynamics, and survey applications (Section 11.2). Next, we discuss other trait-based modeling frameworks and the connections between them (Section 11.3). We then consider the extension of these frameworks to multiple traits and spatial and temporal heterogeneity (Section 11.4). Finally, we conclude in Section 11.5 by considering directions for future research.

11.2 Basic ideas

In this section we outline the basic principles of trait-based theory, considering both density-independent and density-dependent models, feedbacks between ecological/environmental conditions and trait values, and how optimization and evolutionary approaches offer insights into the dynamics and equilibria of such models. Finally, we conclude by describing a range of phenomena uncovered by applying trait-based theory.

Before we start, some words about terminology. With their focus on functional traits, trait-based approaches are, by design, phenotypic approaches. The hierarchical level at which trait variation occurs—within-individual plasticity, within-species genetic variation, or between-species differentiation—is a secondary concern and often ignored. While this is a strength of the approach because it can allow greater generality, it can lead to confusing use of terminology. Here, we will use the term strategy to refer to the trait values of an individual, or of a population or species, when intraspecific trait variation is negligible. For frameworks that are explicitly ecological, we refer to different species as such, but for more general frameworks we use the term populations.

11.2.1 Density-independent models with traits and optimization theory

Exponential growth has been called the first law of population dynamics (Turchin 2001; Pásztor et al. 2016). Such density-independent models form the basis of the simplest approach to trait-based modeling—optimization theory—and are fundamental to understanding more realistic density-dependent models. We begin with the simplest case of an unstructured population i in a constant environment in continuous time, with population density N_i and growth rate r_i:

$$\frac{dN_i}{dt} = r_i N_i \qquad (11.1)$$

The solution of this equation is $N_i(t) = N_i(0)e^{r_i t}$, which approaches zero if $r_i < 0$ and grows to infinity if $r_i > 0$ (assuming no dispersal limitation, that is $N_i(0) > 0$). Equilibrium is possible only when $r_i = 0$, which is infinitely unlikely in the absence of any density-dependent stabilizing mechanism.

Simple as exponential growth may be, we can begin to get ecological insights by considering how a population's growth rate $r_i\left(\vec{x}_i; \vec{E}\right)$ depends on its traits $\vec{x}_i$ and the environment $\vec{E}$ (Geritz et al. 1998). In general, the environment is a multidimensional vector that represents all of the abiotic and biotic factors that affect a population's growth rate, such as resource levels, temperature, and the density of directly interacting species (assumed to be constant in the density-independent case). How r_i depends on traits and the environment is the domain of functional and physiological ecology and is a key element in developing mechanistic trait-based models, including species distribution models (Kearney and Porter 2009).

The critical values of the traits and environmental factors where $r_i\left(\vec{x}_i; \vec{E}\right) = 0$ separate population growth from extinction (Maguire 1973). This can be easily visualized in two dimensions (e.g., two environmental variables, two traits, or one of each), which we call Zero Invasion Plots (Figure 11.1). Figure 11.1A illustrates the classical case of a population with fixed trait values that requires two essential resources, such as nitrogen and phosphorus for plants, so that $\vec{E} = (R_1, R_2)$. Both resources are required for growth, which leads to the L-shaped ZNGI (Tilman 1982). Figure 1B shows a hypothetical situation for a fixed environment where positive growth occurs for a range of values of each trait. This region also depends on an interaction between these traits (such that the viable range of trait 1 depends on the value of trait 2 and *vice versa*). Figure 1C shows the interaction between a single trait and one environmental factor. A horizontal slice through this figure determines the *fundamental niche* of a population with particular trait values. A vertical slice determines what we call the *fundamental community* for a particular environment: species with trait

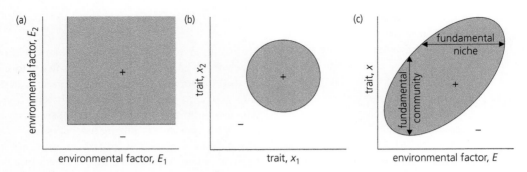

Figure 11.1 Zero Invasion Plots. A: two environmental factors (a ZNGI). B: two traits. C: one environmental factor and one trait. Gray shading denotes positive fitness.

values outside the fundamental community cannot persist even in isolation, so would not be expected to occur absent facilitation.

Now, consider multiple populations, which could represent different species (or, alternatively, different strategies within a species) inhabiting the same environment, governed by Equation (11.1), and growing (i.e., $r_i > 0$). Although these populations do not interact and each has the potential to grow to infinity due to the lack of density dependence, we can still determine the outcome of "competition" among these populations by considering the relative abundance of each population, $p_i = n_i/\sum_j n_j$. Using the quotient rule, we find the dynamics of p_i to be

$$\frac{dp_i}{dt} = p_i \left(r_i - \sum_j r_j p_j \right) = p_i \left(r_i - \bar{r} \right), \qquad (11.2)$$

where $\bar{r}$ is the abundance-weighted average growth rate. This is known as the replicator equation (Hofbauer and Sigmund 1998). As can be seen from the second form of Equation (11.2), a population i with an above-average growth rate ($r_i > \bar{r}$) increases in relative abundance and one with a below-average growth rate decreases. Thus, in the long term, the population with the highest growth rate will dominate the community ($p_i \to 1$), while the relative abundance of all others will decline to zero. This justifies the use of the word *fitness* as a synonym for the *per capita* growth rate, r_i. If multiple populations have equal fitness, we say they are *neutral*, because their relative abundance is determined only by initial conditions.

Instead of a finite number of populations, we now consider a continuum of populations, ordered by their strategy x, which also determines their fitness, $r(x)$. Generalizing the results from the replicator, Equation (11.2), we know that the population with the strategy conveying the greatest fitness will dominate the community in the long term. We can use elementary calculus to find the optimal strategy, x^*, which maximizes fitness given $r(x)$. If x is one-dimensional, we find the maximum by setting the *fitness gradient*, $\frac{dr}{dx}$, equal to zero and solving for x. To be a local maximum, we require the second derivative of fitness to be negative, $\frac{d^2r}{dx^2} < 0$ (Figure 2A). Since there can be multiple local maxima, we have to compare the fitness of all local optima as well as at the ends of the trait space to find the global optimum x^* (Fig. 2B–C).

So far, we have focused on continuous-time models with *unstructured populations*, which can be described by a single variable such as population size or density. However, the theory of *structured populations* (those with e.g., age-, stage-, or size-structure) is well developed, and provides ways to calculate the asymptotic population growth rate r once a stable population structure has been reached. In a discrete-time matrix model, it is the logarithm of the dominant eigenvalue of the Leslie–Lefkovitch matrix (Caswell 2001). Extensions to temporally variable environments also exist: Floquet exponents for periodic systems (Klausmeier 2008) and Lyapunov exponents for aperiodic systems (Metz et al. 1992). Thus, the population growth rate r can be optimized while accounting for all the biological processes contributing to a

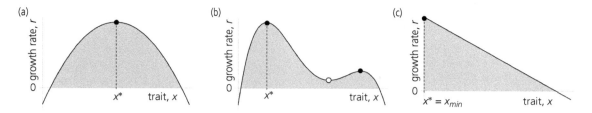

Figure 11.2 Finding local and global maxima on fitness landscapes. A) A single, global optimum. B) Two local optima separated by a fitness minimum. C) A boundary optimum.

population's success, such as individual growth, survival, and reproduction.

11.2.2 Density-dependent models with traits

Density dependence and limiting factors

It has long been recognized that at least some *per capita* vital rates must depend on population density for populations to not to grow to infinity (Turchin 2001). While this density dependence is often modeled as a direct effect of density on *per capita* growth rate, as in the logistic equation, it is often useful to explicitly consider the limiting factors such as resources or predators that mediate density dependence (Chase and Leibold 2003; Meszéna et al. 2006). One important consequence of this environmental feedback loop is the *competitive exclusion principle*: no more species can coexist at equilibrium than there are shared limiting factors (Levin 1970). This sets an upper limit on the diversity that can be maintained in a community, a limit that remains valid in trait-based models.

In particular, when there is only one limiting factor, such as a resource R, stable coexistence is impossible, and a single population will outcompete all others. The break-even resource level R^* of a population i, where its net growth $g_i = 0$, is a simple metric that identifies the best competitor: the population with the lowest R^* will exclude all others. This is known as the R^*-rule (Tilman 1982). Thus R^* combines various physiological parameters into a single metric of competitive ability. In a trait-based setting, the R^*-rule provides a "pessimization" principle analogous to the optimization principles applied to fitness previously (Metz et al. 2008). When R^* is expressed

as a function of traits, calculus can again be used to minimize R^*, and identify the optimal trait values for a given environment (Klausmeier et al. 2004).

If species interacted only through a single limiting factor, ecological communities would be much easier to understand, yet lack diversity, rendering them far less interesting. Luckily this is not the case. When there is more than one limiting factor and populations have differential responses and effects on those factors, then stable coexistence becomes a theoretical possibility. The prototypical species-based competition model is the Lotka–Volterra model, which can be written as

$$\begin{cases} \dfrac{dN_1}{dt} = (r_1 - \alpha_{11}N_1 - a_{12}N_2)\,N_1 = g_1 N_1 \\[2mm] \dfrac{dN_2}{dt} = (r_2 - \alpha_{21}N_1 - a_{22}N_2)\,N_2 = g_2 N_2 \end{cases} \quad (11.3)$$

where r_i are maximum growth rates and α_{ii} and α_{ij} are intra- and interspecific competition coefficients, respectively. The five possible outcomes of competition are: i) species 1 outcompetes 2, ii) species 2 outcompetes 1, iii) species 1 and 2 coexist, iv) either species 1 or 2 excludes the other depending on initial conditions (*founder control*), and v) neutral coexistence. Note that in Equation (11.3), we have introduced g_i to represent the *per capita* growth rate (fitness) of a population, which now combines the maximum exponential growth rate, r, with density dependence.

Invasion analysis

Invasion analysis is a powerful approach to understanding coexistence between two populations (Chesson 2000). The idea is to ask whether each population (termed the *invader*) can invade a monoculture of the other (termed the *resident*) at its equilibrium or other long-term attractor. The invader is assumed to be sufficiently rare that it has no effect on its own per capita growth rate or the residents'. This results in density-independent growth of the invader, which is characterized by its *invasion fitness*, $g_{inv}(E_{res})$. Here the resident at its attractor determines the environment, E_{res}, experienced by the invader (consisting of limiting factors, possibly including its own density). Negative invasion fitness means that the invasion fails, while positive invasion fitness means that it succeeds. If one population has positive invasion fitness but the other has negative, then the first excludes the second (Lotka–Volterra cases i–ii); if both populations have negative invasion fitness, there is founder control (Lotka–Volterra case iv). Finally, if each population has a positive invasion fitness (i.e., they are mutually able to invade), then we say that the two populations *stably coexist* (as in Lotka–Volterra case iii). However, because invasion fitness focuses on the boundaries of the phase space, it does not give us any information on the nature of coexistence in this mutual invasibility case.

The main advantage of invasion analysis is that it is easier to calculate invasion rates than to solve for the coexistence attractor and determine its stability. However, invasion analysis has a few potential shortcomings. First, if there are multiple coexistence equilibria, then the lack of mutual invasibility does not imply that coexistence is impossible (Namba and Takahashi 1993; Priklopil 2012). However, it can be argued that such locally stable coexistence would be vulnerable to stochastic events and that mutual invasibility is more relevant to natural systems. Second, when the resident has multiple attractors, a positive invasion rate does not necessarily imply that the invader persists. Instead the invader can shift the resident from one of its attractors to the other, which then repels the invader, termed the "resident strikes back" scenario (Mylius and Diekmann 2001). Third, it is unclear how to extend invasion analysis to more than two species (Saavedra et al. 2017). Nonetheless, invasion analysis remains a key tool for understanding competition and forms the basis of many trait-based eco-evolutionary modeling approaches to follow.

How to set up density-dependent trait-based models

Having discussed species-based density-dependent models previously, let us now describe how to set up a trait-based model in four easy steps, focusing on non-structured populations for simplicity. First, start with a mechanistic species-based model and identify groups of populations that are functionally similar, which we call *guilds*. Populations within a guild share the same fitness function, which will depend on the same trait(s), but specific trait values may differ between populations. If two populations do have identical trait values, or strategies, they will be selectively neutral (e.g., Lotka–Volterra case v). As an example, one might model predators and prey as two separate guilds (although this decision is part of the art of modeling). Let $\mathcal{G}$ be the number of guilds.

Second, generalize the model to encompass $\mathcal{N}_G$ populations in guild G, indexed by subscripts. For example, let $N_{G,i}$ be the density of the population with the ith strategy in guild G. Any terms that represent interactions between populations or between populations and environmental factors should be replaced by a sum over populations, making no distinction between intra- and inter-specific interactions.

Third, make some model parameters functions of traits (this is the identity function if those parameters are directly considered traits). Together, the model then consists of a set of differential equations of the form $\frac{dN_{G,i}}{dt} = g_G(x_{G,i}; \vec{E}(\vec{N}, \vec{x}))N_{G,i}$, one for each population in each guild. Note that the fitness function g_G of a particular guild now depends on the strategy of the focal population, $x_{G,i}$, as well as environmental factors $\vec{E}$. These in turn depend on the strategies and densities of the rest of the community. Specifically, $\vec{x} = (\vec{x}_1, \vec{x}_2, \ldots, \vec{x}_\mathcal{G})$ and $\vec{x}_G = (x_{G,1}, x_{G,2}, \ldots, x_{G,\mathcal{N}_G})$ describe the set of all traits across guilds, and across populations/strategies within a guild, respectively. Densities are described similarly as $\vec{N} = (\vec{N}_1, \vec{N}_2, \ldots, \vec{N}_\mathcal{G})$ and $\vec{N}_G = (N_{G,1}, N_{G,2}, \ldots, N_{G,\mathcal{N}_G})$. See Boxes 11.1 and 11.2 for examples of how to set up trait-based models.

The final step in setting up a trait-based model is to define a source of trait variation. This choice largely distinguishes various trait-based modeling frameworks, which we compare in Section 11.3. For pedagogical reasons, we will describe adaptive dynamics (which assumes variation arises from small, infrequent mutations) and adaptive statics (adaptive dynamics at equilibrium, without the assumption of small mutations); however, different trait-based approaches often give similar results (see Section 11.3).

It is important to keep in mind that there is usually no unique way of deriving a trait-based model from a species-based one. All of the four steps (identifying guilds, generalizing to multiple populations, making parameters functions of traits, and defining a source of variation) are ultimately determined by the ecological mechanisms identified as relevant by the modeler in that particular context. For example, a trait-based model designed to study the evolution of cannibalism would look different from the competition model derived in Box 11.1, even if both arose from the same single-population model. Similarly, trait-based models studying the emergence of food webs might lump prey and predators into a single guild, unlike Box 11.2.

Invasion analysis of trait-based models

Having defined a trait-based model, how can we analyze it? For simplicity, we will consider a single guild with a single trait here. Begin with a monomorphic resident population with strategy x_1 and find its ecological attractor (assumed here to be an equilibrium for simplicity) and the corresponding environment $\hat{E}(x_1)$, such that $g\left(x_1; \hat{E}(x_1)\right) = 0$. Now consider the fate of a rare population with a different strategy x_0 by calculating its invasion fitness when invading the resident, $g\left(x_0; \hat{E}(x_1)\right)$. As described previously, invasion succeeds if $g\left(x_0; \hat{E}(x_1)\right) > 0$ and fails if $g\left(x_0; \hat{E}(x_1)\right) < 0$. If the new strategy is quite similar to the existing one, then successful invasion implies replacement of the previous resident (Geritz et al. 2002), except at special points described next. This process is then repeated to generate a "trait substitution process." The *fitness gradient*, $\partial g / \partial x_0 |_{x_0 = x_1}$, measures *directional selection* on a resident, given its strategy: if $\partial g / \partial x_0 > 0$ then the trait evolves towards larger values (Figure 11.3A) and if $\partial g / \partial x_0 < 0$ then it evolves towards smaller values (Figure 11.3B). We will call a trait value or

---

Box 11.1   Trait-Based Lotka–Volterra competition

A classic example of a trait-based model arises from the Lotka–Volterra competition model. In it, there is a single guild of competitors and no explicit environmental factors aside from the abundance of competitors. Start with the single-population logistic equation

$$\frac{dN}{dt} = (r - \alpha N)\, N$$

To make it into a trait-based model, we add subscripts for each population i, sum interactions over strategies $j = 1, \ldots, \mathcal{N}$, and make model parameters $r = r(x_i)$ and $\alpha = \alpha(x_i, x_j)$ functions of the focal population's trait x_i and the interacting population's trait x_j. Together, these changes result in:

$$\frac{dN_i}{dt} = \left(r(x_i) - \sum_{j=1}^{\mathcal{N}} \alpha(x_i, x_j)\, N_j \right) N_i = g\left(x_i; \vec{x}, \vec{N}\right) N_i$$

For simplicity, we drop the guild subscript and the explicit consideration of the environment $\vec{E}$ from the general formulation in section 2.2.3. It is commonly assumed that the maximum growth rate r is a unimodal function of x and that α, the strength of competition (competition kernel), declines to zero as a function of the difference in the strategies of the focal and interacting populations. Two functions that satisfy these assumptions are the quadratic $r(x) = 1 - x^2$ and the Gaussian $\alpha(x_i, x_j) = \exp\left[-(x_i - x_j)^2 / \sigma^2\right]$, where σ controls the width of competition kernel.

Motivated by the seminal work of MacArthur and Levins (1967), trait-based Lotka–Volterra models have been used to investigate the conditions under which such models lead to the coexistence of finitely many species with distinct trait values or a continuum of species (Barabás et al. 2012).

Box 11.2 Trait-Based predator-prey interactions

As a more complicated example of how to set up a trait-based model, consider predator-prey interactions. We begin with a classic predator-prey model, the Rosenzweig–MacArthur model (Rosenzweig and MacArthur 1963), where a prey with abundance N is consumed by a predator with abundance P:

$$\frac{dN}{dt} = (r - \alpha N) N - \frac{aN}{1 + haN} P$$

$$\frac{dP}{dt} = \frac{eaN}{1 + haN} P - mP$$

The prey grows at an intrinsic rate r and self-regulates through a competition coefficient α. The predator consumes the prey through a Type II functional response with attack rate a and handling time h, and converts prey abundance into predator abundance with efficiency e. Finally, m sets the mortality rate of the predator.

To convert the previous model into a trait-based model, we first need to identify the guilds at play. A natural choice here consists of introducing two guilds: the prey guild and the predator guild. Their abundances, generalized to multiple populations, are respectively denoted N_i with $i = 1, \ldots, \mathcal{N}_N$ and P_i, with $i = 1, \ldots, \mathcal{N}_P$. Let the fitness function of the prey and the predator depend on traits x and y, respectively. We can then write:

$$\frac{dN_i}{dt} = \left(r(x_i) - \sum_{j=1}^{\mathcal{N}_N} \alpha(x_i, x_j) N_j - \sum_{j=1}^{\mathcal{N}_P} \frac{a(x_i, y_j)}{1 + \sum_{k=1}^{\mathcal{N}_N} h(x_k, y_j) a(x_k, y_j) N_k} P_j \right) N_i$$

$$= g_N \left(x_i; \vec{x}, \vec{y}, \vec{N}, \vec{P} \right) N_i$$

$$\frac{dP_j}{dt} = \left(\sum_{l=1}^{\mathcal{N}_N} \frac{e(x_l, y_j) a(x_l, y_j) N_l}{1 + \sum_{k=1}^{\mathcal{N}_N} h(x_k, y_j) a(x_k, y_j) N_k} - m(y_j) \right) P_j$$

$$= g_P \left(y_j; \vec{x}, \vec{y}, \vec{N}, \vec{P} \right) P_j$$

As in the Lotka–Volterra competition model in Box 11.1, prey growth rate $r(x_i)$ depends on the focal population's trait value and density-dependence, $\alpha(x_i, x_j)$ depends on the trait values of the focal and interacting prey populations. The predators' attack rate $a(x_i, y_j)$, handling time $h(x_k, y_j)$, and conversion efficiency $e(x_i, y_j)$ all depend on the trait values of the predator and prey involved. Note that there are multiple interactions in this model that have been replaced by summations. The first summation in the prey equation adds up competition between prey populations; the second summation adds up predation by different predator populations; and the third summation in the denominator of the functional response adds up time predator j spends handling different prey. Finally, the outer summation in the predator equation adds up energetic gain from different prey populations.

---

strategy $\hat{x}_1$ where directional selection disappears ($\partial g / \partial x_0 = 0$) an *evolutionary equilibrium*, also known as a *singular strategy* (Geritz et al. 1998).

An evolutionary equilibrium is called a (global) *evolutionarily stable strategy* (ESS) if no other strategy can invade it. As in optimization models, an evolutionary equilibrium can be either a fitness maximum, and hence at least locally evolutionarily stable, if $\partial^2 g / \partial x_0^2 \big|_{x_0 = x_1} < 0$ (Figure 11.3C), or a fitness minimum, if $\partial^2 g / \partial x_0^2 \big|_{x_0 = x_1} > 0$ (Figure 11.3D). This quantity $\partial^2 g / \partial x_0^2$, the second derivative of invasion fitness with respect to the trait of the invader, measures the strength of *stabilizing* vs. *disruptive* selection (Figure 11.3C vs. Figure 11.3D). An ESS represents an endpoint of evolution or community assembly. Note that if new strategies are restricted to be similar to existing ones (e.g., due to small mutations), local evolutionary stability is sufficient to prevent

further trait change. However, if large mutations or immigration of different species occur, global evolutionary stability is required (Figure 11.3C vs. Figure 11.3E).

A second form of stability—*convergence stability*—controls whether directional selection leads towards or away from an evolutionary equilibrium (Eshel 1983; Geritz et al. 1998). An evolutionary equilibrium is convergence stable when $\partial^2 g / \partial x_1^2 > \partial^2 g / \partial x_0^2$. Any combination of these two stability conditions (evolutionary and convergence stability) is possible. An evolutionary equilibrium that is both convergence and evolutionary stable (i.e., a fitness maximum) is called a *convergence stable strategy* (CSS), which behaves as we would naively expect an optimum to behave. While fitness minima play a minor role in optimization models, serving only as boundaries between the basins of attraction of alternative optima (Figure 11.2B), they can play a central role in density-dependent models. The most

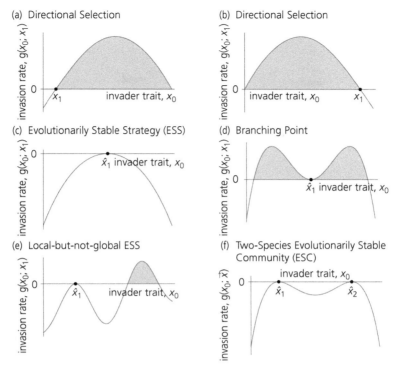

Figure 11.3 Invasion fitness landscapes. Positive invasion fitness is denoted by gray shading. A-B) Directional selection. C) An evolutionarily stable strategy (fitness maximum). D) A branching point (fitness minimum). E) A local-but-not-global ESS. F) A two-species evolutionarily stable community.

interesting case where the two conditions differ is an evolutionary equilibrium that is convergence stable but not evolutionary stable, which is called a *branching point* (Geritz et al. 1998) for reasons discussed below.

Geritz et al. (1998) gives a complete eight-fold classification of the types of stability of monomorphic evolutionary equilibria, both in terms of these second derivatives of invasion fitness and also graphically using *pairwise invasion plots* (PIPs). Whether the invasion of a resident with strategy x_1 by an invader with strategy x_0 is successful or not depends only on the sign of $g\left(x_0; \hat{E}(x_1)\right)$, or $g(x_0; x_1)$ for short. A PIP plots sign$[g(x_0; x_1)]$ as a function of the strategy of the resident and the invader (Figure 11.4). Graphically, convergence stability can be seen along the main diagonal, whereas evolutionary stability is assessed with a vertical line test through the evolutionary equilibrium.

A *mutual invasiblity plot* (MIP) illustrates the pairs of strategies x_1 and x_2 that can stably coexist, i.e.,

$g(x_2; x_1) > 0$ and $g(x_1; x_2) > 0$. It is constructed by superimposing a PIP on its reflection around the 1-1 line, exchanging the role of resident and invader (Figure 11.5). In general, the region of stable coexistence through mutual invasibility (if one exists) does not touch the 1-1 line other than at points corresponding to one-strategy evolutionary equilibria. This implies that, in general, similar species cannot coexist, representing an ecological limit to similarity.

One important exception occurs near branching points, where coexistence of similar strategies is guaranteed. This means that a strategy that successfully invades a resident at a branching point does not exclude it, but coexists with it. These coexisting strategies then experience opposing directional selection and diverge, justifying the name "branching point". The final outcome may be a pair of strategies that prevent invasion (Figure 11.3F), or the development of further branching points leading to a more diverse set of strategies, or other outcomes

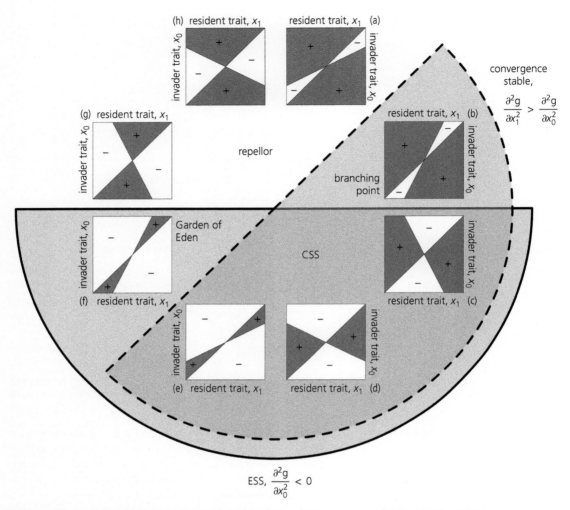

Figure 11.4 The eight-fold classification of pairwise invasibility plots (PIPs). A, G–H) Non-convergence stable repellors. B) An evolutionary branching point is convergence stable but not evolutionarily stable. C–E) Continuous stable strategies (CSSs) are both convergence and evolutionarily stable. F) The Garden of Eden is evolutionarily stable but not convergence stable.

Source: after Geritz et al. (1998)

(see following). A set of strategies (or species) that is both globally uninvasible and convergence stable is described as an *evolutionarily stable community* (ESC); Figure 11.3F illustrates a two-species ESC (Edwards et al. 2018; Kremer and Klausmeier 2017). This scenario assumes no recombination between the two diverging lineages, which may not be valid in sexual species (Waxman and Gavrilets 2005). In general, however, the existence of a branching point indicates that more than one ecological strategy is required to render a community uninvasible.

One important caveat about the previous discussion of the stability of evolutionary equilibria is that all of the conditions based on derivatives are strictly local criteria. Just as a local optimum may not be a global optimum (Figure 11.2B), a local ESS where $\partial^2 g/\partial x_0^2 < 0$ may be invasible by a strategy that is sufficiently different than a resident (Figure 11.3E). In this case, assumptions about the source of new phenotypes matters: under the assumption of small mutations (in adaptive dynamics) or standing genetic variation (in quantitative genetics, see

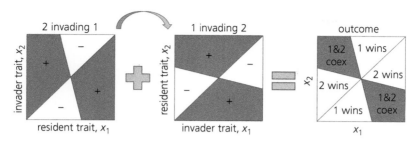

Figure 11.5 A mutual invasibility plot (MIP) shows pairs of strategies than can stably coexist. It is made by exchanging the roles of resident and invader by flipping a PIP on itself.

Source: After Geritz et al. (1998).

Section 11.3), a local-but-not-global ESS would represent a stable equilibrium, whereas larger mutations or immigration of different species from a regional species pool would allow the community to escape such an equilibrium.

Trait-based predictions across environmental gradients

The preceding section offered a detailed description of how to determine the outcome(s) of community assembly/evolution within a community, focusing on particular trait(s), while other model parameters remained fixed. An important application of trait-based approaches is to examine how these outcomes change as these external parameters vary. This can be used to determine how community structure—the diversity and abundance of species present and the value and similarity of their traits—varies with changes in model parameters, including along environmental gradients, a central goal of community ecology.

Other general insights emerge, including revealing how an $\mathcal{N}$-species ESC may lose its evolutionary stability as an environmental parameter varies. Intuitively, one might expect that a member of the ESC loses stability as a branching point emerges; however, except when the model has a particular symmetry, the first bifurcation is a loss of global evolutionary stability, resulting in a local-but-not-global ESS (Figure 11.3E; Geritz et al. 1999). At the same parameter value where the ESC first loses its global evolutionary stability, an $(\mathcal{N} + 1)$-species ESC is created, with the new strategy at zero population density (Figure 11.6). Thus, the system is

discontinuous in traits but continuous in population density at these *evolutionary transcritical bifurcation* points. Alternatively, an $\mathcal{N}$-species ESC may collapse into an $(\mathcal{N} - 1)$-species ESC as the density of one of its members declines to zero. This is a developing area of adaptive dynamics/trait-based theory, sometimes described as the "bifurcation theory of adaptive dynamics".

An efficient way to compute bifurcation diagrams of evolutionary equilibria is as follows (Kremer and Klausmeier 2017). At an initial bifurcation parameter value z, find a (preferably $\mathcal{N} = 1$ species) ESC by simultaneously solving for the abundance $\hat{N}_i$ and trait value $\hat{x}_i$ of each population i such that $g(\hat{x}_i; \vec{x}) = 0$ and $\partial g / \partial x_0 (\hat{x}_i; \vec{x}) = 0$. There are two equations and two unknowns per population, which can be solved numerically using Newton's method. Then vary the bifurcation parameter value z by a small amount δz and solve for the updated evolutionary equilibrium, extrapolating the previous solution(s) as an initial guess. At each value of the parameter z, i) assess global evolutionary stability by checking that $\max g(x_0; \vec{x}) < 0$, and ii) verify that no species has gone extinct ($\hat{N}_i > 0$ for all i). These conditions correspond to passing through an evolutionary transcritical bifurcation point either forward (adding a strategy) or in reverse (removing a strategy). Also, iii) check convergence stability using the Jacobian matrix. If the evolutionary equilibrium is still a convergence stable global ESC with no strategy extinct, continue varying z. Otherwise, stop (refining with a smaller step size δz if necessary). To find the exact bifurcation point, augment the system with the nascent strategy's eco-evolutionary equations

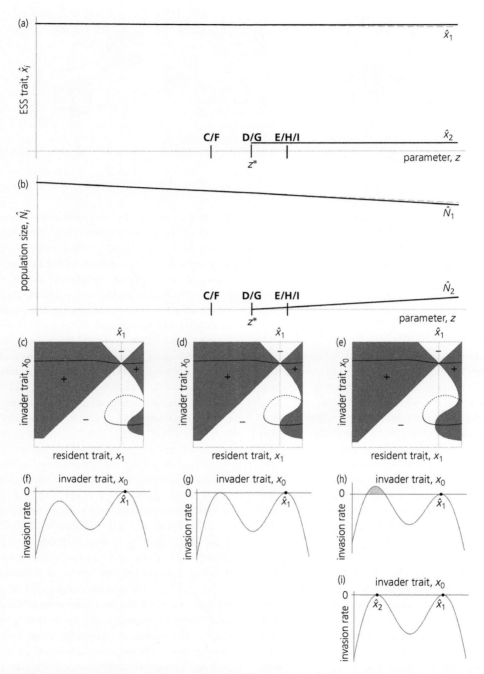

Figure 11.6 A bifurcation diagram showing an evolutionary transcritical bifurcation. A) Equilibrium traits and B) population sizes as a function of an environmental parameter z. C–E) display PIPs occurring C) before, D) at, and E) beyond the bifurcation point z^*. The solid lines on the PIPs represent local maxima of the fitness landscape and the dashed lines represent local minima. F–I) show corresponding fitness landscapes at the F–H) one-species and I) two-species evolutionary equilibria.

$g\left(\hat{x}_{\mathcal{N}+1}\right) = 0$ and $\partial g / \partial x_0 \left(\hat{x}_{\mathcal{N}+1}; \vec{x}\right) = 0$ and two additional unknowns, the trait value of the nascent strategy $\hat{x}_{\mathcal{N}+1}$ and the parameter value where the bifurcation occurs z^{*}. As a new $(\mathcal{N}+1)$-species ESC is created at this point with $\hat{N}_{\mathcal{N}+1} = 0$, this solution provides a natural starting point to be continued as previously shown. The resulting evolutionary bifurcation diagrams summarize predictions of how the evolutionarily stable community structure (trait values, diversity, and population densities) varies with changes in a model parameter, such as along an environmental gradient (e.g., Kremer and Klausmeier 2017).

More complex possible outcomes

Within a given environment, stable evolutionary equilibria are not the only possible outcome of eco-evolutionary models used to study trait-based theory. In this section we provide a non-exhaustive summary of a growing set of dynamical phenomena that have been discovered and which may provide important insights into various ecological systems.

Limit cycles. Similar to their purely ecological counterparts, eco-evolutionary systems can converge towards limit cycles where species' abundances and traits both fluctuate over time. A classic example of these evolutionary cycles happens in the context of predator-prey co-evolution models (Dieckmann et al. 1995; Cortez and Weitz 2014).

Evolutionary suicide. The pessimization principle mentioned earlier illustrates another classic emergent phenomenon of eco-evolutionary models, known more generally as the "Tragedy of the commons" (Hardin 1968). We have described how invasion analysis is used to understand the repeated invasion and replacement of resident populations by invaders with different trait values. This sequence of replacements is determined solely by the fitness of new invaders when rare; nothing ensures that a new invader behaves "optimally" when it has completely replaced the former resident. For example, there is no reason in general for the equilibrium population density of successive invaders to increase. In fact, quite the opposite can happen: evolution can drive a population extinct, either through a continuous decrease in density (Diekmann 2004; Boudsocq et al.

2011) or through a catastrophic tipping point in the presence of an Allee-effect at low densities (Ferrière 2000). These phenomena are considered examples of "evolutionary suicide" or "evolutionary traps".

Branching-extinction evolutionary cycles. Another interesting phenomenon happens when one of the two populations generated by a branching point goes extinct through evolutionary suicide (Dercole 2003). If the surviving population remains in the basin of attraction of the original branching point, it will be driven back towards the branching point and diversify, again setting one population up to experience evolutionary suicide. The succession of these branching and extinction events lead to a stable eco-evolutionary limit cycle.

Alternative evolutionarily stable states. Finally, as in purely ecological models, alternative stable states can occur in eco-evolutionary models in the form of alternative ESSs and ESCs (Kisdi and Geritz 1999; Kremer and Klausmeier 2017). Such eco-evolutionary priority effects mean that the initial trait values of evolving population(s) will influence which ESS/ESC is reached at equilibrium. This once again illustrates that "optimality" in density-dependent trait-based models is a subtle concept, as density-independent models generally only possess one global optimum.

11.2.3 Applications

Previously, we presented a general approach for implementing a trait-based approach using virtually any mechanistic model of community dynamics. It is not surprising then that trait-based approaches have been applied to a broad range of systems in ecology and evolution, to study questions from what determines organism's adaptations to what drives large-scale ecosystem functions. Here we give but a sampling of this extensive literature. Many of the following examples use techniques similar to those already described; others use related methods (see Section 11.3).

This broad spectrum of applications includes a wide range of different types of ecological interactions. In the context of consumer-resource interactions, trait-based models have shown how different resource types influence consumer diversification (Schreiber and Tobiason 2003), as well as revealing optimal allocation strategies for taking up different resources (Abrams 1987) and the effects of resource uptake plasticity (Bonachela et al. 2011). When applied to predator-prey interactions, trait-based approaches have shown how evolution can strongly alter predator-prey cycles (Cortez and Weitz 2014) or even engender them (Abrams and Matsuda 1997), and have helped us understand what drives the evolution of prey defenses (Yoshida et al. 2003; Koffel et al. 2018a). Trait-based models of host-pathogen systems have shown how within-host competition between pathogens is at the origin of their virulence (Van Baalen and Sabelis 1995; Alizon et al. 2013) and how spatial structure can lead hosts to evolve altruistic defense strategies, such as suicide upon infection (Débarre et al. 2012). A diversity of other trophic situations has been investigated, including mixotrophy (Andersen et al. 2015), cannibalism (Dercole and Rinaldi 2002; Hin and de Roos 2019), and intra-guild predation (Patel and Schreiber 2015), the latter two giving rise to a rich set of eco-evolutionary phenomena such as eco-evolutionary cycles and evolutionary suicide. Trait-based approaches have also been applied to positive interactions, e.g., to investigate the emergence and maintenance of facilitation in arid ecosystems (Kéfi et al. 2008), the role of facilitation in primary succession (Koffel et al. 2018b), and the impact of exploiters on the evolution of mutualism (Jones et al. 2009).

Trait-based approaches have made it possible to study the evolution of life-history traits in a diversity of organisms and ecological situations, including the size at maturation of exploited fish stocks (de Roos et al. 2006), the seed size and germination strategies of terrestrial plants (Geritz et al. 1999; Mathias and Kisdi 2002; Levin and Muller-Landau 2000), the foraging behavior of herbivorous arthropods (Egas et al. 2005), and the size and trophic strategies of unicellular planktonic organisms (Chakraborty et al. 2017).

Trait-based approaches have also been used to understand the emergence of community structure. System-specific models have been applied to shade-tolerant trees competing for light in forests subject to disturbances (Falster et al. 2017), phytoplankton-zooplankton systems along nutrient gradients (Sauterey et al. 2017), global distributions of phytoplankton (Follows et al. 2007), and size-structured fish communities (Hartvig et al. 2011). A variety of size-structured food web models have been developed to understand emergent properties such as connectance, omnivory and trophic structure (Loeuille and Loreau 2005; Fuchs and Franks 2010; Banas 2011).

When implemented in ecosystem models with an explicit abiotic environment, trait-based approaches have shed light on how organismal adaptations affect ecosystem processes. Examples include understanding selection patterns on nitrogen-fixing plants and their consequences for N-limitation in ecosystems (Menge et al. 2008; Lu and Hedin 2019), the evolution of plant litter decomposability (Boudsocq et al. 2011; Allison 2012; Barot et al. 2016; Arnoldi et al. 2019), and the determinants of phytoplankton stoichiometry and their effect on oceanic N:P ratios (Lenton and Klausmeier 2007).

11.3 Other trait-based frameworks

As noted in Section 11.2, a plethora of trait-based modeling frameworks have been developed over the years (Abrams 2001; Abrams 2005; Fussmann et al. 2007), which we summarize in Table 11.1/. Some of these frameworks are purely ecological, assuming fixed trait values. Others are purely behavioral/evolutionary, neglecting population dynamics. Finally, many combine ecological and evolutionary dynamics in various ways. These frameworks differ in a number of ways:

- The level of biological organization at which traits vary: within individuals (plasticity, including behavior and physiological acclimation), within species (genetic and non-genetic trait variation), or between species
- The heritability of trait variation
- The degree to which biological details are aggregated (do models track population sizes, trait means, and possibly trait variance/covariances, or entire phenotypic distributions?) (Figure 11.7)
- The relative timescales of different processes
- The source of new phenotypes (mutation or immigration, occasional or continuous)

Despite their differences, these different frameworks are all based on trait-dependent growth

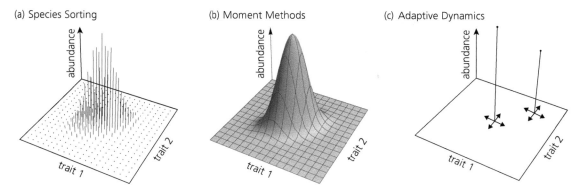

Figure 11.7 Three trait-based modeling frameworks aggregate biological details to different degrees. A) Species sorting. B) Ecological moment methods. C) Adaptive dynamics.

functions g and many can be connected mathematically as limiting cases (Abrams 2001; Lion 2018).

They also can reach similar conclusions about the long-term outcome of community assembly/evolution. When there is a global convergence and evolutionarily stable community, these approaches often tend to similar outcomes. For example, Figure 11.8 shows the outcome of the Lotka–Volterra competition model (Box 11.1) simulated using five different trait-based theoretical frameworks. The ecological quantitative genetics framework initialized with four similar species leads to the four-species ESC predicted by adaptive statics (Figure 11.8A). After a large but finite time, species sorting leads to four distinct clusters of species (Scheffer and van Nes 2006), which are symmetrical (when initial strategies are regularly spaced, Figure 11.8B) or irregular (when strategies are randomly spaced, Figure 11.8C). Community assembly (Figure 11.8D) and adaptive dynamics (Figure 11.8E) also lead to four clusters of species, each containing one or two very similar species, although the transient dynamics vary considerably.

To understand why these distinct frameworks can lead to similar outcomes, consider the oligomorphic dynamics framework (Sasaki and Dieckmann 2011), which tracks the first three moments for a finite number of phenotypic clusters. The "zeroth" moment is the size of population i, $N_i = \int n_i(x)dx$; the first moment is its mean trait, $\bar{x}_i = \int x \cdot n_i(x)dx/N_i$; and the second moment is its trait variance, $V_i = \int (x - \bar{x}_i)^2 n_i(x)dx/N_i$. In the

absence of immigration and mutation, the dynamics of each population are given by

$$\frac{dN_i}{dt} = \int g(x)n_i(x)dx \approx g\,(\bar{x}_i)\,N_i + \frac{1}{2}V_i \frac{\partial^2 g(x)}{\partial x^2}\bigg|_{x=\bar{x}_i} N_i$$

(11.4a)

$$\frac{d\bar{x}_i}{dt} = \frac{1}{N_i}\int x \cdot g(x)n_i(x)dx - \frac{\bar{x}_i}{N_i}\int g(x)n_i(x)dx$$

$$\approx V_i \frac{\partial g(x)}{\partial x}\bigg|_{x=\bar{x}_i}$$

(11.4b)

$$\frac{dV_i}{dt} = \frac{1}{N_i}\int (x - \bar{x}_i)^2 g(x)n_i(x)dx - \frac{V_i}{N_i}\int g(x)n_i(x)dx$$

$$\approx V_i^2 \frac{\partial^2 g(x)}{\partial x^2}\bigg|_{x=\bar{x}_i}$$

(11.4c)

The moment equations in (11.4) are closed by assuming a particular phenotypic distribution, usually normal (Norberg et al. 2001). Assuming small trait variance, each extant species at equilibrium is characterized by $g\,(\bar{x}_i) = 0$ (from Equations 11.4a) and $\frac{\partial g}{\partial x} = 0$ (from Equations 11.4b)—the same conditions defining an evolutionary equilibrium in adaptive dynamics (see Section 11.2). The condition for convergence stability matches the linear stability of Equations 11.4b. Finally, Equations 11.4c shows that trait variance $V_i \to 0$ if $\partial^2 g/\partial x^2 < 0$—exactly the same condition as for evolutionary stability (Taylor and Day 1997). Therefore, it is not surprising that these different frameworks give similar results at equilibrium.

Table 11.1 Comparison of trait-based modeling frameworks.

Modeling Framework	Population Size (N)	Trait Value (x)	Trait Variance (V)	Number of NxV Sets	Source of New Phenotypes	References
Ecological						
Traditional Community Models	dynamic	Fixed	zero	one-few	None	Verhulst 1845; Lotka 1920; Volterra 1926
Species Sorting	dynamic	Fixed	zero	many	None	Chase and Leibold 2003; Follows et al. 2007; Bruggeman and Kooijman 2007
Community Assembly	equilibrated	fixed	zero	dynamic	occasion immigration	Post and Pimm 1983; Rummel and Roughgarden 1985; Law and Morton 1993; Morton and Law 1997
Moment Methods	dynamic	dynamic	dynamic	one	none or continuous immigration	Wirtz and Eckhardt 1996; Norberg et al. 2001; Savage et al. 2007
Intraspecific Variability Theory	dynamic	fixed	fixed	one-few	standing phenotypic variation	Hart et al. 2016
Evolutionary						
Classical Quantitative Genetics	N/A	dynamic	fixed or variable	one	standing genetic variation or continuous mutation	Lande 1976
Optimization Theory	N/A	equilibrated	zero	one	plasticity	Stephens and Krebs 1986; Stearns 1992; Roff 2002
Eco-Evolutionary						
Trait Diffusion Models	dynamic	fixed	zero	infinite	continuous mutation	Levin and Segel 1985; Lehman and Tilman 1997; Merico et al. 2014
Ecological Quantitative Genetics	dynamic	dynamic	fixed	few	standing genetic variation	Abrams 2005
Growth Rate Optimization Theory	dynamic	equilibrated	zero	any	plasticity	Smith et al. 2011
Adaptive Dynamics	equilibrated	dynamic	zero	dynamic	occasional mutation	Geritz et al. 1998
Adaptive Statics	equilibrated	equilibrated	zero	dynamic	everything-is-everywhere	Brown and Vincent 1987; Kremer and Klausmeier 2017, Section 2 of this chapter
Oligomorphic Dynamics	dynamic	dynamic	dynamic	any	continuous mutation	Sasaki and Dieckmann 2011
Drift Equation	equilibrated	dynamic	dynamic	any	none or continuous mutation	Gorban 2007

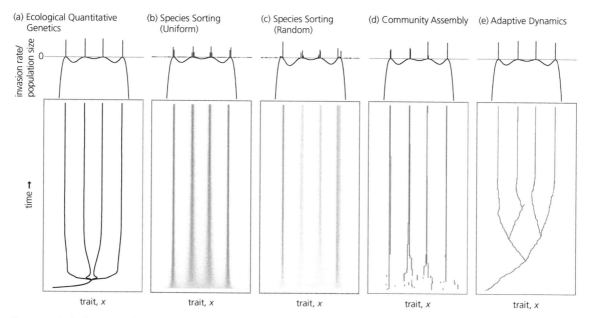

Figure 11.8 The dynamics and long-term outcome of five different modeling frameworks applied to the same trait-based Lotka–Volterra model with a four-species ESC. A) Ecological quantitative genetics. B) Species sorting, with a uniform distribution of species. C) Species sorting, with a random distribution of species. D) Community assembly from a continuous species pool. E) Adaptive dynamics with small mutations.

When do we expect these other frameworks to give significantly different results from the adaptive statics approach we describe in Section 11.2? We are not aware of precise statements, but here are some suggestions based on intuition and experience:

- In the case of a local-but-not-global ESS (Figure 11.3E), the stochastic trait-substitution process of adaptive dynamics will not find a global ESC, whereas a model that allows large mutations or immigration will not get stuck.
- If ecological quantitative genetics or oligomorphic dynamics models are not initialized with a sufficient number of species, they will not find a global ESC. Instead, they will get stuck at a branching point. Furthermore, early trait convergence can reduce the number of distinct species in these simulations, leading to groups of neutral species clustered on a fitness maximum (Edwards et al. 2018).
- If there is no global ESC, then the details of how new strategies arise will be important in determining the non-equilibrium dynamics.

- Increasing immigration or mutation rates (in methods that allow this) will increase the trait variance and eventually affect population size (the "demographic load"; e.g., Ronce and Kirkpatrick 2001) and the number and mean traits of phenotypic clusters.

Frameworks with dynamic trait variances such as ecological moment methods and oligomorphic dynamics may fail at branching points, where $\partial^2 g / \partial x_0^2 > 0$, because the disruptive selection will cause the trait variance to diverge. Ecological moment methods are especially susceptible to this problem because they attempt to represent an entire community with only three pieces of information: total population size, mean trait, and trait variance. Thus, they are not well-suited to situations where there is a multi-species ESC.

These different frameworks make different simplifying assumptions, so no single approach is best for all purposes. Questions that directly concern the source of new phenotypes obviously require a framework that includes those processes. Trait continuum models make the fewest simplifications, but are the most computationally intensive of the listed approaches, intractably so for more than two traits. Models that aggregate these details in order to follow a small number of variables are required. Ecological moment methods are particularly compact, and each moment embodies a major ecological perspective—total population (ecosystem), mean trait (functional), and trait variance (diversity). However, as described previously, they fail at branching points where the variance diverges.

In contrast, the adaptive statics approach presented in Section 11.2 allows for a dynamic number of species. It makes the simplest assumption about the source of new phenotypes ("everything is everywhere"; Baas Becking 1934; De Wit and Bouvier 2006) and is computationally efficient, making it an elegant approach focused on the ecological mechanisms underlying community structure in the absence of mutation or dispersal limitation. However, as an equilibrium approach, it is unable to deal with trait dynamics on any time scale.

Adaptive dynamics takes a long-term perspective to address the evolutionary origins of diversity. However, given its assumption of asexual reproduction, new phenotypes form populations that are demographically independent of their progenitors. This can seem simplistic from a purely evolutionary biology standpoint, as it neglects the genetic, sexual, behavioral, and spatial constraints that can prevent reproductive isolation and assortative mating from occurring, and has been the source of ongoing debate (Doebeli et al. 2005; Gavrilets 2005).

Questions about short-term adaptive responses to environmental perturbations require a framework with trait variances such as ecological quantitative genetics or oligomorphic dynamics. For such questions, we recommend the ecological quantitative genetics approach, which allows species evolution to occur within a community context (e.g., McPeek 2017). Evolution that happens on an ecological time scale can prevent a population whose density is slowly decreasing from going extinct, a phenomenon called "evolutionary rescue" (Gomulkiewicz and Holt 1995). It can also allow persistence in a continuously changing environment if the rate of environmental change is slow enough (Lynch and Lande 1993), although possibly with a tipping point (Osmond and Klausmeier 2018).

Because trait-based approaches can be applied to questions across ecology and evolutionary biology, we need a diverse set of theoretical frameworks. Understanding the relationships among these frameworks (Table 11.1) as well as their strengths and weaknesses is required to choose the best approach for a given question. Devising new ways to reduce the complexity of ecological communities in our models will remain a valuable pursuit.

11.4 Extensions/Complications

The trait-based frameworks we have examined so far were discussed in the simple ecological setting of spatial and temporal homogeneity. Real ecosystems are spatially extended and subject to both externally driven and internally generated temporal fluctuations, and this spatial and temporal heterogeneity is known to be an important determinant of population dynamics and community structure. Furthermore, we have focused on the dynamics of single traits, another vast oversimplification. In this section, we discuss how trait-based theoretical frameworks can be made more realistic, and relevant to more systems, by incorporating temporal and spatial heterogeneity and multiple traits.

11.4.1   Traits in time

The invasion analysis presented in Section 11.2 assumes that a rare, invading population experiences constant conditions (including resident densities and environmental factors). However, these conditions may vary due to externally driven forcing (stochastic or deterministic) or internally generated cycles or chaos. Adaptive dynamics studies of temporally variable systems require calculating an appropriate average invasion rate $\bar{g}_{inv}$, based on the type of variability present within a system and whether there is population structure (Metz et al. 1992). Once the value of $\bar{g}_{inv}$ has been calculated, all the machinery of adaptive dynamics can be used exactly as presented in Section 11.2: calculating (time-averaged) fitness gradients, locating evolutionary equilibria, and determining their convergence and evolutionary stability.

Unstructured populations. In the case of an unstructured population experiencing periodic forcing, we can simply average the instantaneous invasion rate, $g_{inv}\left(x_0; \vec{E}(t)\right)$, over a period:

$$\bar{g}_{inv} = \frac{1}{\tau} \int_0^\tau g_{inv}\left(x_0; \vec{E}(t)\right) dt \qquad (11.5)$$

(Smith and Waltman 1995). It is straightforward to calculate $\bar{g}_{inv}$ when cycles arise from external forcing with known period τ, but potentially harder when cycles are endogenously generated, as the precise value of τ must be determined numerically and may depend on the trait values of resident species. If the environment varies stochastically or chaotically, then the definition of invasion fitness is the limit of Equation (11.5) as $t \to \infty$. In practice, it is usually not possible to calculate this infinite integral to find the exact invasion rate, so an approximation can be obtained by simply averaging g_{inv} over a long interval of time. Note that, because the integral in Equation (11.5) is linear, the gradient of average fitness needed for adaptive dynamics studies, $\partial \bar{g}_{inv}/\partial x_0$, is equivalent to the average of the gradient of instantaneous fitness,

$$\frac{\partial \bar{g}_{inv}}{\partial x_0} = \frac{1}{\tau} \int_0^\tau \frac{\partial g_{inv}}{\partial x_0} dt \qquad (11.6)$$

which may be easier to calculate numerically (Kremer and Klausmeier 2017).

Structured populations. As described in Section 11.2, in a constant environment invasion fitness is given as the dominant eigenvalue of the transition matrix. Intuition might suggest that, in fluctuating environments, invasion rate could be calculated by simply averaging the dominant eigenvalue of the transition matrix over a period in a periodic system (or over a long interval of time in an aperiodic system). However, that turns out to be incorrect. Instead, obtaining invasion rates requires calculating the dominant Floquet exponent (periodic systems; Klausmeier 2008), or more generally, the dominant Lyapunov exponents (aperiodic systems; Metz et al. 1992). In both cases, this must usually be done numerically.

As a final technical note, the definitions of invasion fitness given previously are based on the adaptive dynamics framework, and specifically its separation of time scales. When other trait-based

modeling frameworks are employed (Section 11.3), other approaches are required. For example, in the ecological quantitative genetics approach, the average trait(s) of a population change in response to instantaneous fitness gradients, which depend in turn on the current environment. As genetic variance approaches zero, trait change slows, and quantitative genetics results converge on those of adaptive dynamics. However, with larger genetic variances, rapid evolution is possible. and complex interactions with ecological dynamics may arise (Hairston et al. 2005).

Recently, we used trait-based models to examine the evolutionary stability of species coexistence in variable environments. We used the adaptive statics framework to investigate two fluctuation-dependent coexistence mechanisms (*sensu* Chesson 2000): relative nonlinearity and the storage effect. We found that relative nonlinearity can easily support an ESC of two species (a fast grower and superior competitor), but higher diversity was improbable (Kremer and Klausmeier 2013). The storage effect is a potentially more powerful coexistence mechanism. When the environment alternates periodically between two states and the period of forcing is large, two species can coexist as an ESC under a wide range of conditions (Miller and Klausmeier 2017). When the environment varies continuously, more species can coexist, with a limit to similarity resulting in species with evenly spaced trait values (Kremer and Klausmeier 2017). We also found more baroque outcomes, such as alternative evolutionary attractors (Miller and Klausmeier 2017; Kremer and Klausmeier 2017). When using the quantitative genetics framework, we found that evolutionarily stable coexistence was robust to a small amount of trait variance, but that larger trait variance allowed rapid evolution leading to complex dynamics and species convergence, ultimately undermining species coexistence (Kremer and Klausmeier 2013).

11.4.2 Traits in space

The theoretical framework as described in Section 11.2 implicitly assumes that populations, communities, and ecosystems do not vary in space, or that dispersal between locations is negligible so that spatial patterns can be derived directly from bifurcation diagrams (Section 11.2.2). These assumptions simplify the analysis of trait-based theory when they can be empirically justified for particular organisms, scales, or questions (e.g., in well-mixed planktonic systems). However, accounting for space may be essential when: i) interactions between organisms (and populations) are spatially structured (e.g., competition among terrestrial plants), ii) the trait(s) of interest are directly related to the movement of individuals, or iii) important environmental factors vary in space, such that populations in different locations experience different selective pressures, and dispersal is not negligible. How ecological processes vary in space is the focus of metapopulation, metacommunity, and metaecosystem theories, all of which can be all be integrated with trait-based approaches.

In the adaptive dynamics framework, accounting for space simply consists of adding structure to populations. Rather than considering a single, unstructured population, we instead examine a collection of multiple subpopulations (whose dynamics are driven by local processes), that are coupled together by the exchange of individuals through dispersal. When the subpopulations are discrete, well-separated entities, we call them "patches", and their collective population dynamics can be modelled using matrices similar to Leslie matrices,

$$\frac{d\vec{N}_i}{dt} = \left(G\left(x_i; E\left(\vec{x}, \vec{N} \right) \right) + D\left(x_i \right) \right) \vec{N}_i \qquad (11.7)$$

where $\vec{N}_i$ is a vector of the abundances of population i in different patches, G is a diagonal matrix governing within-patch dynamics and D is a matrix encoding dispersal among patches. In principle, both local processes and dispersal may depend on trait x. Alternatively, it is sometimes more appropriate to model populations as continuously distributed through space (Troost et al. 2005). In this approach, population dynamics can be modeled using systems of partial differential equations called reaction-diffusion systems, which take the form

$$\frac{\partial N_i}{\partial t} = g\left(z, x_i; E\left(\vec{x}(z), \vec{N}(z) \right) \right) N_i + d\left(x_i \right) \frac{\partial^2 N_i}{\partial z^2} \qquad (11.8)$$

where z denotes the spatial dimension, g determines the local dynamics, and the last term allows dispersal (Okubo and Levin 2001). Other approaches vary in their level of detail, from explicitly accounting for the discrete nature of individuals to treating entire populations as either present or absent (e.g., patch occupancy models and cellular automata, see Levins 1969; Durrett and Levin 1998; Klausmeier and Tilman 2002).

Whatever the approach, the fitness of an invading strategy is always given by the dominant eigenvalue of the matrix $(G + D)$ or the linear operator $g + d\ \partial^2/\partial z^2$, which is its asymptotic population growth rate once a stable spatial structure across all subpopulations is reached (Metz et al. 1992; Troost et al. 2005; Van Baalen and Rand, 1998). In the case of reaction-diffusion equations, the linear operator usually needs to be approximated by a matrix. The fitness gradient can be calculated numerically using a finite difference approximation or it can be computed directly using techniques from sensitivity analysis (Caswell 2001), providing additional conceptual insight: under some conditions, the fitness gradient of the population as a whole can be shown to be equal to a weighted average of the local selection gradients, where the weights are the squared abundances of the corresponding subpopulations (Wickman et al. 2017).

Moving from the adaptive dynamics framework to the ecological quantitative genetics framework requires a separate equation for trait dynamics (Kirkpatrick and Barton 1997; Case and Taper 2000; Ronce and Kirkpatrick 2001; Norberg et al. 2012). In the reaction-diffusion setting, this takes the form

$$\frac{\partial x_i}{\partial t} = V \frac{\partial g}{\partial x_0}\bigg|_{x_0 = x_i} + d\left(\frac{\partial^2 x_i}{\partial z^2} + 2 \frac{\partial \log N_i}{\partial z} \cdot \frac{\partial x_i}{\partial z} \right) \qquad (11.9)$$

where the first term captures local directional selection and the second term incorporates gene flow (the second term of which accounts for asymmetric gene flow due to gradients in population density). This powerful framework allows for the investigation of local adaptation, since the trait values of a population depend explicitly on space z.

Applications of spatially-explicit trait-based theory span a diverse set of systems, from bacterial biofilms (Nadell et al. 2016), to social vertebrates and insects (Lehmann et al. 2008), terrestrial plants

(Kéfi et al. 2018), pathogens (Débarre et al. 2012), and plankton in poorly mixed water columns (Troost et al. 2005, Wickman et al. 2017). It has provided a number of important insights into the evolution of species ranges (Kirkpatrick and Barton 1997; Case and Taper 2000), the response of communities to environmental change (Norberg et al. 2012), the maintenance of species diversity in heterogeneous environments (Wickman et al. 2017), and the global distributions of plankton (Follows et al. 2007).

The evolution of dispersal itself is an extensively studied topic. It has long been recognized that spatial variation alone is not sufficient to favor the evolution of dispersal (Hastings 1983; Dockery et al. 1998; Parvinen 1999; Wickman et al. 2017). Only the continuous availability of underexploited patches, either at the edge of an invading population, or maintained by regular disturbance or demographic stochasticity, can turn dispersal into an advantageous trait (Ronce 2007). More subtly, dispersal can evolve as an altruistic behavior (e.g., when it reduces competition among an organism's kin, despite offering no direct benefits).

More generally, spatially-explicit approaches have been essential to the understanding of the evolution of cooperation and a variety of other altruistic traits (Lion and Van Baalen 2008; Lehmann et al. 2008). In completely homogenous systems, altruism is selected against due to the "Tragedy of the commons" (Hardin 1968). Conversely, spatial structure and local dispersal can create "viscous populations", where related individuals tend to cluster in space, favoring the evolution of altruism (Lion and Van Baalen 2008).

11.4.3 Multiple traits

The theory on evolutionary equilibria and their stability presented in Section 11.2 focused on systems with a single trait. In the real world, an organism can be characterized by a myriad of traits that are all simultaneously under selection. Even though trade-offs can constrain the space of possible trait combinations, any given population's strategy is often determined by its specific values of multiple traits. For this reason, a general trait-based theory that applies to multidimensional traits is necessary.

In practice, setting up a trait-based model with multidimensional traits follows the same recipe laid out in Section 11.2.2, except that $\vec{x}_{G,i}$ is now a vector whose coordinates are the collection of traits defining the ith strategy in guild G. Invasion fitness $g\left(\vec{x}_0; \hat{E}\left(\vec{x}_1\right)\right)$ of a mutant $\vec{x}_0$ follows, with the fitness gradient now being a true vector. Evolutionary equilibria are characterized by the trait vectors $\vec{x}_0$ that cancel out the components of the fitness gradient. Because of fitness interactions between traits—selection on one trait usually depends on other traits—finding a multidimensional evolutionary equilibrium implies solving a system of coupled equations. This also applies if the multiple traits belong to separate guilds, such as co-evolving predator-prey systems, as it comes to no surprise that the optimal trait for a prey will depend on the trait of the predator, and vice-versa. Finally, assessing whether these evolutionary equilibria are evolutionarily stable relies on extending the tools presented in Section 11.2.2 to multidimensional space, which is done in practice by checking if the Hessian matrix of the invasion fitness is negative definite for unbounded traits. If the trait space is bounded, constrained optimization has to be used instead.

There is another complication, specific to the multi-dimensional nature of this problem, that involves the idea of convergence stability defined in Section 11.2.2. This problem has been well-explored in the adaptive dynamics context (Leimar 2009; see also Débarre et al. 2014 for a similar approach in ecological quantitative genetics). This complication is subtle, as convergence stability depends on the nature and characteristics of trait variation. In an evolutionary context, genetic variation is usually constrained through correlations—formally encoded in the genetic variance-covariance matrix, also known as the G-matrix of quantitative genetics (Lande 1979)—such that selection on one trait can lead to evolution of another trait, even when the latter is not under selection. Due to these correlations, convergence stability cannot always be solely assessed using the Jacobian of the fitness gradient (the "selection" part), but can also depend on the exact nature of genetic correlations (the "variation" part). To formalize this issue, Leimar (2009) distinguishes between two notions of convergence stability. The first, "absolute convergence stability", imposes very restrictive conditions on the Jacobian of the fitness gradient under which an evolutionary equilibrium will be locally convergence stable under any conceivable adaptive path and G-matrix. The second, "strong convergence stability", places a weaker condition on the Jacobian under which an evolutionary equilibrium will be locally convergence stable under the most probable evolutionary trajectory. This second definition of convergence stability is weaker than the first one: if an evolutionary equilibrium is only strong convergence stable, one could find some very particular series of mutations allowing escape from this equilibrium (Leimar 2009).

Applications of trait-based theories that involve multiple traits are diverse. Two-dimensional trait spaces, resulting in practice from a three-way trade-off between three traits, are a natural starting point. They have been influential in ecology (Grime 1974) and are associated with counterintuitive outcomes, such as the possibility of positive correlations between two traits when the last one is not controlled for (Van Noordwijk and de Jong 1986). A recent example in plants involves the study of optimal allocation between resource competition and the tolerance of and resistance to herbivory—with the latter two traits corresponding to "defense" (Koffel et al. 2018a). We showed that investment in defense is expected to increase along a resource gradient, but that increase in partial resistance, mixed tolerance and resistance, or coexistence of a completely resistant and a tolerant strategy were all possible outcomes, depending on the shape of the allocation trade-off that constrains the three traits. In another two-dimensional example, Falster et al. (2017) showed how a model of plants differing in leaf mass per unit leaf area and height at maturation in a complex forest ecosystem can generate a very diverse community, including a diverse set of shade-tolerant species. In the context of macroevolutionary dynamics, accounting for multiple phenotypic dimensions has been shown to have a strong influence on the structure of the emerging food webs (Allhoff et al. 2015). Using a general model of asymmetric competition, Doebeli and Ispolatov (2017) showed that the

diversity of strategies that coexist at the end of the diversification process scales exponentially with the number of traits considered.

Despite these applications, most trait-based models focus on a single trait or a pair of traits linked by a hard trade-off (effectively one trait). One barrier to multi-trait models is coming up with a manageable way to define the shape of multi-dimensional trade-offs. A possibility is to base them on a common energetic or material currency, so that total allocation to different traits is constant, while functions with flexible shapes encode whether investment in a specific trait has diminishing or accelerating returns (Koffel et al. 2018a). Further investigation of multiple traits—how they affect convergence stability, how to efficiently find eco-evolutionary equilibria, and how to encode multi-dimensional trade-offs—remains an important area for future theoretical development.

11.5 Frontiers of trait-based modeling

11.5.1 Comparisons with empirical systems

One of trait-based theory's advantages, as previously discussed, is its ability to make quantitative predictions about the diversity and distribution of trait values likely to occur within populations and communities, and how these distributions might change across environmental gradients (Sections 11.2.2). In principle, this should provide increased opportunities to test theoretical predictions and models using experimental and observational data. A handful of examples exist, spanning a range of traits, systems, and ecological dynamics. Regarding individual populations and communities in particular environments, examples include studies of the size-dependent flowering strategies of plants (Childs et al. 2003; Rees et al. 2006; Metcalf et al. 2008), the reproductive strategies of female Soay sheep (Childs et al. 2011), and the height and distribution of foliage in herbs and trees (Givnish 1982; King 1990). Considering population and community dynamics through time, successful examples include studies of the predatory-prey cycles exhibited in a rotifer/algae system (Yoshida et al. 2003), and seasonal patterns in aquatic food webs (Boit et al. 2012; Curtsdotter et al. 2019). Across environmental gradients, predictions of trait-based theory have been tested by examining variation in forest productivity along elevational gradients (Enquist et al. 2017; Fyallas et al. 2017), plant allocation to foliage, wood, and fine roots across nitrogen gradients (Dybzinski et al. 2011), and global relationships between the optimal temperature of phytoplankton species and the mean annual temperatures they experience (Thomas et al. 2012). These examples are exciting and highlight the power of trait-based approaches to bridge gaps between the theoretical and empirical world.

However, compared to the extensive (and growing) body of literature focused on theory alone, these empirical tests are few in number. In part, this may reflect challenges posed by the limited availability of high-quality trait data across multiple individuals, species, and environments over time (e.g., Kremer et al. 2017). Excitingly, portions of this constraint are being alleviated through a variety of massive community-wide efforts to compile and publish trait data, especially for terrestrial plants (e.g., TRY database; Kattge et al. 2011). We think, however, that it is more likely that the shortage of examples simply reflects the fact that few teams have attempted to bring together trait-based theory with empirical observations. We hope that the introduction to trait-based theory presented in this chapter will help lower the barriers associated with this challenge, while convincing readers of the value of this opportunity to tighten theoretical-empirical linkages and to advance the field of ecology.

11.5.2 Linking trait- and species-based approaches

In this chapter we have focused on purely trait-based approaches, where a species' performance is defined solely by its traits. This is an effective way to reduce model complexity when the number of relevant traits is less than the number of species. However, achieving this reduction requires knowing the identity (and values) of the relevant traits and how best to incorporate them into process-based models, both of which represent significant challenges. When more species are introduced into

trait-based models (such as ecological quantitative genetics models) than can persist in an evolutionarily stable community (ESC), distinct species may converge on an adaptive peak to become selectively neutral (terHorst et al. 2010; Edwards et al. 2018). This may represent a phenomenon that happens in the real world (McPeek 2017; Edwards et al. 2018), but it is also potentially symptomatic of situations where trait-based models are missing important functional variation among species. Are there hybrid approaches that would allow us to combine trait-based models with species-based models that account for species-specific differences?

One possibility, inspired by Chesson's modern coexistence theory (Chesson 2000), would be to consider introducing species-specific terms that either affect "fitness differences" or are (de-)stabilizing. To allow for fitness differences, we would simply add a species-specific term ϵ_i to a species' growth rate so that

$$\frac{dN_i}{dt} = \left(g\left(x_i; E\left(\vec{x}, \vec{N} \right) \right) + \epsilon_i \right) N_i \qquad (11.10)$$

Theoretically, these fitness-difference terms would simply promote dominance by species with higher ϵ_i values. The real value of this formulation would be in parameterizing the trait-dependent population dynamics of actual species, where species differences that cannot be attributed to the traits considered would be captured by this species-dependent "error term."

If these species-specific effects are instead (de-)stabilizing, the theoretical implications are more interesting and require more intricate model modifications. For example, these terms could represent species-specific sources of negative density-dependence, such as intraspecific competition for mates or specialized natural enemies (Scheffer and van Nes 2006), or positive density-dependence such as Allee effects (Noest 1997). Negative density-dependence inhibits resident species more than invaders (who are naturally at low density), stabilizing coexistence of slightly inferior and neutral species. In contrast, positive density-dependence inhibits rare invaders compared to established residents, leading to more cases of founder control (Section 11.2.2, Lotka–Volterra case iv). A systematic exploration of these effects, as well as broader efforts to integrate trait- and species-based approaches, would be valuable.

11.5.3 Using trait-based theory to improve Earth Systems Models

One frontier where trait-based theory is poised to make important contributions involves earth systems modeling. Earth Systems Models (or ESMs) are spatially explicit models of the dynamic physical and chemical interactions of the earth's land, ocean, and atmosphere (Heavens et al. 2013). They are used to study the past development of our planet's climate and the operation of global biogeochemical cycles. ESMs are also powerful tools for projecting future environmental and ecological conditions under different anthropogenic climate change scenarios, including shifting species ranges and altered ecosystem function (Heavens et al. 2013). While ESMs contain sophisticated descriptions of physical and chemical processes, biological processes (including ecology and evolution) are treated more coarsely or are absent entirely. Historical factors, critical uncertainties (including the absence of a widely-accepted, general model of ecology), data shortages (needed to parameterize and validate biological sub-models), and computational demands (ESMs are already computationally intensive) all contribute to limit the level of biological detail in ESMs. These constraints are problematic, as ecological and evolutionary processes can significantly affect physical and chemical properties, driving feedbacks that regulate the global carbon cycle. Consequently, making more accurate projections of future environmental conditions from regional to global scales depends in no small part on developing more realistic representations of ecology within ESMs. Fundamentally, this is a question of how to model variation in traits (and hence, ecosystem function) through time and space at a global scale. Trait-based approaches offer promising ways to enhance the flexibility and biological diversity of biogeochemical models (Litchman et al. 2015) and ESMs without adding large computational demands.

Currently, the terrestrial and marine components of ESMs typically aggregate Earth's vast functional diversity of individuals and species into somewhere between two and a dozen *functional groups* or *functional types*. All members of a single group are assumed to have fixed identical traits or functions, intended to represent an average individual. Turnover in traits across environments only occurs through changes in the relative abundances of groups, driven by underlying environmental gradients and/or interactions between groups, such as competition or predation. For example, marine systems often contain basic N-P-Z models (where mineral nutrients, N, support a single, generic phytoplankton, P, that is in turn consumed by a generic zooplankton, Z) (e.g., Fasham et al. 1990). Extensions of this basic structure expand the diversity of plankton functional types considered, based on factors including size (e.g., Le Quéré et al. 2005; Stock et al. 2014). Similarly, terrestrial models, termed Dynamic Global Vegetation Models (DGVMs) tend to focus on the dynamics of a handful of plant functional types representing trees and herbaceous species. Predetermined bioclimatic envelopes control the distribution of each functional group, while environmental (and in some cases, competitive) factors control the relative abundance of each group within a given location (Foley et al. 2000; Sitch et al. 2003). Critiques of these approaches include: i) the fact that fixed trait values significantly under-represent the functional variation within and across communities, and ii) interactions between functional groups are over-simplified have been raised in both terrestrial and marine systems (e.g., Van Bodegom et al. 2012; Reichstein et al. 2014; Litchman et al. 2015). Furthermore, there are concerns in terrestrial systems that population demographics and community succession following disturbance are poorly resolved (Fisher et al. 2018), and that fixed bioclimatic constraints of functional groups may severely hamper the ability of DGVMs to predict the effects of climate change, as new, no-analog environments and communities emerge (Van Bodegom et al. 2012).

Trait-based approaches offer promising ways to address these shortcomings, in both marine and terrestrial systems. Efforts to build the next generation of more realistic ecosystem models fall into several groups. This includes adding flexibility to functional groups by replacing fixed trait values with trait-environment relationships that are either empirically parameterized (terrestrial, Zaehle and Friend 2010; Van Bodegom et al. 2012; Verheijen et al. 2015; temperature dependence in marine models, *e.g.*, Stock et al. 2014) or that emerge from various optimality assumptions (terrestrial, Xu et al. 2012; Meir et al. 2015; marine, Smith et al. 2011). In marine systems, both moment methods (Terseleer et al. 2014) and species sorting (Bruggeman and Kooijman 2007; Follows et al. 2007; Ward et al. 2012) have been investigated. Others have adopted a detailed individual- or agent-based approach, where traits vary across individuals, determining their survival, growth, and reproduction, and hence the transmission of their traits to successive generations (terrestrial, Scheiter et al. 2013; Sakschewski et al. 2015; marine, Clark et al. 2011, 2013). This approach allows for trait variation within communities, as well as emergent patterns of trait variation across environments and adaptation to ongoing environmental change, but comes at substantial computation costs. While the goal of these diverse studies is the eventual development of the next generation of more biologically realistic ESMs, few if any have yet been applied at the full scale of an ESM, but rather focus on regional examples. Sorting out which of these approaches, all variously focused on traits, provides the most useful balance between flexibility, feasibility, and reality at different scales and in diverse systems awaits further research.

11.5.4 Final thoughts

As we have seen, trait-based approaches have a long history in ecology and evolution (Section 11.1), extending well before the emergence of trait-based ecology as an identifiable and important paradigm. In recent decades, theoretical frameworks such as adaptive dynamics (Section 11.2) have used evolutionary concepts to provide tools for understanding a diverse set of ecological interactions and systems (Section 11.2.3). An expanding range of trait-based modeling frameworks (Section 11.3), tailored to different situations, may superficially appear quite different, but are in fact they closely related (Table 11.1). Trait-based theory can incorporate complicating factors such as temporal and spatial heterogeneity and multiple traits (Section 11.4).

Future developments of trait-based modeling approaches show great promise in advancing both our theoretical and empirical understanding of ecology, from community structure to global ecosystem dynamics (Section 11.5).

References

Abrams, P., (1983). The theory of limiting similarity. *Annual Review of Ecology and Systematics* 14(1): 359–76.

Abrams, P., (1987). The functional responses of adaptive consumers of two resources. *Theoretical Population Biology* 32(2): 262–88.

Abrams, P.A. and Matsuda, H. (1997). Prey adaptation as a cause of predator-prey cycles. *Evolution* 51(6): 1742–50.

Abrams, P. A. (2001). Modelling the adaptive dynamics of traits involved in inter- and intraspecific interactions: An assessment of three methods. *Ecology Letters* 4(2): 166–75.

Abrams, P. A. (2005). 'Adaptive Dynamics' vs. 'adaptive dynamics'. *Journal of Evolutionary Biology* 18: 1162–5.

Alizon, S., de Roode, J. C., and Michalakis, Y. (2013). Multiple infections and the evolution of virulence. *Ecology Letters* 16(4): 556–67.

Allesina, S. and Tang, S. (2012). Stability criteria for complex ecosystems. *Nature* 483(7388): 205–8.

Allhoff, K. T., Ritterskamp, D., Rall, B. C., Drossel, B., and Guill, C. (2015). Evolutionary food web model based on body masses gives realistic networks with permanent species turnover. *Scientific Reports* 5: 10955.

Allison, S. D. (2012). A trait-based approach for modelling microbial litter decomposition. *Ecology Letters* 15(9): 1058–70.

Andersen, K. H., Aksnes, D. L., Berge, T., Fiksen, Ø., and Visser, A. (2015). Modelling emergent trophic strategies in plankton. *Journal of Plankton Research* 37(5): 862–8.

Arnoldi, J. -F., Coq, S., Kéfi, S., and Ibanez, S. (2020). Positive plant–soil feedback trigger tannin evolution by niche construction: A spatial stoichiometric model. *Journal of Ecology*, 108(1): 378–91.

Baas-Becking, L. G. M. (1934). *Geobiologie; of Inleiding tot de Milieukunde*. [Geobiology; or Introduction to the Science of the Environment]. Den Haag: WP Van Stockum & Zoon NV.

Banas, N. S. (2011). Adding complex trophic interactions to a size-spectral plankton model: Emergent diversity patterns and limits on predictability. *Ecological Modelling* 222: 2663–75.

Barabás, G., S. Pigolotti, M. Gyllenberg, U. Dieckmann, and G. Meszéna. (2012). Continuous coexistence or discrete species? A new review of an old question. *Evolutionary Ecology Research* 14: 523–54.

Barbier, M., Arnoldi, J. F., Bunin, G., and Loreau, M. (2018). Generic assembly patterns in complex ecological communities. *Proceedings of the National Academy of Sciences of the United States of America* 115(9): 2156–61.

Barot, S., Bornhofen, S., Boudsocq, S., Raynaud, X., and Loeuille, N. (2016). Evolution of nutrient acquisition: When space matters. *Functional Ecology*, 30(2): 283–94.

Bazzaz, F. A. and Grace, J. (eds.) (1997). *Plant Resource Allocation*. New York, Elsevier.

Boit, A., Martinez, N. D., Williams, R. J., and Gaedke, U. (2012). Mechanistic theory and modelling of complex food-web dynamics in Lake Constance. *Ecology Letters* 15(6): 594–602.

Bonachela, J. A., Raghib, M., and Levin, S. A. (2011). Dynamic model of flexible phytoplankton nutrient uptake. *Proceedings of the National Academy of Sciences of the United States of America* 108(51): 20633–8.

Boudsocq, S., Barot, S., and Loeuille, N. (2011). Evolution of nutrient acquisition: When adaptation fills the gap between contrasting ecological theories. *Proceedings of the Royal Society of London B: Biological Sciences* 278(1704): 449–57.

Brown, J. S. and Vincent, T. L. (1987). Coevolution as an evolutionary game. *Evolution* 41(1): 66–79.

Bruggeman, J. and Kooijman, S. A. L. M. (2007). A biodiversity-inspired approach to aquatic ecosystem modeling. *Limnology and Oceanography* 52(4): 1533–44.

Case, T. J. and Taper, M. L. (2000). Interspecific competition, environmental gradients, gene flow, and the coevolution of species' borders. *American Naturalist* 155(5): 583–605.

Caswell, H. (2001). *Matrix Population Models: Construction, Analysis, and Interpretation*. (2nd edition). Sunderland, Mass: Sinauer Associates. Inc.

Chakraborty, S., Nielsen, L. T., and Andersen, K. H. (2017). Trophic strategies of unicellular plankton. *American Naturalist* 189(4): E77–90.

Charnov, E. L. (1976). Optimal foraging, the marginal value theorem. *Theoretical Population Biology* 9(2): 129–36.

Chase, J. M. and Leibold, M. A. (2003). *Ecological Niches: Linking Classical and Contemporary Approaches*. Chicago: University of Chicago Press.

Chesson, P. (1990). MacArthur's consumer-resource model. *Theoretical Population Biology* 37(1): 26–38.

Chesson, P. (2000). Mechanisms of maintenance of species diversity. *Annual Review of Ecology and Systematics* 31: 343–66.

Childs, D. Z., Rees, M., Rose, K. E., Grubb, P. J., and Ellner, S. P. (2003). Evolution of complex flowering strategies: an age-and size–structured integral projection model. *Proceedings of the Royal Society of London. Series B: Biological Sciences* 270(1526): 1829–38.

Childs, D. Z., Coulson, T. N., Pemberton, J. M., Clutton-Brock, T. H., and Rees, M. (2011). Predicting trait values and measuring selection in complex life histories: Reproductive allocation decisions in Soay sheep. *Ecology Letters* 14(10): 985–92.

Clark, J. R., Daines, S. J., Lenton, T. M., Watson, A. J., and Williams, H. T. (2011). Individual-based modelling of adaptation in marine microbial populations using genetically defined physiological parameters. *Ecological Modelling* 222(23–24): 3823–37.

Clark, J. R., Lenton, T. M., Williams, H. T., and Daines, S. J. (2013). Environmental selection and resource allocation determine spatial patterns in picophytoplankton cell size. *Limnology and Oceanography* 58(3): 1008–22.

Cortez, M. H. and Weitz, J. S. (2014). Coevolution can reverse predator-prey cycles. *Proceedings of the National Academy of Sciences of the United States of America* 111(20): 7486–91.

Curtsdotter, A., Banks, H. T., Banks, J. E., Jonsson, M., Jonsson, T., Laubmeier, A. N., Traugott, M., and Bommarco, R. (2019). Ecosystem function in predator-prey food webs—confronting dynamic models with empirical data. *Journal of Animal Ecology* 88(2): 196–210.

De Roos, A. M., Boukal, D. S., and Persson, L, (2006). Evolutionary regime shifts in age and size at maturation of exploited fish stocks. *Proceedings of the Royal Society B: Biological Sciences* 273(1596): 1873–80.

De Wit, R. and Bouvier, T. (2006). 'Everything is everywhere, but, the environment selects'; what did Baas Becking and Beijerinck really say? *Environmental Microbiology* 8(4): 755–8.

Débarre, F., Lion, S., van Baalen, M., and Gandon, S., (2012). Evolution of host life-history traits in a spatially structured host-parasite system. *American Naturalist* 179(1): 52–63.

Débarre, F., Nuismer, S. L., and Doebeli, M., (2014). Multidimensional (co)evolutionary stability. *American Naturalist* 184(2): 158–71.

Dercole, F. and Rinaldi, S. (2002). Evolution of cannibalistic traits: scenarios derived from adaptive dynamics. *Theoretical Population Biology* 62(4): 365–74.

Dercole, F. (2003). Remarks on branching-extinction evolutionary cycles. *Journal of Mathematical Biology*, 47(6): 569–80.

Dıaz, S. and Cabido, M. (2001). Vive la difference: Plant functional diversity matters to ecosystem processes. *Trends in Ecology & Evolution* 16(11): 646–55.

Diekmann, O., (2004). A beginners guide to adaptive dynamics. In *Mathematical modelling of population dynamics*. Banach Center Publ, (Vol. 63). Warsaw: Polish Acad. Sci, pp. 47–86

Dieckmann, U., Marrow, P., and Law, R., (1995). Evolutionary cycling in predator-prey interactions:

Population dynamics and the Red Queen. *Journal of Theoretical Biology* 176(1): 91–102.

Dockery, J., Hutson, V., Mischaikow, K., and Pernarowski, M. (1998). The evolution of slow dispersal rates: A reaction diffusion model. *Journal of Mathematical Biology* 37(1): 61–83.

Doebeli, M., Dieckmann, U., Metz, J. A., and Tautz, D. (2005). What we have also learned: Adaptive speciation is theoretically plausible. *Evolution* 59(3): 691–5.

Doebeli, M., and Ispolatov, I. (2017). Diversity and coevolutionary dynamics in high-dimensional phenotype spaces. *American Naturalist* 189(2): 105–20.

Drenovsky, R. E., Grewell, B. J., D'antonio, C. M., Funk, J. L., James, J. J., Molinari, N., Parker, I. M., and Richards, C. L. (2012). A functional trait perspective on plant invasion. *Annals of Botany* 110(1): 141–53.

Durrett, R. and Levin, S. (1998). Spatial aspects of interspecific competition. *Theoretical Population Biology* 53(1): 30–43.

Dybzinski, R., Farrior, C., Wolf, A., Reich, P. B., and Pacala, S. W. (2011). Evolutionarily stable strategy carbon allocation to foliage, wood, and fine roots in trees competing for light and nitrogen: An analytically tractable, individual-based model and quantitative comparisons to data. *American Naturalist* 177(2): 153–66.

Edwards, K. F., Klausmeier, C. A., and Litchman, E. (2011). Evidence for a three-way trade-off between nitrogen and phosphorus competitive abilities and cell size in phytoplankton. *Ecology* 92(11): 2085–95.

Edwards, K. F., Kremer, C. T., Miller, E. T., Osmond, M. M., Litchman, E., and Klausmeier, C. A. (2018). Evolutionarily stable communities: A framework for understanding the role of trait evolution in the maintenance of diversity. *Ecology Letters* 21(12): 1853–68.

Egas, M., Sabelis, M. W., and Dieckmann, U. (2005). Evolution of specialization and ecological character displacement of herbivores along a gradient of plant quality. *Evolution* 59(3): 507–20.

Emlen, J. M. (1966). The role of time and energy in food preference. *American Naturalist* 100(916): 611–17.

Enquist, B. J., Norberg, J., Bonser, S. P., Violle, C., Webb, C. T., Henderson, A., Sloat, L. L., and Savage, V. M. (2015). Scaling from traits to ecosystems: developing a general trait driver theory via integrating trait-based and metabolic scaling theories. *Advances in Ecological Research* 52: 249–318.

Enquist, B. J., Bentley, L. P., Shenkin, A., Maitner, B., Savage, V., Michaletz, S., Blonder, B., Buzzard, V., Espinoza, T. E. B., Farfan-Rios, W., and Doughty, C. E. (2017). Assessing trait-based scaling theory in tropical forests spanning a broad temperature gradient. *Global Ecology and Biogeography* 26(12): 1357–73.

Eshel, I. (1983). Evolutionary and continuous stability. *Journal of Theoretical Biology* 103(1): 99–111.

Falster, D. S., Brännström, Å., Westoby, M., and Dieckmann, U. (2017). Multitrait successional forest dynamics enable diverse competitive coexistence. *Proceedings of the National Academy of Sciences of the United States of America* 114(13): E2719–28.

Fasham, M. J. R., Ducklow, H. W., and McKelvie, S. M. (1990). A nitrogen-based model of plankton dynamics in the oceanic mixed layer. *Journal of Marine Research* 48(3): 591–639.

Fisher, R. A., Koven, C. D., Anderegg, W. R., Christoffersen, B. O., Dietze, M. C., Farrior, C.E., Holm, J. A., Hurtt, G. C., Knox, R. G., Lawrence, P. J., and Lichstein, J. W. (2018). Vegetation demographics in Earth system models: A review of progress and priorities. *Global Change Biology* 24(1): 35–54.

Foley, J. A., Levis, S., Costa, M. H., Cramer, W., and Pollard, D. (2000). Incorporating dynamic vegetation cover within global climate models. *Ecological Applications* 10(6): 1620–32.

Fuchs, H. L. and Franks, P. J. S., (2010). Plankton community properties determined by nutrients and size-selective feeding. *Marine Ecology Progress Series* 413: 1–15.

Fussmann, G. F., Loreau, M., and Abrams, P. A., (2007). Eco-evolutionary dynamics of communities and ecosystems. *Functional Ecology* 21: 465–77.

Fyllas, N. M., Bentley, L. P., Shenkin, A., Asner, G. P., Atkin, O. K., Díaz, S., Enquist, B. J., Farfan-Rios, W., Gloor, E., Guerrieri, R., and Huasco, W. H. (2017). Solar radiation and functional traits explain the decline of forest primary productivity along a tropical elevation gradient. *Ecology Letters* 20(6): 730–40.

Gavrilets, S. (2005). "Adaptive speciation"—it is not that easy: A reply to Doebeli et al. *Evolution* 59(3): 696–9.

Geritz, S. A. H., Gyllenberg, M., Jacobs, F. J. A., and Parvinen, K. (2002). Invasion dynamics and attractor inheritance. *Journal of Mathematical Biology* 44(6): 548–60.

Geritz, S. A. H., Kisdi, É., Meszéna, G., and Metz, J. A. J. (1998). Evolutionarily singular strategies and the adaptive growth and branching of the evolutionary tree. *Evolutionary Ecology* 12(1): 35–57.

Geritz, S. A. H., van der Meijden, E., and Metz, J. A. J. (1999). Evolutionary dynamics of seed size and seedling competitive ability. *Theoretical Population Biology* 55(3): 324–43.

Gilliam, J. F. and Fraser, D. F. (1987). Habitat selection under predation hazard: Test of a model with foraging minnows. *Ecology* 68(6): 1856–62.

Givnish, T. J. (1982). On the adaptive significance of leaf height in forest herbs. *American Naturalist* 120(3): 353–81.

Gomulkiewicz, R., Kingsolver, J. G., Carter, P. A., and Heckman, N. (2018). Variation and evolution of function-valued traits. *Annual Review of Ecology, Evolution, and Systematics* 49: 139–64.

Gorban, A. N. (2004). Selection theorem for systems with inheritance. *Mathematical Modelling of Natural Phenomena* 2(4): 1–45.

Grime, J. P. (1974). Vegetation classification by reference to strategies. *Nature* 250(5461): 26–31.

Hairston, N. G., Jr., Ellner, S. P., Geber, M. A., Yoshida, Y., and Fox, J. A. (2005). Rapid evolution and the convergence of ecological and evolutionary time. *Ecology Letters* 8: 1114–27.

Hardin, G. (1968). The tragedy of the commons. *Science* 162(3859): 1243–8.

Hart, S. P., Schreiber, S. J., and Levine, J. M. (2016). How variation between individuals affects species coexistence. *Ecology Letters* 19(8): 825–38.

Hartvig, M., Andersen, K. H., and Beyer, J. E. (2011). Food web framework for size-structured populations. *Journal of Theoretical Biology* 272(1): 113–22.

Hastings, A. (1983). Can spatial variation alone lead to selection for dispersal? *Theoretical Population Biology* 24(3): 244–51.

Heavens, N. G., Ward, D. S. and Natalie, M. M. (2013). Studying and projecting climate change with earth system models. *Nature Education Knowledge* 4(5): 4.

Hin, V. and de Roos, A. M. (2019). Cannibalism prevents evolutionary suicide of ontogenetic omnivores in life-history intraguild predation systems. *Ecology and Evolution* 9(7): 3807–22.

Hofbauer, J. and Sigmund, K. (1998). *Evolutionary Games and Population Dynamics*. Cambridge: Cambridge University Press.

Jones, E. I., Ferrière, R., and Bronstein, J. L. (2009). Eco-evolutionary dynamics of mutualists and exploiters. *American Naturalist* 174(6): 780–94.

Kattge, J., Diaz, S., Lavorel, S., Prentice, I. C., Leadley, P., Bönisch, G., Garnier, E., Westoby, M., Reich, P. B., Wright, I. J., and Cornelissen, J. H. C. (2011). TRY–a global database of plant traits. *Global Change Biology* 17(9): 2905–35.

Kearney, M. and Porter, W. (2009). Mechanistic niche modelling: Combining physiological and spatial data to predict species' ranges. *Ecology Letters* 12(4): 334–50.

Kéfi, S., van Baalen, M., Rietkerk, M., and Loreau, M. (2008). Evolution of local facilitation in arid ecosystems. *American Naturalist* 172(1): E1–17.

King, D. A. (1990). The adaptive significance of tree height. *American Naturalist* 135(6): 809–28.

Kirkpatrick, M. and Barton, N. H. (1997). Evolution of a species' range. *American Naturalist* 150(1): 1–23.

Kisdi, É. and Geritz, S. A. H. (1999). Adaptive dynamics in allele space: evolution of genetic polymorphism by small mutations in a heterogeneous environment. *Evolution* 53(4): 993–1008.

Klausmeier, C. A. (2008). Floquet theory: A useful tool for understanding nonequilibrium dynamics. *Theoretical Ecology* 1(3): 153–61.

Klausmeier, C. A., Litchman, E., Daufresne, T., and Levin, S. A. (2004). Optimal nitrogen-to-phosphorus stoichiometry of phytoplankton. *Nature* 429(6988): 171–4.

Klausmeier, C. A. and Tilman, D. (2002). Spatial models of competition. In Sommer, U. and Worm, B (eds.), *Competition and Coexistence*. New York, Springer-Verlag, pp. 43–78.

Kneitel, J. M. and Chase, J. M. (2004). Trade-offs in community ecology: Linking spatial scales and species coexistence. *Ecology Letters* 7(1): 69–80.

Koffel, T., Daufresne, T., Massol, F., and Klausmeier, C. A. (2016). Geometrical envelopes: Extending graphical contemporary niche theory to communities and eco-evolutionary dynamics. *Journal of Theoretical Biology* 407: 271–89.

Koffel, T., Boudsocq, S., Loeuille, N., and Daufresne, T. (2018b). Facilitation- vs. competition-driven succession: The key role of resource-ratio. *Ecology Letters* 21(7): 1010–21.

Koffel, T., Massol, F., Daufresne, T., and Klausmeier, C. A. (2018a). Plant strategies along resource gradients. *American Naturalist* 192(3): 360–78.

Kremer, C. T. and Klausmeier, C. A. (2013). Coexistence in a variable environment: eco-evolutionary perspectives. *Journal of Theoretical Biology* 339: 14–25.

Kremer, C. T. and Klausmeier, C. A. (2017). Species packing in eco-evolutionary models of seasonally fluctuating environments. *Ecology Letters* 20(9): 1158–68.

Kremer, C. T., Williams, A. K., Finiguerra, M., Fong, A. A., Kellerman, A., Paver, S. F., Tolar, B. B., and Toscano, B. J. (2017). Realizing the potential of trait-based aquatic ecology: New tools and collaborative approaches. *Limnology and Oceanography* 62(1): 253–71.

Lande, R. (1976). Natural selection and random genetic drift in phenotypic evolution. *Evolution* 30(2): 314–34.

Lande, R. (1979). Quantitative genetic analysis of multivariate evolution, applied to brain: Body size allometry. *Evolution* 33(1, Part 2): 402–16.

Lavorel, S. and Garnier, E. (2002). Predicting changes in community composition and ecosystem functioning from plant traits: Revisiting the Holy Grail. *Functional Ecology* 16(5): 545–56.

Law, R. and Morton, R. D. (1993). Alternative permanent states of ecological communities. *Ecology* 74(5): 1347–61.

Lehman, C. L. and Tilman, D. (1997). Competition in spatial habitats. In Tilman, D., and Kareiva, P. (eds.), *Spatial*

Ecology: The Role of Space in Population Dynamics and Interspecific Interactions. Princeton: Princeton University Press, pp. 185–203.

Lehmann, L., Ravigne, V., and Keller, L. (2008). Population viscosity can promote the evolution of altruistic sterile helpers and eusociality. *Proceedings of the Royal Society B-Biological Sciences* 275(1645): 1887–95.

Leimar, O. (2009). Multidimensional convergence stability. *Evolutionary Ecology Research* 11(2): 191–208.

Lenton, T. M. and Klausmeier, C. A. (2007). Biotic stoichiometric controls on the deep ocean N:P ratio. *Biogeosciences* 4(3): 353–67.

Le Quéré, C. L., Harrison, S. P., Colin Prentice, I., Buitenhuis, E. T., Aumont, O., Bopp, L., Claustre, H., Cotrim Da Cunha, L., Geider, R., Giraud, X., and Klaas, C. (2005). Ecosystem dynamics based on plankton functional types for global ocean biogeochemistry models. *Global Change Biology* 11(11): 2016–40.

Levin, S. A. (1970). Community equilibria and stability, and an extension of the competitive exclusion principle. *American Naturalist* 104(939): 413–23.

Levin, S. A. (1992). The problem of pattern and scale in ecology. *Ecology* 73(6): 1943–67.

Levin, S. A. and Muller-Landau, H. C. (2000). The evolution of dispersal and seed size in plant communities. *Evolutionary Ecology Research* 2(4): 409–35.

Levin, S. A. and Segel, L. A. (1985). Pattern generation in space and aspect. *SIAM Review* 27(1): 45–67.

Levins, R. (1969). Some demographic and genetic consequences of environmental heterogeneity for biological control. *Bulletin of the Entomological Society of America* 15: 237–40.

Lion, S. and van Baalen, M. (2008). Self-structuring in spatial evolutionary ecology. *Ecology Letters* 11(3): 277–95.

Lion, S. (2018). Theoretical approaches in evolutionary ecology: Environmental feedback as a unifying perspective. *American Naturalist* 191(1): 21–44.

Litchman, E. and Klausmeier, C. A. (2008). Trait-based community ecology of phytoplankton. *Annual Review of Ecology, Evolution, and Systematics* 39: 615–39.

Litchman, E., Ohman, M. D., and Kiørboe, T. (2013). Trait-based approaches to zooplankton communities. *Journal of Plankton Research* 35(3): 473–84.

Litchman, E., Tezanos Pinto, P., Edwards, K. F., Klausmeier, C. A., Kremer, C. T., and Thomas, M. K. (2015). Global biogeochemical impacts of phytoplankton: A trait-based perspective. *Journal of Ecology* 103(6): 1384–96.

Loeuille, N. and Loreau, M., (2005). Evolutionary emergence of size-structured food webs. *Proceedings of the National Academy of Sciences of the United States of America* 102(16): 5761–6.

Lotka, A. J. (1912). Evolution in discontinuous systems. I. *Journal of the Washington Academy of Sciences* 2(1): 2–6.

Lotka, A. J. (1920). Analytical note on certain rhythmic relations in organic systems. *Proceedings of the National Academy of Sciences of the United States of America* 6(7): 410–15.

Lotka, A. J. (1934). *Theorie Analytique des Associations Biologique*. Smith, D. P., and Rossert, H. (Trans.) (1998) as *Analyitcal Theory of Biological Populations*. New York, Plenum Press.

Lu, M. and Hedin, L. O. (2019). Global plant–symbiont organization and emergence of biogeochemical cycles resolved by evolution-based trait modelling. *Nature Ecology and Evolution* 3(2): 239–50.

Lynch, M. and Lande, R. (1993). Evolution and extinction in response to environmental change. In Karieva, P., Kingsolver, J., and Huey, R. (eds.), *Biotic Interactions and Global Change*. Sunderland, Mass, USA: Sinauer, pp. 234–50.

MacArthur, R. (1970). Species packing and competitive equilibrium for many species. *Theoretical Population Biology* 1(1): 1–11.

MacArthur, R. and Levins, R. (1967). The limiting similarity, convergence, and divergence of coexisting species. *American Naturalist* 101(921): 377–85.

MacArthur, R. H. and Wilson, E. O. (1967). *The Theory of Island Biogeography*. Princeton: Princeton University Press.

Maguire Jr, B., (1973). Niche response structure and the analytical potentials of its relationship to the habitat. *American Naturalist* 107(954): 213–46.

Mathias, A. and Kisdi, É. (2002). Adaptive diversification of germination strategies. *Proceedings of the Royal Society B: Biological Sciences* 269(1487) 151–5.

May, R. M. (2001). *Stability and Complexity in Model Ecosystems*. Princeton: Princeton University Press.

May, R. M. and Mac Arthur, R. H. (1972). Niche overlap as a function of environmental variability. *Proceedings of the National Academy of Sciences of the United States of America* 69(5): 1109–13.

Maynard Smith, J. (1978). Optimization theory in evolution. *Annual Review of Ecology and Systematics* 9: 31–56.

Maynard Smith, J. (1982). *Evolution and the Theory of Games*. Cambridge: Cambridge University Press.

Maynard Smith, J. and Price, G. R. (1973). The logic of animal conflict. *Nature* 246(5427): 15.

McGill, B. J., Enquist, B. J., Weiher, E., and Westoby, M. (2006). Rebuilding community ecology from functional traits. *Trends in Ecology & Evolution* 21(4): 178–85.

McPeek, M. A. (2017). *Evolutionary Community Ecology*. Princeton: Princeton University Press.

Meir, P., Mecuccini, M., and R. Dewar. (2015). Drought-related tree mortality: Addressing the gaps in understanding and prediction. *New Phytologist* 207(1): 28–33.

Menge, D. N. L., Levin, S. A., and Hedin, L. O. (2008). Evolutionary tradeoffs can select against nitrogen fixation and thereby maintain nitrogen limitation. *Proceedings of the National Academy of Sciences of the United States of America* 105(5): 1573–8.

Merico, A., Brandt, G., Smith, S. L., and Oliver, M. (2014). Sustaining diversity in trait-based models of phytoplankton communities. *Frontiers in Ecology and Evolution* 2(59): 1–8.

Meszéna, G., Gyllenberg, M., Pásztor, L., and Metz, J. A. J. (2006). Competitive exclusion and limiting similarity: A unified theory. *Theoretical Population Biology* 69(1): 68–87.

Metcalf, C. J. E., Rose, K. E., Childs, D. Z., Sheppard, A. W., Grubb, P. J., and Rees, M. (2008). Evolution of flowering decisions in a stochastic, density-dependent environment. *Proceedings of the National Academy of Sciences* 105(30): 10466–70.

Metz, J. A. J., Geritz, S. A. H., Meszéna, G., Jacobs, F. J. A., and van Heerwaarden, J. S. (1996). Adaptive dynamics: A geometrical study of the consequences of nearly faithful reproduction. In *Stochastic and Spatial Structures of Dynamical Systems*, S. J. van Strien and S. M. Verduyn Lunel (eds.), Amsterdam: North Holland, pp. 183–231.

Metz, J. A. J., Mylius, S. D., and Diekmann, O. (2008). When does evolution optimize? *Evolutionary Ecology Research* 10: 629–54.

Metz, J. A. J., Nisbet, R. M., and Geritz, S. A. H. (1992). How should we define 'fitness' for general ecological scenarios? *Trends in Ecology & Evolution* 7(6): 198–202.

Miller, E. T. and Klausmeier, C.A. (2017). Evolutionary stability of coexistence due to the storage effect in a two-season model. *Theoretical Ecology* 10(1): 91–103.

Morton, R. D. and Law, R. (1997). Regional species pools and the assembly of local ecological communities. *Journal of Theoretical Biology* 187(3): 321–31.

Mylius, S. D. and Diekmann, O. (2001). The resident strikes back: Invader-Induced switching of resident attractor. *Journal of Theoretical Biology* 211(4): 297–311.

Nadell, C. D., Drescher, K., and Foster, K. R. (2016). Spatial structure, cooperation and competition in biofilms. *Nature Reviews Microbiology* 14(9): 589–600.

Namba, T. and Takahashi, S. (1993). Competitive coexistence in a seasonally fluctuating environment II. Multiple stable states and invasion success. *Theoretical Population Biology* 44(3): 374–402.

Nash, J. (1951). Non-cooperative games. *Annals of Mathematics* 54(2): 286–95.

Noest, A. J. (1997). Instability of the sexual continuum. *Proceedings of the Royal Society of London B* 264: 1389–93.

Norberg, J., Swaney, D. P., Dushoff, J., Lin, J., Casagrandi, R., and Levin, S. A. (2001). Phenotypic diversity and ecosystem functioning in changing environments: A theoretical framework. *Proceedings of the National Academy of Sciences* 98(20): 11376–81.

Norberg, J., Urban, M. C., Vellend, M., Klausmeier, C. A., and Loeuille, N. (2012). Eco-evolutionary responses of biodiversity to climate change. *Nature Climate Change* 2(10): 747–51.

Okubo, A. and Levin, S. A. (2001). *Diffusion and Ecological Problems: Modern Perspectives*. (2nd edition). New York, Springer-Verlag.

Osmond, M. M. and Klausmeier, C. A. (2018). An evolutionary tipping point in a changing environment. *Evolution* 71(12): 2930–41.

Parker, G. A. and Maynard Smith, J. (1990). Optimality theory in evolutionary biology. *Nature* 348(6296): 27–33.

Parvinen, K. (1999). Evolution of migration in a metapopulation. *Bulletin of Mathematical Biology* 61(3): 531–50.

Pásztor, L., Botta-Dukát, Z., Magyar, G., Czárán, T., and Meszéna, G. (2016). *Theory-Based Ecology: A Darwinian Approach*. Oxford: Oxford University Press.

Patel, S. and Schreiber, S. J. (2015). Evolutionarily driven shifts in communities with intraguild predation. *American Naturalist* 186(5): E98–110.

Poff, N. L., Olden, J. D., Vieira, N. K., Finn, D. S., Simmons, M. P., and Kondratieff, B. C. (2006). Functional trait niches of North American lotic insects: Traits-based ecological applications in light of phylogenetic relationships. *Journal of the North American Benthological Society* 25(4): 730–55.

Polley, H. W., Isbell, F. I., and Wilsey, B. J. (2013). Plant functional traits improve diversity-based predictions of temporal stability of grassland productivity. *Oikos* 122(9): 1275–82.

Post, W. M. and Pimm, S. L. (1983). Community assembly and food web stability. *Mathematical Biosciences* 64(2): 169–92.

Priklopil, T. (2012). On invasion boundaries and the unprotected coexistence of two strategies. *Journal of Mathematical Biology* 64(7): 1137–56.

Rees, M., Childs, D. Z., Metcalf, J. C., Rose, K. E., Sheppard, A. W., and Grubb, P. J. (2006). Seed dormancy and delayed flowering in monocarpic plants: Selective interactions in a stochastic environment. *American Naturalist* 168(2): E53–71.

Reich, P. B., Buschena, C., Tjoelker, M. G., Wrage, K., Knops, J., Tilman, D., and Machado, J. L. (2003). Variation in growth rate and ecophysiology among 34 grassland and savanna species under contrasting N supply: A test of functional group differences. *New Phytologist* 157(3): 617–31.

Reichstein, M., Bahn, M., Mahecha, M. D., Kattge, J., and Baldocchi, D. D. (2014). Linking plant and ecosystem functional biogeography. *Proceedings of the National*

Academy of Sciences of the United States of America 111(38): 13697–702.

Roff, D. A. (2002). *Life History Evolution*. Oxford: Oxford University Press.

Ronce, O. (2007). How does it feel to be like a rolling stone? Ten questions about dispersal evolution. *Annual Review of Ecology, Evolution, and Systematics* 38: 231–53.

Ronce, O. and Kirkpatrick, M. (2001). When sources become sinks: Migrational meltdown in heterogeneous habitats. *Evolution* 55(8): 1520–31.

Roscher, C., Schumacher, J., Gubsch, M., Lipowsky, A., Weigelt, A., Buchmann, N., Schmid, B., and Schulze, E. D. (2012). Using plant functional traits to explain diversity–productivity relationships. *PloS One* 7(5): e36760.

Rosenzweig, M. L. and MacArthur, R. H. (1963). Graphical representation and stability conditions of predator-prey interactions. *American Naturalist* 97(895): 209–23.

Roughgarden, J. (1972). Evolution of niche width. *American Naturalist* 106(952): 683–718.

Roughgarden, J. (1979). *The Theory of Population Genetics and Evolutionary Ecology: An Introduction*. Upper Saddle River, N.J: Prentice-Hall.

Rummel, J. D. and Roughgarden, J. (1985). A theory of faunal buildup for competition communities. *Evolution* 39(5): 1009–33.

Saavedra, S., Rohr, R. P., Bascompte, J., Godoy, O., Kraft, N. J. B., and Levine, J. M. (2017). A structural approach for understanding multispecies coexistence. *Ecological Monographs* 87(3): 470–86.

Sakschewski, B., von Bloh, W., Boit, A., Rammig, A., Kattge, J., Poorter, L., Peñuelas, J., and Thonicke, K. (2015). Leaf and stem economics spectra drive diversity of functional plant traits in a dynamic global vegetation model. *Global Change Biology* 21(7): 2711–25.

Sasaki, A. and Dieckmann, U. (2011). Oligomorphic dynamics for analyzing the quantitative genetics of adaptive speciation. *Journal of Mathematical Biology* 63(4): 601–35.

Sauterey, B., Ward, B., Rault, J., Bowler, C. and Claessen, D. (2017). The implications of eco-evolutionary processes for the emergence of marine plankton community biogeography. *American Naturalist* 190(1): 116–30.

Savage, V. M., Webb, C. T., and Norberg, J. (2007). A general multi-trait-based framework for studying the effects of biodiversity on ecosystem functioning. *Journal of Theoretical Biology* 247(2): 213–22.

Scheffer, M., van Nes, E. H. (2006). Self-organized similarity, the evolutionary emergence of groups of similar species. *Proceedings of the National Academy of Sciences of the United States of America* 103(16): 6230–5.

Scheiter, S., Langan, L., and Higgins, S. I. (2013). Next-generation dynamic global vegetation models: Learning from community ecology. *New Phytologist* 198(3): 957–69.

Schreiber, S. J. and Tobiason, G. A. (2003). The evolution of resource use. *Journal of Mathematical Biology* 47: 56–78.

Sitch, S., Smith, B., Prentice, I. C., Arneth, A., Bondeau, A., Cramer, W., Kaplan, J. O., Levis, S., Lucht, W., Sykes, M. T., and Thonicke, K. (2003). Evaluation of ecosystem dynamics, plant geography and terrestrial carbon cycling in the LPJ dynamic global vegetation model. *Global Change Biology* 9(2): 161–85.

Smith, H. L. and Waltman, P. (1995). *The Theory of the Chemostat: Dynamics of Microbial Competition*. Cambridge: Cambridge University Press.

Smith, S. L., Pahlow, M., Merico, A., and Kirtz, K. P. (2011). Optimality-based modeling of planktonic organisms. *Limnology and Oceanography* 56(6): 2080–94.

Stearns, S. C. (1992). *The Evolution of Life Histories*. Oxford: Oxford University Press.

Stephens, D. W. and Krebs, J. R., (1986). *Foraging Theory*. Princeton: Princeton University Press.

Stock, C. A., Dunne, J. P., and John, J. G. (2014). Global-scale carbon and energy flows through the marine planktonic food web: An analysis with a coupled physical–biological model. *Progress in Oceanography* 120: 1–28.

Suding, K. N., Lavorel, S., Chapin III, F. S., Cornelissen, J. H., Diaz, S., Garnier, E., Goldberg, D., Hooper, D. U., Jackson, S. T., and Navas, M. L. (2008). Scaling environmental change through the community-level: A trait-based response-and-effect framework for plants. *Global Change Biology* 14(5): 1125–40.

Taylor, P. and Day, T. (1997). Evolutionary stability under the replicator and gradient dynamics. *Evolutionary Ecology* 11: 579–90.

terHorst, C. P., Miller, T. E., and Powell, E. (2010). When can competition for resources lead to ecological equivalence? *Evolutionary Ecology Research* 12: 843–54.

Terseleer, N., Bruggeman, J., Lancelot, C., and Gypens, N. (2014). Trait-based representation of diatom functional diversity in a plankton functional type model of the eutrophied southern North Sea. *Limnology and Oceanography* 59(6): 1958–72.

Thomas, M. K., Kremer, C. T., Klausmeier, C. A., and Litchman, E. (2012). A global pattern of thermal adaptation in marine phytoplankton. *Science* 338(6110): 1085–8.

Tilman, D. (1982). *Resource Competition and Community Structure*. Princeton: Princeton University Press.

Troost, T. A., Kooi, B. M., and Kooijman, S. A. L. M. (2005). Ecological specialization of mixotrophic plankton in a mixed water column. *American Naturalist* 166(3): E45–61.

Turchin, P. (2001). Does population ecology have general laws? *Oikos*, 94(1): 17–26.

Turelli, M. (1978). Does environmental variability limit niche overlap? *Proceedings of the National Academy of Sciences of the United States of America* 75(10): 5085–9.

Van Baalen, M. and Sabelis, M. W. (1995). The dynamics of multiple infection and the evolution of virulence. *American Naturalist* 146(6): 881–910.

Van Baalen, M. and Rand, D. A. (1998). The unit of selection in viscous populations and the evolution of altruism. *Journal of Theoretical Biology* 193(4): 631–48.

Van Bodegom, P. M., Douma, J. C., Witte, J. P. M., Ordonez, J. C., Bartholomeus, R. P., and Aerts, R. (2012). Going beyond limitations of plant functional types when predicting global ecosystem–atmosphere fluxes: Exploring the merits of traits-based approaches. *Global Ecology and Biogeography* 21(6): 625–36.

Van Kleunen, M., Weber, E., and Fischer, M. (2010). A meta-analysis of trait differences between invasive and non-invasive plant species. *Ecology Letters* 13(2): 235–45.

Van Noordwijk, A. J. and de Jong, G. (1986). Acquisition and allocation of resources: Their influence on variation in life history tactics. *American Naturalist* 128(1): 137–42.

Verheijen, L. M., Aerts, R., Brovkin, V., Cavender-Bares, J., Cornelissen, J. H., Kattge, J., and Van Bodegom, P. M. (2015). Inclusion of ecologically based trait variation in plant functional types reduces the projected land carbon sink in an earth system model. *Global Change Biology* 21(8): 3074–86.

Verhulst, P. F. (1845). Recherches mathématiques sur la loi d'accroissement de la population. [Mathematical Researches into the law of population growth increase]. *Nouveaux mémoires de l'Académie Royale des Sciences et Belles-Lettres de Bruxelles* 18: 14–54.

Violle, C., Enquist, B. J., Mcgill, B. J., Jiang, L., Hulshof, C., Jung, V., and Messier, J. (2012). The return of the variance: Intraspecific variability in community ecology. *Trends in Ecology & Evolution* 27(4): 244–52.

Violle, C., Navas, M. L., Vile, D., Kazakou, E., Fortunel, C., Hummel, I., and Garnier, E. (2007). Let the concept of trait be functional! *Oikos* 116(5): 882–92.

Volterra, V. (1926). Fluctuations in the abundance of a species considered mathematically. *Nature* 118(2972): 558–60.

Von Neumann, J. and Morgenstern, O. (1944). *Theory of Games and Economic Behavior*. Princeton: Princeton University Press.

Ward, B. A., Dutkiewicz, S., Jahn, O., and Follows, M. J. (2012). A size-structured food-web model for the global ocean. *Limnology and Oceanography* 57(6): 1877–91.

Waxman, D. and Gavrilets, S. (2005). Issues of terminology, gradient dynamics and the ease of sympatric speciation in Adaptive Dynamics. *Journal of Evolutionary Biology* 18: 1214–19.

Westoby, M., Falster, D. S., Moles, A. T., Vesk, P. A., and Wright, I. J. (2002). Plant ecological strategies: some leading dimensions of variation between species. *Annual Review of Ecology and Systematics* 33: 125–59.

Wieczynski, D. J., Boyle, B., Buzzard, V., Duran, S. M., Henderson, A. N., Hulshof, C. M., Kerkhoff, A. J., McCarthy, M. C., Michaletz, S. T., Swenson, N. G., and Asner, G. P. (2019). Climate shapes and shifts functional biodiversity in forests worldwide. *Proceedings of the National Academy of Sciences* 116(2): 587–92.

Wickman, J., Diehl, S., Blasius, B., Klausmeier, C. A., Ryabov, A. B., and Brännström, Å. (2017). Determining selection across heterogeneous landscapes: A perturbation-based method and its application to modeling evolution in space. *American Naturalist* 189(4): 381–95.

Xu, C., Fisher, R., Wullschleger, S. D., Wilson, C. J., Cai, M., and McDowell, N. G. (2012). Towards a mechanistic modeling of nitrogen limitation on vegetation dynamics. *PLoS ONE* 7(5): e37914.

Yoshida, T., Jones, L. E., Ellner, S. P., Fussmann, G. F., and Hairston Jr, N. G. (2003). Rapid evolution drives ecological dynamics in a predator–prey system. *Nature* 424(6946): 303–6.

Zaehle, S. and Friend, A. D. (2010). Carbon and nitrogen cycle dynamics in the O-CN land surface model: 1. Model description, site-scale evaluation, and sensitivity to parameter estimates. *Global Biogeochemical Cycles* 24: GB1005.

CHAPTER 12

Toward a general theory of metacommunity ecology

Dominique Gravel and François Massol

12.1 Introduction

The study of community ecology in a spatial context has a rich history with different roots coming from various disciplines, in particular population biology and geography (MacArthur 1972). Community ecology, as a sub-field of ecology, focuses on the diversity and coexistence of species. One of the hallmarks of spatial community ecology is the theory of island biogeography (TIB), elaborated by MacArthur and Wilson (MacArthur and Wilson 1963), based on a first model they published simultaneously with a very similar study by Levins and Heatwole (1963). The aim of the TIB is to explain various observations emerging from the analysis of biodiversity on islands (e.g., area-diversity and distance-to-mainland-diversity relationships). The thesis defended by the TIB (MacArthur and Wilson 1967) is that most of these observations can reasonably be explained from the balance between island colonization and local extinction processes, and these processes in turn are expected to depend on geographic characteristics such as island size or distance to the nearest continental mass. By recognizing colonization and extinction processes as key drivers of biodiversity at biogeographic scales, MacArthur and Wilson i) were among the first to

propose a mechanistic theory to solve the issue of spatial scale of biodiversity and ii) based their theory on stochastic processes, thus implicitly acknowledging that an average diversity of S does not mean that the S same species should inhabit the site considered at all times.

Since the seminal book of MacArthur and Wilson, the theory on spatial community ecology has followed two main routes: i) a "complex system" approach focusing on species and diversity distributions at different spatial scales, following approaches from landscape ecology, in order to grasp the connection from landscape structure to community and ecosystem processes, e.g., Polis et al. (1997); ii) a "parsimonious assumption" approach aiming at explaining general coexistence mechanisms for community ecology without much attention to the details of the landscape, which in its most recent form is now better known as metacommunity ecology (Holyoak et al. 2005). In recent years, the field of spatial ecology has moved towards a more integrative view, merging both approaches together with a stronger focus on spatially structured food webs to explain coexistence mechanisms and the consequences of species diversity on ecosystem functioning and ecological interaction networks (Massol et al. 2011).

Gravel, D. and Massol, F., *Toward a general theory of metacommunity ecology* In: *Theoretical Ecology: Concepts and Applications*. Edited by: Kevin S. McCann and Gabriel Gellner, Oxford University Press (2020). © Oxford University Press.
DOI: 10.1093/oso/9780198824282.003.0012

The metaecosystem concept and its associated framework (Loreau et al. 2003; Gounand et al. 2018) has notably introduced the ideas that ecological stoichiometry coupled with spatial dynamics might play a very important role in the control of ecosystem productivity (Loreau, 2004; Massol et al. 2011) and limiting factors (resources and natural enemies) shaping species coexistence have to be understood more generally through the prism of biomass fluxes within and among ecosystems (Gravel et al. 2010b,a,b; Massol et al. 2017).

In parallel to the construction of the metapopulation/metacommunity/meta-ecosystem framework, P. Chesson and his collaborators have made crucial contributions to the theory of species coexistence through a completely different approach (Chesson 1994, 2000b,a,b; Snyder and Chesson 2003). In particular, these works have proposed a useful categorization of coexistence mechanisms based on two main classes: on the one hand, some mechanisms can be branded as equalizing because their ultimate effect is to minimize fitness differences between species at large spatial and long temporal scales ; on the other hand, some mechanisms are stabilizing because they tend to increase negative density-dependent interactions within species compared to between-species interactions (also interpreted as niche differentiation). Following the logic of the Lotka–Volterra model, such effects are expected to favor the coexistence of species because they increase the likelihood that the multi-species equilibrium is more stable than the ones lacking one or more species. Some models have implicitly incorporated these ideas into the metacommunity framework through ideas such as the regional similarity hypothesis (Mouquet and Loreau 2002) and the neutral theory of biodiversity (Bell 2000; Hubbel 2001), which basically recasts coexistence theory in the absence of stabilizing mechanisms but with perfect equality between species (Gravel et al. 2006; Adler et al. 2007). Although both equalizing and stabilizing mechanisms work towards species coexistence (i.e., the existence of a feasible equilibrium comprising all considered species), only stabilizing mechanisms actually make this coexistent state resilient to perturbations (Barot and Gignoux 2004). For this reason, the categorization proposed

by (Chesson 2000b) is of particular relevance because it allows for a more precise understanding of the conditions favoring species diversity within a patch and species turnover in space and time.

In this chapter, our first goal is to give the reader a general idea of what metacommunity theory has achieved, what it can explain, and how, and what it has not tackled yet, focusing on theories of community assembly and species coexistence and comparing their predictions. However, going into the details of all predictions and theories linked to metacommunity ecology is way beyond the scope of a single book chapter, see Leibold and Chase (2018) for such an overview). For the purpose of conciseness and consistency, our approach here will be to propose and formalize a single unifying model in the context of patch dynamics (i.e., focusing on species occupancies rather than species abundances) to make predictions on three main statistics (species-species and species-environment correlations as well as spatial species occurrence autocorrelation) that could well capture the distribution shaped by coexistence mechanisms. We will first introduce some theoretical results linked to the Levins metapopulation model and its many offshoots in order to highlight the basic expectations of this model in terms of three correlations describing metacommunity structure: environment-occupancy, first order spatial autocorrelation and co-distribution. We will then resort to simulations to check whether the three proposed statistics are indeed able to discriminate between different scenarios of species coexistence. These results might hopefully guide future empirical and theoretical studies by highlighting relevant signature characteristics of metacommunities as well as weaknesses of occupancy-based metrics, thus kindling future research on appropriate metrics of species coexistence mechanisms.

12.2 A general model for "meta" ecology

We start with the presentation of a single-species model and review elements of metapopulation theory with a unique formalism. The model is developed following the tradition of Levins' model of patch dynamics (Levins 1969). Our objective is to provide a tool that could be used to develop the theory further, but that is also coherent with previous tools.

12.2.1 The heritage of the Levins' model of colonization and extinction dynamics

In population and community ecology textbooks, one of the classic models that is often presented to study spatial dynamics and scaling in biodiversity studies is Levins' metapopulation model. Initially proposed in the context of agronomical research, see Levins (1969), this model has been especially fruitful with many extensions, see the reviews in Hanski (1999) and Britton (2013). Interestingly, the model was developed in parallel to MacArthur and Wilson's theory of island bigeography, which also builds on the same fundamental state variable and processes. Essentially, Levins' model describes the dynamics of expected patch occupancy p, which could be interpreted as a fraction of the landscape that is occupied by the species, as well as the probability to find a population at a given location. The metapopulation is dynamic because of the processes of colonization, which is the result of a propagule landing at a location and establishing a viable population, and extinction, which is the result of a permanent disappearance of all individuals from that locality, either because of stochastic population dynamics or a disturbance. An implicit assumption is that the per capita growth rate is positive in all patches, i.e., that the entire landscape is suitable to establish viable local populations (but see following variants).

We start by deriving Levins' model from its underlying processes (colonization and extinction) and then we add spatial heterogeneity. Let us first consider a large landscape of n patches, each of them with approximately the same quality and size, so that colonization and extinction rates are comparable throughout. We look at the probabilities P_k that k of these patches are occupied. Assuming that propagules landing into a patch can come from any other patch (i.e., global dispersal and perfect mixing), this family of probabilities obeys the following master equation:

$$\frac{dP_k}{dt} = \frac{c}{n}(k-1)(n-k+1)P_{k-1} + e(k+1)P_{k+1} - \left[\frac{c}{n}k(n-k) + ek\right]P_k \tag{12.1}$$

i.e., the number of occupied patches can increase if a colonization happens in one of the $n-k$ empty patches (the associated rate being colonization pressure c/n per occupied patch owing to the division of emigrating propagules between the n possibble destinations, multiplied by the number of occupied patches, k), or can decrease if an extinction happens (with rate e) in one of the k occupied patches. Multiplying both sides of Equation 12.1 by k/n and summing over k yields the following equation for the dynamics of $p = E[k/n]$, with terms in $v = Var[k/n]$:

$$\frac{dp}{dt} = cp(1-p) - cv - ep \tag{12.2}$$

If k were a random variable with binomial distribution, we would have $v = p(1-p)/n$, i.e., vanishing variance with increasing n. In general, we can expect v to decrease with n, so, assuming a large number of patches, the dynamics of p can be approximated by Levins' equation:

$$\frac{dp}{dt} = cp(1-p) - ep \tag{12.3}$$

In this form, it is a one-species model with no underlying spatial heterogeneity. The classic results from this model are easy to obtain:

- there are two equilibria for p, either $p=0$ or $p=1-e/c$;
- the first equilibrium is unstable when $c > e$ and the second is stable, which in ecological terms means that persistence occurs if colonization is larger than extinction; the reverse is true when $c < e$;
- the dynamics of this model are strictly identical to those of a logistic growth model with parameters $r = c - e$ and $K = 1 - e/c$, notably a rate of return to the equilibrium equal to $c - e$.

A very natural improvement to the original model stems from the idea that less than 100 per cent of the available patches are fit for species colonization, i.e., the local intrinsic population growth rate is negative in some locations such that establishment is not feasible even if there are plenty of propagules. The following formalization, introduced by (Nee and May 1992) in a two-species context, adds another parameter to Levins' model, i.e., the proportion of inhabitable patches h:

$$\frac{dp}{dt} = cp(h-p) - ep \qquad (12.4)$$

This model does not change results radically for the one-species, one-habitat type model, i.e., there are still two equilibriums (the second becomes $p = h - e/c$), the critical inequality that must be satisfied for the metapopulation to persist is now $hc > e$, and the rate of return to the non-empty equilibrium is $ch - e$. However, the introduction of this new parameter allows one to model habitat heterogeneity and ecological interactions in a simple way.

12.2.2 Local demography versus regional processes

Levins' metapopulation model and its various offshoots are "macroscopic" models insofar as they concentrate on colonization/extinction dynamics and do not treat population dynamics within a patch. An important implicit assumption of this formalism is that local dynamics are happening much faster than regional dynamics, such that they could be ignored from the model (see Gravel et al. (2010a) for relaxation of this assumption). Essentially, a just-colonized patch is assumed to be identical (on average) to a patch that has been occupied for a long time. Population dynamics are assumed to be fast enough, when compared to colonization/extinction dynamics, for newly formed populations to reach their carrying capacity before the next extinction event in the metapopulation. This assumption is obviously not realistic in all metapopulation settings, especially when there is a strong seasonal forcing on population and colonization/extinction dynamics. A good reading on the limits of this assumption is provided by Keeling (2002) and Eriksson (2013).

12.3 Spatial heterogeneity

Coexistence is impossible in the Levins metapopulation model in the absence of spatial heterogeneity or the possibility of local species replacement. Gause's competitive exclusion principle can easily be reformulated to apply to spatial dynamics by stating that two similar species competing for space cannot coexist. Akin to local dynamics, some form of heterogeneity is required to obtain spatial coexistence. We will see in the next section how differences among species may contribute to it, but first we need to establish how spatial heterogeneity affects single-species metapopulations. This step is necessary to reveal how environmental variation and limited dispersal contribute to affect the equilibrium occupancy of a resident species. In this section we analyze extensions of the single-species Levins model in order to reveal the effects of environmental variation and dispersal limitation on the equilibrium occupancy. Our analysis formalizes how environmental occupancy and spatial correlations may arise and structure species distribution.

12.3.1 Environmental variation

Introducing environmental variation into Levins metapopulation model can be achieved in all generality by making model parameters (i.e., c and e) dependent on patch type and stating the proportion of total patches assigned to each type (i.e., the equivalent of parameter h). For simplicity, consider a metapopulation which comprises two habitat types, say favorable (in proportion π) and unfavorable (in proportion $1 - \pi$). We follow a single species which inhabits this metapopulation, and its metapopulation dynamics are governed by the usual processes of colonization and extinction.

Extinction rate varies between the two habitat types and is equal to e_F in favorable patches and to e_U in unfavorable patches. In the same vein, contribution of occupied favorable patches to colonization (resp. unfavorable) is c_F (resp. c_U). To keep in line with the spirit of approaches proposed earlier (Slatkin 1974; Christiansen and Fenchel 1977; Hanski 1983), unfavorable patches are also considered as potentially more (or less) resistant to colonization through parameter r_U, which describes the probability that colonization can take place.

The differential equations that define the dynamics of species occupancy in both habitat types, (p_U in favorable habitats, p_F in unfavorable ones, and total occupancy $p = p_U + p_F$) according to Levins metapopulation model are:

$$\frac{dp_F}{dt} = (c_F p_F + c_U p_U)(1 - \pi - p_F) - e_F p_F$$

$$\frac{dp_U}{dt} = r_U (c_F p_F + c_U p_U)(\pi - p_U) - e_U p_U \quad (12.5)$$

The main interest of this variant of Levins metapopulation model is that it can predict the expected correlations between species occupancy and patch type, a quantity that we will be interested in later when we will explore statistical moments of metacommunities. To obtain this correlation, we first need to derive expressions for equilibrium occupancies. These are given by the following equations:

$$(1 - \pi - p_F)(c_F p_F + c_U p_U) = e_F p_F$$
$$r_U (\pi - p_U)(c_F p_F + c_U p_U) = e_U p_U \quad (12.6)$$

which can be solved by introducing the variable m defined as:

$$m = 1/(c_F p_F + c_U p_U) \quad (12.7)$$

yielding p_F and p_U:

$$p_F = \frac{1 - \pi}{1 + m e_F}$$
$$p_U = \frac{\pi}{1 + m e_U / r_U} \quad (12.8)$$

The equation on m obtained through system (12.6) is a quadratic equation with solutions:

$$m_{\pm} = \frac{f_F + f_U - \bar{c} \pm \sqrt{(\bar{c} - f_F - f_U)^2 + 4[c_F (1 - \pi) + c_U \pi f_F - f_F f_U]}}{2[c_F (1 - \pi) f_U + c_U \pi f_F - f_F f_U]} \quad (12.9)$$

where $\bar{c} = c_F (1 - \pi) + c_U \pi$, $f_F = e_F$ and $f_U = e_U / r_U$. p can be recovered from Equation (12.9) by summing the two parts of system (12.8), i.e., as:

$$p = \frac{1 - \pi}{1 + m f_F} + \frac{\pi}{1 + m f_U} \quad (12.10)$$

Plugging Equation (12.9) in Equation (12.10) gives a long formula better left hidden. Figure 12.2 presents a more understandable picture of how p varies as a function of statistical moments of the "effective extinction rates", f_x, namely its expectation $\bar{f} = \pi f_U + (1 - \pi) f_F$ and its variance $Var(f) = \pi (1 - \pi)(f_U - f_F)^2$. A larger difference between the two effective extinction rates at a given average effective extinction rate (i.e., going up on Figure 12.1) increases occupancy; conversely, at a given difference of effective extinction rate, increasing the average effective extinction rate (i.e., going right on Figure 12.1) decreases occupancy.

Approximating Equation 12.10 at first order in $Cov[f, c]$ and $Var[f]$, we obtain the following Taylor series approximation for p:

$$p \approx 1 - \frac{\bar{f}}{\bar{c}} + \frac{\bar{f} Cov[f,c]}{\bar{c}^3} + \frac{Var[f]}{\bar{c}^2} \quad (12.11)$$

This expression can also be recovered with a large number of patch types defined by their parameters c_x, e_x and r_x, with $f_x = e_x / r_x$, and the proportion of patches of type x, π_x. The equivalent of system (12.5) then becomes:

$$\frac{dp_x}{dt} = r_x (\pi_x - p_x) \sum_y c_y p_y - e_x p_x \quad (12.12)$$

At equilibrium, Equation (12.12) always implies:

$$p_x = \frac{\pi_x}{1 + f_x / \sum_y c_y p_y} \quad (12.13)$$

and, from Equation (12.12) taken for all x,

$$p = 1 - \frac{\sum_y f_y p_y}{\sum_y c_y p_y} \quad (12.14)$$

Developing the sum at the denominator in terms of $\alpha_x = p_x / \pi_x$ and using Equation (12.13), one obtains:

$$\overline{\alpha c} = E\left[\frac{c_x}{1 + \frac{f_x}{\alpha c}}\right] \approx \frac{\bar{c}}{1 + \frac{\bar{f}}{\overline{\alpha c}}} - \frac{Cov[f,c]}{\overline{\alpha c}\left(1 + \frac{\bar{f}}{\overline{\alpha c}}\right)^2}$$

$$+ \frac{\bar{c} Var[f]}{\overline{\alpha c}^2 \left(1 + \frac{\bar{f}}{\overline{\alpha c}}\right)^3} \quad (12.15)$$

Assuming that $\overline{\alpha c}$ can be decomposed as an average term plus terms in $Cov[f, c]$, $Var[c]$ and $Var[f]$, one finds:

$$\overline{\alpha c} \approx \bar{c} - \bar{f} - \frac{Cov[f,c]}{\bar{c}} + \frac{Var[f]}{\bar{c}} \quad (12.16)$$

With the same type of calculations, we can also obtain the following approximation:

$$\overline{\alpha f} \approx \frac{\bar{f}(\bar{c} - \bar{f})}{\bar{c}} + \frac{(2\bar{f} - \bar{c}) Var[f]}{\bar{c}^3} - \frac{\bar{f}^2 Cov[f,c]}{\bar{c}^2} \quad (12.17)$$

Plugging Equations (12.16) and (12.17) into Equation (12.14) and keeping only sensible terms, we finally recover Equation (12.11).

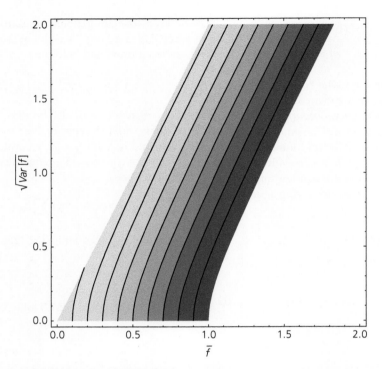

Figure 12.1 Effect of spatial heterogeneity on equilibrium occupancy. The figure illustrates iso-occupancy lines (from 0 to 1, with one line at each 0.1 occupancy increment) as a function of the average effective extinction rate, $\bar{f}$ and the standard deviation of extinction rates, at $\pi = 0.2$, $c_F = c_U = 1$. The area in the top left corner is not possible with only two patch types – it would require negative values for e_F. The area in the bottom right corner leads to $p = 0$.

Based on Equations (12.13) and (12.16), we can also obtain an approximation of p_x:

$$p_x \approx \pi_x \left[\frac{\bar{c} - \bar{f}}{\bar{c} + \Delta f_x} - \frac{\left(f_x Cov\ [f,c]\right)}{\bar{c}(\bar{c} + \Delta f_x)^2} + \frac{f_x Var\ [f]}{\bar{c}(\bar{c} + \Delta f_x)^2} \right]$$

$$(12.18)$$

with $\Delta f_x = f_x - \bar{f}$. Using Equation (12.18), we can get an approximation of the covariance K_x between species occurrence and patch type x occurrence:

$$K_x = p_x - p\pi_x$$
$$\approx -\frac{\pi_x}{(\bar{c} + \Delta f_x)^2}$$
$$\left\{ \begin{array}{l} \left(1 - \frac{\bar{f}}{\bar{c}}\right) Var\ [f] \\ + \left[\left(1 - \frac{\bar{f}}{\bar{c}}\right)\bar{c} + \left(1 - \frac{2\bar{f}}{\bar{c}}\right)\frac{Cov\ [f,c]}{\bar{c}} + \frac{Var\ [f]}{\bar{c}}\right]\Delta f_x \\ + \left[\left(1 - \frac{\bar{f}}{\bar{c}}\right) - \frac{\bar{f}}{\bar{c}} Cov\ [f,c] + Var\ [f]\right]\frac{(\Delta f_x)^2}{\bar{c}^2} \end{array} \right\}$$

$$(12.19)$$

The correlation between species occurrence and patch type x occurrence, κ_x, can be obtained by dividing the right-hand side of Equation (12.19) by $\sqrt{p\left(1 - p\right)\pi_x\left(1 - \pi_x\right)}$ and cutting approximations at the level of variance and covariance terms:

$$\kappa_x \approx -\frac{\sqrt{\pi_x}}{(\bar{c} + \Delta f_x)^2 \sqrt{(1 - \pi)\frac{\bar{f}}{\bar{c}}\left(1 - \frac{\bar{f}}{\bar{c}}\right)}}$$

$$\left\{ \begin{array}{l} \left(1 - \frac{\bar{f}}{\bar{c}}\right) Var\ [f] \\ + \left[\left(1 - \frac{\bar{f}}{\bar{c}}\right)\bar{c} + \frac{\left(1 - \frac{2\bar{f}}{\bar{c}}\right)Cov\ [f,c]}{2\bar{c}} + \frac{Var\ [f]}{2\bar{f}}\right]\Delta f_x \\ - \left[-\left(1 - \frac{\bar{f}}{\bar{c}}\right) + \frac{Cov\ [f,c]}{2\bar{c}^2} - \frac{Var\ [f]}{2\bar{c}f}\right](\Delta f_x)^2 \end{array} \right\}$$

$$(12.20)$$

Independently of Δf_x, environment-occurrence correlations are expected to be negatively affected by the variance in effective extinction rates. A patch type with local extinction rate equal to the metapopulation average would be less occupied than predicted from the product of p and π just because of the variance in extinction rates, which creates a deficit in recolonisation of extinct patches. In other words, for a given average performance, spatial variation in the environment reduces the regional performance of a species. Patch types with larger than average f are expected to have more negative habitat-occurrence correlations due to i) the effect of colonization (the higher the colonization rate, the stronger the effect of Δf_x), ii) the variance in effective extinction rates (the higher the variance, the stronger the effect), and (iii) the covariance between colonization and extinction rates depending on whether the extinction- to-colonisation ratio is lower or higher than $1/2$. If the ratio is lower than $1/2$, a positive covariance means a negative effect of Δf_x on κ_x; conversely, if the f/c ratio is above $1/2$, a positive covariance means a negative effect of Δf_x on K_x. The effect of $(\Delta f_x)^2$ is mainly to decrease the value of the correlation (i.e., becoming more negative), with a modulation by $Cov[\,f, c\,]$ if this quantity is positive.

An important result of Equation (12.20) is that when f_x does not vary among patch types, the environment-occurrence correlations all become equal to zero. This is not so surprising: when only colonization rates out of patches differ, we do not expect more or less productive patches to be occupied more or less often if space is modeled implicitly (i.e., we do not take the clustering of patch types into account). Conversely, when only f_x varies but not c_x, the effects of Δf_x and $Var[\,f\,]$ are quite straightforward: the environment-occurrence correlation decreases with the variation in extinction rates, Δf_x, with the product of both terms, $(\Delta f_x)^2$, and also decreases with the product of this term with $Var[f]$. Since $(\Delta f_x)^2$ and $Var[f]$ are always non-negative, the only term that can produce a positive correlation is the simple Δf_x effects—patch types with less than average extinction rates should have higher correlations. Because of all the negative effects of $(\Delta f_x)^2$ and $Var[f]$, this means that positive environment-occurrence correlations are expected to be less intense than the negative ones—the association, positive or negative, is stronger with

unfavorable environment types than with favorable ones. Or, in other words, we expect a negative correlation between species occurrence, and patch x occurrence even when Δf_x is negative, down to negative values of order $-Var[f]/\bar{c}$.

12.3.2 Dispersal limitation

In this section, we introduce the notion that spatially explicit structure driven by dispersal limitation can induce spatial autocorrelation in species occurrence. Computing the expectation for occurrence autocorrelation is a difficult problem and recent approaches have circumvented this difficulty by applying stochastic differential equation formalism and perturbation analysis (Ovaskainen and Cornell 2006a; Ovaskainen and Cornell 2006b). Here we will focus on a simple toy model that can be approximately solved using pair approximations.

Consider a metapopulation comprising a large number (N) of patches positioned on a circle and assume that colonization processes only take place in a stepping-stone manner (i.e., colonization can only occur from a neighboring patch). We assume that the number of patches is high, so that whole metapopulation extinction due to stochasticity is practically impossible. To analyze the dynamics of such a model metapopulation, we use pair approximations, i.e., we assume that the occurrence of the focal species in a patch can be computed from the knowledge of species occurrence in the two neighboring patches.

To describe the state (occupied, O, or empty, E) of a given patch (with index x) at time t, we use random variable $X_x(t)$. The proportion of patch pairs that are both empty (p_{EE}), both occupied (p_{OO}), or mismatched (p_{EO} and p_{OE}) can be written as follows:

$$p_{EE} = E\left[(1 - X_x)(1 - X_{x+1})\right]$$
$$p_{EO} = p_{OE} = E\left[X_x(1 - X_{x+1})\right]$$
$$p_{OO} = E[X_x X_{x+1}] \qquad (12.21)$$

Quite naturally $p_{EE} + p_{OO} + 2p_{OE} = 1$. Species occupancy is then given by $p = p_{OO} + p_{OE}$.

When a patch x is empty, the pair approximation assumption implies that the probability that its left-hand side neighboring patch is occupied is

$p_{OE}/(p_{OE}+p_{EE})$. Based on this assumption and a colonization rate $c/2$ towards each side of an occupied patch, the differential equations governing the dynamics of the metapopulation are given by:

$$\frac{p_{EE}}{dt} = 2ep_{OE} - cp_{EE}\left(\frac{p_{OE}}{p_{OE}+p_{EE}}\right)$$

$$\frac{p_{OE}}{dt} = \frac{c}{2}p_{EE}\left(\frac{p_{OE}}{p_{OE}+p_{EE}}\right) + ep_{OO}$$

$$- \left[e + \frac{c}{2}\left(1 + \frac{p_{OE}}{p_{OE}+p_{EE}}\right)\right]p_{OE}$$

$$\frac{p_{OO}}{dt} = c\left(1 + \frac{p_{OE}}{p_{OE}+p_{EE}}\right)p_{OE} - 2ep_{OO} \quad (12.22)$$

The equilibrium solution to this set of equations can be explicitly given in terms of e/c:

$$p_{EE} = \frac{2(e/c)^2}{1-(e/c)}$$

$$p_{OE} = p_{EO} = \frac{(e/c)\left[1-2(e/c)\right]}{1-(e/c)}$$

$$p_{OO} = 1 - 2(e/c) \quad (12.23)$$

so that metapopulation occupancy $p = p_{OE} + p_{OO}$ is given as:

$$p = \frac{1-2(e/c)}{1-(e/c)} \quad (12.24)$$

and the autocorrelation between neighboring patch states, $\rho = (p_{OO}-p^2)/p(1-p)$, equals:

$$\rho = \frac{e}{c} \quad (12.25)$$

Plugging $p_{OO} = p^2 + \rho p(1-p)$ and $p_{OE} = (1-\rho)p(1-p)$ into system (12.22), we can deduce:

$$\frac{dp}{dt} = c(1-\rho)(1-p)p - ep \quad (12.26)$$

and from Equations (12.26) and system (12.22):

$$\frac{d\rho}{dt} = c(1-\rho)^2(1-p) - e\rho\frac{\rho}{1-\rho} \quad (12.27)$$

Equations (12.26) and (12.27) yield the equilibrium relationships:

$$(1-\rho)(1-p) = e/c$$

$$(1-\rho)^2(1-p)^2 = \rho e/c \quad (12.28)$$

from which we can also deduce Equations (12.24) and (12.25).

Equations (12.26) and (12.27) are interesting because they highlight the similarities and differences between the model developed here and the spatially implicit Levins model developed previously. In the spatially explicit version, the effective colonization rate becomes multiplied by $1-\rho$, which is the mathematical translation of the fact that colonization is most efficient when occupied, and empty patches are intermingled rather than spatially segregated. Spatially explicit dispersal has two consequences that will be helpful to later understand coexistence. First, it reduces the equilibrium occupancy relative to the standard Levins' model with global dispersal model by an amount equal to e/c. Keeping in mind that the extinction rate has to be smaller than the colonization for persistence, it indicates that the negative effect of dispersal limitation will vanish as colonization rate becomes very large, simply because empty patches are rapidly recolonized. Second, the spatial autocorrelation is always positive and also monotonically decline with colonization rate.

12.4 Coexistence and Persistence

12.4.1 Introducing species interactions

We now move to the most general version of a multi-species version of the Levins model. The model is based on the earlier work of several other authors, including Cohen (1970), Levins and Culver (1971), Slatkin (1974), Hanski (1983), Hanski (1999), and Holt (1996). Its parameterization for specific cases, as we will see, and summarized in Table 12.1 covers different situations such as pre-emptive competition (Levins and Culver 1971), competition-colonization trade-off (Tilman 1994; Hastings 1980), predation (Holt 1996; Gravel et al. 2011b) and mutualism (Klausmeier et al. 2001). The following analysis is based on a two-species scenario for tractability, with the two species labelled 1 and 2, but could easily be extended to multiple species.

See Figure 12.2 and Table 12.1 for description of parameters.

Table 12.1 Summary comparison of different parameterization of the two species model for various cases of inter-specific interactions.

		Sp. 1	Sp. 2	Production	Establishment			Extinction	
Ind. metapop.				b_i	$b_i' = b_i$	s_i	$s_i' = s_i$	e_i	$e_i' = e_i$
Competition	Neutral			$b_1 = b_2$	$b_i' = 0$	$s_1 = s_2$	$s_i' = 0$	$e_1 = e_2$	$e_i' = \infty$
	Col. comp.	Sup.	Weak	b_i	$b_i' = b_i$	s_i	$s_i' < s_i$	e_i	$e_i' = e_i$
	Ext. comp.	Sup.	Weak	b_i	$b_i' = b_i$	s_i	$s_i' = s_i$	e_i	$e_i' > e_i$
	CC-Trade off	Sup.	Weak	$b_1 < b_2$	$b_2' = 0$	$s_1 < s_2$	$s_2' = 0$	e_i	$e_2' = \infty$
	Species sort.			Spatially variable					
Pred.-prey	Bottom-up	Prey	Pred.	$b_2 = 0$	$s_2 = 0$	$s_2 = 0$	s_i'	$e_2 = \infty$	e_i'
	Top-down	Prey	Pred.	$b_2 = 0$	$s_2 = 0$	$s_2 = infty$	$s_i' > 0$	$e_2 = \infty$	$e_1' > e_1$
Plant-poll.	Facultative	Plant	Poll.	$b_2 < b_2'$	$b_2 < b_2'$	$s_2 < b_2'$	$s_2 < b_2'$	$e_2 < e_2'$	$e_2 < e_2'$
	Obligatory	Plant	Poll.	$b_2 = 0$	$s_2 = 0$	$s_2 = 0$	s_i'	$e_2 = infty$	e_i'

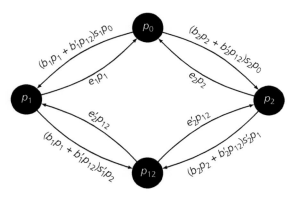

Figure 12.2 Schematic representation of the model.

There are four types of patches to keep track of in a two-species situation: p_1 denotes the fraction of the landscape occupied by species 1 only, p_2 denotes the fraction occupied by species 2 only, p_{12} is the fraction occupied simultaneously by both species and finally, p_0 are empty patches. Following (Hanski 1983), we will simplify notation by defining the quantities $y_1 = p_1 + p_{12}$ and $y_2 = p_2 + p_{12}$. The landscape can only be in one of those states, such that $p_0 = 1 - (p_1 + p_2 + p_{12})$.

Interactions can be represented in various ways, each the result of different local processes. To do so, we first need to decompose colonization in two sub-processes, the propagule production per unit of occupancy, which occurs at rate b_i, and the establishment rate of propagules landing into

a suitable location, which occurs at rate s_i. The traditional definition of an ecological interaction is the effect of a species on the per capita growth rate of another species. If the growth rate is either increased or decreased by the presence of another species, then it should affect the rate at which the population will establish after landing into a patch. This will translate into a modification of the establishment rate in the patches already occupied by the other species, which we will denote s_i'. Since local population dynamics are happening fast relative to regional dynamics, we also need to consider the effect of ecological interactions on the equilibrium population size. Such an effect may either reduce (e.g., in presence of competition or predation) or increase (e.g., in presence of mutualism or a prey) the propagule production, which we will also denote by b_i' Taken all together, this means that ecological interactions may affect the effective colonization rate in the target patch where establishment occurs and in the source patch from which propagules are being produced. The rates of increase of species 1 occupancy due to the colonization of empty patches and already occupied patches will therefore be $(b_1 p_1 + b_1' p_{12}) s_1 p_0$ and $(b_1 p_1 + b_1' p_{12}) s_1' p_2$ respectively.

Following the same logic, ecological interactions may also affect extinction rate via both a modification of the equilibrium population size and the capacity of the species to recover from small local perturbations. Again, we denote by a prime symbol the modified extinction rate e_i' for patches with co-occurrence (p_{12}). The rate of decrease of species 1 occupancy due to its extinction in patches it occupies alone or together with species 2 will therefore be e_1p_1 and $e_1'p_{12}$ respectively. Note that the rate of joint species extinctions is null.

Collecting the terms together and keeping track of all possible pathways between the different states, we get the following set of differential equations:

$$\frac{dp_1}{dt} = (b_1p_1 + b_1'p_{12})\,s_1p_0 - e_1p_1 + e_2'p_{12}$$
$$- (b_2p_2 + b_2p_{12})\,s_2'p_1$$
$$\frac{dp_2}{dt} = (b_2p_2 + b_2'p_{12})\,s_2p_0 - e_2p_2 + e_1'p_{12}$$
$$- (b_1p_1 + b_1'p_{12})\,s_1'p_2$$
$$\frac{dp_{12}}{dt} = (b_1p_1 + b_1'p_{12})\,s_1'p_2 + (b_2p_2 + b_2'p_{12})\,s_2'p_1$$
$$- (e_1' + e_2')\,p_{12} \qquad (12.29)$$

A schematic version of the model is represented in Figure 12.2 and parameters are interpreted for various settings in Table 12.1. Albeit more difficult to analyze than traditional Lotka–Volterra equations for local dynamics, the model is general enough to account for all combinations of positive and negative interactions. Unfortunately it cannot be solved for internal equilibrium except in special cases, but the mutual invasibility can be studied by stability analysis, following (Hanski 1983), a species can invade a metapopulation equilibrium only comprising the other one if this equilibrium is unstable. This technique has the advantage of highlighting the joint effects of interactions via an analysis of the equilibrium occupancy of the resident species and its effect on the invasibility of the interacting species. Doing so, we will be able to map our interpretation on Chesson's formalism of equalizing and stabilizing mechanisms of coexistence.

12.4.2 Technique for invasibility analysis

It is not possible to solve the two-species model for equilibrium except for a few special cases. It is neither possible to compute directly the per capita growth rate of an invading population because of the p_{12} fraction. The approach to investigate invasibility is therefore to use local stability analysis

on the equilibrium where only one species is resident and the other is completely absent (i.e., $\hat{p}_i = 0$, $\hat{p}_{ij} = 0$ and $\hat{p}_j > 0$). In such a situation, the small perturbation that is the object of the analysis is the introduction of the alternative species and the stability analysis tells us if this small perturbation grows (unstable equilibrium, the species invades) or not (stable equilibrium, resistance to invasion). The following analysis was originally derived by Hanski (1983), but here we introduce a few additions due to the model reformulation and the distinction between propagule production (b_i) and establishment (s_i). We will not detail all derivations here but the reader could refer to Hanski's analysis of regional coexistence.

Stability analysis consists of first computing the Jacobian matrix for the previous set of differential equations, evaluating it at the equilibrium points $\hat{p}_i$ and then investigating the Routh–Hurwitz conditions for stability. After some simplifications of the conditions, we find that local stability depends on two inequalities (setting species 2 at equilibrium, species 1 the invader, and with the following definitions $\mu_i = b_i's_i' - b_is_i$):

$$b_1s_1 - b_2s_2 + (\mu_2 - \mu_1)\,\hat{p}_2 - 2e_1 - e_1' - e_2' < 0$$
$$(b_1s_1 - e_2 - \mu_1\hat{p}_2)\,(b_2s_2 + e_1 + e_2' - \mu_2\hat{p}_2)$$
$$< e_1'\left[-(b_1s_1 - e_1) + (b_1s_1 + b_2s_2 - \mu_2)\,\hat{p}_2\right] \quad (12.30)$$

Invasibility will occur if any of these two inequalities is not satisfied. The following analysis for different parameterizations is based on this criterion. Note that coexistence requires this condition to be satisfied at both one-species equilibrium (when each species is resident and the other one absent).

12.4.3 Competition

Fitness inequality and stabilizing interactions

Chesson's theory of coexistence stems directly from MacArthur's heritage formulated in niche theory. Using Lotka–Volterra equations for competitive interactions, it is easy to show that the criteria for stable coexistence depend on the ratio of carrying capacities of the two species and the interaction coefficients among them. Chesson's interpretation of coexistence mechanisms as equalizing and stabilizing directly stems from this condition:

equalizing mechanisms act to reduce the difference in carrying capacities, while stabilizing mechanisms act on the interaction coefficients. For instance, non-linear population dynamics (e.g., a type-II functional response) alter the long-term average carrying capacities via Jensen's inequality, which is interpreted as an equalizing mechanism. Niche differentiation on the other hand reduces the opportunities for species to compete for resources, and thereby reduces the interaction coefficients among them. There is no formal interpretation of these for metacommunities, except by simulations (Roxburgh et al. 2004; Shoemaker and Melbourne 2016).

The previous analysis of equilibrium occupancy with the single-species model was helpful to set-up how different metacommunity settings do affect fitness inequality. The equilibrium occupancy is simply equal to $\hat{p}_i = 1 - e_i/c_i$ for the simple situation where the environment is uniform across the landscape and dispersal is global. Inequality in such a situation therefore only depends on the intrinsic characteristics of the two species. Both environmental variation and dispersal limitations may, however, reduce the equilibrium occupancy, especially when the response to the environment is strong, environmental variation is large, and c_i is low (for a given $\hat{p}_i$). Therefore, species differences in these characteristics may make coexistence more difficult to obtain. (Mouquet and Loreau 2002) already provided a few hints about this situation in their hypothesis of regional similarity, where they conclude that coexistence may be impeded at large dispersal if species are unequal on average across the landscape. Quantification of regional inequality between species is, however, insufficient to conclude about coexistence as we also need to consider the two interspecific interaction coefficients. This is what we will perform in the following analysis of a few cases. In particular, we will look at the boundary conditions between competitive exclusion, unstable coexistence, and stable coexistence over the inequality-interaction space.

Colonization competition (priority effects)

A situation that attracted significant attention of early metacommunity research was the one of colonization competition, also referred as migration competition by Hanski (1983), where interspecific interactions prevent the establishment of an invading species. It is common to refer at this type of interaction as a priority effect (Fukami 2015), where the resident species establishes and changes the environment so that another species coming to that locality cannot establish any further. In our model, this corresponds to the situation where the establishment rate is lower in the presence of competitor than in empty patches (i.e., $s_i' < s_i$). Note that this situation differs from the one where competition reduces propagule production in patches where species co-occur (i.e., $b_i' < b_i$). In order to compare with Chesson's framework based on niche theory, we consider a gradient of niche overlap σ ranging between 0 (no overlap, perfect differentiation) and 1 (perfect overlap) and that each species establishment rate is reduced with increasing overlap, such that $s_i' = s_i \alpha_i (1 - \sigma)$, where α_i is a positive constant indicating the sensitivity of the species to competition. Note that s_i' has to be non-negative.

One of the main questions asked about colonization competition was if it could prevent coexistence and eventually lead to resistance (alternative stable states). The invasibility conditions, specified by inequality 12.30, simplifies considerably for colonization competition. Invasibility of the resident community *res* by an invading species *inv* is feasible if the following inequality is satisfied:

$$\frac{\hat{p}_{inv}}{\hat{p}_{res}} < \alpha_{inv}\sigma \qquad (12.31)$$

As one would guess, it is harder to find stable coexistence with both increasing niche overlap, up to the point where the inferior competitor or the one with the highest occupancy in absence of competition will exclude the other and regain in occupancy (Figure 12.3). Competitive exclusion by the species with the largest regional occupancy will occur if interactions are strong enough. Hanski (1983) also described a situation where priority effects may prevent mutual invasibility and result in unstable coexistence, i.e., a situation where the first species to occupy the landscape resists invasion. This situation is not feasible with the previous definition of competitive interactions, since it is impossible for

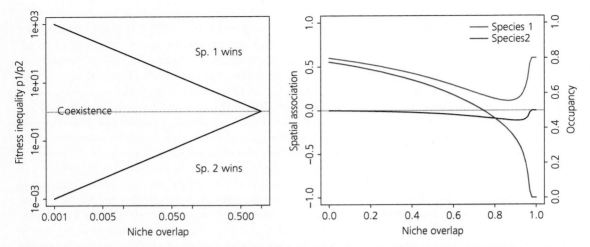

Figure 12.3 Colonization competition. **A)** Regional fitness inequality interaction strength space delimiting where coexistence is feasible. Fitness inequality is computed as the ratio of occupancies of each species in absence of competition. Competition is computed as a function of niche overlap σ such that $s_i' = s_i \alpha_i (1 - \sigma)$, with symetric sensitivities to niche overal, $\alpha s_1 = \alpha s_2$. There is no colonization competition at $\sigma = 0$ and it is impossible to colonize occupied patches because of strong priority effect at $\sigma = 1$. Other default parameters are all symetric except for establishment that is varied to cover the range of occupancies, such that $b_i = b_i' = 1$ and $e_i = e_i' = 1$. **B)** The effect of competition colonization on equilibrium occupancies and on co-occurrence. Here species are slightly unequal by specifying $s_1 = 5$ and $s_2 = 4.5$, other parameters being the same as panel A. Spatial association is the difference between observed co- occurrence and expected co- occurrence under independent distribution, ie $p_{12} - (p_1 + p_{12})(p_2 + p_{12})$.

the two lines to cross on Figure 12.4 (because $\alpha_{inv}\sigma$ could not exceed 1 by definition).

It is interesting to investigate the amount of co-occurrence observed, p_{12}, relative to the expectation if the two species were independently distributed (i.e., $(p_1 + p_{12})(p_2 + p_{12})$), because it may inform on the signature of priority effects on the spatial distribution. Diamond's checkerboard hypothesis (Diamond 1975) arises from the intuition that negatively interacting species will avoid each other in space, which should translate in an observed co-occurrence that is much lower than the random distribution. Diamond's intuition was right, as we see that repulsion increases with interaction strength (Figure 12.4B). That said, the magnitude of the effect is very small relative to the drop in occupancy of both species, in particular of the inferior competitor, such that negative co-occurrence is very unlikely to be detected.One special case of colonization competition that attracted a lot of attention over the years is the neutral model. Hubbell (2001) and Bell (2000) models could be represented in our model by setting all parameters equal and with

strong colonization competition. This situation already attracted the attention of Slatkin (1974) and Hanski (1983), who concluded that coexistence is less and less likely with increasing competition. The zero-sum dynamics represented in Hubbell (2001) model is an extreme case where colonization cannot happen in already occupied patches ($s_i' = 0$). In such a situation the stability of the system is null and therefore make regional abundance subject to a random walk to extinction caused by stochasticity (May 1972; Gravel et al. 2011c). Note that drift is not restricted to this very specific case, it will increase in strength as species inequality reduces and colonization competition increases.

Extinction competition (local exclusion)

Another means by which competitive interactions may affect spatial dynamics is through a modification of the extinction rates. In a situation of pure extinction competition, the two species may colonize all patches, irrespective of their local composition, but then the presence of a competitor may increase the extinction rate, $e_i' = e_i + \alpha_i \sigma$. This

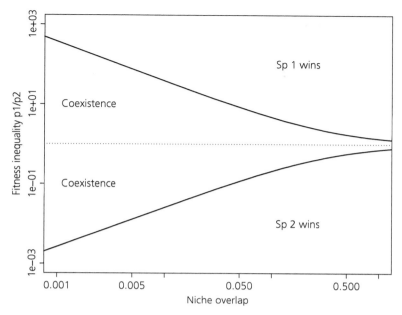

Figure 12.4 Extinction competition. Regional fitness inequality - interaction strength space delimiting where coexistence is feasible under extinction competition. Fitness inequality is computed as the ratio of occupancies of each species in absence of competition. Competition is assumed to be symetric and correspond to a scaling factor I such that $e'_i = e_i + \alpha_i \sigma$, indicating there is instanteous extinction of the weaker competitor at $\sigma = 1$. Other default parameters are all symetric except for establishment that is varied to cover the range of occupancies, such that $b_i = b'_i = 1$ and $e_i = e'_i = 1$.

phenomenon can easily be explained by a reduction in local population size following exploitative or apparent competition, combined with a negative relationship between extinction rate and population size. While the invasion criteria differs significantly from colonization competition, the interpretation of the model is much the same (Figure 12.5). Coexistence is possible if the difference in the occupancies is not too large and competitive interactions not too strong. (Hanski 1983) has shown that priority effects and unstable coexistence are also possible when occupancies are of similar magnitude and interactions very strong, contrary to the original conclusion of (Slatkin 1974).

Competition-colonization trade-off

It is quite challenging to combine both colonization and extinction competition in a single model, but an interesting situation that attracted a lot of attention is one of a trade-off between competitive ability and colonization. While much

credit for this analysis has been awarded to Hastings (1980) and later to Tilman (1994), it is possible to find mentions of it in Skellam (1951) and also in Hanski (1983). Subsequent analyses are found in Pacala and Rees (1998) and Calcagno et al. (2006). The idea is fairly simple and is easily transposed in the model. Basically, one species (labeled species 1) is a strong competitor and therefore could colonize both empty patches and the ones already occupied by the other species, while it is not affected by the presence of the other species. This situation translates in $s_1 = s'_1$ and $e_1 = e'_1$. The other species is a good colonizer of empty patches, but cannot colonize occupied ones, neither defend the ones it already occupies. In such a situation, $s_2 > s_1$ but $s'_2 = 0$, $e_2 < e_1$ and $e'_2 \to \infty$. Coexistence is feasible with this parameterization if the inequality,

$$\frac{s_2}{s_1} > \frac{\hat{p}_1}{1 - \hat{p}_1} + \frac{e_2}{e_1} \qquad (12.32)$$

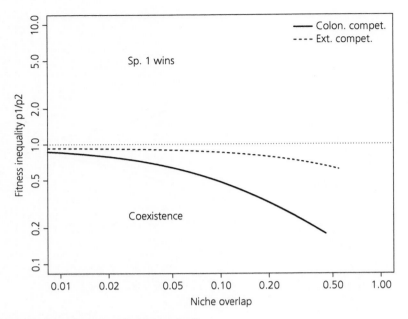

Figure 12.5 Coexistence under the competition-colonization trade-off.

is satisfied. This inequality shows that coexistence is promoted by increasing difference in occupancies between competitors.

What has never been done, however, is its formal interpretation in Chesson's space of fitness inequality and interaction strength, and in particular with less stringent assumption about competitive hierarchies. The aprevious inequality assumes implicitly that competition is unidirectional (against species 2 only) and infinite (the weaker competitor goes extinct instantaneously). Shoemaker and Melbourne (2016) attempted to partition equalizing and stabilizing mechanisms using a combination of stochastic simulations and time series analysis, but the model they used differs significantly from the Tilman–Hastings framework and therefore a formal decomposition of coexistence mechanisms has never been performed. It is nonetheless possible to perform this analysis using a graphical representation of Hanski's analysis (see Figure 12.6 and inequality 12.30). Interestingly, the model formulation allows us to relax some of the most contested assumptions in the Tilman–Hastings model, namely the perfect pre-emption by the strong competitor and the instantaneous

extinction of the weak competitor. While a satisfying first approximation to a trade-off that is commonly observed in nature, these assumptions prevent a more continuous analysis of the effect of interaction strength on coexistence.

The competition-colonization trade-off is a regional coexistence mechanism based on both fitness inequality and species differentiation. As one would guess from inequality (12.30), traits (e.g., energetic investment in seed production) and spatial conditions (e.g., connectivity of the landscape) leading to a strong inequality in occupancies, in favour of the weaker competitor, will promote coexistence. This interpretation contrasts with the general view that stabilizing processes are necessary to promote coexistence and equalizing mechanisms not sufficient. We find that the stronger the niche overlap, the larger the required amount of inequality between species to allow coexistence of the weaker competitor (species 2). In addition, traditional niche differentiation mechanisms reducing the strength of interspecific interactions also promote coexistence. Relaxing the assumption of perfect pre-emption by the stronger competitor and instantaneous

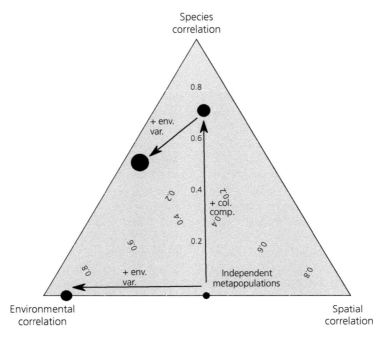

Figure 12.6 Moments for competitive metacommunities. Each dot represents a metacommunity and its size is proportional to the average correlations among the three moments. Species 1 is the strongest regional competitor (because of a higher occupancy). Parameters are: $f_i = f'_i = 1, s_1 = 5, s_2 = 5, s'_i = s_i * (1 - I), e_1 = e'_1 = 1 + d$ and $e_2 = e'_2 = 1 - d$, and $I = 0.85$.

extinction of the weaker competitor both reduce the inequality in occupancies required to promote coexistence. Fitness inequality alone can promote coexistence because there always exists a critical value of s_2 that would allow both species to invade each other, regardless of extinction coefficients (even when $e'_1 = 0$ and $e'_1 = \infty$, in other words when there is immediate extinction of the weak competitor), as long as $\hat{p}_1 < 1$ (Hanski 1983).

Species sorting

Analytical results showing how species sorting may contribute to coexistence with the previous model are impossible to derive, but the few basic principles responsible for the species sorting are easy to understand from the previous findings. Let consider the situation where two competitors have different performances throughout the landscape, either because they respond to different environmental variables or because they differ in their response to a single variable. First, we have previouslly shown for the single species analysis that spatial variation

in the colonization-extinction ratio for each species will decrease their occupancy. This effect of spatial heterogeneity will be further magnified by dispersal limitation and together they may influence regional inequality. Spatial variation of the environment alone may not have an impact on coexistence if it affects occupancies similarly because the inequality will stay unchanged, but it may promote it if it harms more a specialist competitor (which will experience larger spatial variance) than a generalist but weaker competitor. Differences in niche breadth will move away the species pair from the fitness equality line in the coexistence plane. In addition, spatial heterogeneity will reduce opportunities for interactions. Co-occurrence (p_{12}) will be reduced because of spatial sorting and so will the effective importance of exclusion competition. Further, a negative correlation between patches occupied by a species and the colonization rate of the other species ($cor(p_i, s_j)$) will further reduce opportunities for co-occurrence and therefore competitive exclusion. Overall, conditions for coexistence will be made easier with a move toward the left and the center in the inequality/interaction space.

12.4.4 Food webs

The persistence of spatial food webs can also be investigated using the same model. Driven by a simple set of principles, established first by Holt (1996) and Holt (2005) and later generalized by (Calcagno et al. 2011), Gravel et al. (2011b), and Massol et al. (2017). The basic model considers a sequential assembly of a linear food chain made of specialized species, with the bottom-level prey establishing first, followed by a predator and eventually by a top predator. The entire food chain may collapse with the extinction of a low-level species. In the most extreme situation, the predator (labeled species 2) cannot colonize a patch where the prey (labeled species 1) is absent and it goes automatically extinct with the extinction of the prey. These assumptions translate into the model with $s_2 = 0$ and $e_2 = \infty$, but they could be relaxed if one considers that the predator may forage and stay for a short amount of time in unoccupied locations. The spatial dynamics are bottom-up driven in the most simple formulations and therefore $s_1 = s_1'$.

The criterion for the persistence of the prey is the same as an independent metapopulation in the situation where the predator does not harm the dynamics of the prey, i.e., $s_1 - e_1 > 0$. The predator will invade if the following inequality is satisfied:

$$c_2 p_1 > e_2 \qquad (12.33)$$

which indicates that it will persist only if the prey occupancy is large enough relative to the predator extinction rate. The equilibrium occupancy of specialized predators ($p_2 = p_1 - e_2/c_2$) will always be lower than the one of their prey, which eventually will put a limit on the number of trophic levels that can be observed in a region, unless the colonization-extinction ratio scales with trophic level—Holt (2005). A consequence of these assumptions is that the predator will always co-occur with the prey, but the opposite will not always be true. Interestingly, the invasion criteria will remain the same in presence of top-down regulation, where the presence of the predator increases the extinction of the prey ($e_1' > e_1$). Occupancies of both the prey and the predator will, however, be reduced with top-down regulation, and while the predator distribution will remain nested within the one of the prey, the distribution of the prey will be more negatively associated with the one of the predator.

While much of the focus in this section is about two-species mutual invasibility, it is relevant to note a few general results that have been derived for more diverse communities. Persistence of a predator will increase with the generality of its diet, as it is easier to find prey in empty patches and for interactions to rewire following species extinctions (Gravel et al. 2011b). Further, the topology of the regional food web is also affecting the occupancy of the different species because of high order interactions. A predator specializing on a prey with a large occupancy is more likely to persist than a predator selecting a prey with smaller occupancy (Massol et al. 2017). The co-distribution of multiple prey species is also influencing the occupancy of the predator as it affects the total fraction of the landscape that is suitable for colonization (Gravel et al. 2011a). Negative association between prey will increase the persistence of the top predator because of a larger total amount of suitable patches, while positive association will reduce it. On the other hand, in the presence of top-down regulation (a positive effect of the predator on the prey extinction rate), apparent competition may appear at the regional level, reducing total prey occupancy and generating negative association between between them (Holt 2005). The effect of spatial variation in the environment on food web assembly has yet to be studied, but one could easily predict that a positive covariance in the response to the environment between the predator and the prey (i.e., species share the same abiotic niche) will promote the persistence of the predator (Cazelles et al. 2016). More discussion about the impact of spatial dynamics on food web structure and stability is provided as a perspective at the end of the chapter.

12.4.5 Mutualism

The assembly of mutualistic communities follows essentially the same principles as bottom-up predator-prey dynamics (Fortuna and Bascompte

2006; Astegiano et al. 2015), with the distinction that interactions may be mutually beneficial (versus unidirectional for predator-prey) and that mutualists are often facultative. A plant, for instance, will have a much larger colonization rate and potentially a smaller extinction rate in the presence of its mutualist. A specialized pollinator may, however, go extinct from a region if its partner is not abundant enough. In the case of a chain of interactions, it may be expected to see amplification of occupancies, rather than an inefficiency such as the one observed for predators.

12.5 Moments of metacommunities

We now turn to numeric simulations to investigate potential interactions among the different assembly mechanisms that were previously discussed. Simulations also facilitate the investigation of the three moments of metacommunities. The simulation model applies to a large number of patches the two-species model described previously, with the addition of spatial variation in the environment and spatially explicit dispersal. We summarize the spatial structure of metacommunities by looking at three measures of correlation investigated previously: i) **Environmental correlation** reports the spatial association between the occurrence of each species and the environment. Here, because we solve the model for equilibrium occupancies, we compute it as the Pearson correlation between the environment at each patch, E_x, and the expected occupancy, $P_{ix} = p_{ix} + p_{ijx}$. ii) **Spatial correlation** reports the first order spatial autocorrelation between patches. It is computed as the Pearson correlation between occupancies of nearest neighbour patches. iii) **Species correlation** reports the amount of spatial association between species relative to an independent distribution. It is computed as the scaled difference between expected co-occupancy and the independent expectation, $(p_{12} - P_1 P_2)/P_1 P_2$, across all patches. Note that these representations, based on correlations, do not account for shared responses; more sophisticated techniques may solve for partial correlations and allow a complete partitioning of the variation (Ovaskainen et al. 2017; Leibold et al., in review). Here we focus on the correlations to be coherent with previous analytical derivations.

We expect to see situations where synergies among mechanisms could magnify the importance of a given moment, or alternatively antagonism among them may occur. For instance, competitive interactions may force species to occur at locations that are most favourable to them, thereby increasing the environmental correlation. On the other hand, predator-prey interactions may reduce environmental correlation and increase species correlation when the two species share different environmental requirements. We also expect these interactions to be dependent on the spatial contingencies, such as the amount of variance and spatial autocorrelation in the environment and the structure of the connectivity matrix. It was shown for instance that the strength of species sorting in competitive metacommunities may be affected by the landscape structure since short boundaries between environmental types may induce a mass effect as well as dispersal limitations (Ai et al. 2013; Fournier et al. 2017).

We conducted spatially explicit numerical simulations of the model represented in Figure 12.2. We considered a landscape made of $n = 25$ patches. The landscape is simulated as a random geometric graph by distributing patches randomly in a square plane and connections made between the ones distant by less than a threshold value r. For each patch x we consider a local environmental condition E_x that has an average of 0 and a random deviate d_x. For simplicity, and to respect the previous analytical derivations, we consider there are only two types of patches (favorable and unfavorable), and that the local environment only influences equally the extinction parameters e_i and e_i'. We solve the model numerically for equibrium occupancies for all four types and each patch.

12.5.1 Competition

We simulated four scenarios to illustrate interactions among dispersal limitation, environmental heterogeneity and competitive interactions (here limited to colonization competition, but the same results would hold under extinction competition). The basic simulation starts with two independent metapopulations with distinct connectivity landscapes and no underlying environmental variation

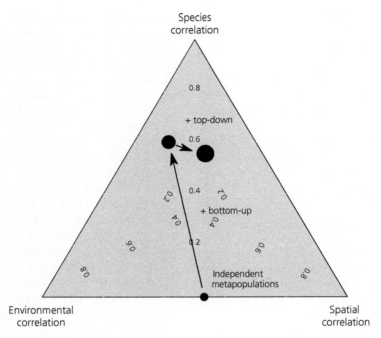

Figure 12.7 Moments for predator-prey interactions. Each dot represents a metacommunity and its size is proportional to the average correlations among the three moments. Species 1 is the predator and species 2 is the prey. The environment is spatially uniform. Parameters are: $f_i = f'_i = 1, s_1 = 0, s_2 = 4, s'_1 = 0, s'_2 = 4, e_1 = 1000, e'_1 = 5, e_2 = 1, e'_2 = 1$ for the bottom-up simulation and $e'_2 = e_2 = 1/(1-I)$ for the top-down situation, where $I = 0.7$

(Figure 12.7). The position of the metacommunity tends to be toward the bottom right of the triangle, dominated by spatial autocorrelation. The exact position of the metacommunity may vary with parameterization and the spatial structure of the landscape, but essentially the only significant correlation is spatial. Some spurious correlation with the environment and between species may, however, happen by chance alone, see Bell (2005), but it will tend to vanish with an increasing number of patches, while it will increase with the amount of spatial autocorrelation in the environment. Not surprisingly, adding variation in the environment moves the location of the metacommunity toward the left of the triangle (species sorting). Alternatively, adding competitive interactions moves the location of the metacommunity toward the top of the triangle, with increasing species correlation. As it would be expected, combining environmental heterogeneity and competition moves the metacommunity toward a more central position; interestingly, the correlations are also

stronger, indicating that both species sorting and negative spatial association get stronger when acting together. Stochastic simulations of a similar model also suggest that some minimal amount of species sorting is required to obtain species correlation because otherwise, competitive exclusion drives spatial distribution and blur any spatial correlation (Leibold and Chase 2018).

12.5.2 Predator-prey interactions

The previous section on coexistence has shown that species correlation may be stronger in the situation of predator-prey interactions because the distribution of specialized predators is nested within the one of their prey. We start again with the same simulation as previously made of two independent metapopulations over a spatially uniform environment. The dependence of the predator on the presence of the prey strongly increases the species correlation. Interestingly, the situation also prevails even if the interaction is strongly asymmetric with top-down regulation: the predator and the prey maintain a positive spatial association, despite the negative effect of the predator on the prey. The distribution of the predator is, however, completely nested within the one of the prey (i.e., $y_1 = p_{12}$ and $p_1 = 0$), while the prey is much more often alone than with the predator. This distinction is important for co-occurrence analysis and we underline that asymmetric indices are much more appropriate to investigate assembly processes and their ensuing patterns (Cazelles et al. 2015).

12.6 Discussion

Our objective in this chapter was to propose a single model unifying different theories of meta-community assembly, from competitive interactions to food webs. The model we presented is a re-interpretation of the one analyzed by Hanski (1983) in his investigation of coexistence in competitive metacommunities, following the earlier work of Cohen (1970), Levins and Culver (1971), and Slatkin (1974). Previous metacommunity theory was based on a wide range of modelling approaches, such as spatialized Lotka–Volterra equations, e.g., Takeuchi (1989); Neuhauser and Pacala (1999), multi-species Levins models, e.g., Hastings (1980); Tilman (1994); Mouquet and Loreau (2002); Holt (2005); Gravel et al. (2011a), individual based models, e.g., Bell (2000); Chave et al. (2002), Markov-chain island-mainland models (Hubbell 2001), point-pattern analysis (Bolker and Pacala 1997), and moment approximations (Chesson, 2000a; Snyder and Chesson 2004). Leibold et al. (2004) proposed a unification of different theories for competitive metacommunities with the definition of four paradigms: neutral, species-sorting, mass effect, and competition-colonization trade-off. The proposition was based on a synthesis of the different theories at that time and free of any modelling approach. This contribution was fundamental to the advancement of the field but now we see the limitations of a verbal theory arising. These include the appreciation that the four paradigms are extreme cases of a more continuous reality (Logue et al. 2011); mechanisms are not exclusive, they can be additive or they could interact (Leibold and Chase 2018); contingencies

such as landscape structure, disturbances, or environmental variation may affect which mechanism dominates community assembly (Ai et al. 2013); species not only interact by competition, they are embedded in a more diversified network of ecological interactions (Cazelles 2016); species are not all equal, and their distributions may be influenced by different processes (Fournier et al. 2017); metacommunity theory needs to provide a wider range of predictions than the traditional opposition between spatial autocorrelation and species-environnement correlation (Leibold et al., in review). Hopefully, the model we presented here will prove general enough to solve at least part of these problems, and be used as a foundation for a new phase of metacommunity research.

A single mathematical formalism allows us to underline the key parameters to investigate, in theory but also in the field. We placed our analysis of coexistence in a fitness inequality and niche overlap space in order to compare regional versus local coexistence mechanisms. We quantified fitness inequality as the ratio of metapopulation carrying capacities (the equilibrium single species occupancy). Equilibrium occupancy is a function of the ratio of extinction to colonization rates in spatially homogeneous environments and we have shown how it is reduced by both spatial variation of the environment and spatially explicit limited dispersal. This quantity proves to be essential to understand coexistence of competitors in a spatially heterogeneous environment, but also bottom-up assembly of food chains. As an extension of the definition for local dynamics, we also define interactions at the regional level as the per patch impact of a species on the colonization and the extinction rates. Indeed, niche overlap reduces local per capita growth rate, a process scaling up at the regional level by its effect on the colonization rate. Similarly, niche overlap reduces equilibrium population size and eventually promotes extinction.

We also proposed a set of three emerging properties to characterize the structure of meta-communities. More specifically, we looked at three moments of the mutlivariate species distribution: i) first-order spatial autocorrelation is a measure of the similarity in species composition among adjacent localities and is mostly driven by the joint effects of disturbances (extinctions) and dispersal limitations; ii) environment-occurrence correlation is a measure of the association between species distribution and the abiotic environment resulting from variation in fitness; iii) species co-distribution is a measure of the spatial association between species and results from various causes, including biotic interactions, shared environmental requirements, and dispersal limitations. Gilbert and Lechowicz (2004) and Cottenie (2005) were the first to describe metacommunity structure with spatial autocorrelation and environment-occurrence correlation. More recently, the development of joint species distribution models (Pollock et al. 2014; Warton 2015) facilitated the analysis of co-distribution and opened new ways to investigate metacommunity dynamics (Zurell et al. 2018). The analysis of co-distribution has a long and rich history in community ecology but was mostly ignored from metacommunity research, but see Bell (2005). Biotic interactions are included in all of the four paradigms of metacommunity dynamics of Leibold et al. (2004), but surprisingly they are not the object of predictions to discriminate them. Various forms of competitive interactions should leave an imprint on species distribution, beyond the checkerboard distribution proposed by Diamond (1975).

Our analysis was not meant to be extensive and future work is, however, needed to identify the circumstances leading to a distinctive co-distribution. We have shown, for instance, that symmetric competition hardly leads to negative spatial association between species, in opposition to Diamond (1975) hypothesis. The onset of competitive exclusion occurs much before negative correlation can be detected from empirical data. We found negative association between competitively interacting species, but measuring this signal in noisy empirical data may require sampling effort much beyond what is typically accessible. Joint species distribution models are powerful tools to quantify co-distribution but they are also limited to the special case of symmetric associations. Asymmetric interactions, in particular antagonistic ones, are impossible to document using covariance or joint probabilities. Rather, conditional probabilities may prove to be more flexible

(and realistic) to describe associations (Cazelles et al. 2015). Shared environmental requirements, indirect interactions, and diffuse interactions are all conditions that are susceptible to mask spatial associations, or alternatively to generate false signal. Investigation of co-distribution in metacommunities should, therefore, be the main object of future metacommunity theory.

Not only does the model we proposed allow development of theory, it could be tested explicitly with measurements of transitions between the different species composition. This analysis was done recently in an investigation of range shifts of temperate forests in North Eastern America (Vissault et al. in review). Forest inventory data was used to document transitions from presence to absence (extinction) and absence to presence (colonization). The model was parameterized across North America and all transitions were conditioned on annual average temperature and precipitations. All of the previous coefficients of species interactions were successfully evaluated, and solving the model made it possible to investigate conditions where competitive interactions limit species range. The model was fitted from dynamical data (transitions) and solved at equilibrium to successfully predict static distribution (current ranges) of both temperate and boreal tree forest. The model was then used to show that stability is the highest in the middle zone, where temperate tree species coexist with boreal ones, and minimal at range limits where interactions are driving one species to the extinction. Trees make a good case for testing such a theory because their spatial dynamics are often driven by disturbances (e.g., canopy gaps, fires) and succession, and because they are also strongly dispersal limited (Hubbell et al. 1999).

12.6.1 Extension to multi-species communities

We focused on pairwise interactions in this chapter but the model we proposed is easy to scale up to entire communities embedded in a diverse network of interactions. The key problem is to represent how interactions add up and influence species dynamics. Tradition in local community ecology is to consider that multiple interactions are additive. In Lotka–Volterra equations, for instance, interactions are summed over the community and a given species has the same effect whether it is alone or in an entire community. If interactions are additive, then it is possible to approximate the total effect of interactions with knowledge of average interaction strength and the covariance between interaction strength and occupancy (Godsoe et al. 2017). Multiple interactions are also additive in consumer resource models (Brose et al. 2006), although they may influence rate of consumption for Type II and Type III functional response and generate non-lineariteis. Cazelles et al. (2016) rather introduced the idea that the effect of other species saturates with increasing diversity in a model of spatial dynamics similar to the one considered here, with the first interaction being the most significant and the subsequent weaker. At the end of the spectrum, (Gravel et al. 2011c) proposed that only the first interaction matter for spatial dynamics, allowing the colonization and the persistence of a consumer if at least one prey is present.

Multi-species analyses have shown that a network approach may be the way to reduce the complexity of spatial community dynamics. With the assumption that a predator requires at least one prey to colonize an area and to persist, one can easily derive the expectation for occupancy as a function of the generality of the diet (Gravel et al. 2011c). As a consequence, generalists are expected to be the first to colonize a new location, documented empirically by Piechnik et al. (2008) and to persist. This per species effect scales up and influences how local network properties and body size distribution are affected by area and isolation (Jacquet et al. 2017). Another important aspect to consider in multi-species communities is the effect of higher-order interactions. A species at the top of the food chain not only needs to find its prey, it will be limited by the distribution of the the prey of its prey; as a result, extinction cascades can occur and influence regional food web dynamics (Holt et al. 1999; Calcagno et al. 2011; Massol et al. 2017). Such a theory has not been explored for competitive interactions, but some principles will nonetheless apply. Generality of a species will influence its persistence in competitive metacommunities, although a reversal should be expected, with the least connected

species being more persistent and the first to colonize empty locations. Further, higher order interactions may also be important for occupancy because of the "enemy-of-my-enemy-is-my-friend" principle.

A set of simple rules also explains how co-distribution scales from a few species to entire networks (Cazelles et al. 2015): i) spatial associations may arise from indirect interactions; ii) associations do not have to be symmetrical; iii) multiple interactions decrease the strength of pairwise associations. Putting these rules together, it was predicted that pairwise associations should tend toward randomness with increasing degree and topological distance between species. As a consequence, species are expected to be independently distributed in species-rich communities. In such a situation, we should expect to find stronger environment-occurrence correlation as well as spatial autocorrelation.

12.6.2 From coexistence to dynamical stability

While species coexistence is a central question of community ecology, another closely connected topic is the issue of community stability. Stability has been defined in a variety of ways, reviewed e.g., by Donohue et al. (2013), and theoretically explored by (Arnoldi et al. 2016), but the central tenet of a stable (meta)community remains the same across definitions: rapidly returning to equilibrium after a perturbation. Coexistence and stability are linked in multiple ways, e.g., since coexistence of species at an equilibrium means that this equilibrium is stable (but all coexistence situations are not at equilibrium), and because coexistence can also be recast as mutual invasibility of all communities lacking one species, which amounts to looking for n communities of $n-1$ species that are unstable to invasions by the nth species.

The question of ecosystem stability is an old-time classic in ecology, dating back at least to (MacArthur 1955). In a provocative paper, (May 1972) challenged the view that species diversity and ecological network complexity contribute positively to ecosystem stability by providing a null model for community stability. He proposed to use random Jacobian matrices to assess whether a randomly assembled set of S species, interacting with connectance c and with Jacobian elements of mean 0 and variance σ^2, could represent a stable ecosystem. The answer was that such a system imposes a strong constraint on all of these factors (May 1972; Allesina and Tang 2012), i.e., $\sigma\sqrt{Sc} < m$ where m is the value of diagonal elements of the Jacobian matrix (feedbacks of species upon themselves). (Allesina and Tang 2012) further elaborated on this theory by providing sophistications of the model, taking into account the proportions of predator-prey mutualistic and competitive interactions, and making a distinction between asymptotic stability and reactivity (Tang and Allesina 2014).

In the same vein, Gravel et al. (2016) explored the question of meta-ecosystem stability using the same framework as the one initially envisaged by May (1972), see also (Coyte et al. 2015 and (Mougi and Konodh 2016). By decomposing links between populations as interactions and dispersal rates, Gravel et al. (2016) evinced a major stabilizing factor arising from spatial structure when dispersal is sufficiently high and patches behave heterogeneously. In this context, dispersal mixes heterogeneous random Jacobian elements together, and these random variables are thus averaged over space, with a sample variance decreasing with sample size (i.e., the number of patches averaged over). With a reduced variance of the average ecosystem, stability is enhanced—in May (1972), the σ that appears in the stability criterion is divided by the number of patches that are being averaged. More generally, even when patch-specific Jacobian elements cannot be considered independent random variables, the σ is still divided by the effective number of independent patches in the meta-ecosystem, this quantity being defined through the number of patches and the correlation of their Jacobians. By simulating spatially structured Lotka–Volterra competitive systems, Gravel et al. (2016) were finally able to show that the result obtained through random matrix modelling also held in random dynamical systems, provided dispersal is not too high—at very high dispersal, patches tend to synchronize and thus, the effective number of independent patches decreases with dispersal.

In the case of the multi-species version of Levins' metapopulation model, stability can be assessed using the same kind of theory. Providing general stability assessment of such models is beyond the scope of this chapter, but we can provide a simple example based on the competitive metacommunity framework used by Calcagno et al. (2006). In this model, each patch can only be occupied by a single species, and occupancy of species i, p_i, is governed by its colonization rate, c_i, the general extinction rate, e, and all the probabilities of successful replacement of species l by species k, η_{kl}:

$$\frac{dp_i}{dt} = c_i\left(h - \sum_j p_j\right)p_i - ep_i + \sum_j \left(c_i\eta_{ij} - c_j\eta_{ji}\right)p_ip_j$$

$$(12.34)$$

If all species are assumed to be present (i.e., non-extinct at the metacommunity scale), the computation of the Jacobian matrix elements J_{ij} is highly simplified:

$$J_{ij} = -c_ip_i^* + \left(c_i\eta_{ij} - c_j\eta_{ji}\right)p_i^* \qquad (12.35)$$

where p_i^* denotes equilibrium occupancies. Following (Tang and Allesina 2014), asymptotic stability of this system, if its Jacobian elements were random, could be obtained by looking at the leading eigenvalue of the Jacobian matrix, as the maximum of $(S-1)E - d$ and $(1+\rho)\sqrt{SV} - E - d$, where E is the mean of non-diagonal Jacobian elements, $-d$ is the mean of diagonal Jacobian elements, V is the variance of non-diagonal Jacobian elements, and ρ is the correlation between Jacobian elements across the diagonal. Since $E < 0$ and $d > 0$ in this system, the leading eigenvalue of a random Jacobian would thus be $(1+\rho)\sqrt{SV} - E - d$. However, for the system to be stable, this would mean that $-E - d$ should at least be negative (otherwise, there is no way the leading eigenvalue could have negative real parts). Using the symmetry of the $c_i\eta_{ij}$ terms in the Jacobian and the equilibrium conditions given by setting the right-hand side of Equation 20.34 equal to zero with all $p_i > 0$, it can be shown that $-E - d$ tends towards $<c_i><p_i>$, i.e., the product of the average colonization rate over all species by the average occupancy of a species, when the number of species goes to infinity. Since this product cannot become negative, this demonstrates that the multi-species competition-colonization version of the Levins cannot be stable by chance alone, and thus a strong constraint on its parameters is needed for the system to be stable, probably inherited from the constraints on parameters needed for the system to be feasible in the first place. Since the system can also be compared to a competitive Lotka–Volterra multi-species one, this result agrees with other recent theoretical approaches aimed at uncovering conditions for the feasibility of large ecological systems (Bastolla et al. 2005; Dougoud et al. 2018; Stone 2018).

The Levins approach to spatial dynamics assumes a disconnection between local and regional time scales. Interestingly, it allows major disturbances to occur locally, leading to one or several extinctions from a patch. Extensions of the Levins model also have the property of very strong elements along the diagonal of the Jacobian, since all species are subject to a very fundamental constraint: they cannot occupy more than the entire landscape. Overshooting is impossible by construction of the model and the nature of spatial dynamics, and therefore it tends to strongly stabilize dynamics. It does not mean, however, that interactions or the spatial arrangement of patches cannot affect stability. Grilli et al. (2015) has investigated, for instance, the impact of spatial network topology on the stability of metapopulations and found that a random arrangement of patches is more stable and persistent than a regular one. The next step would be to develop a formalism to build Jacobian matrices embedding both the network of interactions and the connectivity matrix. It is unclear for now if May's prediction will hold in a spatialized context with patch dynamics. Since spatial dynamics have often found to be stabilizing, see review in Amarasekare (2008), it may be expected to see a reversal of the stability-diversity relationship. (Gravel et al., 2011a), for instance, found with simulations that more diverse and connected food webs are more persistent than simpler ones, in opposition to May's proposition.

12.7 Conclusion

Metacommunity theory has matured and is ready to undertake a new phase in its development. In conclusion, we propose the following three topics at the center of a new research program on community assembly in spatially structured environments.

1. Co-distribution: where and when? New methods are proposed to document biotic interactions from co-distribution, e.g., Pollock et al. (2014); Ovaskainen et al. (2017); Harris (2016) but they suffer from inappropriate integration with metacommunity theory (Zurell et al. 2018). Conditions leading to a distinctive signature of interactions on co-distribution need to be established formally.

2. Diversity-stability in metacommunities. Studies are suggesting that the negative diversity-stability relationship proposed by May (1972) may not apply in metacommunities subject to patch dynamics, such as documented in this chapter. Attention should be given to derive Jacobian matrices from patch dynamics and investigate to what extent food web assembly may stabilize dynamics and solve the stability paradox.

3. Empirical investigation of metacommunity models. The model we proposed is simple enough to be parameterized directly from field data, as exemplified by Vissault et al. (in review). Parameterization of the mdoel and test of its quantitative predictions is required to determine if the proposition is an appropriate representation of spatial dynamics and build further on it. In particular, food web models and the assumption of a sequential community assembly need to be explored.

References

Adler, P. B., Hillerislambers, J., and Levine, J. M. (2007). A niche for neutrality. *Ecology Letters* 10: 95–104.

Ai, D., Gravel, D., Chu, C., and Wang, G. (2013). Spatial structures of the environment and of dispersal impact species distribution in competitive metacommunities. *PLoS ONE* 8: e68927.

Allesina, S. and Tang, S. (2012). Stability criteria for complex ecosystems. *Nature* 483: 205–8.

Amarasekare, P. (2008). Spatial dynamics of foodwebs. *Annual Review of Ecology, Evolution, and Systematics* 39: 479–500.

Arnoldi, J. F., Loreau, M., and Haegeman, B. (2016). Resilience, reactivity and variability: A mathematical comparison of ecological stability measures. *Journal of Theoretical Biology* 389: 47–59.

Astegiano, J., Guimarães, P. R., Cheptou, P. O., Vidal, M. M., Mandai, C. Y., Ashworth, L., and Massol, F. (2015). Persistence of plants and pollinators in the face of habitat loss: Insights from trait-based metacommunity models. *Advances in Ecological Research* 53: 201–57, G. Woodward and D. A. Bohan (eds.), Ch. 5, pp. 201–57. Cambridge, Massachusetts: Academic Press.

Barot, S. and Gignoux, J. (2004). Mechanisms promoting plant coexistence: Can all the proposed processes be reconciled? *Oikos* 106: 185–92.

Bastolla, U., Lässig, M., Manrubia, S. C., and Valleriani, A. (2005). Biodiversity in model ecosystems, I: Coexistence conditions for competing species. *Journal of Theoretical Biology* 235: 521–30.

Bell, G. (2000). The distribution of abundance in neutral communities. *The American Naturalist* 155: 606–17.

Bell, G. (2005) The co-distribution of species in relation to the neutral theory of community ecology. *Ecology* 86: 1757–70.

Bolker, B. and Pacala, S. W. (1997). Using moment equations to understand stochastically driven spatial pattern formation in ecological systems. *Theoretical Population Biology* 52: 179–97.

Britton, N. (2013) Destruction and diversity: Effects of habitat loss on ecological communities. In M. Lewis, P. Maini, and S. V. Petrovskii (eds.), *Dispersal, Individual Movement and Spatial Ecology*. Berlin: Springer-Verlag, pp. 307–31.

Brose, U., Williams, R. J., and Martinez, N. D. (2006). Allometric scaling enhances stability in complex food webs. *Ecology Letters* 9: 1228–36.

Calcagno, V., Massol, F., Mouquet, N., Jarne, P., and David, P. (2011). Constraints on food chain length arising from regional metacommunity dynamics. *Proceedings. Biological sciences/The Royal Society* 278: 3042–9.

Calcagno, V., Mouquet, N., Jarne, P., and David, P. (2006). Coexistence in a metacommunity: The competition-colonization trade-off is not dead. *Ecology Letters* 9: 897–907.

Cazelles, K., Araújo, M. B., Mouquet, N., and Gravel, D. (2016). A theory for species cooccurrence in interaction networks. *Theoretical Ecology* 9: 39–48.

Cazelles, K., Mouquet, N., Mouillot, D., and Gravel, D. (2015). On the integration of biotic interaction and environmental constraints at the biogeographical scale. *Ecography* 39: 921–31.

Chave, J., Muller-Landau, H. C., and Levin, S. A. (2002). Comparing classical community models: Theoretical consequences for patterns of diversity. *The American Naturalist* 159: 1–23.

Chesson, P. (1994). Multispecies competition in variable environments. *Theoretical Population Biology* 45: 227–76.

Chesson, P. (2000a). General theory of competitive coexistence in spatially-varying environments. *Theoretical Population Biology* 58: 211–37.

Chesson, P. (2000b). Mechanisms of maintenance of species diversity. *Annual review of Ecology and Systematics* 31: 343–66.

Cohen, J. E. (1970). A Markov contingency table model for replicated Lotka–Volterra systems near equilibrium. *American Naturalist* 104: 547–59.

Cottenie, K. (2005). Integrating environmental and spatial processes in ecological community dynamics. *Ecology Letters* 8: 1175–82.

Christiansen, F. B. and Fenchel, T. M. (1977). Theories of populations in biological communities. In Fenchel, Tom, *Springer Science & Business Media*. Berlin, New York: Springer-Verlag.

Coyte, K. Z., Schluter, J., and Foster, K. R. (2015), The ecology of the microbiome: Networks, competition, and stability. *Science*, 350: 663–6.

Diamond, J. (1975). Assembly of species communities. In M. Cody and J. Diamond (eds.), *Ecology and Evolution of Communities*. Cambridge: Harvard University Press, pp. 342–444.

Donohue, I., Petchey, O., Montoya, J., Jackson, A., McNally, L., Viana, M., Healy, K., Lurgi, M., O'Connor, N., and Emmerson, M. (2013). On the dimensionality of ecological stability. *Ecology Letters* 16: 421–9.

Dougoud, M., Vinckenbosch, L., Rohr, R. P., Bersier, L. F., and Mazza, C. (2018). The feasibility of equilibria in large ecosystems: A primary but neglected concept in the complexity-stability debate. *PLOS Computational Biology* 14: 1–18.

Eriksson, A., Elias-Wolff, F., and Mehlig, B. (2013). Metapopulation dynamics on the brink of extinction. *Theoretical Population Biology* 83: 101–122.

Fortuna, M. and Bascompte, J. (2006). Habitat loss and the structure of plant-animal mutualistic networks. *Ecology Letters* 9: 278–83.

Fournier, B., Mouquet, N., Leibold, M. A., and Gravel, D. (2017). An integrative framework of coexistence mechanisms in competitive metacommunities. *Ecography* 40: 630–41.

Fukami, T. (2015). Historical contingency in community assembly: Integrating niches, species pools, and priority effects. *Annual Review of Ecology, Evolution, and Systematics* 46: 1–23.

Gilbert, B. and Lechowicz, M. J. (2004). Neutrality, niches, and dispersal in a temperate forest understory. *Proceedings of the National Academy of Sciences of the United States of America* 101: 7651–6.

Godsoe, W., Jankowski, J., Holt, R. D., and Gravel, D. (2017). Integrating biogeography with contemporary niche theory. *Trends in Ecology and Evolution* 32: 488–99.

Gounand, I., Harvey, E., Little, C. J., and Altermatt, F. (2018). Meta-ecosystems 2.0: Rooting the theory into the field. *Trends in Ecology and Evolution* 33: 33–46.

Gravel, D., Albouy, C., and Thuiller, W. (2016). The meaning of functional trait composition of food webs for ecosystem functioning. *Philosophical Transactions of the Royal Society of London B: Biological Sciences* 371(1694), DOI: 10.1098/rstb.2015.0268.

Gravel, D., Beaudet, M., and Messier, C. (2010a). Large-scale synchrony of gap dynamics and the distribution of understory tree species in maple-beech forests. *Oecologia* 162: 153–61.

Gravel, D., Canard, E., Guichard, F., and Mouquet, N. (2011a). Persistence increases with diversity and connectance in trophic metacommunities. *PloS One* 6: e19374.

Gravel, D., Canham, C. D., Beaudet, M., and Messier, C. (2006). Reconciling niche and neutrality: The continuum hypothesis. *Ecology Letters* 9: 399–409.

Gravel, D., Guichard, F., and Hochberg, M. E. (2011b). Species coexistence in a variable world. *Ecology Letters* 14: 828–39.

Gravel, D., Guichard, F., Loreau, M., and Mouquet, N. (2010b). Source and sink dynamics in meta-ecosystems. *Ecology* 91: 2172–84.

Gravel, D., Massol, F., Canard, E., Mouillot, D., and Mouquet, N. (2011c). Trophic theory of island biogeography. *Ecology Letters* 14: 1010–6.

Gravel, D., Massol, F., and Leibold, M. A. (2016). Stability and complexity in model meta-ecosystems. *Nature Communications*, 7: 12457.

Grilli, J., Barabas, G., and Allesina, S. (2015). Metapopulation persistence in random fragmented landscapes. *PLOS Computational Biology* 11: e1004251.

Hanski, I. (1983). Coexistence of competitors in patchy environment. *Ecology* 64: 493–500.

Hanski, I. (1999). *Metapopulation Ecology*. Oxford: Oxford University Press.

Harris, D. J. (2016). Inferring species interactions from co-occurrence data with Markov networks. *Ecology* 97: 3308–14.

Hastings, A. (1980). Disturbance, coexistence, history, and competition for space. *Theoretical Population Biology* 18: 363–73.

Holt, R. (1996), Food webs in space: An island biogeographic perspective. In G. A. Polis and K. O. Winemiller (eds.), *Food Webs: Contemporary Perspectives*. London, UK: Chapman and Hall, pp. 313–23.

Holt, R., Lawton, J., Polis, G., and Martinez, N. (1999). Trophic rank and the species-area relationship. *Ecology* 80: 1495–504.

Holt, R. D. (2005). Food web dynamics in a metacommunity context: Modules and beyond. In M. Holyoak, M. Leibold, and R. D. Holt (eds.), *Metacommunities: Spatial Dynamics and Ecological Communities*. Chicago: Chicago University Press, pp. 68–94.

Holyoak, M., Leibold, M. A., and Holt, R. D. (2005). *Metacommunities: Spatial Dynamics and Ecological Communities*. Chicago: Chicago University Press.

Hubbell, S. (2001). *The Unified Neutral Theory of Biodiversity and Biogeography*. Princeton, NJ: Princeton University Press.

Hubbell, S. P., Foster, R. B., Brien, S. T. O., Harms, K. E., and Condit, R. (1999). Light-Gap disturbances, recruitment limitation, and tree diversity in a neotropical forest. *Science* 283: 554–7.

Jacquet, C., Mouillot, D., Kulbicki, M., and Gravel, D. (2017). Extensions of island biogeography theory predict the scaling of functional trait composition with habitat area and isolation. *Ecology Letters* 20: 135–46.

Keeling, M. J. (2002). Using individual-based simulations to test the Levins metapopulation paradigm. *Journal of Animal Ecology* 71: 270–9.

Klausmeier C. A. (2001). Habitat destruction and extinction in competitive and mutualistic metacommunities. Ecology Letters 4: 57–63.

Leibold, M., Blanchet, G., De Meester, L., Gravel, D., Hartig, F., Peres-Neto, P. J. R., Shoemaker, L., and Chase, J. (in review). Rethinking metacommunity ecology. *Ecology*.

Leibold, M., Holyoak, M., Mouquet, N., Amarasekare, P., Chase, J. M., Hoopes, M., Holt, R. D., Shurin, J. B., Law, R., Tilman, D., Loreau, M., and Gonzalez, A. (2004). The metacommunity concept: A framework for multi-scale community ecology. *Ecology Letters* 7: 601–13.

Leibold, M. A. and Chase, J. M. (2018). *Metacommunity Ecology*. Princeton: Princeton University Press.

Levins, R. (1969). Some demographic and genetic consequences of environmental heterogeneity for biological control. *Bulletin of the Entomological Society of America* 15: 237–40.

Levins, R. and Culver, D. (1971). Regional coexistence of species and competition between rare species. *Proceedings of the National Academy of Sciences* 68: 1246–8.

Levins, R. and Heatwole, H. (1963). On the distribution of organisms on islands. *Caribbean Journal of Science* 3: 173–7.

Logue, J., Mouquet, N., Peter, H., and Hillebrand, H. (2011). Empirical approaches to metacommunities: A review and comparison with theory. *Trends in Ecology and Evolution* 26: 482–91.

Loreau, M. (2004). Does functional redundancy exist? *Oikos* 104: 606–11.

Loreau, M., Mouquet, N., and Holt, R. (2003). Meta-ecosystems: A theoretical framework for a spatial ecosystem ecology. *Ecology Letters* 6: 673–9.

MacArthur, R. (1955). Fluctuations of animal populations, and a measure of community stability. *Ecology* 36: 533–6.

MacArthur, R. H. (1972). *Geographical Ecolog: Patterns the Distribution of Species*. Princeton: Princeton University Press.

MacArthur, R. H. and Wilson, E. O. (1963). An equilibrium theory of insular zoogeography. *Evolution* 17: 373–87.

MacArthur, R. H. and Wilson, E. O. (1967). *The Theory of Island Biogeography*. Princeton: Princeton University Press.

Massol, F., Altermatt, F., Gounand, I., Gravel, D., Leibold, M. A., and Mouquet, N. (2017). How life-history traits affect ecosystem properties: Effects of dispersal in metaecosystems. *Oikos* 126: 532–46.

Massol, F., Gravel, D., Mouquet, N., Cadotte, M. W., Fukami, T., and Leibold, M. A. (2011). Linking community and ecosystem dynamics through spatial ecology. *Ecology Letters* 14: 313–23.

May, R. M. (1972). Will a large complex system be stable? *Nature* 238: 413–14.

Mougi, A. and Kondoh, M. (2016). Food-web complexity, meta-community complexity and community stability. *Scientific Reports* 6: 24478.

Mouquet, N. and Loreau, M. (2002). Coexistence in Metacommunities: The Regional Similarity Hypothesis. *The American Naturalist* 159: 420–6.

Nee, S. and May, R. (1992). Dynamics of metapopulations: Habitat destruction and competitive coexistence. *Journal of Animal Ecology* 61: 37–40.

Neuhauser, C. and Pacala, S. W. (1999). An explicitly spatial version of the Lotka–Volterra model with interspecific competition. *Annals of Applied Probability*. 9: 1226–59.

Ovaskainen, O., Tikhonov, G., Norberg, A., Blanchet, F. G., Duan, L., Dunson, D., Roslin, T., Abrego, N., and Chave, J. (2017). How to make more out of community data? a conceptual framework and its implementation as models and software. *Ecology Letters* 20: 561–76.

Ovaskainen, O. and Cornell, S. J. (2006). Asymptotically exact analysis of stochastic metapopulation dynamics with explicit spatial structure. *Theoretical Population Biology*, 69: 13–33.

Ovaskainen, O. and Cornell, S. J. (2006). Space and stochasticity in population dynamics. *Proceedings of the National Academy of Sciences* 103: 12781–6.

Pacala, S. and Rees, M. (1998). Models suggesting field experiments to test two hypotheses explaining successional diversity. *The American Naturalist* 152: 729–37.

Piechnik, D. A., Lawler, S. P., and Martinez, N. D. (2008). Food-web assembly during a classic biogeographic study: Species' "trophic breadth" corresponds to colonization order. *Oikos* 117: 665–74.

Polis, G. A., Anderson, W. B., and Holt, R. D. (1997). Toward an integration of landscape and food web ecology: The dynamics of spatially subsidized food webs. *Annual Review of Ecology and Systematics* 28: 289–316.

Pollock, L. J., Tingley, R., Morris, W. K., Golding, N., O'Hara, R. B., Parris, K. M., Vesk, P. A., and McCarthy, M. A. (2014). Understanding co-occurrence by modelling species simultaneously with a joint species distribution model (JSDM). *Methods in Ecology and Evolution* 5: 397–406.

Roxburgh, S. H., Shea, K., and Wilson, J. B. (2004). The intermediate disturbance hypothesis: Patch dynamics and mechanisms of species coexistence. *Ecology* 85: 359–71.

Shoemaker, L. G. and Melbourne, B. A. (2016). Linking metacommunity paradigms to spatial coexistence mechanisms. *Ecology* 97: 2436–46.

Skellam, J. (1951). Random dispersal in theoretical populations. *Biometrika* 38: 196–218.

Slatkin, M. (1974). Competition and regional coexistence. *Ecology* 55: 128–34.

Snyder, R. E. and Chesson, P. (2003). Local dispersal can facilitate coexistence in the presence of permanent spatial heterogeneity. *Ecology Letters* 6: 301–9.

Snyder, R. E. and Chesson, P. (2004). How the spatial scales of dispersal, competition, and environmental heterogeneity interact to affect coexistence. *Coexistence American Naturalist* 164: 633–50.

Stone, L. (2018). The feasibility and stability of large complex biological networks: A random matrix approach. *Scientific Reports* 8: 8246.

Takeuchi, Y. (1989). Diffusion-mediated persistence in two-species competition Lotka–Volterra model. *Mathematical Biosciences* 95: 65–83.

Tang, S. and Allesina, S. (2014). Reactivity and stability of large ecosystems. *Frontiers in Ecology and Evolution* 2: 21.

Tilman, D. (1994). Competition and Biodiversity in Spatially Structured Habitats. *Ecology* 75: 2–16.

Vissault, S., Talluto, M., Boulangeat, I., and Gravel, D. (in review) Slow demography and limited dispersal constrain the expansion of north-eastern temperate forests under climate change. *Journal of Biogeography*. Forthcoming.

Zurell, D., Pollock, L. J., and Thuiller, W. (2018). Do joint species distribution models reliably detect interspecific interactions from co-occurrence data in homogenous environments? *Ecography* 41: 1812–19.

CHAPTER 13

Theories of diversity in disease ecology

T. Alex Perkins and Jason R. Rohr

13.1 Introduction

Organisms engaged in parasitic and pathogenic interactions with their hosts represent fundamentally important components of ecosystems. After decades of study, an appreciation has been cultivated for the role of pathogens in regulating host population dynamics (Hudson et al. 1998), shaping host behavior (Rohr et al. 2009; Perkins et al. 2016) and evolution (Best et al. 2008; Boots et al. 2012), facilitating exotic species invasions (Mitchell and Power 2003; Torchin and Mitchell 2004), increasing food web connectance (Lafferty et al. 2006a; Lafferty et al. 2006b), and influencing ecosystem biomass and functioning (Kuris et al. 2008). From an applied point of view, parasites and pathogens are the source of numerous challenges to conservation and human health, with the magnitude of those challenges expected to grow as numerous forms of global change continue their worrisome trends (Lafferty 2009; Martin et al. 2010; Rohr et al. 2011).

Despite the prominent role that parasites and pathogens play in all corners of ecosystems and their considerable entanglement throughout them, the treatment of parasitic and pathogenic interactions in ecological theory has largely been relegated to the study of interactions between a single parasite or pathogen and a single host. This view is perfectly adequate in many systems. In humans,

for example, a number of pathogens that were once zoonotic have now adapted to exclusively circulate among humans (Wolfe et al. 2007). Many of these and other pathogens exhibit strain diversity (e.g., plasmodium and pneumococcus), yet others can, for all intents and purposes, be considered as a single strain in ecological analyses due to the essentially uniform immune response that genetic variants elicit from their hosts (e.g., measles and smallpox viruses) (Lipsitch and O'Hagan 2007). Moreover, this body of theory focused on single-pathogen, single-host systems has led to numerous fundamental advances in population ecology. Many works—including a canonical book (Anderson and May 1992) and a chapter in the third edition of *Theoretical Ecology: Principles and Applications* (Grenfell and Keeling 2007)—have developed, reviewed, and synthesized this body of work exquisitely.

Many parasites and pathogens cannot possibly be understood from a single-host, single-pathogen perspective, however. For every pathogen that has transitioned to exclusive transmission in humans, there are at least as many that circulate in one or more animal species or in animals and humans (Taylor et al. 2001; Wolfe et al. 2007). This diversity of hosts is significant in large part because of heterogeneities among hosts in their susceptibility and infectiousness to a given pathogen (Kilpatrick et al. 2006). Compounding those heterogeneities

Perkins, T. A. and Rohr, J. R., *Theories of diversity in disease ecology* In: *Theoretical Ecology: Concepts and Applications*. Edited by: Kevin S. McCann and Gabriel Gellner, Oxford University Press (2020). © Oxford University Press.
DOI: 10.1093/oso/9780198824282.003.0013

is the structure of contacts between hosts of the same and different species (Paull et al. 2012; Vazquez-Prokopec et al. 2016). In terms of pathogen diversity, it is not uncommon for pathogens to occur as multiple strains, each of which may elicit an immune response from its host that is more effective against itself than other strains (Gupta et al. 1996; Cobey and Lipsitch 2012; Bedford et al. 2015). These strains may interact in other ways, as well. They can engage in exploitative or interference competition, as can pathogens of completely different types (Pedersen and Fenton 2007). Pathogens can also engage in facilitation by temporarily suppressing a host's immune defenses (Mina et al. 2015).

The goal of this chapter is to survey prominent themes in theoretical research on host and pathogen diversity to date. Specifically, we draw attention to theory on the relationship between host diversity and disease and theory on the coexistence of diverse, interacting pathogens. Although there are many valuable contributions to the theory of host and pathogen diversity that do not fall cleanly into either of these two categories, we have chosen to focus on these areas due to the fact that they have received disproportionate attention in disease ecology research. For example, one topic that we have largely ignored that has a great deal of relevance to questions of diversity in host-pathogen interactions is evolution (Levin et al. 1999; Gandon et al. 2001; Grenfell et al. 2004; de Roode et al. 2005). We do, however, describe some important extensions and applications of the two bodies of theory on which we focus, and we comment on potential synergies between and future directions for these two bodies of theory.

Theories related to host and pathogen diversity have been presented in excellent reviews and syntheses before (Rohani et al. 2006; Pedersen and Fenton 2007; Civitello et al. 2015a; Seabloom et al. 2015), but we find it rare for theoretical work related to host and pathogen diversity to be presented alongside one another (Dobson 1990; Holt and Dobson 2006; Keeling and Rohani 2011). By doing so here, and with a focus on both theoretical advances and empirical evidence in support of those advances, we hope to facilitate crosstalk between these areas of research and to provide an accessible entry point for the more general reader of this volume.

13.2 Host diversity

Hypotheses regarding relationships between host diversity and disease have potentially important public health, management, and policy implications because they imply that changes to biodiversity, whether natural and anthropogenic, could increase or decrease human and wildlife diseases. Thus, understanding when, where, and how host diversity affects disease is important because it can facilitate predicting and mitigating disease outbreaks and can influence policy decisions for both biodiversity conservation and public health. Nevertheless, the disease ecology community has become polarized by disagreement over the question of whether host diversity reduces or increases infectious disease risk (Randolph and Dobson 2012; Lafferty and Wood 2013; Ostfeld 2013; Ostfeld and Keesing 2013; Salkeld et al. 2013; Wood and Lafferty 2013; Wood et al. 2014; Civitello et al. 2015a; Civitello et al. 2015b; Salkeld et al. 2015; Levi et al. 2016; Wood et al. 2016; Ostfeld and Keesing 2017; Wilcox 2017).

There are two competing hypotheses regarding the relationship between diversity and disease, the dilution and amplification effect hypotheses. The dilution effect hypothesis proposes that host diversity can reduce the per-host abundance of a particular pathogen and thus reduces the risk of infectious disease caused by that pathogen (Van Buskirk and Ostfeld 1995; Keesing et al. 2010). Consequently, the dilution effect predicts that loss of host diversity should increase infectious disease burden, with the implication that biodiversity conservation (defined as preserving functioning ecosystems with predominantly native species) might reduce infectious diseases. A meta-analysis revealed that much of the published research supports the dilution effect hypothesis (Civitello et al. 2015a). In contrast, some studies support alternatives to the dilution effect (Dunn 2010; Dunn et al. 2010; Randolph and Dobson 2012; Lafferty and Wood 2013; Wood and Lafferty 2013; Young et al. 2013; Wood et al. 2014, 2016), such as no relationship, a highly context-dependent relationship, or an amplification effect—defined by Keesing et al. (2006) as the opposite of the dilution effect, or a positive relationship between host diversity and risk of a particular infectious disease in that host community. Here, we outline the theory for various relationships between host diversity and disease, as well as evidence in support of and against these relationships.

13.2.1 The basics of host diversity–infectious disease theory

Intuitively, host diversity is unlikely to affect pathogens of humans if they rarely interact with non-human hosts or are well controlled in some settings by sanitation, drugs, or vaccines (Wood et al. 2017). Examples include directly-transmitted, specialist pathogens of humans without free-living stages, intermediate hosts, or vectors, such as HIV and the causative agents of human tuberculosis, measles, non-pandemic influenza, and pneumonia (Wood et al. 2017). In contrast, multi-host, wildlife, and zoonotic pathogens, and pathogens with complex life cycles, free-living infectious stages, or generalist vectors are most likely to respond to changes to overall biodiversity. Examples include West Nile virus, hantavirus, and the causative agents of Chagas disease and leptospirosis (Dizney and Ruedas 2009; Suzan et al. 2009; Derne et al. 2011; Kilpatrick 2011; das Chagas Xavier et al. 2012; Gottdenker et al. 2012; Luis et al. 2018). Nevertheless, some of these expectations will need to be re-evaluated as disease ecologists better understand how host diversity (a) regulates the density of susceptible hosts that might then pass directly-transmitted pathogens amongst themselves (Keesing et al. 2006; Strauss et al. 2015; Luis et al. 2018) and (b) influences microbiota that protect against infectious diseases (e.g., Keesing et al. 2010; Johnson et al. 2015; Knutie et al. 2017).

For pathogens that are responsive to host diversity, theory suggests that if the dilution effect occurs, then relationships between host diversity and disease must be non-linear (Figure 13.1). This is because pathogens cannot exist where host richness equals zero given that pathogens rely on hosts for their survival (Ostfeld and Keesing 2000b; Ostfeld et al. 2009; Lafferty and Wood 2013; Wood and Lafferty 2013; Kilpatrick et al. 2017).

Thus, pathogen abundance must initially increase at low levels of host richness before higher levels of richness could theoretically cause a dilution effect (Figure 13.1). For this reason, most dilution effect research has focused on how biodiversity reductions in relatively pristine communities affect disease risk (Van Buskirk and Ostfeld 1995; Schmidt and Ostfeld 2001; Keesing et al. 2006; Ostfeld and Keesing 2012; Levi et al. 2016). In other words, they have focused on the disassembly rather than the assembly of communities. Importantly, the more left-skewed or asymptotic relationships between host diversity and disease are, the more amplification effects should predominate, whereas the more right-skewed they are, the more dilution should predominate (Wood et al. 2016, see Figure 13.1). Additionally, if most communities fall in the right or left portions of unimodal diversity-disease curves, then dilution or amplification, respectively, will be most common, regardless of the direction of the skew (Figure 13.1).

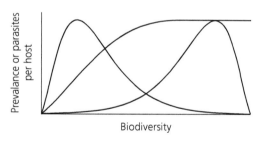

Figure 13.1 Hypothetical relationships between biodiversity and disease risk. The right-skewed distribution suggests that dilution might occur more frequently, but less intensely than amplification, because the relationship is moderately negative over a greater portion of the biodiversity gradient than it is strongly positive. The left-skewed distribution suggests that amplification might occur more frequently but less intensely than dilution, because the relationship is moderately positive over a greater portion of the biodiversity gradient than it is strongly negative. An asymptotic distribution suggests that amplification becomes increasingly moderate with biodiversity. In addition to the shape of biodiversity-disease relationships, the frequency with which each biodiversity level occurs in the environment will also affect the likelihood and intensity of dilution and amplification. These hypothetical curves underscore the importance of documenting the shape of biodiversity-disease relationships, which has rarely been accomplished empirically.

13.2.2 Mechanisms for host diversity–infectious disease interactions

Many of the proposed mechanisms for dilution and amplification include community assembly processes (LoGiudice et al. 2003; Ostfeld and LoGiudice 2003; Keesing and Ostfeld 2015), and thus it is important to cover some basic concepts regarding community assembly and disassembly. Communities are often dichotomized into those that exhibit substitutive assembly, whereby increases in diversity are associated with replacements of individuals because of competition (usually due to a fixed carry capacity for the community), and those that exhibit additive assembly, whereby total density or biomass increases with diversity (Joseph et al. 2013; Mihaljevic et al. 2014). In reality, this is a false dichotomy because theory suggests that all systems should assemble in both an additive and substitutive manner (Mihaljevic et al. 2014). For example, if we start with a system absent of species, then assembly must be additive because species will fill these unoccupied niches and thus will not compete. However, if we assume that niches are not endless, then as open niches are filled and species richness increases, so too do the chances that any new species added to the community will compete with an existing species. Hence, at the inflection point of the species richness versus abundance curve, all communities should shift from additive to substitutive assembly (Mihaljevic et al. 2014). What matters to dilution and amplification mechanisms discussed next is where communities fall on their species richness versus abundance curve.

When communities assemble additively, amplification likely occurs because additional host species will increase the total number of hosts, thus facilitating density-dependent pathogen transmission (Dobson 2004; Rudolf and Antonovics 2005). In contrast, some processes can cause either amplification or dilution. For example, when community assembly is additive, amplification or dilution can occur when competent hosts or non-competent hosts, respectively, are added to communities via the sampling effect—the idea that more diverse communities are more likely to contain a host species that either strongly increases or decreases disease (e.g., Halliday et al. 2017).

However, sampling effects might be less about diversity per se than about species composition or the presence/absence of particular species. In contrast to the sampling effect, the niche complementarity hypothesis depends more directly on diversity per se. It is the notion that coexisting species should often fill different functional roles in a community and thus as diversity increases, regardless of composition, an ecosystem service, such as disease control, should increase (Cardinale et al. 2012; Becker et al. 2014; Rohr et al. 2015; Frainer et al. 2018). The shape of relationships between host diversity and disease will affect whether sampling effects cause amplification or dilution. Right-skewed relationships have more space for scenarios where sampling effects promote dilution and left-skewed relationships have more space to promote amplification.

Dilution is generally expected to occur more frequently when communities reach substitutive assembly, where additional host species must be substituted for individual hosts already present in the community and thus increasing richness does not increase host densities. Given that host densities tend to be relatively constant at this stage of assembly, the frequency of hosts that vary in their competency to transmit pathogens can thus change as new hosts are added. Using a multi-host model, Mihaljevic et al. (2014) considered density- and frequency-dependent pathogen transmission modes crossed with purely additive, purely substitutive, or a saturating host community abundance-richness relationship (starting additive and shifting to substitutive). Importantly, their model revealed that pathogens with frequency-dependent transmission generally show dilution regardless of whether host assembly was additive or substitutive, consistent with other theory supporting the notion that frequency-dependent transmission increases the likelihood of dilution (Dobson 2004; Rudolf and Antonovics 2005; Faust et al. 2017). However, when transmission was density dependent, amplification predominated when communities assembled additively and dilution predominated when they assembled substitutively; thus, the relationship between host richness and disease risk was hump-shaped for the more realistic scenario of a saturating host community abundance-richness relationship—where communities start assembling additively and shift to substitutive assembly as niches fill. Given this theory, if communities are at a substitutive stage of assembly or experience frequency-dependent transmission, dilution seems likely. The biological mechanism often proposed for these patterns is based on the following assumptions: i) either pathogens should experience greater selection to infect abundant than rare hosts or abundant hosts likely make considerable investments into reproduction, growth, and/or dispersal at the expense of defenses against pathogens, or both occur, ii) abundant hosts are more likely to colonize and less likely to be extirpated from ecosystems, and iii) rare hosts displace common hosts when host diversity is high (Ostfeld and Keesing 2000b; Previtali et al. 2012). If these assumptions are true, then abundant and widespread hosts would regularly be amplifying hosts, while hosts with greater diluting potential would be added to communities as biodiversity increases or would be lost from communities when they become fragmented or disturbed (Joseph et al. 2013; Mihaljevic et al. 2014; Johnson et al. 2015; Levi et al. 2016). Under these scenarios, natural community disassembly would regularly cause increases in disease risk.

13.2.3 Evidence in support of proposed mechanisms for host diversity–infectious disease interactions

Several of the assumptions behind the theory for the dilution effect have empirical and observational support (Johnson et al. 2013a; Venesky et al. 2014; Rohr et al. 2015; Liu et al. 2018). For example, a combination of mesocosm experiments and field surveys demonstrated that the most abundant and widespread amphibian hosts are also the most competent hosts for a particular trematode species, supporting the notion that community assembly and disassembly processes function in a manner consistent with the dilution effect for this pathogen (Johnson et al. 2013a). Community (dis)assembly processes also support dilution effects documented for Lyme disease (Ostfeld and Keesing 2000a; LoGiudice et al. 2003; Ostfeld and LoGiudice 2003; Keesing et al. 2010), and in a recent study,

when plant communities were (dis)assembled randomly, dilution was not observed, but when they (dis)assembled naturally, host diversity significantly reduced disease, again highlighting the potential importance of natural assembly processes (Liu et al. 2018). Several other studies support the notion that widespread hosts with "fast-paced" life histories are more susceptible to pathogens when controlling for exposure (Johnson et al. 2012; Han et al. 2015; Sears et al. 2015). This suggests that rare species have an advantage because they are infected less frequently given the same exposure as abundant species, a concept supported in many plant-pathogen systems. For example, Parker et al. (2015) coupled an experiment on forty-four host plant species, with a database on 210 host genera and 212 fungal pathogens, and showed that abundant and phylogenetically common plant species have more infectious disease than rare plant species, particularly those that are phylogenetically distant from common species.

Importantly, this advantage of rarity is also a mechanism for the associational resistance, crop rotation, and Red Queen hypotheses, classic and well-established concepts in plant-herbivore and disease biology, all of which are based on the assumption that communities are in the substitutive portions of their diversity-abundance curves (Lively and Dybdahl 2000; Barbosa et al. 2009; Lively 2010). The associational resistance hypothesis is the well-supported idea that plant host diversity reduces herbivory (Barbosa et al. 2009), in many cases from insects, such as aphids, that have long-term intimate relationships with their host plant (i.e., they are pathogens; Raffel et al. 2008). Whereas the associational resistance hypothesis focuses on the advantages of variation in plant host species in space, crop rotation highlights the value of increasing host plant diversity temporally to reduce pathogen accumulation (Mordecai 2011). The Red Queen hypothesis incorporates a within-species dilution effect (Clay et al. 2008; Ostfeld and Keesing 2012), positing that as a genotype gets more abundant, it faces greater parasitism pressures (Lively and Dybdahl 2000; Lively 2010) so that as the diversity of genotypes within a species increases, per capita disease risk generally declines (e.g., "Red Queen Communities"; Clay et al. 2008).

These examples highlight several mechanisms by which biodiversity can protect against disease both within and among species (see also Civitello et al. 2015a).

13.2.4 Application of theory on host diversity to disease management

Importantly, community assembly theory and field observations suggest that low-diversity communities are a nested subset of their higher-diversity counterparts (Johnson et al. 2013a). This is an example of how diversity and species composition can be correlated (Keesing et al. 2010), a correlation that can make it challenging to disentangle composition from diversity. However, this correlation can also make it easier to manage diseases than if diversity and composition were related to one another idiosyncratically, because managing diversity will by default result in the management of composition (Keesing et al. 2010). As an example, top predators are often added to communities late during community assembly and are often lost from communities first because of their rarity and need for large plots of intact land or water. Owing to these traits, much of the theory behind relationships between host diversity and disease suggests that top predators are frequently diluting species. However, top predator species cannot be added to or sustained in a community without first ensuring that there is an ample abundance and diversity of their prey species, and thus, the nested nature of assembly processes can make it difficult to manage single species or species composition without managing biodiversity.

Both diversity-disease interactions and conservation generally occur at local to regional scales (Kilpatrick et al. 2017) and thus the dependence of dilution and amplification effects on scale can influence the effectiveness of management (Lafferty and Wood 2013; Wood and Lafferty 2013; Kilpatrick et al. 2017). There are several ways in which scale might influence the relationship between biodiversity and disease. Theory suggests that relationships between biodiversity and infectious disease might be strongest at local scales and weaken at larger scales (Johnson et al. 2015) because species interactions that affect dilution and amplification occur

at relatively small spatial scales, whereas abiotic factors like climate tend to predominate as drivers of biological patterns at larger spatial scales (Levin 1992; McGill 2010). Cohen et al. (2016) found support for this hypothesis in amphibian chytrid fungus, West Nile virus, and the bacterium that causes Lyme disease. At large spatial scales, the distribution of pathogens was strongly influenced by climate and human population density, whereas at smaller spatial scales, host richness was a significant predictor of disease prevalence (Cohen et al. 2016). It is also possible that the diluting capacity of a non-competent host might be most observable at small scales where encounter reduction (reducing encounter rate or duration between infected and susceptible individuals; Keesing et al. 2006) can occur, while the amplifying effect of a competent host might be most observable at larger temporal and spatial scales necessary to support definitive hosts and full lifecycle completion of the pathogen (Buck and Perkins 2018). Understanding the scales at which dilution and amplification predominate will be necessary to effectively employ manipulations of biodiversity as a disease management tool.

Whether biodiversity conservation is an effective management tool for protecting against newly introduced pathogens will likely depend on the mechanisms for dilution. Theory suggests that abundant hosts, which are more likely to colonize and less likely to be extirpated from ecosystems, amplify disease risk because: i) pathogens should experience greater selection to infect abundant than rare hosts, ii) abundant hosts make considerable investments into reproduction, growth, and/or at the expense of defenses against pathogens (i.e., trade-offs), or iii) both (Ostfeld and Keesing 2000b; Previtali et al. 2012). However, few studies have attempted to quantify the contribution of these two mechanisms to host competence. If abundant hosts are competent predominantly because pathogens experience greater selection pressure to infect abundant than rare hosts, then biodiversity conservation might not be very effective at preventing outbreaks of novel pathogens because they would be naïve to most of the hosts they encounter and thus would not have experienced selection to infect them yet. In contrast, if abundant hosts are competent predominantly because they invest little in pathogen defenses, then an evolutionary history between a host and pathogen would be less necessary for dilution and thus biodiversity conservation could theoretically be effective at preventing colonization and outbreaks of novel pathogens. Hence, understanding the mechanisms for disease dilution will be crucial for determining whether biodiversity conservation will be effective at managing the hazards and risk of disease emergence (Luis et al. 2013; Hosseini et al. 2017).

13.3 Pathogen diversity

Whereas research on host diversity and infectious disease has revolved around polarizing debate about dilution and amplification, research on pathogen diversity and infectious disease has been somewhat more diffuse. One major focus though has been investigation of interactions among pathogens and their role in mediating a variety of outcomes in multi-pathogen systems: coexistence and competitive displacement, as well as cycling and turnover. An understanding of the conditions under which each of these outcomes occurs in a given system is of great significance, because changes in the factors that promote these outcomes—which can result from introduction of new pathogens, changes in host communities, application of interventions, or evolution—can shift a system's trajectory from one outcome to another. Thus, an ecological understanding of these regimes may hold important clues to how to successfully eradicate certain pathogens and how to prevent the emergence of others.

This body of theory has been developed primarily under two alternative scenarios: a single pathogen with multiple strains or multiple pathogens with a single strain each. Although there can be important differences between pathogen assemblages that fall into these different categories (e.g., the former may involve frequent genetic exchange, whereas the latter does not), there are many similarities among processes that shape these assemblages (Seabloom et al. 2015). These similarities are not surprising given more general similarities between processes shaping ecological and population genetic diversity (Vellend 2010). Accordingly, we draw from examples of

theoretical work on pathogen diversity under both scenarios, and from work that ranges from generic to specific in its emphasis on a particular system.

13.3.1 A community ecology framework for pathogen coexistence

In a general sense, coexistence mechanisms in multi-pathogen systems can be organized around three themes (Bashey 2015). First, pathogen coexistence can be explained through niche differentiation, which involves more intense competition among like than unlike pathogens. Two forms of competitive interactions among pathogens that must be sufficiently weak to allow for co-existence (Rohani et al. 2006) include cross-reactive immunity, which involves one infection eliciting a host immune response that inhibits another (Figure 13.2c), and ecological interference, which involves pathogens reducing host availability for other pathogens through mechanisms unrelated to immunity (Rohani et al. 1998, 2003, and Figure 13.2a). At the same time, pathogens can sometimes facilitate one another through host immunosuppression (Mina et al. 2015). Second, competition-colonization trade-offs can contribute to the maintenance of pathogen diversity, provided that pathogens exhibit variation in traits related to within-host and between-host processes and that variation in those traits is negatively correlated (Hochberg and Holt 1990). The spatially discrete nature of hosts and the necessity of continual colonization of new hosts for pathogen persistence ensure that opportunities for pathogens specializing in competition or colonization are always available. Third, temporal and spatial heterogeneities in the environment experienced by pathogens can promote their coexistence under certain conditions. For example, storage effects occur when pathogens that vary in their responses to a heterogeneous environment transform their success under favorable conditions into persistence under unfavorable conditions through some form of buffering (Chesson 2000). This buffering can be achieved in a variety of ways, including by retreating to an alternative transmission mode when conditions under their primary transmission mode become unfavorable (Roche et al. 2014).

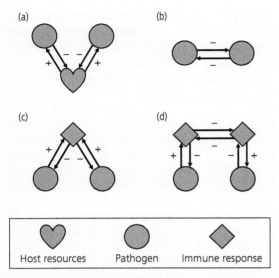

Figure 13.2 Different forms of pathogen interaction. Pathogen interactions can occur either during coinfection of a single host organism by two or more pathogens, or non-concurrently following infection by the first pathogen. (a) Exploitative competition can occur during coinfection when two or more pathogens compete for the same limited host resource. It can also occur non-concurrently if one pathogen kills hosts that can no longer be infected by other pathogens. (b) Interference competition most often occurs between pathogens coinfecting a single tissue type within a host. (c) Apparent competition can occur during coinfection when two or more pathogens stimulate a similar and sufficiently broad immune response. It can also occur non-concurrently when adaptive immunity developed in response to one pathogen is cross-reactive to a subsequent pathogen. (d) Facilitative interactions are also possible, such as when an immune response elicited by one pathogen inhibits a different immune response to another pathogen.

Given how difficult it can be to empirically measure any of several coexistence mechanisms that might be operating, realistic models of pathogen communities offer a valuable tool for gaining insight about the relative contributions of different mechanisms to coexistence in a given system (Mordecai et al. 2016). At the same time, it is critical to develop null models that do not result in coexistence as an artefact of a model's structure or as a result of an unintentionally impactful assumption (Lipsitch et al. 2009). To avoid that, an appreciation for past theoretical research that has established general conditions for coexistence of interacting pathogens is essential.

13.3.2 A diverse web of interactions among pathogens

Mechanisms for pathogen coexistence are usually modulated in one way or another by within-host interactions. Like other organisms, pathogens are known to engage in three major forms of competition: exploitative, interference, and apparent (Mideo 2009, and Figure 13.2a-c). These competitive interactions span what some have portrayed as three "trophic levels," corresponding to host resources (producers), pathogens (consumers), and host immune responses (predators) (Pedersen and Fenton 2007; Graham 2008). Focusing on simultaneous coinfections in humans, Griffiths et al. (2014) found that exploitative competition for host resources shared by two or more pathogens was the most common form of interaction. As an example, multiple species of malaria pathogens and helminths consume red blood cells, in some cases depleting them to such an extent that reductions in the density of competing pathogens result (Budischak et al. 2018). Interference competition between pathogens is also known to occur, although this appears to occur more commonly among pathogens that are physically co-located within certain host tissues (Griffiths et al. 2014). Interactions among pathogens occupying different host tissues or infecting a host at different points in time more typically take the form of apparent competition (Holt 1977), mediated by host immune responses that apply to some degree to two or more pathogens. For example, immune-mediated apparent competition was surmised among helminths infecting the digestive tracts of wild rabbits, due in part to the fact that pathogens occurring downstream in the digestive tract were able to negatively affect pathogens upstream of them (Lello et al. 2004). Despite widespread appreciation for this diversity of interactions among pathogens, pinpointing the nature of and mechanisms for these interactions can be a challenging undertaking (Fenton et al. 2010).

Among other interactions, the ways that pathogens can interact through host immune systems are quite diverse (Pedersen and Fenton 2007). In the context of pathogens infecting a host concomitantly (i.e., coinfection), interactions among even very phylogenetically distant pathogens are possible.

T-helper (Th) cells, which generate signals to activate different types of immune responses, offer one such example. Two major types of these are Th1 and Th2 cells, which elicit immune responses that are effective against intracellular and intercellular pathogens, respectively (Graham 2002). Because both Th1 and Th2 cells originate from the same pool of naive Th cells, an active immune response to one pathogen can inhibit the development of an immune response to another pathogen that infects the host shortly after the first pathogen, at least in the same tissue (Su et al. 2005; Graham 2008, and see Figure 13.2d). Conversely, pathogens that are combatted effectively with signals emanating from the same type of Th cells can lead to a synergized immune response on coinfecting pathogens (Curry et al. 1995; Page et al. 2005, see Figure 13.2c). Depending on which pathogens are involved in coinfection and the order in which two or more infections occur, coinfection can affect transmission dynamics of either or both pathogens and either dampen or exacerbate heterogeneities in the contributions of individual hosts to transmission (Graham et al. 2007).

Beyond coinfection, pathogens infecting a mammalian host can also interact through adaptive immunity developed in response to previous infections by other pathogens (Figure 13.2c). Although pathogen specificity is a hallmark of adaptive immunity, there are reasons to speculate that cross-reactivity of antibody-based adaptive immunity could be fairly common due to evolutionary advantages of an immune system that responds to pathogens that are similar, but not identical, to ones encountered in the past (Fairlie-Clarke et al. 2009). Regardless of their ultimate cause though, capturing the complexities of potential cross-reactivities among the many pathogens that a host faces is a daunting task for theory (Rohani et al. 2006). Cobey (2014) offered one way to simplify this complexity by proposing that a pathogen's "immunophenotype" be defined in terms of the strength, duration, and breadth of a host's immune response to it. These three dimensions can be made to depend on the abundances of other pathogens and various components of the host's immune system. Notably, the immunophenotype of a pathogen can depend on host species, infection history, and current infection and immunological status (Cobey 2014). One even simpler alternative involves tracking the status of hosts with respect to their immunity to each of many strains rather than their full history of infection (Gog and Swinton 2002; Gog and Grenfell 2002). The major advantage of this approach is that it reduces the dimensionality of the state space considerably, although this comes at the cost of the rather specific assumption that cross-reactive immunity renders some hosts completely immune instead of all or some hosts partially immune. Irrespective of the details, ways to address the complexity of pathogen interactions mediated by host immunity through simplifying, but biologically justifiable, assumptions remain an important goal for theory.

13.3.3 Theoretical results about pathogen coexistence

Theoretical results about pathogen coexistence depend a great deal on the properties of the model being used in the analysis. In the simplest models of ecologically similar pathogens, coexistence is a simple question of whether the strength of cross-reactive immunity is below a certain threshold (Keeling and Rohani 2011). From there, conditions for coexistence can quickly become more complicated. White (1998) showed that even the most basic refinements of assumptions about cross-reactive immunity lead to complications that affect criteria for coexistence. Under a model with susceptible-infectious-recovered compartments (SIR, in which hosts gain permanent immunity), conditions for coexistence were sensitive to assumptions about whether past infection results in reduced susceptibility or reduced transmissibility of a subsequent pathogen (White 1998). This distinction is important, because reduced transmissibility blocks transmission but still allows for population immunity to accrue. Under a model with susceptible-infectious-susceptible compartments (SIS, in which hosts are only immune temporarily), coexistence was enabled by differences in the pathogens' abilities to infect partially or completely susceptible hosts (White 1998). This effectively partitions hosts into two distinct resources that can support the coexistence of two pathogens specializing on those resources. Coinfection with another pathogen can add an additional dimension to the way in which hosts are partitioned into distinct resources. Although not capable of fully explaining coexistence of *Streptococcus pneumoniae* strains, Cobey and Lipsitch (2013) found that coinfection with *Haemophilus influenzae* promotes *S. pneumoniae* strain coexistence by disrupting the competitive hierarchy of strains that is typical in the absence of *H. influenzae*. Trade-offs in pathogen fitness in different host or vector species can contribute similarly to pathogen coexistence (Mordecai et al. 2016).

The task of explaining pathogen coexistence in real systems can sometimes be much more formidable than explaining the coexistence of two or three pathogens in a simple model. To explain the coexistence of over ninety strains of *S. pneumoniae*, Cobey and Lipsitch (2012) found that two forms of immunity needed to be invoked. Acting alone, an antibody-based form of immunity that was specific to strains to which an individual had been previously exposed was not sufficient to counteract inherent competitive advantages of certain strains, resulting in greater competitive exclusion than has been observed empirically. When a nonspecific form of immunity based on CD4+ Th cells was added to the model, Cobey and Lipsitch (2012) were able to reproduce observed levels of serotype diversity and to better account for other aspects of *S. pneumoniae* epidemiology, as well. Another consideration that can be important for explaining strain coexistence is the potential for pathogen strains to evolve on relatively fast timescales. In such cases, strong cross-reactive immunity can contribute to stable coexistence of a discrete number of strains, provided that pathogen molecules detected by the immune system respond evolutionarily to that form of diversifying selection. Even in the presence of the homogenizing effect of genetic exchange among strains, Gupta et al. (1996) found empirical support for this theoretical result in the form of more discrete structuring of multilocus, antigenic variants of *Neisseria meningitidis* bacteria than would be expected under random multilocus combinations consistent with observed levels of variation at each locus on its own. Relaxing the assumption of homogeneous mixing of host contacts by Gupta

et al. (1996) amplifies this tendency of strong cross-reactive immunity to promote coexistence of multiple discrete strains, resulting in even greater strain diversity (Buckee et al. 2004; Buckee et al. 2007).

Negative frequency dependence favoring antigenic variants to which host immunity has deteriorated over time has been shown to result in cyclical dynamics that can maintain pathogen diversity through time (Gupta et al. 1998; Gupta and Galvani 1999; Gomes et al. 2002). While these basic results are clear, additional considerations come into play when models are used to explain cyclical dynamics in real systems. Focusing on the bacteria that cause cholera, Koelle et al. (2006) showed that alternating cycles of dominance by either of two serotypes in Bangladesh could be explained by a simple, two-serotype model with strong, but nonetheless partial, cross-reactive immunity. Interestingly, acknowledgment of two serotypes with partial cross-reactive immunity provides an alternative to their previous explanation of cholera dynamics in this setting, which depended on the assumption that immunity is temporary (Koelle et al. 2005). In other words, partial cross-reactive immunity between two strains with alternating cycles offers a plausible explanation for the appearance of temporary immunity when information about strains is not visible in the data (Koelle et al. 2006). Another pathogen that exhibits strain cycling is dengue, which is transmitted by mosquitoes and is well known for the complex interannual dynamics of its four serotypes that affect humans (Cummings et al. 2004). One hypothesis about dengue serotype cycling that has been advanced is that it is driven by antibody-dependent enhancement (ADE), which could enhance the susceptibility and/or transmissibility of an infection with a second serotype, thereby giving a boost to non-dominant serotypes beyond that afforded by herd immunity against the dominant serotype (Ferguson et al. 1999; Cummings et al. 2005; Recker et al. 2009). Although recent evidence does demonstrate ADE of severe disease (Katzelnick et al. 2017), whether ADE is capable of eliciting the effects necessary to drive serotype cycling remains unclear. A more widely accepted alternative hypothesis is that some combination of temporary cross-reactive immunity and seasonal transmission account for serotype cycling (Wearing and Rohani 2006; Adams et al. 2006; Reich et al. 2013; ten Bosch et al. 2016).

13.3.4 Application of theories of pathogen diversity to disease management

One notable body of theoretical work on pathogen diversity that is relevant to disease management assumes that strains circulate independently of one another. This "strain theory" of malaria (Gupta et al. 1994; Gupta and Day 1994) is based on the premise that immunity to a single strain of *Plasmodium falciparum* is long-lasting, but immunity to all strains is negligible. A highly significant, but controversial, prediction of strain theory is that the R_0 for any given strain is relatively low and, thus, intervention coverage thresholds required for eradication are significantly higher if *P. falciparum* is conceptualized as a single- rather than a multi-strain pathogen (Gupta et al. 1994). Given that R_0 estimates for malaria that do not account for strain structure can often be in the range of fifty to a hundred or more (Smith et al. 2007), strain theory makes eradication seem vastly more achievable (Gupta et al. 1994). One critique of this prediction (Dye et al. 1996) used results from a field trial of insecticide-treated bednets that showed little impact on prevalence in humans to argue that intervention coverage would need to be in excess of 96% to achieve eradication, which is far higher than Gupta et al. (1994) envisioned. In response, Gupta and Snow (1996) provided an alternative interpretation of the trial data that is compatible with predictions from strain theory. Recent extensions of strain theory (Artzy-Randrup et al. 2012; He et al. 2018) have used agent-based models to place more emphasis on the highly polygenic nature of *P. falciparum* antigenic repertoires and the important complication that *P. falciparum* undergoes extensive recombination, which raises questions about what the concept of a strain even means for this pathogen (McKenzie et al. 2008).

Another body of theoretical work involving multiple pathogen strains that has received significant attention is that of vaccine escape, which is a phenomenon whereby strains that are not targeted by a vaccine can increase in prevalence due to competitive release from a target strain that has been reduced by vaccination (McLean 1995). This outcome depends critically though on the strength of cross-reactive immunity and the relative competitive abilities of the target and non-target strains prior to vaccination (Gupta et al. 1997). In addition, McLean (1995) found that low vaccination coverage was one reason why vaccine escape might not be observed in a system that otherwise has potential for it. Looking at coverage from a different perspective, Lipsitch (1997) found that vaccination coverage thresholds for elimination of the target strain were lower for a strain-specific vaccine than for a bivalent vaccine, which would affect both strains. Intuitively, this result follows from the non-target strain contributing to the demise of the target strain via apparent competition through naturally-acquired, cross-reactive immunity, while the non-target strain remains resilient to vaccine-derived immunity. Lipsitch (1997) noted that such a scenario may be compatible with the biology of *H. influenzae*. One pathogen for which strain replacement from vaccine escape has been observed empirically is pneumococcus (Hanage et al. 2010). Others with perceived potential for strain replacement include rotavirus (Pitzer et al. 2011), human papillomavirus (Orlando et al. 2012), malaria (Neafsey et al. 2015), dengue (Rodriguez-Barraquer et al. 2014), and pertussis (Nicoli et al. 2015).

The ecological principle underlying vaccine escape, competitive release, is relevant not only to competing strains but also to distinct pathogens engaged in competition. As an example, Lloyd-Smith (2013) assessed the potential of orthopox viruses besides smallpox virus, especially monkeypox virus, to fill the niche vacated by smallpox virus following its eradication in 1980. Although intensive epidemiological investigations in the early 1980s concluded that monkeypox virus was not quite capable of sustained spread ($R_0 = 0.83$) (Fine et al. 1988), more recent epidemiological trends show clear signatures of competitive release not from smallpox virus itself, but from the smallpox vaccine that is no longer in use and thus protects only an aging, and dwindling, population (Rimoin et al. 2010). It is notable that the only two infectious diseases eradicated to date—smallpox and rinderpest—both appear to have competitors encroaching on their vacated niches. Rather than discourage efforts to eradicate diseases, the lesson from these examples is that the possibility of competitive release of other pathogens should not come as a surprise. Instead, preparations for this possibility, along with appropriate research and surveillance, should be undertaken during early stages of planning for eradication campaigns (Lloyd-Smith 2013).

13.4 Are theories of host and pathogen diversity ships passing in the night?

The respective bodies of theory on host and pathogen diversity surveyed previously have been developed largely independently of one another. That is, theories of host diversity have mostly asked how host diversity impacts the disease burden associated with a single type of pathogen, and theories of pathogen diversity have mostly asked how diverse pathogens manage to coexist in a single type of host. Here, we explore a few points of interface between these distinct bodies of theory, with the goal of stimulating further developments at this intersection.

One natural question at the interface of host and pathogen diversity is what impact the former has on the latter. Intuitively, host diversity should promote pathogen diversity by expanding the diversity of niches available to pathogens (Hechinger and Lafferty 2005). One way that this can manifest is in terms of the diversity of host immune repertoires, which models have shown can promote strain diversity (Gupta and Galvani 1999). Support for host diversity as a driver of pathogen diversity by way of niche diversity has also been demonstrated in broader pathogen communities (Johnson et al. 2016). Beyond ideas related to niche diversity, factors that affect the persistence of any single pathogen should also affect pathogen diversity, given that the maintenance of diversity requires the persistence of each constituent species. A number of theoretical studies (Holt et al. 2003; Dobson 2004; Fenton et al. 2015) have demonstrated that host species can easily differ in their individual contributions to a pathogen's persistence. In some cases, a single host species may be sufficient to ensure persistence of a pathogen, whereas in other cases pathogen persistence may only be possible in the presence of multiple host species that are each incapable of sustaining the pathogen on their own. In primates, it has been noted that host species with higher population densities tend to harbor more pathogens (Nunn et al. 2003; Altizer et al. 2007). This finding is consistent with theoretical predictions that higher host density should allow for persistence of pathogens with a wider range of threshold densities for persistence (Dobson 1990).

Another important question at the interface of host and pathogen diversity is what the implications of pathogen diversity are for host health. While the effects of host diversity on host health have been investigated intensely, pathogen diversity has more often been examined as its own object of study rather than as a driver of disease. There are exceptions though. In a simple model of antigenic strain diversity, Abu-Rabbad and Ferguson (2005) showed that there is a monotonically increasing relationship between pathogen diversity and overall pathogen prevalence combined across strains. This relationship was modulated critically though by the strength of cross-reactive immunity, with more intense cross-reactive immunity resulting in lower prevalence. Empirical investigations of the relationship between pathogen diversity and host disease have yielded somewhat different results. An empirical study (Johnson and Hoverman 2012) of six trematode pathogens in an amphibian host found that the relationship between pathogen diversity and host disease depended on whether pathogen communities assembled additively or substitutively, mirroring results about the relationship between host diversity and disease. Specifically, additive assembly increased disease severity, whereas substitutive assembly decreased disease severity in cases where the prevalence of a more virulent pathogen was reduced by increased pathogen diversity (Johnson and Hoverman 2012). In two studies (Johnson et al. 2013b; Rottstock et al. 2014) in which host disease was examined across naturally occurring variation in host and pathogen diversity, greater pathogen diversity was negatively associated with disease, which is more consistent with the notion that pathogen community assembly is substitutive in those systems. In theoretical work going forward, considering pathogen diversity and the dynamic nature thereof may, at a minimum, provide greater insight into the mechanisms underlying relationships between host diversity and disease.

Relationships between host and pathogen diversity are also sensitive to other players in ecological communities. In particular, predators of pathogens offer an additional potential mechanism by which overall biodiversity can mitigate disease risk. Predation on pathogens and parasitized hosts can be an important but overlooked limit on pathogens; for example, comprising an estimated 44% of trophic links in the well-studied Carpinteria Salt Marsh food web (Lafferty et al. 2006b), though most of these links led to pathogen transmission rather than pathogen loss. In one study, increasing tadpole diversity was associated with reduced chytrid fungal loads per frog, and the degree to which tadpole species filter-fed; thus, removing chytrid zoospores from the water was associated positively with their ability to reduce chytrid infections in both transmission experiments and field surveys (Venesky et al. 2014). In another study, the diversity of predators of multiple species of trematode cercariae was associated negatively with trematode infections per host in the field (Rohr et al. 2015). This study used both experiments and mathematical models to demonstrate that the degree to which a species preferred to consume pathogens over hosts determined how strongly that species could dilute disease through pathogen-encounter-reduction mechanisms (Rohr et al. 2015). Many effects of predator diversity on pathogens might actually be species composition effects, but they are good examples for where a sampling effect in diverse communities could tend to increase the chance that pathogen feeders might occur.

13.5 Diversifying the use of theory to address questions of diversity in disease ecology

Theories on host and pathogen diversity in disease ecology have developed over the past three to four decades and have done much to extend understanding of infectious disease dynamics beyond the single-host, single-pathogen paradigm

that preceded it, and still dominates. Many key advances in the theory of multi-host and/or multi-pathogen systems have been underpinned by theoretical developments in community ecology more broadly. In reference to host diversity, community assembly theory has played an important role in clarifying the conditions under which diseases in some host communities are subject to dilution effects and others to amplification effects. In reference to pathogen diversity, modern coexistence theory has been helpful for many who seek to understand what impact each of the very many possible interactions among pathogens have on their mutual persistence. We now turn our attention to questions about the future. What underutilized elements of ecological theory will underlie future advances in our understanding of multi-host and/or multi-pathogen systems? What new theoretical capabilities are needed to meet the most formidable challenges ahead?

One feature of current theory that we find strikingly pervasive is the focus on long-term, equilibrium behavior. As a starting point, using models with stable equilibrium properties to analyze something as inherently complex as a multi-host and/or multi-pathogen system is perfectly reasonable. At some point though, one must wonder what lies beyond models with those properties. Regarding host diversity, we now know a great deal about how changes in host diversity affect the transmission of pathogens that exhibit long-term persistence, but is there similarly general understanding that can be obtained about how changes in host diversity affect diseases prone to epidemics or that are only beginning to emerge? Troublingly, some of the multi-host diseases of greatest concern to human health—such as Lyme disease, West Nile, and yellow fever—exhibit strongly seasonal epizootics with a great deal of poorly understood interannual variation therein. To assume that we fully understand the role of host diversity in those systems would be naive. Regarding pathogen diversity, we now know a great deal about conditions that permit the long-term coexistence of multiple pathogens that circulate in a well-mixed host population, but do we know the extent to which those conditions apply for strongly-immunizing pathogens that persist only at the scale of a metapopulation? In systems such as these, coinfection—a key driver of pathogen interactions in many systems—may be much less common (Vogels et al. 2019). As inspiration for how to advance theory in light of these challenges, one nice demonstration by Lourenço and Recker (2013) showed how more realistic representations of transmission dynamics can alter conclusions about pathogen interactions. They used a spatially explicit, agent-based model of dengue virus transmission to show that stochastic amplification of differences among serotypes was sufficient to recreate many of the same patterns that simpler models could explain only by invoking strong interactions among serotypes. Until possibilities such as these are explored in a greater diversity of systems, much of the theory of multi-host and/or multi-pathogen systems will, in our view, remain provisional.

Another theme of current theory that we have noticed is that the variety of pathogen assemblages that are considered in analyses of multi-pathogen systems is somewhat limited. For example, rather than consider all pathogens in a given community, theoretical investigations often focus on a much smaller subset, such as i) hosts known to harbor a particular type of pathogen (e.g., West Nile virus and its many hosts); ii) strains within a single species of pathogen (e.g., dengue virus serotypes); iii) hosts and/or pathogens that all have a similar mode and dynamic of transmission (e.g., pathogens that all have stable, long-term persistence in a shared set of hosts); iv) a small number of different pathogen types with a documented interaction of specific interest (e.g., helminths and malaria pathogens); or v) a system with a tractable number of multiple hosts and multiple pathogens (e.g., barley yellow dwarf viruses of plants). There are important questions to be addressed in each of these situations, but the fact that the current state of theory is limited to these subsets of the full assemblage of hosts and pathogens must be acknowledged. We find these choices to be reminiscent of the "modules" that have been a focus of theory on food webs (Holt 1997). They may well be instructive in many ways, but they are somewhat myopic in their view of true communities of pathogens and their hosts. There

are, of course, reasonable arguments for restricting the focus of theory in this way. First, it may be the case that interactions beyond the players in these restricted groupings are so minimal as to be insignificant. After all, the specificity to respond to only certain pathogens, or their close relatives, is a hallmark of adaptive immune responses. At the same time though, immune responses can be much less specific in many host species (Wuerthner et al. 2017), a consideration that could lead to greater connectedness in host-pathogen interaction networks than previously appreciated. Second, the analytical tractability of models involving a large number of types quickly diminishes as diversity exceeds that of the more limited assemblages that have been the focus of much work to date. In addition to ways that some models of strain diversity have addressed this issue (Gog and Grenfell 2002; Cobey and Lipsitch 2012), theory from other areas of ecology, such as food webs (McCann 2011), may offer inspiration for future advancements.

Finally, it is worth reflecting on the range of possibilities for how theory—and, more broadly, mechanistic models with a basis in theory—can be used to enhance understanding and management of host-pathogen systems. Many compartmental models offer the ability to obtain formulas describing how various parameters affect conditions for pathogen persistence, which can then be used to describe the contribution of different host species to transmission, explain pathogen coexistence, or inform strategies for pathogen elimination. Models ranging from simple to complex can be used to simulate system dynamics, informing how different biological mechanisms give rise to different observable patterns or how a system might respond to various perturbations from the environment, evolutionary forces, or interventions. Models can be generic and studied without reference to a particular system, or they can be used to extract signals from data not readily apparent in the data itself. Models can also be used for forecasting, an enterprise that directly interfaces models with data, offers a unique opportunity for model comparison and hypothesis testing, and offers direct value for public health (Du et al. 2017; Johnson et al. 2018; Reich et al. 2019). While there are notable exemplars involving multi-host and/or multi-pathogen systems for each of these uses of theory, our perception is that progress in many of these areas is much farther along for single-host, single-pathogen systems than for multi-host and/or multi-pathogen systems. As theories of host and pathogen diversity continue to develop, theoretical ecologists may benefit from looking outward from the narrow literature within existing niches in this area, such as the ones we focused on in this review. Doing so may inject humility and spark creativity, leading to the construction of new and exciting theoretical niches in this field.

Acknowledgments

Funds were provided by grants to T.A.P. from the United States Department of Agriculture National Institute of Food and Agriculture (2019-67,015-28,982) and the National Science Foundation (DEB-1641130) and to J.R.R. from the National Science Foundation (EF-1241889, DEB-1518681, IOS-1754868) and the National Institutes of Health (R01TW010286-01). We thank members of the Perkins and Rohr Labs, as well as Jason McLachlan's ecology class at the University of Notre Dame, for feedback on a draft of the chapter.

References

Abu-Raddad, L. J. and N. M. Ferguson. (2005). Characterizing the symmetric equilibrium of multi-strain host-pathogen systems in the presence of cross immunity. *Journal of Mathematical Biology* 50(5): 531–58.

Adams, B., E. C. Holmes, C. Zhang, M. P. Mammen Jr, S. Nimmannitya, S. Kalayanarooj, and M. Boots. (2006). Cross-protective immunity can account for the alternating epidemic pattern of dengue virus serotypes circulating in Bangkok. *Proceedings of the National Academy of Sciences* 103(38): 14234–9.

Altizer, Sonia, Charles L. Nunn, and Patrik Lindenfors. (2007). Do threatened hosts have fewer parasites? A comparative study in primates. *Journal of Animal Ecology* 76(2): 304–14.

Anderson, Roy M. and Robert M. May. (1992). *Infectious Diseases of Humans: Dynamics and Control*. Oxford: Oxford University Press.

Artzy-Randrup, Yael, Mary M. Rorick, Karen Day, Donald Chen, Andrew P. Dobson, and Mercedes Pascual. (2012). Population structuring of multi-copy, antigen-encoding genes in *Plasmodium falciparum*. *eLife* 1: e00093.

Barbosa, P., J. Hines, I. Kaplan, H. Martinson, A. Szczepaniec, and Z. Szendrei. (2009). Associational resistance and associational susceptibility: Having right or wrong neighbors. *Annual Review of Ecology Evolution and Systematics* 40:1–20.

Bashey, Farrah. (2015). Within-host competitive interactions as a mechanism for the maintenance of parasite diversity. *Philosophical Transactions of the Royal Society B* 370(1675).

Becker, C. G., D. Rodriguez, L. F. Toledo, A. V. Longo, C. Lambertini, D. T. Corrêa, D. S. Leite, C. F. Haddad, and K. R. Zamudio. (2014). Partitioning the net effect of host diversity on an emerging amphibian pathogen. *Proceedings of the Royal Society B* 281: 20141796.

Bedford, Trevor, Steven Riley, Ian G. Barr, Shobha Broor, Mandeep Chadha, Nancy J. Cox, Rodney S. Daniels, et al. (2015). Global circulation patterns of seasonal influenza viruses vary with antigenic drift. *Nature* 523(7559): 217–20.

Best, A., A. White, and M. Boots. (2008). Maintenance of host variation in tolerance to pathogens and parasites. *Proceedings of the National Academy of Sciences* 105(52): 20786–91.

Boots, Mike, Andy White, Alex Best, and Roger Bowers. (2012). The importance of who infects whom: The Evolution of diversity in host resistance to infectious disease. *Ecology Letters* 15(10): 1104–11.

Buck, J. C., and S. E. Perkins. (2018). Study scale determines whether wildlife loss protects against or promotes tick-borne disease. *Proceedings of the Royal Society B* 285: 20180218.

Buckee, Caroline, Leon Danon, and Sunetra Gupta. (2007). Host community structure and the maintenance of pathogen diversity. *Proceedings of the Royal Society B* 274(1619): 1715–21.

Buckee, Caroline O' F., Katia Koelle, Matthew J. Mustard, and Sunetra Gupta. (2004). The effects of host contact network structure on pathogen diversity and strain structure. *Proceedings of the National Academy of Sciences* 101(29): 10839–44.

Budischak, Sarah A., Aprilianto E. Wiria, Firdaus Hamid, Linda J. Wammes, Maria M. M. Kaisar, Lisette van Lieshout, Erliyani Sartono, Taniawati Supali, Maria Yazdanbakhsh, and Andrea L. Graham. (2018). Competing for blood: The ecology of parasite resource competition in human malaria-helminth co-infections. *Ecology Letters* 21(4): 536–45.

Cardinale, B. J., J. E. Duffy, A. Gonzalez, D. U. Hooper, C. Perrings, P. Venail, A. Narwani, G. M. Mace, D. Tilman, D. A. Wardle, A. P. Kinzig, G. C. Daily, M. Loreau, J. B. Grace, A. Larigauderie, D. S. Srivastava, and S. Naeem.

(2012). Biodiversity loss and its impact on humanity. *Nature* 486: 59–67.

Chesson, Peter. (2000). Mechanisms of maintenance of species diversity. *Annual Review of Ecology and Systematics* 31(1): 343–66.

Civitello, D. J., J. Cohen, H. Fatima, N. T. Halstead, J. Liriano, T. A. McMahon, C. N. Ortega, E. L. Sauer, T. Sehgal, S. Young, and J. R. Rohr. (2015a). Biodiversity inhibits parasites: Broad evidence for the dilution effect. *Proceedings of the National Academy of Sciences* 112: 8667–71.

Civitello, D. J., J. Cohen, H. Fatima, N. T. Halstead, T. A. McMahon, C. N. Ortega, E. L. Sauer, S. Young, and J. R. Rohr. (2015b). Reply to Salkeld et al.: Diversity-disease patterns are robust to study design, selection criteria, and publication bias. *Proceedings of the National Academy of Sciences* 112: E6262–2.

Clay, K., K. Reinhart, J. Rudgers, T. Tintjer, J. Koslow, and S. L. Flory. (2008). Red Queen communities. In Richard S. Ostfeld, Felicia Keesing, Valerie T. Eviner (eds.), *Infectious Disease Ecology: The Effects of Ecosystems on Disease and of Disease on Ecosystems*. Princeton, United States: Princeton University Press, pp. 145–78.

Cobey, Sarah. (2014). Pathogen evolution and the immunological niche. *Annals of the New York Academy of Sciences* 1320(July): 1–15.

Cobey, Sarah, and Marc Lipsitch. (2012). Niche and neutral effects of acquired immunity permit coexistence of pneumococcal serotypes. *Science* 335(6074): 1376–80.

Cobey, Sarah, and Marc Lipsitch. (2013). Pathogen diversity and hidden regimes of apparent competition. *American Naturalist* 181(1): 12–24.

Cohen, J. M., D. J. Civitello, A. J. Brace, E. M. Feichtinger, C. N. Ortega, J. C. Richardson, E. L. Sauer, X. Liu, and J. R. Rohr. (2016). Spatial scale modulates the strength of ecological processes driving disease distributions. *Proceedings of the National Academy of Sciences* 113: E3359–64.

Cummings, Derek A. T., Rafael A. Irizarry, Norden E. Huang, Timothy P. Endy, Ananda Nisalak, Kumnuan Ungchusak, and Donald S. Burke. (2004). Travelling waves in the occurrence of dengue haemorrhagic fever in Thailand. *Nature* 427(6972): 344–7.

Cummings, Derek A. T., Ira B. Schwartz, Lora Billings, Leah B. Shaw, and Donald S. Burke. (2005). Dynamic effects of antibody-dependent enhancement on the fitness of viruses. *Proceedings of the National Academy of Sciences* 102(42): 15259–64.

Curry, A. J., K. J. Else, F. Jones, A. Bancroft, R. K. Grencis, and D. W. Dunne. (1995). Evidence that cytokine-mediated immune interactions induced by *Schistosoma mansoni* alter disease outcome in mice concurrently infected with *Trichuris muris*. *Journal of Experimental Medicine* 18 (2): 769–74.

das Chagas Xavier, S. C., A. L. R. Roque, V. dos Santos Lima, K. J. L. Monteiro, J. C. R. Otaviano, L. F. C. F. da Silva, and A. M. Jansen. (2012). Lower richness of small wild mammal species and Chagas disease risk. *PLOS Neglected Tropical Diseases* 6: e1647.

Derne, B. T., E. J. Fearnley, C. L. Lau, S. Paynter, and P. Weinstein. (2011). Biodiversity and leptospirosis risk: A case of pathogen regulation? *Medical Hypotheses* 77: 339–44.

de Roode, Jacobus C., Riccardo Pansini, Sandra J. Cheesman, Michelle E. H. Helinski, Silvie Huijben, Andrew R. Wargo, Andrew S. Bell, Brian H. K. Chan, David Walliker, and Andrew F. Read. (2005). Virulence and competitive ability in genetically diverse malaria infections. *Proceedings of the National Academy of Sciences* 102(21): 7624–8.

Dizney, L. J. and L. A. Ruedas. (2009). Increased host species diversity and decreased prevalence of *sin nombre* virus. *Emerging Infectious Diseases* 15: 1012–18.

Dobson, Andrew. (2004). Population dynamics of pathogens with multiple host species. *American Naturalist* 164 Suppl 5(November): S64–78.

Dobson, A. P. (1990). Models for multi-species parasite-host communities. In Gerald W. Esch, Albert O. Bush, and John M. Aho (eds.), *Parasite Communities: Patterns and Processes*, Dordrecht, Netherlands: Springer, pp. 261–88.

Du, Xiangjun, Aaron A. King, Robert J. Woods, and Mercedes Pascual. (2017). Evolution-informed forecasting of seasonal influenza A (H3N2). *Science Translational Medicine* 9(413).

Dunn, R. R. (2010). Global mapping of ecosystem disservices: The unspoken reality that nature sometimes kills us. *Biotropica* 42: 555–7.

Dunn, R. R., T. J. Davies, N. C. Harris, and M. C. Gavin. (2010). Global drivers of human pathogen richness and prevalence. *Proceedings of the Royal Society B* 277: 2587–95.

Dye, C., J. D. Lines, and C. F. Curtis. (1996). A Test of the Malaria Strain Theory. *Parasitology Today* 12 (3): 88–9.

Fairlie-Clarke, Karen J., David M. Shuker, and Andrea L. Graham. (2009). Why do adaptive immune responses cross-react? *Evolutionary Applications* 2(1): 122–31.

Faust, C. L., A. P. Dobson, N. Gottdenker, L. S. Bloomfield, H. I. McCallum, T. R. Gillespie, M. Diuk-Wasser, and R. K. Plowright. (2017). Null expectations for disease dynamics in shrinking habitat: Dilution or amplification? *Phil. Trans. R. Soc. B* 372: 20160173.

Fenton, Andy, Daniel G. Streicker, Owen L. Petchey, and Amy B. Pedersen. (2015). Are all hosts created equal? Partitioning host species contributions to parasite persistence in multihost communities. *American Naturalist* 186(5): 610–22.

Fenton, Andy, Mark E. Viney, and Jo Lello. (2010). Detecting interspecific macroparasite interactions from ecological data: Patterns and process. *Ecology Letters* 13(5): 606–15.

Ferguson, N., R. Anderson, and S. Gupta. (1999). The Effect of antibody-dependent enhancement on the transmission dynamics and persistence of multiple-strain pathogens. *Proceedings of the National Academy of Sciences* 96(2): 790–4.

Fine, P. E. M., Z. Jezek, B. Grab, and H. Dixon. (1988). The transmission potential of monkeypox virus in human populations. *International Journal of Epidemiology* 17(3): 643–50.

Frainer, A., B. G. McKie, P.-A. Amundsen, R. Knudsen, and K. D. Lafferty. (2018). Parasitism and the biodiversity-functioning relationship. *Trends in Ecology & Evolution* 33(4): 260–8.

Gandon, S., M. J. Mackinnon, S. Nee, and A. F. Read. (2001). Imperfect vaccines and the evolution of pathogen virulence. *Nature* 414(6865): 751–6.

Gog, J. R. and J. Swinton. (2002). A status-based approach to multiple strain dynamics. *Journal of Mathematical Biology* 44(2): 169–84.

Gog, Julia R., and Bryan T. Grenfell. (2002). Dynamics and selection of many-strain pathogens. *Proceedings of the National Academy of Sciences* 99 (26): 17209–14.

Gomes, M.Gabriela M., Graham F. Medley, and D. James Nokes. (2002). On the determinants of population structure in antigenically diverse pathogens. *Proceedings of the Royal Society B* 269 (1488): 227–33.

Gottdenker, N. L., L. F. Chaves, J. E. Calzada, A. Saldaña, and C. R. Carroll. (2012). Host life history strategy, species diversity, and habitat influence *Trypanosoma cruzi* vector infection in changing landscapes. *PLOS Neglected Tropical Diseases* 6: e1884.

Graham, Andrea L. (2002). When T-helper cells don't help: Immunopathology during concomitant infection. *Quarterly Review of Biology* 77(4): 409–34.

Graham, Andrea L. (2008). Ecological rules governing helminth–microparasite coinfection. *Proceedings of the National Academy of Sciences of the United States of America* 105(2): 566–70.

Graham, Andrea L., Isabella M. Cattadori, James O. Lloyd-Smith, Matthew J. Ferrari, and Ottar N. Bjørnstad. (2007). Transmission consequences of coinfection: Cytokines writ large? *Trends in Parasitology* 23(6): 284–91.

Grenfell, Bryan, and Matthew Keeling. (2007). Dynamics of infectious diseases. In Robert May and Angela McLean (eds.), *Theoretical Ecology: Principles and Applications.* 3rd edition. Oxford: Oxford University Press, pp. 132–47.

Grenfell, Bryan T., Oliver G. Pybus, Julia R. Gog, James L. N. Wood, Janet M. Daly, Jenny A. Mumford, and Edward C. Holmes. (2004). Unifying the epidemiological and evolutionary dynamics of pathogens. *Science* 303(5656): 327–32.

Griffiths, Emily C., Amy B. Pedersen, Andy Fenton, and Owen L. Petchey. (2014). Analysis of a summary network of co-infection in humans reveals that parasites interact most via shared resources. *Proceedings of the Royal Society B* 281(1782): 20132286.

Gupta, S. and K. P. Day. (1994). A strain theory of malaria transmission. *Parasitology Today* 10(12): 476–81.

Gupta, S., N. M. Ferguson, and R. M. Anderson. (1997). Vaccination and the population structure of antigenically diverse pathogens that exchange genetic material. *Proceedings of the Royal Society B* 264(1387): 1435–43.

Gupta, S. and A. Galvani. (1999). The effects of host heterogeneity on pathogen population structure. *Philosophical Transactions of the Royal Society* B 354(1384): 711–19.

Gupta, S. and R. W. Snow. (1996). How do bednets influence the transmissibility of *Plasmodium falciparum*? *Parasitology Today* 12(3): 89–90.

Gupta, S., K. Trenholme, R. M. Anderson, and K. P. Day. (1994). Antigenic diversity and the transmission dynamics of *plasmodium falciparum*. *Science* 263(5149): 961–3.

Gupta, Sunetra, Neil Ferguson, and Roy Anderson. (1998). Chaos, persistence, and evolution of strain structure in antigenically diverse infectious agents. *Science* 280(5365): 912–15.

Gupta, Sunetra, Martin C. J. Maiden, Ian M. Feavers, Sean Nee, Robert M. May, and Roy M. Anderson. (1996). The maintenance of strain structure in populations of recombining infectious agents. *Nature Medicine* 2(April): 437.

Halliday, F. W., R. W. Heckman, P. A. Wilfahrt, and C. E. Mitchell. (2017). A multivariate test of disease risk reveals conditions leading to disease amplification. *Proceedings of the Royal Society B* 1340 Oct 25, 284(1865). DOI: 10.1098/rspb.2017.1340.

Han, B. A., J. P. Schmidt, S. E. Bowden, and J. M. Drake. (2015). Rodent reservoirs of future zoonotic diseases. *Proceedings of the National Academy of Sciences* 112: 7039–44.

Hanage, William P., Jonathan A. Finkelstein, Susan S. Huang, Stephen I. Pelton, Abbie E. Stevenson, Ken Kleinman, Virginia L. Hinrichsen, and Christophe Fraser. (2010). Evidence that pneumococcal serotype replacement in Massachusetts following conjugate vaccination is now complete. *Epidemics* 2(2): 80–4.

Hechinger, Ryan F. and Kevin D. Lafferty. (2005). Host Diversity begets parasite diversity: bird final hosts and trematodes in snail intermediate hosts. *Proceedings of the Royal Society B* 272(1567): 1059–66.

He, Qixin, Shai Pilosof, Kathryn E. Tiedje, Shazia Ruybal-Pesántez, Yael Artzy-Randrup, Edward B. Baskerville, Karen P. Day, and Mercedes Pascual. (2018). Networks of genetic similarity reveal non-neutral processes shape strain structure in *Plasmodium falciparum*. *Nature Communications* 9(1): 1817.

Hochberg, Michael E. and Robert D. Holt. (1990). The coexistence of competing parasites. I. The role of cross-species infection. *American Naturalist* 136(4): 517–41.

Holt, Robert D. (1977). Predation, apparent competition, and the structure of prey communities. *Theoretical Population Biology* 12(2): 197–229.

Holt, Robert D. (1997). Community modules. In A. C. Gange and V. K. Brown (eds.), *Multitrophic Interactions in Terrestrial Systems*. Cambridge, United Kingdom: Cambridge University Press, pp. 333–49.

Holt, Robert D. and Andrew P. Dobson. (2006). Extending the principles of community ecology to address the epidemiology of host-pathogen systems. In Sharon K. Collinge, Chris Ray (eds.), *Disease Ecology*. Oxford: Oxford University Press, pp. 6–27.

Holt, Robert D., Andrew P. Dobson, Michael Begon, Roger G. Bowers, and Eric M. Schauber. (2003). Parasite establishment in host communities. *Ecology Letters* 6(9): 837–42.

Hosseini, P. R., J. N. Mills, A. H. Prieur-Richard, V. O. Ezenwa, X. Bailly, A. Rizzoli, G. Suzan, M. Vittecoq, G. E. Garcia-Pena, P. Daszak, J. F. Guegan, and B. Roche. (2017). Does the impact of biodiversity differ between emerging and endemic pathogens? The need to separate the concepts of hazard and risk. *Philosophical Transactions of the Royal Society B* 372:20160129.

Hudson, Peter J., Andy P. Dobson, and Dave Newborn. (1998). Prevention of population cycles by parasite removal. *Science* 282(5397): 2256–8.

Johnson, Leah R., Robert B. Gramacy, Jeremy Cohen, Erin Mordecai, Courtney Murdock, Jason Rohr, Sadie J. Ryan, Anna M. Stewart-Ibarra, and Daniel Weikel. (2018). Phenomenological forecasting of disease incidence using heteroskedastic Gaussian processes: A dengue case study. *Annals of Applied Statistics* 12(1): 27–66.

Johnson, Pieter T. J., and Jason T. Hoverman. (2012). Parasite diversity and coinfection determine pathogen infection success and host fitness. *Proceedings of the National Academy of Sciences* 109(23): 9006–11.

Johnson, Pieter T. J., Daniel L. Preston, Jason T. Hoverman, and Bryan E. LaFonte. (2013b). Host and parasite diversity jointly control disease risk in complex communities. *Proceedings of the National Academy of Sciences* 110(42): 16916–21.

Johnson, Pieter T. J., Chelsea L. Wood, Maxwell B. Joseph, Daniel L. Preston, Sarah E. Haas, and Yuri P. Springer. (2016). Habitat heterogeneity drives the host-diversity-begets-parasite-diversity relationship: Evidence from experimental and field studies. *Ecology Letters* 19(7): 752–61.

Johnson, P. T. J., R. S. Ostfeld, and F. Keesing. (2015). Frontiers in research on biodiversity and disease. *Ecology Letters* 18: 1119–33.

Johnson, P. T. J., D. L. Preston, J. T. Hoverman, and K. L. D. Richgels. (2013a). Biodiversity decreases disease through predictable changes in host community competence. *Nature* 494: 230–3.

Johnson, P. T. J., J. R. Rohr, J. T. Hoverman, E. Kellermanns, J. Bowerman, and K. B. Lunde. (2012). Living fast and dying of infection: Host life history drives interspecific variation in infection and disease risk. *Ecology Letters* 15: 235–42.

Joseph, M. B., J. R. Mihaljevic, S. A. Orlofske, and S. H. Paull. (2013). Does life history mediate changing disease risk when communities disassemble? *Ecology Letters* 16: 1405–12.

Katzelnick, Leah C., Lionel Gresh, M. Elizabeth Halloran, Juan Carlos Mercado, Guillermina Kuan, Aubree Gordon, Angel Balmaseda, and Eva Harris. (2017). Antibody-Dependent enhancement of severe dengue disease in humans. *Science* 358(6365): 929–32.

Keeling, Matt J. and Pejman Rohani. (2011). *Modeling Infectious Diseases in Humans and Animals*. Princeton: Princeton University Press.

Keesing, F., L. K. Belden, P. Daszak, A. Dobson, C. D. Harvell, R. D. Holt, P. Hudson, A. Jolles, K. E. Jones, C. E. Mitchell, S. S. Myers, T. Bogich, and R. S. Ostfeld. (2010). Impacts of biodiversity on the emergence and transmission of infectious diseases. *Nature* 468: 647–52.

Keesing, F., R. D. Holt, and R. S. Ostfeld. (2006). Effects of species diversity on disease risk. *Ecology Letters* 9: 485–98.

Keesing, F. and R. S. Ostfeld. 2015. Is biodiversity good for your health? *Science* 349: 235–6.

Kilpatrick, A. Marm, Peter Daszak, Matthew J. Jones, Peter P. Marra, and Laura D. Kramer. (2006). Host heterogeneity dominates West Nile virus transmission. *Proceedings of the Royal Society B* 273: 2327–33.

Kilpatrick, A. M. (2011). Globalization, land use, and the invasion of West Nile virus. *Science* 334: 323–7.

Kilpatrick, A. M., D. J. Salkeld, G. Titcomb, and M. B. Hahn. (2017). Conservation of biodiversity as a strategy for improving human health and well-being. *Philosophical Transactions of the Royal Society B* 372: 20160131.

Koelle, Katia, Mercedes Pascual, and Md Yunus. 2005. Pathogen adaptation to seasonal forcing and climate change. *Proceedings of the Royal Society B* 272(1566): 971–7.

Koelle, Katia, Mercedes Pascual, and Md Yunus. (2006). Serotype cycles in cholera dynamics. *Proceedings of the Royal Society B* 273(1603): 2879–86.

Knutie, S. A., C. L. Wilkinson, K. D. Kohl, and J. R. Rohr. (2017). Early-life disruption of host microbiota decreases later-life resistance to infections. *Nature Communications* 8: 86.

Kuris, Armand M., Ryan F. Hechinger, Jenny C. Shaw, Kathleen L. Whitney, Leopoldina Aguirre-Macedo, Charlie A. Boch, Andrew P. Dobson, et al. (2008). Ecosystem energetic implications of parasite and free-living biomass in three estuaries. *Nature* 454(7203): 515–18.

Lafferty, Kevin D. (2009). The ecology of climate change and infectious diseases. *Ecology* 90(4): 888–900.

Lafferty, Kevin D., Andrew P. Dobson, and Armand M. Kuris. (2006a). Parasites Dominate food web links. *Proceedings of the National Academy of Sciences* 103(30): 11211–16.

Lafferty, Kevin D., Ryan F. Hechinger, Jenny C. Shaw, Kathleen Whitney, and Armand M. Kuris. (2006b). Food webs and parasites in a salt marsh ecosystem. In *Disease Ecology,* (eds) Sharon K. Collinge, Chris Ray, pp. 119–134. Oxford: Oxford University Press.

Lafferty, K. D., and C. L. Wood. (2013). It's a myth that protection against disease is a strong and general service of biodiversity conservation: Response to Ostfeld and Keesing. *Trends in Ecology & Evolution* 28: 503–4.

Lello, Joanne, Brian Boag, Andrew Fenton, Ian R. Stevenson, and Peter J. Hudson. (2004). Competition and mutualism among the gut helminths of a mammalian host. *Nature* 428(6985): 840–4.

Levi, T., A. L. Massey, R. D. Holt, F. Keesing, R. S. Ostfeld, and C. A. Peres. (2016). Does biodiversity protect humans against infectious disease? *Comment. Ecology* 97: 536–42.

Levin, B. R., M. Lipsitch, and S. Bonhoeffer. (1999). Population Biology, Evolution, and Infectious Disease: Convergence and Synthesis. *Science* 283(5403): 806–9.

Levin, S. A. (1992). The problem of pattern and scale in ecology: The Robert H. MacArthur award lecture. *Ecology* 73: 1943–67.

Lipsitch, Marc. (1997). Vaccination against colonizing bacteria with multiple serotypes. *Proceedings of the National Academy of Sciences* 94(12): 6571–6.

Lipsitch, Marc, Caroline Colijn, Ted Cohen, William P. Hanage, and Christophe Fraser. (2009). No coexistence for free: Neutral null models for multistrain pathogens. *Epidemics* 1(1): 2–13.

Lipsitch, Marc, and Justin J. O'Hagan. (2007). Patterns of Antigenic diversity and the mechanisms that maintain them. *Journal of the Royal Society Interface* 4(16): 787–802.

Liu, X., F. Chen, S. Lyu, D. Sun, and S. Zhou. (2018). Random species loss underestimates dilution effects of host diversity on foliar fungal diseases under fertilization. *Ecology and Evolution* 8: 1705–13.

Lively, C. M. (2010). The effect of host genetic diversity on disease spread. *American Naturalist* 175: E149–52.

Lively, C. M. and M. F. Dybdahl. (2000). Parasite adaptation to locally common host genotypes. *Nature* 405: 679.

Lloyd-Smith, James O. (2013). Vacated niches, competitive release and the community ecology of pathogen eradication. *Philosophical Transactions of the Royal Society B* 368(1623): 20120150.

LoGiudice, K., R. S. Ostfeld, K. A. Schmidt, and F. Keesing. (2003). The ecology of infectious disease: Effects of host diversity and community composition on Lyme disease risk. *Proceedings of the National Academy of Sciences* 100: 567–71.

Lourenço, José and Mario Recker. (2013). Natural, persistent oscillations in a spatial multi-strain disease system with application to dengue. *PLOS Computational Biology* 9(10): e1003308.

Luis, A. D., D. T. Hayman, T. J. O'Shea, P. M. Cryan, A. T. Gilbert, J. R. Pulliam, J. N. Mills, M. E. Timonin, C. K. Willis, and A. A. Cunningham. (2013). A comparison of bats and rodents as reservoirs of zoonotic viruses: Are bats special? *Proceedings of the Royal Society B* 280: 20122753.

Luis, A. D., A. J. Kuenzi, and J. N. Mills. (2018). Species diversity concurrently dilutes and amplifies transmission in a zoonotic host–pathogen system through competing mechanisms. *Proceedings of the National Academy of Sciences* 115(31): 7979–84.

Martin, Lynn B., William A. Hopkins, Laura D. Mydlarz, and Jason R. Rohr. (2010). The effects of anthropogenic global changes on immune functions and disease resistance. *Annals of the New York Academy of Sciences* 1195(May): 129–48.

McCann, Kevin S. (2011). *Food Webs (MPB-50).* Princeton: Princeton University Press.

McGill, B. J. (2010). Matters of scale. *Science* 328: 575–6.

McKenzie, F. Ellis, David L. Smith, Wendy P. O'Meara, and Eleanor M. Riley. (2008). Strain theory of malaria: The first 50 years. *Advances in Parasitology* 66: 1–46.

McLean, A. R. (1995). Vaccination, evolution and changes in the efficacy of vaccines: A theoretical framework. *Proceedings of the Royal Society B* 261(1362): 389–93.

Mideo, Nicole. (2009). Parasite adaptations to within-host competition. *Trends in Parasitology* 25(6): 261–8.

Mihaljevic, J. R., M. B. Joseph, S. A. Orlofske, and S. H. Paull. (2014). The scaling of host density with richness affects the direction, shape, and detectability of diversity-disease relationships. *PLOS One* 9: e97812.

Mina, Michael J., C. Jessica, E. Metcalf, Rik L. de Swart, A. D. M. E. Osterhaus, and Bryan T. Grenfell. (2015). Long-term measles-induced immunomodulation increases overall childhood infectious disease mortality. *Science* 348(6235): 694–9.

Mitchell, Charles E. and Alison G. Power. (2003). release of invasive plants from fungal and viral pathogens. *Nature* 421(6923): 625–7.

Mordecai, E. A. (2011). Pathogen impacts on plant communities: unifying theory, concepts, and empirical work. *Ecological Monographs* 81: 429–41.

Mordecai, Erin A., Kevin Gross, and Charles E. Mitchell. (2016). Within-Host niche differences and fitness trade-offs promote coexistence of plant viruses. *American Naturalist* 187: E13–26.

Neafsey, D. E., M. Juraska, T. Bedford, D. Benkeser, C. Valim, A. Griggs, M. Lievens, et al. (2015). Genetic diversity and protective efficacy of the RTS,S/AS01 malaria vaccine. *New England Journal of Medicine* 373(21): 2025–37.

Nicoli, Emily J., Diepreye Ayabina, Caroline L. Trotter, Katherine M. E. Turner, and Caroline Colijn. (2015). Competition, coinfection and strain replacement in models of *Bordetella pertussis*. *Theoretical Population Biology* 103: 84–92.

Nunn, Charles L., Sonia Altizer, Kate E. Jones, and Wes Sechrest. (2003). Comparative tests of parasite species richness in primates. *American Naturalist* 162(5): 597–614.

Orlando, Paul A., Robert A. Gatenby, Anna R. Giuliano, and Joel S. Brown. (2012). Evolutionary ecology of human papillomavirus: Trade-offs, coexistence, and origins of high-risk and low-risk types. *Journal of Infectious Diseases* 205(2): 272–9.

Ostfeld, R. S. (2013). A Candide response to Panglossian accusations by Randolph and Dobson: Biodiversity buffers disease. *Parasitology* 140: 1196–8.

Ostfeld, R. S. and F. Keesing. (2000a). Biodiversity and disease risk: The case of Lyme disease. *Conservation Biology* 14: 722–8.

Ostfeld, R. S. and F. Keesing. (2000b). Biodiversity series: The function of biodiversity in the ecology of vector-borne zoonotic diseases. *Canadian Journal of Zoology* 78: 2061–78.

Ostfeld, R. S. and F. Keesing. (2012). Effects of host diversity on infectious disease. *Annual Review of Ecology, Evolution, and Systematics* 43:157–182.

Ostfeld, R. S. and F. Keesing. (2013). Straw men don't get Lyme disease: Response to Wood and Lafferty. *Trends in Ecology & Evolution* 28: 502–3.

Ostfeld, R. S., and F. Keesing. 2017. Is biodiversity bad for your health? *Ecosphere* 8(3):e01676.

Ostfeld, R. S. and K. LoGiudice. (2003). Community disassembly, biodiversity loss, and the erosion of an ecosystem service. *Ecology* 84: 1421–7.

Ostfeld, R. S., M. B. Thomas, and F. Keesing. (2009). Biodiversity and ecosystem function: perspectives on disease. In S. Naeem, D. Bunker, A. Hector, M. Loreau, and C. Perrings (eds.), *Biodiversity, Ecosystem Functioning, and Human Well-Being: An Ecological and Economic Perspective*. Oxford: Oxford University Press, Oxford, pp. 209–16.

Page, Kathleen R., Anne E. Jedlicka, Benjamin Fakheri, Gregory S. Noland, Anup K. Kesavan, Alan L. Scott, Nirbhay Kumar, and Yukari C. Manabe. (2005). Mycobacterium-Induced potentiation of type 1 immune responses and protection against malaria are host specific. infection and immunity 73(12): 8369–80.

Parker, I. M., M. Saunders, M. Bontrager, A. P. Weitz, R. Hendricks, R. Magarey, K. Suiter, and G. S. Gilbert. (2015). Phylogenetic structure and host abundance drive disease pressure in communities. *Nature* 520: 542–4.

Paull, Sara H., Sejin Song, Katherine M. McClure, Loren C. Sackett, A. Marm Kilpatrick, and Pieter T. J. Johnson. (2012). From superspreaders to disease hotspots: Linking transmission across hosts and space. *Frontiers in Ecology and the Environment* 10(2): 75–82.

Pedersen, Amy B. and Andy Fenton. (2007). Emphasizing the ecology in parasite community ecology. *Trends in Ecology & Evolution* 22(3): 133–9.

Perkins, T. Alex, Valerie A. Paz-Soldan, Steven T. Stoddard, Amy C. Morrison, Brett M. Forshey, Kanya C. Long, Eric S. Halsey, et al. (2016). Calling in sick: Impacts of fever on intra-urban human mobility. *Proceedings of the Royal Society B* 283: 20160390.

Pitzer, Virginia E., Manish M. Patel, Ben A. Lopman, Cécile Viboud, Umesh D. Parashar, and Bryan T. Grenfell. (2011). Modeling rotavirus strain dynamics in developed countries to understand the potential impact of vaccination on genotype distributions. *Proceedings of the National Academy of Sciences* 108(48): 19353–8.

Previtali, M. A., R. S. Ostfeld, F. Keesing, A. E. Jolles, R. Hanselmann, and L. B. Martin. (2012). Relationship between pace of life and immune responses in wild rodents. *Oikos* 121: 1483–92.

Raffel, T. R., L. B. Martin, and J. R. Rohr. (2008). Parasites as predators: Unifying natural enemy ecology. *Trends in Ecology & Evolution* 23: 610–18.

Randolph, S. E. and A. D. M. Dobson. (2012). Pangloss revisited: A critique of the dilution effect and the biodiversity-buffers-disease paradigm. *Parasitology* 139: 847–63.

Recker, Mario, Konstantin B. Blyuss, Cameron P. Simmons, Tran Tinh Hien, Bridget Wills, Jeremy Farrar, and Sunetra Gupta. (2009). Immunological serotype interactions and their effect on the epidemiological pattern of dengue. *Proceedings of the Royal Society B* 276(1667): 2541–8.

Reich, Nicholas G., Logan C. Brooks, Spencer J. Fox, Sasikiran Kandula, Craig J. McGowan, Evan Moore, Dave Osthus, et al. (2019). A collaborative multiyear, multimodel assessment of seasonal influenza forecasting in the United States. *Proceedings of the National Academy of Sciences* 116(8): 3146–54.

Reich, Nicholas G., Sourya Shrestha, Aaron A. King, Pejman Rohani, Justin Lessler, Siripen Kalayanarooj, In-Kyu Yoon, Robert V. Gibbons, Donald S. Burke, and Derek A. T. Cummings. (2013). Interactions between serotypes of dengue highlight epidemiological impact of cross-reactive immunity. *Journal of the Royal Society Interface* 10: 20130414.

Rimoin, Anne W., Prime M. Mulembakani, Sara C. Johnston, James O. Lloyd Smith, Neville K. Kisalu, Timothee L. Kinkela, Seth Blumberg, et al. (2010). Major Increase in human monkeypox incidence 30 years after smallpox vaccination campaigns cease in the Democratic Republic of Congo. *Proceedings of the National Academy of Sciences* 107: 16262–7.

Roche, Benjamin, John M. Drake, Justin Brown, David E. Stallknecht, Trevor Bedford, and Pejman Rohani. (2014). Adaptive evolution and environmental durability jointly structure phylodynamic patterns in avian influenza viruses. *PLOS Biology* 12(8): e1001931.

Rodriguez-Barraquer, Isabel, Luis Mier-y-Teran-Romero, Ira B. Schwartz, Donald S. Burke, and Derek A. T. Cummings. (2014). Potential opportunities and perils of imperfect dengue vaccines. *Vaccine* 32(4): 514–20.

Rohani, P., D. J. Earn, B. Finkenst.dt, and B. T. Grenfell. (1998). Population dynamic interference among childhood diseases. *Proceedings of the Royal Society B* 265(1410): 2033–41.

Rohani, Pej, Helen J. Wearing, Daniel A. Vasco, and Yunxin Huang. (2006). Understanding host-multipathogen systems: Modeling the interaction between ecology and immunology. In Richard S. Ostfeld, Felicia Keesing, and Valerie T. Eviner (eds.), *Ecology of Infectious Diseases*. Princeton: Princeton University Press.

Rohani, P., C. J. Green, N. B. Mantilla-Beniers, and B. T. Grenfell. (2003). Ecological interference between fatal diseases. *Nature* 422(6934): 885–8.

Rohr, J. R., D. J. Civitello, P. W. Crumrine, N. T. Halstead, A. D. Miller, A. M. Schotthoefer, C. Stenoien, L. B. Johnson, and V. R. Beasley. (2015). Predator diversity, intraguild predation, and indirect effects drive parasite transmission. *Proceedings of the National Academy of Sciences* 112: 3008–13.

Rohr, Jason R., Andrew P. Dobson, Pieter T. J. Johnson, A. Marm Kilpatrick, Sara H. Paull, Thomas R. Raffel, Diego Ruiz-Moreno, and Matthew B. Thomas. (2011). Frontiers in climate change-disease research. *trends in Ecology & Evolution* 26(6): 270–7.

Rohr, Jason R., Autumn Swan, Thomas R. Raffel, and Peter J. Hudson. (2009). Parasites, info-disruption, and the ecology of fear. *Oecologia* 159(2): 447–54.

Rottstock, Tanja, Jasmin Joshi, Volker Kummer, and Markus Fischer. (2014). Higher plant diversity promotes higher diversity of fungal pathogens, while it decreases pathogen infection per plant. *Ecology* 95(7): 1907–17.

Rudolf, V. H., and J. Antonovics. (2005). Species coexistence and pathogens with frequency-dependent transmission. *American Naturalist* 166: 112–18.

Salkeld, D. J., K. A. Padgett, and J. H. Jones. (2013). A meta-analysis suggesting that the relationship between biodiversity and risk of zoonotic pathogen transmission is idiosyncratic. *Ecology Letters* 16: 679–86.

Salkeld, D. J., K. A. Padgett, J. H. Jones, and M. F. Antolin. (2015). Public health perspective on patterns of biodiversity and zoonotic disease. *Proceedings of the National Academy of Sciences* 112: 1-E6261.

Schmidt, K. A. and R. S. Ostfeld. (2001). Biodiversity and the dilution effect in disease ecology. *Ecology* 82: 609–19.

Seabloom, Eric W., Elizabeth T. Borer, Kevin Gross, Amy E. Kendig, Christelle Lacroix, Charles E. Mitchell, Erin A. Mordecai, and Alison G. Power. (2015). The community ecology of pathogens: Coinfection, coexistence and community composition. *Ecology Letters* 18(4): 401–15.

Sears, B. F., P. W. Snyder, and J. R. Rohr. (2015). Host life history and host-parasite syntopy predict behavioural resistance and tolerance of parasites. *Journal of Animal Ecology* 84: 625–36.

Smith, David L., F. Ellis McKenzie, Robert W. Snow, and Simon I. Hay. (2007). Revisiting the basic reproductive number for malaria and its implications for malaria Control. *PLOS Biology* 5(3): e42.

Strauss, A. T., D. J. Civitello, C. E. Cáceres, and S. R. Hall. (2015). Success, failure and ambiguity of the dilution effect among competitors. *Ecology Letters* 18: 916–26.

Su, Zhong, Mariela Segura, Kenneth Morgan, J. Concepcion Loredo-Osti, and Mary M. Stevenson. (2005). Impairment of protective immunity to blood-stage malaria by concurrent nematode infection. *Infection and Immunity* 73(6): 3531–9.

Suzan, G., E. Marce, J. T. Giermakowski, J. N. Mills, G. Ceballos, R. S. Ostfeld, B. Armien, J. M. Pascale, and T. L. Yates. (2009). Experimental evidence for reduced rodent diversity causing increased hantavirus prevalence. *PLOS One* 4(5): e5461.

Taylor, L. H., S. M. Latham, and M. E. Woolhouse. (2001). Risk factors for human disease emergence. *Philosophical Transactions of the Royal Society B* 356(1411): 983–9.

ten Bosch, Quirine A., Brajendra K. Singh, Muhammad R. A. Hassan, Dave D. Chadee, and Edwin Michael. (2016). The Role of serotype interactions and seasonality in dengue model selection and control: Insights from a pattern matching approach. *PLOS Neglected Tropical Diseases* 10(5): e0004680.

Torchin, Mark E. and Charles E. Mitchell. (2004). Parasites, pathogens, and invasions by plants and animals. *Frontiers in Ecology and the Environment* 2(4): 183.

Van Buskirk, J. and R. S. Ostfeld. (1995). Controlling Lyme disease by modifying the density and species composition of tick hosts. *Ecological Applications* 5: 1133–40.

Vazquez-Prokopec, Gonzalo M., T. Alex Perkins, Lance A. Waller, Alun L. Lloyd, Robert C. Reiner Jr, Thomas W. Scott, and Uriel Kitron. (2016). Coupled heterogeneities and their impact on parasite transmission and control. *Trends in Parasitology* 32(5): 356–67.

Vellend, Mark. (2010). Conceptual synthesis in community ecology. *Quarterly Review of Biology* 85(2): 183–206.

Venesky, M. D., X. Liu, E. L. Sauer, and J. R. Rohr. (2014). Linking manipulative experiments to field data to test the dilution effect. *Journal of Animal Ecology* 83: 557–65.

Vogels, Chantal B. F., Claudia Rückert, Sean M. Cavany, T. Alex Perkins, Gregory D. Ebel, and Nathan D. Grubaugh. (2019). Arbovirus coinfection and co-transmission: A neglected public health concern? *PLOS Biology* 17(1): e3000130.

Wearing, Helen J. and Pejman Rohani. (2006). Ecological and immunological determinants of dengue epidemics. *Proceedings of the National Academy of Sciences* 103(31): 11802–7.

White, L. (1998). Cross immunity and vaccination against multiple microparasite strains. *Mathematical Medicine and Biology: A Journal of the IMA* 15(3): 211–33.

Wilcox, C. (2017). The hidden dispute over biodiversity's health benefits. *The Atlantic*. https://undark.org/2017/10/30/biodiversity-disease-human-health/.

Wolfe, Nathan D., Claire Panosian Dunavan, and Jared Diamond. (2007). Origins of Major Human Infectious Diseases. *Nature* 447(7142): 279–83.

Wood, C. L. and K. D. Lafferty. (2013). Biodiversity and disease: a synthesis of ecological perspectives on Lyme disease transmission. *Trends in Ecology & Evolution* 28: 239–47.

Wood, C. L., K. D. Lafferty, G. DeLeo, H. S. Young, P. J. Hudson, and A. M. Kuris. (2014). Does biodiversity protect humans against infectious disease? Ecology 95: 817–32.

Wood, C. L., K. D. Lafferty, G. DeLeo, H. S. Young, P. J. Hudson, and A. M. Kuris. (2016). Does biodiversity protect humans against infectious disease? Reply. *Ecology* 97: 542–5.

Wood, C. L., A. McInturff, H. S. Young, D. Kim, and K. D. Lafferty. (2017). Human infectious disease burdens decrease with urbanization but not with biodiversity. *Philosophical Transactions of the Royal Society B-Biological Sciences* 372: 20160122.

Wuerthner, Vanessa P., Jessica Hua, and Jason T. Hoverman. (2017). The benefits of coinfection: Trematodes alter disease outcomes associated with virus infection. *Journal of Animal Ecology* 86(4): 921–31.

Young, H., R. H. Griffin, C. L. Wood, and C. L. Nunn. (2013). Does habitat disturbance increase infectious disease risk for primates? *Ecology Letters* 16: 656–63.

CHAPTER 14

The impact of temperature on population and community dynamics

David A. Vasseur

14.1 Introduction

Climate change is expected to alter many characteristics of the abiotic environment. These alterations will ultimately be re-expressed as changes in ecological patterns and processes and our ability to understand and predict these changes is one of the great challenges of the current century. In addition to a gradual warming of many of the Earth's ecosystems, concomitant changes in precipitation, the concentrations of organic and inorganic nutrients, and the alteration of habitat (among other things) will interact in important and unforeseen ways. Such interactions have been emphasized in a number of important experiments (e.g., the free-air CO_2 enrichment experiments; Ainsworth and Long 2005) yet, these present a significant challenge to the development of general theoretical approaches for studying population and community dynamics due to the often non-linear, threshold-driven, and context dependent nature of such interactions. Rather, the theoretical foundations in this area have focused more on the integration of singular environmental variables across a range from single populations to complex communities of interacting species.

Of the many environmental variables that impact ecological systems, temperature has proven to be particularly enticing for study, due perhaps to its ubiquitous importance in nature, a strong physical theory upon which to frame its influence, and in many systems, the lack of a feedback cycle between temperature and ecological attributes such as population dynamics. While the global mean temperature has already risen by approximately 1°C and will continue to rise over the coming decades, researchers have also begun to appreciate the potential for variation in temperature beyond the mean change to affect ecological systems. Climate models predict an increase in the temporal variation and autocorrelation of temperature (Easterling et al. 2000; Meehl and Tebaldi 2004; Field et al. 2012), and although there is substantial spatial variation in the extent to which these characters will change, many locations will experience the culmination of these changes as increases in the frequency, intensity, and duration of extreme events.

Population dynamics play a critical role in linking climate change to ecological patterns and process, as they form part of a chain of responses that are linked via ecological interactions and because they are the basis upon which aggregate-level responses at the community or ecosystem level formed. Although the idea that external forces in the environment can influence population dynamics is not new (e.g., Andrewartha 1954), there remains much to be learned about how population dynamics depend on the environment. This lack of understanding is perhaps best exemplified in attempts to forecast population dynamics. While quantitative models have proven useful in some cases, recent work has shown that the forecast horizon, over which sufficiently good predictions can be made, is vastly

Vasseur, D. A., *The impact of temperature on population and community dynamics* In: *Theoretical Ecology: Concepts and Applications*. Edited by: Kevin S. McCann and Gabriel Gellner, Oxford University Press (2020). © Oxford University Press.
DOI: 10.1093/oso/9780198824282.003.0014

reduced in the presence of environmental variation (Petchey et al. 2015). Central to this issue is the fact that there has been little consensus about how environmental variation should interface with population dynamics, especially in circumstances where "the environment" is not a well-specified quantity. This chapter seeks to synthesize efforts to embed temperature variation into models of population and community dynamics, outline the major challenges involved in doing so, and suggest a new paradigm for linking temperature-driven variation in key parameters.

14.2 Population dynamics in varying environments

Form a theoretical perspective, the effect of changing environmental conditions on population dynamics are perhaps best considered through the lens of perturbation theory (Bender et al. 1984). Altered environmental conditions, so long as they do not produce an immediately lethal effect, alter parameters such as the rates of birth and death in a population, thereby dictating a new pattern of population growth, or decline (or stasis) relative to previous environmental states. A large majority of perturbation experiments have considered the role of singular and sustained (long-term) changes to environmental conditions in this context (e.g., Carpenter et al. 2001), and indeed many such experiments have looked at the role of temperature in this manner(Petchey et al. 1999; Barton et al. 2009; O'Connor et al. 2011; Shurin et al. 2012; Fussmann et al. 2014a; Yvon-Durocher et al. 2015). However, it is important to also consider that the same framework is useful for exploring how multiple short-term changes in environmental conditions manifest in population dynamics. Here, the rate at which environmental changes occur, relative to the rate at which the ecological system responds, represents a scalar adjustment that can be applied to any system.

Perhaps the first to study the effect of temporal environmental variation on population growth were Lewontin and Cohen (1969), who examined random variation in the intrinsic growth rate of an exponentially growing population in discrete time,

and Levins (1969) extended their results to random variation in the intrinsic growth rate r and carrying capacity K of the continuous time Logistic model:

$$\frac{dN}{dt} = rN\left(1 - \frac{N}{K}\right). \qquad (14.1)$$

Their results formed the foundation for our understanding of how variation in a biological parameter is reflected in the abundance (N) over time. Levins (1969) demonstrated that when the intrinsic growth rate r varies through time, the population is likely to remain near its carrying capacity K so long as the variance of r is less than its mean, otherwise the population distribution is bimodal with modes at zero and K. When the carrying capacity K is varied, the population remains near the harmonic mean of K; however, the extent to which recent values of K are weighted in the harmonic mean relative to distant values of K *is* determined by the value of r. This final point was revisited later by May (1976), who examined the role of sinusoidal variation in K on population dynamics. May demonstrated that for high values of r, population dynamics would closely track ("environmental tracking") their sinusoidal environments and would approach the same sinusoidal fluctuation (with some associated time lag) as $r \to \infty$ whereas, for low values of r, population dynamics would settle on the harmonic mean of the carrying capacity. The implication is therefore that any variation in K gives rise to a mean population size $\overline{N}$ that increases with r, but is always less than the mean carrying capacity $\overline{K}$ (Figure 14.1). This led to the idea that natural selection should favor genotypes that are best able to track environmental fluctuations when variation in K is small, and select genotypes that integrate across environmental fluctuations when variation in K is large (Boyce and Daley 1980). These findings demonstrate the intertwined roles that model parameters can have with respect to filtering and re-expression of environmental variation in population dynamics and the inherent challenge of dealing with more complex models where multiple parameters may be fluctuating simultaneously.

Much of the early theoretical work on environmental variation assumed a set of rather ideal conditions: i) that environments were stochastic and unpredictable from previous states (e.g., they lacked

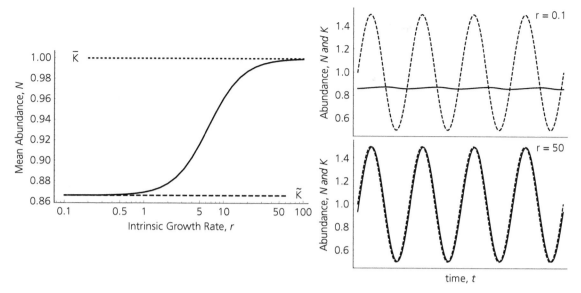

Figure 14.1 Mean abundance exhibited by the logistic model $dn/dt = rN(1 - n/K)$ where $K = 1 + \sin(2\pi t)/2$. At low values of the intrinsic growth rate the mean abundance approaches the harmonic mean carrying capacity $\tilde{K}$ whereas at high values the mean abundance approaches the arithmetic mean carrying capacity $\overline{K}$. The smaller panels show the dynamics of N (solid) and K (dashed) at small and large r. The transition from "averaging" to "tracking" depends on the frequency of oscillations in K, with higher frequencies requiring faster growth rates.

autocorrelation); ii) that variation in the environment mapped linearly onto the biological parameter of interest (e.g., r, K or similar), and iii) that environmental variation was not great enough to generate qualitative changes to the underlying stability of the system. Moving from these idealized conditions to a more natural model of environmental variation that violates one or more of these requirements, improves the biological validity of models but at the same time introduces complexities that interfere with analytical synthesis. Considering the role of temperature in relatively simple models of population dynamics, it is clear that all three of these conditions are easily violated.

Temperature, like many other environmental variables demonstrates strong temporal autocorrelation in aquatic environments and moderate autocorrelation in terrestrial environments (Cyr* and Cyr‡ 2003: Vasseur and Yodzis 2004). Autocorrelation increases the responsiveness of population dynamics to environmental variation (Roughgarden 1975, Tuljapurkar 1982) by concentrating it at longer scales, thereby providing populations more time to mount a response and leading to closer tracking of the environment. This finding led to

the suggestion that environmental autocorrelation could be detrimental for persistence (Ripa and Lundberg 1996, Heino et al. 2000, Heino and Sabadell 2003) by luring populations closer to extinction boundaries. These ideas match closely with those of Levins (1969) and May (1976) whose work on sinusoidal variation represents a special case of autocorrelated variation. In Figure 14.1, the more responsive population demonstrates a much greater range of variation; notably this responsiveness increases not just as function of r but also of the frequency of sinusoidal variation f. However, many counter examples also suggested a beneficial role of autocorrelation for ensuring the persistence of populations (Cuddington and Yodzis 1999; Wichmann et al. 2005) and more recently it has been shown that the effect ultimately depends on the extent to which population dynamics overcompensate for changes in their environmentally determined equilibria (Schwager et al. 2006; Vasseur 2007). Autocorrelation can also act to increase the persistence times of source-sink metapopulations by leveraging the power of exponential growth during long-runs of favorable conditions (Gonzalez and Holt 2002; Roy et al. 2005).

Beyond the general effects of autocorrelation, theoretical work on the relationship between temperature and population dynamics has mainly considered how, and which parameters are sensitive to temperature. Temperature influences population dynamics through a myriad of physiological and behavioral responses that ultimately affect ecologically relevant biological and ecological rates of birth, death and interaction. Peters (1986) provides an incredibly rich summary of the ecological importance of body size and temperature, much of which has ultimately has been formalized as part of the metabolic theory of ecology (Gillooly et al. 2001; Brown et al. 2004). In this framework the effects of temperature are scaled by the Arrhenius relationship $e^{-E_a/kT}$, where E_a is the activation energy, k is Boltzmann's constant, and T is temperature. This relationship generates an increase (or decrease) in biological rates that is approximately exponential over the range of biologically relevant temperatures. While the Arrhenius equation provides a good characterization of cross-species comparisons it does not necessarily characterize the effect that temperature has on the biological rates expressed by individuals or populations. For example, (Eppley 1972) demonstrated that an exponential relationship characterized the overarching rate of maximal phytoplankton production in marine environments, but showed that individual species only approached this curve at their optimum temperature for growth. At the species level, relationships between temperature and production are instead better depicted by the skewed unimodal curves that are commonplace in the study of thermal ecology and oftent described as "thermal performance curves" (Kingsolver 2009); while these curves exhibit an exponential rise over part of the temperature range, they ultimatley slow, reaching a maximum at some optimal temperature and crash quickly at temperatures above the optimum. The incorporation of temperature into studies of population and community dynamics is thus dependent on the scale at which individuals are aggregated into funcional groups—an in issue which will be explored further.

Given the scope of the model (e.g., single population vs. community), temperature variation has the potential to generate both quantitative and qualitative changes in population dynamics. For example, temperature can change the equilibrium or non-equilibrium density of the population, the quasi-equilibrium temporal patterns exhibited by population density (e.g., oscillations), and/or the potential for a population to exist at all. Regardless of the scale at which populations are modeled (single-species or functional groups), temperature has a non-linear effect on biological rates. While it is clear that the non-linearity of these functions can itself generate the possibility for variation to be filtered in non-intuitive ways (Laakso et al. 2001), the non-linearity of responses combined with the co-dependence of many biological parameters on a single variable such as temperature, has provided a rich set of problems to investigate in this area.

Although climate change is expected to alter many aspects of the thermal environment, recent studies have focused on the effects of gradual warming on populations and communities. Here, the equilibrium conditions and population dynamics that are generated at different temperatures are of particular interest. While this approach has proven valuable, there has been some debate about how and where to incorporate temperature sensitivity in models. The wide variety of functional relationships, combined with differences in their sensitivity across model parameters, have led to inconsistency in predictions for the response of populations and communities to warming. In the following section, I review this literature, focusing on models of single populations and consumer-resource systems. I then discuss implications for shorter-term temperature variation by introducing a new framework for modeling temperature-sensitive logistic population dynamics.

14.3 Focusing our paradigm: Which parameters of trophic models should we study?

The level of biological detail that is described in a model changes the number of parameters involved, and with this change, the opportunity to include links to the abiotic environment. My intent now is to employ and summarize the work on a set of simple population and community models that have utility as building blocks for larger and more complicated models of food web dynamics. These models are generally applied to populations of ectotherms and assume a strict mapping of ambient temperature onto body temperature. While it is well known that ectotherms deploy a variety of strategies to decouple their body temperature from ambient temperature, and that this has important ecological consequences (Kearney et al. 2009; Huey et al. 2012; Sears et al. 2016), thermoregulation is not a component of the models described herein. Thermoregulatory behavior can be easily layered on top of the existing set of models by creating a dynamic mapping between ambient and body temperature (e.g., Fey and Vasseur 2016).

It is well accepted that the intrinsic rate of population growth r is sensitive to temperature. In fact, many studies seeking to describe the relationship between performance or fitness and temperature use r as a proxy (Deutsch et al. 2008; Kingsolver 2009; Thomas et al. 2012). r describes the difference between the per-capita rates of birth and death in a population, both of which are an aggregate of other processes that are themselves governed by physiological and ecological temperature dependences. For example, birth rates are influenced by rates of resource acquisition which may be temperature sensitive for various reasons including the effectiveness of membrane transport in microbes, swimming speeds and visual or chemosensory acuity in predators, and enzymatic effectiveness in herbivores, to name only a few. In the absence of other sources of variation, r has little value for studying the effects of temperature since its effect on population dynamics is relatively straightforward. Yet, when populations are coupled via and ecological interactions such as competition and predation, the interplay between the direct and indirect effects of temperature (e.g., those passed through interactions) can yield important insight.

In this spirit, and motivated by the growing body of literature relating metabolic and other biological rates to body size and temperature, Vasseur and McCann (2005) developed and analyzed a basic model of trophodynamics that incorporates the effects of temperature into three key biological rates: the intrinsic rate of increase of a living resource population (r), and the maximum assimilation rate $(1-\delta)J_m$, and the loss rate due to energy

metabolism (m) of its consumer. For tractability, they assumed that temperature increased these three rates according to a Boltzmann–Arrhenius relationship—an approach that has validity when the state variables in the model do not reflect populations of a specific species, but instead reflect characteristic functional groups in a community. Their model followed the classic form of Rosenzweig and MacArthur (1963), adapted to model biomass rather than abundance (Yodzis and Innes 1992), with resource (R) and consumer (C) dynamics are given by:

$$\frac{dR}{dt} = rR\left(1 - \frac{R}{K}\right) - J_m \frac{RC}{R_0 + R}$$
$$\frac{dC}{dt} = C\left[-m + (1-\delta)J_m \frac{R}{R_0 + R}\right].$$

(14.2)

By deriving the equilibrium of this model as a function of temperature, they suggested that in general, both resource and consumers should exhibit declining abundance at warmer temperatures despite greater productivity of the resource, due to a relatively greater increase in the metabolic demand and ingestion rates of consumers. Their findings were predicated on a particular ranking of temperature's effects on the three parameters, drawn from a relatively shallow pool of empirical estimates, and subject to scrutiny regarding where temperature sensitivity entered the model. Equilibrium analysis demonstrates that the effect of warming on the distribution of biomass is largely determined by two key differences among the activation energies of the three biological rates. The difference $(E_J - E_m)$ determines the top-down effect of consumers on resources (positive values lead to reduced resource biomass at warm temperatures; whereas the difference $(E_r - E_m)$ determines the potential for the total biomass in the system to change (with positive values leading to greater biomass). They assumed that the activation of ingestion E_J exceeded the activation energy of consumer respiration E_m which further exceeded the activation energy of resource production E_r and ultimately suggested that the biomass of both resources and consumers should decline with warming (Figure 14.2). In addition, they noted that the stability of the equilibrium could be compromised in warmer environments. Others

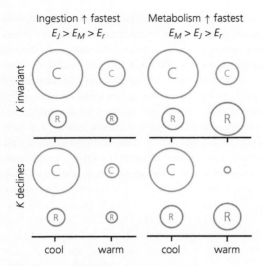

Figure 14.2 Equilibrium abundance exhibited by the Rosenzweig–MacArthur model when three key biological rates vary according to the Boltzmann–Arrhenius relationship. The sizes of circles depict a logarithmic scaling of the amount of biomass at each trophic level. The left-side panels show the pattern that occurs when consumer ingestion increases faster than metabolism while the right-side panels show an alternative arrangement of E_M and E_J. The upper panels show the results when K is invariant, and the bottom panels show the results when K declines with temperature.

later modified the assumptions about the relative relationship between activation energies of the key parameters (O'Connor et al. 2011; Sentis et al. 2017) and experimentally demonstrated that $(E_J - E_m)$ tended to be negative (Rall et al. 2010), which would lead to a reduction in top-down control of resources and a shift toward a resource dominated system (Figure 14.2).

Vasseur and McCann (2005) assumed that the two remaining parameters, the resource carrying capacity (K) and the half-saturation density of the consumer's functional response (R_0), were independent of temperature. One of the primary motivating factors for this assumption is that neither of these are rate parameters; rather, both are threshold values that are defined in units of abundance or biomass density. Threshold parameters generally represent an aggregate of many underlying processes, some of which may be dependent on factors that are extrinsic to the populations described in the model. For example, carrying capacity (K) in (14.2) reflects the extent to which resources com-

pete for resources whose abundance is assumed to be fixed by processes that are extrinsic to the model. While the temperature-dependence of these factors may be challenging to describe, they represent a clear opportunity to improve our understanding of temperature effects on populations and communities.

The assumption regarding the temperature-independence of the half-saturation density R_0 is better understood using the alternative Holling Type II form of the functional response. Under the transformation $J_m \rightarrow h^{-1}$ and $R_0 \rightarrow (ah)^{-1}$ the Michaelis–Menten form of the functional response depicted in (14.2) can be re-expressed using the attack rate (a) and handling time (h) parameters of the Holling Type II. Here it is obvious that a temperature-invariance of R_0 is satisfied so long as a and h have an inverse dependence on temperature. To a first approximation this is a valid assumption. Attack rates of ectothermic consumers should increase with temperature due to increases in movement rates, visual acuity, chemotaxis, and other elements of prey detection and capture (Dell et al. 2011). At the same time, the rate at which consumers handle a unit of resources h^{-1} increases with temperature as ingestion, digestion, and assimilation occur more rapidly. In a meta-analysis of temperature-dependent functional responses that included fifty-six observations on ectothermic consumers, Englund et al. (2011) showed that a and h^{-1} have a near identical response to temperature, reinforcing the assumption that R_0 should be temperature independent. Rall et al. (2012) extended this work to include over 600 functional response estimates from a large diversity of systems, again showing a very close matching of the temperature dependence of a and h^{-1}. More recently, Dell et al. (2014) suggested that this condition could be violated in circumstances where the effectiveness of consumer attacks are influenced by the resource's response to temperature. For example, consumers that engage in active capture or sit-and-wait strategies may have resources that are more elusive in warmer environments, thus slowing or reversing the effect of temperature on attack rates.

In some cases, it may be more appropriate to model the functional response of the consumer-resource model (Equation (14.2)) as a Holling Type III (Holling 1959). A few studies have suggested that warming can induce a shift from Type II to Type III functional responses for the same pair of consumers and resources (Wang and Ferro 1998; Mohaghegh et al. 2001). This change would have considerable implications for both the biomass distribution and stability of the interaction, but it presents a significant challenge to parameterize given the phenomenological nature of the shape parameter. For the zooplankton grazer *Daphia* consuming algae, Uszko and Diehl (2016) demonstrated that, although the functional response was type III over the entire range of temperatures studied, the shape parameter increased with temperature, making the sigmoid rise of the response sharper. The authors suggest that warmer temperatures may cause *Daphnia* to reduce its grazing effort at low food densities to compensate for metabolic losses. While such results may be common among many grazers and predators, few studies have yet to consider the potential for functional changes of this kind.

While there is no disagreement about importance of vital rates in consumer-resource models for determining the impact of temperature for dynamics, the functional forms describing the temperature dependence of these rates has developed considerably. The early work incorporating Arrhenius relationships (e.g., Savage et al. 2004; Vasseur and McCann 2005; O'Connor et al. 2011) assumed that resources and consumers could continue to exhibit increases in their vital rates across a large range of temperatures by assuming, for example, that each represented a broad functional group with relatively diverse thermal sensitivities. When these are replaced by single species, it is well-established that for certain parameters, including measures of fitness and performance, a unimodal relationship that declines sharply beyond an optimum best represents the relationship (Angilletta 2006; Deutsch et al. 2008; Kingsolver 2009). Amarasekare and Savage (2012) demonstrated that the skewed unimodal relationship between *r* and temperature can be derived by assuming that the positive contributions to fitness (e.g., fecundity, developmental or maturation rate) have a symmetric unimodal relationship with temperature while the negative contributions (e.g., mortality

or respiratory energy loss) are driven by an Arrhenius relationship. Although there have been some efforts to incorporate unimodal temperature dependencies into trophic models (Gilbert et al. 2014; Fussmann et al. 2014b; Amarasekare 2015), these are hampered by the potential for thermal asymmetries (Dell et al. 2014). Asymmetries exist when the optimum temperature for one vital rate (e.g., resource intrinsic growth) is mismatched relative to another (e.g., consumer ingestion). For any pair of consumers and resources this asymmetry adds an additional layer of uncertainty that complicates the search for generalities and patterns in response to warming. Before treating the issue of unimodality in temperature responses, it is pertinent to address the potential role of carrying capacity as an additional temperature sensitive parameter.

14.4 Temperature dependence of carrying capacity

Perhaps the more questionable assumption made by Vasseur and McCann (2005) is the temperature invariance of the resource carrying capacity, K. Despite the known importance of this parameter for processes and dynamics at levels of organization from populations to ecosystems (Rosenzweig 1971), there has been surprisingly little study of its temperature dependence (Gilbert et al. 2014). In a study aimed at quantifying the sensitivity of consumer-resource interactions to warming, Fussmann et al. (2014b) surveyed the literature for temperature-scaling relationships and found only five reports on the temperature sensitivity of K (most from microbes). These showed a consistent reduction of K with warming. More recent studies have both confirmed this result (Bernhardt et al. 2018) and supported the idea of temperature invariance (Jarvis et al. 2016). Not surprisingly, theoretical studies that have assumed an increase in K with warming (e.g., Rall et al. 2010; Sentis et al. 2017) tend to show qualitatively different results for trends in biomass and stability compared to studies that assume a decrease or stasis in K (e.g., Savage et al. 2004; Vasseur and McCann 2005; Fussmann et al. 2014b; Binzer et al. 2016; Osmond et al. 2017). Figure 14.2 shows the relative effect of incorporating warming induced reductions in K into consumer-resource models of the form given by Equation (14.2). This addition tends to strongly reduce the biomass of consumer populations, and where top-down control becomes very weak, allow for an increase in resource biomass.

For most species, carrying capacity reflects an aggregate of biotic and abiotic processes, some of which may be temperature-dependent. Schoener (1973) described carrying capacity of a producer as a function of the nutrient supply, the per-capita uptake rate, and the per-capita metabolic rate. Assuming a constant supply of resources, it has been suggested that temperature-induced increases in uptake and metabolism should lead K to decline in warmer environments since fewer individuals can be supported by same flux of resources into the system (Savage et al. 2004; O'Connor et al. 2011; Gilbert et al. 2014). Recently, Bernhardt et al. (2018) extended this logic to include the potential for declining resource body sizes in warmer temperatures (an idea that has been expressed as the temperature-size rule or Bergmann's rule). They demonstrated that temperature induced changes in body mass slow the expected decline in carrying capacity by reducing the per-unit-mass rate of metabolism. They furthermore demonstrated empirical support for this finding in the algae *Tetraselmis tetrahele* over the range 5 to 25°C and under a constant supply of nutrients.

Similar to work on other vital rates, carrying capacity has been shown to have a unimodal response to temperature when such relationships are considered part of the processes underlying carrying capacity. Others have argued that the temperature sensitivity of K might be U-shaped because competition should be strongest at temperatures that are optimal for production (Amarasekare 2015). Uszko et al. (2017) derived a unimodal function for algal carrying capacity based on the temperature dependence of nutrient uptake and respiration of algal cells in the absence of grazers, noting that this function must drop to zero at the upper and lower limiting temperatures for intrinsic algal growth. Considering this requirement, they suggested that carrying capacity could, over the range of biologically relevant temperatures, exhibit invariant, unimodal or a decreasing response to

temperature depending on the interplay of nutrient and light limitation. Lemoine (2019) recently developed this idea further by incorporating both external and internal nutrient dynamics into a model of phytoplankton growth. Here the temperature dependence of K is driven by the interplay among five physiological processes that individually respond to temperature. By randomly combining empirical estimates of the sensitivity of these processes, they found strong support for a unimodal response of K and only rare instances of entirely negative and positive curves over the biologically sensitive range (0–40°C). This fits well to a literature survey of thirty-nine experiments, 53% of which showed a unimodal response of K.

14.5 Unimodal responses and community dynamics

Unimodal thermal response curves are typically described by an exponential increase from a low critical temperature (T_{min}) to an optimum temperature (T_{opt}), beyond which the curve crashes sharply, crossing zero at an upper critical temperature (T_{max}). These critical values provide an additional potential for alterations in the equilibrium stability of populations and communities. For example, in the trophic model (Equation (14.2) extinction of the consumer via a transcritical bifurcation is possible at either low or high temperatures, but not both. Using a model similar to Equation (14.2), but where r, a and h^{-1} are replaced by unimodal functions of temperature (Amarasekare 2015), showed that the upper and lower persistence limits for the consumer are determined by a combination of the critical values of r and a, with those of the more thermally restricted population taking precedence. This work clearly demonstrated the potential for thermal mismatches of consumers and resources to destabilize the system under climate warming. This outcome had been clearly predicted by earlier work comparing the thermal sensitivity of consumption and respiration in urchins and other taxa (Lemoine and Burkepile 2012); declines in the rate of consumption at high temperatures ultimately leads to a "mismatch" between the metabolic requirements and acquisition of energy that makes it impossible for the population to persist. Building on this work Uszko et al. (2017) provide the most complete temperature-dependent model of consumer resource dynamics to date, by incorporating an explicitly derived unimodal function for carrying capacity in addition to unimodal sensitivity of r, a, and h^{-1}. Similar to the work of (Amarasekare 2015), they find that consumer persistence depends strongly on the thermal tolerances of the resource, and that oscillations are likely at temperatures optimal for resource growth. When consumers forage with a Type III functional response oscillations are limited to temperatures near the upper and lower critical temperatures for consumer persistence. Interestingly, they showed that enrichment of the system had only a weak interaction with temperature, with its effects more apparent in warmer temperatures.

14.6 Warming and food webs

Using a tri-trophic model, Binzer et al. (2012) explored the effect of warming and enrichment in size-structured communities whose vital rates (and carrying capacity) were increasing (decreasing) functions of temperature. They found that warming strongly decreased the persistence of the secondary and primary consumer, ultimately leaving only the resource population. However, they found that enrichment could counter the effect of warming, suggesting that a substantial part of the temperature effect in their model was mediated by carrying capacity. Using the niche model of food web construction (Williams and Martinez 2000), these results were extended to dynamic size structured food webs (Binzer et al. 2016). They again found that warming strongly decreased species persistence, particularly at low eutrophication, for food webs where consumers are, on average, one hundred times the mass of their resources. This finding strongly reflected their choice of activation energies (which relied on an extensive database of empirical estimates); here the metabolic loss increased more rapidly than ingestion rate, challenging the ability of many non-basal species to persist. Zhang et al. (2017) took a slightly modified approach, incorporating Arrhenius relationships to describe the effects of warming on parameters, but adding a

thermal niche to the birth rate of populations. They found that species responses to temperature change were not predictable from their own thermal niche but relied more on changes to the food web. They demonstrated that continued functioning of the food web relied on whether the system was open to immigration, such that functional roles could be replaced.

To date, there are no studies that have incorporated unimodal responses in complex food web models. While it is impossible to analytically determine the sensitivity of dynamics to temperature once beyond a fairly simple set of small motifs, it is reasonable to assume that: i) the thermal limits of populations at lower trophic positions can strongly influence those at higher trophic positions, and ii) cascades of extinction may occur when the thermal limits of basal resources or keystone species are surpassed. Although it is a rather straightforward exercise to incorporate unimodal temperature responses into models such as those used by Binzer et al. (2016), doing so remains a rather fruitless effort until we have a better roadmap of how, for example, sensitivity to temperature among the various vital rates changes with body size or trophic position.

14.7 Temperature variation at shorter time scales

The body of literature concerning the impact of temperature on communities has mainly been concerned with equilibrium dynamics and the potential for changes in the equilibrium stability of the system with warming. To realize the predictions made under this framework, temperature change must be sufficiently slow to allow the system to remain sufficiently near to equilibrium at all times. However, many aspects of climate change concern the character of fluctuations in temperature at much shorter time scales than these; time scales that will generate transient dynamics that may have particularly drastic consequences. Recently, the importance of temporal variation in temperature has been highlighted as a key driver of fitness (Helmuth et al. 2014; Vasseur et al. 2014; Stoks et al. 2017), but there has been little work extending this to population, community, and food web dynamics. This is surprising given that much of this work relies on the intrinsic growth rate r as a proxy for fitness and so inherently considers population growth as the underlying metric.

One of the major insights into the work on temperature variation and fitness is that moments when temperature exceeds the upper or lower critical limits of a thermal response curve are key determinants of long-term fitness (Woods et al. 2018). Dealing with these moments from a population dynamic perspective is challenging however, since negative intrinsic growth rates generate inconsistencies in the logistic model of population growth that is the cornerstone of more complex models (Mallet 2012). Because r is multiplied by the factor representing density dependence $(1 - N/K)$, negative values of r lead to an inversion of the effect of density dependence thereby weakening the rate of population decline. Some authors have argued that a functional separation of processes exists when r is negative, such that the effects of density dependence can be neglected during these periods. However, to deal with this challenge others have adopted an alternative form of the logistic model based on Verhulst's original form of the logistic (Long et al. 2007; Mallet 2012):

$$\frac{dN}{dt}\frac{1}{N} = (r - \alpha N).\qquad(14.3)$$

Here, r has a similar but not fully equivalent representation as the intrinsic growth rate of the population (see Schoener 1973), and α represents the intraspecific competition coefficient. I herein refer to as this as the r-α model. The two forms of the logistic model (Equations (14.1), (14.3)) are easily interconvertible since the r-α model has an equilibrium value r/α which is equal to K in the classical r-K formulation. However, this equivalence makes it plainly obvious that environmental variables (such as temperature) that have an effect on r, must also have an effect on K except in the instance where the intraspecific competition coefficient varies in a manner that is exactly compensatory. This is of course an extremely unlikely scenario which furthermore generates unlikely singularities at the critical values where $r = 0$. The more likely scenario, in which r and K change in a correlated fashion has rarely been noted in the literature (see Uszko et al. 2017), but provides a clear constraint that resolves the debate about the form of temperature sensitivity in K.

14.8 Deriving an r-K temperature dependent model

The r-α and the r-K version of the Logistic model can be derived in a variety of ways, but the most common ecological interpretation is based on a density-dependent net difference between births and deaths. Assuming that, either one or both the birth and death rates of a population exhibit linear density dependence, we can derive the following:

$$\begin{aligned}\frac{dN}{dt}\frac{1}{N} &= B - D\\ &= b_0 - d_0 - N(\beta + \delta),\qquad(14.4)\end{aligned}$$

where $B = b_0 - \beta N$ and $D = d_0 + \delta N$ define the per-capita birth and death rates as a function of density according to the density dependence constants β and δ. Here, it is clear that for the r-α model, r is the difference between birth and death rates when $N = 0$ and α is the sum of density dependent effects on birth and death $(\beta + \delta)$. Shifting to r-K terminology, r remains as $b_0 - d_0$ and $K = (b_0 - d_0)/(\beta + \delta)$. From this interpretation of the logistic model, it is clear that if the environment has an effect on the density-independent per-capita rates of birth and death, b_0 and d_0, that these effects should manifest in both r and K of the logistic model (but not in α of the alternative form). If the environment effects only the extent to which density alters per-capita birth and death rates, then K would vary independently of r.

The well-established evidence for a unimodal response of r to temperature (Deutsch et al. 2008; Kingsolver 2009; Thomas et al. 2012; Kremer et al. 2018) in many cases comes from studying the rate of population growth under density-independent conditions. Amarasekare and Savage (2012) demonstrated that this relationship could be reconstructed by assuming a symmetric unimodal relationship between temperature and birth rate, coupled to an Arrhenius relationship for death rate. Building on this set of assumptions, I begin with the following set of equations that incorporate temperature dependence into zero-density per-capita birth and death rates. Assuming no interaction between temperature and density dependence these equations are given as:

$$\begin{aligned}B(T,N) &= b_0(T) - \beta N\\ D(T,N) &= d_0(T) + \delta N,\qquad(14.5)\end{aligned}$$

where $b_0(T) = a_b e^{-s^{-1}(T-b_{opt})^2}$ and the death rate is a simple exponential function of temperature $d_0(T) = a_d e^{zT}$. Here, the a_i are intercepts, b_{opt} is the temperature that optimizes birth rates, s governs the breadth of the birth function, and z scales the effect of temperature (in °C) to mimic the Arrhenius relationship. So long as the parameters ensure that B exceeds D at some temperature, $r(T)$ takes on the familiar unimodal, left-skewed shape that is common to thermal performance curves, with critical temperatures for population growth at $T_{min} < b_{opt}$ and $T_{max} > b_{opt}$. Figure 14.3 shows a three-dimensional plot of $B(T, N)$ and $D(T, N)$; here $r(T)$ is given by the difference between the two planes at $N = 0$ and $K(T)$ is given by the projection of the intersection of the two planes onto temperature. It is easily evident that $r(T)$ and $K(T)$ share their form with respect to temperature since they are related through their derivation according to

$$K(T) = r(T) \cdot (\beta + \delta)^{-1}. \qquad (14.6)$$

Because β and δ are the density-dependent constants, $K(T)$ is simply a constant multiple of $r(T)$; thus, the two curves exhibit a perfect covariance with respect to temperature. The optimum temperature for growth, r_{opt}, corresponds perfectly to the temperature that maximizes population size. K_{opt}

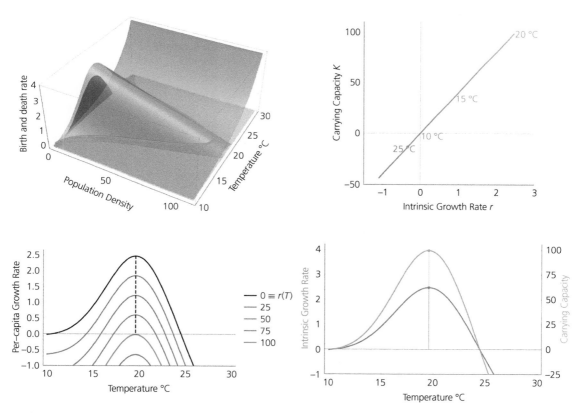

Figure 14.3 The temperature and density dependence of birth and death rate given by Equation 14.5 (green and violet surfaces respectively) interactively determine the joint reliance of r and K on temperature. r(T) is projected in black and K(T) is given by the projection of the intersection of planes (yellow line) onto the bottom plane. Here, density dependence only alters birth rates (e.g., $\delta = 0$) but this has no qualitative effect on the model behavior. In the lower left panel, the temperature dependence of per-capita growth rate (birth–death) is shown for 5 different population densities. The curve when $N = 0$ shows the temperature dependence of r. In the lower right panel, r(T) and K(T) are shown together and the upper-right panel shows their covariance as a function of temperature. In the panels $b_0(T, N) = 3e^{-(T-20)^2/25} - 0.025N$ $b_0(T) = 3e^{-(T-20)^2/25}$ and $d_0(T) = 0.01e^{0.2T}$.

(Figure 14.3). Given the assumptions made here about the nature of birth and death, these optima will always occur at a value less than the optimum for birth b_{opt} (Amarasekare and Savage 2012). Furthermore, it is obvious here that the temperatures at which $r(T)$ and $K(T)$ transition from positive to negative values must be the same. This can be seen in Equation (14.6) where the density-dependence constants have no bearing on the roots of $r(T)$ and $K(T)$. This is visually represented in Figure 14.3 where the curves representing $r(T)$ and $K(T)$ must be equal to zero at precisely the same values. This derivation provides a simple and rather elegant solution to the perceived challenges associated with the scaling of carrying capacity in population and community models. Moreover, it also shows that the r-K version of the logistic model is quite capable of handling negative values of r in a consistent manner; since both $r(T)$ and $K(T)$ switch sign at the same temperature, density dependence is assured to act in the correct manner on per-capita growth rates. It can be shown that this property extends beyond the assumptions made in Equation (14.5) to cases where the strength of density dependence, $\alpha + \beta$, also exhibits temperature sensitivity (see Box 14.1).

14.9 Temperature by density interactions

There are a variety of ways in which temperature might impact the strength of density dependence on population growth. Movement rates of many ectotherms increase in warmer environments (Peters 1986) thereby intensifying opportunities for interactions such as interference competition (Lang et al. 2012). Exploitative competition may also increase if the provisioning of resources is constant since the greater metabolic demand of organisms can lead to a depleted stock of resources. Interactions between temperature and density dependence can also reflect aspects of a biotic resource's response to temperature that arise through its own physiological constraints or interactions with other species.

Box 14.1 describes how the temperature sensitivity of carrying capacity is altered when density dependence is altered by temperature and Figure 14.4 shows an example in which warmer temperatures strengthen density dependence. Although the shift in $K(T)$ modifies the covariance between $r(T)$ and $K(T)$, it does not alter the fact that the two curves intersect zero at precisely the same temperatures (Figure 14.4). The positive

---

Box 14.1 When temperature affects the strength of density dependence

Consistent with the idea that individual resource use increases with temperature, and to provide a working example, the following model exhibits a density dependent reduction in birth rate that increases exponentially with temperature.

$$B(T, N) = a_b e^{-s^{-1}(T - b_{opt})^2} - a_\beta e^{z_\beta T} N$$
$$D(T) = a_d e^{zT}$$

(14.B.1)

Here $r(T)$ remains unchanged from the previous model, but due to the temperature dependence of β, $K(T)$ takes the more complicated form:

$$r(T) = a_b e^{-s^{-1}(T - b_{opt})^2} - a_d e^{zT}$$

$$K(T) = a_\beta^{-1} \left[a_b e^{-s^{-1}(T - b_{opt})^2 - z_\beta T} - a_d e^{T(z - z_\beta)} \right].$$

(14.B.2)

Here, the scaling exponents z_β modifies the optimum of $K(T) \left(\mu_K^{opt} \right)$ relative to that of $r(T) \left(\mu_r^{opt} \right)$. In the case where $z = z_\beta$, indicating that the effect of temperature on death rates and density dependence are the same, the interaction between temperature and density dependence generates a shift in μ_K^{opt} that is equal to $-0.5s \cdot z_\beta\,°C$ (Figure 14.4). This shift is more extreme in cases where $z < z_\beta$. The addition of a temperature and density dependence interaction also reduces $K(T)$ for all values of T (this effect is not demonstrated in Figure 14.4 due to the choice of parameters).

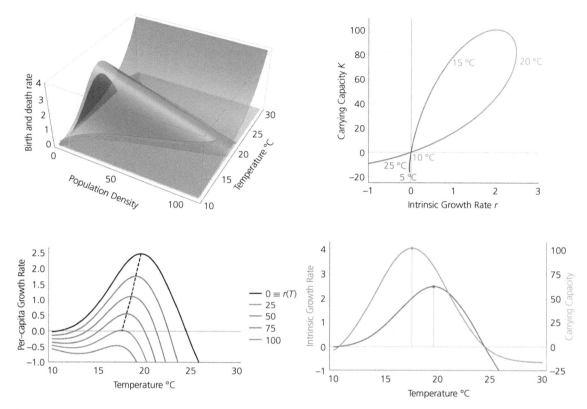

Figure 14.4 The temperature and density dependence of birth and death rate given by Equation 14.B.2 (green and violet surfaces respectively) interactively determine the joint reliance of r and K on temperature. $r(T)$ is projected in black and $K(T)$ is given by the projection of the intersection of planes (yellow line) onto the bottom plane. Here, density dependence alters birth rates interactively with temperature. In the lower left panel, the temperature dependence of per-capita growth rate (birth–death) is shown for 5 different population densities. The curve when $N = 0$ shows the temperature dependence of r. In the lower right panel, $r(T)$ and $K(T)$ are shown together and the upper right panel shows their covariance as a function of temperature. In the panels $b_0 (T, N) = 3e^{-(T-20)^2/25} - 0.0006Ne^{0.2T}$ and $d_0(T) = 0.01e^{0.2T}$.

density-temperature interaction depicted here, demonstrates that cooler temperatures would favor higher carrying capacities at a given r, while warmer temperatures would have reduced K relative to the model without interactions. Furthermore, the model exhibits pronounced differences in the relationship between $r(T)$ and $K(T)$ as the system crosses the upper and lower critical points.

Perhaps surprisingly, an increase in the strengh of density dependence at warmer temperatures leads to a shift in the optimum temperature for growth in more competitive environments (Figure 14.4 lower left). This shift has been observed in experiments where the growth rate of juvenile salmon was measured across a range of food availibity (Brett et al. 1969), and in detailed models

of phtoplankton populations where temperature modified nutrient availability (Thomas et al. 2017). Given that the r-K framework reproduces these imporant and surprising characteristics, further study of this simple framework may provide new insight into how populations respond to variation in temperature.

14.10 Temperature variation, dynamics, and extinction in r-K models

In addition to forming the basis for studies of consumer-resource or food-web dynamics, the r-K models are useful on their own for elucidating the impact of short-term variation on population dynamics. The dynamics of this model can be simulated as a stochastic differential equation (SDE) system (Han and Kloeden 2017), where the dynamics of temperature (T) are given by the stochastic Ornstein-Uhlenbeck (OU) process and the population dynamics (N) are a temperature-dependent deterministic process as defined previously:

$$dT_t = \theta(\mu_T - T_t)dt + \sigma dW_t$$

$$\frac{dN}{dt}\frac{1}{N} = (b_0(T_t) - d_0(T_t))\left(1 - \frac{(\beta + \delta)}{b_0(T_t) - d_0(T_t)}N\right).$$
(14.7)

The Ornstein-Uhlenbeck process generates normally-distributed, temporally-autocorrelated dynamics using a standard Weiner process, dW_t, with volatility σ, that is modified to ensure a tendency to return to the mean value (μ_T). This tendency is given by the reversion rate θ which is herein set at 0.1 to approximate the extent of autocorrelation that naturally occurs in temperature variation (Vasseur and Yodzis 2004). Numerical simulations of the SDE model were simulated as a fine-grained Stratonovich Process in *Mathematica* v. 11.3.

Figure 14.5 shows sample dynamics arising from the two r-K models for three different mean environmental temperatures μ_T. In the temperature-density independent model, when μ_T is set near the modal value of $r(T)$ and $K(T)$ dynamics exhibit

little variability and remain near to the maximum of $K(T)$. Despite the fact that populations are more able to track and therefore embed temperature variation into their dynamics when r is large, here this is offset by relative insensitivity of $K(T)$ near its maximum. At cooler and warmer values of μ_T, $K(T)$ is a more strongly increasing (decreasing) function of temperature, leading to larger variation in $K(T)$. This larger variation translates into greater variation in population dynamics despite a reduction in tracking ability away from the the maximum. As the mean temperature approaches the critical values, the variability in population dynamics becomes small due to the compression of dynamics near zero values and because their ability to track environmental fluctuations is relatively weak. As a confirmation of the key role $K(T)$ plays in determining patterns, the dynamics of the temperature-density dependent model exhibit the least variation around μ_K^{opt}.

Figure 14.6 shows the probability distribution of population size as a function of mean temperature. The interaction of r and K near the upper critical temperature leads to extinctions occuring in environments with mean temperatures substantially less than the critical value. This is a joint effect of the rapid decrease of r and K above the critical value which leads to a strong detrimental effect of

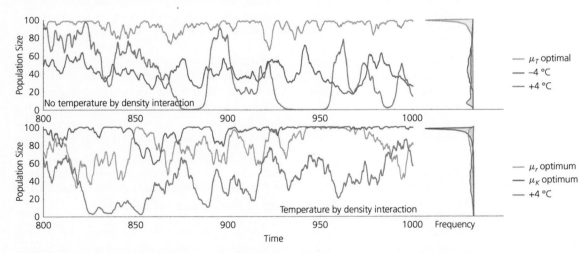

Figure 14.5 Population dynamics for the case without temperature by density interaction (upper) and with temperature by density interaction (lower) when the mean temperature is at the optimum for $r(T)$, and cooler and warmer by 4°C. In the upper panel the μ_T is also the optimum of $K(T)$ whereas in the lower panel the optimum of $K(T)$ is distinct. Histograms at the right show the distribution of population size from $100 < t < 1000$.

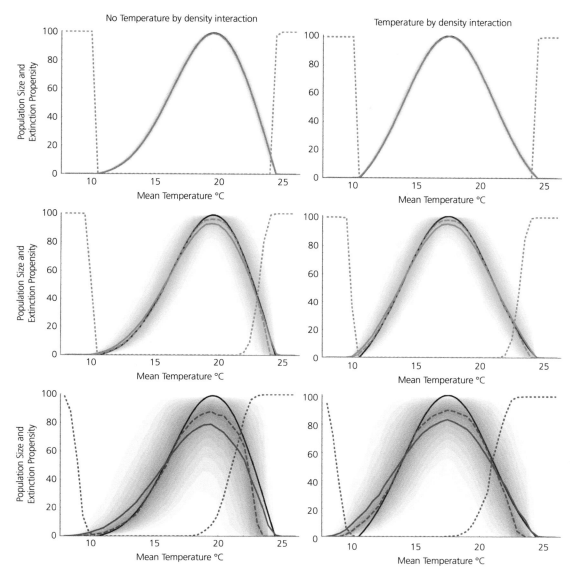

Figure 14.6 Probability densities of population size after 1000 time steps for the Logistic model without (left) and with (right) a density-temperature interaction. Temperature dynamics were simulated by the Ornstein-Uhlenbeck process across a range of mean temperatures with volatility = (top) 0.1, (middle) 0.5 and (bottom) 1.0 and reversion rate = 0.1. Shaded lines denote every 5th quantile of the distribution and the solid line shows the mean. The solid black line is $K(T)$. The dotted line shows the extinction propensity measured as the percentage of replicates that fell below 0.1% of the optimum carrying capacity over the time interval t > 1000.

non-linear averaging (see Vasseur et al. 2014). In contrast, the population is able to tolerate environments with mean conditions at, or even less than the lower critical threshold via a positive effect of non-linear averaging. The fact that both r and K are correlated across these critical points suggests an even greater effect of thermal variability than previous models incorporating only fitness (r) have predicted (Deutsch et al. 2008; Vasseur et al. 2014; Woods et al. 2018).

14.11 Summary and future directions

Including temperature as a driver of key biological rates and ecological thresholds has led to a suite of important predictions about the dynamics of populations and communities. As a whole, these models have driven a more exhaustive study of the rate and functional form of temperature dependence in a variety of key parameters in addition to fueling micro- and mesocosm scale experimental work aimed at understanding the impacts of warming. To date, few studies have taken a close look at the role of shorter-term thermal variability on population dynamics using models that accurately capture the skewed-unimodal nature of temperature responses and none have embedded such dependence into complex food web models. These are both areas deserving further research.

To date, the functional form of temperature dependence of the carrying capacity K, has been challenging to characterize due to the wide variety of assumptions and hypotheses that have been proposed. Recent work, including that developed herein, shows that the sensitivity of K shares a number of key aspects with that of r; notably, the two functions must have the same roots and sign as a function of temperature. Although there is empirical evidence for K as a monotonically increasing, decreasing, and invariant function of temperature, it is possible that these results are capturing results on a subset of the entire unimodal function. More research is needed to better determine how unimodal or more complex interpretations of K relate to the temperature-dependence of intrinsic growth rates.

Body size plays a key role in the determination of a population's carrying capacity and recent work has shown how compensatory changes in body size can play an important role in buffering potential reductions in carrying capacity in warmer environments (Bernhardt et al. 2018). Similarly, changes in body size due to warming have been shown to stabilize consumer-resource interactions (Osmond et al. 2017). Changes in body size due to warming may lead to a host of changes in food webs, particularly when body size determines the strength of trophic interactions in a system. Such changes,

combined with a realistic depiction of the role of temperature on vital rates and carrying capacity, will likely be important in addressing the impact of climate change.

Even in their current form, the relationships that describe the sensitivty of vital rates and thresholds are missing elements that are inherently important in many systems. Thermoregulatory behavior will allow many ectotherms to avoid stressful low and high temperatures, but will potentially incurr the additional cost of reducing their time spent foraging or increasing their vulnerability to predation (Fey and Vasseur 2016; Sears et al. 2016). Within the lifetime of an individual, exposure to critical temperatures can invoke protective measures such as heat shock proteins that diminish the detrimental effects of future exposure (Sinclair et al. 2016). Furthermore, gradual acclimation has been shown to be an important process that decouples acute biological rates from those predicted under chronic exposure to a certain temperature (Sentis et al. 2015; Kremer et al. 2018; Woods et al. 2018). Acclimation may have largely different effects across biologial rates within and across species, challenging our ability to predict the effects of temperature variation, at least in response to temperature variabiliity at shorter time scales. At longer scales, evolution may play a key role in reshaping the thermal responses of parameters. There are thought to be a number of important tradeoffs governing the evolution of thermal performance curves (Angilletta et al. 2003; Bennett and Lenski 2007), but to date, there is no clear best practies on how to constrain evolution in a manner that ensures meaningful theoretical predictions.

There is no doubt that climate change will yield novel environmental conditions that generate qualitative and quantitative changes in population and community dynamics. While temperature may play a key role in certain placers, there are few, if any, ecosystems on Earth where temperature change will occur in isolation of other environmental variables. Research on the interaction of multiple stressors at the population and community level will ultimately serve to provide a more comprehensive picture of ecological systems in the next decade and beyond.

References

Ainsworth, E. A. and S. P. Long. (2005). What have we learned from 15 years of free-air CO_2 enrichment (FACE)? A meta-analytic review of the responses of photosynthesis, canopy properties and plant production to rising CO_2. *New Phytologist* 165: 351–72.

Amarasekare, P. (2015). Effects of temperature on consumer–resource interactions. *Journal of Animal Ecology* 84: 665–79.

Amarasekare, P. and V. Savage. (2012). A Framework for Elucidating the Temperature Dependence of Fitness. *The American Naturalist* 179: 178–91.

Andrewartha, H. G. (1954). *The Distribution and Abundance of Animals*. Chicago, Ill: University of Chicago Press.

Angilletta, M. J. (2006). Estimating and comparing thermal performance curves. *Journal of Thermal Biology* 31: 541–5.

Angilletta, M. J., R. S. Wilson, C. A. Navas, and R. S. James. (2003). Tradeoffs and the evolution of thermal reaction norms. *Trends in Ecology & Evolution* 18: 234–40.

Barton, B. T., A. P. Beckerman, and O. J. Schmitz. (2009). Climate warming strengthens indirect interactions in an old-field food web. *Ecology* 90: 2346–51.

Bender, E. A., T. J. Case, and M. E. Gilpin. (1984). Perturbation experiments in community ecology: Theory and practice. *Ecology* 65: 1–13.

Bennett, A. F. and R. E. Lenski. (2007). An experimental test of evolutionary trade-offs during temperature adaptation. *Proceedings of the National Academy of Sciences* 104: 8649–54.

Bernhardt, J. R., J. M. Sunday, and M. I. O'Connor. (2018). Metabolic theory and the temperature-size rule explain the temperature dependence of population carrying capacity. *the American Naturalist* 192: 687–97.

Binzer, A., C. Guill, U. Brose, and B. C. Rall. (2012). The dynamics of food chains under climate change and nutrient enrichment. *Phil. Trans. R. Soc. B* 367: 2935–44.

Binzer, A., C. Guill, B. C. Rall, and U. Brose. (2016). Interactive effects of warming, eutrophication and size structure: Impacts on biodiversity and food-web structure. *Global change biology* 22: 220–7.

Boyce, M. S. and D. J. Daley. (1980). Population tracking of fluctuating environments and natural selection for tracking ability. *The American Naturalist* 115: 480–91.

Brett, J. R., J. E. Shelbourn, and C. T. Shoop. (1969). Growth rate and body composition of Fingerling Sockeye Salmon, Oncorhynchus Nerka, in relation to temperature and ration size. *Journal of the Fisheries Research Board of Canada* 26: 2363–94.

Brown, J. H., J. F. Gillooly, A. P. Allen, V. M. Savage, and G. B. West. (2004). Toward a metabolic theory of ecology. *Ecology* 85: 1771–89.

Carpenter, S. R., J. J. Cole, J. R. Hodgson, J. F. Kitchell, M. L. Pace, D. Bade, K. L. Cottingham, T. E. Essington, J. N. Houser, and D. E. Schindler. (2001). Trophic cascades, nutrients, and lake productivity: Whole-Lake experiments. *Ecological Monographs* 71: 163–86.

Cuddington, K. M. and P. Yodzis. (1999). Black noise and population persistence. *Proceedings of the Royal Society of London B: Biological Sciences* 266: 969–73.

Cyr∗, H., and I. Cyr‡. (2003). Temporal scaling of temperature variability from land to oceans. *Evolutionary Ecology Research* 5: 1183–97.

Dell, A. I., S. Pawar, and V. M. Savage. (2011). Systematic variation in the temperature dependence of physiological and ecological traits. *Proceedings of the National Academy of Sciences* 108: 10591–6.

Dell, A. I., S. Pawar, and V. M. Savage. (2014). Temperature dependence of trophic interactions are driven by asymmetry of species responses and foraging strategy. *Journal of Animal Ecology* 83: 70–84.

Deutsch, C. A., J. J. Tewksbury, R. B. Huey, K. S. Sheldon, C. K. Ghalambor, D. C. Haak, and P. R. Martin. (2008). Impacts of climate warming on terrestrial ectotherms across latitude. *Proceedings of the National Academy of Sciences* 105: 6668–72.

Easterling, D. R., G. A. Meehl, C. Parmesan, S. A. Changnon, T. R. Karl, and L. O. Mearns. (2000). Climate extremes: Observations, modeling, and impacts. *Science* 289: 2068–74.

Englund, G., G. Öhlund, C. L. Hein, and S. Diehl. (2011). Temperature dependence of the functional response. *Ecology Letters* 14: 914–21.

Eppley, R. W. (1972). Temperature and phytoplankton growth in the sea. *Fishery Bulletin* 70: 1063–85.

Fey, S. B. and D. A. Vasseur. (2016). Thermal variability alters the impact of climate warming on consumer–resource systems. *Ecology* 97: 1690–9.

Field, C. B., V. Barros, T. F. Stocker, D. Qin, D. J. Dokken, K. L. Ebi, M. D. Mastrandrea, K. J. Mach, G. K. Plattner, and S. K. Allen. (2012). Managing the risks of extreme events and disasters to advance climate change adaptation. A Special Report of Working Groups I and II of the Intergovernmental Panel on Climate Change. Cambridge, UK, and New York, N.Y, USA: Cambridge University Press.

Fussmann, K. E., F. Schwarzmüller, U. Brose, A. Jousset, and B. C. Rall. (2014a). Ecological stability in response to warming. *Nature Climate Change* 4: 206.

Fussmann, K. E., F. Schwarzmüller, U. Brose, A. Jousset, and B. C. Rall. (2014b). Ecological stability in response to warming. *Nature Climate Change* 4: 206–10.

Gilbert, B., T. D. Tunney, K. S. McCann, J. P. DeLong, D. A. Vasseur, V. Savage, J. B. Shurin, A. I. Dell, B. T. Barton, and C. D. Harley. (2014). A bioenergetic framework for the temperature dependence of trophic interactions. *Ecology Letters* 17: 902–14.

Gillooly, J. F., J. H. Brown, G. B. West, V. M. Savage, and E. L. Charnov. (2001). Effects of size and temperature on metabolic rate. *Science* 293: 2248–51.

Gonzalez, A., and R. D. Holt. (2002). The inflationary effects of environmental fluctuations in source–sink systems. *Proceedings of the National Academy of Sciences* 99: 14872–7.

Han, X., and P. E. Kloeden. (2017). Stochastic differential equations. In Xiaoying Han and Peter E. Kloeden (eds.) *Random Ordinary Differential Equations and Their Numerical Solution*. Singapore: Springer, pp. 29–36.

Heino, M., J. Ripa, and V. Kaitala. (2000). Extinction risk under coloured environmental noise. *Ecography* 23: 177–84.

Heino, M. and M. Sabadell. (2003). Influence of coloured noise on the extinction risk in structured population models. *Biological Conservation* 110: 315–25.

Helmuth, B., B. D. Russell, S. D. Connell, Y. Dong, C. D. Harley, F. P. Lima, G. Sará, G. A. Williams, and N. Mieszkowska. (2014). Beyond long-term averages: Making biological sense of a rapidly changing world. *Climate Change Responses* 1:6, https://doi.org/10.1186/s40665-014-0006-0

Holling, C. S. (1959). Some characteristics of simple types of predation and parasitism. *The Canadian Entomologist* 91: 385–98.

Huey, R. B., M. R. Kearney, A. Krockenberger, J. A. M. Holtum, M. Jess, and S. E. Williams. (2012). Predicting organismal vulnerability to climate warming: Roles of behaviour, physiology and adaptation. *Philosophical Transactions of the Royal Society B: Biological Sciences* 367: 1665–79.

Jarvis, L., K. McCann, T. Tunney, G. Gellner, and J. M. Fryxell. (2016). Early warning signals detect critical impacts of experimental warming. *Ecology And Evolution* 6: 6097–106.

Kearney, M., R. Shine, and W. P. Porter. (2009). The potential for behavioral thermoregulation to buffer "cold-blooded" animals against climate warming. *Proceedings of the National Academy of Sciences* 106: 3835–40.

Kingsolver, J. G. (2009). The Well-temperatured biologist. *The American Naturalist* 174: 755–68.

Kremer, C. T., S. B. Fey, A. A. Arellano, and D. A. Vasseur. (2018). Gradual plasticity alters population dynamics in variable environments: Thermal acclimation in the green alga *Chlamydomonas Reinhartdii*. *Proc. R. Soc. B* 285: 20171942.

Laakso, J., V. Kaitala, and E. Ranta. (2001). How does environmental variation translate into biological processes? *Oikos* 92: 119–22.

Lang, B., B. C. Rall, and U. Brose. (2012). Warming effects on consumption and intraspecific interference competition depend on predator metabolism. *Journal of Animal Ecology* 81: 516–23.

Lemoine, N. P. (2019). Considering the effects of temperature x nutrient interactions on the thermal response curve of carrying capacity. *Ecology* 100(4): e02599.

Lemoine, N. P. and D. E. Burkepile. (2012). Temperature-induced mismatches between consumption and metabolism reduce consumer fitness. *Ecology* 93: 2483–9.

Levins, R. (1969). The effect of random variations of different types on population growth. *Proceedings of the National Academy of Sciences* 62: 1061–5.

Lewontin, R. C. and D. Cohen. (1969). On population growth in a randomly varying environment. *Proceedings of the National Academy of Sciences* 62: 1056–60.

Long, Z. T., O. L. Petchey, and R. D. Holt. (2007). The effects of immigration and environmental variability on the persistence of an inferior competitor. *Ecology Letters* 10: 574–85.

Mallet, J. (2012). The struggle for existence. How the notion of carrying capacity, K, obscures the links between demography, Darwinian evolution and speciation. *Evolutionary Ecology Research* 14: 627–65.

May, R. M. (1976). *Theoretical Ecology, Principles and Applications*. Oxford: Blackwell Scientific.

Meehl, G. A. and C. Tebaldi. (2004). More intense, more frequent, and longer lasting heat waves in the 21st century. *Science* 305: 994–7.

Mohaghegh, D. Clercq and Tirry. (2001). Functional response of the predators Podisus maculiventris (Say) and Podisus nigrispinus (Dallas) (Het., Pentatomidae) to the beet armyworm, Spodoptera exigua (Hübner) (Lep., Noctuidae): Effect of temperature. *Journal of Applied Entomology* 125: 131–4.

O'Connor, M. I., B. Gilbert, and C. J. Brown. (2011). Theoretical predictions for how temperature affects the dynamics of interacting herbivores and plants. *The American Naturalist* 178: 626–38.

Osmond, M. M., M. A. Barbour, J. R. Bernhardt, M. W. Pennell, J. M. Sunday, and M. I. O'Connor. (2017). Warming-Induced changes to body size stabilize consumer-resource dynamics. *The American Naturalist* 189: 718–25.

Petchey, O. L., P. T. McPhearson, T. M. Casey, and P. J. Morin. (1999). Environmental warming alters food-web structure and ecosystem function. *Nature* 402: 69–72.

Petchey, O. L., M. Pontarp, T. M. Massie, S. Kéfi, A. Ozgul, M. Weilenmann, G. M. Palamara, F. Altermatt,

B. Matthews, J. M. Levine, D. Z. Childs, B. J. McGill, M. E. Schaepman, B. Schmid, P. Spaak, A. P. Beckerman, F. Pennekamp, and I. S. Pearse. (2015). The ecological forecast horizon, and examples of its uses and determinants. *Ecology Letters* 18: 597–611.

Peters, R. H. (1986). *The Ecological Implications of Body Size*. Cambridge: Cambridge University Press.

Rall, B. C., U. Brose, M. Hartvig, G. Kalinkat, F. Schwarzmüller, O. Vucic-Pestic, and O. L. Petchey. (2012). Universal temperature and body-mass scaling of feeding rates. *Philosophical Transactions: Biological Sciences* 367: 2923–34.

Rall, B. C., O. Vucic-Pestic, R. B. Ehnes, M. Emmerson, and U. Brose. (2010). Temperature, predator–prey interaction strength and population stability. *Global Change Biology* 16: 2145–57.

Ripa, J. and P. Lundberg. (1996). Noise colour and the risk of population extinctions. *Proc. R. Soc. Lond. B* 263: 1751–3.

Rosenzweig, M. L. (1971). Paradox of enrichment: Destabilization of exploitation ecosystems in ecological time. *Science* 171: 385.

Rosenzweig, M. L. and R. H. MacArthur. (1963). Graphical representation and stability conditions of predator-prey interactions. *The American Naturalist* 97(895): 209–23.

Roughgarden, J. (1975). A simple model for population dynamics in stochastic environments. *The American Naturalist* 109: 713–36.

Roy, M., R. D. Holt, and M. Barfield. (2005). Temporal autocorrelation can enhance the persistence and abundance of metapopulations comprised of coupled sinks. *The American Naturalist* 166: 246–61.

Savage, V. M., J. F. Gillooly, J. H. Brown, G. B. West, and E. L. Charnov. (2004). Effects of body size and temperature on population growth. *The American Naturalist* 163: 429–41.

Schoener, T. W. (1973). Population growth regulated by intraspecific competition for energy or time: Some simple representations. *Theoretical Population Biology* 4: 56–84.

Schwager, M., K. Johst, and F. Jeltsch. (2006). Does red noise increase or decrease extinction risk? Single extreme events versus series of unfavorable conditions. *The American Naturalist* 167: 879–88.

Sears, M. W., M. J. Angilletta, M. S. Schuler, J. Borchert, K. F. Dilliplane, M. Stegman, T. W. Rusch, and W. A. Mitchell. (2016). Configuration of the thermal landscape determines thermoregulatory performance of ectotherms. *Proceedings of the National Academy of Sciences* 113: 10595–600.

Sentis, A., A. Binzer, and D. S. Boukal. (2017). Temperature-size responses alter food chain persistence across environmental gradients. *Ecology Letters* 20: 852–62.

Sentis, A., J. Morisson, and D. S. Boukal. (2015). Thermal acclimation modulates the impacts of temperature and enrichment on trophic interaction strengths and population dynamics. *Global Change Biology* 21: 3290–8.

Shurin, J. B., J. L. Clasen, H. S. Greig, P. Kratina, and P. L. Thompson. (2012). Warming shifts top-down and bottom-up control of pond food web structure and function. *Philosophical Transactions of the Royal Society of London B: Biological Sciences* 367: 3008–17.

Sinclair, B. J., K. E. Marshall, M. A. Sewell, D. L. Levesque, C. S. Willett, S. Slotsbo, Y. Dong, C. D. Harley, D. J. Marshall, and B. S. Helmuth. (2016). Can we predict ectotherm responses to climate change using thermal performance curves and body temperatures? *Ecology Letters* 19: 1372–85.

Stoks, R., J. Verheyen, M. Van Dievel, and N. Tüzün. (2017). Daily temperature variation and extreme high temperatures drive performance and biotic interactions in a warming world. *Current Opinion in Insect Science* 23: 35–42.

Thomas, M. K., M. Aranguren-Gassis, C. T. Kremer, M. R. Gould, K. Anderson, C. A. Klausmeier, and E. Litchman. (2017). Temperature–nutrient interactions exacerbate sensitivity to warming in phytoplankton. *Global Change Biology* 23: 3269–80.

Thomas, M. K., C. T. Kremer, C. A. Klausmeier, and E. Litchman. (2012). A global pattern of thermal adaptation in marine phytoplankton. *Science* 338: 1085–8.

Tuljapurkar, S. D. (1982). Population dynamics in variable environments. II. Correlated environments, sensitivity analysis and dynamics. *Theoretical Population Biology* 21: 114–40.

Uszko, W. and S. Diehl. (2016). Temperature dependence of the Type III functional response in Daphnia. Ph.D dissertation. Umeoa University.

Uszko, W., S. Diehl, G. Englund, and P. Amarasekare. (2017). Effects of warming on predator–prey interactions—a resource-based approach and a theoretical synthesis. *Ecology Letters* 20: 513–23.

Vasseur, D. A. (2007). Populations embedded in trophic communities respond differently to coloured environmental noise. *Theoretical Population Biology* 72: 186–96.

Vasseur, D. A., J. P. DeLong, B. Gilbert, H. S. Greig, C. D. G. Harley, K. S. McCann, V. Savage, T. D. Tunney, and M. I. O'Connor. (2014). Increased temperature variation poses a greater risk to species than climate warming. *Proceedings of the Royal Society B: Biological Sciences* 281: 20132612.

Vasseur, D. A. and K. S. McCann. (2005). A mechanistic approach for modeling temperature-dependent consumer-resource dynamics. *The American Naturalist* 166: 184–98.

Vasseur, D. A. and P. Yodzis. (2004). The color of environmental noise. *Ecology* 85: 1146–52.

Wang, B. and D. N. Ferro. (1998). Functional responses of *Trichogramma Ostriniae (Hymenoptera: Trichogrammatidae)* to *Ostrinia nubilalis (Lepidoptera: Pyralidae)* under laboratory and field conditions. *Environmental Entomology* 27: 752–8.

Wichmann, M. C., K. Johst, M. Schwager, B. Blasius, and F. Jeltsch. (2005). Extinction risk, coloured noise and the scaling of variance. *Theoretical Population Biology* 68: 29–40.

Williams, R. J. and N. D. Martinez. (2000). Simple rules yield complex food webs. *Nature* 404: 180.

Woods, H. A., J. G. Kingsolver, S. B. Fey, and D. A. Vasseur. (2018). Uncertainty in geographical estimates of performance and fitness. *Methods in Ecology and Evolution* 9: 1996–2008.

Yodzis, P. and S. Innes. (1992). Body size and consumer-resource dynamics. *The American Naturalist* 139: 1151–75.

Yvon-Durocher, G., A. P. Allen, M. Cellamare, M. Dossena, K. J. Gaston, M. Leitao, J. M. Montoya, D. C. Reuman, G. Woodward, and M. Trimmer. (2015). Five years of experimental warming increases the biodiversity and productivity of phytoplankton. *PLoS biology* 13: e1002324.

Zhang, L., D. Takahashi, M. Hartvig, and K. H. Andersen. (2017). Food-web dynamics under climate change. *Proc. R. Soc. B* 284: 20171772.

CHAPTER 15

Alternative stable states, tipping points, and early warning signals of ecological transitions

John M. Drake, Suzanne M. O'Regan, Vasilis Dakos, Sonia Kéfi, and Pejman Rohani

15.1 Introduction

15.1.1 Tipping points in dynamical systems

Biological populations and ecosystems commonly exhibit *alternative stable states*. For instance, some species display cooperative behavior such as group foraging or coordinated defense. If the cooperative behavior is necessary for the growth of populations at small sizes, such that there is a *critical population size* below which the population cannot persist, then the population is said to exhibit a *strong Allee effect* (Allee et al. 1949; Courchamp et al. 1999). Above this threshold, the population will approach a carrying capacity. Another example comes from the dynamics of shallow lakes, which are often found in either a clear state dominated by aquatic vegetation or a turbid state dominated by algae (Scheffer et al. 1993). The transition between these two states is typically controlled by nutrient inputs or top down regulation through trophic cascades (Carpenter et al. 2008). Transitions between alternative stable states may, of course, arise by a direct change of state. For instance, a subcritical population subject to Allee effects may be supplemented with enough individuals to exceed the critical size. In this case, the dynamical tendencies of the population have not changed, but its size has been adjusted so that it now tends upward, toward carrying capacity, rather than downward toward extinction. A less obvious cause for transition among alternative stable states is the slow drift in some external condition, such as the influx of phosphorus to a lake, that changes the system's dynamical tendencies. In this case, the system may move to a point where qualitative features, such as stable states, appear or disappear. The points at which these qualitative changes occur, e.g., a particular level of phosphorus loading, are tipping points that govern the possible behaviors of the system. Changes in the system state associated with such tipping points are *critical transitions*.

Drake, J. M., O'Regan, S. M., Dakos, V., Kéfi, S., and Rohani, P., *Alternative stable states, tipping points, and early warning signals of ecological transitions*
In: *Theoretical Ecology: Concepts and Applications*. Edited by: Kevin S. McCann and Gabriel Gellner, Oxford University Press (2020). © Oxford University Press.
DOI: 10.1093/oso/9780198824282.003.0015

To derive a theory for critical transitions, we begin by considering a general model for the growth of an isolated population with carrying capacity N,

$$\frac{dn}{dt} = A(n,t) = b(n,t) - d(n,t), \qquad (15.1)$$

where $n(t)$ is the population, $b(n, t)$ is birth rate and $d(n, t)$ is death rate. The model has equilibrium states at the equilibrium $n^* = 0$ and where $b(n,t) = d(n,t)$ at some time t. Our theory is concerned with critical transitions that occur over long time scales, for example, gradual variations in demographic parameters due to shifts in phenotypic, behavioral or life history traits as a result of climate change, or increases in anthropogenic pressures such as harvest effort or land use. To model gradual changes appropriately, we couple Equation (15.1) to another equation describing underlying changes in system parameters. For instance, assuming gradual changes in the birth rate, we have

$$\frac{\partial b(n,t)}{\partial t} = \varepsilon f(t), \qquad (15.2)$$

where $f(t)$ is a continuous, non-zero function of t. The rate of change is determined by ε and its magnitude is assumed to be small relative to the population dynamics, such that $0 < \varepsilon \ll 1$. Equations (15.1) and (15.2) together form a *fast-slow system* (Kuehn 2015). This model assumes that the birth rate changes slowly over long time scales. A system with nonlinear feedback will typically exhibit parameter-dependent stable steady states. For instance, in (15.1) possible states include *extinction* (if $n^* = 0$ is the stable equilibrium) and the *carrying capacity*, the value $n^* = N$ such that $b(N,t) = d(N,t)$ (if $n^* = N$ is the stable equilibrium). Typically, critical transitions occur when the slow change in $b(n, t)$ causes (15.1) to go through a *bifurcation* (Strogatz 2014). Because (15.1) and (15.2) are coupled, such a bifurcation is sometimes called a *dynamic bifurcation* (Hale 1984).

How do we study such models? Typically, ε will be so small that for short periods of time it will be acceptable to make the simplifying assumption that r is unchanging over a time interval of interest. This is the assumption of *separability of time scales*. Thus, for short time intervals, we will consider only Equation 15.1 (or its stochastic counterpart, see the following) and not the full fast-slow system. In this case, we can use the tools of linear stability analysis. For a system in one dimension with the form $\frac{dn}{dt} = A(n)$, we consider a fixed point n^* and

let $\xi(t) = n(t) - n^*$ be a small perturbation from n^*. To determine whether ξ grows or decays we note that $\frac{d\xi}{dt} = A(n) = A(n^* + \xi)$. Now, $A(n^* + \xi)$ is expressed in terms of the Taylor expansion $A(n^* + \xi) = A(n^*) + A'(n^*)\xi + O(\xi^2)$. Ignoring the $O(\xi^2)$ terms, defining the eigenvalue $\lambda = A'(n^*)$, and noting that $A(n^*) = 0$, we have the approximation $\frac{d\xi}{dt} = \lambda\xi$ with solution $\xi(t) = \xi e^{\lambda t}$. Thus, if the eigenvalue $\lambda < 0$, the perturbation will decay to zero and the point n^* is stable. Alternatively, if $\lambda > 0$ the system diverges from its equilibrium, n^*, which is unstable. A bifurcation occurs at $\lambda = 0$, which is a tipping point of the system (Strogatz 2014).

15.1.2 Early warning signals

Early warning signals are statistical features of systems that anticipate the approach to a tipping point (Scheffer et al. 2009). They arise from the interaction between noise and the tendency of the nonlinear system to return to its asymptotic states. Many statistical features are qualitatively identical when the system is sufficiently close to a tipping point, leading to a great deal of interest in identifying model-independent early warning signals that could be exploited to create early warning systems—information systems to provide advance warning of the approach to a critical transition. Such model-independent indicators are primarily due to *critical slowing down*, which refers to the loss of resilience (Scheffer et al. 2015), which is the tendency of the system to return more slowly to its steady state as the bifurcation is approached. The autocovariance function and dependent statistical summaries such as the variance, autocorrelation coefficient or power spectrum are then affected in predictable ways as the system approaches the critical point. The source of noise driving such early warning signals may be intrinsic (e.g., *demographic stochasticity*) or extrinsic (e.g., *environmental stochasticity*, which are environmental fluctuations that affect the demographic events experienced by all individuals). In both cases, the state of the system n must be considered a random variable. Accordingly, the deterministic representation of the system used in the previous section will no longer be adequate. Instead, the system is represented by stochastic differential equations. In one dimension,

$$dn = A(n,\theta)dt + \sqrt{B(n,\theta)}dW. \qquad (15.3)$$

This equation consists of two terms, one for the *mean field*, $A(n, \theta)$, and a second for the *fluctuations*, $\sqrt{B(n,\theta)}$. $W(t)$ is a Wiener process or Brownian motion process, meaning that incremental changes ΔW are normally distributed with mean 0 and variance Δt. Typically, the mean field is dependent on both the state of the system and some unobservable parameters, collected in the vector θ. Separating the mean field and fluctuations, the mean field can also be written as a differential equation $\frac{dn}{dt} = A(n, \theta)$, which is sometimes referred to as the "deterministic skeleton" but is just as readily interpreted as the mean flow in a "fully" stochastic system. As the fluctuations go to zero, this representation reduces to a deterministic equation. Different sources of noise (e.g., demographic and environmental stochasticity) give rise to different forms for the fluctuations (O'Regan and Burton

2018). An example of a stochastic differential equation in ecology is provided in Box 15.1.

In one dimension, under continuity and boundary conditions that are typically satisfied (or approximately satisfied) for ecological systems, n will approach a stationary (or quasi-stationary) distribution,

$$P(n) = \frac{\mathcal{N}}{B(n,\phi)} \exp\left(2\int_0^n \frac{A(x,\theta)}{B(x,\theta)}dx\right), \quad (15.4)$$

where $\mathcal{N}$ is a normalization constant that ensures $\int_1^\infty P(n)dn = 1$ (Nisbet and Gurney 1982; Gardiner 2009). Numerous other statistical properties may be derived. Importantly, the eigenvalue of the mean field equation, $\lambda = \frac{d}{dn}A(n,\theta)$, evaluated at an equilibrium n^* not only gives the stability of the equilibrium in the deterministic sense elaborated previously, but is also a key determinant of the

---

Box 15.1 Example: A stochastic logistic model

To illustrate the use of a stochastic differential equation in ecology, we consider a stochastic version of the familiar logistic model for regulated population growth. A stochastic logistic growth equation may be obtained by substituting $A(n,\theta) = rn(1 - n/K)$ and $B(n,\theta) = gn$ into Equation 15.3 to obtain

$$dn = rn(1 - n/K)dt + \sqrt{gn}\,dW.$$

We numerically solve the model for two different parameter combinations using Euler's method (Allen 2011). For these solutions, the intrinsic rate of increase, r, was set to 1.0

and 0.2, respectively. In both cases, the carrying capacity, K, was set to 100 and the diffusion parameter, g, was set to one. The logistic model exhibits a transcritical bifurcation at $r = 0$, at which point the equilibrium at carrying capacity loses stability and extinction becomes the attracting state. Thus, the difference between the two simulations is not in the long run average state (for these values of r both solutions fluctuate around $n^* = 100$) but in (15.1) the speed at which they grow from near extinction at the start of the simulation, and (15.2) the damping of perturbations around carrying capacity.

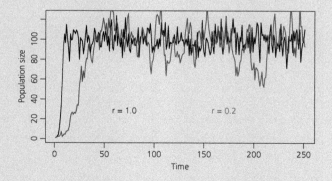

continued

Box 15.1 *Continued*

It is immediately apparent from these simulations that *r* governs more than just the speed of population growth, however. Specifically, the model that is closer to the bifurcation (*r* = 0.2, blue line) exhibits a solution that is more variable, with long sojourns away from the carrying capacity, compared with the model with the model where *r* = 1.0.

The following plot shows a histogram of the distribution of population sizes visited by each simulation in the period from Time 50 to Time 250 (to allow for the transient growth at the start of the simulation to disappear). As expected, the sample variance in the population with *r* = 0.2 is much larger than in the population with *r* = 1.0.

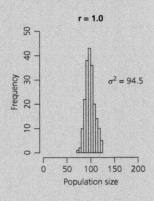

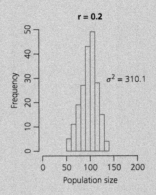

Additionally, the blue line (*r* = 0.2) appears to exhibit longer "runs" than the black line (*r* = 1.0). This is a feature of the

greater autocorrelation in the model closer to the tipping point. This is verified by inspection of the autocorrelation function.

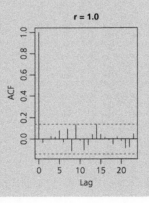

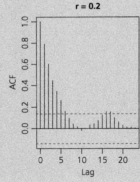

properties of the stochastic system. For instance, we derive a linear approximation to (15.3) by retaining leading terms of the Taylor expansions of $A(n, \theta)$ and $B(n, \theta)$ about n^*, yielding an Ornstein–Uhlenbeck equation,

$$d\xi = \lambda \xi dt + \sqrt{B(n^*, \theta)}\, dW. \tag{15.5}$$

Recall that $\lambda < 0$ because n^* is stable by assumption. Equation (15.5) additionally arises formally from the *Van Kampen system size expansion*, described in Section 2. The stationary or quasi-stationary variance of (15.5) is,

$$\sigma^2 \approx \frac{B(n^*, \theta)}{2|\lambda|}. \tag{15.6}$$

Thus, as the tipping point at $\lambda = 0$ is approached, the variance diverges (i.e., the denominator in Equation (15.6) become smaller and smaller as λ becomes less and less negative, causing the entire expression to blow up). This feature, where the eigenvalue is in the denominator of a formula for the theoretical variance, is a ubiquitous feature of stochastic systems. This is the cause of the observation that the variance of a stochastic system typically increases as a critical transition is approached (Gilmore 1981).

Another related concept is the *potential function*, a function $U(n)$ taking the form,

$$U(n) = \int_{n*}^{n} f(s)ds, \qquad (15.7)$$

so that $\frac{dn}{dt} = -U'(n)$. The potential is a curve or surface in n that has it's minimum at the equilibrium n^* giving rise to the "ball and cups" heuristic (Figure 15.1) (Scheffer et al. 2001; Nolting and Abbott 2016). A system starting at any point n will move "downhill" in this diagram, which is particularly useful for visualizing the behaviors of bistable systems (which exhibit "double well" potentials) and transitions that may occur when a parametric change in $U(n)$ causes one of the bistable states to be lost. Typically, this corresponds to a saddle-node bifurcation. The resulting *cusp catastrophe* can give rise to sudden system shifts of large magnitude and *hysteresis*, a phenomenon in which the steady state of a system may depend on its history. The cusp catastrophe, in particular, has motivated a lot of theory on critical transitions in ecology and is a widely accepted explanation for existence of alternative stable states in shallow lake ecosystems (Scheffer et al. 1993).

Identifying $A(n, \theta)$ with $-U'(n)$, and assuming the fluctuations to be independent of the population size n, we can also write Equation 15.3 as

$$dn = -U'(n)dt + \sqrt{B(\theta)}\,dW. \qquad (15.8)$$

This representation shows that important features of that shape, such as the direction of motion from any given point and the location of any equilibria, are independent of the noise, which is measured by $\sqrt{B(\theta)}$. As previously demonstrated, one may derive the stationary probability density of states, which is commonly expressed in the form

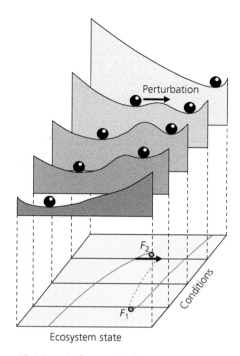

Figure 15.1 Potential functions (at different parameterizations) of a bistable system exhibiting a saddle-node bifurcation illustrate the concept of alternative stable states. Depending on conditions, the system can persist in a "high" state, a "low" state, or exhibit alternative stable states. Solid blue lines in the bifurcation diagram depict stable equilibria. The dashed blue line is an unstable branch. Tipping points (saddle-node bifurcations) occur at F_1 and F_2. Reprinted by permission from *Nature*, Scheffer et al. (2001.)

$$P(n) = \mathcal{N} \exp\left(-\frac{2U(n)}{B(\theta)}\right), \qquad (15.9)$$

where the normalization constant is $\mathcal{N} = 1/\int_0^\infty \exp\left(-\frac{2U(n)}{B(\theta)}dn\right)$. From this formula comes the proposal that by interpreting measurements of the system state over time as samples from (15.9) one might reconstruct the potential $U(n)$, the qualitative features of which provide insight into the critical behaviors of the system (Ditlevsen and Johnsen 2010; Livina et al. 2010). For instance, if the system exhibits two alternative stable states, then the histogram of measurements will be bimodal (Gilmore 1981). These and many other properties of simple stochastic systems are elaborated in Nisbet and Gurney (1982) and Gardiner (2009).

15.1.3 Bifurcation delay

In many applications, a key question is when the system will undergo a transition between alternative stable states. Importantly, this may not coincide with a bifurcation in the system's mean field. In systems where there are two coexisting stable equilibria, a change in the basin of attraction can occur due to sufficiently large change of state without any movement in the underlying attractor. Similarly, as the fast system moves closer and closer to a bifurcation, the size of displacement necessary to make this change gets smaller and smaller. As a consequence, in bistable systems the shift from one basin of attraction to another is very likely to occur before the bifurcation in the mean field due to a stochastic perturbation (Scheffer et al. 2015). On the other hand, in other systems, particularly those where the tipping point corresponds to a transcritical bifurcation or Hopf bifurcation, the change in system state may not occur until some time after the bifurcation in the system's mean field, a situation referred to as *bifurcation delay* (Berglund and Gentz 2006; Dibble et al. 2016).

15.2 Theory

15.2.1 Birth-death processes

As hinted at previously, the key to anticipating critical transitions is understanding the interaction between the deterministic fast-slow dynamics and stochasticity. In this section, we elaborate on this idea and develop the quantitative theory of critical transitions for some canonical ecological models.

First, we consider the effects of demographic stochasticity, i.e., variation among individuals in the timing of reproduction and death, on the change in the size of a population. More precisely, we consider changes in population size in a small increment of time Δt, and model the intrinsic population fluctuations with a continuous-time Markov chain. Table 15.1 indicates the changes in population size that occur in a small increment of time, Δt, which comprise a *birth-death Markov process*.

For example, the probability of an increase in the population size in a small time increment depends only on the current birth rate $b(n, t)$, and not on previous values of the birth rate. Letting $\Delta t \to 0$, the events in the birth-death process can be described more concisely via a *master equation* for the probability distribution $P_n(t)$ of n individuals at time t,

$$
\begin{aligned}
\frac{dP_n(t)}{dt} &= d_{n+1}^t P_{n+1}(t) + b_{n-1}^t P_{n-1}(t) - b_n^t P_n(t) \\
&\quad - d_n^t P_n(t), \quad n = 0, 1, \ldots, N \\
&= T(n|n+1) P_{n+1}(t) + T(n|n-1) P_{n-1}(t) \\
&\quad - (T(n+1|n) + T(n-1|n)) P_n(t), \quad (15.10)
\end{aligned}
$$

consisting of $N + 1$ differential equations. At $n = 0$ and $n = N$, we define the transition probabilities appropriately (Table 15.1). Equation (15.10) can be solved analytically if the rates b_n^t and d_n^t are constant or linear (Van Kampen 2007) or if the rates are nonlinear, it may be solved numerically if the population size is not too large (e.g., less than 1,000; Keeling and Ross (2008)).

Since a master equation for an ecological birth-death process often has density-dependent birth and death rates b_n^t and d_n^t, we use an analytical approximation called the *Van Kampen system-size expansion* (Van Kampen 2007). Crucially, the expansion hinges on the assumption that the population size N is *large*, which ensures that the fluctuations (jumps between states n, Table 15.1) are small relative to the population size. The

Table 15.1 Transition probabilities associated with changes in number of individuals n. Note that $T(0|-1) = T(1|0) = T(N|N+1) = T(N+1|N) = 0$ since the system is closed.

Event	Change in state	Master Equation Term	Transition probability per unit time Δt
Birth	$n \to n + 1$	$T(n+1|n)$	$b(n, t)\Delta t = b_n^t \Delta t$
Death	$n \to n - 1$	$T(n-1|n)$	$d(n, t)\Delta t = d_n^t \Delta t$
No change	$n \to n$	–	$1 - (b(n, t) - d(n, t))\Delta t$

advantage of the expansion is that it leads to a stochastic differential equation for the fluctuations, from which leading indicators of critical transitions can be obtained.

The expansion assumes that the discrete random variable n can be approximated with a continuous random variable,

$$n = N\phi(t) + \sqrt{N}\psi(t), \tag{15.11}$$

where ψ is a continuous random variable describing fluctuations that scale with the square root of the population size N and $\phi(t)$ is a function determined by the Van Kampen system size expansion. Substituting Equation (15.11) into the master equation and computing the Van Kampen expansion yields the following system of equations that decouple the mean field dynamics from the stochastic fluctuations and therefore approximate the evolution of the probability distribution $P_n(t)$ through time,

$$\frac{d\phi(t)}{dt} = \alpha(\phi, t), \tag{15.12}$$

$$\frac{\partial \Pi(\psi, t)}{\partial t} = -\frac{\partial}{\partial \phi}(\alpha(\phi, t))\frac{\partial(\psi\Pi)}{d\psi}$$
$$+ \frac{1}{2}(\beta(\phi, t))\frac{\partial^2 \Pi}{\partial \psi^2}. \tag{15.13}$$

Equation (15.12) describes the dynamics of the population proportion, $\phi = n(t)/N$, through time. Equation (15.13) represents the evolution of the probability distribution $P_n(t) = \Pi(\psi, t)$. It is a Fokker–Planck equation with drift coefficient $\alpha(\phi, t)$, and diffusion coefficient $\beta(\phi, t)$. The drift coefficient determines the rate of return to the system state $\phi(t)$, and the diffusion term describes the strength of random perturbations. Essentially, the transformation to the new variables ϕ and ψ via the system-size expansion yields a normally distributed description for the probability distribution $P_n(t)$ (Van Kampen 2007). The description is most appropriate far from the boundaries. Further, if $n(t)$ is small, the Gaussian description breaks down. It is from the Fokker–Planck equation that we obtain a stochastic differential equation that provides a route to leading indicators. Letting $\lambda(\phi, t) = \frac{\partial}{\partial \phi}(\alpha(\phi, t))$, the Fokker–Planck equation describing the evolution of the random variable $\psi(t)$ (15.13) is equivalent to the stochastic equation (Allen 2011),

$$d\psi = \lambda(\phi, t)\psi dt + \sqrt{\beta(\phi, t)}dW. \tag{15.14}$$

Equation (15.14) can be Fourier transformed to yield the power spectrum (Nisbet and Gurney 1982), and integrating the power spectrum yields expressions for stationary variance and lag-τ autocorrelation. Alternatively, taking expectations of the solution of Equation (15.14) will also give expressions for stationary variance and lag-τ autocorrelation (Gardiner 2009; Allen 2011) in the limit $t \to \infty$. Table 15.2 summarizes the expressions for these summary statistics.

In what follows, we apply the theory to two representative examples of ecological tipping points: i) overharvesting representing a catastrophic transition, and ii) a non-catastrophic transition in Levins metapopulations. In each case we assume intrinsic noise, and therefore we can apply this framework. We then investigate the agreement between the leading indicators theoretically derived using this method with the same statistics measured from exact simulations. We note that neither of the following examples has a double-well potential, and therefore, are not bistable systems in the sense of having two positive alternative stable states. They were chosen for demonstration based on analytical tractability. (Bistable systems with a cusp catastrophe involve solving a cubic polynomial for the steady states and, although typically tractable, involve much more algebra.)

15.2.2 Case Study 1: The Logistic model with harvesting

First, we consider a model of overharvesting,

$$\frac{dn}{dt} = rn\left(1 - \frac{n}{N}\right) - hN, \tag{15.15}$$

where r is the per capita growth rate of the population $n(t)$, N is its carrying capacity and hN is a constant rate of harvest effort. The model has two steady states (Figure 15.2a),

Table 15.2 Leading indicator statistics.

Lag-1 Autocorrelation	Variance	Power spectrum
$\exp(-\|\lambda(\phi, t)\|)$	$\frac{\beta(\phi, t)}{2\|\lambda(\phi, t)\|}$	$\frac{\beta(\phi, t)}{\|\lambda(\phi, t)\|^2 + \omega^2}$

(a)   Harvest model

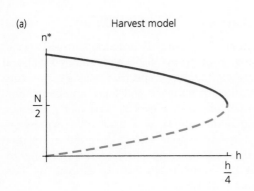

(b)   Levins metapopulations

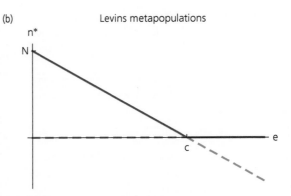

Figure 15.2 Bifurcation diagrams for each model. The logistic model with harvesting exhibits a saddle-node bifurcation at $h = r/4$. The Levins metapopulation model has a transcritical bifurcation at $e = c$. Solid blue branches indicate stable steady states and dashed red branches are unstable steady states. Parameters for the harvest model: $r = 1, N = 50, h = [0, 1/4]$. Parameters for the Levins model: $c = 2, N = 50, e = [1, 3]$.

$$n_{1,2} = \frac{N}{2}\left[1 \pm \sqrt{1 - \frac{4h}{r}}\right].$$

If $h < r/4$, n_2 is stable and n_1 is unstable. The model exhibits a saddle-node bifurcation at $h = r/4$, where the stable steady state (solid blue branch in Figure 15.2a) and the unstable steady state (dashed red branch) collide and disappear. Consequently, if $h > r/4$ then the population collapses to extinction (Brauer and Kribs 2015).

To model the gradual approach to extinction from overharvesting, we assume the harvest effort h increases gradually over time at rate h_1 from an initial harvest effort of h_0,

$$h(t) = \begin{cases} h_0 + h_1 t, & 0 < t_h \\ r/4 & t \geq t_h. \end{cases} \quad (15.16)$$

The time the critical threshold $h = r/4$ is attained is denoted by $t_h = (r/4 - h_0)/h_1$. Modeling gradual increases in harvest effort yields the following fast-slow system,

$$\frac{dn}{dt} = rn\left(1 - \frac{n}{N}\right) - hN \quad (15.17)$$

$$\frac{dh}{dt} = h_1. \quad (15.18)$$

We write the fast-slow model as a continuous-time Markov chain (Table 15.3), which can be expressed as a master Equation (15.10). Applying the Van-Kampen system size expansion to the master equation yields the following equations,

$$\frac{d\phi(t)}{dt} = r\phi(t)(1 - \phi(t)) - h(t), \quad (15.19)$$

$$\frac{\partial \Pi(\psi, t)}{\partial t} = -(r - 2r\phi(t))\frac{\partial(\psi\Pi)}{d\psi}$$
$$+ \frac{1}{2}(r\phi(t)(1 - \phi(t)) + h(t))\frac{\partial^2\Pi}{\partial\psi^2}, \quad (15.20)$$

where $\phi(t) = n(t)/N$. Equation (15.20) can be expressed as a stochastic differential equation,

$$d\psi = (r - 2r\phi(t))\psi dt$$
$$+ \sqrt{r\phi(t)(1 - \phi(t)) + h(t)}dW, \quad (15.21)$$

which can be analyzed through Fourier transformation or by taking expectations of its solution to yield the stationary statistics in Table 15.4.

To understand behavior of the statistics as the critical threshold is approached, it is instructive to consider the steady state approximation, where the rate of change of harvest effort (Equation (15.18)) is set to zero. To obtain the steady state, Equation (15.19) is set to zero and solved for steady states $\phi_{1,2}$. The stable state ϕ_2 is $1/2\left(1 + \sqrt{1 - 4h/r}\right)$, and the saddle-node bifurcation occurs at the critical threshold $h = r/4$. By Fenichel's theorem (Fenichel 1979), the fast-slow dynamics will approach those of the model with constant bifurcation parameter h evaluated at the steady state as h_1 approaches zero. The steady state approximation assumes the peak of the probability distribution is located at the steady

Table 15.3 Transition probabilities for the models (15.17)–(15.18) and (15.25)–(15.26) associated with changes in number of individuals n.

Harvest Model Event	Change in state	Transition probability per unit time Δt
Birth	$n \rightarrow n + 1$	$rn\,(1 - n/N)\,\Delta t = b_n^t\,\Delta t$
Death	$n \rightarrow n - 1$	$h(t)N\Delta t = d_n^t\,\Delta t$
No change	$n \rightarrow n$	$1 - \left(rn\,(1 - n/N) - h(t)N\right)\,\Delta t$

Levin's Model Event	Change in state	Transition probability per unit time Δt
Birth	$n \rightarrow n + 1$	$cn\,(1 - n/N)\,\Delta t = b_n^t\,\Delta t$
Death	$n \rightarrow n - 1$	$e(t)n\Delta t = d_n^t\,\Delta t$
No change	$n \rightarrow n$	$1 - (cn\,(1 - n/N) - e(t)n)\,\Delta t$

Table 15.4 Leading indicator statistics for models (15.19)–(15.20) and (15.27)–(15.28).

Model	Lag-1 Autocorrelation	Variance	Power spectrum
Harvest Model	$\exp\left(-|r - 2r\phi(t)|\right)$	$\dfrac{r\phi(t)(1-\phi(t))+h(t)}{2|r-2r\phi(t)|}$	$\dfrac{r\phi(t)(1-\phi(t))+h(t)}{|r-2r\phi(t)|^2+\omega^2}$
Levin's Model	$\exp\left(-|(c-e(t))-2c\phi(t)|\right)$	$\dfrac{c\phi(t)(1-\phi(t))+e(t)\phi(t)}{2|(c-e(t))-2c\phi(t)|}$	$\dfrac{c\phi(t)(1-\phi(t))+e(t)\phi(t)}{|(c-e(t))-2c\phi(t)|^2+\omega^2}$

state ϕ_2 rather than at $\phi(t)$. The stochastic differential equation for the fluctuations about the steady state, which is equivalent to Equation (15.20) evaluated at the steady state, is an Ornstein–Uhlenbeck process,

$$d\psi = (r - 2r\phi_2)\,\psi dt + \sqrt{r\phi_2\,(1 - \phi_2) + h}\,dW. \tag{15.22}$$

Substituting the steady state approximation into the expressions for the early warning signals in Table 15.4 allows us to examine the limiting behavior of the indicators. As h approaches $r/4$ from the left, the lag-1 autocorrelation approaches 1 since the eigenvalue $r - 2r\phi_2$ approaches zero as ϕ_2 tends to $1/2$ and the power spectrum exhibits greater power in lower frequencies. The variance blows up to infinity as $\phi_2 \rightarrow 1/2$ and h approaches the threshold $r/4$ from the left,

$$\lim_{h \rightarrow r/4^-} \frac{r\phi_2\,(1 - \phi_2) + h}{2\,|\,r - 2r\phi_2\,|} = \frac{\frac{r}{4} + \frac{r}{4}}{2\,|\,0\,|} = +\infty.$$

Leading indicators in Table 15.4 were obtained numerically using the fast-slow solution and the steady state approximation. The analytical predictions for the leading indicator behavior using the steady state approximation are predictive of

the behavior of the fast-slow indicators. Figure 15.3 shows the trends in the leading indicators as the harvest rate increases to the critical threshold. Lag-1 autocorrelation and variance increase as predicted, and the power spectrum moves towards lower frequencies. These changes in the summary statistics are indicative of the critical slowing down that signals the impending bifurcation.

15.2.3 Case Study 2: The Levin's metapopulation model

Next we consider Levin's metapopulation model (Levins 1969),

$$\frac{dn}{dt} = cn\left(1 - \frac{n}{N}\right) - en, \tag{15.23}$$

where $n(t)$ is the population size, c is the per capita colonization rate, e is the per capita extinction rate and N is the number of patches. The model has two steady states, $n_1 = 0$ and $n_2 = (1 - e/c)\,N$, and n_2 is stable if colonization rate is greater than extinction rate. The model has a transcritical bifurcation point at $c = e$, where the steady states meet and exchange stability (Figure 15.2b). Equation (15.23) also represents a model of overharvesting with per

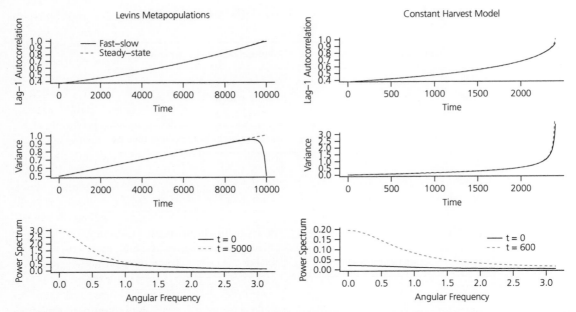

Figure 15.3 Trends in leading indicators of population extinction for two ecological models. The solutions of the fast-slow models were obtained numerically using the lsoda ODE solver in R. For autocorrelation, the theoretical results obtained using the steady state approximations (dashed line) are virtually indistinguishable from exact numerical solutions of fast-slow models (solid line). For variance, the theoretical result is excellent for the harvest model all the way to the bifurcation point and for Levins for most of the range, but there is a discrepancy in the vicinity of the tipping point. For both models, the power spectrum shows a "red shift" from relatively even distribution over all frequencies at $t = 0$ to dominance by low frequencies close to the bifurcation. Parameters for the Levins model: $c = 2$, $e(t) = 1 + 0.0001t$, $\phi_{L0} = 0.5$, $t_e = 10000$; Parameters for the harvest model: $r = 1$, $h(t) = 0.01 + 0.0001t$, $\phi_{H0} = 0.99$, $t_h = 2400$.

capita growth rate of c and per capita harvest effort e (Brauer and Kribs 2015).

We assume that the per capita extinction rate slowly increases over time to eventually equal the colonization rate, that is,

$$e(t) = \begin{cases} e_0 + e_1 t, & 0 < t_e \\ c & t \geq t_e \end{cases} \quad (15.24)$$

where $t_e = (c - e_0)/e_1$ is the time that the critical threshold $e = c$ is reached. Equation (15.23) may be recast as a fast-slow system,

$$\frac{dn}{dt} = cn\left(1 - \frac{n}{N}\right) - en \quad (15.25)$$

$$\frac{de}{dt} = e_1. \quad (15.26)$$

Again we write Equations (15.25) and (15.26) as a continuous-time Markov chain, with transitions between states as described in Table 15.3. The Van-Kampen system-size expansion yields

$$\frac{d\phi(t)}{dt} = c\phi(t)(1 - \phi(t)) - e(t)\phi(t), \quad (15.27)$$

$$\frac{\partial \Pi(\psi, t)}{\partial t} = -(c - e(t) - 2c\phi(t))\frac{\partial(\psi\Pi)}{d\psi} + \frac{1}{2}(c\phi(t)(1 - \phi(t)) + e(t)\phi(t))\frac{\partial^2 \Pi}{\partial \psi^2}, \quad (15.28)$$

where $\phi(t) = n/N$. Writing (15.28) as a stochastic differential equation,

$$d\psi = (c - e(t) - 2c\phi(t))\psi dt + \sqrt{c\phi(t)(1 - \phi(t)) + e(t)\phi(t)} dW, \quad (15.29)$$

and applying the usual analysis, we obtain leading indicators of population extinction (Table 15.4).

Once more, it is instructive to use the steady state approximation to gain insight into limiting behavior of the leading indicators as the critical threshold is approached, and detection of critical slowing down prior to metapopulation collapse. The stable steady state is $\phi_2 = 1 - e/c$, and we let the extinction rate approach the colonization rate from the left. The eigenvalue $c - e - 2c\phi_2 = -(c - e)$ approaches zero as e approaches c from the left and consequently, lag-1 autocorrelation approaches 1 and the power spectrum is again indicative of greater power in lower frequencies. Rather than blowing up however, the variance increases to 1 as e approaches c from the left,

$$\lim_{e \to c^-} \frac{c\phi_2 (1 - \phi_2) + e\phi_2}{2 \mid c - e - 2c\phi_2 \mid} = \lim_{e \to c^-} \frac{(c - e)\frac{e}{c} + \frac{e}{c}(c - e)}{2(c - e)}$$
$$= \lim_{e \to c^-} \frac{e}{c} = 1. \qquad (15.30)$$

The trends in the fast-slow leading indicators obtained from solving Equations (15.25)–(15.26) numerically are similar to the steady state approximations (Figure 15.3). However, close to the threshold, the fast-slow variance does not match the limiting value of 1 obtained using the steady state approximation. Unlike model (15.15), the Levin's metapopulation model undergoes a critical transition at $n = 0$, and as the metapopulation teeters on the verge of extinction, Equation (15.28) obtained from the van Kampen expansion of the master equation will not be an accurate description of the fluctuation dynamics. Trends in leading indicators far from the boundary $n = 0$ are accurate, but there is loss of accuracy near the boundary. The limiting behavior of variance at the tipping point for this model can only ever be an approximation and result (15.30) should be interpreted cautiously, but perhaps more importantly, this result predicts that, far from the boundary, variance increases as extinction rate increases.

15.3 Empirical evidence

Concurrent with the development of theory and simulation studies on early-warning indicators of critical transitions, there is also a growing body of empirical evidence (Scheffer et al. 2012, 2015; Litzow and Hunsicker 2016). The idea is that by measuring changes in recovery rate, variance, autocorrelation, or power spectra of the ecological state dynamics, we can detect the onset of critical slowing down (CSD) that precedes a critical transition. The

characteristic signatures of these indicators, as presented in Section 15.2, can then be used to signal loss of stability and the potential risk of a tipping point. Most empirical examples come from long-term monitoring data (usually time series) of ecological systems that have already experienced a regime shift. In fewer cases, spatial statistics have been used, either through derivation of the spatial pattern induced by loss of resilience or through space-for-time substitution comparing indicators along a stress gradient. On the other hand, there is only a handful of studies where specific experiments have been developed to test the indicators by actually causing a regime shift in situ (Table 15.5). The majority of these studies focuses on systems of single populations. Both observational and experimental work so far have aimed to provide "proof-of-principle" evidence for the possibility of detecting approaching instabilities, and there are well developed approaches for their practical application (Dakos et al. 2012). Operationalizing these indicators would allow for practical applications, for instance ranking ecosystems according to their resilience (for instance along a gradient), or monitoring over time the resilience of a given ecosystem and its propensity to shift (Scheffer et al. 2015).

In what follows, we highlight a few of the empirical examples from lab and field experiments as well as observational data that make use of either temporal or spatial data sets to infer for a system its proximity to a tipping point.

15.3.1 Lab experiments

Slowing down before the collapse of a photoinhibited phytoplankton population

Some of the clearest demonstrations of early-warnings prior to tipping points come from controlled population experiments in the lab. For example, Veraart et al. (2012) measured critical slowing down in a phytoplankton population that was stressed to extinction. In a chemostat, a monoculture of cyanobacterium was exposed to a slow (daily) increase in light conditions. During the course of the experiment the population was disturbed by diluting its standing density by a fixed amount, and the population was left to recover

Table 15.5 Examples of studies that have estimated early-warning signals on empirical and experimental data organized according to the type of ecological study system, the type of transition involved, and the type of indicators analyzed. Note that the list is not exhaustive and under-represents the fact that so far there are more observational than experimental studies available.

System type	Transition	Indicators	Reference
Empirical			
marine fish populations	population decline	Temporal	Krkošek and Drake 2014
marine community	community compositional shifts	Temporal	Beaugrand et al. 2008
intertidal community	shifts in dominance	Temporal	Benedetti-Cecchi et al. 2015
marine/terrestrial populations	shifts in abundance	Temporal	Bestelmeyer et al. 2011
lake plankton community	eutrophication	Temporal	Burthe et al. 2016
avian population	extinction threshold	Temporal	Hefley et al. 2013
marine fish populations	stock collapses	Temporal	Litzow et al. 2013
tree individuals	tree mortality	Temporal	Camarero et al. 2015
lake paleo-communities	eutrophication	Temporal	Wang et al. 2012
marine phytoplankton	community compositional shifts	Temporal	Wouters et al. 2015
lake plankton community	community compositional shifts	Temporal	Gsell et al. 2016
lake paleo-communities	anoxia shift	Temporal	Belle et al. 2017
marine fish populations	overexploitation	Temporal	Hshie et al. 2006
intertidal community	community compositional shift	Spatial	Hewitt and Thrush 2010
marine community	community compositional shift	temporal/spatial	Lindegren et al. 2012
avian/zooplankton community	spatial discontinuities	temporal/spatial	Sundstrom et al. 2017
salt marsh vegetation	shift to bare tidal flat	temporal/spatial	van Belzen et al. 2017
drylands	desertification	spatial patterns	Kefi et al. 2007
Experimental			
lake community	trophic cascade	Temporal	Batt et al. 2013
lake community	trophic cascade	Temporal	Carpenter et al. 2011
lake community	algal bloom	Temporal	Pace et al. 2015
yeast population	Allee effect collapse	Temporal	Dai et al. 2012
zooplankton population	population extinction	Temporal	Drake and Griffen 2010
phytoplankton population	photoinhibition	Temporal	Veraart et al. 2012
whale populations	overexploitation	Temporal	Clements et al. 2015
phytoplankton population	population extinction	Temporal	Jarvis et al. 2016
zooplankton population	population decline	Temporal	Wissel 1984
drylands	desertification	Temporal	Bestelmeyer et al. 2013
intertidal community	shifts in dominance	Spatial	Rindi et al. 2017
yeast population	Allee effect collapse	Spatial	Dai et al. 2013

back to equilibrium. These disturbance-recovery experiments were conducted every four to five days until light intensity reached a threshold at which the population was not able to sustain its growth (after around four weeks from the start of the experiment) (Figure 15.4a). At that critical light intensity, where the positive effect that the population is exerting on its growth by protecting itself via shading is compromised, the population becomes photoinhibited and collapses to extinction (Huisman and Weissing 1994). Along this trajectory to extinction, it was shown that the measured recovery rate of the population decreased over time. This is a direct result of critical slowing down that occurred prior to population collapse (Figure 15.4b).

Slowing down prior to extinction of zooplankton populations

In a different lab experiment, Drake and Griffen (2010) "pushed" a zooplankton population to extinction by slowly deteriorating its environment. The deterioration was simulated by progressively reducing the available food fed to the experimental populations. Specifically, the authors used sixty populations of a freshwater cladoceran (*D. magna*) that they randomly assigned to a stressed

(deteriorating environment) and control (constant environment) treatment. After an initial period to allow for the population to achieve quasi-stationarity, the populations of the stressed treatment received progressive reductions in food in roughly monthly intervals. The authors monitored the abundance of all populations for both treatments on a weekly basis. The experiment lasted for over a year, until the last populations in the stressed treatment went extinct. It was observed that the populations in the deteriorating environment went extinct (but at different time points and levels of food), while most populations in the control treatment survived (Figure 15.4c). Although the transition to population extinction was gradual rather than catastrophic, the authors estimated early warning indicators (coefficient of variation, autocorrelation, skewness, and spatial correlation)

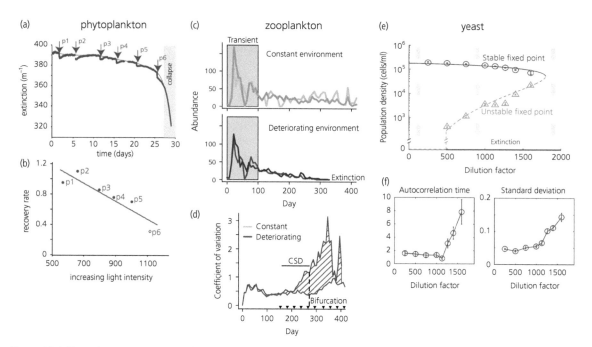

Figure 15.4 Three microcosm experiments showed evidence of critical slowing down. A photoinhibited phytoplankton population was perturbed at multiple points during the slow increase in light intensity (left). The recovery rate is a direct measurement of system stability, corresponding inversely to the magnitude of the eigenvalue in a theoretical model. A progressively food-limited population exhibited excess variance in replicates subject to progressive reduction in food supply compared with control populations reared in a constant environment (middle; "CSD" indicates the period of critical slowing down). A yeast system exhibiting cooperative behavior displayed stability properties reminiscent of a saddle-node bifurcation (right). Populations initiated along the upper stable branch showed an increasing pattern in autocorrelation and variance as the dilution factor approached the critical point.

Modified with permission from Scheffer et al. (2015).

from the ensemble of all populations at each weekly observation time point for both treatments. By comparing the changes in the indicators between the stressed and control treatments it was found that the early warning signals identified a change in the dynamics of the zooplankton populations during the deterioration of their environments. Moreover, in the case of the coefficient of variation, this indicator showed a strong increase prior to extinction demonstrating for the first time that critical slowing down occurs with noncatastrophic transitions as well as catastrophic ones (Figure 15.4d).

Slowing down before the extinction of yeast populations with an Allee effect

Perhaps the most complete experimental demonstration of identifying tipping points using generic early-warning signals comes from a yeast population experiment (Dai et al. 2012). In this system, growth is facilitated by a cooperative effect within a population: yeast cells can metabolise sucrose outside the cell so that other cells in the population can benefit. This positive population effect however requires some minimum cell density, below which the effect is compromised and the population can go extinct. Such threshold behavior is characteristic of an Allee effect which means that at low population density per capita growth rate becomes negative (Allee et al. 1949). Dai et al. (2012) followed the dynamics of laboratory yeast populations at increasing levels of dilution rate (paralleling the harvest model derived in Section 15.2) to identify the threshold at which the yeast population collapsed to extinction due to the Allee effect (Figure 15.4e). The top figure shows how the exact critical density threshold was estimated for each dilution rate below which the population would not survive but go extinct. Following these steps, it was possible to empirically characterize the fold bifurcation, including the two alternative states and the unstable saddle between them (Figure 15.4e). Based on this bifurcation diagram, the authors monitored the density dynamics of replicate yeast populations for a range (but constant level) of eight dilution rates and estimated the average variance, coefficient of variation, autocorrelation, and skewness of the dynamics for each dilution rate. All early-warning indicators but skewness exhibited a systematic increase prior

to the collapse of the yeast population providing strong evidence that critical slowing down can provide warning of the impending transition in the system (Figure 15.4f).

15.3.2 Field experiments

Early-warning experiments outside the control conditions of the lab are scarce, as they are difficult to perform (Dakos et al. 2015). One of the very few studies that attempted to identify tipping points based on critical-slowing down signals at community level in the field comes from Paul and Peter US lakes in Wisconsin (Carpenter et al. 2011). During the course of three years, Carpenter et al. (2011) gradually added large-mouth bass in Peter Lake that was dominated by planktivorous fish populations. Their aim was to manipulate Peter Lake in order to induce a trophic cascade that would overturn the fish community from planktivore to piscivore dominance. The mechanism behind this regime shift is based on bass releasing pressure of planktivores feeding on juvenile bass resulting in higher recruitment of bass drawing planktivores to low densities and making piscivores eventually dominant. Models had indicated the possibility of a catastrophic transition caused by this trophic cascade mechanism that could be anticipated by early-warning signals (Carpenter et al. 2008). Indeed, the authors witnessed this shift in dominance during their experiment, while this regime shift was not documented in the nearby lake, Paul that they used as a reference. During the experiment, different variables were monitored (piscivores and planktivores abundances, zooplankton and chlorophyll as proxy of phytoplankton) for both manipulated and reference lakes. A series of indicators (return rate, variance, skewness, spectral properties) were measured on all of these variables and they were compared between the reference and manipulated lake. This comparison suggested that variance of planktivores (that were main part of the actual trophic cascade) increased before and during the regime shift. More interestingly, high-frequency chlorophyll dynamics exhibited a shift to low frequency power spectra compared to the control as expected from theory. These findings actually implied that early-warning signals from high-frequency monitored ecosystem variables could potentially be useful for monitoring resilience at the whole ecosystem level (Batt et al. 2013).

15.3.3 Observational studies

Detecting climatic transitions along time series

Lab and field experiments, like the ones described previously, provide relatively long and high resolution time series for estimating early-warning signals. However, this quality of information is lacking for most natural ecological systems. Thus, most research on unmanipulated systems has comprised retrospective analysis of past records, such as paleoreconstructions of the Earth's climate.

Although the climate appears to have been exceptionally stable during the Holocene, in fact this is an exception as it has been punctuated by sudden events that triggered abrupt transitions between contrasting climatic states. Among the most prominent of these events are the end of the greenhouse Earth more than 34 million years ago (the Eocene to Oligocene transition) when the Earth shifted from a tropical climate to a state with ice caps, the abrupt (recurring) transitions at the end of each glacial period, or the most recent termination and restart of the thermohaline circulation that marked the Younger Dryas period (around 12,000 years ago). Such transitions are not just past singular events. Contemporary concerns about the possibility of abrupt transitions have been raised for a series of climate tipping elements (Lenton et al. 2007), like the weakening of the thermohaline circulation, that could trigger to a similar disruption as it did in the past (Caesar et al. 2018). In view of this possibility, the operational challenge is to detect such approaching instabilities before they become irreversible.

Dakos et al. (2008) attempted this by analysing paleoclimatic records that describe 8 of the most important documented past abrupt climatic transitions using indicators based on critical slowing down. They showed that in all of these cases critical slowing down did precede the transitions. For example, in the case of the exit from the Younger Dryas, the authors used a paleorecord of grayscale from a sediment core at the Cariaco basin in the Caribbean that is proxy for changes of the thermohaline circulation (Figure 15.5a). By focusing

only the part of the record that preceded the transition to the end of the Younger Dryas (roughly around 11,500 years ago), and after filtering the data with a smoothing function to remove the long term slow trends, it can be assumed that the resulting residuals are capturing the fluctuations of the system (in this case the thermohaline circulation) to natural disturbances. Thus, the autocorrelation of the residuals is an indirect measure of the strength of recovery of the system to its average state. In this record, Dakos et al. (2008) used a window equal to half the size of the record to estimate the autocorrelation (at the first lag, AR1) of the residuals (Figure 15.5a). By sliding this window along the time series, one can retrieve the evolution of AR1 as function of time (Figure 15.5b). An increase in AR1 along this period could signal that the thermohaline circulation was slowing down towards a critical threshold that would mark a shift to another state. Indeed, the authors found the trend of the indicator to be positive (Figure 15.5b) and statistically significant when compared to trends estimated in randomly generated trajectories of AR1 from various null models (Dakos et al. 2012).

But, is an increase in AR1 to be expected prior to the collapse of the thermohaline circulation? In the same study, a climate model of intermediate complexity was used to simulate the effect of a slow increase of freshwater input into the North hemisphere (due to ice melt for instance) that can weaken the circulation and lead to its collapse (Figure 15.5c). By focusing on the pre-transition period and following the steps already described, a similar rise in AR1 was found (Figure 15.5d). The positive trends in AR1 both in the empirical observational and modelled data from this study provided the first clear evidence that climatic transitions can be preceded by slowing down and that these indicators could be potentially used to monitor the risk of future tipping events.

15.4 Spatial indicators of resilience

Although most of the work to date on early warning signals has focused on temporal indicators, there are analogous spatial signatures. A number of ecosystems are characterized by striking spatial patterns, such as boreal peatlands, mussel beds,

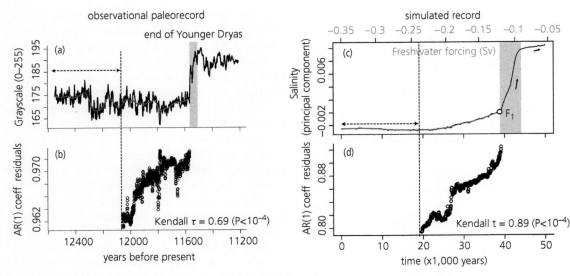

Figure 15.5 Time series of abrupt climate shifts reflecting the onset and termination of the thermohaline circulation. (a) Reconstructed paleodata of the end of the Younger Dryas, and (c) simulated time series generated by the CLIMBER-2 climate model. (b, d) In both empirical and simulated cases the system slowed down before the transition, as revealed by an increasing trend in autocorrelation AR1 of the residuals after removing the slow trend estimated by a Gaussian kernel function (smooth red line). Gray bands identify transition phases, arrows mark the width of the moving window used to compute slowness. Point F_1 denotes a fold bifurcation at which the circulation disrupts due to the small changes in freshwater intrusion (Sv). High positive values of Kendall τ mean a strong positive trend in AR1.

Modified with permission from Dakos et al. (2008).

mud flats, savannas, coral reefs and dryland ecosystems (Rietkerk and van de Koppel 2008). Because these patterns are well-known to change along stress gradients, it has been suggested that the shape and size of these patterns could be used as indicators of ecosystem degradation (von Hardenberg et al. 2001; Rietkerk et al. 2004). Recently, Chen et al. (2019) have shown that the eigenvalues of the covariance among measurements taken at multiple locations provide a signature of critical slowing down. Importantly, this *spatial eigenvalue* is robust to environmental heterogeneity, which might have been expected to obscure spatial patterning due to the loss of system-wide resilience.

15.4.1 Critical slowing down spatial indicators

Critical slowing down also arises in spatial systems (Dakos et al. 2011). One way to understand this is to picture two neighboring units connected by diffusion that can locally experience a critical transition to an alternative state. Close to the transition, the two units will become more like each other because

critical slowing down increases the relative effect of diffusion. As a result, the spatial recovery from disturbance (Dakos et al. 2011) and spatial propagation of perturbations (Dai et al. 2013) will be slow. This ultimately translates to an increase in *spatial correlation* (Dakos et al. 2010), an increase in *spatial variance* (Guttal and Jayaprakash 2009; Donangelo et al. 2010), or a peak in *spatial skewness* (Guttal and Jayaprakash 2009).

15.4.2 Two broad types of patterns in drylands

Key ideas

The idea that spatial patterns can be used as indicators of ecosystem degradation has been especially well studied in drylands, theoretically and empirically (von Hardenberg et al. 2001; Rietkerk et al. 2004). Dryland ecosystems are characterized by patches of vegetation in a matrix of bare soil (Figure 15.6).

Broadly speaking, two categories of vegetation patterns can be found in drylands: i) regular, periodic, *Turing-like* vegetation patterns that resemble

Figure 15.6 Picture from a Mediterranean landscape in Cyprus showing the typical patchiness of the vegetation cover in these ecosystems. Photo credit: F.D. Schneider.

designs seen on animal coats (von Hardenberg et al. 2001; Rietkerk et al. 2004), and ii) *irregular patterns*, where patches of all sizes are present in the system and the distribution of patch sizes tend to follow heavy tail distributions (Scanlon et al. 2007; Kéfi et al. 2007).

Patch-based indicators

It has been shown that early warning signals based on critical slowing down may not work in spatially structured ecosystems with periodic patterns

(Dakos et al. 2011). In such cases, looking at the patterns themselves may provide an interesting alternative. Under increasing stress, models have shown that regular vegetation patterns change from homogeneous vegetation cover to gaps, labyrinths, spots and, finally, desert (von Hardenberg et al. 2001; Rietkerk et al. 2004; Kéfi et al. 2010). In mathematical models, some of these patterns always occur in the bistable region (i.e., they coexist with stable homogeneous desert) (Kéfi et al. 2010). This means that when the system is degrading, it goes through the full succession of patterns, whereas when it is regenerating after a collapse, the system eventually goes back to exhibiting labyrinths, gaps or homogeneous vegetation, but not to spots. This implies that spot patterns arise only from the degradation of a pattern with a higher cover and that they indicate proximity to a discontinuous shift toward a desert, in ecosystems where resource-concentration drives the feedback between vegetation and soil water availability (Rietkerk et al. 2004; Kéfi et al. 2010). It is however noteworthy that spot patterns can also emerge from different ecological mechanisms. Thus, observing spot patterns in nature is not sufficient to infer that an ecosystem is close to a discontinuous shift. Knowing the underlying ecological mechanism is also necessary.

In ecosystems exhibiting irregular vegetation patterns, models have shown that patch size distributions deviating from a power law, toward fewer large patches than expected for a pure power law, indicate proximity to transitions (Kéfi et al. 2007; Kéfi et al. 2011). Whereas a system far from transition is characterized by the presence of patches of all sizes, a system tends toward a limited range of patch sizes (intermediate and small) when stressed. This is because the largest patches fragment into smaller ones, while the smallest patches die due to the high level of stress. More practically, along a transition to desertification, the distribution of vegetation patch sizes goes from spanning clusters (vegetation patches crossing the whole system), to power laws, to truncated power laws and finally to an exponential distribution (Kéfi et al. 2011).

Empirical evidence

This observation of sequential pattern formation leads to the idea that dryland ecosystems may be ranked by their resilience to environmental change by focusing on the patch size distribution. Kéfi et al. (2007) investigated how the spatial organization of vegetation is influenced by the degree of external stress in field data from three grazed Mediterranean arid ecosystems in Spain, Greece and Morocco. In each of these ecosystems, data was collected on three sites with different levels of livestock grazing. In each of the nine (3×3) sites, the authors analysed the number and sizes

of vegetation patches, and plotted the number of patches, $N(S)$, as a function of size, S. They then fitted these *patch-size distributions* to two different models: a power law,

$$N(S) = CS^{\gamma} \qquad (15.31)$$

and a truncated power law,

$$N(S) = CS^{\gamma} \exp\left(-\frac{S}{S_x}\right), \qquad (15.32)$$

where γ is the estimated scaling exponent of the model, S_x the patch size above which $N(S)$ decreases faster than in a power law, and C is a constant.

In the field sites with the lowest grazing pressure, the patch-size distributions were best fitted by heavy tail distributions resembling a power law. This power-law relation implies that vegetation patches were present over a wide range of size scales, with many small patches and relatively few large ones. This is consistent with another study published which found power law distributions in vegetation patch size across Africa (Scanlon et al. 2007). As herbivory increased in the three ecosystems, the distributions deviated increasingly from a pure power law, because of the fragmentation of the large patches as well as the loss of the smallest patches from the ecosystem (Kéfi et al. 2007).

This is consistent with theoretical results which suggest that for high cover, the patch size distribution is characterized by the presence of *spanning clusters*, very large patches of the size of the system itself (Kéfi et al. 2011). As the cover decreases, spanning clusters of occupied cells first disappear at a point that is referred to as the percolation point of occupied cells. Interestingly, at this point there is a drastic change in system-wide connectivity, as the probability that a spanning patch appears in the system changes dramatically, but other ecological variables of interest, such as the fraction of occupied cells, vary smoothly with no apparent shift. Power laws emerge at this point. From the percolation point, the large patches are progressively lost, leading to deviations from power laws. These deviations become stronger as the system approaches extinction, and the tail of the distribution exhibits increasingly fewer large patches than at the percolation point. The sequence of patch size

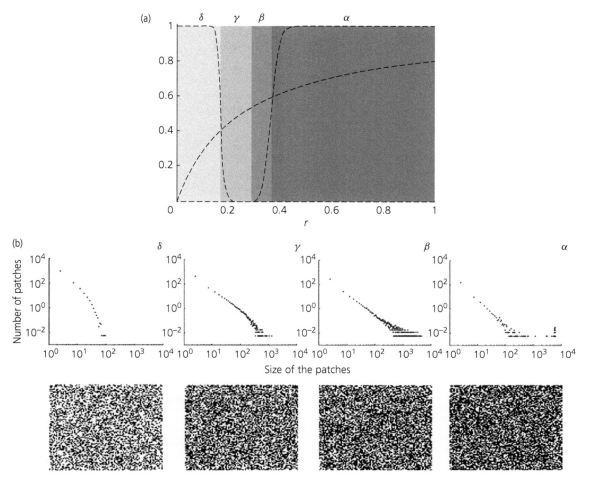

Figure 15.7 Succession of patch size distributions in a model along a gradient. (a) Each of the grey areas corresponds to a different region. Full line: fraction of occupied cells in the lattice at steady state. Dashed left line: percolation probability of empty cells. Dashed right line: percolation probability of occupied cells. (b) Patch size distributions of occupied cells at steady state on a log–log scale, and the corresponding snapshots of the system at the end of the simulations for each of the four regions shown in (a). Black: occupied cell. White: empty cell.

Figure from Kéfi et al. (2011).

distributions with decreasing cover can be characterized by four distinct patterns: i) spanning clusters of vegetation, ii) power laws (Equation 15.31), iii) truncated power laws (Equation 15.32), iv) truncated power law (Equation 15.32) with spanning clusters of empty sites Kéfi et al. (2011) (Figure 15.7). Simultaneously, as the cover keeps decreasing, the probability that spanning clusters of empty cells appear in the system increases.

Furthermore, theory suggests that this succession of patterns occurs both along continuous and discontinuous transitions (Kéfi et al. 2007). The combination of model and data analysis suggest that increasing deviations from pure power laws in the patch size distribution of vegetation in drylands may indicate that the ecosystem is degrading and approaching the desertification point. As well-resolved spatial data is becoming increasingly available at low cost due to improved technology (such as remote sensing), further tests of these theories will help further validate these theoretical results and clarify to what extent they can actually be used as management tools, in drylands, and more generally in spatially structured ecosystems.

15.4.3 Structural early warning signals

In addition to space, ecological systems are structured by many features. For instance, populations may be structured by age, sex, physiological condition, or behavior. Species in communities are structured by the connections they share with other species in food webs. Such structure is important to the dynamics of the system when it affects the change in system state, for instance when encounter between males and females is required for reproduction or there is consumption by herbivores or predators. The existence of spatial early warning signals suggests that structural measurements such as body size spectrum, food web connectance, or species abundance distribution might also contain signatures of criticality. There is, however, little theory on such *structural early warning signals*. Tirabassi et al. (2014) have shown that time series data can be used to estimate interaction networks that are informative about structural changes in a vegetation model and Cavaliere et al. (2016) studied how links among individuals changed systematically in the collapse of cooperation networks. Finally, Dakos (2018) has investigated how some species or food web modules may provide more information about the approach to a critical point than others, suggesting that the best indicators of ecological collapse may be theoretically informed *sentinels*. More work is needed in this area.

15.5 Conclusion

The theory of alternative stable states, tipping points, and early warning signals of ecological transitions has been developed with increasing sophistication over the last two decades. The models presented here are methodologically instructive, but relatively simple, both in their structure and in the number of interacting state variables. Importantly, these models illustrate that there is more to be understood about the stochastic phenomena associated with classical ecological models. Although some of these phenomena

are qualitatively universal (e.g., the increase in autocorrelation associated with a critical transition), the specific properties of many models, especially more complex models, remain poorly understood. Numerous empirical examples of alternative stable states and associated early warning signals have been identified in concert with these theoretical advances. However, empirical evidence remains largely specific to particular settings and has frequently led to identifying additional complexities that affect the manifestation of critical phenomena in real systems. We view this as a healthy feedback between theory and evidence. Despite these qualifications, the use of stochastic early warning signals to monitor ecological systems approaching a tipping point is a promising development in ecological theory. We suggest that future work be guided with a view toward operationalizing these concepts, including the development of better theory about the observability of critical slowing down and the performance of field projects to demonstrate the effectiveness of early warning signals at scale.

Acknowledgments

We thank Kevin McCann and an anonymous reviewer for comments on an earlier version of this manuscript. JMD and PR were supported by the National Institute of General Medical Sciences of the National Institutes of Health under Award Number U01GM110744. The content is solely the responsibility of the authors and does not necessarily reflect the official views of the National Institutes of Health.

References

Allee, W. C., Emerson, A. E., Park, O., Park, T., and Schmidt, K. P. (1949). *Principles of Animal Ecology*. Philadelphia: Saunders.

Allen, L. J. S. (2011). *An Introduction to Stochastic Processes with Applications to Biology*. Boca Raton, Fla: CRC Press.

Batt, R. D., Carpenter, S. R., Cole, J. J., Pace, M. L., and Johnson, R. A. (2013). Changes in ecosystem resilience detected in automated measures of ecosystem metabolism during a whole- lake manipulation. *Proc. Natl. Acad. Sci. U.S.A.*, 110(43): 17398–403.

Berglund, N. and Gentz, B. (2006). *Noise-Induced Phenomena in Slow-Fast Dynamical Systems: A Sample-Paths Approach. Probability and Its Applications.* 1st edition. London: Springer-Verlag.

Brauer, F. and Kribs, C. (2015). *Dynamical Systems for Biological Modeling: An Introduction.* Boca Raton, Fla: Chapman and Hall/CRC.

Caesar, A. L., Rahmstorf, S., Robinson, A., Feulner, G., and Saba, V. (2018). Observed fingerprint of a weakening Atlantic Ocean overturning circulation. *Nature* 556: 1–19.

Carpenter, S. R., Brock, W. A., Cole, J. J., Kitchell, J. F., and Pace, M. L. (2008). Leading indicators of trophic cascades. *Ecol. Lett.* 11(2): 128–38.

Carpenter, S. R., Cole, J. J., Pace, M. L., Batt, R., Brock, W. A., Cline, T., Coloso, J., Hodgson, J. R., Kitchell, J. F., Seekell, D. A., Smith, L., and Weidel, B. (2011). Early warnings of regime shifts: a whole-ecosystem experiment. *Science* 332(6033): 1079–82.

Cavaliere, M., Yang, G., Danos, V., and Dakos, V. (2016). Detecting the collapse of cooperation in evolving networks. *Sci. Rep.* 6: 30845.

Chen, S., O'Dea, E. B., Drake, J. M., and Epureanu, B. I. (2019). Eigenvalues of the covariance matrix as early warning signals for critical transitions in ecological systems. *Sci. Rep.* 9: 2572.

Courchamp, F., Clutton-Brock, T., and Grenfell, B. (1999). Inverse density dependence and the allee effect. *Trends Ecol. Evol.* 14(10): 405–10.

Dai, L., Korolev, K. S., and Gore, J. (2013). Slower recovery in space before collapse of connected populations. *Nature* 496(7445): 355–8.

Dai, L., Vorselen, D., Korolev, K. S., and Gore, J. (2012). Generic Indicators for Loss of Resilience Before a Tipping Point Leading to Population Collapse. *Science* 336(6085): 1175–7.

Dakos, V. (2018). Identifying best-indicator species for abrupt transitions in multispecies communities. *Ecological Indicators* 94: 494–502.

Dakos, V., Carpenter, S. R., Brock, W. A., Ellison, A. M., Guttal, V., Ives, A. R., Kéfi, S., Livina, V., Seekell, D. A., van Nes, E. H., and Scheffer, M. (2012). Methods for detecting early warnings of critical transitions in time series illustrated using simulated ecological data. *PLoS ONE*, 7(7): e41010.

Dakos, V., Carpenter, S. R., Nes, E. H. V., and Scheffer, M. (2015). Resilience indicators: Prospects and limitations for early warnings of regime shifts. *Philosophical Transactions of the Royal Society B-Biological Sciences,* 370:20130263.

Dakos, V., Kéfi, S., Rietkerk, M., van Nes, E. H., and Scheffer, M. (2011). Slowing down in spatially patterned ecosystems at the brink of collapse. *American Naturalist* 177(6): E153–166.

Dakos, V., Scheffer, M., van Nes, E. H., Brovkin, V., Petoukhov, V., and Held, H. (2008). Slowing down as an early warning signal for abrupt climate change. *Proceedings of the National Academy of Sciences of the United States of America* 105(38): 14308–12.

Dakos, V., van Nes, E., Donangelo, R., Fort, H., Scheffer, M., and Nes, E. H. V. (2010). Spatial correlation as leading indicator of catastrophic shifts. *Theoretical Ecology* 3(3): 163–74.

Dibble, C., O'Dea, E. B., Park, A. P., and Drake, J. M. (2016). Waiting time to infectious disease emergence. *J. R. Soc. Interface*, 13: 20160540.

Ditlevsen, P. D. and Johnsen, S. J. (2010). Tipping points: Early warning and wishful thinking. *Geophys. Res. Lett.* 37(19): L19703.

Donangelo, R., Fort, H., Dakos, V., Scheffer, M., and Van Nes, E. H. (2010). Early warnings for catastrophic shifts in ecosystems: Comparison between spatial and temporal indicators. *International Journal of Bifurcation and Chaos* 20(2): 315–21.

Drake, J. M. and Griffen, B. D. (2010). Early warning signals of extinction in deteriorating environments. *Nature* 467(7314): 456–9.

Fenichel, N. (1979). Geometric singular perturbation theory for ordinary differential equations. *Journal of Differential Equations* 31: 53–98.

Gardiner, C. (2009). *Stochastic Methods: A Handbook for the Natural and Social Sciences.* Springer Series in Synergetics, 4th edn. Berlin Heidelberg: Springer-Verlag.

Gilmore, R. (1981). *Catastrophe Theory for Scientists and Engineers.* New York: Wiley.

Guttal, V. and Jayaprakash, C. (2009). Spatial variance and spatial skewness: leading indicators of regime shifts in spatial ecological systems. *Theoretical Ecology* 2(1): 3–12.

Hale, J. K. (1984). Introduction to dynamic bifurcation. In Salvadori, L., (ed.), *Bifurcation Theory and Applications.* Berlin, Heidelberg: Springer.

Huisman, J. and Weissing, F. J. (1994). Light-limited growth and competition for light in well- mixed aquatic environments—An elementary model. *Ecology* 75(2): 507–20.

Keeling, M. J. and Ross, J. V. (2008). On methods for studying stochastic disease dynamics. *J. R. Soc. Interface* 5(19): 171–81.

Kéfi, S., Eppinga, M., de Ruiter, P., and Rietkerk, M. (2010). Bistability and regular spatial patterns in arid ecosystems. *Theoretical Ecology* 3(4):257–69.

Kéfi, S., Rietkerk, M., Alados, C. L., Pueyo, Y., Papanastasis, V. P., ElAich, A., de Ruiter, P. C., Alados, L., and Ruiter, P. C. D. (2007). Spatial vegetation patterns and imminent desertification in mediterranean arid ecosystems. *Nature* 449(7159): 213–17.

Kéfi, S., Rietkerk, M., Roy, M., Franc, A., de Ruiter, P. C., and Pascual, M. (2011). Robust scaling in ecosystems and the meltdown of patch size distributions before extinction. *Ecol. Lett.* 14(1): 29–35.

Kuehn, C. (2015). *Multiple Time Scale Dynamics*. Cham: Springer.

Lenton, T. M., Held, H., Kriegler, E., Schellnhuber, H. J., Hall, J. W., Lucht, W., and Rahmstorf, S. (2007). Tipping elements in the Earth's climate system. *PNAS* 105(6): 1786-1793.

Litzow, M. A. and Hunsicker, M. E. (2016). Early warning signals, nonlinearity, and signs of hysteresis in real ecosystems. *Ecosphere* 7(12).

Levins, R. (1969). Some demographic and genetic consequences of environmental heterogeneity for biological control. *Bulletin of the Entomological Society of America*, 15 (3): 237–240.

Livina, V. N., Kwasniok, F., and Lenton, T. M. (2010). Potential analysis reveals changing number of climate states during the last 60 kyr. *Clim. Past* 6: 77–82.

Nisbet, R. M. and Gurney, W. S. C. (1982). *Modelling Fluctuating Populations*. New York: Wiley.

Nolting, B. C. and Abbott, K. C. (2016). Balls, cups, and quasi-potentials: Quantifying stability in stochastic systems. *Ecology* 97(4): 850–64.

O'Regan, S. M. and Burton, D. L. (2018). How stochasticity influences leading indicators of critical transitions. *Bull. Math. Biol.* 80(6): 1630–54.

Rietkerk, M., Dekker, S. C., de Ruiter, P. C., and van de Koppel, J. (2004). Self-organized patchiness and catastrophic shifts in ecosystems. *Science* 305(5692): 1926–9.

Rietkerk, M. and van de Koppel, J. (2008). Regular pattern formation in real ecosystems. *Trends in Ecology & Evolution* 23(3): 169–75.

Scanlon, T. M., Caylor, K. K., Levin, S. A., and Rodriguez-Iturbe, I. (2007). Positive feedbacks promote power-law clustering of kalahari vegetation. *Nature* 449: 209–212.

Scheffer, M., Bascompte, J., Brock, W. A., Brovkin, V., Carpenter, S. R., Dakos, V., Held, H., van Nes, E. H., Rietkerk, M., and Sugihara, G. (2009). Early-warning signals for critical transitions. *Nature* 461(7260): 53–9.

Scheffer, M., Carpenter, S., Foley, J. A., Folke, C., and Walker, B. (2001). Catastrophic shifts in ecosystems. *Nature* 413(6856): 591–6.

Scheffer, M., Carpenter, S. R., Dakos, V., and van Nes, E. (2015). Generic indicators of ecological resilience: Inferring the chance of a critical transition. *Annual Review of Ecology, Evolution, and Systematics* 46(1): 145–67.

Scheffer, M., Carpenter, S. R., Lenton, T. M., Bascompte, J., Brock, W., Dakos, V., van de Koppel, J., van de Leemput, I. A., Levin, S. A., van Nes, E. H., Pascual, M., and Vandermeer, J. (2012). Anticipating Critical Transitions. *Science* 338(6105): 344–8.

Scheffer, M., Hosper, S. H., Meijer, M. L., Moss, B., and Jeppesen, E. (1993). Alternative equilibria in shallow lakes. *Trends Ecol. Evol.* 8(8): 275–9.

Strogatz, S. (2014). *Nonlinear Dynamics and Chaos*, (2nd edn.) Boulder, Colorado: Westview Press.

Tirabassi, G., Viebahn, J., Dakos, V., Dijkstra, H. A., Masoller, C., Rietkerk, M., and Dekker, S. C. (2014). Interaction network based early-warning indicators of vegetation transitions. *Ecological Complexity* 19: 148–57.

Van Kampen, N. G. (2007). *Stochastic processes in physics and chemistry*. Amsterdam, Netherlands: North-Holland.

Veraart, A. J., Faassen, E. J., Dakos, V., van Nes, E. H., Lürling, M., and Scheffer, M. (2012). Recovery rates reflect distance to a tipping point in a living system. *Nature* 481(7381): 357–9.

von Hardenberg, J., Meron, E., Shachak, M., and Zarmi, Y. (2001). Diversity of vegetation patterns and desertification. *Physical Review Letters* 87: 198101.

CHAPTER 16

Areas of current and future growth

Kevin S. McCann and Gabriel Gellner

We are currently in a time of significant environmental change, and with the continued growth of the human population this change is unlikely to subside. While applied research has always played some part of ecological research, modern research in both empirical and theoretical ecology has seemed to increasingly consider how this global change has altered the structure and function of ecological systems. When we both started practicing ecology, the divide between what was seen as fundamental and applied was large. Now, these boundaries seem to be blurring and the massive changes unfolding before us seem to have led researchers to re-examine classical theory from perspectives previously only largely glossed over (i.e., applied issues motivate fundamental theory now).

Climate change research has pushed empirical ecologists to recognize that organisms are broadly responding to the associated changing seasonal signals of climate change by altering their phenology. So extensive has this work become, that recent meta-analyses have patterns across whole ecosystems, and these responses can be larger in some ecosystems relative to others. This behooves theory to really understand the role of seasonal timing in everything from coexistence, to interaction strength, the frequency of diseases, and the cycling of nutrients and materials. For this reason, it is hard not to imagine a large growth in theory that looks more at seasonality. While seasonality has certainly been considered, it has historically been intermittent and ignored by ecology in general and has yet to make its way to ecology textbooks beyond

the recent work on empirical phenology patterns. Nonetheless, understanding the role of seasonality is a fundamental need brought on by an emerging and growing applied problem.

In a manner similar to seasonality, ecosystem theory is not well-represented in any of the theoretical ecology (TE) books, including this one. Here, meta-ecosystem theory is referred to in Gravel and Massol's important emerging piece, yet still, despite the amazingly long and excellent empirical work done in ecosystem ecology, a base of theory hardly exists. There is the well-known and excellent book by DeAngelis (1992), and a lot of modeling done on NPZ (nutrient-phytoplankton-zooplankton) or NPZD (where D is detritus), but this well-done ocean research has yet to integrate well into the general tenets of ecology. Again, with global change occurring and intersecting with the nutrient and carbon cycles in critical ways, it seems this is a time for ecology as a field to follow in the footsteps of DeAngelis and others to bring the generalities of this research to bear on both fundamental and applied research. While this has been pushed by the largely empirical stoichiometry literature, more needs to be done to tie nutrients to the currency of energy and vice-versa.

Several areas of recent theoretical growth come out of a modern research paradigm that is interested in crossing scientific boundaries (e.g., socio-ecology). Again, pushed by a world where we realize the connections are ultimately important and feedback to alter the system. As such, placing humans and their actions in a dynamic role in

McCann, K. S. and Gellner, G., *Areas of current and future growth* In: *Theoretical Ecology: Concepts and Applications*. Edited by: Kevin S. McCann and Gabriel Gellner, Oxford University Press (2020). © Oxford University Press.
DOI: 10.1093/oso/9780198824282.003.0016

ecosystems is on the rise. In applied problems, these socio-ecological intersections often lead to "wicked problems" where optimization as a society is multi-dimensional and far from obvious. These problems, which are ultimately higher dimensional dynamical problems with feedbacks, are often economic, social, and deeply connected to human behavior. While this area exists and is thriving, it seems as though it will only grow in the coming decades. In our opinion, it is still youthful enough that the ideas from this, that we are aware of, have not yet percolated into textbooks—a litmus test for the lasting success of a coherent set of ideas in ecology.

While we have already referred to global change and how it will lead some areas of research, it is clear that theoretical ecology is branching out to extend its current theory to embrace changing conditions. This has happened relatively strongly at the population level but has been done in a less convincing and thorough manner at the community, food web, and ecosystem levels. A number of chapters reflect this current trend of looking at stochasticity, transients, and structural change in populations to whole ecosystems. Global impacts are driving the recognition of multiple stressors, and theory has followed suit. This is consistent with the interest in stochasticity, to consider the implications of multi-stressors or perturbations on the stability and functioning of ecological systems. This new area has argued that the long-lasting reliance on local stability is not enough.

Although strictly speaking, bioinformatics is not theory but rather the analysis and manipulation of large amounts of data, it has been coupled to theory frequently (e.g. job searches seem to regularly do this). Nonetheless, theory will need to grow in order to embrace the use of large amounts of data in ecology, socio-ecology, and disease ecology. Further, many theoreticians are also adept at programming, allowing them to be both theoreticians and bioinformaticians. Often, large data exercises seem to want to remove themselves from theory ("the models are just too simple and not realistic enough"). Disease ecology, in many areas, has shifted away from theory, and yet there is a clear role for simultaneously doing both theory and more detailed applied approaches, with one informing the other. This is part of a long tactical versus strate-

gic modeling argument but one that should not be forgotten. Additionally, the intersection of bioinformatics and theory is potentially rich. Tools of the bioinformatics approach are useful for implementation into high data theory (e.g., May's complex matrices) and potentially for applications of theory (e.g., deep learning and fisheries). Here, we would argue that the intersection of these different but technically overlapping research areas ought to drive advances.

With the growing population, food production is becoming a massive global issue. This is a socio-ecological problem, and it is so large and growing as to demand its own comments. One clear aspect of food production is that it makes ecosystems into agro-ecosystems, (human-dominated ecosystems). These agro-ecosystems impact both adjacent ecosystems and distant ecosystems because of the connectivity of nature's ecological systems. The Lake Erie dead zone for example, was once largely the manifestation of urban effluents before sewage treatment, whereas now its massive and growing dead zone is more directly related to agriculture in the surrounding USA and Canadian watersheds. Water, here, is nature's transport system and, not surprisingly, there is a growing frequency of these dead zones globally. Due to the connectivity and the complex of feedbacks, this is another area ripe for theoretical input and guidance. It will also require bioinformatic approaches, and numerous other aspects could use the aid of ecological theory or its existing tools. For example, even the aspect of understanding how climate and spatial arrangements (e.g. homogeneity or heterogeneity) alter the stability of yield and economics is a problem core to the tools of the theoretical ecologist. Note, much of the connections in space are at the ecosystem level so theory at the ecosystem scale is critical and needs to be incorporated into the general toolbox of ecologists.

One aspect of recent trends, started some time back by Peter Yodzis and Ulf Dieckmann, involves considering how biological constraints, like body size allometry, impact ecological dynamics. Constraints are the "reality" filters of complex dynamical systems theory and are playing an increasingly big role in ecological theory (see Brose's Chapter 9 for example). One can imagine that constraints may be ultimately tied to whole food web theory matrix techniques for example, that ensure these matrices are also "feasible" an area that has always plagued general community matrix theory.

To end the book, we note that we have missed things that are clearly important and being developed. Namely, while eco-evolutionary theory is within the trait chapter of Klausmeier, Kremer and Koffel, it is arguably largely missing in this book, likely reflecting an unfortunate bias towards our own strengths. Clearly eco-evolutionary theoretical developments are currently being developed, and we imagine and hope that future versions of theoretical ecology will reveal strong growth in this important area. Much work is being developed related to evolutionary response to global change (e.g., evolutionary rescue). Again, consistent with the themes being developed in this book, we would argue that this multi-disciplinarian approach to theory (evolution and ecology, agriculture and ecology, economics and ecology, society and ecology) have become part of the toolbox of modern ecology and modern theoretical ecology and likely will play a massive role in future theoretical development.

Glossary

activation energy the energy which must be provided to a system of reactants in order to generate a reaction. The activation energy determines the relationship between temperature and vital rates in the Arrhenius equation

adaptive dynamics a trait-based theoretical framework that allows for the emergence of community structure, assuming infrequent, small mutations of existing strategies

additive assembly total density or biomass increases with diversity as a community assembles because additional species do not replace species that are already present

adult-driven population cycles cycles in a structured consumer population exploiting a shared resource that arise because adult consumers are competitively superior and require lower resource densities for their survival than juveniles. These stage-structured population cycles are distinct from classical predator-prey cycles and result from ontogenetic asymmetry

Arrhenius equation a formula for the temperature dependence of biological and ecological rates, originally developed to describe rates of chemical reactions.

autocorrelation the relationship among subsequent observations in a temporal (or spatial) sequence. Positive autocorrelation refers to a tendency for subsequent observations to fall on the same side of the arithmetic mean

biomass overcompensation an increase in the biomass of a particular life history stage of a consumer population when its mortality increases, resulting from the relaxation of density dependence. This overcompensation occurs irrespective of whether mortality of the entire population or of a particular life history stage increases

branching point an evolutionary equilibrium that is convergence stable but not evolutionary stable

carrying capacity the number of individuals in a population at which the rate of per-capita increase via births and immigration is equal to the rate of per-capita loss via death and emigration

causality (cause-and-effect relationship) refers to a relationship between two variables, objects, events and states of affairs, by which a cause contributes to occurrence of an effect. Following three conditions are important in definitions of most causality measures: (1) the cause occurs before its effect, (2) there exists the correlation between the cause and its effect, and (3) the correlation between the cause and its effect do not disappear in face of any confounding variables.

community matrix the community matrix describes the linearized dynamics around a fixed point of an ecological community. It is calculated evaluating the Jacobian matrix of the dynamical system at the fixed point. A fixed point is locally stable if all the eigenvalues of the community matrix have negative real part

community all the biological species living in a defined locality

competitive exclusion the process by which a species is driven to extinction by competition with other species; no more species can coexist at equilibrium due to limiting factors

contemporary niche theory a theoretical framework that employs a graphical approach to determine community structure based on zero net growth isoclines (ZNGIs), which summarize the response of organisms to their environment, and impact vectors, which summarize the effect of organisms on their environment

contingent competitive exclusion competitive exclusion that depends on the initial densities of a species and its competitors

convergence stability when directional selection pushes a strategy toward an evolutionary equilibrium.

convergence stable strategy (CSS) an evolutionary equilibrium that is both convergence and evolutionary stable

cross-reactive immunity immunity developed in response to infection by one type of pathogen also confers some degree of protection against a different type of pathogen

degree distributionn the degree of a node in a undirected network is the number of nodes it connects to. The degree distribution is the probability of observing a node with a given degree

density feedback the tendency of the per capita population growth rate of a species to increase or decrease as a result of changes in the density of that same species, or a different species from the same guild, mostly due the effects of species density on an intermediary such as a resource or a natural enemy on which per capita growth depends

density dependence changes in individual life history rates, for example, rates of somatic growth, development, maturation and mortality, brought about by changes in overall population density. This negative feedback effect of population density on individual life history rates can operate directly (direct density dependence) or indirectly, for example, through depletion of a shared resource that individuals forage on (delayed density dependence)

density-dependent transmission pathogen transmission is a function of the number of infected individuals per unit space

directional selection when there is a non-zero fitness gradient

diversity maintenance the process by which the diversity of species is maintained over time

ecological drift the tendency of species with equal average fitnesses, that are also not ecologically differentiated, to drift in abundance due to the cumulative effects of random perturbations of population density

emergent Allee effect an Allee effect of a predator on a structured prey population that emerges from the change in stage- or size-structure of the prey with increasing mortality. The predator experiences positive density dependence at low density (an Allee effect) because the density of its preferred prey stage increases through biomass overcompensation despite a decreasing overall prey density

emergent facilitation the (mutual) facilitation between two stage- or size-selective predators of the same structured prey population, which emerges from the changes in prey stage- or size-structure that the predators induce

emergent predator exclusion the phenomenon that a stage- or size-selective predator of a structured prey population goes extinct with increasing productivity of the resources that the prey forages on, because the increased resource productivity changes the prey population structure in a way that is detrimental for predator persistence

environmental or *E*-state the set of variables that characterize the environment in which the individuals in a structured population model live and that determine together with the individual or *i*-state the development, reproduction and mortality of the individuals as well as their interaction with the environment

environmental tracking the expression of a pattern of population dynamics that is similar to that exhibited by the forcing environment, usually at some temporal lag

equilibrium an ecosystem state (for a point equilibrium) or set of states (for cycles or chaos) in which the system will remain in perpetuity unless perturbed. An equilibrium can be stable or unstable; see the following points. A system is considered to be "at equilibrium" if it is in one of these states/sets of states and there is zero population growth

evolutionarily stable community (ESC) an evolutionary equilibrium (usually of >1 species) that is globally evolutionarily stable and convergence stable

evolutionarily stable strategy (ESS) an evolutionary equilibrium that is evolutionary stable, either locally (cannot be invaded by nearby strategies) or globally (cannot be invaded by any other strategy)

evolutionary equilibrium a trait value or set of trait values where there is no directional selection; also known as a singular strategy

evolutionary transcritical bifurcation a bifurcation where an evolutionary equilibrium loses its global evolutionary stability

feasibility a fixed point is feasible if all its components are positive.

fitness gradient the change in fitness with respect to change in a trait value, $\partial g/\partial x_0|_{x_0=x_1}$; it summarizes the directional selection, a strategy experience

fitness a synonym for the per capita growth rate, g_i; see also invasion fitness

food chain a linear pathway in a food web defining the progress of organic matter from lower to higher trophic levels

food web the set of all links between the species in a community defining which species feed on which other species

forecast horizon the dimensional distance in time for which useful forecasts can be made. This is generally quite low for ecological variables due to various kinds of stochasticity and uncertainties about model structure and data

founder control an outcome of competition where whichever species reaches equilibrium first excludes the other

frequency-dependent transmission pathogen transmission is a function of the proportion of infected individuals per unit space

functional response the relationship between the density of resources or prey and the number consumed per consumer/predator in a unit of time. Temperature has strong effects on numerous aspects of the functional response

global stability a solution is globally stable within a given domain D when a system returns to the equilibrium after a perturbation of any given magnitude, with the requirement only that the perturbation does not take the system outside the domain D

gradual acclimation non-genetic phenotypic changes that are too slow to closely track the environmental changes that drive them, yet too fast to be considered ecologically irrelevant

growth isocline a curve or surface in Euclidean space with axes being population densities, or other quantities affecting per capita population growth, for which a particular species has zero population growth

guilds groups of species that are functionally similar in a community, which share a fitness function such that species with identical trait values are neutral

half-saturation density the density of resources or prey at which half of the maximal ingestion of a consumer or predator is achieved. The half-saturation density is a parameter of the Monod formulation of the Holling type II functional response

harmonic mean a summary statistic that is commonly applied in situations when the average of rates is desired. The harmonic mean is the reciprocal of the arithmetic mean of the reciprocals of the individual observations. The harmonic mean is always less than the arithmetic mean

individual or *i*-state the set of variables or traits that characterize individuals in a structured population model and that determine together with the environmental or *E*-state the development, reproduction and mortality of the individual as well as its interaction with its environment

interaction coefficient the rate at which the per capita growth rate of a species changes relative to its maximum value as the density of the species (intra specific interaction) or of a different species (interspecific interaction) changes

interspecific competition competition, usually for shared resources by individuals of different species

invade a population that is rare, attempting to establish among a resident community; grows or declines exponentially

invasibility criterion the judgement that species in a guild coexist if it is possible for each of them to increase from low density in the present of the other guild members not necessarily at low density

invasion analysis a popular approach to understanding coexistence between two populations, based on whether each population can invade monoculture of the other on its ecological attractor

invasion fitness fitness of a population when it is rare in an environment set by any resident population(s)

juvenile-driven population cycles cycles in a structured consumer population exploiting a shared resource that arise because juvenile consumers are competitively superior and require lower resource densities for their survival than adults. These stage-structured population cycles are distinct from classical predator-prey cycles and result from ontogenetic asymmetry

life history theory predicts how organisms should optimize their allocation to growth, survival, and reproduction

limiting similarity limits on how similar the trait values of species can be and yet allow them to coexist

linear stability analysis use of a linear approximation near an equilibrium point to compute the rate of exponential growth or decay in a small displacement from that equilibrium. When the linear approximation is written in matrix form, it is known as the Jacobian matrix and its dominant eigenvalue gives this exponential rate

local stability a fixed point is locally stable if, starting starting from an arbitrarily close initial condition, dynamics converge to the fixed point

locally stable equilibrium an equilibrium that is returned to in the long run after sufficiently small perturbations

metabolic theory a concept that extends the relationship between metabolic rate, body size and temperature to describe patterns at other levels of organization

mutual invasiblity plot (MIP) illustrates the pairs of strategies x_1 and x_2 that can stably coexist

natural enemy partitioning the tendency for different members of guild to be most susceptible to different natural enemies

neutral populations with identical fitness

neutrally stable equilibrium an equilibrium forming one of a continua of equilibria such that perturbation from the equilibrium leads to another equilibrium nearby with no tendency to return to the initial equilibrium

niche overlap the degree to which species are similar in their use of the environment with regard to those components associated with density feedback

non-equilibrium system any population, community, or ecosystem that is experiencing transient and/or stochastic dynamics, and is therefore not currently at equilibrium

non-linear averaging the average value of a non-linear function that is generated when the independent variable is distributed across a range of values. Non-linear averages typically differ from the function value at the average of the independent variable

nonlinear dynamics refers to temporal changes of variables that are generated by a deterministic rule where the outputs show disproportional response to the changes of the inputs. In nonlinear dynamics, small differences between initial states often diverge exponentially (called sensitivity to initial conditions), making their long-term behaviors unpredictable

ontogenetic asymmetry differences in, for example, ingestion rate, maintenance rate, or resource and habitat use between individuals of different body sizes or life-history stages that translate into differences in individual competitiveness

optimal foraging theory predicts how organisms should optimize foraging for different resources

optimization theory a framework that assumes that organisms will maximize their fitness, or a fitness proxy

Ornstein–Uhlenbeck (OU) process a stochastic differential equation which combines a random-walk with a tendency to return to a central value. OU processes can be used to generate temporally-autocorrelated dynamics to represent temperature or other environmental variables

overall interaction the geometric mean of the relative interaction coefficients of two species in a community

pairwise invasion plots (PIPs) used in adaptive dynamics to classify one-species evolutionary equilibria, these plot the sign of $g(x_0; x_1)$ as a function of the traits of a resident and an invader population

per capita growth rate the rate of change of population density per unit time, per unit density

permanent coexistence an outcome for deterministic models in which all species rise above some minimum positive density in the long run from any state in which no species are extinct

physiologically structured population model a structured population model that represents individuals by a set of individual state or i-state variables and describes the life history of the individual (development, reproduction and mortality) as well as its interaction with the environment dependent on these i-state variables and on the state of the environment the individual lives in. The population level model emerges by bookkeeping these individual life history dynamics

population or p-state the mathematical object in a structured population model that represents the distribution of the individuals in the population over all possible individual states. This can be a vector of densities, if the individuals are classified in discrete life history stages, or a continuous distribution in case the individual state can adopt values in a continuous range

potential function a function that describes how a dynamical system in any given state will change in the absence of external perturbation. It can be thought of as a surface, and the system's state as a ball rolling on this surface. The ball will roll downhill, away from unstable equilibria (peaks in the surface) and toward stable equilibria (wells). It will roll more slowly on flat spots and more quickly on steep parts of the surface

random matrix a random matrix is a matrix whose coefficients are random variables. As such, instead of studying a given matrix, results obtained using random matrix theory describe the "typical behavior" of an entire class of matrices whose coefficients are sampled from a given distribution

rank (of a matrix) the rank of a matrix is the number of linearly independent columns (or, equivalently, rows) in the matrix. For square matrices, the rank is also equivalent to the number of non-zero eigenvalues. A square matrix is said to be of full rank if the rank is equal to its size, or, equivalently, if all the eigenvalues are different from zero

relative average fitness the ratio of species average fitnesses of two different species in a guild

relative limitation ratio the ratio of interspecific to intraspecific interaction coefficients

resident a population that is not an invader, i.e., which has reached its ecological attractor

resource partitioning the situation in which the different species in a guild are most heavily dependent on different resource species, or more formally have linearly independent utilization functions

saddle an unstable equilibrium that is attracting from some states and repelling from others; the dynamics may approach a saddle before ultimately moving away

species average fitness a quantity defined for each member of guild predicting which species in any subset of the guild would ultimately dominate, excluding the others, in the absence of a coexistence mechanism

species diversity the number of species in a defined area, or more generally a measure that increases with the both the number of species and the evenness of their abundances

spectral density the spectral density is the probability density function associated with the eigenvalues of a random matrix ensemble. It describes the probability of observing an eigenvalue with a given magnitude

spectrum the spectrum of a matrix is the set of eigenvalues

stabilizing/disruptive selection selection that respectively disfavors (or favors) trait values that are more extreme than the focal strategy's, causing trait variance to decrease (or increase)

stable coexistence the tendency of all species in a guild to increase following perturbation to low density, avoiding extinction with positive invasion fitness

state dependency in the context of community ecology, "state dependency" means that effects of species or environment on another species may depend on the system state, which may vary with time, space and biological or non-biological environments

stable equilibrium an equilibrium that is returned to in the long run following a perturbation, including both locally stable and globally stable equilibria

state space the set of possible values for state variables of interest. If we're interested in the dynamics of a population, the state variable is population density and state space is a one-dimensional line from 0 to ∞. If we're interested in two interacting populations, state space is two-dimensional, representing pairs of population densities

stationary environmental variation environmental variation that can be characterized by long-term stable frequencies of events, and therefore having a central tendency defined by a fixed mean, and spread defined by a fixed variance

stochastic differential equation a differential equation in which one of more of the terms is a stochastic process

stochastic random, with respect to the process being studied

storage effect a coexistence mechanism arising in a variable environment from the three-way interaction of the response of population growth to environmental change, changes in competition and species densities. It is the mechanism allowing temporal partitioning to promote species coexistence

strategy the trait values of a population (or species, in some cases)

structural stability a system is considered to be structurally stable if any smooth change in the model or in the value of its parameters does not change its dynamical behavior (such as the existence of equilibrium points, limit cycles, or deterministic chaos). In Chapter 7, the relevant dynamical behavior is the stable coexistence of species and structural stability is reinterpreted as the area in parameter space compatible with both a dynamically stable and feasible equilibrium

structured population model a model that represents a population by its composition in terms of, for example, the sex-, age-, stage-, or size-structure of its individuals as well as by the abundance of these different types of individuals

substitutive assembly increases in diversity are associated with replacements of individuals because of competition (usually due to a fixed carrying capacity for the community); thus, the addition of an individual of one species replaces an individual(s) of another species

temporal niche the way in which a species uses the environment over time

temporal partitioning the presence of differences between species in their temporal niches

thermal performance curve the relationship between a measure of organism or population performance (e.g., swimming speed; growth rate) and temperature. These curves are typically unimodal and skewed to reflect a rapid reduction in performance above the modal temperature

thermoregulation the ability of an organism to maintain its body temperature at a value different than its surrounding environment

top-down control/effect the extent to which a consumer or predator determines the structure and biomass of the resource/prey community

trade-off relationships between non-independent traits that constrain their variation

trait any measurable characteristic of an individual; functional traits are those that affect performance and ultimately fitness. See also strategy

transcritical bifurcation a point in parameter space where an equilibrium point exchanges its stability with another equilibrium point as a parameter is varied. When temperature varies, stable consumer-resource systems may transition to stable resource-only systems (consumer extinction) via a transcritical bifurcation

transient dynamics dynamics that occur in a system that is not at equilibrium.

trophic level the position of species in a food web defined by the maximum number of species that organic matter passes through before being consumed by the species

universality the spectrum of a random matrix is universal if it does not depend on the full distribution from which the coefficients are drawn, but rather only on a few moments of the distribution

unstable equilibrium an equilibrium state that a dynamical system will naturally diverge away from, unless perturbed toward it. However, if the ecosystem is precisely in this state, it will remain there in perpetuity unless perturbed. It may be a point equilibrium, or a more complex dynamic such as an unstable limit cycle or chaotic repellor

utilization function a function defining the consumption rate of each resource by a particular consumer species measured per unit resource, and per unit consumer species

Index

Note: Tables, figures, and boxes are indicated by an italic *t*, *f*, and *b* following the page number.

for resources 12–15
and species sorting 209–10
symmetric 214
competition load 102
competition matrices 99–101, 102, 112
direct 98, 104, 114
effective 98, 104, 105, 109, 110
mean field 101
symmetric 109
competitive exclusion 167, 205, 209,
212, 214, 230
contingent 8, 11
local 120
and spatial dynamics 198
competitive interactions 7, 204, 207,
211, 212, 214
and correlation 83*b*
and extinction rates 206
interspecific 97
pathogens 227, 228
competitive load 105, 109
competitive metacommunities 211,
215
coexistence in 213
moments for 209*f*
competitive relationships 5
competitive release 231, 232
competitive systems 99–104, 114, 216
complex ecological networks 75,
134–42
complexity-stability debate 77, 118
connectance of systems 75
connective stability 100*b*
conservation 162, 222, 226, 227
constraints 36, 83*b*, 286
biological 2
dynamical stability 113
mouth-size 121
constructive interference 37
consumer dynamics 19*b*
consumer-resource interactions 2, 36,
60, 137
consumer-resource models 30, 30*b*,
32*b*, 34–6, 70, 249
consumer-resource systems 43,
44*f*, 46
consumers 150
abundance at warmer
temperatures 247
extinction 250
consumption 250
contemporary niche theory 164
contingent exclusion 8*f*, 10*f*, 12
control theory 36
convergence stability 170, 183, 184
convergent cross mapping, and
multivariate S-map 124–5

co-occurrence 148–9, 204, 206, 209
cooperative behavior 263
covariance matrices 82
crawl-bys 47
critical population size 263
critical slowing down 273, 278
critical threshold 270
critical transitions 263, 264, 268,
273–7
C-R models *see* consumer-resource
models
crop rotation 225
cross-reactive immunity 227
cusp catastrophe 267
CV *see* coefficient of variation
cyanobacterium 273
cyclopoids 127

D

Daphnia 249
data 156
DeAngelis, Donald 37
death 116
death rates 53, 252, 253*f*, 254*f*,
255*f*, 268
decomposition 30*b*, 37*f*
defense 120, 184
degree distribution 85, 150, 151,
153, 154
delay-differential equations 56–7
delayed feedback loops 36
delayed logistic model 29*b*
delays *see* lags
demographic stochasticity 268
dengue 230, 231, 234
densities 168
density dependence 50, 55, 167, 185
density-dependent functional
responses 109
density-dependent integral projection
models 58
density-dependent trait-based
models 167–75
density feedback 21
density-independent models, with
traits and optimization
theory 165–7
destructive interference 37*f*
deterministic density dependence 50
deterministic skeleton 265
detritus 156
feedback 38
recycling 37
developmental stages 121
diagonal elements 79
Diamond's checkerboard
hypothesis 206

Dieckmann, Ulf 286
diet analyses 122
diffuse coevolution 93
diffusion coefficient 269
diffusion parameter 265*b*
dilution effect 222, 223, 224, 225,
226, 233
Dirac delta function 80*b*, 81*b*
direct competition matrices 98, 104
discrete models 33
discrete Ricker model 32, 34*f*
disease ecology 4, 221–42, 286
diseases, spread in contact
network 88
dispersal
evolution of 183
limitation 201–2
diversity-disease interactions 226
Drake, John 4
drift coefficient 269
Drosophila 120
drylands, vegetation spatial
patterns 278–82
dynamical stability 99, 100*b*, 109, 113,
114, 215
dynamic bifurcation 264
dynamic complex networks 138
dynamic energy budget models 60
dynamic global vegetation
models 186
dynamics 40
of an ecological community 3, 76*b*
Dyson, Freeman 78

E

early warning signals 4, 264–7, 282
Earth Systems Models 186–7
eco-evolutionary theory 287
ecological dynamics, interspecific
interactions and 116–19
ecological interference 227
ecological moment methods 179, 180
ecological networks 143–60
eco-physiology 163
ecosystem degradation 278
ecosystem theory 285
ectotherms 247, 248, 258
edges *see* links
EDM *see* empirical dynamic
modelling (EDM)
effective competition matrices 98,
104, 112
effective growth rates 98, 107
effective interspecific
competition 104, 105
eigenvalues 79
eigen-vectors 79